The Limits of Law

The Limits of Law

Essays on
Democratic Governance

Peter H. Schuck

Yale University

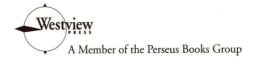

Westview
PRESS
A Member of the Perseus Books Group

The essays in this book are reprinted with permission of the publications in which they originally appeared:

Chapter 1 "Legal Complexity: Some Causes, Consequences, and Cures," 42 Duke L.J. 1–52 (1992)

Chapter 2 "Multi-Culturalism Redux: Science, Law, and Politics," 11 Yale Law & Policy Rev. 1–46 (1993)

Chapter 3 "Some Reflections on the Federalism Debate," Yale Law & Policy Rev. 1–22 (1996)

Chapter 4 "The Politics of Regulation," 90 Yale L.J. 702–725 (1981)

Chapter 5 "When the Exception Becomes the Rule: Regulatory Equity and the Formulation of Energy Policy Through an Exceptions Process," 1984 Duke L.J. 165–200 and 289–300

Chapter 6 "Law and Post-Privatization Regulatory Reform: Perspectives from the U.S. Experience," Luigi Manzetti, ed., *Regulatory Policy in Latin America: Post-Privatization Regulation* (Coral Gables, Fla.: North-South Center Press at the University of Miami; distributed by Lynne Rienner Publishers, 2000)

Chapter 7 "Against (and for) Madison: An Essay in Praise of Factions," 15 Yale Law & Policy Rev. 553–597 (1997)

Chapter 8 "Delegation and Democracy: Comments on David Schoenbrod," 20 Cardozo L. Rev. 775–793 (1999)

Chapter 9 "To the *Chevron* Station: An Empirical Study of Federal Administrative Law," 1990 Duke L.J. 985–996 and 1054–1061

Chapter 10 "The Thickest Thicket: Partisan Gerrymandering and Judicial Regulation of Politics," 87 Colum. L. Rev. 1325–1384 (1987)

Chapter 11 "Mass Torts: An Institutional Evolutionist Perspective," 80 Cornell L. Rev. 941–989 (1995)

Chapter 12 "Public Law Litigation and Social Reform," 100 Yale L.J. 1763–1786 (1993)

Published in 2000 in the United States of America by Westview Press, 5500 Central Avenue, Boulder, Colorado 80301-2877, and in the United Kingdom by Westview Press, 12 Hid's Copse Road, Cumnor Hill, Oxford OX2 9JJ

Find us on the World Wide Web at www.westviewpress.com

A CIP catalog record for this book is available from the Library of Congress.
ISBN 0-8133-6758-1(pb); 0-8133-6759-X (hc)

The paper used in this publication meets the requirements of the American National Standard for Permanence of Paper for Printed Library Materials Z39.48-1984.

10   9   8   7   6   5   4   3   2   1

Contents

Part II   Institutions and Processes

Part III   Mapping the Limits of Law

Introduction and Acknowledgments

My thesis in this book is simpler to state than to prove.

Law confronts unprecedented challenges today as it seeks to order an astonishingly dynamic American society. It is not meeting these challenges as well as it must—or even as well as it might. Many of law's failures betray its limits as a mechanism for governing such a society. Some of these limits inhere in law's very nature. Others are more contingent, reflecting the particular ways in which Americans have thought about and deployed law in order to manage bewildering social change. Whatever the source of law's limits, they are certain to grow even more problematic as the pace of transformation quickens and as the social, economic, cultural, and technological conditions that law seeks to regulate become more unruly and difficult to control.

Law faces a crisis of legitimacy—if not today, then soon enough. This crisis is not measured simply by the declining public confidence in government and other political institutions including the legal profession and the media. In fact, as I argue in Chapter 7, American society is governed better today than in the past and better than in most other complex post-industrial polities. Our public officials and lawyers have never been better trained, nor our media more professional. Nor can the crisis be accurately measured by the level of public participation in government; as Chapter 7 also shows, participation is lower in some respects, higher in others. Indeed, the most remarked-upon index of nonparticipation, nonvoting in federal elections, does not appear to be dysfunctional.[1] The presidential impeachment drama of 1998–1999 suggests (at least to me) that the rule of law in general, and the Constitution in particular, are no less venerated by Americans today than they were in the past.

The looming crisis of legitimacy, I believe, will not come from law's corruption, a tarnishing of its ideals, or a diminished yearning for its dominion. No serious person doubts that the polity's principal function is to secure a just order and that law is an essential mechanism for attaining it. Instead, law's legitimacy will erode if and when a widespread belief takes hold that law has become *incompetent* in discharging this fundamental function. As social complexity grows, secular values proliferate, and aspirations for justice deepen, Americans will look more than ever to law as the solution to social conflicts and as the guarantor of civic virtue.

Just as competition dominates all aspects of life—biology, economy, politics, culture, religion, social status, and group relations—so must it affect our choice of strategies for social ordering. Law is by no means the only such strategy (although it frames all of the others), nor are all forms of law alike in their effects. Law makes markets viable and interacts with social norms in subtle and important ways. If law falters, social progress is impeded. Markets and norms will rush to fill the gap left by law's failure, of course, but they may prove to be even less effective at social governance than an incompetent law. We must always choose among or combine imperfect systems even as we try to improve their performance.

Our first task, then, is to seek a richer understanding of law's limits. Part I of this book elaborates several of the most daunting constraints and challenges that law faces today. (Law's bright promise, having allured mankind since the earliest human communities, needs less of an introduction.) Chapter 1 maps law's complexity, and Chapter 2 compares law to the parallel cultures of science and politics with which it increasingly interacts. Chapter 3 explores the extraordinary social diversity of American society, a great and steadily growing problem for regulatory law.

The next nine chapters, in Part II, examine how public law functions in its various institutional forms and settings. Three chapters concern administrative regulation. Chapter 4 critiques James Q. Wilson's classic schema for the analysis of regulatory politics. Chapter 5 uses regulatory policy as a prism for studying the mythic conflict between law as a system of rules, and equity as a solvent for law's categorical rigidity, suggesting alternate ways to manage the conflict. Chapter 6 describes the constitutional and institutional relationships between law and markets in the United States, showing how regulatory reform seeks to alter these relationships.

Two chapters focus on legislation. In Chapter 7, I juxtapose the perennial vilification of special interest groups ("factions," as James Madison termed them in his canonical *Federalist* No. 10) against the extensive legal protections that they enjoy. I proceed to advance and defend a controversial claim—that these groups have vastly improved our law, politics, and policies—and I propose certain reforms to improve this pluralist system. In Chapter 8, I defend the common legislative practice, condemned by most commentators, of enacting statutes that delegate broad lawmaking authority to administrative agencies under ambiguous standards.

Four chapters concern lawmaking through court adjudication. Chapter 9 presents the results of a statistical study of the patterns and actual outcomes of judicial review of federal administrative agency decisions, focusing on the lower courts' response to the U.S. Supreme Court's *Chevron* ruling, a landmark of contemporary administrative law. Chapter 10 examines the courts' role in regulating various aspects of the electoral process through constitutional adjudication. Chapter 11 traces and analyzes the emergence of the mass toxic tort case, a decidedly modern form of lawmaking that exhibits many features of public law litigation. Chapter 12 reviews an important empirical study that rejects the common notion that Supreme Court decisions in public law litigation are responsible for much social change.

Part III, the concluding essay (Chapter 13), is entitled "The Limits of Law." It distills, extends, and generalizes the main lessons of the preceding chapters. Combining a schematic, structural analysis of law with specific examples, I limn its characteristic shortcomings as an instrument of public policy. By stripping away the law's majestic veneer to reveal the prosaic machinery that lies beneath, I invite more realistic expectations of it. I then systematically compare law to social norms and economic markets, its main competitors in the ancient struggle to manage human affairs, analyzing the incentives that fuel each of them, as well as their economies of information, transaction costs, and moral legitimacy. The essay (and book) concludes by proposing some general principles that might help policymakers to exploit law's strengths while also relegating it to its proper place in the larger project of social governance.

This concluding essay is published here for the first time. The twelve other essays were written mainly for academic audiences in law and the social sciences over a period of almost two decades, many of them quite recently. I believe that even the oldest ones, however, remain salient to the continuing public debate over law's role in society. With the permission of the journals where they first appeared, I republish them here in essentially their original form, except for excised portions of the essays in Chapters 5, 6, and 9 in which most general readers would have little interest or that are duplicative. The original footnotes have been converted into endnotes. They have been numbered consecutively here even in Chapters 5 and 9; hence some of the cross-references in the endnotes for these chapters refer to notes that are not included here. Chapter 6 retains the original social science reference format.

I wish to acknowledge the generous support of the Yale Law School, my intellectual community for twenty years, of the New York Law School, my home away from home for the past three spring semesters, and of New York University Law School, which provided generous administrative support in the very final stages of this project. I am also grateful to Leo Wiegman, my editor at Westview Press.

I dedicate this book to Marcy, whose steadfast love, unlike law, knows no limits.

Note

1. Benjamin Highton & Raymond E. Wolfinger, The Political Implications of Higher Turnout (Institute of Governmental Studies Working Paper No. 99–5).

Part I
Constraints and Challenges

1

Legal Complexity

Some Causes, Consequences, and Cures

Introduction

Simplicity is a compelling virtue. Poets praise it.[1] Artists pursue it.[2] Moralists preach it.[3] Monastics live it.[4] Even today—*especially* today, as simplicity becomes more elusive—we more ordinary folk pay it at least verbal homage.

Scholars' views of simplicity are, well, more complex. On the one hand, simplicity cuts across our intellectual grain. We have a strong taste for complexity; indeed complexity amounts to a craft value—a point to which I shall return. On the other hand, scholars embrace simplicity (at least in its more sophisticated forms) out of professional ideology and custom. Recognizing that the cost of information is a crucial constraint on greater complexity, scholars view simplification as a necessary concession to our limited knowledge. This insight yields many fruitful implications.[5] Scholars perceive another of simplicity's virtues, this one at the meta-scientific level. There, the principle of Ockham's Razor asserts that simpler theories possess greater methodological, epistemological, and aesthetic elegance and value.[6]

I propose to explore complexity, simplicity's obverse—and more specifically, *legal* complexity. Of course, any attempt to analyze this subject systematically is fraught with difficulties. After all, legal complexity is hard to define, much less measure. It arises in a multitude of different contexts that may have little in common, contexts in which its meanings are likely to be different and its consequences not readily traceable. The task of distinguishing when it is a cause of some other condition from when it is an effect of some other cause, always difficult, is especially so because of complexity's frequent association with cognate concepts such as uncertainty. Even when its effects can be isolated, evaluating them is not a straightforward matter. In short, those who attempt to generalize about, and hence to simplify, a subject this subtle and intricate should reflect upon the words of the curmudgeonly Henry Adams,

3

who denounced simplicity as "the most deceitful mistress that ever betrayed man."[7]

For all its pitfalls, however, the effort to analyze legal complexity seems a worthy enterprise. This is certainly not because legal complexity is a new subject. In fact, it is an ancient concern,[8] one that has continued to obsess lawyers, policymakers, social critics, editorial writers, and men and women in the street, who almost invariably condemn legal complexity in the most caustic terms.[9] Yet despite the cascade of public and professional criticism, consideration of legal complexity in the academy is still in an embryonic stage; the subject remains more narrowly conceived than its importance warrants.

I define a legal system as complex to the extent that its rules, processes, institutions, and supporting culture possess four features: density, technicality, differentiation, and indeterminacy or uncertainty. I hasten to concede that one might well conceive and define it in other terms. An alternative and potentially useful definition, for example, might center on whether the people who are subjected to a legal rule, process, or institution perceive and experience it as complex, instead of on the objective qualities that a more detached viewer might ascribe to it (as my definition does).[10] Still, I suspect that the four qualities on which I focus capture most, if not all, of what people would mean if they were to think about legal complexity.

Density and technicality are chiefly aspects of the system's rules. *Dense* rules are numerous and encompassing. They occupy a large portion of the relevant policy space and seek to control a broad range of conduct, which causes them to collide and conflict with their animating policies with some frequency. An example of a dense legal regime is that governing pension administration,[11] which cuts across and seeks to integrate a wide variety of legal specialties.

Technical rules require special sophistication or expertise on the part of those who wish to understand and apply them. Technicality is a function of the fineness of the distinctions a rule makes, the specialized terminology it employs, and the refined substantive judgments it requires. The Internal Revenue Code[12] is probably the leading example of technical rules.

A legal system is *institutionally differentiated* insofar as it contains a number of decision structures that draw upon different sources of legitimacy, possess different kinds of organizational intelligence, and employ different decision processes for creating, elaborating, and applying the rules. Product safety, for example, is institutionally differentiated in that it is governed by statutory provisions, regulatory standards promulgated by several different agencies and private technical organizations, tort litigation, and common law contract principles.[13]

The final feature—*indeterminacy*—is a quality both of rules and of legal processes and institutions. Indeterminate rules, processes, and institutions are usually open-textured,[14] flexible, multi-factored, and fluid. The familiar reasonableness standard in tort law is an example of an indeterminate rule. Turning on diverse mixtures of fact and policy, indeterminate rules tend to be costly to apply and their outcomes are often hard to predict. Indeterminacy's relation to legal complexity is itself complex. Ironically, rules and institutions that are designed to reduce the law's indeterminacy may actually *increase* it, due to the cumulative effect of their density, technicality, and differentiation.[15] Indeterminacy, then, may be a consequence, as well as a defining feature, of complexity.

Although I have been discussing complexity as if it were a fixed essence, it is of course nothing of the sort. Indeed, I have just defined it as a composite of four variables. As such, it can only be located on a continuum ranging from extreme simplicity at one end to extreme complexity at the other. Thus a legal rule, process, or institution is neither simple nor complex; it is only more or less simple or complex compared to some other actual or ideal one. Complexity is multi-dimensional, and its dimensions cannot easily be measured, much less weighted. Hence it is neither possible nor desirable to attempt to classify something precisely as simple or complex. I shall therefore use the terms in a loose, relativistic sense, always assuming that other things remain equal. As long as my general analysis persuades, little should turn upon how any particular legal phenomenon is classified.[16]

Even so, some examples may help to sharpen the categories a bit. At the extremes, the rule that the President of the United States must be at least 35 years old[17] is simple, whereas the rule against perpetuities[18] is complex. Unlike the presidential age rule, the rule against perpetuities is embedded in a dense forest of norms, is notoriously indeterminate and highly technical (neither rule is institutionally differentiated). Moving away from the poles, tort law's reasonableness standard is moderately complex. Although neither dense nor technical, it is notably indeterminate, involving interaction among judge, jury, private groups, and often a legislature or agency. Precisely because contract rules generally seek to facilitate private choices, they tend to be fairly simple. Tax law, while including many bright-line rules, is quite complex; its rules are dense, technical, and elaborated through a differentiated system of agencies and tribunals.[19]

For all the broad-gauged interest in legal complexity, legal scholars have largely confined their analyses of this phenomenon to two aspects: (1) its transaction costs, including legal uncertainty; and (2) certain of its sources, especially litigation incentives, judicial decisions, and rule form.[20] These analyses are valuable and form the basis for much that follows; nevertheless, one is struck by their narrowness. Legal complexity, after all, has consequences that go well beyond transaction costs, and has sources besides litigation incentives and judicial lawmaking. Its forms, costs, structural causes, limits, and possible reform raise important social issues that need to be explored in greater depth and breadth.

My argument consists of four linked claims, which I develop and defend in turn in Parts I through IV. The first two claims—that legal complexity is increasing, and that this is problematic for a system of justice—are not, I think, particularly controversial. Of course, I can no more demonstrate the first (growing complexity) by merely citing examples than I can prove increased regulatory burdens by counting pages in the *Federal Register* (although many have purported to do so). Still, I hope in Part I to satisfy any doubters by showing that this trend appears in the forms, subject matter, goals, interpretation, and remedial structure of legal norms in a variety of areas.

My second claim, that complexity is problematic for a system of justice, will likewise command widespread agreement. Numerous commentators, for example, point to the administrative and transaction costs that complexity generates.[21] Although this point is correct as far as it goes, it deflects attention from two other kinds of complexity-induced problems, which I call *governance* and *delegitimation* costs. These have received much less attention, perhaps because they are less palpable and involve "softer" responses of a psychological and emotional nature; I seek to remedy this neglect in Part II.

My third claim speaks to the causes of legal complexity and is therefore more controversial. Scholars analyzing legal complexity have largely defined it in terms of uncertainty and other transaction costs, broadly defined.[22] According to them, much complexity originates in the ways in which litigation incentives and adjudication affect the form of rules. Although this approach seems correct as far as it goes, it ignores another important set of causes, which I call the "political economy of complexity." As discussed in Part III, this consists of the professional skills, career ambitions, and craft values that drive the dominant producers and rationalizers of law—here I refer not only to judges but also to legislators and their staffs, administrators, litigators, and legal scholars—to choose more, rather than less, legal complexity.

My final claim, presented in Part IV, is that the growing costs of legal complexity generate powerful behavioral responses in the direction of legal simplification[23]—first among private decisionmakers, then among public officials, and relatively late in the game, among legal scholars[24]—and that these responses can be used not only to define complexity's limits but also to deduce general principles for evaluating particular reform proposals. I conclude in Part V by identifying some specific simplification options that should be seriously considered.

An important caveat going to my normative argument is in order. As Henry Adams's epigram[25] and Jerry Brown's flat tax proposal remind us, simpler is not always better.[26] Legal complexity sometimes produces fairer, more refined, more efficient, even more certain, forms of social control.[27] The question always is: All things considered, are the benefits of a given level of complexity worth its costs? There is no general answer to this question, of course, and I do not seek to answer it for any particular legal phenomenon. By the same token, complexity should not be seen as a symbol of what is wrong with American law more generally. Indeed complexity is both a weakness and a strength. My goals, then, are more limited and theoretical: to enrich the discourse on complexity's causes and consequences, to suggest some possible cures, and to derive some criteria for knowing when to pursue simpler law.

This caveat—that simpler law is not always better law—is important because I shall say a great deal about complexity's *costs* but little about its *benefits*. I wish to be clear about this bias, lest it be misunderstood. It is purposeful; indeed it connects with my central point. Because the political economy of lawmaking presses the law toward greater complexity with little regard to whether any particular complexity is worth its costs, we end up with more complexity than we need (by some more objective account). This constitutes a kind of structural imbalance, which we can only hope to redress by urging the producers, rationalizers, and administrators of law to keep simplicity's more elusive virtues and complexity's corresponding vices constantly in mind.

I. The Growth in Legal Complexity

The legal system as a whole exhibits a marked tendency to become more complex, a feature that it appears to share with other systems, physical and social.[28] In the case of the law, this tendency is certainly not inexorable, as the replacement of writ pleading with much simpler code pleading and the replacement of tort law in the workplace with workers' compensation systems demonstrate.[29] Nor does complexity grow at the same rate and at the same time in all areas of the law.[30] Yet for all these qualifications, the strength and generality of this trend are striking. One can discern it *throughout* the legal system—in the form, subject matter, goals, interpretation, and remedial infrastructure of legal norms.

A. *The Form of Legal Norms*

Many legal norms evolved from relatively precise, acontextual, determinate, and hard-edged forms to relatively ambiguous, contextual, indeterminate, and open-ended ones. These two types of forms are sometimes referred to as rules and standards.[31] Rules are not always simple, and standards are not always complex, but these formal categories do describe paradigmatic, antipodal types. They express distinctive ways in which the law views, values, argues about, and influences the nature of social relationships. Further, these formal types affect substance, shaping both particular legal outcomes and the balance among competing social ideals and practices.

A movement from rules to more complex standards has been evident for some time. At the "meta-law" level, the evolution of legal norms from common law principles to statutes to administrative regulation, although animated in part by a quest for greater certainty, has only produced more open-ended complexity. Efforts to achieve greater certainty have generally failed, as the history of administrative law demonstrates. A generation of scholars, officials, and reformers urged that agencies make policy through rulemaking rather than the traditional case-by-case adjudication, in large part because of the greater certainty that rules were thought to afford. But in a longitudinal study of administrative law court decisions, Don Elliott and I found that during the last twenty years rulemaking made only minor inroads.[32] Indeed we found a *retreat* from rulemaking back to adjudication in several important policy sectors.[33]

The movement toward administrative rulemaking is intimately connected to the increased resort to administrative *discretion* as a dominant legal modality,[34] and the exercise of discretion in turn generates more legal complexity. Although the legal system employs many techniques to constrain and guide discretion—statutory language, judicial review, legislative oversight, public participation, and procedural requirements are examples—the pervasive delegation of discretion to agencies (and to courts) means that the resulting legal regime is almost certain to become more dense, technical, institutionally differentiated, and indeterminate than if the legislature had simply promulgated a rule itself. There are often compelling public interest reasons to confer discretion, even given the risk that it will sometimes be abused. Greater legal complexity, however, should be seen as one more consequence of doing so.

Even tort law, which is administered by courts rather than discretionary agencies and which has traditionally been one of the simpler legal specialties, has become more complex. Its relatively fixed rules—for example, the no-duty rule, the impact rule limiting emotional distress claims, the rule restricting recovery of lost profits—are steadily giving way to more indeterminate standards shaped by more differentiated institutions.[35] An especially striking example is found in the well-known *Tarasoff* case, in which the California Supreme Court, after imposing a specific duty to *warn* foreseeable victims, amended its opinion to substitute a duty to *exercise reasonable care* to protect them, a vaguer, more general duty that has spawned much confusion.[36] Another example from the same court is found in *Rowland v. Christian*,[37] in which the court jettisoned the ancient categorical rules governing the duties that landowners owe to those injured on their property, in favor of a general reasonableness standard applicable even to trespassers. Also, judicial recognition of relatively open-ended cancerphobia claims, traditionally dismissed as too speculative, is now widespread.[38]

This discussion of legal forms is not meant to suggest that they have moved in only one direction, from simple rules to more complex standards. Some notable and interesting counter-examples exist. Consider the Federal Sentencing Guidelines, which established a generally binding grid for judges' sentencing decisions.[39] Albert Alschuler and others have criticized this reform as a misguided attempt to achieve some of the virtues of clear, simple rules, especially horizontal equity, by reducing the largely standardless discretion that sentencing judges previously enjoyed. To Alschuler, the Guidelines are characteristic of a more general style of contemporary legal thought in which numerous cases are aggregated and treated uniformly despite their real differences.[40] Other instances of simplification-through-aggregation can also be cited.[41] Still, the dominant trend is toward legal forms that create more discretion and complexity, not less.

B. The Subject Matter of Legal Norms

The administrative state grew out of the effort to regulate areas of activity previously governed primarily by informal or contractual norms, and other areas previously regulated at lower levels of intensity or lower levels of government. It elaborated new bodies of law bearing all of complexity's hallmarks. Dense norms occupied much of the field of activity. Regulatory law also brought more technicality; specialized lawyering became so essential that the profession had to reorganize along new lines. New institutions—highly differentiated agencies and the diverse structures to which they give rise[42]—proliferated. Meant to increase certainty, regulation actually reduced it on balance because of its greater ambition and its preservation of much of the common law regime.

Two examples will suffice to illustrate the point. Before *Baker v. Carr*[43] and the Voting Rights Act of 1965,[44] the federal law of voting rights was relatively simple, concerned largely with reapportionment, fraud, and egregious forms of intentional racial discrimination. Today, however, this body of law also involves the detailed federal regulation and review of thousands of state and local election laws involving structures of representation, voting rules, annexations, municipal finance, and the allocation of legislative business.[45] Bewilderingly complex law penetrates even private law fields. Employment and employee benefits law, for example, is now a dense mixture of private contracting, common law adjudication, statutory norms, detailed agency regulation, and informal control through legislative oversight.[46]

C. The Goals of Legal Norms

Before the age of statutes,[47] the administrative state, and an avowedly policymaking judiciary, the policy ends invoked by American lawmakers were generally modest. Legislatures' principal goals were to facilitate private ordering and to establish public policies to buttress that system,[48] while common law courts usually hewed to a formalistic conception of judging that emphasized (at least at the level of judicial rhetoric) a fidelity to *stare decisis* and legislative intent, rather than articulated an instrumentalist stance.[49]

The New Deal changed all that, and the change it wrought accelerated in the decades that followed. New legislative goals, largely implemented by administrative agencies, included health and safety, equal opportunity, income redistribution, financial security for the elderly, stabilization of markets, development of infrastructure, governmental reform, and many more. This transformation of public and private law invited judges to abandon even the pretense of formalism.[50] Spurred on by many legal scholars,[51] they openly embraced a conception of role, a style of thought, and a rhetoric of decision that legitimated judicial policymaking in a variety of areas.

Once judges adopted an explicitly policy-oriented style, the more complex character of their new course quickly became clear. Leaving the familiar, secure terrain of formalism for the more exhilarating but perilous realm of policy-making, a larger number of decision-relevant goals came into view. This multiplicity of goals necessitated new legal doctrines capable of encompassing and harmonizing them. In tort law, for example, the courts pursued cost-internalizing and loss-spreading goals, "inventing" the doctrine of enterprise liability in the process.[52]

The same imperatives led courts in both private and public law to adopt certain common decision methodologies that vastly complexify the system. Important examples include interest-balancing,[53] sequential burden-shifting,[54] and broad but incomplete, spasmodic deference to other institutions.[55] By requiring judges to balance numerous diverse, and inevitably conflicting, policy goals, these doctrines are bound to be both technical and indeterminate. Institutional differentiation only magnifies this complexity, for the doctrines must be applied by agencies to whom the courts accord ill-defined deference and with whom they share adjudicatory power.

D. The Interpretation of Legal Norms

The interpretation of legal texts is an ancient problem, as the Talmud vividly demonstrates. Still, today's Babel-like cacophony of legal hermeneutics is unprecedented. For whatever reason—the influence of post-modernist literary theories on legal thought,[56] the related emphasis on interpreting norms contextually, the triumph of realism and instrumentalism over formalism in law, a more general delegitimation of traditional sources of authority—a plethora of competing approaches has thrown the field open.[57] No clear winner is likely to emerge anytime soon. Meanwhile, the technicality and indeterminacy of statutory norms grows.

An example of this growth is the fate of post-*Chevron*[58] judicial review of statutory interpretations by administrative agencies, one of the three principal pillars of the "new textualism."[59] In *Chevron*, the Supreme Court promulgated a two-part test for judicial review of agency interpretations of statutes,[60] an approach that sought to render administrative law more simple and certain by constraining the interpretive freedom of lower courts. But less than a decade later, the doctrine's growing complexity has already undermined that purpose. Contrary to *Chevron's* intention, the rate at which the D.C. Circuit overturned agency interpretations actually rose in the years immediately following the decision;[61] and even the Supreme Court has been unable to apply its own test consistently.[62]

E. The Remedial Infrastructure of Legal Norms

Legal norms are supported and vivified by an adversary process, a court system, and an enforcement apparatus which have grown more complex with the emergence of mass litigation, a bureaucratized judiciary, and highly differentiated remedies. The remedial system, for example, is now redundant in many respects. This redundancy can be seen in the increasing overlap between tort and contract, tort and workers' compensation, and public and private enforcement mechanisms.

Tort adjudication tends to be more complex than contract adjudication involving similar parties and subject matter.[63] Yet courts increasingly recognize tort causes of action for losses that traditionally sounded only in contract, and that are *still* remediable in contract—product liability[64] and liability for pure economic loss are examples.[65]

Similarly, tort litigation over injuries already covered by workers' compensation systems continues, despite the fact that workers' compensation systems are supposed to produce simpler, swifter, and more certain compensation for workplace injuries.[66] The result is an immensely complex hybrid claiming system.[67]

The complex mixture of public and private enforcement is exemplified by our environmental protection system. An intricate system, it is replicated at three levels of government. At each level, it combines officially enforced criminal sanctions, civil penalties, and administrative actions with privately enforced remedies against enforcement officials as well as polluters.

II. The Problematics of Legal Complexity

Should we view legal complexity as a problem? If we suppose that legal rules are largely epiphenomenal, reflecting the underlying social conditions to which they relate, then we might want law's complexity to keep pace with society's. Social complexity is growing remorselessly. Interdependencies increase. Cultures and markets fragment. Values and technologies change. Bureaucracies expand. Under these conditions, a denser, more intricate legal system may be both inevitable and desirable.

This is true, I believe, but only up to a point. A more complex law entails many significant transaction costs which must be accounted for. Such law tends to be more costly and cumbersome to administer, more difficult for lawmakers to formulate and agree upon, and more difficult to reform once established. Administrators and subjects of such law must invest more in order to learn what it means, when and how it applies,[68] and whether the costs of complying with it are worth incurring. Other costs of administering a complex legal system include those related to bargaining about and around the system's rules and litigating over them.[69]

Thus, legal complexity magnifies transaction costs by generating uncertainty.[70] Although complexity does not alone generate all of the costs—some would exist even in a simple legal system with simple rules[71]—it is clearly an important source of them. Just *how* costly legal complexity is depends in part upon our incentives and our capacities to comply, which are in turn shaped by our values, intelligence, technology, and social control mechanisms.

Complexity-induced costs can be both inefficient and unfair. In fields as diverse as agency regulation, trusts and estates, and torts, complexity can inhibit beneficial transactions, impose dead-weight losses, create frustrating delays, consume the energies of talented individuals, breed new and difficult-to-resolve disputes, and discourage compliance.[72] Promoting passivity and entrenching the status quo, legal complexity can stultify a society that often depends on vigorous action in solving problems.[73] Complexity's costs, moreover, impose disproportionate burdens on the poor by raising prices and necessitating the services of lawyers and other professionals trained in the management of complexity.[74]

Complexity alters our incentives and tests our capacities, straining their limits. But complexity increases while the constraints on our capacities—especially social values and intelligence—are relatively fixed, at least in the short run. At some point, complexity's demands are bound to outstrip our capacities to manage it, creating a gap between them; and unless the forces propelling complexity can somehow be reversed, this gap will widen.

Transaction costs generally, including those associated with complexity, have received much scholarly analysis—and for good reason. Like friction in mechanics, they are ubiquitous and limit the system's performance. But scholars have paid less attention to two other kinds of complexity-induced costs, which I shall emphasize here. *Governance costs* arise from the need to formulate and gain agreement on complex rules. *Delegitimation costs* occur when rules become so complex that their intelligibility and legitimacy decline.[75]

A. Governance Costs

When a rule must be agreed upon by a number of rulemakers, its formulation entails costs; the more numerous those whose assents are necessary, the more costly the agreement will be.[76] A legal system that is complex in any of the senses I have defined will multiply these governance costs.

Guido Calabresi's image of a legal landscape constituted by the existing rules and practices[77] helps to show why. As the body of rules grows more dense, the legal landscape becomes more thickly populated and harder to traverse. Concealed declivities, sudden detours, arterial congestion, unexpected cul-de-sacs, puzzling signs, and jarring encounters abound. Because integrating new rules with existing ones becomes tricky and dangerous, the system must develop another layer of meaning: rules about rules.[78] In this locale, it is no longer enough to know one's location and destination; one cannot survive without a great deal of local knowledge about when the buses run, whether cabs will venture into certain neighborhoods, which vendors are trustworthy, and where it is safe to walk. People with a choice do not venture out unattended. Experienced guides equipped with maps and special know-how are essential, for only the initiated can lead a newcomer through the honeycomb of enclaves, each with its local patois, exotic cuisine, peculiar customs, and belligerent pride.[79]

A legal landscape this complex engenders several kinds of governance costs that have generally been overlooked. First, those who make legal rules become more risk averse. Even fervent reformers hesitate to alter a landscape that is so hard to read; they know that in a more polycentric legal world, any change will have ripple effects, ramifying widely, swiftly, and unpredictably throughout the system's web.[80] When the risks of error are magnified, rulemakers are more likely to adhere to even an unsatisfactory status quo.[81] This increased risk aversion surely contributes to the bleak policymaking deadlock, the sense of drift, that exists today in so many policy fields.

Institutional differentiation spawns legal indeterminacy, another governance cost. The proliferation of policymaking institutions multiplies the sources of innovation, information, and legitimacy—precious resources in any social system. On the other hand, this diversity also encourages conflict and raises decision costs.[82] The only way to reach agreement among institutions may be to adopt open-ended, multi-factored or otherwise indeterminate legal standards. These standards do not really reduce conflict but simply use delegated authority to move the policy conflict from one rulemaking locus to others, usually agencies and courts.[83]

Delegated standards thus increase the delegate's cost of decision, especially if it is itself a collegial or otherwise differentiated body. Judge Patricia Wald of the District of Columbia Circuit recently underscored this point when she defended the concededly problematic *Chevron* test to those who would prefer a more refined, complex standard:

> Judges of radically different political and social viewpoints can only reason together on the basis of a few relatively simple propositions that they can all agree govern, so that disputes can be narrowly focused on their application. The *Chevron* decision, warts and all, has accomplished this. . . . Were we to switch to a broader framework of what is good regulatory policy or which of thirty canons apply, our debates would be less focused, our work would be more complex, and our differences would more frequently prove irreconcilable. A simple decisional framework may be essential to collegial decisionmaking in a court of widely differing views.[84]

B. Delegitimation Costs

I have been discussing costs of legal complexity borne in the first instance by those who must administer the system.[85] But if the complex legal landscape contains many pitfalls for the governors, it is *terra incognita* for the governed. In a society that values negative liberty[86] and personal "space," the density of the legal system—the penetration of law into every corner of human life, or what has been called "hyperlexis"[87]—is bound to be a source of deep resentment.[88] When rules are indeterminate, their precise meanings cannot be easily grasped, nor can their applications be readily predicted. Confusion and uncertainty follow. If the rules are technical, they will often be opaque to the common mind, common sense, common experience, and even common morality.[89]

Intelligible only to experts, the law is likely to mystify and alienate lay citizens whose intelligence it often seems designed to mock. When this Delphic law also emerges from an institutional black box that is itself dense and difficult to comprehend, its legitimacy—the sense of "oughtness" that the lawmakers hope will attach to it—is diminished.

The fact that these characteristics of the complex legal regime seem to be objective may for a time earn it acquiescence, even support. But as we shall see, complexity is not neutral in its effects; it advantages some groups and disadvantages others,[90] a fact that is well understood by those who seek to influence the shape of the law. Once citizens begin to suspect that these advantages and disadvantages are unfairly, rather than randomly, distributed, and that this distribution is purposeful rather than adventitious, they will come to view complexity in an altogether different, less tolerant light. Profound cynicism about and alienation from the legal system may result.

One cannot measure these delegitimation costs directly, of course, much less know the extent to which legal complexity is their cause. Historical studies indicate that popular disgust with legal complexity and a quest for simplification was an important factor leading to the adoption of code pleading in this country.[91] This successful reform of the formal law—what John Langbein calls "legal implosion"—is surely exceptional. More commonly, I suspect, the public suffers excessive complexity in silence, responds with informal simplifications,[92] or simply fails to comply.

The literature reveals remarkably little empirical inquiry into the link between complexity and noncompliance. Our ignorance extends even to the tax field, where understanding this relationship is an important policy priority.[93] There is evidence, however, that these delegitimation costs are great. Taxpayers bewildered by tax law's complexity and uncertainty appear more likely to violate it.[94] Voluntary compliance, so critical to the tax law's integrity, depends upon its intelligibility. "Erosion of taxpayer morale," James Eustice observes, "is not an unimportant side effect of all this confusion—if taxpayers think the whole system is unknowable, the temptation to use self help to fashion their own private tax shelters becomes well nigh irresistible."[95]

There is ample evidence of delegitimation costs in fields other than tax. A Rand study of corporate responses to modern product liability law, for example, found that the law emitted such noisy, random, and confusing signals to manufacturers that it had little effect on the product design decisions it was supposed to influence.[96] New York's hypertechnical signature and petition requirements nearly kept Paul Tsongas, a genuine presidential contender, off the primary ballot, a result that was averted, ironically, only by invoking another technicality.[97] Recently, in some Latin American societies, legal complexity has helped to produce an immense illegal sector.[98] In the United States, complexity has helped to delay, and in some cases defeat, the implementation of many important regulatory statutes.[99]

Again, however, these weighty objections to complexity would not necessarily be decisive in any particular situation. A simpler regime, after all, might be even worse. I underscore the disadvantages of complexity here only because the rulemaking process systematically obscures them.

III. The Political Economy of Legal Complexity

Legal complexity clearly has many causes. The economy has grown larger and more interdependent. The social conditions that the law seeks to regulate have grown more difficult to understand and control. Higher levels of education and professionalism have increased the public's taste and tolerance for complexity in all social institutions, including the legal system. All of the components of the legal world—law, lawyers, litigation, legal commentary, legal techniques, problems deemed fit for legal regulation—have expanded enormously.[100]

One must not assume, however, that more social complexity leads inexorably to more legal complexity. The two are closely related, of course, but one does not always follow from the other. Complexity, like most other things, is subject to the law of diminishing returns. Social actors manifestly understand this. Research in experimental psychology and organizational behavior indicates that they radically simplify their complex decision environments in order to make them manageable, and that this strategy is both rational and typical.[101] Instances abound in which legal simplification seems the best, or at the least a plausible, response to social complexity. I discuss some of these examples in Part IV.

Beyond a certain point, then, legal complexity is simply not preordained by social complexity. In a real sense, we choose it. Why and in what sense do we choose it? One can argue that the social choice for complexity is not a conscious one. In this "external rationality" account, legal complexity is not so much the goal of any individual actor's choice as it is the indirect consequence of a multitude of decisions made on other grounds, such as a desire to address a new condition or to accommodate a hard case. These decisions then combine to yield a complexity that survives because individual actors lack the incentive to change it. This external rationality story surely explains a good deal of legal complexity.

I wish to offer a different account—one of *internal* rationality. In this story, the main producers, rationalizers, and administrators of law—legislators and their staff, bureaucrats, litigants, lawyers, judges, and legal scholars—generally benefit from legal complexity while bearing few of its costs.[102] On balance, they prefer a complex system and hence choose rules and institutions that tend to support and perpetuate it. This is not to deny that an aroused public opinion can occasionally be mobilized to demand greater legal simplicity, and that this demand may sometimes carry the day, as the code pleading movement did in the nineteenth century. It is to claim, rather, that the burden of political inertia usually ensures legal complexity's triumph.

I noted earlier that the benefits and costs of complexity are not evenly distributed and that this uneven distribution is hardly an accident. Political actors understand this fact and seek to exploit it, even if they cannot always precisely gauge the relevant magnitudes and distributions.[103] The beneficiaries of complexity are many. They include groups that are relatively well equipped to cope with complexity and for whom complexity can create a competitive advantage outweighing its costs, groups that complexity insulates from public accountability, and groups that supply the services that complexity renders valuable. I shall specifically discuss these groups in a moment.

Those who ultimately bear complexity's costs, of course, are even more numerous. These cost bearers have an incentive to press politicians and other law producers to simplify the rules of the game—but they constitute an exceedingly diffuse group. Free rider and other obstacles to political organizing will likely dissipate most of their energies and pressures.

Only those cost bearers with the most at stake—insurers and other institutional litigators, narrowly focused regulated interests, and the like—are left to demand simplification, yet they labor under a serious political disadvantage. Given their obvious economic stakes in underlying substantive issues (say, mass tort claims or natural gas prices), political opponents can easily stigmatize their complaints about complexity as self-serving and pretextuous. Complaints about complexity will seem especially disingenuous in a political ethos like ours that increasingly demands disinterested, public interest arguments for policy change.[104] In contrast to the cost bearers, the beneficiaries of complexity can drape themselves in lofty public interest goals, such as securing the individual's right to a day in court, preventing the shrewd from circumventing the law, and heading off problems before they arise.

Thus, the political economy of legal complexity contains some structural elements favoring its survival and flourishing. When the interests of law producers are added to the equation, one can readily predict that many worthy simplification reforms will die on the vine and that others will succeed only if they happen to coincide with the interests of politically powerful groups or with the government's own fiscal stakes.[105]

Legislators and Their Staff. Legislators might prefer legal complexity for four self-interested, electorally related reasons. Complexity can help them to (1) confer divisible policy benefits on constituents; (2) confer divisible non-policy benefits; (3) enhance their power over bureaucrats; and (4) ease the legislature's collective action problem.

Complex statutes enable legislators to create private goods, conferring divisible policy benefits on one or a few groups without having to confer them on all. Legislators who wish to target a statutory policy to favor (or disfavor) particular interests can employ a number of complexifying techniques. For example, they can multiply and refine policy categories, classify groups, and establish new institutional power centers. In these ways, they can hope to calibrate their political support, achieving a level of control that simpler, less discriminating statutes do not usually permit. Complexity can also help to obfuscate certain political goals (such as wealth redistribution) that would invite opposition to policies that seemed to implicate them. Tax legislation is notorious for this.[106] Recent immigration legislation accomplished a similar sleight-of-hand. Without quite naming the Irish, the statute created a special new preference for them and concealed it in a remarkably complex and opaque formula.[107]

In addition to (or instead of) targeting policies at particular constituencies, complex laws also create opportunities for legislators to engage in targeted intervention at the law application stage. This "casework" with the relevant bureaucracy permits legislators to confer highly visible, selective benefits on favored constituents without limiting their own freedom of action on larger, politically riskier policy issues. Legislators can, for example, oppose a new benefits policy yet intervene on behalf of constituents later on when the agency denies their claims. Indeed, a prominent political scientist has argued that legislators create complex new programs and bureaucracies in part *so that* they can intervene selectively later on when problems materialize.[108]

Complex laws also enable legislators to exercise influence over the personnel, policies, and budgets of the agencies and the programs that they create.[109] Such influence is politically valuable in itself, and is also essential in assuring bureaucratic compliance. The potential for this influence provides a powerful motive for legislators to enact complex statutes, and also explains much of their post-enactment activity.[110]

Legal complexity can help legislators avoid collective action problems that a simpler law might well exacerbate. Legislators who wish to reduce conflict, minimize rulemaking costs, and reach consensus in the face of their strong incentives to behave opportunistically often resort to complex legislative forms. Examples include logrolls, omnibus bills, ambiguous provisions, and delegation of rulemaking authority to other more specialized institutions.[111] Ironically, then, legal complexity can help to solve politicians' problems by creating new problems for their constituents.

A final consideration concerns legislators' staff aides. In recent decades, their number has increased dramatically.[112] This growth, coupled with other changes in legislative operations at all levels of government, has led to staff dominance of much of the legislative process and output.[113] Although their incentives largely parallel those of their elected employers, staff members also have strong personal, professional, and careerist reasons to draft more complex bills. Complex legislation enables staff members to enlarge and exhibit their professional and technical expertise, deepens legislators' dependency on their advice, magnifies their influence over policy and administration, and enhances their personal satisfaction and career prospects.[114]

Perhaps the most revealing evidence of the legislative impulse toward complexity is its ability to prevail even when a constituency for simplification exists and public pressures for reform are strong. The Tax Reform Act of 1986,[115] which was sold to the public as a simplification measure, has actually increased the law's complexity in important respects.[116] This outcome is not as paradoxical or unusual as it might seem. Politics, fairness, and economic efficiency often require policymakers to adopt grandfather rules, side payments, subsidies, and other transitional and compensatory mechanisms in order to move from a complex regime to a simpler one.[117]

Bureaucrats.   For somewhat different reasons, agency officials possess strong incentives to elaborate legal networks that meet all of my complexity criteria.[118] By filling most of the relevant policy space with rules, agencies constrain the ability of regulatees to either elude agency jurisdiction or circumvent agency standards. Dense rules are designed to foreclose such tactics. Indeterminate rules also serve important bureaucratic interests. Although costlier for agencies to apply and for regulatees to apprehend, they nevertheless possess a virtue that often proves decisive: they preserve agencies' future freedom of action in policy environments dominated by uncertainty and the need for flexibility.[119]

Agencies need no special incentives to elaborate technical rules; the nature of their tasks ordinarily ensures that their rules will usually be intelligible only to cognoscenti in the field. In addition, technical rules promote agency autonomy.[120] Being more opaque to the generalist institutions like Congress and the media that seek to influence it, such rules make agencies more difficult to control and help obscure their pursuit of controversial policies. The same is true of complex procedures that make agency decisions more costly to challenge. Finally, agencies are not merely instances of institutional differentiation; they are also causes of it. Their endemic need to mobilize outside information and political support prompts them to proliferate new entities: coordinating mechanisms, advisory committees, administrative review panels, technical support groups, intergovernmental bodies, a specialized bar, a specialized press, and many others.[121] These entities then take on lives of their own, which interact with agency activities to promote additional complexity.

These agency interests in complexity are mirrored in the interests of some of those in the private bureaucracies that agencies regulate. For every new regulatory program or legal complexity, there is a set of corporate officials whose jobs and occupational advancement depend upon understanding, complying with, and managing it.[122] This cohort does not ordinarily dominate a company's decisionmaking process; but it does act as a kind of pro-complexity Trojan Horse inside the corporate structure, weakening somewhat management's more reflexive, cost-conscious resistance to complexity.

Litigants, Lawyers, and Judges.   As noted earlier, the question of how the litigation process shapes legal rules has received considerable scholarly attention.[123] Indeed, of all the causes of legal complexity, litigation dynamics appears to be the only one that *has been* analyzed systematically.

Some scholars, like Jason Johnston and Carol Rose, argue that incentives endogenous to the litigation process generate a pattern of perpetual oscillation between bright-line and open-ended rule forms.[124] Others, however, discern an inexorable trend toward indeterminacy. Priest and Klein, for example, show that disputes turning on determinate rules will be settled rather than litigated (regardless of their content), which assures that the rules litigants bring to court are at the indeterminate end of the spectrum.[125] Making a related point, Anthony D'Amato argues that because a rule is easier to challenge than to defend, and a rule that disadvantages tends to invite challenge, the resulting litigation systematically favors the evolution of more indeterminate rules.[126] Henderson and Eisenberg also claim that indeterminate rules tend to favor plaintiffs, but for different reasons. They emphasize that such rules, by creating jury questions, enhance the settlement value of plaintiffs' claims, and that this trend is a one-way ratchet: courts, having adopted indeterminate rules, find it hard to go back to more precise ones.[127] Richard Epstein likewise sees a firm trend toward indeterminacy, but ascribes it to the incentives of lawyers, who seek to maximize demand for their services by promoting more complex rules that invite expert interpretation and manipulation.[128] Michelle White argues that tax lawyers, like tax accountants and the Internal Revenue Service, have vested interests in a complex tax law, although each group favors a different level of complexity.[129] Boris Bittker suggests that since tax experts' analytical and critical skills account for much of the law's complexity, they cannot be expected to make it simpler and more enforceable.[130]

Some litigation models view judges as merely ratifying the moves of the parties and their lawyers, whereas other models ascribe greater importance to judges' own goals and their discretion to pursue them.[131] I endorse the latter, having suggested elsewhere that the jury reduces the cost to judges of innovating—of rejecting, refining, or distinguishing precedent. With a jury, judges can innovate secure in the knowledge that it will be up to anonymous jurors to determine the concrete meaning and consequences of the change.[132] Judicial innovations tend to make the law more complex,[133] although there are certainly exceptions.[134] Some judicial innovations are dictated by traditional criteria, but many others reflect different motives. The judge may wish to reduce her boredom, call attention to herself in order to attract support from special interests,[135] or burnish her reputation for creativity, independence, and professional skill with lawyers, academics, journalists, and other court-watchers. Doctrinal innovations, moreover, are also likely to enhance what D'Amato has called the "information value" of a decision.[136]

Although the interests favoring complexity are systematic and powerful, they are not monolithic. Some litigants, lawyers, and judges do have countervailing interests in promoting simpler law, at least some of the time. Because litigants bear many of the costs of a complex adjudication process, some of them will be disadvantaged by complex substantive rules—although it must be added that most clients play little or no role in the formulation of legal arguments.[137] Contingency fee lawyers, who must bear most of the costs of litigating under complex rules and procedures, may prefer simplicity out of narrow self-interest.[138] Even lawyers who would benefit financially from a more complex law may nevertheless support simplification reforms for public interest reasons.[139] As for judges, simple rules are easier to administer and generate fewer disputes, an important consideration for overwhelmed courts.

My claim, then, is not that the interests of litigants, lawyers, and judges in legal complexity are invariably and unalterably opposed to greater simplicity in law. It is only that these interests tend to predominate, and that this fact is an important reason for the growth in legal complexity.

Legal Scholars. Like other denizens of the legal culture, but for altogether different reasons, legal scholars are drawn to legal complexity. Earlier, I called it a craft value. Like our competing attraction to elegantly simple theories, complexity is aesthetically pleasing. We delight in stories that are richer, more encompassing, and more satisfying than simplicity generally permits. This taste, moreover, is not merely aesthetic. It also reflects a uniquely scholarly commitment, which views and seeks to understand reality as an intricate array of fields on which congeries of forces interact in hard-to-predict ways. This commitment, as much as anything else, distinguishes scholars from other well-educated, sophisticated folks.[140]

There are reasons to think that this distinctive scholarly commitment to complexity, always great, is growing apace in the law schools. Creativity—the discovery of new information, the elaboration and testing of novel hypotheses, and the subversion of traditional paradigms—is the supreme academic virtue, the stuff of which Nobel laureates, scholarly superstars, and distinguished university departments are made. Perhaps because legal scholars are generally less interested than their natural and behavioral science colleagues in discovering new data and testing theories,[141] they have been that much busier seeking to elaborate novel theories and subvert traditional paradigms.

Three "schools" of legal theory have dominated recent legal scholarship, although they do not begin to exhaust the set of approaches to legal analysis. These schools—legal process/judicial policymaking, Critical Legal Studies (CLS), and law and economics—occupy the academy's ideological center, left, and right, respectively.[142] No general characterization of these schools can fully capture the diversity and nuanced positions within them. Still, a common theme is that their approaches, if seriously pursued, would tend to make the law more complex. This tendency I believe reflects more the logic of the scholars' theories than any normative commitment on their part to legal complexity *per se.* I now turn to a discussion of this tendency.

The "new" legal process/judicial policymaking scholars, of whom John Hart Ely is perhaps the exemplar in public law, stress the need to maintain the integrity of the lawmaking process through three principal norms. First, different institutions have distinctive roles to play in the legal system, roles derived from the institutions' particular legitimating forms and norms and technocratic capacities. Second, these institutions should employ utilitarian, instrumental rationality methodologies in their interpretation of legal materials. Finally, the acid test of the law's integrity, and the source of its legitimacy, is procedural regularity.[143]

Taken seriously and taken together, these three norms—institutional competence, purposivism, and proceduralism—militate in favor of greater legal complexity. The *institutional competence* norm implies differentiation in decisionmaking institutions. It dictates that legislatures make social policy judgments, courts interpret and apply the law, juries find facts, agencies apply technical expertise, private interests order their relationships in the shadow of law, and so on. The *purposivism* norm implies that the law will be interpreted to further multiply, often conflicting policy goals. The *proceduralism* norm implies that legal rights will be surrounded by extensive process safeguards. Purposivism and proceduralism will generate (in my terms) dense, indeterminate rules.

CLS scholarship rejects the formalistic premises of the legal process school, emphasizing instead the importance of law's subjectivity, contextuality, and indeterminacy.[144] In this view, conditions that putatively simple rules treat as objective and determinate are actually social constructions privileging certain perspectives and groups, constructions that do not exist apart from the interpreter's subjectivity. CLS scholars maintain that rules, like all texts, are inherently ambiguous, contextual, and manipulable.[145] The legal system that they constitute, being wholly epiphenomenal, reflects and advances the interests of the already powerful. In these related senses, then, *all* legal rules and systems are, and must be, complex, and the mystification induced by the law's complexity can be used to secure a kind of passive acquiescence in—a bogus legitimation of—the system.

Law and economics scholars are more ambivalent about legal complexity than are scholars from the other two schools. On the one hand, perhaps the most valuable contribution of law and economics to the analysis of law is its systematic attention to the costs of legal complexity as it affects efficiency.[146] Efficiency requires minimizing the transaction costs that complexity generates, as well as minimizing the efficiency-distorting practices that complexity may facilitate, such as the strategic use of legal procedures, rent-seeking rules, and uncertainty itself.[147]

On the other hand, any serious pursuit of efficiency (not to speak of equity) will often require complex rules. After all, the goals and constraints relevant to a given policy are likely to be numerous, and the legal rules, in order to be efficient, must take account of, and be tailored to, each of them. Accomplishing this may necessitate a system of multi-factored rules, multiple defenses, complex party structures, sequential burden-shifting, and so on. In their quest for elegantly simple theories, even the best law and economics scholars sometimes overlook the complexity of efficiency. Richard Posner's insistence that the common law contributory negligence rule is efficient is perhaps the clearest example of this error.[148] In fact, efficient deterrence requires a well-calibrated comparative fault system, often long causal chains, new damage categories, and rules that are sensitive to risk preference and insurance market factors. No simple rule or set of rules can satisfy all of these constraints.

The fact that legal scholars tend to prefer complexity says nothing, of course, about the extent to which this preference actually affects the law. Indeed if the law schools are as increasingly isolated from the legal profession and hence from the rest of society as some have claimed,[149] scholars' influence may be negligible. Nevertheless, courts' growing reliance upon recent law school graduates as judicial clerks, coupled with their growing reliance upon academic scholarship (and a more theoretical scholarship at that),[150] assures that scholars' theories—and their proclivities for complexity—will continue to influence the law's direction.

Let me be clear that my explanation accepts the claim that genuine public interest concerns may demand complexity. It may be, for example, that a simple rule in a given situation would require too many exceptions or be evaded too easily. I also recognize that legal actors who prefer legal complexity *on balance* may nonetheless feel countervailing pressures for simplicity. This is especially true of bureaucrats and others who must administer law in the face of complexity's costs. Moreover, as my external rationality theory[151] posits, legal actors may not always (or even usually) think in such explicit terms about the choice for or against complexity. Finally, my internal rationality story[152] is neither better than nor inconsistent with either an external rationality account or the significantly narrower internal rationality accounts favored by some law and economics scholars, which stress how litigation incentives shape law into more complex forms. Given our ignorance about the precise causes of legal complexity, *all* of these stories are plausible. Those who would reduce that ignorance need all the help we can get.

My claim, then, is a modest one, albeit far-reaching in its implications for reform. It is that the influentials who systematically shape the legal and political processes have strong personal, professional, and ideological interests in legal complexity that are often effective in securing these interests in the formal law.

IV. The Limits of Legal Complexity

I have argued that the forces favoring legal complexity are broadly based, powerful, and systemic. Does this mean that the law will continue to move inexorably along this path, becoming ever more dense, indeterminate, technical, and institutionally differentiated? The answer, clearly, is "no." In nature, the momentum of objects in motion is limited by friction and gravity. In politics, the momentum of triumphant forces is limited by events, organizational dynamics, competition, and new ideas. In the legal system, the momentum of complexity is limited by the responses to complexity's rising costs by those who bear them.

Still, these costs are not always immediately apparent, and those benefited by complexity have strong incentives to employ rhetorical and political tactics to conceal, disguise, or reconceive them. The costs may be rationalized in terms of some transcendent ideal,[153] or even depicted as benefits.[154] The policy-making process, moreover, tends to increase complexity. Officials often misdiagnose problems and adopt operationally complex reforms. The response to many regulatory failures—natural gas price controls, for example—is more extensive regulation rather than reconsideration of the underlying regulatory strategies.[155] The enormous costs of mass tort litigation have led to procedural fixes such as consolidated trials and class actions which only generate new uncertainties, legal challenges, delays, and unfairness.[156]

Complexity's costs, then, can be ignored, rationalized, and multiplied for a time, perhaps for a long time. Eventually, however, they become insupportable. The political momentum and behavioral incentives reach a critical juncture; countervailing pressures for simplification begin to affect both the law and how people respond to the law. I believe that we have reached that point. Many producers and consumers of the law now act as if the returns to complexity were diminishing. They are devising strategies to contain, circumvent, and turn complexity to their own advantage.[157]

The reaction against legal complexity proceeds in two domains, at different tempos. My discussion of its political economy[158] indicated that in the public sphere of formal law, the forces favoring complexity control the relevant processes and norms and usually overwhelm the simplifiers. In the informal domain, however, the responses to complexity need not be mediated by or effectuated through politics or formal legal changes. Instead, they can seek to avoid or reduce these costs through informal simplifications of various kinds. We can distinguish at least three informal strategies: contract, unilateral simplification, and withdrawal.

Contract.   Cost bearers often circumvent legal complexity by contracting around it, agreeing with others who also stand to benefit from a less complex system to substitute and be bound by a new, simpler regime. There are many familiar examples of this simplification strategy. Disputants agree to use arbitration, mediation, or other alternative dispute resolution approaches that they regard as less costly than litigation.[159] Contracts specify a particular choice-of-law rule, measure of damages, or liability standard, rather than leaving such issues to a court and jury. Jeffrey O'Connell's various "neo no-fault" proposals employ this approach.[160] So does negotiated rulemaking, a form of regulatory proceeding in which participants attempt to reach a consensus, including an agreement not to challenge the negotiated rule in court.[161]

Unilateral Simplification.   Instead of contracting around complexity, cost bearers may act unilaterally, substituting their own, simpler set of practices for the more burdensome ones that the law prescribes. H. Laurence Ross's study of insurance adjustment practices showed that insurers followed adjustment decision patterns that deviated markedly—and invariably in the direction of greater simplicity—from the formal rules and procedures dictated by the tort system and by insurance contracts.[162] Robert Ellickson's recent study of dispute settlement practices utilized by ranchers and farmers in Shasta County, California, revealingly entitled *Order Without Law*, analyzed the conditions under which neighbors resolved their disputes according to informal, extralegal norms that had little to do with the formal rules of property law. He found—not surprisingly—that they were much more likely to do so when the stakes were small relative to the costs of the legal system, and when the rules otherwise governing the dispute were technically complex, such as water law.[163]

Other research has unearthed unilateral simplification in the area of public law. My own study of the Department of Energy found evidence that procedural complexities, many of them mandated by judicial and executive order, had magnified the costs of using informal rulemaking as the mode for energy policymaking. As these costs rose, the agency decided—with mixed results—to abandon rulemaking in favor of policy development largely in the form of adjudications by a special office authorized to grant exceptions to rules.[164] A recent study of the National Highway Traffic Safety Administration found an even more dramatic abandonment of rulemaking in favor of adjudication taking the form of vehicle recalls. The authors attribute this unilateral shift to what I call institutional differentiation—there, the uncertainties, procedural barriers, delays, and other costs entailed by having the agency's rules reviewed by courts ignorant of the agency's regulatory tasks.[165]

Withdrawal. At the extreme, unilateral simplification in the face of complexity costs takes the form of partial or complete withdrawal from the field. A notorious example is the liability insurance availability crisis of the mid–1980s. According to most analysts, it contributed to a reduction or cessation of risky but socially valuable activity in fields as diverse as after-school sports programs, day care, general aviation, contraceptive research, vaccines, and obstetrical care.[166] Many other less familiar instances of legal complexity driving out desirable activity could also be cited.

How durable are these formal and informal simplification strategies in the face of the powerful forces favoring legal complexity? Unfortunately, this question is very difficult to answer. Complexity's costs and benefits are remarkably dynamic, responding to shifts in technology, public attitudes, politics, and other social vectors. For example, telecommunications law, only recently simplified by a technologically driven deregulation, already faces re-regulation forces.[167] A similar cycle may occur in medical malpractice law, where simplifying—and often arbitrary—caps and defenses have been established[168] that may engender a complexifying backlash instigated by consumer groups.

As these examples suggest, legal simplicity—no less than complexity—also has its cost-driven limits. For this reason, the equilibrium between complexity and simplicity is likely to move back and forth along the continuum over time.

But this pattern of oscillation does not mean that the formal and informal regimes will reach identical equilibria. In the informal context, the equilibrium will be quite sensitive to changes in costs and benefits, while the formal law equilibrium will be sensitive to such changes only as they are institutionalized through the political influence of different groups.[169]

If legal complexity usually takes hold in the formal law regime and cost-justified simplicity finds a niche in the informal, why not just rely on private incentives to generate informal simplicity where it is warranted? Would that approach leave any problems that simplicity-minded law reformers would still need to address? The answer, I think, is "yes." Many cost-justified simplicity strategies cannot flourish unless the law formally affirms, protects, and promotes them.

Some simplifications—deregulation of financial services is an example—cannot be implemented without changes in the law because the complexity is now legally mandated.[170] In such cases, any informal simplification strategy short of unilateral withdrawal will probably be illegal.[171] Even when the complexity is voluntary, however, some simplifications cannot reap their full advantages unless they are established by law. Adverse selection problems, for example, may undermine any noncompulsory insurance schemes. Some of Jeffrey O'Connell's imaginative contractual no-fault proposals, which seek to elide the political obstacles to legislation, may suffer from this difficulty.[172] Free rider problems may also discourage even the beneficiaries of simplicity from investing in such a strategy unless the law assures them that others will do likewise. Another point, related to these market failures, is that formal, more or less comprehensive schemes may be needed to achieve scale economies or other efficiencies. The Canadian health insurance system's universality, for example, apparently derives some of its advantages from lowering administrative costs and what I have called delegitimation costs.[173]

Finally, even absent these problems, contracts to simplify will not be entered into unless there is some assurance that the formal law will enforce them. Medical malpractice law provides an important example. At least viewed *ex ante*, providers and patients would probably *both* be better off with any of a large number of simpler liability regimes.[174] Under the current state of the law, however, they cannot contract for them with any expectation that their informal simplifications will be upheld by the courts.[175] This is also true for many other fields of activity[176]—river canoe rentals, for example—as evidenced by the frequency with which providers unilaterally withdraw from those fields despite the existence of simpler alternatives that would probably leave most or all parties better off.

V. Toward Legal Simplification: A Strategy for Reform

What, then, should public-spirited reformers do about legal complexity? Does the preceding analysis provide any analytical leverage for our choices about the amount of complexity that is appropriate to a given legal problem?

Improving the balance between complexity and simplicity requires three levels of analysis. At the first level, we can try to assess complexity's costs and benefits more comprehensively, as I attempted to do earlier in drawing attention to governance and delegitimation costs.[177] At the second level of analysis, we can seek general principles to guide our future balancing choices. Again, the earlier discussion is instructive. By scrutinizing the informal simplification strategies that groups adopt in order to minimize complexity's costs, we can gain a clearer understanding of what those costs are, as well as of the likely benefits of adopting simpler alternatives. More to the point, we can deduce from these cost-minimizing strategies some useful criteria for determining both *where* to look for promising simplification opportunities and *how* to implement reform. I shall call these balancing criteria the cost distribution, audience, mimicking, and user fee principles.

The Cost Distribution Principle.   The earlier discussion of the political economy of complexity indicated that the *de jure* complexity level partly reflects the control that law producers exercise over its development, and that it is therefore unlikely to be socially optimal. If law producers can easily externalize complexity costs to diffuse, poorly organized interests, they will be even less inclined to adopt simpler, less costly alternatives.[178] This suggests a criterion that reformers can use to discern when simplification efforts may be fruitful. By studying how complexity costs are distributed, reformers can identify situations in which these costs are disproportionately borne by groups that face high obstacles to political organization, and in which the benefits of complexity flow primarily to well-organized groups. In these situations, complex arrangements may persist for no better reason than that powerful groups are advantaged by them and can free-ride on weaker, more diffuse cost bearers.

The Audience Principle.   Boris Bittker has suggested another criterion for identifying potentially fruitful areas for simplification. Call it the "audience principle." It holds that the complexity of a rule should be tailored to the sophistication and cost-bearing capacities of those who will have to interpret and implement it. Bittker notes that complex tax rules are less problematic if they are addressed to experts who must apply them to uncommon transactions than if they are addressed instead to numerous lay people who must understand and apply them to common transactions.[179] Bittker's criterion, while concerned with the plight of individual taxpayers, would apply as well to other mass administration areas, such as welfare, voter registration, pension administration, and social insurance, where simplification might have a large payoff. The audience principle, moreover, would be concerned with effects on small businesses as well as on individuals.

Another application of this audience criterion emphasizes the fact that some subjects of legal regulation seem more closely linked to basic democratic values than others. In contrast to Bittker's point about the administrative costs of complexity in different settings, the focus here is on how complexity affects the democratic morale and self-government in different settings. One would expect that the public's perception of the law's legitimacy is jeopardized more by the needless and perhaps strategic complexity of, say, rules on voting and political competition[180] than by the complexity found in, say, the regulation of food and drug products.

The Mimicking Principle. In addition to knowing *where* to simplify, we need to know *how* to simplify. By studying the ways in which people contract around the formal law, we can often obtain good information about its inefficiencies, including its excessive complexities.[181] As a presumptive balancing principle, we should consider altering the formal law to mimic the informal simplification strategies. This principle, however, can serve only as a first approximation; if the informal strategies offend public norms or are products of market failures or strategic behavior, the formal law should not mimic them.

Making the formal law and informal practice more congruent is not necessarily superfluous. As long as private incentives alone are unlikely to generate the desired complexity level,[182] the fact that some informal simplification has occurred does not mean that the resulting level is now optimal. Having the formal law affirm, protect, and promote simplification may still be socially beneficial.

Unfortunately, even the most desirable informal practices cannot always be successfully mimicked by the law. Samuel Gross explains some of the reasons why this is so:

> Informal norms of behavior suffer from the limitations of their advantages: their relative flexibility, and their responsiveness to interests that legal systems are hard-pressed to regulate—trust, reputation, civility, etc. Because of these features, such norms may operate very well in practice, and yet be too vague, too complex, too changeable, or too personal to enact as laws, or even fully to articulate.[183]

The User Fee Principle. Where feasible, lawmakers should seek to tax the special beneficiaries of legal complexity for the special costs associated with those benefits. I use the word "special" in recognition of the fact that it is usually very difficult to isolate, allocate, and quantify most complexity costs, and that the effort to do so will seldom be worth its cost. Still, some situations exist in which marginal complexity costs can be accurately calculated and assigned. For example, the Federal Rules of Civil Procedure authorize the court to assess a party with the costs of any excessive discovery it has occasioned.[184] The court may also shift some of a defendant's litigation costs to a plaintiff who rejects a settlement offer and then fails to recover more than the offered amount at trial.[185] It may be feasible to apply this principle in other situations in which the political economy of complexity can be more closely aligned with the public interest in both achieving an efficient level of complexity and in fairly distributing its costs. A crude effort in this direction is exemplified by statutes that exempt from certain regulatory requirements companies below a certain size.[186] In part, the theory of such exemptions seems to be that imposing the same compliance costs on large and small businesses would put the latter at a competitive disadvantage, which would be both unfair and inefficient.

At the third level of analysis in improving the complexity-simplicity balance, we can ask whether these criteria point to any *specific* reforms that seem likely to promote justice by reducing the administrative, transaction, governance, and delegitimation costs of legal complexity.[187] Some promising simplification proposals do exist. Whether they can deliver what they promise and whether they are politically feasible are questions, of course, that must await more detailed analysis. Before dismissing them as naïve, however, we should remember that a reform that is politically unattainable now may become more attractive later as the pressure of events, competition, attitudinal shifts, and other changes alter its cost-benefit profile.

Many simplification reforms focus primarily on reducing uncertainty-related *transaction costs*. One approach is to adopt clearer, simpler rules. If bargaining costs are low and the rule is merely a default that the parties may displace by contract, almost *any* transparent rule may be an improvement.[188] Commercial law reform proposals, of course, often take this approach.[189] Since transparent rules are more certain and easily administered, however, they can be superior even if the rules are not mere defaults and their bargaining costs are high. The Keeton-O'Connell no-fault auto insurance plan exemplifies this position,[190] as do certain elements of Paul Weiler's recent medical malpractice reform proposal.[191] Clear "safe harbor" rules that establish periods of repose in the products liability field[192] or acceptable practice in the medical malpractice area[193] also reduce uncertainty-related transaction costs.

Simpler legal rules may reduce *governance costs*, not just transaction costs. Returning to Fuller's spider web metaphor for the legal system,[194] policymakers may be less risk averse if they think that innovating in an area that they *do* govern will not reverberate in others that they do not. This consideration, for example, should counsel courts against extending tort principles into the realm governed largely by private contractual arrangements under the Uniform Commercial Code.[195] Similarly, less institutional differentiation might reduce the legal indeterminacy that such differentiation tends to spawn. In tort cases, for example, technical standards issued by regulatory agencies and satisfying certain conditions could be made presumptively binding on juries.[196] Jury discretion could be constrained by using scheduled damages to compensate pain and suffering, consortium, and other nonpecuniary losses.[197]

Simpler legal rules may also reduce *delegitimation costs*. Scheduled damages, for example, could limit the great inequities resulting from allowing different juries to award very different damages to victims who are in fact similarly situated.[198] No-fault systems could reduce the delay and capriciousness of tort litigation, which by denying timely compensation to deserving accident victims delegitimates the system. Sometimes, however, a more complex rule may be needed to produce a simpler, more equitable law. For example, I have proposed that judges with large asbestos caseloads abandon the exceedingly simple first-come, first-served rule for scheduling trials in favor of a more complex rule that would sequence claims according to the seriousness of plaintiffs' present injuries, after applying medical criteria.[199]

Although the proposals I have just mentioned are directed primarily at the tort system, the critique of legal complexity extends far beyond this area to all areas of public policy. The focus of simplification reformers, then, should be broad indeed. At its most general level, their goal should be to increase the supply of socially valued activities by reducing the complexity-related costs of performing them. For example, voter registration—an inconvenient, time-consuming process in many jurisdictions—could be facilitated by simply linking it to applications for a driver's license.[200] A similar technique can be used to encourage people to consent to donating their organs in the event of a fatal accident.[201] Pruning away the needlessly, indeed cynically, complex signature and petition requirements from New York's election law would prevent partisans from exploiting its complexity to foster costly litigation and deny serious candidates access to the ballot.[202]

A large number of far-reaching simplification reform proposals in the area of public law involve deregulation.[203] Financial services, international trade, energy, and biotechnology are attractive candidates for such reform. Other proposals fall under the rubrics of incentive-based regulation. Environmental protection furnishes many opportunities for reforms of this kind, including emissions trading and pollution taxes.[204] Performance-based management is an analogous reform within bureaucracies.[205] Still other proposals involve a change in the mix of market and regulatory forces, as in public education and health care.[206] More generally, policymakers should institutionalize a periodic review designed to purge laws of their unwanted encrusted complexities. Several techniques now in use for other purposes—for example, legislative revision commissions, sunset reviews, and regulatory and small business impact statements—might serve as fruitful models.

Few legal simplification efforts, of course, work in precisely the way they were envisioned, as the experiences with airline deregulation and sentencing guidelines demonstrate.[207] Efficient markets, moreover, are neither easy to establish and maintain nor unproblematic in their operation. What makes such reforms at least plausible, then, is not that they are perfect, but rather the fact that centrally coordinating innumerable individual and firm decisions fairly and efficiently has proved to be an unmanageably complex task.[208] In retrospect, the earlier faith that improvements in information technology and other management techniques would enable bureaucracies to keep pace with complexity in these areas seems hopelessly fatuous. If anything, complexity's resistance to centralized control seems to have increased over time.

VI. Conclusion

An analysis of legal complexity, then, holds important lessons for lawmakers, citizens, and scholars. The professional producers, rationalizers, and administrators of law must think more carefully about the complex rules and systems that they have tended to prefer. Perhaps a more systematic view of the causes and consequences of complexity may bring them to different conclusions about its merits in one legal realm or another.

Given the political economy of complexity, however, law producers are unlikely to take this more systematic view on their own unless citizens insist upon it by rewarding law producers when they devise worthy simplifications and penalizing them when they embed excessive complexity in the law. We know that the case for simplicity in law can occasionally carry the day politically. The deregulation of surface transportation[209] and energy production,[210] the Paperwork Reduction Act,[211] and the "bubble" approach to pollution control[212] are examples, flawed though they surely are in some respects. Sustaining these simplification victories over time, and refining them as their imperfections become manifest, will be more difficult.

We scholars also have a crucial role to play in the campaign to domesticate legal complexity. Our professional detachment, analytic training, and commitment to understanding complexity equip us to conduct relatively sophisticated, broad-gauged studies of its effects in different legal settings, of the strategies that people adopt in its shadow, and of the merits of proposed reforms that seek to strike a superior balance.[213] But we are educators as well as scholars. As we learn more about legal complexity's consequences, we should infuse that learning into the political economy of complexity, reminding anyone who will listen about the elusive virtues of simplicity in law.

Notes

1. "And, as the greatest only are, [i]n his simplicity sublime." ALFRED LORD TENNYSON, ODE ON THE DEATH OF THE DUKE OF WELLINGTON 6 (1852).

2. "Art, it seems to me, should simplify. That, indeed, is very nearly the whole of the higher artistic process. . . . " WILLA CATHER, ON WRITING 102 (1949).

3. "Embrace simplicity. . . . " LAO-TZU, THE WAY OF LAO-TZU (Wing-tsit Chan trans.), *reprinted in* JOHN BARTLETT, FAMILIAR QUOTATIONS 64 (Emily M. Beck ed., 15th ed. 1980).

4. "Our life is frittered away by detail. . . . Simplify, simplify." HENRY D. THOREAU, WALDEN 91 (J. Lyndon Shanley ed., 1971) (1854).

5. Herbert Simon, for example, noted the irrationality of complex, formally rational decisionmaking in organizations, and developed a fundamental distinction between optimizing and "satisficing" behavior. HERBERT SIMON, ADMINISTRATIVE BEHAVIOR xxviii–xxxi (3d ed. 1976). In the political sphere, Charles Lindblom described, and sought to justify, incremental behavior—what he called "partisan mutual adjust-

ment"—in terms of the need to reduce information and other decisionmaking costs. *See* CHARLES E. LINDBLOM, THE INTELLIGENCE OF DEMOCRACY: DECISION MAKING THROUGH MUTUAL ADJUSTMENT 21–84 (1965); Charles E. Lindblom, *The Science of "Muddling Through"*, 19 PUB. ADMIN. REV. 79 (1959). Ronald Coase analyzed how various kinds of complexity affect firms' structure and their pursuit of efficiency. *See* Ronald H. Coase, *The Nature of the Firm*, 4 ECONOMICA N.S. 386 (1937), *reprinted in* THE NATURE OF THE FIRM (Oliver E. Williamson & Sidney G. Winter eds., 1991); Ronald H. Coase, *The Problem of Social Cost*, 3 J.L. & ECON. 1 (1960) [hereinafter Coase, *The Problem of Social Cost*]. Oliver Williamson extended Coase's insights in a variety of ways. *See, e.g.,* OLIVER WILLIAMSON, MARKETS AND HIERARCHIES: ANALYSIS AND ANTITRUST IMPLICATIONS (1975).

6. For an elaborate historical development of this point, see THOMAS S. KUHN, THE STRUCTURE OF SCIENTIFIC REVOLUTIONS (1962).

7. HENRY ADAMS, THE EDUCATION OF HENRY ADAMS 441 (1918).

8. As Roscoe Pound noted in 1906, "[d]issatisfaction with the administration of justice is as old as law." Roscoe Pound, *The Causes of Popular Dissatisfaction with the Administration of Justice*, 40 AM. L. REV. 729, 729 (1906), *reprinted in* 8 BAYLOR L. REV. 1, 1 (1956). Several of the problems that Pound discussed, such as the law's procedural focus and the "sporting theory of justice," are elements of legal complexity, although he did not use that precise phrase.

9. *See, e.g.,* WALTER K. OLSON, THE LITIGATION EXPLOSION (1991).

10. Even parties subject to the same rule and engaged in the same transaction—the law governing an insurance contract, for example—might well perceive its level of complexity very differently, depending on their information and other resources and their stakes in and experience with the rule. Another aspect of the difference between these "objective" and "subjective" definitions of complexity is nicely illustrated by the *Tarasoff* litigation, discussed *infra* note 36. There, the therapists understood the court's rule to require them to warn those in danger, even though the rule in fact imposed only a general duty of care, which might or might not include a warning—a confusion facilitated by the court's alteration of its original decision. I am grateful to Marc Galanter for raising this point and these examples.

11. 29 U.S.C. ss 1001–1461 (1988).

12. 26 U.S.C. (1988).

13. *See generally* JERRY MASHAW & DAVID HARFST, THE STRUGGLE FOR AUTO SAFETY (1990); *see also* Competitive Enter. Inst. v. National Highway Traffic Safety Admin., 956 F.2d 321 (D.C. Cir. 1992) (dispute between automobile lobby and NHTSA over fuel economy standards).

14. This concept is developed in H.L.A. HART, THE CONCEPT OF LAW 124–32 (1961).

15. *See* Boris I. Bittker, *Tax Reform and Tax Simplification*, 29 U. MIAMI L. REV. 1, 2 (1974).

16. How, for example, should a system of scheduled damages for pain and suffering be classified relative to the existing system of largely indeterminate, jury-prescribed awards? In my discussion of these systems in Part IV, I treat the former as simpler than the latter. I do so because the former is relatively determinate and institutionally undifferentiated (the jury has much less to decide), and requires a less technical set of doctrines for controlling the jury. On the other hand, a schedule system could be quite complex, depending on how it is designed. Classification, then, is manifestly a matter of judgment.

17. U.S. CONST. art. II, s 1, cl. 4.

18. *See* Lucas v. Hamm, 364 P.2d 685 (Cal. 1961) (holding that rule against perpetuities so complicated that attorney of ordinary skill who misunderstands it cannot be

held liable for malpractice), *cert. denied,* 368 U.S. 987 (1962). The modification of this rule proposed in the Uniform Statutory Rule Against Perpetuities, adopted in a number of jurisdictions, exemplifies one approach to legal simplification—here, through a savings clause principle of wait-and-see. *See* Uniform Statutory Rule Against Perpetuities prefatory note, *reprinted in* John H. Langbein & Lawrence W. Waggoner, Selected Statutes on Trusts and Estates 674, 674 (1992).

19. Some claim—perhaps hyperbolically, certainly antagonistically—that the Federal Sentencing Guidelines are approaching the level of complexity of the Tax Code. *See, e.g.,* José A. Cabranes, The Federal Sentencing Guidelines: A Dismal Failure 6 (remarks at the University of Chicago Law School, January 15, 1992) (on file with author); *see also* Albert W. Alschuler, *The Failure of Sentencing Guidelines: A Plea for Less Aggregation,* 58 U. Chi. L. Rev. 901 (1991).

20. On legal uncertainty, see Anthony D'Amato, *Legal Uncertainty,* 71 Cal. L. Rev. 1 (1983); Werner Z. Hirsch, *Reducing Law's Uncertainty and Complexity,* 21 UCLA L. Rev. 1233 (1974). Some scholars have analyzed the optimal level of rule precision or determinacy. Ehrlich and Posner define precision in terms of the number and simplicity of the facts to which legal consequences attach, Issac Ehrlich & Richard A. Posner, *An Economic Analysis of Legal Rulemaking,* 3 J. Legal Stud. 257, 261 (1974), whereas Colin Diver defines it in terms of transparency, accessibility, and congruency, Colin S. Diver, *The Optimal Precision of Administrative Rules,* 93 Yale L.J. 65, 67 (1983). Many scholars have noted the transaction costs of complex rules. *See, e.g.,* sources cited *supra* note 5. Another group has explored how rule forms evolve through litigation, a genre summarized and extended in Jason S. Johnston, *Uncertainty, Chaos, and the Torts Process: An Economic Analysis of Legal Form,* 76 Cornell L. Rev. 341 (1991).

21. Complex litigation, including mass toxic torts, is perhaps the most widely discussed example. *See, e.g.,* Richard A. Posner, Economic Analysis of Law 542–47 (4th ed. 1992); Peter H. Schuck, Agent Orange on Trial: Mass Toxic Disasters in the Courts (enlarged ed. 1987); D'Amato, *supra* note 20, at 10; Hirsch, *supra* note 20, at 1241–45; Peter H. Schuck, *The Worst Should Go First: Deferral Registries in Asbestos Litigation,* 15 Harv. J.L. & Pub. Pol'y 541, 553–68 (1992).

22. *See, e.g.,* sources cited *supra* notes 20–21.

23. As discussed in Part III, *infra,* this simplification is more often *de facto* than *de jure.*

24. My analysis of the political economy of legal complexity in Part III may help to explain this interesting lag among academics.

25. *See supra* text accompanying note 7.

26. The absurdity of a thoroughgoing legal simplicity was captured by Swift in his description of Brobdingnag's legal system:

> No Law of that Country must exceed in Words the number of Letters in their Alphabet, which consists only in two and twenty. But indeed, few of them extend even to that Length. They are expressed in the most plain and simple Terms, wherein those People are not mercurial enough to discover above one Interpretation. And to write a Comment upon any Law is a capital Crime. As to the Decision of civil Causes, or Proceedings against Criminals, their Precedents are so few, that they have little Reason to boast of any extraordinary Skill in either.

Jonathan Swift, Gulliver's Travels 130 (Scholars' Facsimiles & Reprints 1976) (1726).

27. *See, e.g.,* Bittker, *supra* note 15, at 1–2; Paul L. Joskow & Alvin K. Klevorick, *A Framework for Analyzing Predatory Pricing Policy,* 89 YALE L.J. 213 (1979). As Bittker points out, the reverse can also be true: simple language can be a source of complexity. Bittker, *supra* note 15, at 2.

28. This may reflect a more secular, perhaps even universal, dynamic affecting such systems. *See generally* NICHOLAS GEORGESCU-ROEGEN, THE ENTROPY LAW AND THE ECONOMIC PROCESS (1971); TALCOTT PARSONS, THE SOCIAL SYSTEM (1951).

29. Even here, however, one is also struck by the tendency of the simpler substitutes to grow more complex over time.

30. Consider the deep structural differences between tort law (decentralized, common law), patent law (technology-driven, statutory), administrative law (process-oriented), property law (transaction-oriented), and constitutional law (structure-oriented). Given such differences, the similarity of the rhythm and character of change in these fields is unexpected. Moreover, particular doctrines may oscillate between simpler and more complex forms. *See* Johnston, *supra* note 20 at 346.

31. *See, e.g.,* Ehrlich & Posner, *supra* note 20, at 258; Duncan Kennedy, *Form and Substance in Private Law Adjudication,* 89 HARV. L. REV. 1685, 1687–88 (1976). Carol Rose calls them "crystals" and "mud." Carol M. Rose, *Crystals and Mud in Property Law,* 40 STAN. L. REV. 577, 578–79 (1988).

32. Peter H. Schuck & E. Donald Elliott, *To the* Chevron *Station: An Empirical Study of Federal Administrative Law,* 1990 DUKE L.J. 984, 1014–15 (in 1984–1985, the high point in absolute terms for rulemakings during the study period, they constituted only 6.5% of cases coded as rulemakings, ratemakings, or adjudications; excluding agencies that did not use rulemaking at all, rulemakings constituted only 9.4%; the share of rulemaking declined between 1975 and 1984–1985). This study, it should be noted, measured rulemakings only indirectly, by counting circuit court cases involving such proceedings.

33. *See id.; see also infra* text accompanying notes 164–65.

34. *See generally* KENNETH C. DAVIS, DISCRETIONARY JUSTICE: A PRELIMINARY INQUIRY (1969).

35. Even bright-line rules can become indeterminate around the edges. In the areas cited in the text, for example, courts applying relatively clear rules stretched their meanings in order to find: a special relationship as the predicate to imposing a legal duty, *e.g.,* Farwell v. Keaton, 240 N.W.2d 217, 222 (Mich. 1976); impact, *e.g.,* cases cited in RICHARD EPSTEIN ET AL., CASES AND MATERIALS ON TORTS 1055–56 (4th ed. 1984); and foreseeable economic loss, *e.g.,* People Express Airlines v. Consolidated Rail Corp., 495 A.2d 107, 116–18 (N.J. 1985). For an example of stretching in administrative law, see Peter H. Schuck, *When the Exception Becomes the Rule: Regulatory Equity and the Formulation of Energy Policy Through an Exceptions Process,* 1984 DUKE L.J. 163.

36. *Compare* Tarasoff v. Regents of Univ. of Cal., 529 P.2d 553 (Cal. 1974) (Tarasoff I), *withdrawn,* 551 P.2d 334 (Cal. 1976) *with* Tarasoff v. Regents of Univ. of Cal., 551 P.2d 334 (Cal. 1976) (Tarasoff II). *See* Daniel J. Givelber et al., *Tarasoff, Myth and Reality: An Empirical Study of Private Law in Action,* 1984 WIS. L. REV. 443, 465–68 (showing confusion in therapists' understanding of difference between *Tarasoff I*'s duty to warn and *Tarasoff II*'s more general duty). Subsequent cases have glossed *Tarasoff II* with a complex, even more indeterminate set of principles. *E.g.,* Hamman v. County of Maricopa, 775 P.2d 1122, 1128 (Ariz. 1989) (extending duty to any foreseeable victim, not just target of specific threat); Hedlund v. Superior Court, 669 P.2d 41, 46–47 (Cal. 1983) (where threat was against mother, finding duty extended to child who suffered emotional

harm while seated next to mother who was attacked; theory of recovery also included malpractice, although child was not defendant's patient); Petersen v. State, 671 P.2d 230, 236–37 (Wash. 1983) (finding duty extended to motorists injured in drug-related automobile accident caused by defendant's patient).

37. 443 P.2d 561 (Cal. 1968). Jason Johnston not only views this decision as moving from a relatively bright-line rule to a balancing rule producing uncertainty, but also as reducing the rule's efficiency. Johnston, *supra* note 20, at 379–82.

38. *See* discussion and sources cited in SCHUCK, *supra* note 21, at 31.

39. 18 U.S.C. ss 3551–3580 (1988).

40. Alschuler, *supra* note 19, at 904–08.

41. One important example is hospital reimbursement under Medicare according to diagnostically related groups. *See* Social Security Amendments of 1983, Pub. L. No. 98–21, s 601, 97 Stat. 65, 149–63 (codified at 42 U.S.C. s 1395ww) (establishing prospective payment system under which payments to hospitals are based on fixed cost estimates rather than on the actual cost of providing care). Another example is the Social Security disability insurance grid system, which was challenged and upheld in Heckler v. Campbell, 461 U.S. 458 (1983).

42. *See infra* text accompanying notes 119–23.

43. 369 U.S. 186 (1962).

44. Pub. L. No. 89–110, 79 Stat. 437 (codified at 42 U.S.C. ss 1971, 1973–1973p).

45. For the most recent example in the Supreme Court, see Presley v. Etowah County Comm'n, 112 S. Ct. 820 (1992). In addition to showing the expansion of subject matter, this case also exemplifies how institutional differentiation can increase complexity. Here, the Court declined to grant its customary deference to the Justice Department's construction of the Voting Rights Act, adding a new source of indeterminacy.

46. *See generally* JOHN H. LANGBEIN & BRUCE A. WOLK, PENSION AND EMPLOYEE BENEFIT LAW 579–614 (1990).

47. *See* GUIDO CALABRESI, A COMMON LAW FOR THE AGE OF STATUTES 1 & n.1 (1982).

48. *See* Richard B. Stewart, *The Reformation of American Administrative Law*, 88 HARV. L. REV. 1669, 1671–81, 1715–16 (1975).

49. Judges, of course, often alluded to the law's purposes at some level of generality. It is a matter of degree. For a fundamental dispute over that degree (among other disputes), compare MORTON J. HORWITZ, THE TRANSFORMATION OF AMERICAN LAW, 1780–1860, at 16–30 (1977) with A.W.B. Simpson, *The Horwitz Thesis and the History of Contracts*, 46 U. CHI. L. REV. 533 (1979) (disagreeing, *inter alia*, with Horwitz's interpretation of opinions) and Gary T. Schwartz, *Tort Law and the Economy in Nineteenth-Century America: A Reinterpretation*, 90 YALE L.J. 1717, 1721 (1981) (opinions reveal "rudimentary level" of instrumentalism, consistent with various purposes).

50. *See* BRUCE A. ACKERMAN, RECONSTRUCTING AMERICAN LAW (1984); Stewart, *supra* note 48, at 1678–81.

51. *See, e.g.*, Abram Chayes, *The Role of the Judge in Public Law Litigation*, 89 HARV. L. REV. 1281 (1976); Owen M. Fiss, *The Forms of Justice*, 93 HARV. L. REV. 1 (1979).

52. George L. Priest, *The Invention of Enterprise Liability: A Critical History of the Intellectual Foundations of Modern Tort Law*, 14 J. LEGAL STUD. 461, 463 (1985).

53. *See, e.g.*, T. Alexander Aleinikoff, *Constitutional Law in the Age of Balancing*, 96 YALE L.J. 943 (1987); Jerry L. Mashaw, *The Supreme Court's Due Process Calculus for Administrative Adjudication in* Mathews v. Eldridge: *Three Factors in Search of a Theory of Value*, 44 U. CHI. L. REV. 28 (1976).

54. *See* Wards Cove Packing Co. v. Atonio, 490 U.S. 642, 648, 658 (1989) (altering burden-shifting formula to increase plaintiff's burden) (effectively overruled by the Civil Rights Act of 1991, Pub. L. No. 102–166, 105 Stat. 1071); Texas Dep't. of Community Affairs v. Burdine, 450 U.S. 248 (1981) (refining burden-shifting formula for all Title VII cases); McDonnell Douglas Corp. v. Green, 411 U.S. 792, 802–06 (1973) (establishing formula for shifting burden of proof between parties in Title VII race discrimination cases); *In re* "Agent Orange" Prod. Liab. Litig., 597 F. Supp. 740, 832 (E.D.N.Y. 1984) (using burden-shifting to solve indeterminate defendant problem), *aff'd*, 818 F.2d 145 (2d Cir. 1987), *cert. denied*, 484 U.S. 1004 (1988); Sindell v. Abbott Labs., 607 P.2d 924 (Cal.) (allowing liability of DES manufacturers to be based on market share rather than on specific evidence of causation of harm), *cert. denied*, 449 U.S. 912 (1980); Martin v. Abbott Labs., 689 P.2d 368, 381 (Wash. 1984) (adopting market share alternate liability theory); Collins v. Eli Lilly Co., 342 N.W.2d 37, 53 (Wis. 1984) (considering market share when apportioning liability to each defendant), *cert. denied*, 469 U.S. 826 (1984). This approach (sequential burden-shifting) is designed to elicit information for the court in service of deterrence, compensation, and other policy goals.

55. These institutions include legislatures, administrative agencies, juries, and private organizations. On deference to legislatures, see, e.g., INS v. Cardoza-Fonseca, 480 U.S. 421, 452–55 (1987) (Scalia, J., concurring in the judgment) (arguing that courts should adopt a "plain meaning" approach to statutory interpretation); H.J., Inc. v. Northwestern Bell Tel. Co., 492 U.S. 229, 251–56 (1989) (Scalia J., concurring in the judgment) (elaborating on the "plain meaning" approach). On deference to agencies, see, e.g., Thomas W. Merrill, *Judicial Deference to Executive Precedent*, 101 YALE L.J. 969 (1992); Cass R. Sunstein, *Law and Administration After* Chevron, 90 COLUM. L. REV. 2071 (1990); and the recent Supreme Court decisions in Presley v. Etowah County Comm'n, 112 S. Ct. 820, 831–32 (1992), and Lechmere, Inc. v. NLRB, 112 S. Ct. 841, 847–48 (1992). On deference to juries, see Peter H. Schuck, *The New Judicial Ideology of Tort Law, in* NEW DIRECTIONS IN LIABILITY LAW 4, 10–12 (Walter Olson ed., 1988). On deference to private organizations, see Consumer Product Safety Act, 15 U.S.C. ss 2056(b), 2058(b) (authorizing Consumer Product Safety Commission to rely on privately developed safety standards and to issue proposed rules based on such standards); Occupational Safety and Health Administration Standards for Air Contaminants, 29 C.F.R. s 1910.1000 (1991) (imposing limits on 428 workplace hazards, and basing limits on consensus standards previously developed by private industry associations); and Janet Gilboy, Government Use of Private Resources in Law Enforcement (1992) (unpublished manuscript, on file with author). These deference doctrines often operate differently than their authors intend. *See infra* Section I(D).

56. *See* RICHARD POSNER, LAW AND LITERATURE: A MISUNDERSTOOD RELATION (1988).

57. The rise of a "new textualism" signals uneasiness about, indeed a reaction against, this new interpretive freedom. *See, e.g.,* William N. Eskridge, Jr., *The New Textualism*, 37 UCLA L. REV. 621 (1990); Jerry L. Mashaw, *Textualism, Constitutionalism, and the Interpretation of Federal Statutes*, 32 WM. & MARY L. REV. 827 (1991).

58. Chevron U.S.A. Inc. v. Natural Resources Defense Council, Inc., 467 U.S. 837 (1984).

59. The others are clear statement requirements and "plain meaning" interpretation. Mashaw, *supra* note 57, at 828–29.

60. Courts must first ask whether Congress has addressed the precise question at issue, and if they find that it has not, must then ask whether the agency's interpretation of the statute is reasonable. 467 U.S. at 842–43.

61. Whereas the D.C. Circuit initially decreased deference afforded to such interpretations, the affirmance rate in other circuits rose. Schuck & Elliott, *supra* note 32, at 1041–42.

62. Merrill, *supra* note 55, at 980–85. Two decisions in the Court's most recent Term indicate that this failure continues, further magnifying the doctrine's indeterminacy. Presley v. Etowah County Comm'n, 112 S. Ct. 820 (1992) (declining to defer to administrative interpretation of Voting Rights Act of 1965); Lechmere, Inc. v. NLRB, 112 S. Ct. 841 (1992) (reversing administrative order for employer to cease barring union organizers from premises).

63. This is true for several reasons. First, tort law's standard of care and measure of damages are more open-ended. Second, the existence of a tort law duty may be an issue whereas the existence of a contract usually is not. Third, causation is often difficult to ascertain. Finally, pre-dispute legal counseling and documentary evidence are less commonly available in tort law.

64. *See* U.C.C. s 2–715 (1990) (providing that following a breach of contract the buyer may recover not only for loss of a product's economic value but also for "injury to person or property proximately resulting from any breach of warranty.")

65. Accountants' liability is an important area of expansion. *Compare, e.g.,* Ultramares Corp. v. Touche, 174 N.E. 441 (N.Y. 1931) *with* H. Rosenblum, Inc. v. Adler, 461 A.2d 138 (N.J. 1983). *See generally* John A. Siliciano, *Negligent Accounting and the Limits of Instrumental Tort Reform,* 86 Mich. L. Rev. 1929 (1988). Although the contract remedy may require a series of linked privity-based actions, modern civil procedure makes this a relatively straightforward matter.

66. Tort law has become far more pro-plaintiff since then, but the tort system's complexity and costs have also increased markedly.

67. *See* Richard A. Epstein, *The Legal and Insurance Dynamics of Mass Tort Litigation,* 13 J. Legal Stud. 475, 488–95 (1984) (arguing for exclusive reliance on the workers' compensation system through reinstatement of the privity limitation in tort law); Paul C. Weiler, *Workers' Compensation and Product Liability: The Interaction of a Tort and a Non-Tort Regime,* 50 Ohio St. L.J. 825 (1989).

68. As Bittker has noted in the tax context, these costs will be quite different depending on the audience. *See infra* text accompanying notes 179–80.

69. Many of these costs are classified as "transaction costs." For some taxonomies, see Robert C. Ellickson, *The Case for Coase and Against "Coaseanism,"* 99 Yale L.J. 611, 614–15 (1989); Guido Calabresi, *The Pointlessness of Pareto: Carrying Coase Further,* 100 Yale L.J. 1211, 1232–34 (1991). The systematic positive and normative analysis of how transaction costs affect legal rules is a pillar of modern legal scholarship. *See, e.g.,* Posner, *supra* note 21; Guido Calabresi & A. Douglas Melamed, *Property Rules, Liability Rules, and Inalienability: One View of the Cathedral,* 85 Harv. L. Rev. 1089 (1972); Coase, *The Problem of Social Cost, supra* note 5.

Legal complexity and legal uncertainty are cognate concepts, but uncertainty is actually contingent on complexity, which as I have noted depends in turn upon other characteristics of the legal system. *See supra* page 3. The Internal Revenue Code, for example, is a complex legal (sub)system that contains many relatively certain rules. *See supra* text accompanying notes 12, 19.

70. While uncertainty (or indeterminacy) is largely a function of complexity as I have defined it, *see supra* note 69, uncertainty may have other sources as well, as when a simple rule is perceived and treated as complex by those who are subject to it. *See supra* note 10 and accompanying text.

71. To pick an extreme example, even if the liability rule for traffic accidents was that pedestrians always win, and even if everyone knew the rule, the costs of organizing a market on which these entitlements could be traded would be exceedingly high.

72. Louis Kaplow has developed several models of legal complexity that take into account its effects on the incentives of potential violators and enforcement agencies to acquire (and in the violators' case, reveal) information. *See* LOUIS KAPLOW, A MODEL OF THE OPTIMAL COMPLEXITY OF RULES (National Bureau of Economic Research Working Paper No. 3958, 1992).

73. For a striking example, see Robert A. Kagan, *Adversarial Legalism and American Government*, 10 J. POL. ANALYSIS & MGMT. 369 (1991) (illustrating costs of adversarial legalism with case study of the dredging of Oakland Harbor).

Such inefficiencies, of course, may have virtues as well as vices, as Samuel Gross reminds us. *See* Samuel R. Gross, *The American Advantage: The Value of Inefficient Litigation*, 85 MICH. L. REV. 734, 748–56 (1987).

74. *See* Hirsch, *supra* note 20, at 1246–47.

75. A governance cost can readily be viewed as a kind of transaction cost, but it is not useful to characterize a delegitimation cost in that way.

76. JAMES M. BUCHANAN & GORDON TULLOCK, THE CALCULUS OF CONSENT: LOGICAL FOUNDATIONS OF CONSTITUTIONAL DEMOCRACY 106 (1962); Ehrlich & Posner, *supra* note 20, at 267.

77. CALABRESI, *supra* note 47, at 3–7.

78. *E.g.*, Administrative Procedure Act, 5 U.S.C. ss 551, 552a–559, 701–706 (1988); Regulatory Flexibility Act, 5 U.S.C. ss 601–612 (1988).

79. This fierce localism is a vision worthy of G.K. Chesterton. *See* GILBERT K. CHESTERTON, THE NAPOLEON OF NOTTING HILL (1904).

80. Lon L. Fuller, *The Forms and Limits of Adjudication*, 92 HARV. L. REV. 353, 395–404 (1978) (describing concept of polycentricity).

81. This is a logical implication from official risk aversion. I discuss the phenomenon in PETER H. SCHUCK, SUING GOVERNMENT: CITIZEN REMEDIES FOR OFFICIAL WRONGS 70–71 (1983).

82. With respect to private actors, see, e.g., Henry Hansmann, *When Does Worker Ownership Work? ESOPs, Law Firms, Codetermination, and Economic Democracy*, 99 YALE L.J. 1749, 1780–83 (1990). With respect to public actors, see *infra* text accompanying notes 107–11.

83. *Compare* Jerry L. Mashaw, *Prodelegation: Why Administrators Should Make Political Decisions*, 1 J.L. ECON. & ORGANIZATION 81, 97 (1985) (arguing that "[e]limination of discretion at one choice point merely causes the discretion that had been exercised there to migrate elsewhere in the system") *with* THEODORE J. LOWI, THE END OF LIBERALISM: THE SECOND REPUBLIC OF THE UNITED STATES (2d ed. 1979) (criticizing failure of Congress to make policy decisions); *see also* James S. Eustice, *Tax Complexity and the Tax Practitioner*, 45 TAX L. REV. 7, 11 (1989) (leaving unanswered tax policy questions to courts shifts complexity problem without eliminating it).

84. Patricia M. Wald, Comment, *The "New Administrative Law"—With the Same Old Judges in It?*, 1991 DUKE L.J. 647, 668–69 (footnote omitted).

85. These costs, of course, flow through to the rest of us, in the forms described earlier: blocked transactions, deadweight losses, delays, litigation, heightened risk aversion, and conflict among governing institutions. Again, this does not deny that some of these effects entail countervailing benefits. Litigation, for example, is a public good in-

sofar as it creates precedents that clarify and refine the law for the use of others, a benefit that is, of course, especially valuable in connection with complex rules. To the extent that the rules are more complex than they need to be, however, this is a bootstrapped benefit.

86. This concept is elaborated in ISAIAH BERLIN, *Two Concepts of Liberty, in* FOUR ESSAYS ON LIBERTY 118 (1969).

87. "Hyperlexis," a term coined by Bayless Manning, describes "the pathological condition caused by an overactive law-making gland." Bayless Manning, *Hyperlexis: Our National Disease,* 71 NW. U. L. REV. 767, 767 (1977).

88. *See, e.g.,* OLSON, *supra* note 9, at 1–11; Michael J. Cacace, *The Nation's Love-Hate Relationship with Lawyers,* FLA. B.J., Oct. 1991, at 94, 94–95.

89. This common sense, common morality criterion is akin to what Anthony D'Amato calls "natural law" and John Finnis calls "practical reasonableness." D'Amato, *supra* note 20, at 49–51 (citing JOHN FINNIS, NATURAL LAW AND NATURAL RIGHTS 100–27 (1980)).

90. *See infra* Part III.

91. Alison Reppy, *The Field Codification Concept, in* DAVID D. FIELD: CENTENARY ESSAYS 17, 21–25 (Alison Reppy ed., 1949).

92. *See infra* Part IV.

93. For a discussion of some of the methodological obstacles to such studies, see Susan Long & Judyth Swingen, *An Approach to the Measurement of Tax Law Complexity,* J. AM. TAX ASS'N, Spring 1987, at 22, 25 (proposing six indices of complexity); Joel Slemrod, *Complexity, Compliance Costs, and Tax Evasion, in* 2 TAXPAYER COMPLIANCE 156, 178 (Jeffrey A. Roth & John T. Scholz eds., 1989) (reviewing methodological issues; "only recently has research been focused on the relationship between complexity, compliance costs, and tax evasion").

94. *E.g.,* Jeffrey A. Roth et al., *Understanding Taxpayer Compliance: Self Interest, Social Commitment, and Other Influences, in* 1 TAXPAYER COMPLIANCE, *supra* note 93, at 71, 129 ("Of the seven guilt neutralization mechanisms investigated by Thurman . . . the justification, 'It is okay to claim an undeserved tax deduction when you are not really sure what the rule is,' was the most widely accepted and most consistently related to compliance.")

95. Eustice, *supra* note 83, at 19 (but citing no empirical support for proposition); *see also* JOHN F. WITTE, THE POLITICS AND DEVELOPMENT OF THE FEDERAL INCOME TAX 62 (1985) (arguing that complexity "makes the task of enforcement significantly more difficult, and it makes it easier to plead ignorance or error when the intent was truly fraud").

> Humorist Dave Barry imagines that taxpayer noncompliance has something to do with the fact that the tax code is larger than the average taxpayer's home and nobody in the entire world really understands it because it was apparently written by hostile mutant non-English-speaking lawyers from space, plus it is revised about every 25 minutes, plus it is used to take taxpayers' money away and turn it over to a federal government that routinely spends it on activities like declaring National Deviled Ham Awareness Month. Nah, that couldn't be it. It's probably some kind of chemical disorder in the taxpayers' brains.

Dave Barry, *Schedule 936850345-D,* INT'L HERALD TRIB., Apr. 4–5, 1992, at 18.

96. GEORGE EADS & PETER REUTER, DESIGNING SAFER PRODUCTS: CORPORATE RESPONSES TO PRODUCT LIABILITY LAW AND REGULATION 27–29 (1985).

97. *See* Michael Specter, *Once Again, New York's Arcane Election Laws Shape Race,* N.Y. Times, Feb. 28, 1992, at B1 (candidates subject to summary removal from ballot for spelling errors on ballot, incorrect ordering of witness sheets, wrong type of clips used to bind pages, etc.); Michael Specter, *Now It's a Technicality That Keeps Tsongas and Brown on Ballot,* N.Y. Times, Mar. 11, 1992, at A18 (lawsuit challenging Tsongas dismissed on technicality).

98. *See, e.g.,* Hernando de Soto, The Other Path: The Invisible Revolution in the Third World (1989); Peter H. Schuck & Robert E. Litan, *Regulatory Reform in the Third World: The Case of Peru,* 4 Yale J. on Reg. 51 (1986).

99. *See, e.g.,* Robert Pear, *U.S. Laws Delayed by Complex Rules and Partisanship,* N.Y. Times, Mar. 31, 1991, at A1 (noting delays in legislation on the homeless, air pollution, waste storage, etc.).

100. *See, e.g.,* Marc Galanter, *Law Abounding: Legalization Around the North Atlantic,* 55 Mod. L. Rev. 1 (1992).

101. *See, e.g.,* Judgment Under Uncertainty: Heuristics and Biases (Daniel Kahneman et al. eds., 1982); Lindblom, *supra* note 5, at 80; Simon, *supra* note 5, at 81–83.

102. Although I mean to use self-interest here in a fairly strong, nontautological sense, I recognize the often valid criticism, directed at some versions of "public choice" theory, that self-interest can be defined self-referentially and nonfalsifiably. *See, e.g.,* Jerry L. Mashaw, *Explaining Administrative Process: Normative, Positive, and Critical Stories of Legal Development,* 6 J.L. Econ. & Organization 267, 269–72 (1990); Symposium, *The Theory of Public Choice,* 74 Va. L. Rev. 167 (1988). By rooting their self-interest in rather conventional professional, careerist, and economic goals, I hope to minimize the force of this objection.

103. *See infra* text accompanying notes 106–17.

104. *See generally* Steven Kelman, Making Public Policy: A Hopeful View of American Government 248–70 (1987) (examining the role of public spirit in the political process).

105. For two such examples see *supra* note 41.

106. *See, e.g.,* Richard L. Doernberg & Fred S. McChesney, *On the Accelerating Rate and Decreasing Durability of Tax Reform,* 71 Minn. L. Rev. 913 (1987) (public choice model attributing recent increase in the rate of tax reform to shorter-term "contracts" between legislators and private interests); Daniel Shaviro, *Beyond Public Choice and Public Interest: A Study of the Legislative Process as Illustrated by Tax Legislation in the 1980s,* 139 U. Pa. L. Rev. 1 (1990) (criticizing public choice model and emphasizing prestige and symbolism explanations of recent legislation).

107. Immigration Act of 1990, s 132(c), 8 U.S.C. s 1153 note (Supp. II 1990) (providing that no less than 40% of the visas during a three-year transitional period must go to "the foreign state the natives of which received the greatest number of visas issued under section 314" of the 1986 law). That "foreign state" was Ireland. *See* Donatella Lorch, *Organizing for Visas: Irish, Lottery and Luck,* N.Y. Times, Oct. 12, 1991, at 31, 33.

108. Morris P. Fiorina, Congress: Keystone of the Washington Establishment 44–47 (2d ed. 1989).

109. *See, e.g.,* Matthew D. McCubbins et al., *Administrative Procedures as Instruments of Political Control,* 3 J.L. Econ. & Organization 243 (1987).

110. By placing complex procedural constraints upon an agency's decisionmaking process, politicians are able to respond to potential deviations from the status quo prior to the implementation of a change in policy, and thereby retain effective control over

agency decisions. Matthew D. McCubbins et al., *Structure and Process, Politics and Policy: Administrative Arrangements and the Political Control of Agencies*, 75 VA. L. REV. 431 (1989).

111. *See supra* text accompanying notes 80–83.

112. The number of aides serving on members' personal staffs in the U.S. House of Representatives rose from 4,055 in 1967 to 7,569 in 1989; the number serving on members' staffs in the U.S. Senate rose from 1,749 to 3,837 in the same period. NORMAN J. ORNSTEIN ET AL., VITAL STATISTICS ON CONGRESS, 1991–1992, at 126 (1992).

113. For some revealing case studies, see BRUCE A. ACKERMAN & WILLIAM T. HASSLER, CLEAN COAL, DIRTY AIR (1981); MICHAEL J. MALBIN, UNELECTED REPRESENTATIVES (1980). For a discussion of the concerns raised by the explosion in Congressional staffing, see FIORINA, *supra* note 108, at 118–21.

114. *See* MALBIN, *supra* note 113, at 172–78 (discussing workload which in part reflects complexity).

115. Pub. L. No. 99–514, 100 Stat. 2085 (codified as amended in scattered sections of 26 U.S.C.).

116. *See* Doernberg & McChesney, *supra* note 106, at 958–59. This is especially true of the intricate, detailed transitional rules necessary to implement the new policy against real estate tax sheltering. *See* C. EUGENE STEUERLE, THE TAX DECADE: HOW TAXES CAME TO DOMINATE THE PUBLIC AGENDA 116–17 (1992).

117. *See* Depository Institutions Deregulation and Monetary Control Act of 1980, Pub. L. No. 96–221, 94 Stat. 132 (codified in scattered sections of 12 U.S.C.); Garn-St. Germain Depository Institutions Act of 1982, Pub. L. No. 97–320, 96 Stat. 1469 (codified in scattered sections of 12 U.S.C.); Railroad Revitalization and Regulatory Reform Act of 1976, Pub. L. No. 94–210, 90 Stat. 31 (codified as amended in scattered sections of 45, 49 U.S.C.); Airline Deregulation Act of 1978, Pub. L. No. 95–504, 92 Stat. 1705 (codified in scattered sections of 49 U.S.C.); Motor Carrier Act of 1980, Pub. L. No. 96–296, 94 Stat. 793 (codified in scattered sections of 49 U.S.C.); Bus Regulatory Reform Act of 1982, Pub. L. No. 97–261, 96 Stat. 1102 (codified in scattered sections of 49 U.S.C.).

118. Their success in doing so is of course the subject of innumerable jeremiads against regulation. *See, e.g.*, WILLIAM A. NISKANEN, JR., BUREAUCRACY AND REPRESENTATIVE GOVERNMENT (1971).

119. Agencies may also want the rules to leave some flexibility for the regulated even at the price of some uncertainty. Johnston points out that even when agencies issue relatively precise rules, the courts' refusal to recognize compliance with such rules as a defense to tort liability has, if anything, added to the complexity and uncertainty faced by regulatees. Johnston, *supra* note 20, at 366.

120. *See* JAMES Q. WILSON, BUREAUCRACY: WHAT GOVERNMENT AGENCIES DO AND WHY THEY DO IT 244–48 (1989) (technical task structures make agencies more independent of congressional control).

121. *See* Thomas O. McGarity, *The Internal Structure of EPA Rulemaking*, LAW & CONTEMP. PROBS., Autumn 1991, at 57 (describing the structural and decisionmaking apparatus of the Environmental Protection Agency).

122. *See* MASHAW & HARFST, *supra* note 13, at 117 (auto manufacturers devote substantial resources to regulatory affairs offices, which coordinate compliance with health, safety, and related requirements).

123. *See supra* note 20 and accompanying text.

124. Johnston, *supra* note 20, at 371. Carol Rose, focusing on property law, also perceives oscillation, but for her it is driven by judges who muddy the crystalline rules to protect the

"fools" ensnared by them, and by legislators and transactors who must then try to restore a regime of crystals in the interests of efficiency. Rose, *supra* note 31, at 603–04.

125. George L. Priest & Benjamin Klein, *The Selection of Disputes for Litigation*, 13 J. LEGAL STUD. 1 (1984).

126. D'Amato, *supra* note 20, at 23–24.

127. James A. Henderson, Jr. & Theodore Eisenberg, *The Quiet Revolution in Products Liability: An Empirical Study of Legal Change*, 37 UCLA L. REV. 479, 515 (1990); *see also* Theodore Eisenberg & James A. Henderson, Jr., *Inside the Quiet Revolution in Products Liability*, 39 UCLA L. REV. 731 (1992).

128. Richard A. Epstein, *The Political Economy of Product Liability Reform*, 78 AM. ECON, REV. pt. 2, at 311, 313 (1988). Johnston criticizes Epstein's view on several grounds. Lawyers, he says, can only realize this goal through their clients' litigation. Although he does not go on to say that lawyers never subordinate the clients' interests to their own, he does argue that the lawyers might benefit more from oscillation than from a steady trend toward indeterminacy. Johnston, *supra* note 20, at 371–72.

129. Michelle J. White, *Why Are Taxes So Complex and Who Benefits?*, 47 TAX NOTES 341 (1990).

130. Bittker, *supra* note 15, at 10–11. For a Bittkeresque parody of the notion that the Code's complexity reflects nothing more than profit-maximizing by tax professionals, see Boris I. Bittker, *James S. Eustice*, 45 TAX L. REV. 1 (1989).

131. *See* Priest & Klein, *supra* note 125 (supporting the former model); Henderson & Eisenberg, *supra* note 127 (supporting the latter model).

132. Schuck, *supra* note 55, at 11. A recent example of this is the *en banc* decision of the California Supreme Court in Mitchell v. Gonzales, 819 P.2d 872 (Cal. 1991), in which the court replaced the "but for" test for cause-in-fact in negligence actions with the "substantial factor" test, which is somewhat less determinate and could send more cases to the jury.

133. *See, e.g.,* Wex S. Malone, *Ruminations on Cause-in-Fact*, 9 STAN. L. REV. 60, 99 (1956) ("Thus distinction is heaped upon distinction and law becomes increasingly and unnecessarily complex.")

134. *See, e.g.,* INS v. Chadha, 462 U.S. 919 (1983) (moving to institutional simplification); Vermont Yankee Nuclear Power Corp. v. Natural Resources Defense Council, Inc., 435 U.S. 519 (1978) (moving to less density); Miller v. California, 413 U.S. 15 (1973) (moving to less technical rule); Baker v. Carr, 369 U.S. 186 (1962) (moving to more bright-line rule).

Perhaps the most notable simplifying innovation is the current effort to simplify asbestos and some other mass tort litigation. This, however, should be seen as the extreme case in which complexity's limits have manifestly been reached, and I therefore discuss it in Part IV.

135. Most American judges are elected, and in some states reelection can be a very risky and expensive business. *See, e.g.,* John T. Wold & John H. Culver, *The Defeat of the California Justices: The Campaign, the Electorate, and the Issue of Judicial Accountability*, 70 JUDICATURE 348 (1987); Peter Applebome, *Texas Court Fight Puts Focus on Elected Judges*, N.Y. TIMES, Jan. 22, 1988, at B4.

136. D'Amato, *supra* note 20, at 19–22 (describing information value as a measure of the divergence of an actual message or result from an anticipated message or result).

137. *See generally* DOUGLAS E. ROSENTHAL, LAWYER AND CLIENT: WHO'S IN CHARGE? (1977) (describing relationship between lawyers and their clients in personal injury

cases); *see also* DONALD L. HOROWITZ, THE JUROCRACY (1977) (describing powerful role of lawyers in administering government programs). This is less true of corporate clients, who can draw upon their own in-house legal expertise and who also are repeat players.

138. For an economic model that predicts that contingency fee lawyers are the group tending to prefer the simplest law, see Michelle J. White, Legal Complexity (June 30, 1989) (unpublished manuscript on file with author).

139. Robert Gordon, while noting that "historically lawyers have sacrificed income repeatedly" in order to advance other goals, argues that this form of professional public spiritedness has declined over time. Robert W. Gordon, *The Independence of Lawyers*, 68 B.U. L. REV. 1, 40, 48 (1988).

140. The most important of these groups are the media (whose attitudes toward complexity are shaped by the technical constraints), policymakers (whose biases toward complexity are not intellectual), and what used to be called the intelligentsia (when Marxism was more in fashion).

141. *See generally* Peter H. Schuck, *Why Don't Law Professors Do More Empirical Research?*, 39 J. LEGAL EDUC. 323 (1989).

142. For a recent, perspicuous discussion of the three schools, see William N. Eskridge, Jr. & Gary Peller, *The New Public Law Movement: Moderation as a Postmodern Cultural Form*, 89 MICH. L. REV. 707 (1991). My characterizations of these schools in this section draw heavily upon this account.

143. *Id.* at 709–23.

144. *Id.* at 764–84.

145. *See, e.g.,* PETER GOODRICH, READING THE LAW 16–19 (1986); Eskridge & Peller, *supra* note 142, at 765–66.

146. For an example, see POSNER, *supra* note 21.

147. A controversial example is cited by Peter Huber, who states that "[p]laintiffs' lawyers can profit handsomely from the disorder and inherent unpredictability" that are caused by what Huber calls "the right-field slouch"—an asymmetrical curve of verdicts in which, because of a few enormous recoveries, the mean verdict is much higher than the median. Peter Huber, *Junk Science and the Jury*, 1990 U. CHI. LEGAL F. 273, 291.

148. *See* Gary T. Schwartz, *Contributory and Comparative Negligence: A Reappraisal*, 87 YALE L.J. 697, 703–10 (1978).

149. *See* Harry H. Wellington, *Challenges to Legal Education: The 'Two Cultures' Phenomenon*, 37 J. LEGAL EDUC. 327 (1987). A recent but still unpublished empirical study of the contents of law reviews lends some support to Wellington's view. Michael J. Saks, Law Journals: Their Shapes and Contents, 1960 and 1985: Address Before the AALS Symposium on Legal Scholarship (Jan. 6, 1989) (law reviews in 1985, as compared with those in 1960, are more dominated by scholars than practitioners, are more critical of existing doctrine, and are more useful to policymakers and theorists than to practitioners).

150. Saks, *supra* note 149 (mean number of citations of law review articles in judicial opinions rose 59% from 1960 to 1985). *But see* Lawrence Friedman et al., *State Supreme Courts: A Century of Style and Citation*, 33 STAN. L. REV. 773, 812–17 (1981) (noting a growing citation of law reviews, but little use of social science).

151. *See supra* text accompanying note 101.

152. *See supra* note 102 and accompanying text.

153. An example is courts' insistence that "the cost of protecting a constitutional right cannot justify its total denial." Bounds v. Smith, 430 U.S. 817, 825 (1977).

154. An example is consumer groups' celebration of the egregiously inefficient tort system for assuring "a day in court" which few can actually obtain.

155. *See* STEPHEN BREYER, REGULATION AND ITS REFORM 240–60 (1982).

156. *E.g.*, JUDICIAL CONFERENCE AD HOC COMMITTEE ON ASBESTOS LITIGATION, REPORT TO THE CHIEF JUSTICE OF THE UNITED STATES AND MEMBERS OF THE JUDICIAL CONFERENCE OF THE UNITED STATES 17–22 (1991); SCHUCK, *supra* note 21, at 262–68; Richard Epstein, *The Consolidation of Complex Litigation: A Critical Evaluation of the ALI Proposal*, 10 J.L. & COM. 1 (1990); Roger H. Trangsrud, *Mass Trials in Mass Tort Cases: A Dissent*, 1989 U. ILL. L. REV. 69 (1989). These costs have led to substantive law changes as well. Lester Brickman, *The Asbestos Litigation Crisis: Is There a Need for an Administrative Alternative?*, 13 CARDOZO L. REV. 1819, 1840–68 (1992).

157. A recent example in the marketplace is the airline industry's radical simplification of a fare structure that had become so complex that passengers and their agents had great difficulty in dealing with it. Bridget O'Brien & James S. Hirsch, *Simplifying Their Fares Proves More Difficult than Airlines Expected*, WALL ST. J., June 4, 1992, at A1 (competition for passengers is preventing airlines from maintaining simple structure). *But see* Edwin McDowell, *Airfare Plan Fails, American Admits*, NEW YORK TIMES, Oct. 17, 1992, at A41; David Field, *Pricing Plan Crumbles as Other Airlines Add Innovations*, WASH. TIMES, Oct. 14, 1992, at C1.

158. *See supra* Part III.

159. Society, of course, may have a different view of the relevant costs and benefits of such techniques. For a provocative view on this question, see Owen M. Fiss, *Against Settlement*, 93 YALE L.J. 1073 (1984).

160. Jeffrey O'Connell, *A "Neo No-Fault" Contract in Lieu of Tort: Preaccident Guarantees of Postaccident Settlement Offers*, 73 CAL. L. REV. 898, 906–08 (1985).

161. *See* Negotiated Rulemaking Act of 1990, 5 U.S.C. ss 581–590 (Supp. III 1991).

162. *See* H. LAURENCE ROSS, SETTLED OUT OF COURT. THE SOCIAL PROCESS OF INSURANCE CLAIMS ADJUSTMENT (1970).

163. ROBERT C. ELLICKSON, ORDER WITHOUT LAW: HOW NEIGHBORS SETTLE DISPUTES 257 (1991). Ellickson cites other milieus, involving interacting social groups, in which similar simplification incentives operate. *See id.* at 189–206.

164. Schuck, *supra* note 35, at 194–96; *see also* Peter L. Strauss, *Rules, Adjudications, and Other Sources of Law in an Executive Department: Reflections on the Interior Department's Administration of the Mining Law*, 74 COLUM. L. REV. 1231, 1254–58 (1974).

165. *See* MASHAW & HARFST, *supra* note 13, at 147–71.

166. *E.g.*, INSTITUTE OF MEDICINE, MEDICAL PROFESSIONAL LIABILITY AND THE DELIVERY OF OBSTETRICAL CARE 38–42 (1989); THE LIABILITY MAZE: THE IMPACT OF LIABILITY LAW ON SAFETY AND INNOVATION (Peter W. Huber & Robert E. Litan eds., 1991); TORT LAW AND THE PUBLIC INTEREST: COMPETITION, INNOVATION, AND CONSUMER WELFARE 55–68 (Peter H. Schuck ed., 1991); George L. Priest, *The Current Insurance Crisis and Modern Tort Law*, 96 YALE L.J. 1521 (1987).

167. *See, e.g.*, Consumer Television Consumer Protection Act of 1992, Pub. L. No. 102–385 (passed Oct. 9, 1992).

168. PAUL C. WEILER, MEDICAL MALPRACTICE ON TRIAL 19–69 (1991).

169. This difference between the two regimes helps to explain why simplifications in the formal law regime may not forestall further simplifications in the informal one. If my analysis of the political economy of complexity is correct, politicians will tend to strike their balance at a higher complexity level than society in general or cost-bearing

groups in particular might wish. Even though Virginia lawmakers decided to replace tort law for birth-related neurological injuries with a no-fault system, obstetricians and patients will still search for other strategies that yield even better complexity equilibria. *See id.* at 153–54 (criticizing Virginia no-fault plan).

170. *See, e.g.,* Glass-Steagall Act of 1933, ch. 89, 48 Stat. 162 (codified as amended in scattered sections of 12 U.S.C.).

171. Indeed in some regulated industries, even unilateral withdrawal may be illegal unless the regulatory agency formally authorizes it. *See* 15 U.S.C. s 717f(b) (1988) (requiring pipeline operators to obtain approval of Federal Energy Regulatory Commission before abandoning natural gas pipelines or facilities); 49 U.S.C. s 10903(a) (1988) (requiring railroads to obtain approval of Interstate Commerce Commission before discontinuing service along rail lines).

172. *See* O'Connell, *supra* note 160, at 908–10 (acknowledging adverse selection problems of "neo no-fault" approach and proposing ways of addressing them).

173. *See* Theodore R. Marmor & Jerry L. Mashaw, *Canada's Health Insurance and Ours: The Real Lessons, the Big Choices,* Am. Prospect, Fall 1990, at 18, 22.

174. For discussion of some of the variables bearing on this question, see Neil K. Komesar, *Injuries and Institutions: Tort Reform, Tort Theory, and Beyond,* 65 N.Y.U. L. Rev. 23, 38–47 (1990) (distribution and magnitude of impacts and stakes among actual and potential victims and injurers affects effectiveness of different systems of risk control).

175. *E.g.,* Tunkl v. Regents of Univ. of Cal., 383 P.2d 441 (Cal. 1963). Even if unenforceable as such, a limited liability contract may nevertheless have some value to the provider (and thus to the patient)—for example, by discouraging suits or furnishing evidence of knowledge of a risk. I am indebted to Boris Bittker for pointing this out.

176. *See, e.g.,* Wagenblast v. Odessa Sch. Dist., 758 P.2d 968 (Wash. 1988) (invalidating release form concerning interscholastic sports accidents).

177. *See supra* Sections II(A), (B). Another example of a more comprehensive calculus is Samuel Gross's analysis of the benefits of some complexity-induced inefficiencies. *See* Gross, *supra* note 73.

178. An example is consumers who cannot externalize their costs to insurers or to other groups that can organize to protect their own (and indirectly, consumers') interests.

179. Bittker, *supra* note 15, at 5.

180. *See, e.g., supra* note 97 and accompanying text.

181. Indeed, that possibility may be an important reason for selecting a particular legal rule based on informal practice. *See, e.g.,* Ian Ayres & Robert Gertner, *Strategic Contractual Inefficiency and the Optimal Choice of Legal Rules,* 101 Yale L.J. 729 (1992).

182. *See supra* text accompanying notes 170–76.

183. Gross, *supra* note 73, at 756.

184. Fed. R. Civ. P. 26(c), 37(a)(4).

185. Fed. R. Civ. P. 68.

186. *See, e.g.,* Americans with Disabilities Act of 1990, 42 U.S.C. s 12111(5)(A) (Supp. II 1990).

187. Again, I assume that complexity's beneficiaries will fully exploit any gains from it without our help.

188. *See* Ayres & Gertner, *supra* note 181, at 737.

189. *Id.* at 765.

190. Robert E. Keeton & Jeffrey O'Connell, Basic Protection for the Traffic Victim 5–10 (1965) (under such plans, the issue is occurrence of accident and injury, not fault).

191. WEILER, *supra* note 168, at 114–32.

192. *See, e.g.,* ARIZ. REV. STAT. ANN. s 12–551 (1991) (product liability actions must be commenced within 12 years of sale); CONN. GEN. STAT. ANN. s 52–577(a) (1991) (product liability actions must be commenced within 10 years after defendant parted with the product); TENN. CODE ANN. s 29–28–103(a) (1991) (product liability actions must be commenced within 10 years of date of purchase); *see also* Robert A. Van Kirk, Note, *The Evolution of Useful Life Statutes in the Products Liability Reform Effort,* 1989 DUKE L.J. 1689.

193. *See, e.g.,* 42 U.S.C. s 1320c–6(c) (1988) (exempting physicians and providers from civil liability for actions taken on account of or in compliance with norms applied by peer standards review organizations).

194. *See supra* note 80 and accompanying text.

195. *See* JAMES A. HENDERSON, JR. & AARON D. TWERSKI, PRODUCTS LIABILITY: PROBLEMS AND PROCESS 279–80 (1987); Morris G. Shanker, *Strict Tort Theory of Products Liability and the Uniform Commercial Code,* 17 CASE W. RES. L. REV. 5 (1965).

196. *See* SCHUCK, *supra* note 21, at 291.

197. *See* AMERICAN LAW INSTITUTE, ENTERPRISE RESPONSIBILITY FOR PERSONAL INJURY 199–230 (1991) (considering a similar "scale" approach to the calculation of pain and suffering damages); James F. Blumstein et al., *Beyond Tort Reform: Developing Better Tools for Assessing Damages for Personal Injury,* 8 YALE J. ON REG. 171, 177–86 (1991); Randall R. Bovbjerg et al., *Valuing Life and Limb in Tort: Scheduling "Pain and Suffering,"* 83 NW. U. L. REV. 908 (1988–89); Peter H. Schuck, *Scheduled Damages and Insurance Contracts for Future Services: A Comment on Blumstein, Bovbjerg, and Sloan,* 8 YALE J. ON REG. 213, 216–19 (1991).

198. *See* Bovbjerg et al., *supra* note 197, at 923 (providing data indicating that within each of eight "severity levels" of tort claims the highest valuation of damages is generally scores of times higher than the lowest); Schuck, *supra* note 21, at 559–67. This "demoralization cost" engendered the demand for sentencing guidelines in the context of criminal law. *See supra* note 19.

199. *See* Schuck, *supra* note 21.

200. *See* S. 250, 102d Cong., 1st Sess. (1991) (proposed National Voter Registration Act of 1991, also known as the "Motor Voter" bill, under which voter registration would take place during driver's license application and renewal); H.R. 4366, 102d Cong., 2d Sess. (1992) (providing for voter registration at time of driver's license application and renewal). Professor Raymond Wolfinger has studied the effects of complex voter registration procedures and argued that simpler procedures would strengthen the legitimacy of the electoral process without having significant partisan effects. RAYMOND E. WOLFINGER & STEVEN J. ROSENSTONE, WHO VOTES? 80–88 (1980); *see also* Peverill Squire et al., *Residential Mobility and Voter Turnout,* 81 AM. POL. SCI. REV. 45, 57–58 (1987) (proposing simplified registration procedure).

201. *See, e.g.,* CONN. GEN. STAT. ss 14–42(b), 19a–279(b) (1990) (requiring state to give drivers an opportunity to indicate on driver's licenses whether they wish to donate organs in event of fatal accident).

202. *See supra* note 97 and accompanying text.

203. For a summary of such proposals, see Ronald Cass, *Privatization: Politics, Law and Theory,* 71 MARQ. L. REV. 449 (1988).

204. *See* Bruce A. Ackerman & Richard B. Stewart, *Reforming Environmental Law,* 37 STAN. L. REV. 1333, 1341–51 (1985).

205. *See generally* DAVID OSBORNE & TED GAEBLER, REINVENTING GOVERNMENT: HOW THE ENTREPRENEURIAL SPIRIT IS TRANSFORMING THE PUBLIC SECTORS (1992)

206. *See* John E. Chubb & Terry M. Moe, Politics, Markets & America's Schools 199–201 (1990); Paul Starr, The Logic of Health Care Reform (forthcoming 1992).

207. *See supra* text accompanying notes 39–40.

208. There is abundant evidence of other societies' inability to manage it, from the strong privatization movements in virtually all Western European nations to the collapse of centrally administered economies in Eastern Europe and other parts of the world.

209. *See, e.g.,* Motor Carrier Act of 1980, Pub. L. No. 96–296, 94 Stat. 793 (codified in scattered provisions of 49 U.S.C.); Railroad Revitalization and Regulatory Reform Act of 1976, Pub. L. No. 94–210, 90 Stat. 31 (codified as amended primarily in 45, 49 U.S.C.).

210. *See, e.g.,* Natural Gas Policy Act of 1978, Pub. L. No. 95–621, 92 Stat. 3350 (codified in scattered provisions of 15 U.S.C.).

211. Pub. L. No. 96–511, 94 Stat. 2812 (codified as amended in 5, 20, 30, 42, 44 U.S.C.).

212. Chevron U.S.A. Inc. v. Natural Resources Defense Council, Inc., 467 U.S. 837 (1984). For an analysis of *Chevron,* see Cynthia R. Farina, *Statutory Interpretation and the Balance of Power in the Administrative State,* 89 Colum. L. Rev. 452, 458–61 (1989).

213. *See, e.g.,* Richard A. Posner, The Federal Courts: Crisis and Reform (1985); Stephen D. Sugarman, Doing Away with Personal Injury Law (1989).

2

Multi-Culturalism Redux

Science, Law, and Politics

The very word justice *irritates scientists. No surgeon expects to be asked if an operation for cancer is just or not. No doctor will be reproached on the grounds that the dose of penicillin he has prescribed is less or more than* justice *would stipulate.*[1]

A third of a century has now passed since the British writer C.P. Snow sounded an alarm about the "two cultures" problem.[2] By "culture," he meant both a course of intellectual development and "a group of persons living in the same environment, linked by common habits, common assumptions, a common way of life"[3]—definitions that will adequately serve my purposes here. Snow wrote of the "gulf of mutual incomprehension" yawning between the cultures of science and of literature, which he called "traditional" culture. Literary intellectuals' misunderstanding of science, he noted, often verged on "hostility and dislike."[4]

With the clairvoyance of hindsight, we can now see that Snow aimed at the wrong target.[5] Misunderstandings between science and literature today are rather a sideshow, peripheral to the main event. Science's clashes with two[6] *other* cultures, law and politics, seem far more consequential given the speed of technological change, the growth of the administrative state's authority to control it, and the coercive power of legal and political authority.[7]

One is tempted to draw an analogy between this cultural conflict and the bitter religious and ethnic struggles that roil most countries and many American cities today. Like these other struggles, the science-law-politics conflict is fundamentally cultural; the ultimate prize is the power to shape how society thinks, feels, lives, values, and chooses. Like religio-ethnic confrontations, this conflict unfolds simultaneously at various levels: in obscurity (individual scientific research, legal argument, policy analysis) and in the glare of public view (NIH budget debates, Supreme Court decisions, regulatory legislation). And like them, the conflict—even when it goes unrecognized—lies near the center of our most important public debates.

The analogy to religious and ethnic struggles, of course, can only take us so far. Unlike the combatants in Bosnia, the Punjab, and South Central Los Angeles, the partisans of science, law, and politics generally recognize that their professional cultures are neither monolithic nor wholly self-defining, and that their social interdependence runs deep. They bear a common allegiance to the democratic institutions charged with regulating multi-cultural conflicts. They do not dispute their competitors' legitimacy *within the proper spheres* of each. While their cultural chauvinism is often vehement, it is not violent—except rhetorically. Finally, precisely because these battles usually occur within a legislative chamber or courtroom over a discrete, often narrowly technical policy issue, the combatants can more easily forget that something much greater—a normative world-view—is actually at stake.

This article has three parts. Part I sets the stage for my analysis of this multi-cultural conflict. There I describe two notorious disputes, Bendectin and Agent Orange, which exemplify some of the patterns that I shall discuss.

Part II extends the theme of cultural conflict beyond the litigation context by sequentially analyzing and comparing science, law, and politics along three dimensions: their central values; their distinctive incentive structures and decision techniques; and their characteristic biases, especially their orientations toward the tension between professional and populist values.

In Part III, I consider how we should approach the multi-culturalism problem in public policymaking, especially where science issues are involved. After noting that these conflicts are not only inevitable but socially desirable in a democratic-liberal-technocratic polity,[8] I advocate a criterion of cultural competence for allocating decisional authority over multi-cultural issues. I suggest that by empowering one culture's distinctive decision-making rules and institutions to control the issues lying at that culture's core, the relevant scientific, legal, and political values can be integrated with greater synergy and less waste. I conclude by exploring some specific reform implications of the analysis, including the creation of new inter-cultural "bridging" institutions.

Before turning to the cases, some preliminary observations about the discussion that follows are in order. First, I treat multi-culturalism generally and more specifically in terms of the character of the three cultures, and the relations among them. I am primarily interested, however, in the relationship between science and law, a priority reflected in the discussion in Parts I and III. My reasons are fairly straightforward. Politics-law and politics-science conflicts are ubiquitous and are resolved through the fluid, workaday processes of political give-and-take. Subject to constitutional limits, politicians hold the trump cards and can impose whatever solutions they like. In a crucial sense, politics is a meta-culture, regulating other cultures and their interactions. Politicians' collisions with law and with science are therefore ubiquitous and receive constant attention and sophisticated commentary. In both Agent Orange (and to a lesser extent, Bendectin), for example, politics was the forum to which those dissatisfied with the law's handling of scientific issues could and did ultimately appeal. Conflicts between science and law, moreover, are more obscure and less visible to the public eye. These cultures are more technical and less open-textured than politics; hence their own internal structures and requirements, which are poorly understood by outsiders, constrain the solutions to their conflicts, which become matters primarily for insiders. Thus, public discourse about them is relatively parochial and impoverished.

Second, although the law intersects with scientific and technical analysis at almost every turn,[9] I am primarily interested in two other legal domains in which science plays an especially prominent role. The first is the public law of "social regulation"—environmental protection, occupational safety and health law, consumer product safety, and the like—in which government agencies develop and enforce general legal standards in order to promote public health. This domain is exemplified by the Bendectin litigation. The second is the private law of toxic torts in which individuals sue alleged polluters and product distributors for compensation for harm, usually personal injuries.[10] Here, I offer the Agent Orange case as the example. In both domains, advocates and decision-makers must mobilize and interpret uncertain scientific data in support of legal arguments and authoritative decisions about risk assessment and risk distribution in society. I focus on social regulation and toxic torts because the differences among science, law, and politics are most profound, controversial, and problematic in these areas.

Third, I shall emphasize cultural *conflict*. By doing so, I do not mean to deny that these three cultures exhibit some important commonalities.[11] For example, each culture is centrally concerned with solving problems, though, of course, not of the same kind or in the same way. Each culture is also highly professionalized; in order to join and succeed, its members must acquire an arcane knowledge, practice special techniques and skills, and subscribe to a distinctive set of norms, a world view common to the group. Each culture seeks to enhance the group's social power, its command of resources and values. Finally, each culture is supported by and indispensable to the modern state's effectiveness.

Still, the cultures' divergences are more striking than their commonalities. Science, law, and politics are not merely unique ways of living and thinking but also represent radically different modes of legitimating public decisions. Each invokes distinct values in support of its claims to exercise authority. Science appeals to the capacity of technical rationality and specialized expertise to generate and test empirically falsifiable propositions.[12] Law appeals to the capacity of universal, abstract, binding principles to produce justice.[13] Democratic politics appeals to the capacity of participation, accommodation, and accountability to justify the state's coercive authority.[14] Each, then, invokes a distinctive conception of truth or, less grandly, of how to achieve the good. The three cultures, then, compete at several different levels.[15] They are encoded in diverse public symbols, appeal to discrete conceptions of decisional legitimacy, express their own rhetoric, and develop their own power bases. And because each culture is embedded in different governmental institutions, each must face special structural and constitutional obstacles to resolving multicultural tensions.[16] This cultural competition is socially desirable in many ways, but unless it is creatively managed—the subject of Part III—it may also occasion great social cost.

The Bendectin and Agent Orange litigations with which I begin are hardly typical cases, but neither are they anomalous or anachronistic. They exhibit some of the deep normative and political conflicts that divide the scientific, legal, and political cultures. Such conflicts are certain to intensify in the future. Science's remarkable advances in instrumentation, methodology, theory, and data constantly generate new ethical and regulatory dilemmas which only a combination of law and politics can resolve. It unleashes a cascade of new products and new technologies which create new risks that often justify social control.[17] Science's growing capacity to postpone death, for example, raises the most delicate questions about the quality and cost of life, while its emerging genetic wizardry engenders new value conflicts and Faustian bargains.[18]

Law and politics, for their parts, are chronically ambitious, constantly striving to extend their jurisdictions to regulate scientific activities that were previously autonomous. This ambition is fortified by changing social attitudes about risk and expertise that weaken public deference to science. Recent disputes over products and technologies—asbestos, breast implants, video terminal displays, computer keyboards, cigarettes, electromagnetic fields, and many others—prefigure further political and legal growth. They presage a future of constant cultural collisions, pressures for regulatory controls, and novel personal injury litigation.

In order to explain the problematic handling of disputes like Bendectin and Agent Orange, it arguably is not necessary to resort to the somewhat elusive notion of cultural conflict at all. In this view, a simpler, more parsimonious explanation would be that the law is just not very competent in resolving complex scientific disputes very well. This explanation, however, would merely raise a more basic question: why are legal rules and institutions still applied to such disputes when they have proved to be problematic in resolving them? The answer to this question, I believe, begins with the notion that the law approaches this adjudicative task in a culturally bound, hence normatively loaded, way, which confirms the law in viewing it simply as an old task arising in a new context. The law uses traditional methods not because it is mindless or hidebound but because these methods encode its most cherished, distinctive values.

The notions of culture and cultural conflict are certainly not the only, and may not even be the best, concepts for understanding the problematic outcomes that one increasingly observes at the intersection of law, science, and politics. Culture is a notoriously slippery concept, as the bitter controversy among social scientists over the existence of a "culture of poverty" reveals. As I have just suggested, however, the idea of law's incompetence in dealing with science is even more question-begging. In attempting to understand both the law's stubborn insistence on doing new things in the old ways and its continuing difficulty in comprehending and integrating the quite different modes of science and of politics, the idea of culture—of a unique way of viewing, valuing, and manipulating the world—seems as serviceable as any.

I. Two Case Studies

Fortunately for our purposes, the twists and turns of the Bendectin and Agent Orange litigations have been comprehensively documented. They continue today, fifteen years after the first cases in each litigation were filed.[19] In each case, science, law, and (to a lesser extent) politics were obliged to enter into a kind of shotgun marriage. In each, this awkward union was consummated not in nuptial bliss but in a bitter estrangement, as the unwilling partners pursued quite different, often incompatible directions. I do not claim that these litigations are altogether paradigmatic of the science-law-politics conflict. Like all mammoth cases, they are unusual in certain respects. I claim only that we can learn something from them about how one important social decision modality, namely court litigation, often addresses multi-cultural issues.

A. Bendectin

Bendectin[20] was an anti-nausea drug marketed from 1956 until 1983 to some 30 million pregnant women for morning sickness until the manufacturer removed it from the market, citing the high cost of litigation over the drug. As recently as 1980, the Food and Drug Administration (FDA) approved Bendectin as safe and effective. Since 1977, when the first Bendectin case was filed, more than 2100 suits have been brought alleging birth defects or infant deaths caused by the drug. In each of the 27 cases that went to trial (25 of them before a jury and one consolidating more than 800 claims) the central factual issue was Bendectin's "general causation"—its capacity to cause the *kinds* of injuries alleged by the plaintiffs. As is true in many but not all toxic tort disputes, this issue was made vastly more difficult in the Bendectin cases by the absence of either a pathognomonic ("signature") disease or a generally accepted biological theory of causation. In almost all of these cases, essentially the same scientific evidence on causation—consisting of epidemiological, *in vivo, in vitro*, chemical structure, and secular trend studies—was presented in much the same way, usually by the same expert witnesses. *At trial*, many Bendectin plaintiffs won jury verdicts; indeed, their success rates were comparable to those obtained in products liability cases generally. Some of these jury verdicts were enormous; the most recent, rendered in September 1991, awarded $33.75 million in compensatory and punitive damages.

The plaintiffs' success at trial, however, was utterly at variance with the great weight of the scientific evidence on the drug's teratogenicity (i.e., its capacity to cause birth defects). This body of evidence grew larger, more rigorous, more consistent, and more unequivocal as the 1980s wore on.[21] It strongly suggested to virtually all disinterested scientists that Bendectin was unlikely to have caused the alleged birth defects and that any remaining doubt on this score was probably irreducible. Moreover, since 1987, the federal appellate courts (where most of the litigation has occurred) have firmly endorsed this view of the evidence, taking the unusual step of reversing plaintiffs' verdicts instead of simply remanding them for new trials. The difference between the judges' and the juries' views of the plaintiffs' claims in these cases is striking.[22]

This scientific and judicial consensus exonerating Bendectin makes it all the more remarkable that the rate of plaintiff victories at trial did not decline appreciably during the late 1980s and early 1990s. In fact, the two most recent Bendectin trials, far from following this consensus, actually produced a hung jury and the stunning $33.75 million award just mentioned. Thus science and the law (at least as applied in jury verdicts) have gone off in opposite directions.

In an effort to explain this divergence, Professor Joseph Sanders recently scrutinized the trial transcripts of a cross-section of Bendectin cases, hoping to determine how the trial lawyers actually used and presented scientific evidence on causation.[23] His analysis focuses on the peculiar nature of the legal process which filters and translates the scientific record into expert testimony at trial.[24]

Five aspects of the process, Sanders finds, were especially problematic in encouraging legal fact-finding to diverge from the scientific evidence offered in the Bendectin cases. First, expert witnesses were selected and deployed in ways that made it hard for the fact-finder, whether jury or judge, to evaluate and differentiate between their testimonies.[25] Second, the nature of the experts' testimony made all of the science seem to be of equal worth and relevance.[26] Law's fact-finders are not blind, Sanders observes; instead they lack "depth perception." Third, cross-examination seldom clarified the strengths and weaknesses of witnesses' scientific testimony; instead, it ritualistically centered on their putative biases and trivial misstatements. Fourth, Sanders notes, the nature of the evidence and the structure of the legal issues made it easier for the plaintiffs in Bendectin and other toxic tort cases to arrange the evidence into a coherent, persuasive story than for the defendants to do so.

Finally, Sanders suggests that the juries in Bendectin and other toxic tort cases may have discounted the kind of purely statistical evidence on causation, including epidemiological studies, upon which the defendants in these cases must often rely. Citing recent psychological experiments indicating that juries evaluate evidence according to how well it "fits" into each of the competing stories before them, he concludes that this may systematically advantage the plaintiffs in such cases. While plaintiffs can prevail even if the jury believes from the statistical evidence that the defendant's product can cause only a very small fraction of the birth defects, defendants can prevail only if the jury believes that the drug is incapable of causing *any* of them.

Because science and the jury-made law of Bendectin have taken diametrically opposed paths,[27] the *politics* of Bendectin has been free to move in several directions. This litigation is now one of the "bloody shirts" waved by partisans in order to mobilize public support in the struggle over products liability reform. It has become a *cause celebre* for diverse interests. To those who favor new restrictions on liability, for example, the Bendectin experience demonstrates how a safe, socially valuable drug can be forced off the market by malleable tort doctrines, costly nuisance claims, "junk science," and irrational jury verdicts.[28] To those who favor expanding (or at least retaining) existing liability levels, however, Bendectin shows that a lay jury, not an elite court, is the appropriate institution for resolving factual conflicts over expert scientific testimony on causation.[29] The two sides talk past each other precisely because, as discussed in Part II, each speaks the language and invokes the values of a different culture. In order to achieve mutual intelligibility, they must turn to a third, hopefully more *integrative* culture—politics. As we shall also see, however, politics is not always a faithful translator.

B. Agent Orange

The Agent Orange[30] litigation exemplifies an intriguingly different relationship among science, law, and politics. Like the Bendectin litigation, it was launched in the late 1970s and continues today, although the main action in Agent Orange ended in the late 1980s. The case was spawned by America's involvement in the Vietnam War, a watershed in American politics, and became a controversy of immense proportions, involving a plaintiff class of 2.4 million people (ultimately producing about 250,000 individual claims), much of the chemical industry, and the U.S. Government. In addition to the $180 million required to settle the class action, the main parties (not counting the government) incurred litigation costs that certainly exceeded $110 million. Because of the case's connection to the war and its high public profile, it also occasioned intense political and organizational activity by veterans groups at the federal and state levels, a factor that distinguishes it from the more fragmented Bendectin litigation.

As with Bendectin, the central issue of fact was general causation—whether the dioxin contaminant of Agent Orange could have caused the veterans' cancers and other chronic diseases in light of the amount and conditions of their exposure to it. Because the injuries could not be traced to a single cause (as in the case of asbestosis), but instead could have been produced by a number of different factors, proof of causation was peculiarly dependent on naked statistical evidence rather than on direct evidence of exposure to the single causal agent. It was also more difficult to establish the soldiers' levels of exposure to Agent Orange under highly variable wartime conditions than to measure a woman's exposure to a drug, like Bendectin, taken under prescription. The plaintiffs' diseases had long latency periods in Agent Orange; in Bendectin, however, they were manifest at birth.

Causation, then, was even harder to resolve here than it was in Bendectin. But the body of scientific evidence bearing on Agent Orange's toxic effects was also larger, including numerous animal and epidemiological studies. In theory, the latter were especially valuable for inferring causation; they were based on human populations and reflected a kind of "natural experiment" (since only individuals in Vietnam had been substantially exposed to Agent Orange). Some of these epidemiological studies, moreover, were unusually large and well-designed.[31]

All Agent Orange cases were in effect consolidated in a single federal court, obviating the prospect of the inconsistent verdicts that so plagued the Bendectin litigation. After settling the class action, the judge, Jack Weinstein, turned to the several hundred remaining "opt-out" cases. Having studied and mastered the scientific evidence to a degree that few other judges would even attempt, Judge Weinstein ruled that the animal studies were not helpful in proving the etiology of the plaintiffs' conditions, that "the only useful studies having any bearing on causation" were the epidemiological studies, that the best of these were negative, and that plaintiffs' scientific experts had not even discussed them. Since plaintiffs' experts' conclusions about causation were based wholly on their examination of individual medical records, which Judge Weinstein deemed irrelevant to proof of causation in such a case, he flatly excluded their testimony and dismissed the opt-out plaintiffs' cases. This dismissal was upheld by the appellate court, albeit on grounds other than the causation evidence.[32]

Judge Weinstein's rulings on the causation evidence in Agent Orange have raised fundamental issues about the appropriate boundaries between the domains of science and law. May a judge, trained as a lawyer, simply reject on its scientific merits the testimony of reputable scientists concerning a complex causal issue within their professional ken? May he exclude from the jury's consideration a large body of scientific evidence simply because he thinks that the jury might misunderstand it? May he insist that only epidemiological evidence, with all its flaws, constitutes acceptable proof of causation? May he treat as "negative" epidemiological evidence that most scientists would say is merely "inconclusive"? Does the fact that he could exclude testimony based on novel methods or principles mean that he may also exclude novel scientific opinions based on *conventional* methods or principles?

These issues are highly controversial in the legal culture. The manner in which the courts resolved them in Agent Orange and Bendectin has affected the courts' handling of causation evidence in other toxic tort cases, establishing a kind of "epidemiological threshold" that plaintiffs must cross in order to avoid having their claims dismissed.[33] As in Bendectin, the tensions between science and law on these questions have created special opportunities for politicians. Despite (or perhaps because of) Judge Weinstein's firm conclusion that the scientific evidence did not establish Agent Orange's causal responsibility for human cancers, and despite subsequent epidemiological studies and other analyses that tended to confirm the accuracy of his conclusion,[34] political pressures induced the Veterans Administration, and then Congress, to grant permanent disability benefits to veterans suffering from two forms of cancer.[35]

My point is not that Judge Weinstein was correct and the VA and Congress wrong. Indeed, they may *all* have been correct, since each was responding to a somewhat different question and thus operating under a different standard of proof.[36] The more pertinent point is that when neither scientific nor legal technocrats can furnish authoritative answers to problems arising at the increasingly crowded intersection of science and law, we must expect politicians to bridge the gap, using the uncertainty as a reason (perhaps a pretext) to supply their own answers.

Why are authoritative answers at the science-law frontier so elusive that politicians must intervene? The inherent complexity of the problems is aggravated by the short time frames that public law and public opinion frequently demand and the limited problem-solving resources that they provide. Often— as when the issue is whether exposure to low levels of a chemical caused a tort plaintiff's cancer—the question is "trans-scientific" (to use physicist Alvin Weinberg's term): although it can be formulated in scientific terms, it cannot be conclusively answered by science alone. In these cases we must also look to other, non-scientific criteria of decision.[37]

This trans-science problem, however, is minimized in the Bendectin and Agent Orange cases.[38] Although expert witnesses can almost always be found to create an issue of fact, the scientific conclusion was not in genuine doubt in either of these cases.[39] By the time the courts had to rule in them, mainstream science had reached a reasonably firm consensus that the evidence did not establish causation.[40] The real issue in these cases, then, was not the scientific consensus on causation but rather science's authority, legitimacy, and intelligibility in the larger, transcendent worlds of law and politics.

Even so, the fact that the legal outcomes in Bendectin and Agent Orange turned out to be consistent with the best available science is only mildly reassuring, for in both cases this convergence required extraordinary judicial interventions—reversal of jury verdicts in Bendectin and close technical scrutiny of expert testimony in Agent Orange. With less audacious courts, both cases could easily have gone the other way.[41] These narrow victories remind us that important social decisions can be distorted when agents of one culture control decisions more properly governed by another culture operating under quite different rules. Such mismatches of authority and competence will often produce costly decision processes that generate substantive outcomes of doubtful legitimacy, if not outright error.[42] Cultural imperialism can be as problematic in domestic policymaking as in world politics.

Although defining and defending each culture's appropriate jurisdiction are hard tasks, as I discuss in Part III, the difficulties in defending whatever jurisdictions are defined are even greater. The combatants in public policy struggles will always attempt to obscure whatever jurisdictional lines have been drawn. Special interests—whether engaged in institutional design, justificatory rhetoric, litigation, or legislative-bureaucratic politics—strategically deploy some expedient mixture of scientific "facts," legal "principles," and political consensus norms. Jurisdictional line drawing is pointless unless these lines can be defended, in which case trans-cultural understanding, respect, and cross-fertilization become even more imperative to reduce the now greater risk that each culture will wall itself off into a dangerous isolation.

II. The Competing Cultures

Before I proceed, a caveat. In order to contrast science, law, and politics, one must characterize the three cultures in ways that are stylized but hopefully not caricatured. The generalizations I make about each culture are subject to important exceptions, qualifications, and distinctions. Although I note these refinements, my approach—which exaggerates the purity, consistency, and exclusivity of each culture's normative structure—risks some over-simplification. If one hopes to identify the major lines of cultural cleavage, anticipate the conflicts that they are increasingly engendering, and consider how they might be ameliorated, this risk cannot be avoided altogether.

I organize the analysis of each culture around three different dimensions: (1) the central values to which members of the culture subscribe; (2) the incentive structures that animate the culture's members and the decision techniques that they typically employ; and (3) the characteristic biases and orientations of the culture.

A. Science

1. Central Values.   Given Snow's purpose, one might have expected him to be a kind of anthropologist of the scientific culture, probing its deep structure. In fact, he tells us rather little about it. Scientists, he observes, are optimistic and practical, concerned above all else with understanding nature and solving problems.[43] He maintains that they read few literary books and have underdeveloped imaginations.[44] He notes, however, that the scientific culture is not monolithic, suggesting that pure scientists have little more in common with engineers and other applied scientists than with literary intellectuals.[45] Snow surely exaggerates here, for whatever the differences among scientific subcultures, there *is* a core of beliefs, training, and techniques common to those who are recognized as scientists by the scientific community, at least as conventionally defined.[46]

What constitutes this common core? Peter Huber, an engineer-lawyer who is a militant scientific positivist and a caustic critic of the law's treatment of scientific evidence, asserts that "[t]he scientific ideal stands in sharp contrast to the windy agnosticism of the modern philosopher, litigator, or social engineer."[47] Huber holds that the modern scientist is not dogmatic but is instead "a credulous skeptic—skeptic in that he demands serious evidence and proof; credulous in that he concedes, not just offhandedly but very systematically, that every measurement, correlation, analysis, or theory may contain some margin of error, which may in turn conceal important but unrecognized new truth."[48] Science, Huber insists, is the domain of systematic verification to which social purposes are quite irrelevant.[49]

Other commentators, less tendentious than Huber, are also less certain of science's detached, ahistorical objectivity. Sheila Jasanoff, reviewing the work of historians and sociologists of science, notes three of their major findings.[50] First, scientific facts are not immanent in an objective reality waiting to be discovered by any scientists who look in the right place. Instead, they are constructed and validated through a social process dominated by those in the scientific community who possess authority to do so. Second, this validation process is itself shaped by the scientific paradigms, the shared assumptions and prejudices of the professional community that dominate the thought of a particular period. These paradigms hold sway for reasons that may have less to do with their intrinsic merit than with their support of existing social structures, including the scientific establishment. Third, the authority to validate science rests in part on boundary-drawing and other strategic behavior by scientific disputants, behavior that can effectively exclude their less influential competitors.

To these findings, one might add another so obvious that it may easily escape notice. For most scientists, the search for particular facts is not guided solely by their autonomous, spontaneous curiosity. Instead, the search is constrained and channeled by the resources available for research, which in turn reflect the priorities of politicians, corporations, foundations, and other sources of funding for science.

This insistence on the contingent, socially constructed, and validated, resource-constrained character of scientific paradigms and propositions, especially in areas of great uncertainty or in which dominant views are firmly institutionalized, is an important antidote to the more transcendent, universal pretensions of certain conceptions of science. But it would be equally wrong to conclude from the fact of science's social embeddedness that its culture is as flexible, indeterminate, and relativistic as those of law and politics. In its professional norms and aspirations, and to some extent in its actual performance, science is committed to a conception of truth (though one that is always provisional and contestable) reached through a conventional methodology of proof (though one that can be difficult to apply and interpret) based upon the testing of falsifiable propositions.[51]

2. Incentives and Techniques.   What motivates scientists to behave as they do in their professional settings? Like other highly educated people, of course, they are driven by a desire for professional recognition, economic security, social influence, job satisfaction, and intellectual stimulation, among other things. But some of the goals that motivate them are peculiar, if not unique, to the scientific culture. Perhaps most important, scientists subscribe to and are actuated by rigorous standards of empirical investigation and proof; to deviate from these standards is to be deemed professionally incompetent, or worse. Scientists also define themselves in part by their membership in larger scientific communities that both contribute to, and are entitled to exploit, their own work. These principles of peer review invigorate and enforce their adherence to a norm of extreme caution (Huber's "credulous skepticism").

These values and incentives lead to a distinctive set of scientific practices and techniques. I have just noted the importance of peer review. Other practices reflect science's changing context. The team approach to research, for example, has become the norm as science fragments into a large number of increasingly narrow technical specialties and as intricate research problems cut across these specialty boundaries. Today, much research requires a large investment of time, money, staff, and other resources for which scientists must vigorously compete, yet the payoffs in basic knowledge or in practical application are highly uncertain and often far in the future. Contemporary science, then, is a high-risk activity requiring large aggregations of capital and talent as well as techniques for diversifying the risks of failure. For all these reasons, much scientific enterprise has grown more collaborative, corporate, and dependent upon government support.[52] In most fields, the solitary investigator is becoming an inspiring relic of an increasingly anachronistic, Renaissance vision of science. Today, teamwork is more the norm.[53]

In addition, the time frame of science is relatively open-ended. It is true, of course, that competitive pressures often demand speed where a discovery may have important commercial applications, as in pharmaceutical research. Nevertheless, science—especially basic research—tends to move in its own, largely autonomous rhythms. These rhythms are dictated by the pace of technological development and dissemination, the availability of resources for further investigation, and the process of consensus formation among scientists. Imposing arbitrary deadlines cannot accelerate these factors.

3. Biases and Orientations.   Like all cultures, science nurtures certain biases, blind spots, and predispositions. Most scientists receive an intensely technical training, face strong incentives to follow highly specialized career paths, and must keep up with voluminous research literatures that are often more specialized still. Generalist scientists today are few and far between. These conditions foster a decidedly narrow, technocratic perspective. Their hunger for the respect of other scientists, buttressed by peer review, causes the vast majority to shun advocacy of controversial positions on technical issues in the mass media or other nonprofessional public forums, including courtrooms and legislative hearings. Doubtful about lay understanding and fearful of being misinterpreted, they tend to be far more comfortable reporting on their work in the precise, qualified, technical language of the peer-reviewed journal than holding press conferences to announce their latest findings to reporters whose scientific training may not extend much beyond a course in biology taken many years ago. Skittish about active involvement in politics and wary of lawyers and other professional advocates who do not subscribe to their distinctive canons, they prefer the familiar environments of the laboratory, the seminar room, and the specialized scientific meeting to the courtroom or talk show.[54]

Experimental scientists are preoccupied with the process of unearthing hard facts; their goal is discovery, their master techniques are the analysis of data and the testing of theories. Unlike lawyers and politicians, there is little in their training, professional norms or work environment that gives them a sophisticated understanding of social value conflicts or equips them even to address such conflicts. The political process that pits science against other normative systems is the bailiwick of specialized science bureaucrats. For most practicing scientists, however, politics is *terra incognita*. Scientists' uneasiness around politicians is really a special case of their more general suspicion of populism. One defining feature of any culture is its orientation toward the roles of expert and lay judgments in conferring legitimate authority on decisions, and science is no exception. Its distinctive position can be illustrated if we imagine a spectrum along which attitudes about the sources of legitimate decision-making authority are arrayed, with professional autonomy at the left-hand pole and lay decision making on the right-hand pole.[55] Science, with its technocratic commitments to rigorous method, objectivity, and expert judgment, would occupy the professional autonomy pole; pure science would be on the extreme left and applied science to its right. As we shall see in our discussion of the other two cultures, expert bureaucracy would lie a bit further to the right, law—divided into non-jury and jury components—would lie somewhere near the middle, while political bureaucracy would be located nearer the lay decision-making pole. (The market and familism are included in order to fill out the extreme right-hand position.)

As this spectrum suggests, science harbors a deep aversion to populist legitimations of decision-making authority; many dangerously false claims have been propagated in the name of public opinion. Science exalts instead the trained expert who possesses esoteric knowledge and who adheres to values and methods that ordinary people can scarcely understand. The scientific spirit of "credulous skepticism" rejects folk wisdom and conventional assumptions that cannot pass through the profession's fine-meshed empirical screen.[56]

These broad generalizations about the culture of science, of course, describe what is in fact a far more complex social reality. Many exceptions should prop-

TABLE 2.1 Decisionmaking Authority in Different Cultures

Pure science	Applied science	Expert bureaucracy	Law non-jury	Law jury	Political bureaucracy	Market and Family
- - - -	- - - -	- - - -	- - - -	- - - -	- - - -	- - - -

Professional autonomy ← → Lay decisionmaking

erly be noted. For example, scientist-writers like Stephen Jay Gould[57] and C.P. Snow himself exhibit a broad humanistic vision reflecting their deep familiarity with the literary culture. Scientists like Barry Commoner and Samuel Epstein are ardent controversialists who gravitate eagerly to the public forum;[58] many others are also perfectly delighted when the science reporter from the *New York Times* or even *USA Today* calls to discuss their work. Certain distinguished scientists turn out to be fine science bureaucrats as well; examples include Maxine Singer and Rene Dubos. The canons of scientific proof are not as clear-cut as they seem; they contain (and conceal) difficult issues of methodology and interpretation, as the many disputes over environmental carcinogens attest.[59] And there are always scientists—some "clinical ecologists," for example—who flagrantly violate those canons.[60]

Some distinctions should also be drawn. For example, the conventional contrast between "hard" and "soft" sciences tracks important divisions that belie the merely superficial unity of the scientific culture.[61] Although physicians are scientifically trained, they do not approach data in the same manner as do practicing scientists.[62] Theoretical and experimental scientists do quite different things and think in different ways. Even within a particular scientific specialty or sub-specialty, practices and values are likely to vary among countries, regions, and even research groups in the same locality. Although it is common to speak of the scientific "community" (and I do so here), such usage is a rather quaint way to describe what has in fact become a fragmented profession.

In addition to these exceptions and distinctions, some qualifications are in order. Science has changed a great deal since the time that Snow wrote. Peer review has come under severe criticism as an inadequate and sometimes corrupt method of regulating a given profession.[63] Moreover, despite (or perhaps because of) the remarkable success of many branches of science in improving the conditions of life, the gap between the demand for and the supply of research funds has widened. This development has significantly altered the norms and practices of science. It is no longer enough for scientists to describe and analyze interesting phenomena: in order to justify continued financial support, even pure researchers must demonstrate how others will be able to use their work. Science is no longer the self-contained, autonomous enclave it once was. Instead, researchers must increasingly interact with and satisfy the outside interests on whom they have come to depend. But even recognizing these exceptions, qualifications, and changes, the theory and practice of science exhibit enough normative coherence and behavioral regularity that one can fairly speak of science as a culture, as a way of seeing, thinking, valuing, and acting that distinguishes it from other cultures, particularly law and politics.

B. Law

If the scientific culture, with its emphasis on rigorous methodology and proof, is arcane and remote from public view and common experience, the legal culture—or at least much of it—is to the average citizen more conspicuous (e.g., the imagery of trial), part of the vernacular (the language of rights), and numbingly familiar (the preparation of tax returns).[64]

1. Central Values.   Law's version of truth only dimly resembles the version advanced by science. Indeed, the notion of verifiable truth to which scientists appeal in their experiments and research bears almost no relationship to the conception of truth ordinarily pursued in legal proceedings. Legal principles are normative propositions about which particular states of the social world *should* be sought, not positive statements about how the natural or social world *does in fact* work. Legal principles seek and find their justification in arguments derived from a bewildering array of social policy goals: fairness, efficiency, administrative cost, wealth distribution, and morality, among others. Legal decision-makers balance these goals in non-rigorous, often intuitive ways that are seldom acknowledged and sometimes ineffable.[65] Moreover, courts explicitly invoke other considerations in support of their decisions that are essentially social policies in disguise.[66] Even the classic principle of *stare decisis*, for example, appeals to the policies of predictability, expectations, and decision cost minimization. The practice of analogical reasoning appeals to the policy of treating like cases alike. The principle of deference to particular institutions appeals to the policy of specialized, expert decision making.

This difference between science and law entails a fundamental distinction between the pursuit of "truth" (science's province) and the pursuit of "justice" (law's province).[67] I hasten to add that this familiar distinction is one of degree only. Both paradigms are ideal types, abstractions employed to isolate some of their essential features rather than to represent a far more complex reality. In this connection, I have noted that scientific fact-finding is not wholly objective; its data, methods, interpretation, and authoritativeness are contextual, contingent, and often controversial.[68]

By the same token, the justice sought by law is not purely subjective, not simply in the eye of the beholder. It is true, of course, that notions of justice do vary with time and place, and that the most bitter, protracted debates in any society revolve around its meaning. But justice does contain a more objective component. Ultimately, its normative claims depend upon the truth value—defined in a relatively rigorous, scientific sense—of the empirical propositions that at least implicitly underlie those claims. Law's legitimacy, at least in the long run, rests in part upon its ability to generate outcomes that are more or less correct. To be "correct," an outcome must comport with the common morality and common sense of the lay community, and also command the respect of the relevant communities of experts. If instead these lay and expert communities come to view the legal system's errors of fact or law as systematic or otherwise substantial, they are bound to call law's integrity and utility into question.

How much may law deviate from scientific truth before its legitimacy is jeopardized? Like conceptions of justice, a society's tolerance for legal error is a variable, not a constant. Changes in public attitudes, political discourse, and scientific opinion can alter the level of legal error that society, and hence the law, will accept.[69] The *Bendectin* litigation illustrates the point. In a few of the early cases, juries found that Bendectin caused birth defects; some juries even awarded punitive damages against the producer. As studies casting doubt on the drug's causal responsibility proliferated in the early to mid–1980s, the scientific community responded by strongly criticizing the evidence on which these findings had been based. In time, this criticism undermined, and in some cases reversed, the earlier decisions. More important, it contributed to a more general discrediting of the tort system. This system, after all, managed to discover the error only after Bendectin had been driven off the market, depriving consumers of an often effective and unique remedy for a serious condition, and only after its manufacturer had incurred more than $100 million in legal fees.[70] The law's repudiation of bad science in the *Bendectin* litigation thus came tragically late.

Today, the law seems to be demanding greater reliability of scientific claims before it will honor them, although evidence of this shift remains fragmentary. Some courts, perhaps emboldened by Judge Weinstein's exhaustive scrutiny of the expert medical testimony in the *Agent Orange* case,[71] have recently insisted upon greater rigor in the law's use and interpretation of scientific evidence, especially on the issue of causation in toxic tort cases.[72] A swelling chorus of scientifically informed commentary has also criticized the law's traditional approach to technical evidence.[73] Even more significant in the long run, perhaps, the Environmental Protection Agency is currently conducting a thorough reevaluation of its diverse risk assessment methodologies, a review prompted in part by widespread criticism of that approach by many prominent scientists and economists.[74]

These convergences between the standards of truth in science and in law are noteworthy and on the whole encouraging, but the more general point remains: the two cultures characteristically pursue fundamentally different ends—verifiable fact for the one, and justice for the other. This difference also implies that science and law have different orientations toward the distributive consequences that their activities generate. Many individual scientists, of course, care deeply about whom their findings benefit and burden, yet the culture of science in principle must take a dispassionate stance on that question. The canons of science, after all, dictate that if research uncovers a new truth, scientists must not suppress it but should instead let the chips fall where they may. In principle, at least, how society ultimately decides to use (or misuse) scientific facts is a separate question about which they may feel strongly but usually possess no special expertise.

In contrast, the legal culture is anything but neutral about the distribution of outcomes, even in principle. It is normative to its core. The law, of course, defines rights and duties with desired substantive outcomes very much in view when it protects property, proscribes criminal conduct, exacts taxes, supports wars, demands equal treatment for similarly situated groups, and regulates social and economic relationships. Practicing lawyers are expected to advocate their clients' biases and implement their agendas; failure to do so may constitute professional malpractice. Academic lawyers routinely elaborate legal theories designed to promote values they personally prefer. Among those in the field of law, only judges are expected to put aside their normative goals when those goals conflict with the properly understood rule of law.

2. Incentives and Techniques.   The incentives that motivate legal actors are varied but largely conventional. In this respect, the law is no different than other cultures. Some of the incentives that shape lawyers' conduct, however, are distinctive to their professional milieus. For practicing lawyers, the decisive incentive is the need, consistent with both self-interest and professional ethics, to effectively represent the client's interests, whatever those interests may be. The lawyer's income (if not always her psychic well-being) is enhanced by her willingness to subordinate her personal policy views to those of her client. Somewhat paradoxically, this substantive self-abnegation actually reinforces, and then rationalizes, the legal culture's singularly powerful normative thrust by ensuring that any client that can afford to hire a lawyer can enjoy some access to the policy-making and adjudicative processes, where it can press its claims.[75] Where the scientist's "clients" are verifiable facts waiting to be revealed and used, the lawyer's are social interests seeking gratification and advancement.

Lawyers' strong client orientation also colors how incentive structures in the two cultures treat uncertainty and complexity. Paradigmatically, science progresses by generating new data and hypotheses that often undermine the then-dominant theories. When this occurs, the resulting uncertainties and complexities may persist for a long time; although these uncertainties often contain the seeds for new progress, they must first germinate.[76] Despite this tendency toward uncertainty and complexity, however, science's ultimate goals are precisely the opposite: it seeks the most parsimonious theory that can both explain all existing data and yield testable new hypotheses.

In contrast, legal actors are more agnostic about whether and to what extent certainty and simplicity are virtues in law. For practicing lawyers, it all depends on their clients' interests, which may militate in favor of certainty on one issue, uncertainty on another, and a shifting balance over time on a third. For judges, it depends on how they balance various goals of the legal system— for example, the competing policies of having clear rules and of responding flexibly to equitable considerations in individual cases. Legislators and bureaucrats, who also face countervailing incentives, will tend to favor legal complexity and uncertainty because it helps them both to resolve intricate political and policy disputes and to develop special expertise that confers autonomy, prestige, and power over decisions.[77]

The law is usually in much more of a hurry to decide than science is. Ironically, however, law's findings, although less reliable and tested than those of science, are treated as more final and authoritative. Law operates under pressure to resolve particular disputes speedily and conclusively. Once it finds facts (and confirms them on appeal), those findings are considered *res judicata*—final for the law's purposes, however erroneous they may be in fact. Science, in contrast, seeks to develop a professional consensus on the truth of its propositions. This consensus often takes a long time to assemble, yet even then it is conditional, always open to revision on the basis of new data or theories.[78]

Richard Cooper, a former general counsel of the FDA, has analogized cross-examination in the courtroom to peer review in the scientific journal, noting that cross-examination is simply a more concentrated form of review suitable to the law's more hurried, arbitrary pace.[79] Many scientists, however, would surely reject any analogy between scrupulous peer review and what they view as the truth-obscuring manipulations and tricks of the interrogating attorneys. Most scientists would probably also be dubious about permitting juries to hear and rely upon scientific evidence that has not previously been published in a peer-reviewed professional journal—an issue raised by a Bendectin case pending before the U.S. Supreme Court.[80]

The legal culture, of course, is hardly indifferent to the dangers of making premature decisions on the basis of incomplete information. Judges fashion many legal principles—for example, procedural rules allocating evidentiary burdens,[81] and substantive rules defining the legal consequences of knowledge and ignorance[82]—in order to create incentives to produce, use, and disseminate information that policymakers may need. Agencies and legislatures also seek to stimulate new information that can help to solve legal problems.[83]

Nevertheless, judges are obliged to adjudicate the disputes that come before them promptly and on the basis of the best evidence that can then be adduced, even if that evidence seems wholly inadequate to support a scientific claim.[84] Judges do not ordinarily have the luxury of deferring a decision until additional studies are conducted, the data are more conclusive, and a firm scientific consensus is reached. Instead, they must decide on the basis of uncertain, incomplete evidence, a circumstance that Cooper likens to "a jury verdict reached midway during a trial."[85] The law's demand for an immediate resolution of disputes, he observes, may force it "to choose among competing scientific theories, a choice that legal decision-makers are not competent to make, and that scientists are not ready to make."[86] Although agencies usually enjoy greater control over their dockets and decision priorities than do courts, they too are under considerable compulsion—occasionally judicial, sometimes legislative, often political—to act promptly despite data gaps that would dismay a research scientist and implementation gaps that would astonish an engineer.

I have already noted the central importance of peer review in science. Peer review is much more peripheral to lawyers, however, and the structure of incentives that shapes their behavior reflect its marginality. Lawyers are hardly indifferent to their reputations among fellow lawyers; client referrals as well as professional recognition and pride are at stake. Moreover, the institution of appellate review is a kind of peer-administered control structure. But the legal culture has not developed peer review systems genuinely analogous to science's refereed journals, grant review committees, and academic appointments processes. Law's highly competitive, public-oriented, adversary system contributes to this difference. Scientists participate in a truly global community of peers, yet they may achieve world renown (even Nobel Prizes) by impressing a very small set of experts in a narrow sub-specialty with their quiet, painstaking, imaginative work. Lawyers' reputations, in contrast, depend on a more localized notoriety among less sophisticated audiences dominated by lay clients with largely economic interests. More than in science, the legal culture (or at least a good part of it) richly rewards combativeness, self-promotion, and an aggressive, vivid personality—although these qualities are by not means unknown among top scientists.

The incentive structures in science and law, however, do not simply reflect their different client orientations, attitudes toward complexity and uncertainty, and peer review systems. They also reflect differences in how the two cultures are organized and financed. While the number of scientific investigators is quite large, science is administered predominantly through a relatively "clustered" structure consisting of a comparatively small number of leading universities, research institutes, and corporations. Within this structure, considerable coordination occurs through sub-specialty journals, professional conferences, and the funding decisions of a limited number of sources.

Legal activity is not nearly so coordinated. Hundreds of thousands of lawyers act daily on behalf of millions of clients. They make claims and deploy arguments that are utterly fragmented except insofar as the law provides clear rules or unambiguous principles of decision, and not simply a conventional rhetoric of rights. Formal legal institutions such as legislatures, courts, and agencies do provide some coordination and guidance to lawyers, their clients, and others. In some respects, however, these institutions simply increase the chaos; they too are radically decentralized (within both the federal system and each state system). Their pronouncements are often susceptible to competing interpretations, and they provide multiple access and decision points for any legal actors who are dissatisfied with one or another interpretation.

3. Biases and Orientations.   Law, like science, has its characteristic blind spots and preoccupations. The differences between the two cultures in this respect are fortified by their members' distinctive training. Scientific education is largely didactic and constructive; it emphasizes the transmission of information, the techniques of theory-building, and the modes of empirical investigation. Legal education, in contrast, is essentially deconstructive and dialogic; it emphasizes the malleability of facts, the plasticity of legal doctrine, the indeterminacy of legal texts, and the power of rhetorical skill. Decades after specialty and subspecialty training became common for doctors, moreover, lawyers continue to be trained and practice as generalists. Their mere admission to the bar usually entitles them to practice law in any field they like with no legal requirement for specialty certification.[87] Most American judges are also generalists not only because of the nature of their legal education but also because of the general jurisdiction of their courts. Indeed, unlike their colleagues in civil law countries, they receive no special training to be professional judges. The legal culture exhorts both judges and ordinary lawyers to have a broad, synthetic, social vision rather than a narrow, insular, technocratic one.

On the other hand, lawyers' central role in the adversary system can foster a kind of truculent tendentiousness that can encourage them to take frivolous positions, overlook or obscure complexities, and give short shrift to other points of view. They can do so with the easy conscience of advocates who confidently assume that any extreme claims they make will be countered by others no less extreme and will then be resolved by judges who understand this exercise in hyperbole and routinely make allowances for it. Their professional penchant for advocacy and rhetoric, intensified by the financial interest that many have in disputes and litigation, often promotes conflict rather than resolving it. Commentators have noted that the adversary process is far better at deconstructing scientific claims than at reconstructing "the communally held beliefs that reasonably pass for truth in science."[88] Few scientists feel comfortable in this contentious milieu. Most find it particularly repugnant both as an intellectual process for seeking truth and as a matter of personal and professional style.[89]

Finally, the fact that law is both authoritative and suppletive—that it both legitimates official actions and facilitates private ones—creates other biases. Because much law must be predicted, understood, and applied by many ordinary people with limited resources, simplicity is often a compelling legal virtue. Law cannot afford to be as nuanced as the realities it seeks to shape;[90] it necessarily draws lines and creates categories that force many legal decisions into a binary mold; one is either in or out of the category, and it matters a great deal which.[91]

This rather arbitrary binary classification, so characteristic of legal thought and so evident in the Bendectin and Agent Orange cases, is utterly alien to science. Where the practicing lawyer or judge speaks casually of chemical A being (or not being) a carcinogen, or of action B having "caused" condition C, the careful scientist is much more circumspect. To her, causal relationships are only stochastic predictions, not categorical facts. In science, the goal is not to facilitate socially useful action at low cost, as it sometimes is in law, but instead to understand the world in all its complexity. For science, theoretical simplification—the slice of Ockham's Razor[92]—is not a condition of normativity but merely one technique for deepening and extending this understanding.

In part (but only in part), this tendency toward categorical reductionism in the law reflects its commitment to the jury as a lay decision-maker in many disputes. In no other legal system in the world does the jury play so large a legal and political role.[93] Invoking populist premises, the legal culture depicts it as the embodiment of common sense and yeoman virtue; it institutionalizes a mode of *knowing*, of which experts and other elites who suffer from "trained incapacity" (in Philip Selznick's apt phrase) are thought to be incapable. Lay jurors are often the triers of even complex facts,[94] and much legal doctrine enshrines the cognitive and behavioral standards of ordinary people (the "man on the Clapham omnibus," in one formulation),[95] rather than expert standards, as the test of legally approved conduct. Finally, the jury affirms populist values by exercising certain *political* functions, serving as the voice of common morality, a bulwark of common liberty, and a decentralized organ of popular government, one that is constantly refreshed.[96] The jury thus reflects the legal culture's singular compromise between professional autonomy, which in science counts for everything, and popular sovereignty, which in science counts for little (but trouble).[97]

C. Politics

Politics, the pursuit and exercise of the coercive, prescriptive, and symbolic powers of the state, lies near the core of all social life, appearing in many forms and venues. Here, I am principally interested in how politicians approach those public policies whose legitimacy draws heavily on scientific authority and on scientific propositions about the natural world. As noted earlier, my paradigmatic examples are regulation of the safety of foods, drugs, consumer products, the environment, and the workplace.[98]

Politics relates symbiotically to both science and law but in different ways. Science has its own politics, often fierce and bitter, in which scientists pursue power, recognition, and resources from the government, the profession, and other sources.[99] Just as scientists often play politics, politicians also have many opportunities to exploit the prestige and symbols of science in order to fortify their empirical claims, legitimate and build public support for their decisions, and clothe themselves in the mantle of scientific truth.

1. Central Values.   Like all cultures, politics pursues a mix of values some of which are unique to its particular way of life.[100] In a liberal democratic polity like ours, which purports not to privilege particular visions of the good, these are chiefly process values, although they are deployed in pursuit of substantive ends. Three of these process values seem paramount. The *participation* norm holds that individuals should be empowered, in the interest of human dignity, to play some meaningful role in shaping decisions that affect their vital interests. The *accountability* norm demands that officials be held politically responsible to the public for their actions. The *conflict management* norm emphasizes that other values can be achieved only if social conflicts are kept within tolerable limits.

2. Incentives and Techniques.   These values engender an equally distinctive set of political incentives and decision techniques. Virtually all academic models of politics, as well as many less systematic commentaries, posit that politicians are primarily, if not exclusively, driven by the need to build and maintain a winning electoral coalition. No sophisticated political analyst, of course, doubts either that most politicians' definition of the winning coalition is complex enough to accommodate other personal and ideological goals which they possess, or that politicians sometimes take positions on issues that cannot easily be explained simply in terms of conventional calculations of electoral advantage. But even when the electoral imperative is narrowly conceived, it explains their actions better than any other single factor.

From this preoccupation with election, certain behavioral strategies follow, most of which[101] sharply differentiate the political culture from the scientific and legal ones. One important difference relates to the cultures' audiences and thus to the form of discourse that is possible. Unlike scientists and judges, who mainly address their professional colleagues and can employ technical and theoretical kinds of arguments, politicians speak to a lay and largely uninformed electorate. Often, they can only reach the voters through media that, while sometimes more sophisticated than the voters, are also severely constrained by the voters' limitations of time, understanding, and interest.

Instead of the nuanced, abstract arguments deployed in the scientific and legal cultures, then, political rhetoric is relatively crude and particularistic. Where both scientific and legal discourses are designed to pursue truth through the elaboration of principles, the point of political discourse ultimately is to persuade. Rhetorical strategies that would be professionally unacceptable in science and often in law—explicit appeals to sentiment, ideology, or interest—are standard tactics in politics, where the "mobilization of bias" is both normal and normative.[102]

In addition to a distinctive audience and rhetoric, politics has its own time horizon. Especially when compared to science, but even when contrasted with law, political decisions tend to be spasmodic and impulsive. They are shaped by deadlines that seem highly arbitrary from almost any other perspective—especially that of a scientific model of decision making in which evidence is gathered, alternative hypotheses are considered, and a deliberate, rational judgment is reached. The political culture often demands swift action, and when it does it will not tolerate delay, even if prudence might counsel otherwise. The pace of mass democratic politics is driven by the insistent rhythm of public opinion, which will not be temporized.

Another distinction of the political culture relates not to discursive method but to decisional technique. In theory and largely in fact, scientific hypotheses are confirmed or refuted by experimentation, and judicial rulings proceed by reasoned elaboration of established principles.[103] In contrast, the paradigmatic decision technique in liberal democratic politics is bargaining to a consensus,[104] a process that is complex, amorphous, and continuous. Numerous participants form constantly shifting alliances and deploy a fluid mixture of rewards, threats, special interest claims, public interest ideals, and evocative symbols. Because the process is so open-ended in time, participation, and issue-space, political outcomes are not merely unpredictable; they are also opaque and hard to identify. Even the enactment of legislation, itself a protracted affair, is only a shadowy guide to what it will become. Its meaning will depend upon its future implementation.

These defining features of political behavior shape the criteria for evaluating that behavior. Political bargains can be criticized on a variety of procedural and substantive grounds. But the complaint that an outcome is inconsistent with earlier ones, which often will be a decisive objection in science and law, carries far less weight in the political culture. In the political environment, change is an effective rallying cry, flexibility is a crucial resource, and policy innovation is a desideratum. Inconsistency in politics is as likely to be an asset as a liability. By the same token, the complaint that a political decision lacks strong empirical support is also often beside the point. Such evidence may be unavailable when the decision must be made, or if it is available, may well be subject to controversial, normatively charged interpretations. Even beyond this, constitutional principles do not ordinarily prevent a legislature from deciding against the weight of the evidence; in most policy areas, any "rational basis"—even one hypothesized by the reviewing court—will suffice.[105]

3. Biases and Orientations. As these last observations suggest, politics also has its characteristic blind spots. A notable one is its abhorrence of firm principle. This, of course, is seldom publicly acknowledged as such; instead, it is portrayed and celebrated as a benign commitment to consensus and compromise. We can better understand this bias by comparing it with how firm principle is treated in science and law.

Science, by its very nature, demands that its practitioners rigorously observe certain canons of investigation and verification, and that they accept, or at least respect, its substantive principles until they can disprove them. Legal principles, while not verifiable in any scientific (or other) sense, are also treated as presumptively binding. In law's normative hierarchy, they govern conduct unless and until they are contradicted by other principles of an equal or higher dignity.

In the political culture, however, compromise of principle is not merely inevitable and habitual; it is also *normative*. A successful practitioner of politics must possess both a taste and a talent for compromise. House Speaker Sam Rayburn's well-known advice to the novice—"if you want to get along, go along"—remains a fundamental precept of the politician's creed. Many politicians, of course, do not view compromise as an abandonment of principle but instead justify it as simply a tactic employed in the service of a larger principled strategy, much as a sailboat caught in an unfavorable wind must tack back and forth in order to reach its destination. Doubtless this is often true. But however one views this conduct, the result is much the same: compromise of principle is essential to the profession of politics.

Another distinctive bias of politics is its populism—its appeal to the superior virtues of common people. We have already seen that this populism is anathema to science. The legal culture's use of the jury and the veneration of its findings, as well as the election of many judges, manifest a limited but important commitment to populism. Though law is more populist than science, politics is even more populist than law. In law, expertise is often privileged. For example, qualified expert witnesses may offer opinion testimony in many circumstances in which lay witnesses may not.[106] Scientific treatises and other authoritative works may be admitted under an exception to the hearsay rule.[107] Professional custom constitutes the standard of care in malpractice cases, and the business judgment rule governs most corporate transactions. Judges are obliged to set aside those jury verdicts that they deem irrational or contrary to the weight of the evidence.

Our political culture embraces many of the populist premises that science and to a lesser degree law repudiate. It maintains the principle that the legitimacy of public decisions must rest primarily upon bases other than the professional status, esoteric knowledge, or special expertise of the decisionmaker. This principle applies regardless of whether the decision-maker is a regulatory bureaucracy, corporation, or individual official.[108] It affirms that however much technocracy can contribute to public deliberations, the popular will is the ultimate touchstone of policy. It insists, sometimes to the point of outright pandering, that the people know best even when it is clear that they do not. This principle goes well beyond a grudging, realistic recognition that in a democracy the voters have the last word; it is also fundamentally normative. It elevates the wisdom of popular judgments, their superiority to those of the experts, and the independent integrity of the political process, to the level of central articles of the democratic faith.

Although it is not inaccurate to speak of a political culture, as I have done, it is also useful for certain purposes to differentiate broadly between two political subcultures: elected officials and their political appointees, on the one hand, and the career civil service, especially in its lower, more technical reaches, on the other. I characterized these two groups earlier as "political" and "expert" bureaucrats—a crude but serviceable distinction.[109] In terms of their attitudes toward lay participation in decision making, political bureaucrats, whom democratic theory supposes to be exquisitely responsive to electoral concerns, lie near the lay decision-making end of the spectrum, far from science. The expert bureaucrats lie closer to the professional autonomy pole; their fidelity to programmatic clients, bureaucratic traditions, and professional canons competes with the norms of hierarchical authority and responsiveness to the electorate.[110]

Both of the political biases which I have noted—aversion to principle, and obeisance to populism—are visibly at work in the *Agent Orange* and (to a lesser extent) *Bendectin* cases. While scientific principles eventually proved capable of resolving these cases to most toxicologists' satisfaction, these principles bore less dignity in the political world where lay judgments often dominate professional ones. In Congress, where populism routinely trumps science and rewrites the law, neither the scientific fact that Agent Orange did not harm the veterans nor the legal conclusion that this denied them any right to compensation was decisive. In the Bendectin cases, the sequence of events made politics' subordination of scientific values less salient. Some politicians rebuked the FDA's scientist-bureaucrats for overriding lay jurors' populist wisdom in the early cases, but the manufacturer's withdrawal of the drug from the market in 1983 quickly mooted the point.

III. Looking Ahead

Multi-cultural conflicts among the legal, political, and scientific cultures should not be a cause for regret. They are not only inevitable, but they serve essential social functions. They raise certain competing interests to the level of public consciousness and debate, which no wise polity can afford either to suppress or to ignore. They encourage social innovation and policy flexibility by infusing the polity with a varied array of legitimating norms and problem-solving techniques, making it difficult for any single world-view to always dominate. They also increase and refine our stock of social information, supplying policymakers with values, ideology, imagery, and problem-solving techniques whose diversity makes them all the more valuable. No single culture, moreover, can possibly mobilize all of these social resources all of the time. For example, the scientific ethos, which gained sway during the New Deal period, yielded some ground to the participatory politics of the Great Society, which in turn led to the more demanding legal controls of the late 1960s and early 70s.[111] In the 1980s we reached a more fluid, transitional stage, which recognized the values of all three cultures to some degree but in which none was clearly ascendant.

As the Bendectin and Agent Orange cases illustrate, the mix of values necessary to resolving multi-cultural conflicts is not fixed but changes over time. Moreover, the cultures interact in complex, often unexpected, ways. In the Bendectin cases, for example, scientific values came to dominate purely legal ones after the mid–1980s, as the scientific evidence in support of the drug's safety grew steadily more conclusive and the courts became more uneasy about permitting juries to exercise their legally sanctioned power to deviate from that conclusion in individual cases. In the Agent Orange cases, Congress infused new political values into an earlier legal-scientific consensus when it decided to compensate veterans whose injuries the court had found, relying on the best available science, to be insufficiently linked to the herbicide. In that litigation's intricate blend of science, law, and politics, each culture insisted on its own centrality while opportunistically borrowing values from the others.

This cultural eclecticism was most evident on the causation issue. Organized groups—the chemical industry, the veterans, and the U.S. government—recruited scientists to buttress their political and legal interests. The scientists were then obliged to set their cultural norms of discourse and proof to one side as they had to testify in the less scientific terms—for example, "more probable than not"—that the legal rules demanded. The lawyers, while mobilizing scientific data and methodology in the form of expert testimony, also looked to politicians and bureaucrats to help resolve the dispute. The politicians and bureaucrats, for their part, funded epidemiological studies and paid their verbal respects to the scientific evidence, then awarded veterans benefits with little regard to its findings.

These cases demonstrate that in the fluid worlds of politics and policymaking, the relevant cultural boundaries are poorly marked and evanescent, so much so that we constantly cross them without even knowing it. We may find it expedient to draw careful lines in order to preserve for each a core domain, a clearly defined jurisdiction within which each culture's special values and procedures can govern. While I suggest some line-drawing criteria below, the fact is that the most interesting and important conflicts, such as those in the Agent Orange cases, will occur near the cultures' peripheries where these domains touch and begin to overlap, and where the optimal mix remains highly uncertain.

We have seen that many questions that society poses to science are really "trans-scientific" in nature.[112] In the same way, other questions that we delegate to politicians and to judges are trans-political and trans-legal, respectively. But although cultural boundaries will become more permeable as society grows more complex and undertakes more ambitious goals, we must not conclude reductively that these boundaries are simply formal constructions that we can safely ignore or transgress. Notwithstanding their permeability, science, law, and politics remain coherent cultures. When one of them addresses a question that it is normatively and technically competent to answer, and does so through a process that conforms to its distinctive competencies, society should strongly presume that its answers are valid and legitimate, and those challenging them should bear a very heavy burden of proof.

What, then, are the contours of each culture's appropriate sphere? Which issues is each competent to decide? Here, the conventional concepts of core and periphery are helpful, though not decisive in the hard cases. Setting epistemological quibbles to one side, some issues may be said to be (or treated *as if* they were) scientific, legal, or political at their core, although not at their periphery. Because a cultural sphere's contours are not self-defining or immanent but are instead shaped by evolving social values, purposes, and perceptions of appropriateness, the domains of core and periphery shift over time and in different contexts.

Consider some examples. The operation of clinical testing laboratories was long-treated as a matter within the core of scientific activity. Social concerns about rising health care costs and incompetent diagnoses, however, moved clinical laboratories out toward the periphery of science where they overlap with law and politics, which now subject them to extensive regulation. Occasionally the movement is in the other direction. Recombinant DNA research, a controversial political topic during the 1970s, was originally subjected to strict legal controls. As its benefits became more apparent and its risks all but vanished, however, DNA research gravitated to the legal and political peripheries and beyond. Shedding the earlier controls, it entered the realm of essentially unrestricted science.

As these examples suggest, the three cultures commonly converge at their peripheries when confronted with a multi-cultural issue. This convergence demands a complex decision-making structure that can somehow integrate the values of several conflicting cultures in pursuit of a satisfactory, if often contingent, resolution. It must negotiate the relative weights of the conflicting values in a more or less *ad hoc* fashion since they ordinarily cannot be specified in advance. Such a system is inevitably messy and to some degree indeterminate, but this is a condition of liberal-democratic-technocratic society that we simply must learn to live with and manage better.

While recognizing that the power to characterize issues as scientific, legal, or political is often the power to determine who will decide them and what the ultimate outcome will be, this allocation should be relatively unproblematic where an issue lies at a culture's core, that is, where it involves a quintessentially scientific, legal, or political question.[113]

Nevertheless, current legal arrangements often confound such an allocation even in the clearest core cases. The central question in the Bendectin cases—whether and under what circumstances the drug causes birth defects when taken during pregnancy—is scientific at its core, in at least the following four senses. First, it is a question about a factual relationship, with few "value" elements. Second, the scientific community has reached a consensus on how this question should be formulated, which methodologies are appropriate for answering it, and what counts as evidence. Third, no objective person—scientist, lawyer, or politician—really believes that this answer should turn on who asks the question or who administers the experiments. Finally, neither law nor politics seriously disputes that this is indeed a scientific issue in all of these senses.

Some, however, will view even these propositions as socially constructed conventions rather than as objective truths. The propositions are not self-evident; they raise hard questions that deserve—and in the sociology and history of science are receiving—serious responses.[114] For example, what is a "fact"? Who belongs to the "scientific community"? Is its self-constituting character an invitation to narrow-mindedness or even corruption? Who gets to decide these questions? Questions like these, which emphasize the social constructedness, contingency, and political pedigree of ostensibly scientific facts, are important cautions against adopting what Sheila Jasanoff calls "a naively positivist image of science."[115]

These questions can lead to valuable insights. But we should not carry their logic so far as to preclude rational, coherent discourse about science—or indeed about any other salient social practice that needs to be better understood. If the necessary terms of discourse are themselves contingent social constructs that are devoid of intelligible meaning, then rational discourse becomes impossible. We place ourselves in an infinite regress culminating in analytical inconclusiveness and prescriptive paralysis. This frustrating prospect, of course, cannot refute the social constructedness of science; that a conclusion is dismal does not mean that it is wrong. It should encourage us, however, to search for other strategies, even though they are imperfect.[116]

Two pragmatic considerations further justify viewing the causal issue in the Bendectin cases as a core scientific one. First, even if the propositions supporting this view are merely social conventions, they are so widely accepted as to be canonical. Indeed, if Bendectin's causation is not a scientific question, it is difficult to imagine one that is. Second, society has made remarkable material progress by treating such issues precisely as if they were scientific at their core to view science as essentially an epiphenomenon of politics and law would be to place these gains (and future ones) in serious jeopardy.

I have argued that a core scientific issue like causation should be authoritatively decided within the scientific culture by institutions that this culture designates as appropriate to the task, subject only to controls (such as judicial review) that are designed to advance, or at least are consistent with, the particular cultural values in question (such as factual accuracy). In the Bendectin cases and many others like it, the Food and Drug Administration (FDA) is that institution.

This is not to say, of course, that the FDA fully instantiates the scientific ideal. Criticism of that agency for being unduly influenced by regulated firms and for lacking sufficient technical expertise and enforcement resources has long been a staple of American regulatory politics. But this cannot be a decisive consideration, for in our system the same is true of virtually all government institutions. For better or for worse, the FDA is the agency that the public has empowered to make authoritative judgments of this kind on its behalf. In recent years, moreover, its technical and enforcement resources have been significantly enhanced due in part to its uncommonly strong leadership. Its counterparts in Europe receive a level of deference from their publics and courts that no American agency is likely to enjoy; the more competitive, fragmented, populist character of our politics assures that even technical agency decisions will be vigorously contested.[117] Nevertheless, we should strive to justify greater public and judicial deference both by strengthening the agency's scientific base and by increasing the authoritativeness of its decisions for juries in tort cases.

In Bendectin, however, well-settled legal principles prevented the court from according any greater deference to the FDA's finding on the causation question than to an individual's (or a juror's) flip of a coin. As I and others have argued elsewhere, it is hard to justify this repudiation of the cultural competence principle,[118] which is rather like permitting English majors to authoritatively answer complex physics problems on which important social consequences turn. If they get it right, it is purely by accident.

The cultural competence norm should be equally decisive in the political and legal cultures. In order to maintain the integrity and patrol the boundaries of the *political* culture against unwarranted intrusions by law, the courts have adopted certain self-denying principles and stratagems—for example, the political question doctrine[119] and the so-called "passive virtues."[120] These safeguards, however, are notoriously weak; courts, both "liberal" and "conservative," commonly breach such boundaries. As for core *legal* issues, few if any would exist in a purely democratic, majoritarian polity, where all issues are subject to political resolution. Liberal constitutionalism, however, carves out a significant legal core by placing certain activities, such as speech, beyond the reach of politics, and by barring governmental actions, such as bills of attainder, that lack sufficient generality to control legislative abuse.[121]

I have noted, however, that the most interesting multi-cultural issues—especially conflicts between science and law—lie not at the core of one culture but near the periphery of several. Here, the problem is not to allocate the issue to one culture and then protect its decisional autonomy and integrity, but rather to ensure that the culture with ultimate decisional authority infuses into its decision process the relevant values of the other cultures. Thoughtful, imaginative scholars have advanced and carefully dissected many interesting proposals for accomplishing this integration with respect to science-law conflicts. Since it would be idle for me to rehearse these proposals, I shall simply group the various approaches.

Administrative Law. Many of the administrative law innovations since the 1960s have been designed to assimilate diverse cultural values into the decision process of agencies. These include increased rule-making, broadened participation and hearing rights, heightened judicial review, greater access to information and to the decision process, technical advisory groups, and the like.[122]

Expert Testimony. Another approach to reform emphasizes the manner in which scientific evidence is not only discovered and prepared, but also presented to and constraining of the trier of fact (usually a jury). Such proposals usually involve some alteration in the form, timing, neutrality, sponsorship, screening, criticism, or review of expert testimony.[123] The Supreme Court is now considering (in a Bendectin case) one such proposal: the revival of the so-called *Frye* standard for the admission of scientific evidence.[124] Another proposal, advanced by John Monahan and Laurens Walker under the rubric of "social frameworks," would authorize courts to instruct juries with respect to established social scientific facts that recur from case to case (as in Bendectin), much as they now instruct juries with respect to binding legal principles.[125]

Trier of Fact. Other proposals are concerned with the nature and technical qualifications of the entity that determines the facts in court litigation or administrative regulation. They must address the different statuses that expert and lay judgments enjoy in science and in law, differences which make it difficult to agree upon a suitable composition, function, and control mechanism for this entity. Such proposals usually advocate the use of specialized juries, a new allocation of fact-finding duties between judge and jury, or some form of "science court" or other expert tribunal.[126]

Positivism. Another approach encourages scientists and judges to characterize and differentiate their decisions in a way that distinguishes sharply between questions of fact and questions of value. The notion is that by isolating facts and values and explicitly calling decision-makers' attention to this distinction, decisions can be reviewed and legitimated in ways that are democratically and technocratically appropriate to their epistemological nature.[127]

Cross-Cultural Understanding. The most uncontroversial proposal stresses the importance of greater tolerance and acceptance of the diverse values and perspectives that different cultures bring to the decision process. The notion is that educating scientists, lawyers, and politicians about each other's value systems and modes of thinking will enhance the quality and political acceptability of social decisions. In this spirit, exchange programs bring scientists to Capitol Hill and executive branch agencies, while law students and political science majors are encouraged to enroll in university science and technology studies programs and to participate in interdisciplinary education. Judge Howard Markey of the U.S. Court of Appeals for the Federal Circuit, which handles patent, copyright, trademark, and other technical issues, is a typical advocate of this strategy: "We need to think long and hard," he writes, "about the future of a society as technologically oriented and as law-soaked as ours when our scientists and lawyers cannot even talk to each other."[128]

These approaches to managing multi-cultural issues all have the attractive features emphasized by their proponents. Each, however, is also problematic in important respects. While many of the ideas about opening up the administrative process to diverse interests have already been instituted, they have not been notably successful.[129] Most expert testimony reforms threaten the deeply embedded (though highly contestable) norms of the adversary system of proof. Attempts to transform the trier-of-fact are likely to be political nonstarters. This is especially true of efforts to alter the jury, one of our legal system's sacred cows, in the name of expertise, one of our political system's *betenoirs*.[130] Positivist reforms rest upon a fact-value distinction that is both controversial in principle and often objectionable in practice. A rigid, categorical positivism is especially vulnerable when applied to policy approaches like risk regulation, whose social authority rests heavily on political forms of legitimation.[131] Even cross-cultural understanding, an obviously desirable goal, risks sensitizing us to underlying normative differences without doing much to resolve them. Indeed, emphasizing a culture's own distinctiveness may actually reinforce its chauvinistic impulses and intensify cultural conflict. My earlier analogy to heightened ethnic consciousness is hardly reassuring in this regard.

Moreover, each of these remedial approaches (save the last) would collide at the most fundamental level with certain structural, constitutional, and normative features of our public law system. Competing governmental organs institutionalize the three cultures in different degrees. Technocratic expertise, the paradigmatic scientific value, is primarily the domain of executive branch agencies, although Congress has sought greater technical parity in recent years.[132] Principled decision making is both a judicial and bureaucratic virtue. But because this value is threatened in bureaucracies, it is ultimately enforced in the courts, where it can operate under less cultural stress. Participation and accountability, preeminent political values, are primarily the province of Congress and the executive agencies. Still, some courts have tried to secure them through a variety of substantive and procedural public law doctrines.[133]

Bridging Institutions.   If the chasms that separate the cultures are structural as well as normative and political, we must try to design *new* institutions capable of bridging them. These institutions should expose each culture's own blind spots, broaden its relevant knowledge base, and augment its modalities of proof. They should acknowledge, and then seek to undermine, the smug certitudes and parochialism that afflict all cultures: national, ethnic, or professional.

Science bureaucrats, for example, can experiment with new ways to incorporate political valuation techniques into ostensibly and inertially technocratic agency choices. Former EPA administrator William Ruckelshaus attempted this when he allowed industrial communities to vote on tradeoffs of economic and environmental values before setting pollution standards.[134] Judges and lawyers should devise evidentiary procedures—putting expert testimony in written form, for example[135]—that will make scientists more comfortable in the hearing room or court rather than causing the best of them to shun public forums. Courts should also adopt procedures better suited to gathering and analyzing political and scientific information bearing on the consequences and implementation costs of their far-reaching decisions.[136] Politicians should organize policy-making structures in order to achieve better mixes of empirical validity, legal legitimacy, and political accountability. Elected officials, for example, can provide technocratic regulators with more specific decision criteria that formulate questions that science can actually answer—questions, for example, about the number of life-years saved; the number and severity of injuries avoided per dollar spent or job lost; and regulatory risks in comparison to risks currently accepted by the public, as revealed in their everyday choices.[137] Such an approach not only should improve the means-ends rationality of policy decisions but should also strengthen political control and accountability of those decisions.

These proposals are of course modest. But managing multi-cultural issues near the peripheries has proved so difficult that considerable humility by reformers is warranted. Only culturally eclectic reforms have a reasonable chance of gaining the necessary political support; monocultural ones are likely to fail. Some proposals that I have mentioned—increasing the use of written testimony on direct examination to improve both the accuracy and intelligibility of scientific evidence, for example—promise to strengthen scientific and legal values without sacrificing political ones, a kind of Pareto-superior move.[138] On the other hand, most of them—including the more fundamental changes like greater use of court-appointed experts or eliminating juries—may succeed in advancing the values of one (or two) of the cultures only by appearing to subordinate the values of the other(s), which is more problematic.[139]

But even the most controversial reforms may be propelled forward by the cyclical changes in the culture that move beneath the surface of normal politics. The most important turn of this meta-cultural cycle, of course, occurred during the New Deal when the cultures of science and bureaucratic politics waxed at the expense of the more traditional judicial-legal culture. Then, a growing faith in technocratic expertise converged with (and itself encouraged) fundamental institutional reforms that supplanted much common law adjudication and common law thinking with a system of policy-oriented, technocratic, and electorally-sensitive administration.

The relative autonomy of this "public science," however, did not survive the convulsions of the 1960s. A more highly politicized, legalistic society, one increasingly suspicious of the neutrality and benignity of a science allied with power, insisted on new political and legal controls on technocratic decision making in public agencies and in private laboratories affected with a public interest. Whether or not these controls have proved effective is a surpassingly important social question, but it is beside the present point about cultural cycles: the time for a triumphant, hegemonic culture of public science came and then went.

IV. Conclusion

Conceivably, we are on the verge of another tectonic cultural change. If the themes of the 1992 presidential campaign are any guide, the American public has become both skeptical about much judicial and political regulation and optimistic about the potential social gains from market-driven, scientific and technological innovation. Perhaps this bespeaks a new *zeitgeist* that will once again exalt and institutionalize scientific values in public policymaking. Perhaps unified Democratic Party control over the political branches (and in time possibly the courts) will allay suspicions, which flourished during the era of divided government in the 1970s and 1980s, that scientific values serve as little more than pretexts and camouflages for the pursuit of narrow partisan, bureaucratic, or ideological advantage.[140]

But even if the time is propitious for this new consensus, it is safe to predict that science will never enjoy the degree of autonomy that its remarkable achievements, tantalizing promise, and methodological self-discipline[141] might seem to have earned for it. If past is prologue, law and politics will continue to rein in even a resurgent science despite the innovation costs, lost opportunities, and policy errors that crude controls often entail. Science will have to make its case at the bars of public opinion and administrative law as well as in the laboratory and the market for technology.

The public forum, however, is precisely where law and politics enjoy the greatest tactical advantage; it is here that their cultural values, so often incompatible with scientific canons, tend to prevail. They alone possess the extraordinary powers to conclusively choose, coerce, and legitimate social action. Unfortunately, power, knowledge, and wisdom seldom coincide in the real world. Law and politics, like science, offer partial, biased, and distorted solutions to multi-cultural issues.[142] Nevertheless, the values to which politics and law appeal—legal principle, public tradition and symbolism, populist ideology, and democratic consent—will increasingly carry the day, subordinating scientific rigor and independent inquiry to demands for political relevance and public control.

In the epigraph to this article, Karl Menninger asserts that scientists find the word "justice" irrelevant to most of their work. To many lawyers and politicians, however, the notion of objective scientific truth is a parochial conceit, sometimes useful to one's client or cause but otherwise not to be taken too seriously. From these mutual suspicions, valuable lessons may be drawn. Scientists must remember that it is lawyers and politicians who formulate the public rules for our complex society. Lawyers must remember that the project of science demands, and generally deserves, a kind of freedom to which legal controls will often be inimical. Politicians must remember that science, which has become the motor of this social progress,[143] is to some irreducible degree an elite enterprise that cannot flourish under the incubus of a militant populism. Ordinary citizens must remember that the ideals of scientific advance, fair process, and democratic legitimacy are all precious and indispensable, and must hope that this multi-cultural competition can somehow unite them.

Notes

1. KARL MENNINGER, THE CRIME OF PUNISHMENT 17 (1968).
2. C.P. SNOW, THE TWO CULTURES (1965). For a legal scholar's ruminations about a two cultures problem within legal education, see Harry Wellington, *Challenges to Legal Education: The 'Two Cultures' Phenomenon,* 37 J. LEGAL EDUC. 327 (1987).
3. *Id.* at 62–64.
4. *Id.* at 4.
5. Snow's generally elegant, insightful essay also fails on other grounds. For example, he never satisfactorily explained why the misunderstanding between science and literature was problematic enough to justify his small book, not to mention the much larger commentary that immediately followed in its wake. The flood of responses provoked by his book made him feel (as he later recalled) "uncomfortably like the sorcerer's appren-

tice." *Id.* at 54. From the controversy stirred by his lecture, he inferred that his ideas on the subject "were not at all original but were waiting in the air." *Id.* at 54–55.

He also failed to specify the links between intellectuals' attitudes toward science and politicians' willingness to support it. Thus, Snow failed to lay a foundation for his conviction that the anti-scientific attitudes emerging among intellectuals threatened science's political support and thus its capacity to improve the conditions of life. *Id.* at 90–97. Moreover, the course of history has proved his prediction proved quite wrong, as the enormous growth since the 1950s in the NIH, NSF, and NASA budgets attest. Of course it is possible that even more resources would have been forthcoming, absent the antipathy that he described.

Nor did Snow identify the *causes* of the science-literature schism. He did observe that scientists were more optimistic; they distinguished, as the traditionalists did not, between the tragedy of the human condition and the melioristic potential of social action. *Id.* at 6–7. But instead of asking why this difference had arisen, he contented himself with suggesting that scientists' greater commitment to problem-solving had something to do with it. *Id.* at 7.

6. It hardly need be said that my choice of *three* cultures is somewhat arbitrary. If greater analytical precision were the goal, one could easily multiply the number. Indeed, as I shall discuss, each of the three contains important subcultures. For example, Snow and many others have distinguished between pure and applied science. *Id.* at 31. I note some other distinctions. *See infra* text accompanying note 45. Professor Jasanoff has extended this distinction to that between research and regulatory science. Sheila Jasanoff, The Fifth Branch: Science Advisers as Policymakers 6 (1990).

Snow noted that his two cultures could as easily have been 102 or 2002. Snow, *supra* note 2, at 9, 66. Similarly, my three cultures could be subdivided or increased with little difficulty. A more rigorous or taxonomic purpose would require more refined distinctions. For present purposes, however, taxonomic precision is less important than broad thematic coherence, which a proliferation of categories might diminish.

7. As to relative consequentiality, my colleague Owen Fiss has made a similar point about the effects of applying literary theory to the interpretation of legal texts. Owen M. Fiss, *Objectivity and Interpretation*, 34 Stan. L. Rev. 739 (1982).

8. Democratic, liberal, and technocratic values, of course, can and often do clash with each other. For one exploration of these value clashes (analyzed under other labels), see Jerry L. Mashaw, Bureaucratic Justice: Managing Social Security Disability Claims (1983).

9. For example, the law of intellectual property, especially patents, takes its very content from science, both pure and applied. The law of evidence often demands scientific support for the use of certain techniques, such as DNA typing and epidemiology, and for the drawing of particular inferences from testimony, such as causation. Medical malpractice cases usually involve (indeed, they may require) testimony by scientific experts. Antitrust litigation relies heavily upon technical economic analysis of product markets. Employment discrimination law often looks to statistical analyses of labor markets for evidence of bias.

10. For an extensive but (in the author's words) selective bibliography on toxic torts, see Robert F. Blomquist, *An Introduction to American Toxic Tort Law: Three Overarching Metaphors and Three Sources of Law*, 26 Val. U. L. Rev. 795, 802–05 n.29 (1992).

11. The relationship between law and politics is especially close. Indeed, many would say—some *have* said—that law and politics are essentially indistinguishable. *See,*

e.g., David Kairys, *Legal Reasoning, in* THE POLITICS OF LAW 11, 17 (David Kairys ed., 1982) (asserting that "law is simply politics by other means"). I do not agree with Kairys' use of the word "simply".

12. *See generally* KARL R. POPPER, THE LOGIC OF SCIENTIFIC DISCOVERY 32–33 (1961) (emphasizing testability and falsifiability criteria); THOMAS KUHN, THE STRUCTURE OF SCIENTIFIC REVOLUTIONS (2d ed. 1970) (discussing the testing of paradigms).

13. *See generally* RONALD DWORKIN, LAW'S EMPIRE (1986); H.L.A. HART. THE CONCEPT OF LAW (1961); IMMANUEL KANT, THE PHILOSOPHY OF KANT: IMMANUEL KANT'S MORAL AND POLITICAL WRITINGS (Carl J. Friedrich ed. & Theodore M. Greene et al. trans., 1949).

14. ROBERT A. DAHL, A PREFACE TO DEMOCRATIC THEORY (1956).

15. Snow was not evenhanded in appraising the scientific and traditional cultures. To be sure, be maintained that each was impoverished in its own way; scientists possessed under-developed imaginative faculties, while literary intellectuals were blind to the beauty and utility of the natural order. Nevertheless, no reader of *The Two Cultures* can doubt which of them he thought the more benighted and taxable with the heavy burdens of change. Whereas literary intellectuals were "natural Luddites," scientists were by nature progressive, leading society toward a luminous future. SNOW, *supra* note 2, at 22.

Snow's harsh indictment of traditional culture was misguided, I think, in its failure to recognize how that culture was essential to the social legitimacy and power of science. It was the traditional culture, after all, that succeeded in first exposing and then softening the harsh rigors of the Industrial Revolution. To see that this is so, one need only consider how traditionalist writers like Blake, Dickens, Disraeli, the early Marx, Whitman, and Upton Sinclair influenced reform in Britain and the U.S. These humanists, Luddites or not, helped to palliate and domesticate the profound technological and social changes that industrialism had wrought. By doing so, they rendered these changes more acceptable to the public.

16. *See* discussion *infra* text accompanying notes 131–133.

17. As Peter Huber has argued, the fact that the risks are new does not mean that they are greater than those which they may have displaced. Peter Huber, *The Old-New Division in Risk Regulation,* 69 VA. L. REV. 1025 (1983).

18. *See, e.g.,* LEON R. KASS, TOWARD A MORE NATURAL SCIENCE: BIOLOGY AND HUMAN AFFAIRS (1985); *see also* JUDITH AREEN ET AL., LAW, SCIENCE AND MEDICINE ch. 7 (Death and Dying), ch. 8 (Reproduction and the New Genetics) (1984); Gina Kolata, *Ethicists Struggle to Judge the 'Value of Life',* N.Y. TIMES, Nov. 24, 1992, at C3; Norman Frost, *Regulating Genetic Technology: Values in Conflict, in* 3 GENETICS AND THE LAW (Aubrey Milunsky & George J. Annas eds., 1985).

19. *See* Ivy v. Diamond Shamrock Chems. Co., 781 F. Supp. 902 (E.D.N.Y. 1991) (concerning Agent Orange), *appeal pending,* No. 92–7275 (2d Cir.); Daubert v. Merrell Dow Pharmaceuticals, Inc., 951 F.2d 1128 (9th Cir. 1991) (concerning Bendectin), *cert. granted,* 113 S. Ct. 320 (Oct. 13, 1992) (No. 92–102).

20. The discussion that follows borrows heavily from a still unpublished account of the Bendectin litigation, Joseph Sanders, From Science to Evidence: The Testimony of Causation in the Bendectin Cases (1992) [hereinafter Sanders] (on file with author), which in turn draws on Joseph Sanders, *The Bendectin Litigation: A Case Study in the Life Cycle of Mass Torts,* 43 HASTINGS L.J. 301 (1992). *See also* Michael D. Green, *Expert Witnesses and Sufficiency of Evidence in Toxic Substances Litigation: The Legacy of Agent Orange and Bendectin Litigation,* 86 NW. U. L. REV. 643 (1992); PETER HUBER, GALILEO'S REVENGE: JUNK SCIENCE IN THE COURTROOM ch. 7 (1991).

21. This was partly because investigating Bendectin's effects was easy relative to many other drugs. Green, *supra* note 20, at 677–78. Green, a chronicler of the Bendectin litigation, agrees with Sanders that "the scientific record on Bendectin's teratogenicity by the mid-to-late 1980s had become unusually rich." *Id.* at 677.

22. Michael Green points out that all of the plaintiffs' jury verdicts occurred either in Washington, D.C. (4), Philadelphia (1), or Texas (2), while juries found for Merrell Dow (or hung) throughout the rest of the country. He believes that the plaintiff verdicts were influenced by juries' wealth redistribution motivations. Letter from Michael D. Green, Professor of Law, University of Iowa, College of Law, to Peter H. Schuck, Simeon E. Baldwin Professor, Yale Law School (Dec. 17, 1992) (on file with author).

23. Sanders, *supra* note 20. Much of Sanders' analysis, though not his application to Bendectin, follows Samuel R. Gross, *Expert Evidence*, 1991 Wis. L. Rev. 1113.

24. Another possible explanation for the divergence between science and legal outcome is incompetent lawyering. This seems doubtful, however, since each side chose to use the same small group of lawyers repeatedly throughout the litigation. A third possible explanation, incompetent juries, would be hard to distinguish from Sanders' legal process explanation.

25. For example, those who actually conducted the research tended to be neglected in favor of "secondary" experts; those who testified repeatedly tended to give more highly polished testimony; and the same number of experts tended to testify on both sides of an issue, creating an illusion of equal evidentiary weight. Sanders, *supra* note 20, at 24–36.

26. For example, the process and sequence through which expert testimony was introduced appeared to give equal weight to different kinds of studies that actually have different probative value, such as *in vitro* and epidemiological studies. *Id.* at 37–42.

27. According to Sanders, the science in Bendectin was also influenced by its intersection with the law in that the litigation affected the volume of research on the topic and caused scientists to become politicized on this issue. Letter from Joseph Sanders, Professor of Law, University of Houston Law Center, to Peter H. Schuck, Simeon E. Baldwin Professor, Yale Law School (Jan. 11, 1993) (on file with author).

28. The epithet "junk science," which has entered the political lexicon, was apparently coined by Peter Huber. See HUBER, *supra* note 20, at 2.

29. At least one prominent plaintiff's lawyer and defender of the tort system has been critical of the Bendectin litigation. Paul Rheingold, *It's Time to Change the System on Junk-Science, Quack-Expert Issues*, MANHATTAN LAW., Nov. 1–7, 1988, at 13.

30. The account that follows is taken largely from PETER H. SCHUCK, AGENT ORANGE ON TRIAL: MASS TOXIC DISASTERS IN THE COURTS (enlarged ed. 1987). *See also* Green, *supra* note 20, at 659–61.

31. Interview with Dr. Jan Stolwijk, Professor of Epidemiology, Yale School of Public Health, in New Haven, Conn. (Oct. 23, 1985).

32. SCHUCK, *supra* note 30, at 226–44, 301.

33. *See* Green, *supra* note 20, at 672.

34. *See, e.g.,* Marilyn Fingerhut et al., *Cancer Mortality in Workers Exposed to 2,3,7,8-Tetracholorodibenzo-p-Dioxin*, 324 NEW ENG. J. MED. 212 (1991); Warren E. Leary, *High Dioxin Levels Linked to Cancer*, N.Y. TIMES, Jan. 24, 1991, at A16 (stating that Fingerhut study found increased incidence of soft-tissue sarcomas in workers with dioxin levels in their blood of 3600 parts per trillion (ppt), but found no excess cancer in workers with levels of 640 ppt; Vietnam veterans exposed to Agent Orange had levels of 45 to

400 ppt); Warren E. Leary, *Higher Risk of Rare Cancer Found for Vietnam Veterans*, N.Y. TIMES, Mar. 30, 1990, at A10 (noting that veterans showed no increased rate of five suspect cancers, but did show increased rate of sixth cancer, non-Hodgkin's lymphoma, but that rate of this cancer was highest among sailors on ships, who had least exposure to Agent Orange); Keith Schneider, *Panel of Scientists Finds Dioxin Does Not Pose Widespread Cancer Threat*, N.Y. TIMES, Sept. 26, 1992, at 9 (stating that EPA-convened panel finds human cancer risks confined to chemical workers and victims of dioxin-related industrial accidents). In mid–1991, an Illinois appeals court threw out a $16.28 million jury verdict against Monsanto, the manufacturer of a chemical containing a tiny quantity of dioxin, for a train spill of the chemical in Missouri which occasioned one of the longest jury trials in American history. The court's ruling reflected the fact that the jury did not find that dioxin had caused plaintiffs any actual injury. Kemner v. Monsanto Co., 576 N.E.2d 1146 (Ill. App. Ct. 1991).

35. Adam Clymer, *Bill Passed to Aid Veterans Affected by Agent Orange*, N.Y. TIMES, Jan. 31, 1991, at B6 (stating law covers non-Hodgkins lymphoma and soft-tissue sarcoma). This law also granted disability benefits for chloracne, a condition that had previously been found to be caused by dioxin exposure. Since then, the VA has also granted benefits to certain victims suffering from peripheral neuropathy. *See Vietnam Veterans to Get Benefits for Ailment Tied to Agent Orange*, N.Y. TIMES, July 3, 1991, at B6.

36. For Judge Weinstein, the question was whether the veterans should be able to shift their losses to the chemical companies (and, ultimately, to the government), and the standard was therefore relatively demanding ("preponderance of the evidence"). For the VA, it was whether its statute required, permitted, or precluded its paying compensation for certain illnesses. For Congress, it was simply a policy question, essentially unconstrained by any legal standard, as to whether certain illnesses should be compensated.

37. *See* Wendy Wagner, *Trans-Science in Torts*, 96 YALE L.J. 428, 431 n.20 (1986).

38. We should remember that for all their complexity, they were "easy" cases in this limited sense. Multi-cultural conflict often takes much more intractable forms.

39. Another example of such a case is Wells v. Ortho Pharmaceutical Corp., 615 F. Supp. 262 (N.D. Ga. 1985), involving the alleged teratogenicity of a contraceptive jelly. It is discussed in these very terms in Gross, *supra* note 23, at 1121–24.

40. The qualifications are necessary even here because some contrary scientific testimony, which plaintiff proffered but the lower courts excluded, purports to discredit the defendant's negative studies. The excludability of this testimony is now at issue before the Supreme Court. *See* Daubert v. Merrell Dow Pharmaceuticals, Inc., 951 F.2d 1128 (9th Cir. 1991) (excluding testimony of Dr. Shanna Helen Swan), *cert. granted*, 113 S. Ct. 320 (Oct, 13, 1992) (No. 92–102). For a discussion of the excludability controversy, see Eliot Marshall, *Supreme Court to Weigh Science*, 259 SCIENCE 588 (1993).

41. As it was, the outcome in Bendectin came only after a socially valuable drug was removed from the market. *See infra* text accompanying note 70.

42. American policymaking may be uniquely pathological in these respects. Whether the substantive issue is regulation of toxic substances, nuclear power plants, occupational safety and health, or environmental protection more generally, important policy decisions are fiercely contested, always open to reconsideration, and subject to competing criteria of justification. *See, e.g.*, RONALD BRICKMAN ET AL., CONTROLLING CHEMICALS: THE POLITICS OF REGULATION IN EUROPE AND THE UNITED STATES 301–02, 312–13 (1985); JOSEPH BADARACCO, JR., LOADING THE DICE (1985); STEVEN KELMAN,

REGULATING AMERICA, REGULATING SWEDEN: A COMPARATIVE STUDY OF OCCUPATIONAL SAFETY AND HEALTH POLICY (1981); EUGENE BARDACH & ROBERT KAGAN, GOING BY THE BOOK: THE PROBLEM OF REGULATORY UNREASONABLENESS (1982); DAVID VOGEL, NATIONAL STYLES OF REGULATION: ENVIRONMENTAL POLICY IN GREAT BRITAIN AND THE UNITED STATES (1986).

43. SNOW, *supra* note 2, at 6–7.

44. *Id.* at 12–13.

45. *Id.* at 31–32. Today, the colloquial appellations "hard" and "soft" as applied to the natural and social sciences denote important differences in their training, methodologies, public support, and prestige.

46. This qualification about the conventional definition of scientific communities follows recent research findings in the field of sociology of science. *See infra* text accompanying notes 50–51. This work emphasizes that scientific "facts," like the scientific enterprise itself, are socially constructed; they are recognized as facts only if (in a recent formulation) "they are produced in accordance with prior agreements about the rightness of particular theories, experimental methods, instrumentation techniques, validation procedures, review processes, and the like. These agreements, in turn, are socially derived through continual negotiation and renegotiation among relevant bodies of scientists." Non-science institutions—including legal fact-finders like judges and juries—also participate in the construction of science. Sheila Jasanoff, *What Judges Should Know About the Sociology of Science*, 32 JURIMETRICS J. 345, 347, 356–58, & sources cited (1992). This issue is discussed in greater detail at *infra* text accompanying notes 113–116.

47. HUBER, *supra* note 20, at 221.

48. *Id.* at 222.

49. *Id.* at 221–22; *see also* Steven Goldberg, *The Reluctant Embrace: Law and Science in America*, 75 GEO L.J. 1341, 1343 (1987). Huber's formulation recalls Robert K. Merton's earlier notion of "organized skepticism" as a central element of the scientific ethos. ROBERT K. MERTON, SOCIAL THEORY AND SOCIAL STRUCTURE 542 (1968).

50. *See* JASANOFF, *supra* note 6, at 12–14; *see also* Jasanoff, *supra* note 46.

51. For one consensus statement of this faith, see Amicus Brief of 72 Nobel Laureates, 17 State Academies of Science, and 7 Other Scientific Organizations in Support of Appellees at 23–24, Edwards v. Aguillard, No. 85–1513 (U.S. 1993).

52. Even so, basic science operates with relative freedom from the "day-to-day judicial and political constraints common elsewhere in American society." Goldberg, *supra* note 49, at 1364.

53. Nevertheless, a reaction against "big science" seems to have set in recently. This is visible not only in the public sector, where massive high-technology projects such as the supercollider and Star Wars have encountered much scientific and congressional opposition, *see* Malcolm W. Browne, *Budget Plans Worry Some Scientists*, N.Y. TIMES, Apr. 11, 1993, at 20, col. 3, but also in the private sector, where many market-driven firms—be they giants like Bell Labs and IBM or small biotech and software start-ups—have decentralized their research and development activities on the theory that scientific innovation is more likely to flourish in less bureaucratic settings. It is generally accepted that new jobs are disproportionately generated by smaller firms.

54. Partly for this reason, "[l]egal control of technology provides something more of a jolt to the scientist than it does to the lawyer." Goldberg, *supra* note 49, at 1368.

55. On this point, I am indebted to Bruce Ackerman, who has elaborated a somewhat analogous distinction between the ideal types of "scientific policy-maker" and "ordi-

nary observer." BRUCE ACKERMAN, PRIVATE PROPERTY AND THE CONSTITUTION 10–20 (1977).

56. Given this bias, it is not surprising that scientists (other than science bureaucrats) find Congressman John Dingell's ongoing crusade to "cleanse" science of its elitist practices and pretensions incomprehensible, which may explain why they have been so ineffectual in opposing it. *See* Robert Cook, *A Capital Collision*, NEWSDAY, May 9, 1989, at 3; Bernard D. Davis, *Fraud vs. Error: The Dingelling of Science*, WALL ST. J., Mar. 8, 1989, at 14.

57. *E.g.*, STEPHEN J. GOULD, BULLY FOR BRONTOSAURUS: REFLECTIONS IN NATURAL HISTORY (1991).

58. Barry Commoner's involvement in the public forum has included running for President in 1980. Philip Shabecoff, *Commoner Says Victory is Not Object of His Drive*, N.Y. TIMES, Oct. 30, 1980, at B19. Dr. Samuel Epstein's participation in the public arena has included numerous appearances before Congress testifying on a variety of scientific issues. *See* CONGRESSIONAL INFORMATION SERVICE INDEX (listing at least 17 appearances by Dr. Epstein as a witness at congressional hearings since 1974).

59. *E.g.*, Gio B. Bori, *Overturning the Verdict on Carcinogens*, WALL ST. J., Aug. 27, 1992. Indeed, last year the National Toxicology Program's [NTP] Board of Scientific Findings issued an advisory review of NTP in which it suggested that the scientific methodology upon which the NTP relies in classifying compounds as carcinogens may not present any significant threat of cancer to human beings. *See also What Price Cleanup*, N.Y. TIMES, Mar. 21–26, 1993 (series of five articles highlighting some of the mistakes of American environmental policy).

60. See, e.g., discussion of Bertram Carnow in HUBER, *supra* note 20, at 92–93. For a recent lampoon-editorial on this subject, see Daniel E. Koshland, Jr., *The Great Overcoat Scare*, 259 SCIENCE 1807 (Mar. 26, 1993).

61. *See supra* note 45.

62. According to one research scientist who also treats patients, clinicians tend to be much less rigorous; they tend to seek only enough data to enable them to be comfortable with their best clinical judgments. Telephone Interview with Dr. Leonard Milstone, Associate Professor of Dermatology, Yale University School of Medicine (Dec. 22, 1992).

63. *See, e.g.*, Symposium, *Guarding the Guardians: Research on Editorial Peer Review*, 263 JAMA 1306 (1990) (cited in Amicus Brief of the American Association for the Advancement of Science and the National Academy of Sciences at 16, Daubert v. Merrell Dow Pharmaceuticals, Inc., No. 92–102 (U.S. filed Jan. 19. 1993) [hereinafter Amicus Brief]). For present purposes, however, the more important point is that "[e]ven the most vocal critics of the peer review system do not . . . recommend that it be dismantled." Amicus Brief, *supra*, at 16–17.

64. I do not mean to deny, of course, that much of the legal culture is inaccessible to non-lawyers, a phenomenon that has provided grist for satirists and critics throughout the ages. I am simply comparing law to science in this regard.

65. *See generally* MICHAEL POLANYI, PERSONAL KNOWLEDGE (1958).

66. The relationship between principles and policies is developed in RONALD H. DWORKIN, TAKING RIGHTS SERIOUSLY (1977).

67. These labels, of course, are conventional. *See* John Thibaut & Laurens Walker, *A Theory of Procedure*, 66 CAL. L. REV. 541 (1978). Those authors view "truth" as concerned with cognitive conflicts and "justice" as concerned with conflicts of interest. *Id.* at 543–44.

68. *See supra* text accompanying notes 50–51.

69. Even in criminal procedure, where a libertarian bias favoring false negatives over false positives is particularly strong ("it is better that nine guilty defendants go free than that one innocent defendant be wrongfully convicted"), there are social limits to the bias. This is indicated by the intense, continuing debates over the appropriate standards for bail and preventive detention, the minimum size of the jury, and the scope of the *habeas corpus* remedy. In civil law, bitter controversies over the location and shifting of burdens of proof likewise demonstrate how society's views concerning permissible error levels change over time. A recent example is s 105 of the Civil Rights Act of 1991, Pub. L. 102–166, which amended s 703 of the Civil Rights Act of 1964, 42 U.S.C. s 1981 (amending 42 U.S.C. s 2000e–2), to overrule the Supreme Court's decision in Wards Cove Packing Co. v. Atonio, 403 U.S. 642 (1988).

70. For a pithy discussion of this episode, see HUBER, *supra* note 20, at 111–29. The high litigation costs, unfortunately, are not peculiar to Bendectin. They have been much higher in Agent Orange cases, *see* SCHUCK, *supra* note 30, at 5, and in asbestos cases, *see* Schuck, *The Worst Should Go First: Deferral Registries in Asbestos Litigation*, 15 HARV. J.L. & PUB. POL'Y 541, 553–68 (1992).

71. *See generally* SCHUCK, *supra* note 30.

72. Green, *supra* note 20, at 666.

73. *E.g.,* Troyen A. Brennan, *Causal Chains and Statistical Links: The Role of Scientific Uncertainty in Hazardous-Substance Litigation*, 73 CORNELL L. REV. 469, 494–500 (1988) (discussing cases); Bert Black & David E. Lilienfeld, *Epidemiological Proof in Toxic Tort Litigation*, 52 FORDHAM L. REV. 732 (1984); Peter Huber, *Safety and the Second Best: The Hazards of Public Risk Management in the Courts*, 85 COLUM. L. REV. 277 (1985). For a scientist's critique of science's own approach to such evidence, see Alvan R. Feinstein, *Scientific Standards in Epidemiological Studies of the Menace of Daily Life.* 242 SCIENCE 1257 (1988) (criticizing much current methodology).

74. *See* Robin Shifrin, Note, *Not By Risk Alone: Reforming EPA Research Priorities*, 102 YALE L.J. 547, 553 (1992).

75. This access is subject to the increasingly rigid constraints of standing doctrine. *E.g.,* Lujan v. Defenders of Wildlife, 112 S. Ct. 2130 (1992).

76. KUHN, *supra* note 12.

77. For a detailed discussion of this point, see Peter Schuck, *Legal Complexity: Some Causes, Consequences, and Cures*, 42 DUKE L.J. 1, 27–31 (1992).

78. As Michael Green puts it, "[t]he notion of refusing to reconsider a determination that one knows is wrong would drive scientists even wilder than trotting out the concept of justice." Letter from Michael D. Green to Peter H. Schuck, *supra* note 22.

79. Richard M. Cooper, *Scientists and Lawyers in the Legal Process*, 36 FOOD DRUG COSM. L.J. 9, 19 (1981).

80. Daubert v. Merrell Dow Pharmaceuticals, Inc., 951 F.2d 1128 (9th Cir. 1991), *cert. granted*, 113 S. Ct. 320 (Oct. 13, 1992) (No. 92–102).

81. *See, e.g.,* 9 JOHN H. WIGMORE, EVIDENCE IN TRIALS AT COMMON LAW s 2509 (Chadbourn rev. 1981) (discussing *res ipsa loquitur* doctrine).

82. *E.g.,* Beshada v. Johns-Manville Prods. Corp., 447 A.2d 539, 546–49 (N.J. 1982) (striking state-of-the-art defense in asbestos cases); Feldman v. Lederle Lab., 479 A.2d 374, 386 (N.J. 1984) (limiting *Beshada*), *rev'd on other grounds*, 592 A.2d 1176 (N.J. 1991).

83. One method the legislatures and agencies have used to address these legal problems is "technologyforcing" statutes and regulations. *See* BRUCE A. ACKERMAN &

WILLIAM T. HASSLER, CLEAN COAL/DIRTY AIR 101 (1981). Standard-setting agencies may force development of new technologies where costs of compliance with a new standard would be exceedingly high using existing technologies or where compliance is simply infeasible using current technologies. Examples of such technology-forcing regulations include OSHA's standards for occupational exposure to vinyl chloride, coke oven emissions, lead, and cotton dust. *See* James C. Robinson & Dalton G. Paxman, *Technological, Economic, and Political Feasibility in OSHA's Air Contaminants Standard,* 16 J. HEALTH POL. POL'Y & L. 1, 6–7 (1991). Courts have generally upheld these technology-forcing methods. *See* Huber, *supra* note 17, at 1060–62.

84. *See, e.g.,* Ferebee v. Chevron Chem. Co., 736 F.2d 1529, 1534–35 (D.C. Cir.), *cert. denied,* 469 U.S. 1062 (1984).

85. Cooper, *supra* note 79, at 25.

86. *Id.*

87. I am aware of one limited exception. In order to prosecute a patent claim before the Patent Office, one must be certified as a specialist. 37 C.F.R. s 10.10 (1988). This requirement, however, does not apply to the litigation of patent claims in the courts.

88. *See* Jasanoff, *supra* note 46, at 353; *see also* Sanders, *supra* note 20, at 44.

89. *See, e.g.,* Sanders, *supra* note 20, at 30.

90. *See generally* Schuck, *supra* note 77.

91. Thus a defendant is either guilty or not guilty, negligent or not, in breach of the contract or statute or in compliance with it. One's agent is either a servant or an independent contractor. The court either has jurisdiction over a case or lacks it. The will is either valid or invalid. The AFDC claimant is either eligible for the benefit or she is ineligible.

92. *See* WEBSTER'S THIRD NEW INTERNATIONAL DICTIONARY 1501 (1976) ("the philosophic rule that entities should not be multiplied unnecessarily").

93. *See generally* Peter H. Schuck, *Mapping the Debate on Jury Reform, in* THE VERDICT ch. 9 (Robert E. Litan & Marc Whitehead eds., forthcoming 1993).

94. Indeed, juries are still constitutionally permitted to decide questions of law in Maryland and Indiana. *See* VALERIE P. HANS & NEIL VIDMAR, JUDGING THE JURY 157 (1986). Judges, the other triers of fact, also reflect populist values to some extent. In many states, they are selected by political parties and voters, not by their professional peers. Mary T. Wickham, Note, *Mapping the Morass: Application of Section 2 of the Voting Rights Act to Judicial Elections,* 33 WM. & MARY L. REV. 1251, 1252 & n. 14 (1991) (listing jurisdictions that elect their judges).

95. Hall v. Brooklands Auto Racing Club, 1 K.B. 205, 224 (1933).

96. For reflections on how well the civil jury fulfills these expectations, see generally the contributions in THE VERDICT, *supra* note 93. On the jury's political functions, see Akhil R. Amar, *The Bill of Rights as a Constitution,* 100 YALE L.J. 1131 (1991).

97. This formulation is too cute. It is not meant to suggest, of course, that scientists are not committed to democratic values, or that science could continue to thrive in the absence of political freedom or broad public support. I mean only that science *qua* science—as a culture that investigates the world in a particular way—does not depend on popular sovereignty, and that a militant populism often threatens it. For science, any political system permitting genuinely free inquiry will do.

98. *Supra* text accompanying notes 9–10.

99. *See, e.g.,* JAMES D. WATSON, THE DOUBLE HELIX: A PERSONAL ACCOUNT OF THE DISCOVERY OF THE STRUCTURE OF DNA (1980). The fight between the United States team led

by Robert Gallo and the French team led by Luc Montagnier for recognition as the first to identify the virus that causes AIDS, further exemplifies the politics involved in scientific research. *See* Marlene Cimons, *Bad Blood; Two Groups of AIDS Researchers—One American. One French—Are Fighting More Than Just the Disease*, L.A. TIMES MAG., May 25, 1986, at 16.

100. This contradicts the assertion by one commentator (who, as a federal judge, should know better) that "[s]cience and law are all we have." Howard T. Markey, *Science and Law: The Friendly Enemies*, 30 IDEA 13 (1989).

101. Most, but not all. Credit-claiming, for example, pervades each of the three cultures, although not in the same way and to the same extent. Politicians, the quintessential entrepreneurs, trumpet their virtues to the public without reserve or shame. Scientists, more tempered by the professional dictates of collaboration, peer review, and caution, are more circumspect. They must seek to burnish their reputations with peers and funding agencies, yet, they are wary of premature claims that can be decisively discredited. Lawyers and judges are constrained by ethical canons from conventional advertising, so they avidly seek (and find) imaginative alternative forms of self-promotion.

102. E.E. SCHATTSCHNEIDER, THE SEMI-SOVEREIGN PEOPLE 29–30 (1960) (asserting that political interest groups are themselves "a mobilization of bias in preparation for action") (emphasis omitted).

103. Actually, even legal realists recognize that most cases are easy for courts to resolve. *See, e.g.,* BENJAMIN N. CARDOZO, THE NATURE OF THE JUDICIAL PROCESS 164 (1921) (stating that in a majority of cases, legal precedent mandates a single outcome).

104. In this respect, politics resembles the decentralized, competitive character of markets, but one should not exaggerate the similarities. Although politics and markets are highly interdependent—market forces shape political competition, and *vice versa*—they organize and justify their decisions in altogether different ways. Additionally, their goals, techniques, and ideology also differ. There are pervasive, endemic tensions between a centralized, aggregative, cooperative system of political power and resource allocation and a fragmented, individualistic, competitive market system. ROBERT A. DAHL & CHARLES E. LINDBLOM, POLITICS, ECONOMICS, AND WELFARE: PLANNING AND POLITICO-ECONOMIC SYSTEMS RESOLVED INTO BASIC SOCIAL PROCESSES (1953); OLIVER E. WILLIAMSON, MARKETS AND HIERARCHIES (1975).

In contrast, the structures of science and law are more similar to market structures. Like markets, science and law are each driven by intense competition among decentralized decision-makers animated in part by private goals and a broader public interest in productive efficiency.

105. McGowan v. Maryland, 366 U.S. 420, 426 (1961) ("statutory discrimination will not be set aside if any state of facts reasonably may be conceived to justify it").

106. *Compare* FED. R. EVID. 701 *with* FED. R. EVID. 702.

107. FED. R. EVID. 803(18).

108. Populist politics, of course, reflects many factors, including our democratic institutions, our Horatio Alger myth of individualism, and our anti-hierarchical, anti-authoritarian, anti-intellectual traditions. *See* RICHARD HOFSTADTER, ANTI-INTELLECTUALISM IN AMERICAN LIFE (1963).

109. *See supra* text accompanying notes 55–56.

110. *E.g.,* William H. Simon, *Legality, Bureaucracy, and Class in the Welfare System*, 92 YALE L.J. 1198 (1983); Gary J. Greenberg, *Revolt at Justice, in* INSIDE THE SYSTEM 105, 195–210 (Charles Peters & Timothy J. Adams eds., 1970).

111. Clearly, changing partisan divisions within the federal government also had a great deal to do with these cycles, but this hardly refutes my observation, since the political parties differed with respect to the weight that should be accorded to different cultures' values and decisions.

112. *See supra* text accompanying note 37.

113. Multi-cultural issues, of course, do not come to us neatly and objectively labeled; indeed, the labels are themselves social constructions whose meanings are contingent upon how people succeed in deploying them. *See supra* note 46 and text accompanying notes 50–51.

114. *Id.*

115. *See* Jasanoff, *supra* note 46, at 356.

116. In this connection it seems revealing that Professor Jasanoff, a sophisticated expositor of the sociology of science view, employs terms like "science" and "scientist" as if they possessed some core, objective meaning not altogether contingent upon the speaker's idiosyncratic conceptions. *Id. passim.*

117. *See supra* note 42.

118. *See, e.g.,* SCHUCK, *supra* note 30, at 291.

119. *See, e.g.,* Nixon v. United States, 113 S. Ct. 732 (1993); Steven L. Carter, *From Sick Chicken to* Synar: *The Evolution and Subsequent De-Evolution of the Separation of Powers,* 1987 B.Y.U.L. REV. 719; Peter H. Schuck, *The Thickest Thicket: Partisan Gerrymandering and Judicial Regulation of Politics,* 87 COLUM. L. REV. 1325, 1377–84 (1987).

120. *See* ALEXANDER M. BICKEL, THE LEAST DANGEROUS BRANCH: THE SUPREME COURT AT THE BAR OF POLITICS (1962). The classic response to Bickel is found in Gerald Gunther, *The Subtle Vices of the "Passive Virtues"—A Comment on Principles and Expediency in Judicial Review,* 64 COLUM. L. REV. 1 (1964).

121. An example is the kind of legislative veto invalidated by the Supreme Court in INS v. Chadha, 462 U.S. 919 (1983). There, Congress exercised the power to reverse a quintessentially legal decision, one that adjudicated the legal rights of a lone individual whose personal liberty was being infringed upon by the government. This is a paradigmatic instance in which our constitutional tradition of due process proscribes politics from invading the adjudicatory function.

122. *See generally* STEPHEN G. BREYER & RICHARD B. STEWART, ADMINISTRATIVE LAW AND REGULATORY POLICY: PROBLEMS, TEXT, AND CASES (3d ed. 1992). Unfortunately, some of these administrative law innovations have not been successful. *See, e.g.,* Clayton P. Gillette & James E. Krier, *Risk, Courts, and Agencies,* 138 U. PA. L. REV. 1027, 1061–99 (1990) (arguing that proposals to increase the scope of agency authority at the expense of judicial scrutiny are premature); Jerry L. Mashaw, *Improving the Environment of Agency Rulemaking: An Essay on Management, Games, and Legal and Political Accountability,* LAW & CONTEMP. PROBS. (forthcoming 1993).

123. *E.g.,* Gross, *supra* note 23, at 1208–30; Richard Marcus, *Discovery Along the Litigation/Science Interface,* 57 BROOK. L. REV. 381 (1991); *see* E. Donald Elliott, *Toward Incentive-Based Procedure: Three Approaches for Regulating Scientific Evidence,* 69 B.U.L. REV. 487 (1989); E. Donald Elliott, *The Future of Toxic Torts: Of Chemophobia, Risk as a Compensable Injury, and Hybrid Compensation Systems,* 25 HOUS. L. REV. 781 (1988); HUBER, *supra* note 20, ch. 11.

124. Daubert v. Merrell Dow Pharmaceuticals, Inc., 951 F.2d 1128 (9th Cir. 1991), *cert. granted,* 113 S. Ct. 320 (Oct. 13, 1992) (No. 92–102).

125. *See generally* JOHN MONAHAN & LAURENS WALKER, SOCIAL SCIENCE IN LAW: CASES AND MATERIALS ch. 5 (2d ed. 1990).

126. *E.g.*, James A. Martin, *The Proposed "Science Court,"* 75 MICH. L. REV. 1058 (1977); Stephen Sugarman, *The Need to Reform Personal Injury Law: Leaving Scientific Disputes to Scientists,* 248 SCIENCE 823 (1990); Cooper, *supra* note 79; Milton R. Wessel, *Science, Technology and the Law in America: A Plea for Credibility in Dispute Resolution,* 22 JURIMETRICS J. 245 (1981); *see also* Schuck, *supra* note 93.

127. *E.g.*, David L. Bazelon, *Science and Uncertainty: A Jurist's View,* 5 HARV. ENVTL. L. REV. 209 (1981); COMMITTEE ON RISK & DECISION MAKING, NATIONAL RESEARCH COUNCIL, RISK AND DECISION MAKING: PERSPECTIVES AND RESEARCH 31–34 (1982).

128. Markey, *supra* note 100, at 18; *see also* Leon Rosenberg & Guido Calabresi, *Law and Medicine,* 32 YALE L. REP. 12 (1986) (dialogue between medical school and law school deans about effects of malpractice litigation). Stephen Goldberg's proposal for "science counselors," who would help scientists to be more sensitive to the social implications of their research and its applications, is a variant of this approach. Goldberg, *supra* note 49, at 1379–87.

129. *See supra* note 121.

130. *See, e.g.*, Schuck, *supra* note 93.

131. These observations are not inconsistent, I think, with the kind of pragmatic, positivistic reforms that I recommend below. *See supra* text accompanying notes 114–16.

132. There has been a rapid growth of congressional staff agencies. MICHAEL J. MALBIN, UNELECTED REPRESENTATIVES 4, 9–24 (1980) (four congressional support agencies: Library of Congress, General Accounting Office, Office of Technology Assessment, and the Congressional Budget Office increased significantly in both size and importance between 1945 and 1980); NORMAN J. ORNSTEIN ET AL., VITAL STATISTICS ON CONGRESS 1989–1990 xv, 127, tables 5–1 & 5–8 (after explosive growth in the 1970s, size of congressional staffs has stabilized in recent years). In February 1991, the Carnegie Commission on Science, Technology and Congress released a report recommending ways to improve the means by which Congress gets advice on science and technology issues. *Congress Needs Higher-Quality Information to Handle Scientific, Technological Issues, Carnegie Commission Group Says,* PR NEWSWIRE, Feb. 13, 1991, *available in* LEXIS, Nexis Library, PRNews File. In contrast, the courts have made no attempt to keep pace with the technical resources of either the agencies or Congress. *See, e.g.*, Baltimore Gas & Elec. Co. v. NRDC, 462 U.S. 87, 103 (1983) ("[A] reviewing court must remember that the Commission is making predictions within its area of expertise, at the frontiers of science. When examining this kind of determination, as opposed to simple findings of fact, a reviewing court must generally be at its most deferential.").

133. *E.g.*, Baker v. Carr, 369 U.S. 186 (1961) (alleged denial of equal protection due to state's failure to reapportion legislative seats is justiciable constitutional claim); United States v. Students Challenging Regulatory Agency Procedures (SCRAP), 412 U.S. 669 (1973) (broad citizen standing to challenge regulatory decisions). *But see, e.g.*, Lujan v. National Wildlife Fed'n, 497 U.S. 871 (1990) (narrowing citizen standing).

134. William Ruckelshaus, *Risk in a Free Society,* 14 ENVTL. L. REP. 10190, 10192–93 (1984).

135. *See* sources cited *supra* note 123.

136. For a discussion of one such approach, see PETER H. SCHUCK, SUING GOVERNMENT: CITIZEN REMEDIES FOR OFFICIAL WRONGS 188–89 (1983) (decree implementation analysis).

137. For recommendations along these lines, see ACKERMAN & HASSLER, *supra* note 83; Albert L. Nichols & Richard Zeckhauser, *OSHA after a Decade: A Time for Reason, in* CASE STUDIES IN REGULATION: REVOLUTION AND REFORM 203 (1981); Sidney A. Shapiro &

Thomas O. McGarity, *Reorienting OSHA: Regulatory Alternatives and Legislative Reform*, 6 YALE J. ON REG. 1, 37 (1989) (calling for the increased use of performance standards). A very limited move in this direction has been taken by the U.S. Senate when it passed the Government Performance and Results Act, which is pending in the House.

138. *See, e.g.*, Gross, *supra* note 23, at 1215–18. The pending proposed Federal Rule of Civil Procedure 26(a)(2)(B) will, if adopted (which appears probable) require a written report by an expert whom a party expects to testify. FED. R. CIV. P. 26(a)(2)(B) (submitted by the Judicial Conference to the Supreme Court, Nov. 27, 1992) (copy on file with author). Neither the proposed rule nor the commentary on it mentions the question of this report's admissibility. *Id.* commentary at 99–101.

139. *See* Gross, *supra* note 23, at 1208–32.

140. Although much has been made of the corrosive effects of divided government, *e.g.*, James Sundquist, *Needed: A Political Theory for the New Era of Coalition Government in the U.S.*, 103 POL. SCI. Q. 613 (1988), the truth of the matter is far more complex, as seen in the first few weeks of the Clinton administration, during which conflicts erupted between the new Democratic President and the Democratic chairmen of the Senate Judiciary, Armed Services, and Finance committees. *See* Ruth Marcus & David S. Broder, *President Takes Blame for Rushing Baird Selection; Clinton Says He Knew of Problem Before Nomination*, WASH. POST, Jan. 23, 1993, at A1 (Biden and Clinton clash over Baird nomination); Michael Wines, The Gay Troop Issue: This Time, Nunn Tests A Democrat, N.Y. TIMES, Jan. 30, 1993, at 1 (Nunn and Clinton disagree on the issue of admitting homosexuals into the military); Mary McGrory, *Confirmation Shalalacking*, WASH. POST, Jan. 17, 1993, at C1 (Moynihan criticizes Clinton-nominee Shalala's lack of emphasis on Social Security and welfare reform at her confirmation hearings); *see also* DAVID R. MAYHEW, DIVIDED WE GOVERN: PARTY CONTROL, LAWMAKING, AND INVESTIGATIONS, 1946–1990 (1991) (noting that the incidence of major legislation and investigations is unaffected by divided government); Martin Shapiro, *APA: Past, Present, Future*, 72 VA. L. REV. 447 (1986) (finding that divided government affects theories of the proper relationship among branches).

141. These scruples are neither universal nor always availing, as the incidence of scientific fraud demonstrates. *See, e.g.*, Marcus, *supra* note 123, at 388–90.

142. Indeed, the additional myopia engendered by their ultimate decisional power may magnify the deficiencies of legal and political solutions.

143. For a recent decidedly negative view of this development, see BRYAN APPLEYARD, UNDERSTANDING THE PRESENT: SCIENCE AND THE SOUL OF MODERN MAN (1992).

3

Some Reflections on the Federalism Debate

Introduction

A just polity requires two main features: the proper distribution of governmental power within and among its political entities, and a pervasive public virtue. The two are closely related. In an election year when both features are being called into question in the U.S., this symposium could not be more timely.

Not since the New Deal—perhaps not since the Civil War—have we so thoroughly scrutinized and debated the institutions and practices of "our federalism" (as the Supreme Court affectionately calls it).[1] Today, federalism is being reconstructed in all branches and at all levels of government through a variety of forms: statutes, administrative and judicial arrangements, court decisions, and new private sector responsibilities.[2]

Broadly speaking, federalism can devolve power in two directions; it can move public power *downward* to the states,[3] and it can disperse power *outward* to private actors. This "privatization"[4] is often excluded from the notion of federalism, yet there are sound analytic reasons to include it. Downward devolution and outward privatization are not sharply distinct categories. Instead, they overlap.[5] Each is a potentially valuable instrument in federalism's toolbox.

The federal government's authority in peacetime probably crested during the energy crisis of the late 1970s. Even at its high water mark, however, the national state apparatus remained radically incomplete, deeply contested, and always vulnerable to retrenchment. Today, the public entertains serious doubts about whether the national government can solve complex social problems. The public believes, rightly or wrongly, that national solutions have already been tried and that they have largely failed.[6] Although the public's confidence in state governments is only somewhat greater than its trust in Washington,[7] we can be certain that the states, once having retrieved authority, will not readily relinquish it absent some grave, hard-to-foresee national emergency. The stakes in the current federalism debate, therefore, are high indeed.

93

Most of the symposium papers focus on specific legal and policy domains—environmental regulation, welfare policy, torts, and individual rights—as well as exploring some theoretical perspectives on federalism. The papers consider how, why, and with what consequences devolution is occurring in so many areas. This introduction will look across (and peer beneath) these particular domains, identifying some common themes and developments that the welter of detailed, policy-specific analysis might otherwise obscure.

My argument can be briefly stated. Many policy elites regard the current federal system, which entrenches broad state authority that competes with the national government for resources and legitimacy, as a case of arrested political development, a kind of pulmonary embolism in the body politic. To them, federalism is an anachronistic relic of an ancient and unjust constitutional order; it is the institutional vestige of a localism long since marginalized by the emergence of a modern and universalizing culture based on mass education, a vast suburbanized middle class, and a popular culture shaped by national media and technologies. In this view, federalism today lacks normative justification and impedes the full realization of a strong and effective national polity.

I believe that these policy elites—who include most liberal activists and many Washington-oriented analysts and prestigious academics[8]—are wrong. The "genius" (as it was formerly called) of federalism was once an article of national faith confidently proclaimed by politicians and professors across the land, but beginning in the 1930s several events cast dark shadows over this traditional piety. The Depression severely tested it, the South's massive resistance to *Brown v. Board of Education* savagely mocked it, and the Great Society and Nixon eras interred it under a mountain of nationalizing policy initiatives. Federalism had nourished some of America's most repellent and repressive political regimes, most notably in the deep South: lynchings tolerated if not abetted by state officials, governors barring black children from entering public schools, Bull Connor's dogs attacking civil rights demonstrators in Alabama, widespread poverty and disease in the Mississippi Delta, corrupt and insular Bourbon courthouse machines. These harsh images of federalism are fixed in our minds like insects caught in amber.[9]

But whatever injustices federalism worked in the past, it is a very different system today. Neither the federal government nor the states are even remotely what they were during the civil rights era, when many of our strongest impressions of the federal system were first formed.[10] Federalism now serves both as an instrument of the modern administrative state and as a rather flexible institutional accommodation to the extraordinary diversity of American society and to the challenges that this diversity poses for national unity. This diversity-accommodating aspect of federalism receives too little attention from commentators. Although inter-state differences help to explain federalism's remarkable durability, we still lack a determinative theory—constitutional considerations aside—for deciding which of those differences the federal government should tolerate or encourage and which of them it should limit or override altogether. We are left in the fluid and highly compromised realm of normal politics where, for at least the next few years, the system is likely to accord greater deference to inter-state differences and less weight to the value of national uniformity.

American federalism, like our politics and society more generally, has evolved in a generally progressive direction during the last thirty to forty years.[11] In noting this generally reformist tendency, of course, I do not mean to praise it in all of its particulars. We surely would have had to invent a robust federal system if our Constitution and subsequent political development had not bequeathed one to us, but we just as surely would have designed it very differently. The present configuration of state jurisdictions has little to recommend it besides historical pedigree; our political map was drawn with blood and iron, not by experts in public administration. The existing allocation of responsibilities among the different levels of government is irrational in many respects.[12]

Still, history, pragmatic compromise, and our remarkable social diversity have their just claims on our political structures and practices. If federalism is far from being an ideal system, it nevertheless remains a great source of social strength and political cohesion that help to bind a congeries of disparate peoples to the nation by accommodating their passionately parochial interests. It is also a system that more severely divided societies would do well to emulate, albeit in their own fashions.

My paper develops this argument by exploring five themes or developments that bear on contemporary federalism: (1) the *pervasiveness of devolution* in the U.S.; (2) devolution's *global character*; (3) the growing *social diversity* that is devolution's driving force; (4) the complex relationship between *technological change* and devolution; and (5) the *cognitive demands* on government created by the federal system. The analysis is neither systematic nor rigorous; I employ neither overarching theory nor refined analytical framework. My purpose here is not to prove hypotheses but to frame and provoke the discussion that will follow at this symposium.

I. The Pervasiveness of Devolution

The pressure to devolve power from the center to the periphery is a nearly universal phenomenon in contemporary society. It is by no means confined to the political sphere; indeed, it is proceeding far more rapidly and irreversibly in the economic and social realms. Although status quo interests almost always resist devolution and often succeed in delaying or defeating it, the pressures to devolve power in complex social systems are relentless. This is true whether those pressures are driven by efficiency goals, concerns about protecting liberty, or communitarian ideals. In a democracy, the devolutionary impulse inevitably extracts important concessions from the center. Even in the most totalitarian regime, this impulse manages to find informal, symbolic, and clandestine outlets for rebellion and diversity.[13]

A. *Devolution by the Federal Government*

Under one banner or another, the assertion of states' rights has been a central political motif in the U.S. throughout our long, spasmodic process of national consolidation. At the same time, a citizenry perennially suspicious of private concentrations of economic power demanded national political institutions capable of controlling it.[14] Mass education, mass media, and mass mobility disseminated more cosmopolitan values and created something like a common national culture. Recurrent wars and international and economic crises spawned large, professional bureaucratic establishments.

These developments all strengthened the hand of those forces calling for a more active central state. Nevertheless, they also generated a strong backlash against the new cosmopolitanism. Powerful counter-cultural movements, which appealed to the deep populist strains long endemic in American life, firmly rejected the new cosmopolitanism—and its reified political apparatus in Washington—in favor of more parochial, differentiated cultures and politics. As I discuss below, demographic and technological changes have accelerated this cultural fragmentation, increasing the demand for a federal structure capable of fully representing this diversity. All branches and levels of government have responded to this demand in diverse public policy domains.

The practice of outward devolution by the federal government to the private sector has been even more important than downward devolution to the states.[15] Since the late 1970s, Congress has privatized numerous activities and entities that were once federally regulated or owned. The most significant examples are the transportation industry, whose air and surface modes are now largely free of federal regulation, and the telecommunications industry, which was substantially deregulated in January 1996. The sale of Conrail, the growing use of market-based incentives in regulation under the Clean Air Act and other laws, and the auctioning of certain federally-regulated communication spectra are additional instances. As noted immediately below, privatization of at least portions of public pension systems may also be on the policy horizon.

B. *Devolution by Congress*

Congress, of course, is leading this decentralizing project. The President has now signed a far-reaching reform of the AFDC program that will give the states much greater policymaking authority over eligibility criteria, benefit levels, and other programmatic elements, as well as enlarged administrative responsibilities.[16] Congress is also more receptive to proposals to distribute benefits through vouchers or similar near-cash techniques. This receptivity even extends to programs like Medicare and Social Security pensions in which the states have played little or no policy or fiscal role. Some of these proposals, which are likely to receive growing support, would effect devolution through privatization.[17] In other policy areas such as manpower training, education, and transportation, Congress has moved toward block grants and looser restrictions on other levels of government. Finally, Congress enacted legislation in 1995 to eliminate future unfunded federal mandates to state and local governments.

C. Devolution by the Executive Branch

The executive branch has initiated downward devolution of its own. During the 1980s and 1990s, agencies have used their administrative authority to delegate more policy responsibility to their state and local counterparts. The Reagan and Bush Administrations, although often stymied in their "new federalism" initiatives by Democratic congresses, did manage to consolidate some categorical programs, to reduce regulatory restrictions in certain areas, and otherwise to enlarge state discretion. Despite criticism from the left, the Clinton Administration has continued such efforts, which include a permissive use of the waiver authority under section 1115 of the Social Security Act to allow states to experiment with changes in AFDC, Medicaid, and child welfare policies.[18]

D. Devolution by the Federal Courts

Even the federal courts have become downward devolutionists. Judicial deference to local preferences has taken several different forms. Procedurally, they have encouraged the federal judicial districts to experiment with local rules in order to promote more efficient modes of civil discovery and case management.[19] Doctrinally, they have reaffirmed the continuing centrality of state law even in nationwide mass tort litigation,[20] Fifth Amendment Takings Clause jurisprudence,[21] constitutional torts,[22] and much federal product safety regulation.[23] The Supreme Court has also recently limited federal power to exercise authority even in areas in which Congress has asserted a national interest.[24]

E. Devolution by the States

The states, too, have increasingly embraced both downward and outward devolution. Changes in public education, perhaps the most politically explosive area of state-provided services, are especially revealing of the dynamics of contemporary federalism. As in the past, New York City may be the leading edge of reform. The city is moving to decentralize regulatory authority in personnel and other educational policy areas to the individual school level, thus by-passing, and perhaps eliminating altogether, the large-district community boards.[25] The state, however, can only effectuate this radical devolution of power by first re-centralizing it.

The devolution of education policymaking takes other forms as well. A number of states have created so-called "charter schools," which may be operated by independent public or private entities. Such schools, which may receive public funds, operate with great autonomy, free of local school board controls.[26] Wisconsin and some other states have authorized pilot programs, soon to be expanded (but also under court challenge), that enable children to use state-funded vouchers to pay private school tuition.

An increasingly common and far-reaching form of state-level privatization is for states to devolve extensive powers of self-government to common-interest housing developments governed by homeowner associations.[27] In an instance of sub-state level devolution, New York City has delegated to privately-run "business improvement districts" a broad range of authority to provide important municipal services to businesses and residents and to impose tax-like user fees for those services.[28]

F. Devolution Within the Private Sector

Decentralization by for-profit enterprises is of special interest because the way in which private firms internally organize their resources often prefigures change, *mutatis mutandis*, in the slower-moving public sector. Since 1980, the most notable trend in industrial organization has been the practice by large integrated enterprises of replacing highly-centralized management structures with looser, more decentralized ones organized around market-driven, multi-skill, flexible production and localized profit centers. Within the firm, authority structures and resource allocations are increasingly determined by the dictates of time- and cost-efficient information flows and market incentives, rather than by formal corporate ownership patterns.[29] The recent organizational transformations of AT&T, IBM, and many other industrial giants represent desperate efforts to meet the challenges posed by more nimble, market-responsive competitors. Their strategies include many elements of downward and outward devolution: breakup into smaller units; delegation of initiative and policymaking to lower-level, more market-sensitive employees; tactical out-sourcing; and elimination of middle management layers.

II. The Global Character of Devolution

There is much talk today about the demise of the nation-state.[30] Many commentators claim (and ardently hope) that traditional notions of national sovereignty are being rendered increasingly artificial by the growing integration of the world economy, the rise of transnational legal regimes, the spillover effects of environmental pollution, the irrelevance of national borders to massive immigration flows, and the need for international cooperation to control the dangerous conduct of rogue states. Proponents of this view cite the creation during the post-World War II era of numerous supra-national entities to coordinate international trade regimes, collective security arrangements, environmental accords, and political cooperation. They point to the European

Union, which integrates all of these purposes into a multi-state structure that even provides for a supranational "European citizenship."

In fact, however, the nation-state is not only flourishing but proliferating, and it is devolution, the essence of federalism, that is reinvigorating it. One kind of global devolution—indeed one of the greatest devolutions in world history—has occurred in the wake of the sudden dissolution of the Soviet empire. Like the breakup of the Ottoman, Austro-Hungarian, British, and French empires earlier in this century, this event has spawned a profusion of new (or long-suppressed) entities extending in a broad arc from the Baltic and Central and Eastern Europe through Central Asia.

These entities, which claim a nation-state status that is often precarious or even fictive, in turn face devolutionary pressures from their own ethnic and religious minorities. The emergent states of the former Yugoslavia, the Chechnyan uprising against Russia, and insurgencies in a number of African states provide vivid examples of this phenomenon. The forces of devolution also stalk more well-entrenched prey, roiling long-established nation-states like Canada and Mexico; even strong states like the U.K., Spain, and Belgium are vulnerable to the militant demands of separatist movements. In order to survive, such nation-states must either suppress their minorities, which is difficult for democratic regimes (or even authoritarian ones) to do, or adopt a form of federalism or more modest power-sharing arrangement. The American states' demand for devolution, therefore, is part of a global *zeitgeist*. The powerful centrifugal forces exerted by diversity are propelling this change.

A second type of global devolution is actually the result of aborted or incomplete supranational projects. The most important example, of course, is the European Union after the (at least temporary) failure of Maastricht. Its gradual expansion—from the customs union created by the Treaty of Rome to common market to regional residency and work zone to the guarantee of voting rights in local (and EU) elections—proceeded without major interruption until the early 1990s and culminated in the Maastricht accords. Unmistakable danger signals, however, had already appeared. When the Dublin and Schengen agreements sought to fashion a common immigration, refugee, and border control policy, a number of EU members refused to accede.

The European currency and common monetary policies envisioned by Maastricht are proving elusive. Some of the most powerful EU states have serious reservations about both timing and feasibility, and even Germany is faltering. They foresee the loss of autonomy, political risks, and short-term economic dislocations that a common monetary policy will entail. They also fear enhancing the more general authority of the central EU bureaucracy.

Just as "Washington" has become a readily serviceable, all-purpose political epithet deployed by those who are dissatisfied with national policies and demand the devolution of power to the states, so "Brussels" is now a rhetorical metaphor for meddlesome bureaucratic empire-building, corrosive cosmopolitanism, and insidious challenges to national sovereignty. Devolution—the effort to retrieve powers now exercised by Brussels, and the refusal to grant new ones—is among the most significant political currents in Europe today. Across the Atlantic, complaints about NAFTA—more strident during the presidential campaign—are echoing this devolutionary credo, but with an American accent.

III. Diversity and Devolution

The Founders, as Samuel Beer reminds us, contrived a constitutional system of federalism in the hope of advancing three fundamental civic virtues: liberty, community, and utility.[31] But they did not write on a clean slate. They designed their federal system for a society that was geographically far-flung and, especially by the standards of the day, remarkably heterogeneous in demographic, religious, linguistic, cultural, and political terms. The dynamics and distribution of settlement during the colonial period had assured that the emerging civil society, once united in a national polity, would exhibit an unprecedented diversity.[32] The states, and the federal system that both reflected and reinforced the states' political identities and social cultures, are the institutional expressions of this diversity.

The characteristic of America that has most struck its more acutely perceptive visitors across the centuries is the polyglot, eclectic, improvisational character of its civil society. This diversity, which is greater today than ever before, has many sources and dimensions but it ultimately rests on demographic foundations. Demographic heterogeneity entails cultural differentiation, which in turn spawns many other, more meaningful differences. The heterogeneities of ethnicity, language, and national origins that are such striking features of contemporary American society are a direct consequence of recent immigration patterns and a pluralistic political culture that tolerates—and in some ways encourages—the maintenance (in some forms) of these differences.

The post–1965 migration flow to the U.S. has little in common with the pre–1965 flows that created the still-dominant population stock. One example will suffice to make the point: in 1965, there were barely one million Asian-Americans; by 1990 the total had increased more than sevenfold, to 7.3 million—or almost 3% of the U.S. population. The Asian-American grouping, moreover, consists of numerous subgroups—Chinese, Filipino, Japanese, Indian, Korean, Vietnamese, Cambodian, Laotian, and others—with different languages, cultures, socioeconomic profiles, and experiences in the U.S.[33] Much the same is true for some of the other ethnic groupings now constituted by the U.S. Census.[34]

The U.S. is also the most religiously diverse nation in the world. It is not simply that the world's religious traditions, great and small, are all well represented here. It is also that each of the main religious groupings—Christian,

Jewish, Islamic, Hindu, and Buddhist—contains confessional sub-groups that are bewildering in their variety. They differ from one another liturgically, doctrinally, organizationally, demographically, and in their geographic distributions. This religious diversity also is a function of immigration patterns. Immigrants who brought with them quite different cultural, linguistic, and confessional traditions found it desirable to establish churches here that were parochial in those senses. Thus, Catholic immigrants from France, Bavaria, Italy, Puerto Rico, and South America preferred to worship with co-religionists from the old country.

The fierce dissenting ethos of American Protestantism, refined through almost four centuries of struggle and fragmentation, is a powerful and independent cause of religious diversity that has precipitated a vast number of Protestant denominations and sects. Even the non-Protestant religions in the U.S. have been profoundly influenced by these fractionating pressures. American Judaism, for example, has split into at least four streams, most of which have no real counterparts among Jews in other countries. Such centrifugal tendencies are by no means confined to liberal, congregational groups. They extend as well to the more hierarchical Catholic and Orthodox churches and the rapidly growing evangelical sects. In most cases, the churches' worshipers, liturgies, and other practices in the U.S. are far more heterogeneous than they are anywhere else in the world. This religious diversification, moreover, continues. For every church amalgamating with others today, many more are born afresh or separate from parent congregations.

This American diversity also possesses a strong regional aspect. States (and the regions in which they cluster) differ in many important ways, not just superficial ones like accents, dress, and sports team allegiances. It is this regional heterogeneity that our political institutions in general, and the system of federalism in particular, were meant to respect and preserve. The states are distinct from one another with respect to most of the variables that affect and thus differentiate their political behavior: wealth, public services, cultural institutions, age, distribution and urbanization of the population, economic development, climate, ethnic and religious patterns, partisan division, political structure, style and culture, and the like. The pronounced residential concentration of new, culturally diverse immigrants in a small number of metropolitan areas magnifies this regional distinctiveness.[35] Many local communities in the more internally diverse states exhibit a similar distinctiveness.

Diversity among the states might seem artificial given the fact that their existing boundaries were established for a number of historical reasons that had precious little to do with the kinds of economic and other factors that a rational, omnipotent institutional designer seeking to craft a just and efficient federal system would emphasize today. But these state-forging circumstances, however historically contingent, left their indelible marks on the populations of the different states. By now, each state possesses a distinctive social character and political culture.[36]

These local distinctions turn out to be remarkably durable. Two examples drawn from the politically-salient area of health policy—one relating to professional standards, the other to individual behavior—will illustrate the point. Medical education, specialty certification, technology, product marketing, research, and (increasingly) legal standards of care are highly national in character. Even so, local diversities dominate. When providers have more than one option for treating a medical condition, the treatment they use and the prices they charge vary enormously from region to region. Moreover, these regional differences persist even after one controls for differences in medical resources, insurance, and other such factors. Persistent region-specific professional cultures overwhelm the strong pressures for national uniformity.[37]

Sharp inter-state differences in health status and individual behaviors also persist. In his book *Who Shall Live?*, economist Victor Fuchs notes that the contiguous states of Nevada and Utah enjoy roughly the same levels of income, schooling, urbanization, climate, and resources devoted to medical care, and are alike in many other respects as well, yet "their levels of health differ enormously. The inhabitants of Utah are among the healthiest individuals in the United States, while the residents of Nevada are at the opposite end of the spectrum."[38] Fuchs attributes these disparate health outcomes to life style differences—not only tobacco and alcohol consumption but also marital status and geographical stability linked to religious beliefs and practices.[39]

Such persistent differences constitute the distinctive engine and problematic of federalism. Different states' inhabitants exhibit famously divergent public attitudes and policy preferences on a wide variety of policy issues. This is true whether the policy domain is one over which the states enjoy broad discretion with respect to funding levels and programmatic content (such as AFDC, Medicaid, and public education),[40] one in which the states' role is highly constrained by federal prerogatives (such as the treatment of immigrants),[41] or one in which the federal government expressly seeks to reduce or eliminate state-to-state and locality-to-locality inequalities (such as compensatory education and food stamps).

The political acceptability of these inequalities in states' spending and program characteristics, which reflect variations in their tax bases and in their citizens' values, is of course a core issue in the federalism debate. Those who advocate greater uniformity hope to override these differences in pursuit of the nationalist, egalitarian ideals that have dominated modern American political discourse but that have never been fully accepted or institutionalized. Devolutionists, in contrast, regard inter-state differences as benign, even desirable; they wish to accord them full, or at least fuller, expression.

But however this debate is resolved, the normative question will remain. Some differences among states reflect citizens' deeply-held values or important local interests that they want their policymakers to affirm and preserve, while others are more expendable. Which inter-state differences are so normatively compelling that the federal government must countenance their continuation rather than suppress them in the interest of national uniformity?

To this central question, the Constitution provides only a partial answer. It bars the federal government from overriding inter-state differences that are protected by the Bill of Rights, that do not affect interstate commerce, or that other structural limitations on national power immunize. For the rest, however, the Constitution leaves the question to be resolved in the pulling and hauling of normal politics. Even in this realm, to be sure, a quasi-constitutional background norm holds that the federal government should tolerate inter-state differences unless there is a compelling reason to override them.[42] Still, this is no more than a default rule, a rebuttable presumption. The fundamental normative question remains: Which conditions will suffice to rebut this presumption of state diversity?

This question is especially difficult because in principle, and sometimes in fact, *each* level of government—federal, state, and local—is capable of protecting diversity values. The ability and willingness of a particular level to do so depend primarily on the nature of the conflict that the diverse interests implicate and on the political and legal cultures which prevail at that level. Small racial and religious minorities, for example, can often receive greater legal protection at the federal level than at the state level.[43] A concern for diversity, therefore, does not always justify devolution. Indeed, as the case of civil rights enforcement famously demonstrates, such a concern may justify entrusting the primary authority and responsibility to the center.

Still, there should be at least one easy answer to the question of which state differences the federal government should be able to suppress: it should reduce those differences which, if permitted to be the subject of inter-state competition, will engender a so-called "race to the bottom." This answer might seem to be an easy one because such a race, by its very nature, would undermine *both* local and national values. For reasons that I discuss below, however, neither the race-to-the-bottom theory nor criteria such as allocative or governmental "efficiency" can resolve the suppression-by-difference question. After all, the federalism debate directly implicates competing conceptions of nationhood, and the efficiency criterion begs most of the important issues.

IV. Technological Change

If the diversity of American life leaves us uncertain about how we should treat inter-state differences, technology—by facilitating the expression of those differences—is deepening this normative indeterminacy. In this way technology is raising the stakes in a federal system designed, among other purposes, to give diversity political and institutional form.

Technology's precise effects on diversity are complex and changing, hence still poorly understood. In part, this is because technology triggers multiple and competing effects on diversity that we can scarcely glimpse today, much less evaluate. Although some of these changes might work to homogenize our culture and make centralized authority more palatable to the public, technology also enhances social diversity. Civil libertarian fears notwithstanding, past predictions of technology-based authoritarian control in the U.S. have proved as exaggerated as they are common. New technologies promise to enlarge individual choice, redefine social relationships, and transform markets in ways that will encourage individuals and groups to express existing diversities and to cultivate new ones. Although these changes will not necessarily produce a more desirable society—more choices do not always yield better ones—a responsive federalism must strive to reflect and integrate the resulting diversities.

Many of the most important social effects of technology are quite unexpected, even to their creators. Three examples—air conditioning, television, and computers—will illustrate the point.

Air conditioning transformed American politics and society by making many areas of the country attractive to individuals and businesses that otherwise would not have located there.[44] It encouraged a vast population shift in the U.S. in which millions of Americans, many of them retirees and young adults from northern and midwestern states, moved to states that had been thinly populated and had tended to practice a traditionalist courthouse politics. The migrants brought with them different values, traditions, and policy preferences that imposed new demands on state governments. This migration, by diversifying and enlarging the population of those states, helped to transform their politics in various ways. Many of these states were forced to modernize their political structures, and they developed a more competitive, issue-oriented politics. These political changes in the Sunbelt states exerted reform pressures on other states, which must compete for population and tax base. These changes, in turn, altered congressional and presidential politics and thus the terms of the federalism debate.

The transformative social effects of television are so widely acknowledged as to be a cliche. For my purposes, however, what is most interesting about TV is that, despite widespread fears (or hopes) that it would standardize popular culture and encourage a uniformity of speech and outlook, it has not done so. This is not to deny the obvious fact that millions of American viewers of network TV watch the same sports events and entertainment shows, hear the same speech patterns, laugh at the same jokes, receive the same news reports, and observe the same celebrities. Nor do I mean to deny the equally obvious fact that much TV programming is as banal and coarse as we, its viewers, often are.

Still, the diversity-enhancing power of this medium is at least as impressive as its propensity toward uniformity. The notorious decline of the Big 3 networks in favor of a bewildering variety of cable channels, upstart networks, foreign language offerings, public TV, and multimedia applications of the TV screen has spawned extraordinarily heterogeneous programming for viewers.

Even after discounting the hype that often pervades discussion of our telecommunications future, it seems clear that our electronic destiny is diversity, not uniformity.[45]

The personal computer, along with the automobile, may prove to be the most diversity-enhancing technology of all.[46] Already, the rapid proliferation of chat groups, home pages, World Wide Web databases, and multimedia linkages have vastly increased the ability of users to indulge their most arcane and specialized interests (and fantasies), from aardvarks to Zoroastrianism. Moreover, the broad diffusion of electronic mail over the Internet and Web is enabling individuals to conduct conversations with one another at a low and steadily declining cost. These developments, which are certain to spread in the years ahead, will inevitably increase individuals' choices about their (literal) connections to others and about what they wish to read, see, hear, feel, and learn. These expanded domains of choice will in turn generate an even more fundamental change in *consciousness*—in our conviction, surely exaggerated but nonetheless deeply felt, that our identities are both controllable and readily transformable.

Such technologies, with the social shifts that they portend, may fundamentally alter the terms of the federalism debate—albeit in complex ways. The same computer-based technologies that will enlarge individual choice can also enable policymakers to gather, retrieve, integrate, manipulate, and analyze immense quantities of data at relatively low cost. In the past, arguments for central planning, industrial policy, and other national interventions in the economy have been premised on our growing power to exploit such technologies to rationalize public policies. With such data-processing and analytical power, the argument goes, more effective national regulation should be possible even in the face of growing social diversity. I believe that this argument is false, but this is beside the point, which is that computer technologies are transforming the crucial variables that any federal system must reflect.

One of these variables is the effect of physical location on the choices and prospects of an individual or firm. For example, the ability to communicate with others quickly and cheaply on a computer screen enables one to enjoy many of the economic and cultural advantages of New York City while living in South Dakota and enjoying its lower tax rates. More choices of this kind, and the lower cost of gratifying them regardless of location, will greatly complicate the Tiebout effect, in which individuals distribute themselves among communities according to their differing preferences concerning the mix of taxes and services offered by those communities.[47]

In this way (and in others), technology could exacerbate the existing competition among jurisdictions, encouraging them to adopt beggar-thy-neighbor policies. This would tend to accelerate the much-discussed "race to the bottom." By freeing consumers and employers to locate anywhere at lower opportunity costs, technology increases the pressure on high-amenity, high-tax states like New York to reduce their regulatory and fiscal burdens in order to retain their more mobile population, employment, and tax bases. On the other hand, such an exodus would leave New York unable to provide those amenities to remote consumers as well as to resident ones.[48] Here, as elsewhere, a Prisoners' Dilemma dynamic drives behavior. The would-be free-riders could defeat their own purposes, making themselves and others in the community worse off than if they could agree on a cooperative strategy. The resulting equilibrium might easily be sub-optimal. The conventional solution to this problem is for the national government to adopt tax and subsidy policies that can defuse the competition among states and localities. Most federalism theorists emphasize this justification for an active national policy role in a federal system,[49] and some national policies do indeed function to keep inter-state rivalries within tolerable limits.

But federalism, I maintain, is far more than a judicious policy response to the risk of races to the bottom. First, it is not at all obvious that such races would occur unless Washington supplied corrective policies. In fact, theoretical models of the race-to-the-bottom dynamic predict a variety of possible outcomes under a number of plausible scenarios, while the empirical data are inconclusive as to actual outcomes.[50] Beyond this indeterminacy, the risk of such a race is more normatively ambiguous and complicated than many advocates for national regulation suggest. These advocates emphasize the game-theoretic Prisoner's Dilemma, yet they often overlook another economistic phenomenon that can produce a compensating advantage: The same competitive dynamic that might cause states to race to the bottom can also constrain the states' perverse incentives to adopt sub-optimal spending and regulatory policies, incentives that both public choice theory and political experience suggest are powerful indeed.

Efforts to impose national uniformity, moreover, entail their own disadvantages. Uniformity mandated at the "wrong" level, or administered incompetently even at the "right" one, may well be worse than heterogeneous outcomes among the states. Washington's efforts to regulate inter-state competition suffer from a variety of recurrent flaws. Its policy instruments are crude, perhaps too crude for the necessary fine-tuning. Grants to states and localities, for example, tend to distort those jurisdictions' own taxing and spending policies.[51] Careful administration may reduce these distortions (e.g., a maintenance of effort requirement) but this may simply create new distortions in the process (e.g., locking the state into an outdated and undesirable pattern of expenditure).

Moreover, the optimal balance between federal and state preferences, initiative, and accountability is elusive. Even where federal categorical grants to states might be justified as targeted mechanisms to internalize state-created externalities, they tend to be policy-intrusive and administratively cumbersome. At the same time, federal officials resist broader functional grants that surrender policy control and funding to state officials, who may have different political and policy priorities and whose expenditures may be more closely disciplined by their taxpayers-voters. Washington often responds more slug-gishly than states to the changing social conditions, market forces, and local imperatives that should inform public policy. In areas as diverse as workfare in AFDC, managed care in Medicaid, charter schools in public education, and more efficient forms of public utility regulation, the states and localities are usually the first to devise new programmatic innovations, and those innova-tions are often progressive.[52] Finally, Congress, no less than the states, pos-sesses strong incentives to use national policymaking authority to "cheat" on the federalist bargain.[53] Devolution of national authority to the states can help to limit such cheating, just as it can help to control the states' incentives to over-spend and over-regulate.

I wish to be clear that in pointing to these deficiencies of national authority in a federal system, I do not mean to deny that such authority can sometimes be justified as a way to constrain socially destructive races to the bottom. My point, rather, is that, one cannot reach a sound overall judgment about how best to allocate policymaking and fiscal responsibilities between the two levels of government until one analyzes many important, empirically-based factors that militate in favor of devolution to the states.

V. The Cognitive Demands of Devolution

Broadly speaking, we may distinguish between two ways in which a federal policymaking institution can decentralize national power. The most common way might be called "default decentralization." Here, the federal policymaker simply allows the power to make and implement decisions that might consti-tutionally be made at the national level to remain instead where it already is—with a lower level of government or with private actors. The other way might be called "affirmative decentralization," in which the federal policymaker actively delegates—downward or outward—power that she is presently exer-cising.

Most of the debate about federalism concerns the appropriateness, scope, and terms of affirmative decentralization. In order to affirmatively decentral-ize power in a coherent fashion, that power must first be centralized, rational-ized (i.e., organized for delegation with certain ends in view), and then dele-gated. Ordinarily, the first and third steps will not be particularly problematic; after all, the power in question is usually centralized to a considerable degree already, and the delegation, once arranged politically, can then be ordered into effect.[54] It is the intermediate step—rationalization of the power to be dele-gated—that is the most difficult. To rationalize a power before delegating it, the federal policymaker must gain a deep, nuanced, fully contextual under-standing of the policy problem to which the power is to be addressed. Only then can the terms of the delegation be carefully and functionally tailored.

One dimension of this rationalization process is easily overlooked. I refer to its cognitive-sympathetic aspect, by which I mean the ability of the power-delegating institution to project itself—through an act of imaginative identification—into the institutional mind of the lower-level delegate who must ultimately exercise that power.

Consider, for example, the area of AFDC policy. In order to meet the cognitive-sympathetic needs of a rationalized delegation of policymaking authority, the federal decisionmaker—Congress, welfare bureaucracy, or court—must be able to comprehend the decisionmaking context of local officials who administer the program at the "retail" level. The former must understand the nature of the latter's resource constraints, political culture, operating routines, and ways of thinking about their tasks—all of which are often radically different from their own. Federal policymakers must imagine the intricate microcosmic interactions between front-line local agency caseworkers and their clients, take into account the informal norms that those interactions generate, and shape the ensuing delegation accordingly.

This perspectival chasm is exceedingly difficult to bridge, even under the best of circumstances. The problem is not simply that federal delegators are remote from the local delegates in both time and space; it is also that the two groups inhabit quite different institutional, motivational, and hence valuational worlds.[55] If we wish to improve federalism's performance, we must somehow ameliorate this problem. Whether federal agencies are permitted to retain or enlarge their existing authority or are required to devolve it downward or outward, they must learn to infuse lower-level values and perspectives into their policy decisions or into their rationalization of the power to be delegated, as the case may be.[56] A number of fairly standard techniques can advance this cognitive-sympathetic project. Examples include more extensive federal consultations with local officials, greater regionalization of federal administration, incorporation of local norms into federal policy decisions, intergovernmental personnel exchanges and training that expose policymakers to conditions and constraints in the field (and vice-versa), liberal use of waiver authorities to encourage local policy variations and experiments, and systematic evaluation and dissemination of their results.

Conclusion

As American federalism enters its third century, it exhibits a remarkable durability and vitality. It flourishes not only because of the political inertia of established institutional structures and vested interests (although they certainly play their part), but because Americans remain deeply divided over public policy issues of all kinds.[57] We need political institutions that reflect these divisions; we also need institutions that suppress and soften them. It may seem ironic to urge that policy elites should respect the extraordinary diversity of American society in the name of national unity, but any contradiction is only superficial. A sound federalism must both mirror our differences and mute them, and the precise balance that it strikes between these two national imperatives must constantly change as our values and interests change. Today devolution is firmly in the saddle. For the foreseeable future, American federalism will surely accord to inter-state differences greater programmatic scope and political legitimacy than they have enjoyed since the New Deal. Just as surely, however, any new equilibrium will be fiercely contested and inevitably transitory. We may safely schedule another symposium on federalism five years hence.

Notes

1. The Court used the phrase in Younger v. Harris, 401 U.S. 37, 44 (1970). Its provenance is traced in Mary Brigid McManamon, *Felix Frankfurter: The Architect of "Our Federalism,"* 27 GA. L. REV. 697 (1993).

2. Congress has already enacted some far-reaching reforms, including the unfunded mandates legislation. Even more fundamental changes may reach the President's desk in the coming months. How they will leave his desk, of course, is another matter. When the voters render their initial verdict on these developments in November, the *vox populi* (or at least the *vox* that the politicians claim to hear) will probably demand a slower pace and narrower scope in these changes.

3. States, in turn, may transfer some of this authority downward to their localities. This possibility merits more public attention than it has so far received. For example, New York Governor George Pataki has proposed devolving to the state's counties much of the authority over AFDC that he hopes the state will receive from Congress.

4. Privatization can take a number of different forms. These include de-regulation, market-based regulation, sale of governmental assets to private entities, cash or near-cash subsidies to consumers with which they purchase privately-provided goods and services, contracting-out public services to private providers, and others. *See* Ronald Cass, *Privatization: Politics, Law, and Theory,* 71 MARQ. L. REV. 449, 451–52 (1988).

5. Privatization, after all, is only one of many possible ways to decentralize governmental power. When government decides to privatize, it is simply choosing to rely primarily on private incentives rather than bureaucratic ones. The public goals of a privatization policy—liberty, diversity, empowerment of sub-national communities, and pursuit of efficiency—are often the same ones that a policy of downward devolution is intended to achieve. Both public decentralization and privatization policies combine public and private initiatives, authorities, and resources. The precise mix of public and private participation is always a central policy design question.

For certain purposes, one might wish to distinguish the privatization of existing governmental authority from a social policy decision to allow activity that has not yet been "publicized" to remain in the private sector. How such "non-publicization" differs—conceptually, normatively, and empirically—from the privatization of existing governmental authority is an interesting question. In the increasingly liminal policy world in which public and private imperceptibly shade into one another, it is also a very important one, but I shall not address it here.

6. For the view that this loss of public confidence is simply a temporary, cyclical phenomenon, see generally E.J. DIONNE, JR., THEY ONLY LOOK DEAD: WHY PROGRESSIVES WILL DOMINATE THE NEXT POLITICAL ERA (1995). I regard this as wishful thinking. Any concessions to states' rights now will be difficult to dislodge in the future.

7. According to a recent joint survey by the Washington Post, Harvard University, and the Kaiser Family Foundation, while in 1964 three in four Americans trusted the federal government all or most of the time, today only one in four does so. This change is part of a more general decline in Americans' trust—in one another and in our institutions. Richard Morin & Dan Balz, *Americans Losing Trust in Each Other and Institutions*, WASH, POST, Jan. 28, 1996, at A1. The respondents indicated a higher level of trust in state governments, a finding that apparently is consistent with other surveys. *See* Eric Schmitt, *Senate Approves Bill to Phase Out Farming Subsidies*, N.Y. TIMES, Feb. 8, 1996, at A1 ("Many public opinion surveys show that people have more trust in state government than in the Federal Government.") (quoting Professor Larry Sabato).

8. It is striking in this regard that public law scholars at elite law schools (often described, accurately and tellingly, as "national" institutions) show little interest in state law, politics, and culture. For example, administrative law courses at these schools and the leading casebooks focus almost entirely on federal agencies. The vast body of state administrative law goes largely unmentioned. On this point, see Peter H. Schuck, *Introduction, in* FOUNDATIONS OF ADMINISTRATIVE LAW 6 (Peter H. Schuck ed., 1994). Much the same is true with respect to constitutional law. Courses in local government law are largely concerned with the general principles that govern municipal organization, finance, and regulation. Apparently, only one law school program in the U.S. focuses on the law of a particular locality. Telephone Conversation with Prof. Ross Sandler, Director, Center on New York City Law, New York Law School, Feb. 23, 1996.

9. Wade Henderson, director of the Washington office of the NAACP, recently stated: "Many African-Americans remember that 'states' rights' were code words for the states' denial of basic civil rights. We are concerned that this history not return in the context of welfare reform." Robert Pear, *Governors' Plans on Welfare Attacked*, N.Y. TIMES, Feb. 14, 1996, at A12. Hostility to federalism, moreover, is not confined to liberals and blacks—and certainly not to Americans. Nationalizing elites in most countries fear that federalism and the social diversity that it protects and reinforces are state-fragmenting conditions that only the centralization of power can cure. Even the leaders of a country like Canada, with its strong federalist tradition, fear that its national unity is now in jeopardy. *E.g.*, Charles Truehart, *It's Official, Canada Adrift on Quebec*, WASH. POST, Mar. 2, 1996, at A15. For other examples of nation-states grappling with the challenge of diversity, see generally DONALD L. HOROWITZ, ETHNIC GROUPS IN CONFLICT (1985). Some of Horowitz's examples, such as Nigeria, have since opted for more authoritarian solutions.

10. On changes in the states, see generally CARL VAN HORN, THE STATE OF THE STATES (3d ed., 1996); LARRY SABATO, GOODBYE TO GOOD-TIME CHARLIE: THE AMERICAN GOVERNOR TRANSFORMED, 1950–1975 (2d ed., 1983). On changes in the federal government, see generally THE NEW POLITICS OF PUBLIC POLICY (Marc K. Landy & Martin A. Levin eds., 1995).

11. I support this claim in the concluding section of Peter H. Schuck, *Alien Ruminations*, 105 YALE L.J. 1963 (1996) (book review).

12. For an extended argument on this point, see generally PAUL E. PETERSON, THE PRICE OF FEDERALISM (1995).

13. The literature on the day-to-day experiences of those living, working, and governing in communist states is rich with examples of such low-visibility outlets. Two classics in this genre are MILAN KUNDERA, THE UNBEARABLE LIGHTNESS OF BEING (Michael H. Heim trans., 1984), and ALEKSANDER SOLZHENITSYN, ONE DAY IN THE LIFE OF IVAN DENISOVICH (Gillon Aitken trans., 1970).

14. *See generally* THEDA SKOCPOL, PROTECTING SOLDIERS AND MOTHERS: THE POLITICAL ORIGINS OF SOCIAL POLICY IN THE UNITED STATES (1992); STEPHEN SKOWRONEK, BUILDING A NEW AMERICAN STATE: THE EXPANSION OF NATIONAL ADMINISTRATIVE CAPACITIES, 1877–1920 (1982).

15. Privatization is a global phenomenon. *See generally* Amy L. Chua, *The Privatization-Nationalization Cycle: The Link Between Markets and Ethnicity in Developing Countries*, 95 COLUM. L. REV. 223 (1995).

16. *See* Robert Pear, *Senate Passes Welfare Measure, Sending it for Clinton's Signature*, N.Y. TIMES, Aug. 2, 1996, at A1. The extent to which they will also receive or raise the funds necessary to discharge these new welfare program responsibilities, of course, is a more doubtful matter. The Food Stamp program, at least for the near term, will retain its current structure of uniform national standards and funding, albeit at lower benefit levels. The federal-state shared responsibility for Medicaid has not been significantly changed in the law.

17. *See, e.g.*, Robert Pear, *Plan to Put Part of Social Security into Stock Funds*, N.Y. TIMES, Feb. 17, 1996, at A1.

18. *See generally* U.S. General Accounting Office, GAO/HEHS–96–44, MEDICAID SECTION 1115 WAIVERS: FLEXIBLE APPROACH TO APPROVING DEMONSTRATIONS COULD INCREASE FEDERAL COSTS (1995) (summarizing waiver projects). On the other side, the right has criticized the administration for resisting certain state innovations, including some of Wisconsin's more radical reforms. *See* Robert Pear, *Clinton Wavers After Backing Welfare Plan*, N.Y. TIMES, June 14, 1996, at A1.

19. *See, e.g.*, Title I of the Judicial Improvements Act of 1990, 104 Stat. 5089, 5089–98.

20. *See generally* LINDA S. MULLENIX, MASS TORT LITIGATION (1995) (ch. 3).

21. *See* Lucas v. South Carolina Coastal Council, 505 U.S. 1003, 1029 (1992) (suggesting that state nuisance law has traditionally guided determinations of when state governments may effect regulatory takings without compensation).

22. *See* DeShaney v. Winnebago County Dep't of Social Services, 489 U.S. 189, 201–02 (1989).

23. *See* Medtronic, Inc. v. Lohr, 116 S. Ct., 64 U.S.L.W. 4625 (1996).

24. *See, e.g.*, Seminole Tribe of Fla. v. Florida, 116 S. Ct. 1114, 1119 (1996); United States v. Lopez, 115 S. Ct. 1624, 1632–33 (1995) (striking down, on Commerce Clause grounds, statute making possession of firearms near schools federal crime). Some other decisions have used narrowing statutory interpretations to accomplish this limitation. *See, e.g.*, New York v. United States, 505 U.S. 144, 169–70 (1992); Gregory v. Ashcroft, 501 U.S. 452, 464–67 (1991). For a recent review of these and other of the Court's federalism decisions, see Jenna Bednar & William N. Eskridge, Jr., *Steadying the Court's "Unsteady Path": A Theory of Judicial Enforcement of Federalism*, 68 S. CAL. L. REV. 1447 (1995).

25. Joseph Berger, *Board of Education: A Thing of the Past?*, N.Y. TIMES, Feb. 18, 1996, at A39.

26. Peter Applebome, *Start of Charter School Shows Flaws in Concept*, N.Y. TIMES, Mar. 6, 1996, at B9 (reporting that as of December 1995, twenty states had authorized charter schools).

27. *See generally* EVAN MCKENZIE, PRIVATOPIA: HOMEOWNER ASSOCIATIONS AND THE RISE OF RESIDENTIAL PRIVATE GOVERNMENT (1994); Robert C. Ellickson, *Cities and Homeowner Associations*, 130 U. PA. L. REV. 1519 (1982).

28. On business improvement districts, see Thomas Lueck, *Owners Challenging Business District*, N.Y. TIMES, Nov. 29, 1995, at B1. The voting rules for the governance of

such districts are under challenge. *See* Kessler v. Grand Central Partnership, 95 Civ. 10029 (SAS) (filed S.D.N.Y. Nov. 28, 1995).

29. *See, e.g.,* ARNALDO BAGNOSCO & CHARLES F. SABEL, SMALL AND MEDIUM-SIZED ENTERPRISES (1995); MICHAEL J. PIORE & CHARLES F. SABEL, THE SECOND INDUSTRIAL DIVIDE (1984).

30. *See generally* KENICHI OHMAE, THE END OF THE NATION STATE: THE RISE OF REGIONAL ECONOMIES (1995); Claudio Grossman & Daniel D. Bradlow, *Are We Being "Propelled Towards A People-Centered Transnational Legal Order?,* 9 AM. U.J. INT'L. L. & POL'Y 1 (1993).

31. *See generally* SAMUEL H. BEER, TO MAKE A NATION: THE REDISCOVERY OF AMERICAN FEDERALISM (1993).

32. *See generally* BERNARD BAILYN, THE PEOPLING OF BRITISH NORTH AMERICA (1986).

33. *See, e.g.,* Felicity Barringer, *Immigration Brings New Diversity to Asian Population in the U.S.,* N.Y. TIMES, June 12, 1991, at A1. *See generally* YEN LE ESPIRITU, ASIAN AMERICAN PANETHNICITY: BRIDGING INSTITUTIONS AND IDENTITIES (1992). As a result of immigration's demographic effects, the *U.S.* population is also younger than other leading industrial nations—another diversity-enhancing attribute.

34. I say "constituted by the *U.S.* Census" in recognition of the utter artificiality of some of these groupings.

35. The top six states of intended residence for immigrants in 1993 accounted for over 70% of immigrants admitted that year. This pattern of concentration has continued since 1971. 1993 STATISTICAL Y.B. IMMIGR. NATURALIZATION SERV. 21–22. New immigrants also are beginning to settle in significant numbers even in ethnically homogeneous "heartland" communities. *See* Steven A. Holmes, *In Iowa Town, Strains of Diversity,* N.Y. TIMES, Feb. 17, 1996, at 6.

36. This diversity is perhaps most apparent during the presidential primary season, when political and media commentators have occasion to call special attention to it.

37. Gina Kolata, *Sharp Regional Incongruities Found in Medical Costs and Treatments.* N.Y. TIMES, Jan. 30, 1996, at C3.

38. VICTOR R. FUCHS, WHO SHALL LIVE?: HEALTH, ECONOMICS, AND SOCIAL CHOICE 52 (1974).

39. *Id.* at 52–54.

40. See data in PETERSON, *supra* note 12, at 44.

41. Nathan Glazer, for example, recently has shown that Massachusetts is far more attentive to the interests of immigrants, both legal and illegal, than is Texas. Nathan Glazer, *Governmental and Nongovernmental Roles in the Absorption of Immigrants in the United States, in* PATHS TO INCLUSION: THE INTEGRATION OF MIGRANTS IN THE UNITED STATES AND GERMANY (P. Schuck et al. eds., forthcoming 1997). Texas, in turn, is viewed in another comparison as being more solicitous than California. Scott McCartney and Karen Blumenthal, *Texas Strives to Avoid California's Mistakes, and It Is Prospering,* WALL ST. J., Sept. 13, 1995, at A1; *see also* PETER SKERRY, MEXICAN AMERICANS: THE AMBIVALENT MINORITY (1993) (arguing that Mexican immigrants and Mexican-Americans have made more progress in San Antonio, Texas, where they have faced greater racial discrimination, than in Los Angeles, California, where they have faced less).

42. Traditionally, this norm was quite widely accepted. Between 1960 and the early 1990s, however, it weakened considerably. In the current Congress, it has again become robust.

43. The heightened constitutional protection accorded to "discrete and insular minorities" under the *Carolene Products* standard is an example. *See* United States v. Carolene Prods. Co., 304 U.S. 144, 152 n.4 (1938). Likewise, state constitutional rights are premised on the notion that individuals can often expect greater protection at the state than at the local level.

44. This fact, so obvious once one takes note of it, was pointed out to me by Professor Nelson Polsby.

45. Communications technology is expanding diversity in other ways. Through highly specialized advertising and targeted media, product manufacturers and service providers can now identify and create market niches based on ethnic, regional, gender, and other specialized appeals, and then hopefully move into broader cross-over markets. Tortilia products, for example, began with a narrow following in some southwestern states. By 1994, sales exceeded $2.4 billion annually; the fastest-growing market was the Midwest. Linda Wong, Executive Director and General Counsel of Rebuilding Los Angeles, Remarks at Immigration and World Cities conference, Columbia University (Feb. 10, 1996).

46. At least for those who can afford to gain access to it. The cost of a PC has steadily declined even as its power and capabilities have increased. A much-discussed, frequently-predicted shake-out in the manufacturing sector of the industry may reduce competition somewhat and slow the pace of these pro-consumer changes, but they will probably continue nonetheless. If so, cost is unlikely to prevent any but the most destitute of American families from affording a bottom-of-the-line PC. Utilization, of course, is a separate question.

47. *See generally* Charles M. Tiebout, *A Pure Theory of Local Expenditures*, 64 J. POL. ECON. 416 (1956).

48. According to a recent report by the Regional Plan Association, in New York City—indeed, in the New York metropolitan region as a whole—this scenario is already unfolding. Kirk Johnson, *Report Sees Major Decline for New York Region*, N.Y. TIMES, Feb. 14, 1996, at A1.

49. *See, e.g.*, Jerry L. Mashaw & Susan Rose-Ackerman, *Federalism and Regulation, in* THE REAGAN REGULATORY STRATEGY 111, 117–18 (George C. Eads & Michael Fit eds., 1984). *See generally* PETERSON, *supra* note 12; Bednar & Eskridge, *supra* note 24.

50. Professor Klevorick's literature review makes this plain. Alvin K. Klevorick, *The Race to the Bottom in a Federal System: Lessons from the World of Trade Policy, in* YALE LAW & POLICY REVIEW/YALE JOURNAL ON REGULATION, SYMPOSIUM: CONSTRUCTING A NEW FEDERALISM 177, 179–81 (1996).

51. Under certain conditions, such grants might even be unconstitutional. *See* Lynn A. Baker, *Conditional Federal Spending After Lopez*, 95 COLUM. L. REV. 1911, 1916 (1995).

52. *See, e.g.*, Douglas J. Besharov, *The Hope of a New Approach*, WASH. POST, Dec. 3, 1995, at C1 (describing states' recent welfare reforms). Although some state reforms are designed primarily to save money, it is hard to explain these changes simply on the basis of that rationale. The states often provide more benefits at greater cost than federal law requires.

53. *See* Bednar & Eskridge, *supra* note 24, at 1467–81.

54. Subject, of course, to the usual implementation obstacles. These may be significant, although not so great as when the national government seeks to centralize power that was previously decentralized. *See, e.g.*, MARTHA DERTHICK, AGENCY UNDER STRESS:

THE SOCIAL SECURITY ADMINISTRATION IN AMERICAN GOVERNMENT (1990) (discussing federalization of state programs for support of aged, blind, and disabled into SSI).

55. One thinks of Robert Cover's famous discussion of different *nomoi*—worlds "of right and wrong, of lawful and unlawful, of valid and void." Robert Cover, *Nomos and Narrative*, 97 HARV. L. REV. 4, 4 (1983). For my purposes, however, the more useful typologies are Robert Merton's distinction between cosmopolitans and parochials, James Q. Wilson's contrast of the investigatory worlds of FBI and DEA agents, and Michael Lipsky's contrast between "street-level bureaucrats" and their superiors at agency headquarters. *See generally* MICHAEL LIPSKY, STREET-LEVEL BUREAUCRACY (1980); ROBERT MERTON, SOCIAL THEORY AND SOCIAL STRUCTURE (3d ed. 1968); JAMES Q. WILSON, THE INVESTIGATORS: MANAGING FBI AND NARCOTICS AGENTS (1978). On the liability implications of these differences in perspective, see PETER H. SCHUCK, SUING GOVERNMENT: CIVIL REMEDIES FOR OFFICIAL WRONGS (1983), especially chs. 6 and 7.

56. There is a corresponding need for local officials to learn to view themselves as part of the national policy system, which must sometimes transcend even the most deeply-rooted parochial differences. A more radical, institutional approach to altering the balance of national and local interests and values would restructure representation in the U.S. Senate to include multi-state, regional, or even national constituencies. *See* Peter H. Schuck, *Industrial Policy's Obstacles.* N.Y. TIMES, Sept. 7, 1983, at A23.

57. The durability of these divisions over time, as revealed in public opinion surveys, is remarkable. *See generally* BENJAMIN I. PAGE & ROBERT Y. SHAPIRO, THE RATIONAL PUBLIC: FIFTY YEARS OF TRENDS IN AMERICA'S POLICY PREFERENCES (1992).

Part II
Institutions and Processes

4

The Politics of Regulation

Perhaps only a political scientist would regard as "controversial" the proposition that there is a politics of regulation.[1] Consider some recent events: Congress nearly emasculated the Federal Trade Commission.[2] Deregulation initiatives[3] generated fierce and protracted opposition from regulated interest. New regulatory proposals,[4] and once-obscure regulatory appointments, produced hard-fought battles. Even regulatory-reform proposals directed at administrative technique and judicial review—hardly the stuff of which political controversy is ordinarily made—became mired in prolonged conflict.[5] In truth, regulation has become the Stalingrad of domestic political warfare.

How is this battle actually being waged? What is at stake? What is the likely outcome? In *The Politics of Regulation,* Harvard political scientist James Q. Wilson seeks to shed light on these questions. He has commissioned nine essays on individual regulatory and enforcement programs, adding a magisterial essay of his own that attempts to integrate the major implications of the case studies into a broad theoretical perspective on regulatory politics and behavior. To the meager regulatory theories that now underlie discourse on the subject, Wilson would add more enriching fare.

I. Economic Regulation

By insisting on a distinctive politics of regulation, Wilson is not simply reiterating the obvious. He is stalking bigger game: the "economic" theory of regulation advanced by the economist George Stigler,[6] and "political" theories advanced by political scientists such as Theodore Lowi[7] and Marver Bernstein.[8]

In classic Chicago-school fashion, Stigler's theory holds that regulation is wholly epiphenomenal. The activity of regulation is not actuated by autonomous political or ideological factors; rather, it reflects the play of market forces. In this view, firms seek to preserve or expand their market shares by de-

---

The Politics of Regulation. Edited by James Q. Wilson. New York: Basic Books, Inc., 1980. Pp. xii, 468.

manding protection from competition. Politicians, responding to this demand, supply influence, legal authority, and a regulatory apparatus that imposes costs, often at prohibitive levels, on actual or potential competitors of the regulated firms. The agency, by building walls around the regulated sector, resembles a medieval lord who protects the economic interests of those sellers fortunate or prescient enough to have already gained shelter within the citadel. Consumers must either pay the monopolistic prices that the sheltered firms can command or manage to do without. Of course, politicians in the legislature and in the agency can prescribe legal rules capable of constraining the market power of regulated firms. In deciding whether and how to exercise this control, however, politicians seek to maximize their self-interest. They know that organizational and political activity generates different costs and benefits for different interests,[9] that regulated firms can better bear those costs and reap those benefits than consumers, and that firms can more easily furnish politicians what they most desire—political, programmatic, and financial support of various kinds, and a secure job upon retirement from public life.[10] Accordingly, politicians succor the regulated firms and neglect the consumer. The agency becomes the communications center of an ongoing cartel, the signaling apparatus for a legalized conspiracy in restraint of trade. The relationship of regulatory agency to regulated industry becomes one of abject subordination, a debasement reflected in rhetorical metaphors: "indentured servant," "tool," and "captive."

In contrast to Stigler's concern with the *economic* calculations of politicians and regulated firms, other students of regulation emphasize techniques of *political* influence: the formation of coalitions, the weaving of intricate networks of influence over agency officials, the appointment of sympathetic officials, the interplay of legal rules and discretion, and the manipulation of symbols.[11] Yet political and economic theories of regulatory behavior predict much the same thing: domination by regulated interests over the personnel, policies, and performance of regulatory agencies.

Since the mid–1960s, this shared academic view of regulatory behavior has shaped the attitudes of policymakers, scholars, "public interest" activists, journalists, and ordinary citizens. Doubtless, this influence is attributable less to the popularity of the *Bell Journal of Economics and Management Science* and of the classics of antipluralist political science than it is to the efforts of enterprising, politically active observers of regulation, who have found congenial the theorists' descriptive propositions, if not always their policy prescriptions. Ralph Nader and his epigones,[12] "consumer oriented" congressional committees and their burgeoning staffs,[13] investigative journalists,[14] and others in positions of influence have distilled from these theories several essential premises that constitute a kind of reformer's creed. First, the behavior of a regulatory agency, and indeed of government in general, is determined by the political power of those interests seeking to influence it. Second, the political power of those interests depends on their economic resources (for example, dollars, lawyers, control over jobs) and on their special access to politicians. Third, regulatory politics is at bottom a Manichean struggle between a discrete and powerful "corporate interest" and an equally well-defined, but politically feeble, consumer (or "public") interest. Finally, that struggle, which is nothing but the interaction of those two vectors of force, leads to only one, melancholy outcome.

This creed, elaborated and embellished in a rhetoric suitable for public consumption, was rendered as a theory of agency "capture." The theory soon acquired the commanding status of conventional wisdom, confidently asserted and rarely questioned. So powerful did its dominion become that an entire generation of congressional staffers, political activists, journalists, and students has come to political maturity armed with its certitudes.

The capture theory could not have taken hold as it did, of course, had it not accurately and vividly described the conditions of many, perhaps most, regulatory agencies in the early 1970s. Certainly, the symptoms of regulatory pathology to which we have become so accustomed—stifled competition, gross inefficiency, hostility to public participation in agency processes, frustration of innovation, administrative chaos and delay, secrecy, absence of long-range planning, and indifference to competing social objectives—amply justified the jeremiads of the agencies' critics, as most of the case studies in the Wilson volume confirm. George Stigler, Theodore Lowi, and Ralph Nader could find overwhelming evidence for their indictments in the Civil Aeronautics Board's refusal to certify new trunk lines,[15] its unauthorized imposition of a route moratorium,[16] and its flagrantly illegal administration of the fare structure.[17] Similar support could be found in the Food and Drug Administration's failure to implement the efficacy requirements of the 1962 drug legislation,[18] and in much other regulatory misbehavior.

Nevertheless, even the most ardent capture theorist should have been struck by certain persistent anomalies and contradictory data. Many old-line regulatory agencies, for example, had succeeded admirably in performing some of the statutory tasks that Congress had thrust upon them. They had nurtured fledgling transportation industries in a developing economy, created a vast and intricate communications network to unify a far-flung people, and protected regional and rural interests in an increasingly urban society. If some inefficiency was the price of these achievements, who could say that the redistributional gains did not justify it?[19] Who could say that messy political, administrative, and operational facts not easily incorporated into economists' models did not appropriately shape agency behavior? If the agencies now seemed anachronistic, was that because conditions had changed or because economists' theories had changed?

More important, the capture theory could not readily explain certain stubborn regulatory patterns. The Federal Power Commission (FPC), for example, had long maintained rates for interstate natural gas far below the levels prevailing in the intrastate market, thereby discouraging production and encouraging wasteful uses,[20] hardly a strategy calculated to endear the FPC to politically well-connected producers. If the FPC was indeed captured, its captors must have been those consumers in the nonproducing states fortunate enough to be hooked into a utility system with long term supply contracts. Similarly, the Securities and Exchange Commission (SEC) had become the scourge of the corporate community, regulating it vigorously in the interests of the uninformed investor. The Office of Civil Rights (OCR), established in the Department of Health, Education, and Welfare shortly after the enactment of the 1964 Civil Rights Act, had been remarkably effective in securing the racial integration of southern schools by the early 1970s despite well-organized, politically potent opposition.[21] Did consumers of natural gas, small investors, and southern blacks possess economic power or political influence that had somehow escaped notice, an influence capable of dictating policy? Were the FPC, SEC, and OCR merely exceptions that proved the rule of agency subservience to the regulated? Or was the conventional wisdom simply wrong?

The answer was not long in doubt. The anomalies proliferated so rapidly during the Nixon-Ford years that the capture theory's predictions became more exception than rule. Administrations profoundly sympathetic to corporate interests actively supported or acquiesced in a veritable flood of new regulatory programs that business bitterly opposed.[22] Between 1970 and 1975, at least thirty important regulatory statutes were enacted, establishing new agencies and vastly expanding the authority of existing ones.[23] In many of those measures, the hands of Ralph Nader and of other capture theorists were plainly visible.[24] When the Carter Administration acceded to power in 1977, this regulatory establishment, swollen to unimagined dimensions, was entrusted to many former (and perhaps future) public interest activists.[25] Strongly committed to the ideologies of consumerism, environmentalism, and community action, those individuals accepted uncritically the premises of the capture theory, even though they had devoted their careers to struggling against its political implications. Their official positions now confirmed its inadequacy. Far from feeling indentured to the regulated industries, those officials were profoundly suspicious of them, if not actually hostile. They quickly seized the opportunity to act on those suspicions.[26]

The capture theory was devastated by these remarkable developments;[27] even refinements in the theory could not rehabilitate it. It was plausible to think, for example, that agencies that regulate many industries, such as the Federal Trade Commission and the Environmental Protection Agency, might be less vulnerable to capture than those that regulate only one, but this notion left unexplained the deregulation policies of several single-industry agencies, such as the Federal Communications Commission under Chairman Charles Ferris, the Interstate Commerce Commission under Chairmen Dan O'Neal and Darius Gaskins, and the Civil Aeronautics Board under Chairmen John Robson, Alfred Kahn, and Marvin Cohen.[28] Another contention, that changes such as deregulation are merely cosmetic, was belied by the fierce opposition that those policy shifts in fact aroused among some of America's most powerful corporations and unions and their congressional allies.[29]

Prevailing theories, it appears, cannot begin to explain much of the observed political reality of the last decade. How, then, are we to understand it? Wilson provides us with some guidance, but we cannot evaluate his offering without first considering an element of regulatory politics to which his essay devotes surprisingly little attention: the changing character of regulation since 1965.

II. Social Regulation

I have mentioned the striking fact that many who most vigorously attacked the performance and legitimacy of the regulatory apparatus prior to 1977 soon found themselves in firm control of its machinery. From their official perches, they administered a regulatory domain vastly enlarged through their own heroic efforts. Is this result paradoxical? I think not. It rather reflects dynamic forces that animated the regulatory explosion of the 1970s and will, *mutatis mutandis,* continue to shape the regulatory politics of the 1980s. Three forces are especially noteworthy. First, a distinctive mode of public intervention, so-called "social" regulation, has emerged with unique political, social, and economic characteristics. Second, markets have evolved in ways highly subversive of old-line "economic" regulation and highly conducive to social regulation. Third, important institutions have developed in ways likely to sustain and augment these forces.

Social Regulation.   Proponents of the new regulation, many of whom adhere to the capture theory, stress that it differs fundamentally from the old regulation of the New Deal era.[30] They point out that "economic" or cartel regulation of a market was designed to control rates, entry, and basic patterns of service, that by suppressing competitive forces, such regulation often generated substantial efficiency losses and distributional inequities, and that its legal and administrative machinery was so susceptible to industry manipulation that it amounted to "corporate socialism," pernicious in origin[31] and perverse in execution. The newer "social" regulation, in contrast, was designed to enhance health, safety, the environment, equal opportunity, and the quality of life. By internalizing the social costs generated by private decisions, it would minimize them. Innovative legal and administrative arrangements would ensure that capture did not occur. Social regulation would not simply yield economic efficiency; it was, above all, an essential element of a just and humane society, protecting those most vulnerable to the depredations inevitable in an industrial setting. With perfect consistency, then, reformers could oppose economic regulation and support social regulation.

If the aspirations implicit in the theoretical foundations of social regulation could readily be implemented, the politics of regulation would almost certainly have taken a very different form than it has. In fact, this account, though accurate as far as it goes, neglects important political, economic, and administrative dimensions of social regulation that determine the nature and scope of regulatory conflict. Of these, I shall discuss four.

First, most programs of social regulation confer exceedingly broad regulatory authority, often extending to all industries in the society, all firms doing business with the government, or all federally assisted activities. The ambit of social regulation, then, far exceeds that of classic economic regulation, which embraced firms within only a single industry. Cross-industry jurisdiction may well reduce the likelihood that the agency will be captured by any particular industry, but it also raises certain obstacles to effective regulation: the need for (and paucity of) information, expertise, resources, and political support, and the need to fine-tune policies and rules to accommodate the far greater diversity of the regulated domain. When those high demands are not met, regulatory failure, igniting intense political controversy, is likely.[32]

Second, social regulation entails many of the same kinds of undesirable consequences as economic regulation, while spreading those consequences across far larger sectors of the economy. The costs of complying with uniform standards, whether those of the Environmental Protection Agency or of the Interstate Commerce Commission, are similar in character. They often render marginal firms unprofitable, discourage new entry and investment, stifle innovation, regressively tax consumers when passed on in product prices, diminish consumer choice, surround capital investment decisions with great uncertainties, and violate norms of horizontal equity. This is not to deny that social regulation often generates benefits; doubtless it does, although available data do not establish conclusively or even persuasively that benefits always exceed costs.[33] The point here is that those costs are no less problematic simply because the regulation is social rather than economic. If anything, the contrary is true.[34]

Third, social regulation seeks to advance many ends—for example, life, health, racial equality, ecological balance—that cannot readily be objectively valued. Even if a satisfactory method for doing so existed, any effort to quantify explicitly those ends or to trade them off against others would be highly vulnerable to political attack as callous, indifferent to human suffering, and subservient to corporate interests.[35] Because those ends are embraced with special, even theological, fervor and are couched in the constraint-denying language of "rights,"[36] social regulation often assumes a highly ideological, uncompromising character that encourages efforts to expand and to perfect regulatory controls with little regard to costs.[37]

Fourth, quite apart from the nature of its ends, the types of risks with which social regulation is increasingly concerned—for example, the dangers of environmental or biological insults, of invidious discrimination, of offenses to one's personal integrity[38]—are often difficult to identify, or literally invisible. In an important sense, their very existence may be a function of precarious scientific judgments, the state of laboratory technology, and ill-defined or inconsistent public attitudes towards uncertainty. The contingent, evanescent character of these risks, the fundamental human values that they implicate, and the large number of people affected ensure that the politics of regulating these risks will be volatile. They will be rooted less in fact and analysis than in theory and *ipse dixit*, less in reasoned inferences from human experience than in extrapolations from transitory and inevitably speculative laboratory findings. The question, "How high shall the rate of return to natural gas producers be?" is a formidable intellectual and political problem, but the question, "How safe shall the air be?" is far more controversial and elusive. Finally, the unusual difficulty in predicting outcomes of health, safety, and other social regulation tends to create a broad zone of uncertainty and subjective judgment in which regulators' redistributive efforts, inefficient as such schemes may be, will nonetheless flourish.[39]

To the extent, then, that social regulation supplements or supplants economic regulation, regulatory struggle assumes new, more polarizing forms that yield less readily to persuasion, compromise, and other conventional processes of political accommodation.

Changing Patterns of Market Failure.   The legitimacy of economic and social regulation is anchored in different kinds of market failure. The former is usually premised, rightly or wrongly, on the existence of a natural monopoly, the risk of "destructive competition," the ability of producers to extract rents, or the need to allocate scarcity.[40] Social regulation, in contrast, is ordinarily justified by the need to correct externalities, improve information, override socially pernicious preferences, redress inequalities in bargaining power, or ensure that services purchased with public funds meet minimum standards.[41]

The demand for regulation during the 1970s has reflected a new configuration of market failures and new public attitudes towards those failures. In this changed context, traditional market-failure justifications for economic regulation are increasingly suspect. Technological advances have eliminated certain apparent market failures, unleashing vital economic forces in industries long thought to be unsuited to competition. Electronic funds-transfer systems, for example, have made sluggish, artificially segmented financial institutions both fiercely competitive and increasingly innovative. Cablecasting and other technologies have rendered obsolete the scarcity justification for restriction of broadcasting franchises by the Federal Communications Commission. A host of telecommunications entrepreneurs are successfully eroding AT&T's "natural monopoly" in microwave transmission.[42]

Similarly, fears that unregulated industrial concentration would cause poor market performance have been somewhat allayed by a "new learning" stressing the importance of scale efficiencies, international competition, and other market-strengthening conditions.[43] Finally, chronic inflation has increasingly come to be viewed as a special kind of market failure for which price controls, the conventional nostrum of economic regulation, would be a poor remedy.[44]

In short, structural changes in the economy have seriously undermined the theory and practice of economic regulation.

Social regulation, in contrast, responds to very different conditions. The kinds of market failure that purport to justify social regulation are now more prevalent, not less. In an interdependent, urban society, externalities are ubiquitous. Urbanization implies that one's activities are more likely to affect one's neighbors, and to do so in ways that cause social and private welfare to diverge. The level of these externalities, however, is not simply a function of such physical or geographical variables. It also reflects more fundamental changes in public preferences and attitudes. Regulation of smoking in public areas, for example, has not become politically salient simply because of research demonstrating adverse health effects upon nonsmokers (that link was always suspected), or because *per capita* smoking has increased (it has actually declined). Rather, nonsmokers have grown less tolerant of smokers, and have acquired the numerical strength to work their will in legislative arenas. Other consumption decisions that in an earlier day were considered entirely a private affair are today thought to affect the welfare of the larger society, even in the absence of any physical interaction. Whether those responses reflect increased altruism or greater officiousness, the universe of such "merit" goods and bads, thought to justify public efforts to influence consumption patterns, has steadily grown. And one form of intervention leads almost inexorably to others. Thus, health care for the poor was originally subsidized as a merit good. Once public dollars were involved, however, health care quickly became a highly regulated activity.[45]

Objective conditions and attitudinal changes have conspired to create or to exacerbate other kinds of market failure. The pronounced separation of production and consumption in a technologically sophisticated society, for example, has left consumers poorly informed about much that they consume and relatively ill-equipped to evaluate nonobvious risks.[46] Moreover, society increasingly values public goods, such as clean air and equal justice, that the market cannot adequately provide, and rejects a distribution of income thought to affect market behavior in undesirable ways.

Taken together, these long-run changes in social conditions and preferences suggest that, while the kinds of market failure that have traditionally supported economic regulation are receding in importance, those thought to justify social regulation are proliferating rapidly. To the extent that disputes over economic and social regulation implicate different interests, conditions, issues, processes, and dimensions of conflict, these developments imply a fundamental transformation in the politics of regulation now and in the future.

Institutional Environment.   Social regulation, I have maintained, is a broad, surging current fed by powerful tributaries. It is possible, however, that this current could be dammed or diverted. Regulation, after all, possesses its own characteristic shortcomings—Charles Wolf has labeled these "non-market failures"[47]—and the contemporary politics of regulation demonstrates that the existence of regulatory failure has become widely acknowledged. Despite these realities, however, the institutions that increasingly shape our politics—public interest organizations, national media, Congress, and government bureaucracies—seem far more likely, at least in the long run, to propel the regulatory tide than to restrain it.

An influential sector of nonprofit organizations staffed by a cadre of effective political activists has, in a few short years, radically altered the *dramatis personae* and scope of regulatory debate.[48] Due largely to their success in advocating legal reforms and developing new fundraising practices, their effective access to the political process, as Wilson observes, has been dramatically increased in the last decade or two.[49] Many of these groups have strong vested interests—ideological, political, and economic—in maintaining and expanding social regulation, especially those programs that they helped to establish. Their position will be buttressed by more conventional allies: regulated interests sheltered or nourished by the program,[50] industries whose products or services would be needed to comply with regulatory standards,[51] and labor unions whose members' jobs and wage levels are thought to be protected by the program.[52] Groups with growing demographic importance and political power, such as blacks, Hispanics, and the elderly, seem likely to demand additional protection from the depredations of both marketplace and bureaucracy.

The editorial and reportorial content of the national media tends to be liberal, cosmopolitan, critical of existing institutions and social conditions, and sympathetic to the reformist agenda. The debunking of established authority and institutions, the ideology of secular humanism, and the pursuit of social reform are the warp and woof of network news and public-affairs programming. These influences have almost certainly guided the public's political consciousness toward those values.[53] A conservative administration, especially one of avowedly parochial orientation, will provide even more grist for the adversary journalist's mill.

Fueled by an extraordinary profusion of staff resources,[54] Congress has become a powerful engine of social regulation. Members of the congressional committees with responsibility for an established program tend to possess strong personal, political, and policy interests in its continuation and growth. Important new regulatory statutes are unlikely to be enacted in the wake of the 1980 elections, but this seems less significant than the fact that ample, not-yet-exploited regulatory authority is already on the books. Indeed, far-reaching regulations, carrying multibillion dollar price tags, are already scheduled for issuance in the early 1980s.[55]

Short-term political appointees, like members of Congress themselves, cannot easily contain this dynamic process. Many regulations are mandated by existing law. Others are justified by the plausible and conservative, albeit often illusory, purpose of improving the effectiveness of those controls already in place.[56] Moreover, one need not subscribe to reductionist theories of bureaucracy to recognize that the career officials who administer a regulatory program tend to have personal and professional stakes in its survival and success, however measured, and to identify intensely with its goals. Finally, mounting budgetary pressures, which will intensify if congressional or constitutional limits on spending are adopted, tempt hard-pressed officials to accomplish important political and policy objectives by extracting private expenditures through regulation rather than through direct expenditure of scarce public funds.[57]

None of this is to say, of course, that the outcome of any particular regulatory struggle is preordained or that regulatory growth is inexorable. The instances of deregulation, largely confined thus far to the realm of economic regulation, testify eloquently to the contrary. So do some early actions of the Reagan administration. Nevertheless, the interests supporting regulation will often prevail, especially where the struggle is waged in the administrative and judicial arenas, in which they are more influential, rather than in the legislative arena.

III. Wilson's Theory of Regulatory Politics

Wilson wishes to clear away the intellectual debris left by this whirlwind of change, and to fashion in its stead a theoretical framework that can better account for the raging political battles over regulation. He advances somewhat ambivalent claims for his construction. Eschewing any pretense to rigor, assuring us that the "discipline" of political science is "as inelegant, disorderly, and changeable as its subject matter,"[58] he nonetheless aspires to identify "continuities, if not cosmic generalizations" about regulation.[59] Indeed, he hopes to approach "[a] complete theory of regulatory politics."[60] This confusion is heightened by Wilson's failure to clarify precisely what it is that his generalizations are supposed to explain.[61]

A "complete theory of regulatory politics," or even a comprehensive set of "continuities," would seek to explain at least the following phenomena: the appearance of a regulatory proposal on the political agenda; the ability of that issue to attain priority over all the other issues pressing for recognition and resolution by the political system; the adoption of the proposal in a particular legislative or administrative form; its subsequent institutionalization in an administrative milieu; the staffing patterns for the regulatory program; the substantive decisions resulting from the regulatory activities; and the program's evolution, which occasionally leads to its eventual demise.

The essays in Wilson's book cast a somewhat uneven light on these matters, illuminating some and neglecting others. The chapter on electric utility regulation, for example, presents a rather confusing, apolitical picture of its political origins. Utility tycoon Samuel Insull, we are told, advocated *state* regulation of his industry "as an alternative to local competition and political bargaining."[62] Several obvious questions are ignored: Why would a local utility like Commonwealth Electric not have preferred regulation at the municipal level, which was within the orbit of its influence? Why did Insull, contrary to other utility entrepreneurs, not fear municipal ownership?[63] Why did industrial and commercial consumers of power, presumably influential advocates for stringent regulation, play no discernible political role? Despite such omissions, however, the book as a whole provides an important corrective to reductionist explanations of regulatory origins. Its case studies, for example, reveal that some agencies, such as the Civil Aeronautics Board, were created as a result of political pressures from the regulated industry,[64] that some, such as the Shipping Board, now the Federal Maritime Commission, were established over the industry's fierce opposition,[65] and that others, such as the Office of Civil Rights, began without regulated interests being much involved one way or the other.[66]

Wilson's most distinctive contribution to regulatory theory is his effort to systematize this diversity. Constructing a four-cell matrix based on the distribution of the costs and benefits of any particular regulatory scheme,[67] Wilson distinguishes four "political situations" that reflect different patterns in which issues are generated and coalitions formed. *Majoritarian politics* occurs when both costs and benefits are widely distributed; the Social Security and Sherman Acts are offered as examples.[68] In this mode, interest-group activity is minimal, presumably because of organizational "free-rider" problems.[69] *Interest-group politics* occurs when both costs and benefits are narrowly distributed; the labor laws and the Shipping Act are mentioned.[70] Here, specialized but highly motivated interests compete; typically, the result is compromise. *Client politics* occurs when costs are widely distributed but benefits are concentrated; state licensing laws are cited.[71] Ordinarily, the special interests that benefit have the field to themselves, as the cost-bearing consumers or taxpayers have little incentive to organize in opposition. Finally, *entrepreneurial politics* occurs when benefits are widely distributed and costs are highly concentrated; environmental and auto-safety regulation are given as examples. In this mode, a political entrepreneur like Ralph Nader or Estes Kefauver somehow manages to mobilize diffuse public concerns and to overcome strong resistance by the regulated sector.[72]

This typology is both original and provocative,[73] suggesting patterns of regulatory behavior far richer and more complex than those conjured up by the bromidic axioms of capture theory. Emphasizing the importance of the motivations of regulatory officials, Wilson uncovers further layers of meaning in regulatory behavior. Thus, he distinguishes among *careerists* motivated by organizational bureaucratic concerns; *politicians* ambitious for higher appointive or elective office; and *professionals* responsive to norms and interests emanating from the larger occupational community outside the agency.[74] This analysis is buttressed by two excellent case studies—one on the Antitrust Division of the Justice Department,[75] the other on the Federal Trade Commission[76]—that demonstrate how agency routines, case selection, interbureau conflict, and regulatory policies are shaped by the distinctive training, professional orientation, and career paths of staff lawyers and economists. Analyses of the Office of Civil Rights and of the airline-deregulation controversy also remind us that academic theories and politically unconventional ideas can profoundly influence the course of administrative law and regulatory *realpolitik*.

Despite these considerable virtues, however, Wilson's analytical construct is ultimately of little value to one who would *predict* regulatory behavior rather than simply explain it *ex post*. Most of the important questions remain unanswered and many new ones are raised. Thus, Wilson suggests that entrepreneurial politics has become a common feature of regulatory life,[77] yet that hardly constitutes a theory or even an explanation. The political arena, after all, has always been thick with policy entrepreneurs: congressional staffers searching for a "big issue," special interest lobbyists stalking competitive advantage or special benefits, public interest advocates pursuing their visions of reform, and journalists hoping to develop a long-running front-page story. Why do some flourish while others go out of business? Why did that quintessential policy entrepreneur, Ralph Nader, strike oil with auto safety and wholesome meat regulation, but drill dry holes with corporate chartering, tax reform, and proposals for a consumer protection agency? If regulatory legislation is often preceded by "scandal" or "crisis," as Wilson suggests,[78] what factors determine which events are so characterized and which are not?

The answers to these questions probably have much to do with the modes of political discourse to which different kinds of regulatory issues lend themselves, and with the ways in which the mass media, a formidable influence that Wilson scarcely mentions, choose to treat such issues. Some regulatory issues are more susceptible to vivid and simplified presentation than others. A congressional hearing at which the diseased lungs of deceased coal miners are exhibited is gripping theater; the consequences of other, equally insidious environmental insults are less dramatically conveyed. As with any market commodity, the demand for entrepreneurship waxes and wanes; popular appetites for apocalypse, crisis, outrage, and reform evidently can become surfeited.

Wilson's typology also begs important questions. He correctly observes that values in political life are not given, but emerge only in the course of political processes.[79] This truth, however, necessarily implies that actors often cannot know *a priori* what counts as a cost or a benefit to them. Evaluation not only precedes, but grows out of, political action. Moreover, the very identity of costs and benefits, not merely their distribution, will often be opaque at each stage of the regulatory process. Any regulated industry experiences a configuration of costs and benefits that is complex and in constant flux and redefinition. The "oil industry" is in fact a congeries of producers, pipelines, refiners, resellers, jobbers, retailers, dealers, brokers, and other groups selling to an even more diverse array of users. Not only do the interests of those groups clash, but each is itself extremely heterogeneous, with interests varying according to geographical location, product mix, historical marketing pattern, and a host of other attributes. For Wilson's typology to be at all serviceable, one must first know how broadly or narrowly the costs and benefits of regulation will be distributed in the myriad, constantly changing markets that the constellations of these groups create. That knowledge, needless to say, would be devilishly hard to come by.

And even if we assume that a discrete, well-defined market can be isolated for analysis, what do we really know of the regulatory costs and benefits? If social science has established anything during the last decade, surely it is that regulation of complex markets and institutions produces many unpredictable, uncontrolled consequences.[80] And passing the rather awesome empirical questions of what a regulation's effects will be and which of those effects should count as costs and as benefits, it remains a matter of singular difficulty to determine who in fact will ultimately bear them. Who, for example, will bear the costs of complying with regulations requiring certain federally assisted hospitals to provide uncompensated care to the poor?[81] The hospital's donors? Its employees? Its uninsured patients? Blue Cross subscribers in the community? Those ill persons turned away as a result? Overcrowded municipal hospitals?[82]

If the answers to the distributional questions are not straightforward ones, how are we to apply Wilson's typology at all? Perhaps we could observe which organizations favor a particular regulatory proposal and which oppose it, and could then simply infer the actual distribution of costs and benefits from that configuration of interests. But in order to pursue that strategy, we would need to wait until the lines were drawn and the armies massed; at that point, Wilson's matrix could only confirm what we already knew. To put the dilemma another way, the matrix could come into play as a plausible predictive device only when either we can answer a number of questions that are unlikely, in the interesting cases, to be answerable, or we are prepared to make extremely simplistic assumptions about the probable consequences of a regulatory proposal.[83] Still, for all its indeterminacies and gaps, Wilson's analysis of regulatory politics remains the most sophisticated account of this quotidian phenomenon that we possess, a telling commentary on the impoverished state of our contemporary political theory.

IV. The Courts and Regulation

Regulatory politics without the courts is like *Hamlet* without—Polonius. Yet Wilson and his collaborators apparently attach importance only to those relatively infrequent occasions on which courts adjudicate a regulatory dispute, and simply lament the case-by-case, uncertainty-enhancing character of judicial review of regulatory actions.[84] The influence of the courts on the regulatory process, however, although easily exaggerated (especially by lawyers), is more systematic. In conjunction with Congress and the agencies, courts embed regulatory conflicts in particular procedural structures. In their own right, courts clothe an agency's policy judgments in the legitimating mantle of principle, an especially important function in those situations in which exercises of broad, legislative-type discretion, rather than adjudications, are under review. Indeed, Congress would not, and constitutionally perhaps could not, confer broad decisional authority upon the agencies unless it were confident that Article III courts would confine exercises of that authority within statutory and constitutional limits.[85] In a number of respects, then, courts form essential parts of the institutional background against which allocations of regulatory power are made, evaluated, and legitimated.

Even at the more mundane level of reviewing particular regulatory decisions, courts may influence regulatory politics in important ways. First, courts define the nature of the decisionmaking process by prescribing how regulatory issues are to be raised and resolved. Although often procedural and technical in form, such judicial decisions may nevertheless have far-reaching substantive implications. Thus, by insisting that an administrative decision employ certain procedures, a court may affect the interests that are represented, the record that is developed, the weight to be accorded agency expertise, and the appropriateness of political influences on the substantive outcome.

In addition, courts influence what resources and remedies are available to participants in the regulatory process. By deciding which interests have standing to challenge agency action, when litigation costs may be shifted between parties, to which types of information participants may have access, and under which circumstances private citizens may proceed directly against a regulated firm, courts redesign the political process and environment in which the agency exercises regulatory power.

Courts also define the contours of the agency's regulatory discretion. By deciding which issues an agency may or must resolve and which criteria of decision constrain it, the court in effect allocates regulatory power between legislature, court, agency, and citizens. Indeed, by construing the agency's discretion very narrowly, the court may effectively determine a policy decision. And when a court compels a reluctant agency to enforce statutory rights, it shifts the balance of power among those private interests affected by the agency's authority.[86]

Finally, and more generally, courts constitute a significant strategic resource, for the mere availability of judicial review is an important weapon in regulatory conflict. Each element ancillary to judicial review of a regulatory decision—the delay, the expense, the probability of particular substantive outcomes, the imposition on the dispute of judicial forms of resolution—advantages certain interests at the expense of others.

In each instance, courts influence the structure and substance of regulatory politics in ways that have little to do with the analytical categories employed by Wilson's distributional matrix, but instead reify a conception of appropriate judicial role. That conception in turn reflects the court's confidence in a particular agency's decision processes, the extent to which the issue seems to demand the specialized expertise that an agency may be thought to possess, and the particular functions—among those discussed above—that the court feels obliged to perform.

The chief architects of administrative law, most notably the Court of Appeals for the District of Columbia Circuit, have not yet embraced any consistent conception of judicial role in the review of increasingly complex regulatory decisions.[87] In view of the competing values at stake and the diverse factors affecting agency decisionmaking, they are unlikely to do so in the future. It is all the more striking, then, that several of the regulatory reform proposals that have attracted political support envision a significantly enhanced role for the courts in the regulatory process.[88] Not the least of the ironies of the recent conservative triumph may well be a new spasm of judicial activism in administrative law, one precipitated by a Congress determined to use the courts as a weapon in the regulatory battles of the 1980s.

V. The Zeitgeist and Regulation

In the end, the politics of regulation turns less on the dynamics of coalition formation, the behavior of regulatory officials, or the rulings of courts, important as these are, than on the dominant vision of the larger society in which nationally organized interests, policy entrepreneurs, bureaucrats, and courts are merely highly specialized, and often unrepresentative, manifestations. That vision encompasses a conception of the good society and of the place of the citizen in that society, a notion of the proper boundaries between public and private, and of the appropriate domains of community norms and individual freedom. That vision, whatever its content, ultimately prescribes the tolerance within which conventional regulatory politics can be conducted.

Any politics of regulation surely must be directed first and foremost to these fundamental questions of individual autonomy and social purpose. Significantly, it is this "metapolitics" of regulation that has been transformed in recent decades. One regrets, then, that Wilson, after acknowledging the importance of ideas to regulatory politics, leaves it at that. Ideology thus remains as so much unexplained variance, as a black box. Yet it seems clear that a new public philosophy has deeply eroded the traditional, ideological restraints upon the objects and intrusiveness of regulatory intervention—restraints based, perhaps, on notions of federalism, of limits of law, of individual responsibility, or of unacceptable levels of "non-market failure." Until quite recently—and long after economic regulation had become a prominent component of our public law—it remained almost inconceivable that problems of sexual harassment in the workplace,[89] the conduct of behavioral research,[90] and the editorial policies of magazine publishers,[91] to select some recent examples, would be subject to national rules and potential legal sanctions. Such interventions, however, have become commonplace, suggesting that any limits to

the utopian sweep of the regulatory vision are evidently limits of political expediency, not of principle. Transitory, elastic, and highly vulnerable to mo-
mentary shifts in the winds of public opinion, those boundaries cannot readily withstand the long term pressures to extend regulation's reach.

What is the source of those sparks that so readily ignite the regulatory tin-
der? Doubtless there are many, but a few seem especially significant. First,
American society has for the past fifteen years experienced the continuous exigencies of war, economic turmoil, and social change. These conditions are
perennially the most dependable precursors and powerful progenitors of sta-
tism. Dislocations in energy markets spawned a vast regulatory system,
thrusting governmental power, and thus political conflict, into the very core of
the nation's economic decisionmaking apparatus. Persistent inflation growing
out of war-related deficits precipitated three years of extensive wage-price
controls, with a legacy of encompassing regulation in increasingly critical economic sectors, such as health care.[92] Newly mobilized social groups have
pressed their claims for equal treatment, and in some cases preference,
through civil rights regulations.[93]

Second, the ineffectiveness of much regulation has encouraged its expansion, confirming the cynic's observation that nothing succeeds like failure. The
failure of natural gas price regulation did not prevent its extension to the previously unregulated intrastate market.[94] Similarly, the inability of state certifi-
cate-of-need laws to contain hospital costs has led both to the expansion of
their regulatory jurisdiction to cover physicians' offices and specialized non-
hospital facilities, and to rate or revenue controls over hospitals.[95] This "tar-
baby effect," as it has aptly been called,[96] has been observed in many other regulatory contexts, and its causes—political risk-aversion on the part of
regulators, the desire to control the unanticipated consequences of existing
regulation, redistributive efforts, and considerations of horizontal equity[97]—
are persistent and systematic.

Third, as discussed above, powerful elements of American society have acquired a considerable vested interest in the continuation and expansion of regulation, and a transformed reality has lent plausibility to their alarums of market failure. Finally, and perhaps most importantly, American society appears
to have come to a new view of the role and possibilities of law and politics in
the pursuit of the good society. Until quite recently, Americans regarded inequalities, dashed hopes, and personal misfortunes not as pervasive social injustices to be extirpated but as discrete obstacles—due to the will of God, the
victim's own deficiencies, or simple bad luck—to be surmounted by individual effort or endured with stoic resignation. Even if a condition were regarded
as intolerable, a federal regulatory statute would have seemed a most unlikely
instrument of reform.

Today, in contrast, injustices are readily perceived, their tractability is
widely assumed, and collective intervention by legal rule appears to be the
remedy of choice. As our perception of imperfection has grown, our tolerance

for it has diminished. These attitudes no doubt reflect a complex evolution in morality, ideas, and politics. Whatever their cultural sources, they have fused in a melioristic, not to say utopian, ambition to reform a disagreeable social reality through the affirmative application of public power. That impulse has virtually obliterated the moral, constitutional, and political boundaries that once contained it, and the social consensus that once domesticated it.[98] In shaping the human and institutional materials standing between that energizing impulse and that beckoning vision of social justice, however, we are limited to the same old tools: politics, law, and administration.[99] If past is indeed prologue, there is precious little reason to believe, but much reason to hope, that those crude instruments can be made equal to the increasingly demanding tasks that will be set for them.

Notes

1. *See* Wilson, *The Politics of Regulation,* in THE POLITICS OF REGULATION 357, 357 (J. Wilson ed. 1980) [book hereinafter cited without cross-reference].

2. *See* Federal Trade Commission Improvements Act of 1980, Pub. L. No. 96–252, 94 Stat. 374 (1980); HOUSE COMM. ON INTERSTATE AND FOREIGN COMMERCE, FEDERAL TRADE COMMISSION IMPROVEMENTS ACT OF 1979, H.R. REP. No. 181, 96th Cong., 1st Sess. 9 (1979) (recommending legislative veto of agency rules, exemption of savings and loan associations from agency jurisdiction, and prohibition of agency actions under Lanham Trademark Act); SENATE COMM. ON COMMERCE, SCIENCE, AND TRANSPORTATION, FEDERAL TRADE COMMISSION ACT OF 1979, S. REP. No. 500, 96th Cong., 1st Sess. 5–7 (1979) (proposing limitation of FTC regulation of insurance business, commercial advertising, and used car warranties).

3. *E.g.,* Motor Carrier Act of 1980, Pub. L. No. 96–296, 94 Stat. 793 (1980); Railroad Transportation Policy Act of 1980, Pub. L. No. 96–448, 94 Stat. 1895 (1980).

4. *E.g.,* Comprehensive Environmental Responses, Compensation, and Liability Act of 1980, Pub. L. No. 96–510, 94 Stat. 2767 (1980); 42 C.F.R. ss 124.501–.607 (1979) (Hill-Burton Act regulations). The Hill-Burton Act regulations were challenged in American Hosp. Ass'n v. Harris, 477 F. Supp. 665 (N.D. Ill. 1979) (denying motion for preliminary injunction against regulations taking effect).

5. *E.g.,* S. 401, 97th Cong., 1st Sess. (1981) (Regulatory Cost Reduction Act of 1981) (providing, *inter alia,* for judicial review of regulatory impact analysis); S. 67, 97th Cong., 1st Sess. (1981) (Administrative Procedure Act Amendments of 1981) (providing for de novo review of agency interpretations of statutes, eliminating any presumption of validity of agency regulations, and imposing more demanding standard of review on agency actions). Each of these measures was the subject of considerable controversy during the Ninety-sixth Congress, S. 67 having actually passed the Senate.

6. *See* Stigler, *The Theory of Economic Regulation,* 2 BELL J. ECON. & MANAGEMENT SCI. 1 (1971).

7. *See* T. LOWI, THE END OF LIBERALISM 125–56 (1969).

8. *See* M. BERNSTEIN, REGULATING BUSINESS BY INDEPENDENT COMMISSION 263–67 (1955).

9. *See* M. OLSON, THE LOGIC OF COLLECTIVE ACTION 21, 33–36 (rev. ed. 1971).

10. *See* Posner, *The Federal Trade Commission,* 37 U. CHI. L. REV. 47, 85–86 (1969); Stigler, *supra* note 6, at 12–13.

11. *See, e.g.,* M. Bernstein, *supra* note 8, at 278–79; M. Edelman, The Symbolic Uses of Politics 188–94 (1977); H. Friendly, The Federal Administrative Agencies 1–26 (1962); T. Lowi, *supra* note 7, at 288–97.

12. *See, e.g.,* R. Fellmeth, The Interstate Commerce Omission 311–25 (1970); J. Turner, The Chemical Feast 3–4 (1970).

13. *See, e.g.,* House Subcomm. on Oversight and Investigations, Comm. on Interstate and Foreign Commerce, Federal Regulation and Regulatory Reform, H.R. Doc. No. 134, 95th Cong., 1st Sess. (1976); Senate Comm. on Governmental Affairs, 95th Cong., 1st Sess., Study on Federal Regulation (Comm. Print 1977) (five volumes).

14. *See, e.g.,* L. Kohlmeier, The Regulators 29–128 (1969); M. Mintz & J. Cohen, America, Inc. 237–53 (1971).

15. *See* Behrman, *Civil Aeronautics Board,* in The Politics of Regulation at 75, 88.

16. *See id.* at 97–98.

17. *See* Moss v. CAB, 430 F.2d 891, 902 (D.C. Cir. 1970) (tariffs established through cooperation of airlines and CAB without public notice and hearing were unlawful).

18. *See* American Pub. Health Ass'n v. Veneman, 349 F. Supp. 1311, 1317 (D.D.C. 1972).

19. Welfare economists traditionally define a point B as Pareto superior to point A if efficiency gains are so great that gainers *could* compensate losers and still be better off at point B than at point A. Politicians, however, may properly conclude that such a move is not acceptable unless the losers are *actually* compensated by the gainers, and that where this transfer is not feasible, point A is to be preferred to point B despite B's greater efficiency.

20. *See* S. Breyer & P. MacAvoy, Energy Regulation by the Federal Power Commission 69–72 (1974).

21. *See* Rabkin, *Office for Civil Rights,* in The Politics of Regulation at 304, 312–13.

22. For example, the Nixon Administration actively supported federal regulation of environmental quality and occupational health and safety, albeit in a somewhat different form than the statutes ultimately enacted by Congress. *See* Kelman, *Occupational Safety and Health Administration,* in The Politics of Regulation at 236, 241–42; Marcus, *Environmental Protection Agency,* in The Politics of Regulation at 267, 273.

23. *See* Lilley & Miller, *The New "Social Regulation,"* Pub. Interest, Spring 1977, at 49.

24. *See, e.g.,* Katzmann, *Federal Trade Commission,* in The Politics of Regulation at 152, 177, 423 nn.61–63 (reorganization of FTC in early 1970s reflected recommendations of Nader report and ABA Commission study); Marcus, *supra* note 22, at 270–72 (1970 clean-air amendments significantly influenced by Ralph Nader).

25. Prominent examples include Joan Claybrook, a fierce critic of the automobile industry who became its safety regulator as head of the National Highway Traffic and Safety Administration; Michael Pertschuk, who designed much of the consumer legislation of the 1960s and 1970s as a Senate aide and became chairman of the Federal Trade Commission; and Carol Tucker Foreman, a consumer activist and *bete noire* of the food industry who became its regulator as Assistant Secretary for Food and Consumer Affairs in the Department of Agriculture.

26. *See, e.g.,* Association of Nat'l Advertisers, Inc. v. FTC, 627 F.2d 1151, 1155–56 (D.C. Cir. 1979), *cert. denied,* 447 U.S. 921 (1980) (upholding refusal of FTC Chairman Pertschuk, who advocated regulation of television advertising in speeches, interviews, and periodicals, to excuse himself from rulemaking proceedings).

27. Wilson, *supra* note 1, at 361–63.

28. *See* Behrman, *supra* note 15, at 104–20 (discussing CAB deregulation).

29. *See id.* at 117–20. Preliminary indications are that their opposition may not have been myopic. *See* Pace, *'80 Airlines Loss to be a Record,* N.Y. Times, Dec. 26, 1980, s D, at 1, col. 6 (domestic airlines reported losses of between $150 and $200 million during 1980).

30. *See* M. GREEN & N. WAITZMAN, BUSINESS WAR ON THE LAW at iii (1979).

31. For the classic exposition of the theory that regulation was advanced at the behest of large corporations in order to frustrate competition, see G. KOLKO, RAILROADS AND REGULATION 1877–1916 (1965), and G. KOLKO, THE TRIUMPH OF CONSERVATISM (1963). The historical accounts in *The Politics of Regulation* tend to support Wilson's conclusion that recent scholarship "demolish[es]" Kolko's argument. Wilson, *supra* note 1, at 365 n.9.

32. *See* Schuck, *Regulation: Asking the Right Questions,* 11 NAT'L J. 711, 711–17 (1979).

33. *See, e.g.,* L. BACOW, BARGAINING FOR JOB SAFETY AND HEALTH 24–50 (1980); T. SOWELL, AFFIRMATIVE ACTION RECONSIDERED 34–39 (1975). On the other hand, the data typically fail to establish conclusively that benefits do not exceed costs. *See* Schuck, *supra* note 32, at 711–12. Given limitations on information and on the conclusiveness of cost-benefit analysis of most programs of social regulation, perhaps the most that can be said is that there are strong reasons to doubt that all social regulation is worth what it costs.

34. Because of the broad sweep of environmental and workplace regulation, the costs of even small or isolated inefficiencies in such efforts could loom quite large relative to those of a clearly inefficient program of economic regulation, such as surface transportation regulation by the Interstate Commerce Commission. This is especially true for environmental regulation, which often requires extensive capital investment. Thus, the welfare loss associated with the ICC railroad regulation was estimated at $742 million per year as of 1972. *See* Levin, *Railroad Rates, Profitability and Welfare Under Deregulation* (forthcoming 12 BELL J. ECON. (1981)). In contrast, the costs of meeting a single proposed environmental standard, that for ozone, was estimated by the Council on Wage and Price Stability in the range of $14.3 to $18.8 billion per year, with no demonstrated gains in long-term health effects. *See* Council on Wage and Price Stability, Report of the Regulatory Analysis Review Group 2 (Oct. 16, 1978) (on file with *Yale Law Journal*). The Environmental Protection Agency has estimated the costs of meeting its New Source Performance Standard for coal-fired utilities to be $4.1 billion in 1995. In their recent study, Ackerman and Hassler concluded that this standard will in fact exacerbate air pollution in certain parts of the country. *See* Ackerman & Hassler, *Beyond the New Deal: Coal and the Clean Air Act,* 89 YALE L.J. 1466, 1540–41 (1980).

35. *See, e.g.,* M. GREEN & N. WAITZMAN, *supra* note 30, at 63–75 (criticizing use of market incentives and cost-benefit analyses to determine allocation of health, safety, and environmental protection).

36. *Cf.* R. DWORKIN, TAKING RIGHTS SERIOUSLY at xi (1978) (possession of rights permits individuals to trump collective goals).

37. *See* Schuck, *The Graying of Civil Rights Law: The Age Discrimination Act of 1975,* 89 YALE L.J. 27, 85–91 (1979).

38. *See, e.g.,* Basic HHS Policy for Protection of Human Research Subjects, 46 Fed. Reg. 8,386–91 (1981) (to be codified in 45 C.F.R. ss 46.101–.124).

39. R. ZECKHAUSER, USING THE WRONG TOOL 9–11 (1981). An interesting implication of Zeckhauser's analysis appears to be that regulators bent upon redistribution will often refrain from seeking to improve their information.

40. *See* Breyer, *Analyzing Regulatory Failure: Mismatches, Less Restrictive Alternatives, and Reform,* 92 HARV. L. REV. 547, 553–60 (1979) (reviewing market failure justifications for economic regulation).

41. *See* M. GREEN & N. WAITZMAN, *supra* note 30, at 7–17 (reviewing market failure justifications for social regulation).

42. *See* Breyer, *supra* note 40, at 599–603.

43. *See generally* INDUSTRIAL CONCENTRATION (H. Goldschmid, H. Mann, & J. Weston eds. 1974).

44. *See* M. KOSTERS, CONTROLS AND INFLATION 109–17 (1975). It is a striking confirmation of the ill repute in which economic regulation is increasingly held that persistent double-digit inflation has led to few calls, even by politicians of the left, for reimposition of wage-price controls.

45. *See, e.g.,* National Health Planning and Development Act of 1974, 42 U.S.C. ss 300e–4, 300k–300t (1976 & Supp. III 1979) (establishing national health planning and development programs); Social Security Amendments of 1972, s 249F, 42 U.S.C. ss 1320c to 1320c–19 (1976 & Supp. III 1979) (establishing Professional Standards Review Organization).

46. One court made this observation in the following way:

Advances in the technologies of materials, of processes, of operational means have put it almost entirely out of the reach of the consumer to comprehend why or how the article operates, and thus even farther out of his reach to detect when there may be a defect or a danger present in its design or manufacture.

Micallef v. Miehle Co., 39 N.Y.2d 376, 385, 348 N.E.2d 571, 577, 384 N.Y.S.2d 115, 121 (1976).

47. Wolf, *A Theory of Non-Market Failure,* PUB. INTEREST, Spring 1979, at 114.

48. *See* A. MCFARLAND, PUBLIC INTEREST LOBBIES 2–4 (1976); D. MAYHEW, CONGRESS: THE ELECTORAL CONNECTION 177–78 (1974); Schuck, *Public Interest Groups and the Policy Process,* 37 PUB. AD. REV. 132, 133–34 (1977).

49. Wilson, *supra* note 1, at 385–86.

50. These need not be corporate entities, but may include the "helping professions" and others whose services are demanded by the program. *See, e.g.,* M. DERTHICK, UNCONTROLLABLE SPENDING FOR SOCIAL SERVICES GRANTS 113 (1975) (HEW officials administering state grants needed protection against professional social workers as well as politicians).

51. These may include manufacturers of pollution control equipment, lawyers, accountants, and the like.

52. *See* Behrman, *supra* note 15, at 117 (airline labor "vehemently opposed" to regulatory reform or deregulation).

53. *See* E. EPSTEIN, NEWS FROM NOWHERE 200–36 (1973).

54. *See* M. MALBIN, UNELECTED REPRESENTATIVES 9–19 (1980).

55. *See, e.g.,* Clark, *If Reagan Wants to Trump the Regulators, Here's OMB's Target List for Openers,* 13 NAT'L J. 94 (1981). President Reagan's 60-day freeze on the issuance of new regulations, 46 Fed. Reg. 11,227–28 (1981), does not apply to the independent regulatory agencies. Its long-term impact remains to be seen.

56. *E.g.,* Natural Gas Policy Act of 1978, Pub. L. No. 95–261, 92 Stat. 3352 (codified at 15 U.S.C. ss 3301–3432 (Supp. III 1979)).

57. *See, e.g.,* C. DeMuth, Regulatory Costs and the "Regulatory Budget" 6–7 (Dec. 1979) (unpublished Faculty Project on Regulation, John F. Kennedy School of Government, Harvard University).

58. Wilson, *supra* note 1, at 363.

59. *Id.* at 391.

60. *Id.* at 372.

61. Wilson affirms that "[a]nyone who purports to explain the behavior of regulatory agencies must first make clear what behavior is worth explaining." *Id.* at 372. Wilson himself fails to do so, however, noting only that "industry-serving behavior"—an ambiguous and problematic concept in its own right—is too narrow a focus. *Id.* at 372–73.

62. Anderson, *State Regulation of Electric Utilities,* in THE POLITICS OF REGULATION at 3, 6.

63. *See id.* at 6–7.

64. *See* Behrman, *supra* note 15, at 79–85.

65. *See* Mansfield, *Federal Maritime Commission,* in THE POLITICS OF REGULATION at 42, 43–48.

66. *See* Rabkin, *supra* note 21, at 309–12, 335–37.

67. Wilson, *supra* note 1, at 366–67.

68. *Id.* at 367–68.

69. *See* M. OLSON, *supra* note 9, at 14–15.

70. Wilson, *supra* note 1, at 368, *But cf.* Mansfield, *supra* note 65, at 47 (Shipping Act enacted under conditions of majoritarian politics).

71. Wilson, *supra* note 1, at 369–70. In noting that the origins of the Civil Aeronautics Board and state public utility commissions differ from the predicted pattern of client politics, *id.* at 369, Wilson indirectly acknowledges that his categories do not adequately explain the complexities of regulatory politics.

72. *Id.* at 370–71.

73. For an earlier elaboration of Wilson's typology, see Wilson, *The Politics of Regulation,* in SOCIAL RESPONSIBILITY AND THE BUSINESS PREDICAMENT 135, 141–46 (J. McKie ed. 1974).

74. Wilson, *supra* note 1, at 374–82.

75. Weaver, *Antitrust Division of the Department of Justice,* in THE POLITICS OF REGULATION at 123.

76. Katzmann, *supra* note 24, at 152.

77. Wilson, *supra* note 1, at 370.

78. *Id.* at 371.

79. *Id.* at 363.

80. *See, e.g.,* S. BREYER & P. MACAVOY, *supra* note 20, at 121–24 (Federal Power Commission regulation benefited some consumers but not others; natural gas price regulation produced harmful shortages).

81. 42 C.F.R. ss 124.501–607 (1979).

82. *See* Note, *The Hill-Burton Act, 1946–1980: Asynchrony in the Delivery of Health Care to the Poor,* 39 MD. L. REV. 316, 367–74 (1979) (discussing distribution of costs of uncompensated care).

83. Wilson also leaves unanswered the question of whether his typology is meant to describe the politics of regulatory legislation, of postenactment regulatory administration, or both. The political forces shaping each of those processes will often be quite different.

84. Wilson, *supra* note 1, at 390.

85. *See, e.g.,* Johnson v. Robison, 415 U.S. 361, 366 (1974); Ethyl Corp. v. EPA, 541 F.2d 1, 68 (D.C. Cir.), *cert. denied,* 426 U.S. 94 1 (1976) (en banc) (Leventhal, J., concurring). *But see* Panama Canal Co. v. Grace Line, Inc., 356 U.S. 309, 318 (1958) (when agency's

duty to act depends on inference from "large or loose statutory terms," construction of statute committed to agency discretion).

86. *See* Adams v. Richardson, 480 F.2d 1159, 1161 (D.C. Cir. 1975) (ordering HEW to begin compliance reviews and enforcement proceedings after finding agency "derelict in [its] duty to enforce Title VI").

87. *See, e.g.*, Ethyl Corp. v. EPA, 541 F.2d 1, 66–69 (D.C. Cir.), *cert. denied*, 426 U.S. 941 (1976) (en banc) (Bazelon, J., and Leventhal, J., concurring).

88. *See* note 5 *supra* (citing recently introduced congressional bills).

89. *See* 45 Fed. Reg. 74,676–77 (1980) (to be codified in 29 C.F.R. s 1604.11).

90. *See* 46 Fed. Reg. 8,386–91 (1981) (to be codified in 45 C.F.R. s 46.101–124).

91. *See* Pound, *2 Publishers Accuse U.S. Election Agency of Rights Violations*, N.Y. Times, Feb. 16, 1981, at 1, col. 4.

92. *See, e.g.*, Emergency Petroleum Allocation Act of 1973, 15 U.S.C. ss 751–760h (1976 & Supp. III 1979); National Health Planning and Resources Development Act of 1974, 42 U.S.C. ss 300k–300t (1976 & Supp. III 1979).

93. *See* Schuck, *supra* note 37, at 29 n.14.

94. *See* Natural Gas Policy Act of 1978, Pub. L. No. 95–261, 92 Stat. 3352 (codified at 15 U.S.C. ss 3301–3432 (Supp. III 1979)).

95. *See, e.g.*, MD. ANN. CODE art. 43, ss 568H–568Z (1980); N.Y. PUB. HEALTH LAW ss 2803, 2807–2808 (McKinney 1971 & Supp. 1976–77); H.R. 2626, 96th Cong., 1st Sess. (1979) (Hospital Cost Containment Act). *See generally* U.S. CONGRESSIONAL BUDGET OFFICE, CONTROLLING RISING HOSPITAL COSTS (1979) (discussing state and federal proposals).

96. *See* McKie, *Regulation and the Free Market: The Problem of Boundaries*, 1 BELL J. ECON. & MANAGEMENT SCI. 6, 9 (1970).

97. Wilson, *supra* note 1, at 377.

98. For a somewhat analogous analysis attempting to explain an asserted increased failure by the Supreme Court in constitutional adjudication, see Deutsch, *Neutrality, Legitimacy, and the Supreme Court*, 20 STAN. L. REV. 169, 223–29 (1968).

99. *See* J. PRESSMAN & A. WILDAVSKY, IMPLEMENTATION 161–62 (1973); Schuck, *supra* note 32, at 19–20.

5

When the Exception Becomes the Rule

Regulatory Equity and the Formulation of Energy Policy Through an Exceptions Process

For almost a decade (and as recently as 1981), the Department of Energy (DOE) exceptions process—a process by which a person, firm or entity subject to a valid statutory or administrative rule is relieved from the legal obligation to comply with that rule because of the special features of the situation—was an extraordinarily important regulatory device. The DOE's Office of Hearings and Appeals (OHA),[1] which administered the exceptions process, routinely shifted hundreds of millions of dollars in cross-subsidies among refiners and made economic life-and-death decisions concerning thousands of business firms and local communities. With the official termination of price and allocation controls on January 21, 1981, the DOE shifted into low gear (some would say neutral) and legislative proposals were introduced to abolish or reorganize the Department.[2] Despite these developments, the DOE exceptions process is not simply a historical curiosity whose significance vanished with the lines at gas stations. It remains an innovation of singular interest to students of administrative process.

Even if the process were utterly moribund, it would be worth studying in its own right. OHA remains quite active. Its caseload, although well below the levels that prevailed during the motor gasoline crisis of 1979, continues to be substantial.[3] Moreover, some of its most controversial cases, involving large policy issues and enormous sums of money, are still pending.[4] Even if a reorganization of the DOE occurs, these pending cases will have to be resolved. It is also quite possible, perhaps even probable, that controls will be reimposed at some future date. So long as the United States economy continues to be vulnerable to shocks resulting from developments in the Middle East, future energy price controls cannot be ruled out.[5] Indeed, Iran's protracted war with

139

Iraq raises the possibility of convulsive political changes and resulting short-ages in international oil markets, developments that might lead to a new call for controls.

The continuing concerns about regulatory rigidity and the demands for regulatory reform also make research on the exceptions process timely. Changes in administrative law and many proposals for reform increasingly favor policy development through rules and more formal, judicial-type rule-making procedures. If those trends persist, as appears likely, administrative techniques will be needed that encourage flexible accommodations to diverse and complex conditions within an increasingly rule governed system. A prop-erly structured exceptions process might address that need.

This article examines the pursuit of regulatory equity through an administrative "exceptions process." Such a process relieves a person, firm, or entity subject to a valid statutory or administrative rule from the legal obligation to comply with the rule. It does so by issuing a formal exception, waiver, or similar form of special relief from the rule's application based upon the special features of the applicant's situation.[6]

The article consists of four parts. Part I explores the tension between the con-ceptions of justice represented by rules and by equity, highlighting the ways in which this tension is expressed in a regulatory context. Part I concludes by posing broad questions about the exceptions process that the study will at-tempt to address. Part II examines the exceptions process in energy regulation through four case studies of exceptions decisionmaking at the DOE, as ad-ministered by the Office of Hearings and Appeals. Each case study illustrates certain themes or tendencies that seem endemic to an exceptions process of this kind. Drawing upon the case studies and other sources, Part III analyzes and evaluates the essential features of the DOE's exceptions process, conclud-ing with a discussion of the exceptions process as a "safety valve." Part IV summarizes the study by offering tentative answers to the questions posed at the end of Part I.

It should be emphasized at the outset that this is a study of only one excep-tions process and, as the reader shall see, a distinctive one at that. Such a study cannot generate clear implications for other exceptions processes in other agencies with other regulatory tasks, for the truth of any nontrivial general-ization about the exceptions process cannot be shown to extend beyond the particular DOE example. Such is the awesome power of social science!

Nevertheless, an in-depth study of a particular administrative process can be valuable. It can support at least a qualitative appraisal of the variables im-portant to the performance of that kind of process. It can highlight the rela-tionships between the various elements of such a process, and the values im-plicated by those relationships. Even if such a study lacks unequivocal normative conclusions, it can still identify problem areas and suggest plausi-ble approaches to reform. In the end, however, the chief argument in favor of detailed case studies of administrative process is that they are likely to be superior to the alternatives—conventional wisdom, unconventional intuition, and a methodological rigor and comprehensiveness that the subject matter does not permit.

I. Regulation and Equity

Federal agency rules that prescribe private conduct are, of course, ubiquitous techniques of social control. Although commonplace, however, they are also relatively novel. As recently as twenty years ago such rules were largely confined to the Internal Revenue Service and the independent regulatory commissions created during the New Deal era. But between 1970 and 1975, Congress established seven major new regulatory agencies and enacted more than 30 grants of broad regulatory authority.[7] Today, rules have joined grants-in-aid, taxes, subsidies, jawboning, and aggressive use of the media as instruments by which the federal government attempts to conform private behavior to declared public policies.

Although the proliferation of such rules began to slow in the late 1970's as regulatory reform efforts took hold, especially in 1981 when the Reagan Administration assumed power,[8] this may prove to be but a pause in a long-term tide of regulatory intervention. The growth of rules, after all, seems to reflect deep-seated changes in American society—far-reaching demographic and political shifts, a deepening awareness of ecological complexity, and fundamental economic, moral, and institutional transformations. Social goals that rules (and sometimes *only* rules) seem capable of achieving have become more salient. These goals include eliminating discrimination against vulnerable groups, perfecting markets, strengthening national cohesion and uniformity, redistributing wealth, and making policy more "rational" and predictable.[9]

Rules increasingly dominate our collective life. They are the gears in the machinery of modern government. In principle, at least, rules are both instruments of power and brakes upon its exercise. They assist citizens in controlling the activist state because rules specify rights and facilitate remedies for violations. By particularizing citizens' duties, rules also enable the state to influence the conduct of citizens. And rules help both citizens and the state to conduct their affairs on the basis of some common, predictable assumptions concerning the norms and conditions that will prevail.

Rules, then, are necessary conditions of any fully developed, contemporary conception of a just administrative process. But they are not sufficient. Justice also demands that the rigor of rules be tempered by other considerations. So long as values exist that cannot readily be formulated as rules and anomalous cases arise that rules fail to anticipate, rules will constitute an incomplete technology of justice.[10] As the social domain in which rules govern expands, the occasions of such rule-based injustice will multiply, perhaps exponentially. In such situations, the infusion of equity into the regulatory process—what I shall refer to as "regulatory equity"[11]—will become an ever more vital component of the administrative process.

A. The Limits of Rules

That rules cannot fully achieve justice is an ancient theme in legal theory. Aristotle distinguished between "legal" justice, based upon general rules, and "equity," which corrects what is merely legally just.[12] That distinction has been reflected in many important institutional and doctrinal developments. Examples include the equitable jurisdiction of courts; the evolution of many rigid common law rules into more flexible standards, such as "reasonableness," in which equity is "built-in";[13] and the open-ended, indeterminate standards contained in much modern legislation.

Regimes of rules and of equity are based upon fundamentally different conceptions of justice; each conception, taken alone, is radically incomplete. The regime of rules is general and prescriptive. It requires at a minimum that a decisionmaker accurately apply general, clearly articulated norms to fairly established facts. In contrast, the regime of equity is specific and ad hoc. It requires that any such norms be subordinated to an overriding standard of contextual fairness—that is, fairness to individuals in light of their particularized situations. Rules respond to the gravitational pulls of backward-looking precedent, forward-looking policy, or outward-looking analogies and notions of legal equality. Equity resonates to the inward-looking concerns of the immediate, to the riveting force of the particular, the situational. Those who value rules emphasize the need for commonality, regularity, continuity, and order. Those who esteem equity stress the importance of individuality (we are unique), spontaneity (we are not bound by the past), responsiveness (our needs change), and freedom (our course is not predetermined). Whereas rules exalt formal categories, equity is profoundly suspicious of abstraction and seeks to free diversity from the delusive discipline of order. Equity speaks not to the typical case—indeed, it may even deny that such a thing exists—but rather to the exotic, the unexpected, the exigent. Its distinctive techniques are neither comprehensive vision, synoptic analysis, nor disembodied principle, but sound judgment, contextual analysis, and an intuitive "feel" for what is fair under the circumstances.

Rules glorify precisely those technocratic values—predictability, stability, uniformity, and control—about which equity is most skeptical; they systematically overlook or override certain particularities of time, place, and context. Our sense of justice, however, often demands that these particularities receive greater recognition and weight than rules ordinarily accord them. We can readily imagine sets of facts that come well within a rule's terms yet seem to call for a different disposition. When such an instance occurs, justice seems to call for suspending the rule in that case, without necessarily calling its general validity into question. Equity, too, entails certain risks, but they are the risks of uncertainty, irrationality, favoritism, diversity, and incoherence—precisely those that an increasingly rationalistic, centralized, control-oriented society wishes to minimize. The tension in our law between rule and equity, then, can never be eliminated. It will persist, as Thurman Arnold noted, "[s]o long as men require a moral and logical ideal to satisfy their impulses toward mercy and common sense."[14] The quest for regulatory equity is a search for an appropriate means to harmonize these eternally conflicting values.

Any complex system of rules that aspires to justice must make some provision for regulatory equity. Although classes of cases always exist in which rules create injustice, this does not explain what it is about a case that places it within those classes. It fails to reveal which characteristics demand that the rule be suspended rather than applied, and which reasons or motives make an appeal to equity seem appropriate. The following discussion attempts to provide that explanation.

The limits of rules define the boundaries of regulatory equity. Broadly speaking, three general categories of conditions or reasons may mark those limits. The need for regulatory equity may derive from certain features of the rule itself, from the institutional context in which the rule is developed and applied, and from situational needs of the decisionmaker that may have nothing to do with the rule's own features or context.

1. The Character of Rules.   Like any structure for deciding particular cases, a regime of rules necessarily dispenses imperfect justice—imperfect in the sense that decisions derived from it must reflect whatever limitations rules possess *qua* rules. This discussion addresses four potential limiting features: form, knowledge, comprehensiveness, and articulation. Every rule has at least some limitations. These may often be reduced (at some cost) but can never be wholly eliminated, for they inhere either in the nature of rules or in the complexity of reality. Insofar as these limitations remain, perfect justice solely through a regime of rules is unattainable.

a) Limitations of Form   Three formal attributes of a rule determine the extent to which it can achieve its purposes without equity's assistance: its generality (the number of cases to which it is meant to apply), its transparency (the degree to which it evokes uniform interpretations in different minds),[15] and the number of unweighted factors that it makes relevant to its application. These attributes are empirically as well as analytically distinct. For example, a very general rule may have ambiguous language and prescribe multiple unweighted factors. As the twenty-sixth amendment demonstrates,[16] however, a rule need not have either of these attributes.

The ancients recognized that rules' formal imperfections can cause injustice. Aristotle maintained, for example, that the law could not achieve true justice in part because it "takes the usual case."[17] But the relationship between the form of rules and the content of justice is more intricate than this categorical statement suggests. Judges seldom take "the usual case," preferring instead to formulate the narrowest rule that can connect the facts of a dispute to some source of decisional legitimacy, such as a precedent, statute, constitution, or "natural right." The level of generality at which legislators and regulators frame rules is often a matter of conscious policy choice; it is influenced by the significance they accord to predictability, equal treatment, flexibility, incremental policy development, and other values in a particular context.[18]

Transparency and the number of unweighted decision factors also affect a rule's efficacy. A rule may be so opaque, or may enumerate so many unweighted factors, that it cannot generate reasonably predictable outcomes. As Aristotle wrote, "when the thing is indefinite the rule also is indefinite."[19] A rule that "undesirable behavior" is tortious, for example, would afford no hint as to what conduct might be actionable, even if one could predict with confidence how cases at the extremes (e.g., murder, marriage) would be decided. Such a provision fails to perform even minimally those functions—bounding administrative discretion, predictability, encouraging equal treatment, facilitating legislative and judicial review—that constitute rules' distinctive contribution to a just legal regime.

A rule that is too transparent may also be unable to attain its purpose. Consider the following example: "If a Ford strikes a Buick on July 16, 1985, the driver of the Ford shall pay $100 to the driver of the Buick." This rule is stunningly determinate, indeed so much so that it may well deny due process or equal protection by practically assuring that virtually identical driving behavior will have very different legal consequences, depending upon happenstance.[20]

Any given rule, then, expresses an inescapable tension between the virtues and vices of each of its formal elements. A more general rule controls more cases but only by subjecting more diverse phenomena to its homogenizing prescriptions. A vaguer, more ambiguous rule permits greater flexibility in adapting to new or unanticipated conditions but only by reducing the predictability and uniformity of outcomes. A multifactored rule, especially one that fails to weight the factors, enriches the administrator's ability to discriminate among complex phenomena but diminishes the rulemaker's (or reviewing court's) control over particular decisions. Regulators can only transcend these limitations by looking beyond the regime of rules to the ethos of equity.

b) Limitations of Knowledge   We are extraordinarily ignorant of the intricate web of cause, consequence, and circumstance in which our intentions and actions are shaped and executed. But however little we know of the world as it is, we know even less of the world that will be. A regime of rules, of course, is directed to the future. To Aristotle, equity meant deciding cases as the "legislator himself would have said had he been present, and would have put into his law if he had known."[21] In this view, when cases arise that the rule did not envision and to which it cannot justly be applied, equity must effect what the rulemaker's want of prescience makes necessary; it must suspend or reformulate the rule (Aristotle does not indicate which) to achieve a just outcome in the unforeseen case.

This notion of the relationship between imperfect knowledge and equity seems quite incomplete, at least in the regulatory context. Imagine a perfectly prescient rulemaker. She fully comprehends the implications of all rules that she might issue, foresees all changes that might occur, and anticipates all cases that may arise in the future. Is it clear, as Aristotle implies, that this clairvoyant seer would formulate a rule resolving in advance all cases yet to come? And if she would, would this achieve perfect prescriptive justice, rendering equity superfluous? The answer to both questions, it would seem, is no. She might believe, for example, that by framing a rule today that will anticipate and correctly decide tomorrow's case, she would incur unacceptable political costs in attempting to persuade others to accept that rule. She might therefore prefer to proceed incrementally, issuing a more limited but noncontroversial rule now and deferring the resolution of future cases to a later day. If she also faced high information costs in formulating a rule capable of fully anticipating the future, she might find an incremental strategy even more attractive.

Aristotle also seems to have been wholly concerned with rules formulated by rulemakers who not only are ignorant of the future but also proceed as if they were *unaware* of their ignorance. Yet some rulemakers *are* aware of their ignorance and guard against it in fashioning rules. Both kinds of rules demonstrate the need for regulatory equity, but each implies somewhat different responses to that need. Unanticipated ignorance, of course, is commonplace; we seldom know precisely what we don't know. Attempting to resolve unforeseen cases through rules never designed to apply to them will lead to harsh, absurd outcomes unless equity can palliate them. Of course, rulemakers who are unaware of their own ignorance may not perceive the contingent need for regulatory equity, much less provide an institutional means to achieve it. They may still pursue equity, but will not ensure that certain mechanisms for attaining it are available.

Ignorance of the future can often be anticipated and its most deleterious effects blunted. Even if regulators cannot map the future in detail, they can sometimes discern the broad contours of contingency that must be faced and design rules to conform to that dimly perceived topography. Suppose, for example, that an official must regulate a rapidly evolving technology, such as telecommunications. She knows or strongly suspects that the activity will present a very different face in twenty years than it does today. She anticipates that technology, industry structure, market conditions, and consumer preferences will change significantly but she cannot predict with confidence the precise nature of those changes. Unwilling to rely upon highly speculative forecasts, but aware of the uncertainty problem, she has several options. She may decide to proceed incrementally, eschewing rules in favor of policymaking through case-by-case adjudication. She may instead promulgate rules containing vague language or multiple, unweighted decision criteria, thereby preserving flexibility for the volatile future. Alternatively, she may devise a more determinate rule to govern what she thinks the future will bring but create an auxiliary administrative process that can provide equitable relief from the rule whenever appropriate. Each of these approaches recognizes the substantial claims that equity may assert against an uncertain future.

c) Limitations of Comprehensiveness   A rule does not always govern autonomously, even within its well-defined boundaries. Dominion over its subjects may be hotly contested. Professor Dworkin illuminates this point by distinguishing between rules, policies, and principles.[22] Although developed for an altogether different purpose, Dworkin's distinction nevertheless suggests several ways in which noncomprehensive rules may demand regulatory equity. For Dworkin, a rule is a standard that is absolute, "applicable in an all-or-nothing fashion";[23] it prescribes a particular result if the particular facts that it stipulates are present. A principle, however, is a standard that asserts a requirement of morality; it does not prescribe a particular outcome but merely "states a reason that argues in one direction."[24] Its reach depends upon its weight or importance. In contrast, each rule has equal weight, at least for purposes of resolving conflicts between them.[25] Finally, a "policy" is a standard that sets a social goal to be pursued.[26]

Rules, principles, and policies often compete to influence or control the outcome of administrative decisions. First, the sheer volume of rules promulgated and administered by an agency increases the risk that any rule that seems to cover a particular set of facts will encounter another rule with its own plausible claim of coverage. The agency, of course, can resolve such a conflict, but only on the basis of some *other* ground of decision. Second, policy is really an amalgam of conflicting policies (in Dworkin's sense of the term) that reflect its multiple statutory objectives, its diffuse political constituencies, and the programmatic and administrative realities within which it must work. A rule, then, may not only contradict other rules but also conflict with policies not fully embodied in rules, policies as firmly within the agency's charge as those that underlie that rule. Here, too, only some overriding criterion—whether a rule, principle or policy—can ultimately resolve such conflicts. Finally, an agency's rules are part of a continuing, intense conversation with the legislature, courts, and society at large concerning the scope and meaning of the agency's purposes and methods. That conversation leads to appropriate accommodation of rules and equity and clarifies the values that each represents.[27]

Threats to the comprehensiveness and autonomy of an agency's rules, consequently, come from several quarters—from conflicts between rules, from policies and principles that exemplify other values, and from other institutions. These sources of tension reflect moral, administrative, and political imperatives to which an agency must somehow respond. For example, when the Occupational Safety and Health Administration is challenged to justify an occupational safety standard that imposes heavy costs upon regulated firms, it cannot simply point to its broad statutory authority to develop rules that minimize risks to workers. Even before an agency promulgates a statutorily authorized rule, it must take account of competing policies (e.g., the objective of maintaining a viable industrial sector) and competing principles (e.g., a worker's health is not protected if her employer is forced out of business).[28] Equity is one integrating technique.

d) Limitations of Articulation   In our legal culture, the legitimacy of a rule—and perhaps its validity as well—ordinarily requires that the reasons adduced in its support be justified in terms of some preexisting, appropriate premise of decision, some rule or principle whose generality, by transcending the particular case, avoids the risks of arbitrariness inherent in ad hoc decisionmaking. It is not sufficient that the decisionmaker either flips a fair coin[29] or admires one of the parties.

The norm that legal decisions should be reduced to writing[30] is designed in part to secure and reinforce this rational element of legitimacy. The obligation to render a written decision subjects one to an intellectual discipline, a public process of justification, in which one must struggle to link rules, principles, evidence, inference, and logic into a chain of reasoning that can command general respect. But although the articulation of reasons grounded in general rules is a noble aspiration of our legal system, many regulatory decisions fail to fulfill it.[31] The norm of reason-giving is not nearly as well-established for regulators as for judges. Agencies sometimes provide reasons when they are not legally obligated to do so, but their articulation is often cursory, conclusory, and of little use to one seeking to evaluate a decision's substantive rationality.

Although the law often *permits* decisionmakers to refrain from providing reasons, the nature of certain decisions may actually *preclude* them from doing so. Several situations illustrate this predicament. First, an administrator may apply a clear and indeterminate rule and reach a decision that seems justified, though not required, and yet be unable to elucidate precisely how she reasoned from the one to the other. Either because a governing norm requires it or because complex policy considerations demand it, the administrator may feel obliged to take many unweighted factors into account. Here, the reasons that support the ultimate decision would include at least an explanation of each factor, an assessment of the decision's empirical relationship to the real world, and a description of the implicit weighting scheme by which the agency integrated the factors into a decision. In principle, the decisionmaker could reconstruct her mental operations, make them explicit, and place them on public view so that the elements of her decision can be scrutinized and evaluated. In practice, however, she probably could not identify, much less articulate, all of those elements, either to herself or to others.[32]

In the situations described above decisionmakers can in principle base their decisions on identifiable general rules. In other situations, however, decisionmakers cannot devise a general rule from which to derive and rationalize decisions. To put the point another way, there are decisions the justice or correctness of which cannot intelligibly be measured by their consistency with a rule. Professionals frequently make decisions of this kind. Physicians, for example, must sometimes diagnose illness or prescribe therapies without being able to anchor those decisions in a general rule or principle, yet they feel confident that they are correct and that professional colleagues would do likewise. Experienced social workers or lawyers sometimes encounter problems that do not fit readily within conventional categories, yet they will often devise particular solutions that seem "just," "appropriate," or simply "feel right."

Decisions of this kind can arise for two reasons. First, certain decisions require a high degree of specialized judgment and are virtually immune from any nonprocedural, objectively verifiable criticism. The central ingredient of such decisions—an idiosyncratic, intuitive, essentially subjective apprehension of reality—is inaccessible, indeed antithetical, to generalization. Second, certain decisions are designed to be wholly discretionary. They do not necessarily require ineffable or intuitive judgment; indeed, it may be perfectly possible to specify the controlling factors in the form of a general rule. Wholly discretionary decisions perform a social function they could not perform if they were systematized and regularized by rules. They are auxiliary components of a complex administrative system whose routine activities—here, the application of rules to particular facts—generate pressures that threaten the system's continuing viability or integrity. These pressures may include dissatisfaction with the rule's policy, perceived inequities in the rule's initial application, changes in circumstances, and the like. When such pressures exceed the level that the system is designed to tolerate, the wholly discretionary decision comes into play. Like a safety valve in a mechanical system, discretion relieves pressure by assuming some of the system's functions and altering how it performs others.

The pardoning power, deployed through executive clemency, dramatically exemplifies this safety valve function. This power is plenary, exercised without any governing or even constraining standards.[33] Pardoning decisions are not "intuitive" as that term is generally used; their standardlessness is not inherent in the kinds of judgments demanded by pardoning decisions. Such decisions *could*, both in principle and in practice, be regulated by rules. Criminal sentencing and parole decisions, for example, which do not demand fundamentally different kinds of judgments than pardoning decisions, are sometimes constrained by substantive rules.[34] Arguably, rules would make executive clemency more predictable, accurate, visible, and rational than its present, wholly discretionary character permits.

But structuring the pardoning power through rules would impair its ability to give justice individual form and to soften the remaining rigidities of an already discretionary criminal process. To do so would not merely alter outcomes (for better or for worse) but would fundamentally change the nature of the pardon decision, undermining its very raison d'etre. Executive clemency, after all, is not designed to enhance horizontal equity among prisoners or to yield predictable decisions. It seeks extraordinary justice in particular cases, not ordinary justice in the general run of cases. Far from generating expectations in prisoners, executive clemency decisions are socially valued precisely because they deny the legitimacy of such expectations.[35] An exercise of clemency is an expression of mercy, an act of grace, an acknowledgement of the insufficiency of rules. It cannot be transformed into its opposite without abandoning its distinctive claim to advance a radically different conception of justice.

Wholly discretionary decisions obviously risk favoritism, arbitrariness, and abuse, conditions inimical to the rule of law. Moreover, their standardlessness renders review by superior authority very difficult. Therefore, wholly discretionary decisions are usually confined to situations in which those risks are minimal; they affect persons whose status is already so degraded that an unfavorable decision will leave them little or no worse off than if no such decision process had been available at all.[36] This "what do I have to lose?" condition is notably absent in conventional regulatory schemes, where predictability and the protection of property rights and expectations are especially important values.[37]

2. The Institutional Context of Rules.   A regime of rules is embedded in a set of institutional arrangements through which general prescriptions are developed, promulgated, applied, evaluated, and perhaps modified. The ability of such a regime to achieve justice without recourse to equity depends upon the institutions charged with performing these rule-sustaining functions. Because certain institutions are especially hospitable to rule-based justice and others to equity, the legal system can affect how equitable considerations shape a rule's application by entrusting it to the ministrations of one kind of institution rather than another.

The organization, ideology and operating procedures of common law courts, especially those engaged in private adjudication, encourage judges to be more preoccupied with the interests of particular litigants than with those of the larger society. Regulatory agencies, however, tend to weigh policy and programmatic considerations more heavily, even when they adjudicate.[38] As Part II will demonstrate, this distinction reflects differences in the institutional purposes, types of rules, decision procedures, and organizational forms and settings of courts and agencies.

Legislatures present a somewhat more complex pattern. Their most characteristic output, the public bill, ordinarily takes the form of a general rule. This is not surprising. Generality not only minimizes the risk and appearance of legislative favoritism but also captures substantial "economies of scale" in legislative production. Legislatures, however, have also established specialized organs to dispense particularistic justice. Private bills, which typically prescribe results intended for only one or a small number of beneficiaries, are ordinarily processed under unique procedures.[39] Public bills, of course, are sometimes drafted to achieve decidedly particularistic results—for example, so called "Christmas tree" tax amendments designed to benefit one or relatively few companies. Even there, however, special procedures are needed to minimize abuse.[40]

The relationship between different conceptions of justice and the institutions created to implement them is not simply a matter for institutional designers in the legislative and executive branches. Courts also influence this relationship, most notably by elaborating a common law of administrative process designed to render agency decisionmaking more regularized, generalized, visible, and susceptible to judicial scrutiny and control.[41] To facilitate judicial review, for example, courts have encouraged agencies to use rules. This, in turn, increases the need for regulatory equity to supplement and refine those rules. On the other hand, when adjudicating in a common law mode, courts tend to avoid rule-like decisions that might constrain their future flexibility.

3. The Situational Needs of Rulemakers.   Both the inherent imperfections of rules and the particular institutional settings in which they are developed and applied may create lacunae in the structure of regulatory justice that only equity can fill. But not all demands for equity are so systematic. Some are ad hoc, reflecting the incentives that confront particular rulemakers in particular circumstances. Two of these circumstances are particularly important: the need to win political support for agency decisions and the need to process a large volume of cases with scarce administrative resources.

An official may wish to issue or enforce a rule that is politically controversial. In order to mobilize sufficient support for the rule, she may need to satisfy potential opponents either that it will not apply to them or, in the event that it does, that they will not be adversely affected by it. For a number of reasons, the rule may need to be quite general in form; hence, it may be impossible to allay the concern of potential opponents. In such situations, the official may couple the rule with some equitable process by which those adversely affected can hope to obtain relief from its burdens.[42] Moreover, by assuring that a rule will not preclude consideration of special factors that may arise, such a process may also make the rule easier to defend in court.[43]

Regulatory equity can also be a tactical response to the reality of scarce administrative resources. The time, personnel, and budget required to enforce broad rules on a case-by-case basis may be extremely costly and the resulting benefits meager. Nonetheless, officials may want the rule on the books where it can encourage some voluntary compliance and project a coherent regulatory posture. Under those circumstances, they may be inclined to retain the rule but grant relief to classes of the regulated, such as small firms, if that will conserve administrative resources without undermining the actual or perceived integrity and viability of the regulatory program as a whole.[44]

B. Regulatory Equity and Discretion

There is an intimate relationship between regulatory equity, in the sense in which that concept is used here, and discretion. Discretion, according to its chief expositor, Professor Kenneth Davis, exists "whenever the effective limits on [an official's] power leave him free to make a choice among possible courses of action or inaction."[45] An equitable standard, by its very nature, creates some discretion in the official who applies it; a number of different outcomes will be consistent with that standard. Discretion, therefore, affords decisionmakers leeway within which they can give equitable considerations some weight when they apply a rule.

But regulatory equity and discretion are by no means identical concepts. Regulatory equity is an objective or goal of the legal system, while discretion is a legal form or technique, a means to that end. Discretion is necessary to achieve regulatory equity but it is not an end in itself. The relationship between discretion and regulatory equity is revealed in the different techniques through which regulatory decisions can assimilate equitable considerations, the role of discretion in each of those regulatory techniques, and its somewhat different role in an exceptions process.

First, regulatory equity may be achieved through *rule formulation*. A rule can be written to include equitable standards, such as "reasonableness," that invite situation-specific judgments when it is applied. A rule can also be fine-grained, dividing the regulated population into a large number of discrete categories each of which is treated differently.[46] An existing rule, of course, can also be reformulated or repealed so that it no longer applies to situations that experience has shown to deserve special treatment.

Second, regulatory equity may, within certain limits, be achieved through *rule interpretation*. Thus, an agency that has occasion to decide what a rule means or to whom it applies can take equitable considerations into account when it renders that decision. In stressing certain facts rather than others or in manipulating the level of generality at which elements of the rule are to be pitched, for example, the agency enjoys considerable latitude about whether to include or to exclude particular parties. Certain regulatory methods facilitate this individualization of rules through interpretation. For example, the requirement that a license or permit be obtained before a particular activity is undertaken is often designed to allow situational factors to be incorporated into the decision as to whether and under what conditions the license or permit should be granted.[47]

Third, regulatory equity can be introduced through *rule enforcement*. This is not quite the same as rule interpretation. Even in situations in which the language and purpose of the rule may be perfectly clear and may be unambiguously applicable to a particular firm or person, agency officials may consider situational factors in deciding whether, when, and in what manner to enforce the rule against a particular violator.

Finally, regulatory equity can be introduced by creating a *formal exceptions process* for the explicit purpose of considering applications for relief from particular rules. Whether the relief that this process grants is described as an exception, waiver, special relief, variance, or exemption, the technique is essentially the same. An exceptions process, as we shall see, also employs rule formulation, rule interpretation, and rule enforcement techniques in performing its tasks.

Discretion plays an essential but distinctive role in each of these regulatory equity techniques. When a rule is formulated, discretion may be implanted in the standards contained in it. The role of discretion in rule interpretation is often more ambiguous and only implicit. The official interpreting the rule, for example, may not be willing to acknowledge, indeed may not be aware, that she is making certain choices, such as selection of the relevant facts, that neither precedent nor logic strictly compels. Decisions as to which rules to enforce and against whom obviously require that discretion be exercised, but that discretion may be quite separate from whatever discretion is contained in the formulation or interpretation of the rule itself. The latter may be perfectly transparent and nonproblematic. Indeed, prosecutorial discretion is often governed by factors, such as resource constraints and compliance patterns, that have nothing to do with the rule's meaning.

In a formal exceptions process, discretion plays yet another role. There, the process itself assumes that the rule, as formulated and interpreted, does apply to a particular situation and presumably will be enforced as such. In that context, discretion does not operate upon the rule but is only invoked to determine whether that situation qualifies for special dispensation under the legal standards governing exceptions relief.

It is tempting to view this as a distinction without a difference, to conclude that the use of discretion in the exceptions process simply effects a reformulation, reinterpretation, or nonenforcement of the rule. This view, however, ignores several important points. The first concerns the moral meaning of rules. It is one thing to say that a rule does not apply to A, and quite another to say that the rule does apply to A but will be suspended in A's case for certain equitable reasons. In the first case, A's conduct (and that of others similarly situated) is being justified rather than condemned. The moral content of the rule, therefore, is being altered. In the second case, however, the moral content of the rule is affirmed; it continues to condemn the proscribed *conduct* but excuses A from *liability or stigma* on the basis of circumstances peculiar to A as an individual (and others similarly situated).[48]

A second distinction between discretion that acts directly upon a rule and discretion that is used in an exceptions process to decide whether relief from a concededly applicable rule should be granted, relates to the institutional structure within which the decisions are made. An explicit exceptions process, where one exists,[49] can assume many different organizational forms. This article is principally concerned with only one, in which an agency establishes an exceptions office that is to some extent structurally separate and independent from the program office that issues and administers the rules from which relief is sought.[50] This kind of structural separation of rule and equity may express not only a fundamental psychological ambivalence about the values that each embodies but also a principle of organizational function.[51] As we shall see, this separation also has important policy consequences,[52] and thus applying discretion to the exceptions process rather than to the rule has important practical effects as well.

C. Regulatory Equity and Judicial Equity

The pursuit of equity in the regulatory process has certain obvious parallels to the more familiar, traditional phenomenon of judicial equity through case-by-case adjudications.[53] Both processes are animated by similar concerns about the limited ability of rules alone to achieve justice in particular cases. Both reflect some similar values and possess some common features. For example, each resolves particular disputes through adjudications that are legitimated in part by the use of explicit reasoned justifications subject to review by higher authority. Each process is informed through oral and written arguments developed through adversarial techniques. Each recognizes the relevance and authority of statutes, rules, prior cases, and other decision materials.

The significance of these similarities between agency and court adjudication is increasing at a time when Congress characteristically leaves courts to adjudicate without much statutory or constitutional guidance. Nevertheless, the differences between the ways in which courts and agencies deploy equitable values are at least as important as the apparent similarities, underscoring the distinctive character of regulatory equity. They also suggest why a specialized administrative organ or arrangement is often necessary to infuse regulatory equity into the administrative process.

1. Institutional Purpose.   The dominant purposes of courts and agencies differ.[54] Characteristically, courts adjudicate the rights and obligations of disputants on the basis of principled justifications and distinctions derived from previously adopted legal norms. It is true, of course, that courts often advert to considerations of social policy, and to the predicted consequences of a decision for persons and interests not before the court. This occurs not only in public law litigation but increasingly in private law litigation as well. Despite the relevance of extra-litigation factors, however, the canons of the judicial craft and the requirements of judicial legitimacy continue to focus the court's analysis upon the claims of the parties before it. This naturally inclines the court toward a situational, particularistic orientation rather than toward more generalized policy prescriptions. When a court seeks equity, it does so by refining existing principles, carving out exceptions to them, or developing competing ones embodying a different array and weighting of values.

A regulatory agency, in contrast, is an engine of continuous social policy formulation and implementation. Although obliged to render neutral, principled decisions with respect to individual disputes brought before it, an agency's principal purpose is to effectuate an externally created but bureaucratically internalized legislative purpose, usually the protection of certain collective values or group interests. Thus, the Civil Aeronautics Board was established to promote the interests of the nascent airline industry, the Equal Employment Opportunity Commission to advance the rights of minorities, and the Environmental Protection Agency to safeguard the environment. This orientation encourages agencies systematically to undervalue particularized justice in favor of the social interests and policy goals that they are required to pursue through their regulatory programs. These interests and goals usually transcend those of the particular parties before them.[55]

2. Types of Rules.   Common law adjudication often requires judges to devise new principles or rules where existing ones cannot fairly resolve a dispute or where no plausibly applicable rule exists at all. But the rules that courts elaborate through case-by-case adjudication typically differ in important respects from those that agencies develop in rulemaking—and even from those that they apply in agency adjudication. Agency rules are limited only by the very permissive contours of a typically broad and ambiguous statutory standard. An agency is permitted, even expected, to promulgate legislative-type rules that reflect the exercise of discretion, judgment, specialized knowledge, and political choice. Thus, agency rules often plunge into new policy realms, boldly occupying unfamiliar terrain and mapping it through a more or less comprehensive set of prescriptions. In such cases, justification need not rest upon principle, except insofar as the statute broadly supplies one; it is ordinarily enough that the rule not be inconsistent with the statutory standard and that it meet minimal standards of rationality. Policy considerations, as mediated by agency "expertise," are thought to supply the necessary ingredients of decision.

In contrast, the kinds of rules that courts develop through case-by-case adjudication tend to cling parasitically to familiar moorings, only incrementally modifying solutions that have already been framed. Although it is commonplace for an agency to decide, for instance, that trucks on interstate highways shall be no more than 65 feet in length, it would be extremely unusual for a court to devise such a rule itself. That is the kind of particularized choice that a democratic society does not expect unelected generalist judges to make.[56]

There is an intriguing irony here, one highly relevant to the problem of regulatory equity. Although conceived as broad exercises of discretion, agency rules often take the form of relatively rigid, detailed prescriptions. Particularized justice cannot be achieved directly through such forms but only through an auxiliary mechanism, such as an exceptions process. Judicial rules, in contrast, are fashioned by tribunals whose discretion is systematically, indeed constitutionally, limited. Courts steadfastly refuse to acknowledge that they exercise discretion even (perhaps especially) when they clearly do. Yet the rules that emerge from this relatively constrained process usually take the form of general formulations whose flexible contours can easily accommodate the palliating impulses of situational justice. Agencies tend to spawn hard-edged rules that resist the solvent of further discretion; an equitable capacity must therefore be added. Courts, while eschewing discretion, tend to produce tractable, malleable rules capable of absorbing equitable claims as they arise in individual cases.

3. Decision Procedures.   Given their distinct purposes and products, it is hardly surprising that the procedures and doctrines of courts and regulatory agencies differ significantly; procedures, after all, are intended to reinforce an institution's dominant goals even as they are shaped by those goals. Most court adjudication, for example, is structured to focus attention narrowly upon the claims of individual litigants rather than upon a decision's larger social consequences. The rules of evidence, the boundaries of the record, and principles such as those governing standing, ripeness, and intervention, for example, all reinforce this traditional, constrained view of the judicial function. Divergences from this model, of course, are increasingly countenanced, even encouraged. This does not mean that the model is incoherent or fails to describe most of what courts do, but only that it is under pressure to adapt to new functions traditionally associated with agencies and legislatures.[57]

For most regulatory agencies, however, individual dispute resolution is decidedly ancillary to the discretionary, policy development function,[58] a fact strikingly revealed in those agencies, most notably the National Labor Relations Board (NLRB), that rely upon adjudications almost exclusively as a mode of decision.[59] The powerful interest in yoking an agency's procedures to its policy objectives is demonstrated by the broad administrative discretion to reverse policy direction and abandon precedent *retroactively*[60] through adjudication despite the potential injustice to individual parties. Agencies are also permitted to adjudicate without the procedural safeguards of independence and objectivity characteristic of courts.[61] Far from being a source of illegitimate bias, the regulatory agency's policy commitments, its pervasive politicization, are mobilized so that the agency may better achieve its purposes.[62] The agency thus systematically subordinates the values of neutrality, principled decision-making, and particularized justice to the demands of a politicized, pragmatic policy instrument that seeks to transform certain domains of reality in prescribed ways.

4. Organizational Forms and Settings.   Even in an age of burgeoning judicial caseloads and complex forms of litigation, a court remains a remarkably solitary decisionmaker.[63] In the federal courts, at least, judges ordinarily employ only a small retinue of law clerks and researchers to assist them; in state courts, even a single clerk may be a luxury. Judges' physical and intellectual isolation mirror the traditional, limited conception of their function. Judging is viewed as a lonely, insulated, highly personalized task in which one applies logical and analytical powers, the corpus of legal rules, distillations of principle, and divinations of equity to the record. The record—principally evidence and arguments—has already been intentionally circumscribed by the procedures and conventions of litigation. Legal arguments are abstracted from the larger world of political struggle and social consequences, and drawn into the artificially confined world of the courtroom and the particular parties.

The contrast between this relatively closed, unpopulated milieu and the dense, teeming environment in which regulatory officials make decisions could hardly be more striking. From their perches in the organizational hierarchy, regulators preside over a swarm of bureaucratic, policy-generating activity. Their decisionmaking machinery, unlike that of judges, is highly differentiated—by function (e.g., policy development, enforcement, research), by programmatic subject matter (e.g., water, air, pesticides), by geography (e.g., field operations, state and local programs), and by other dimensions of specialization (e.g., legal counsel, economic analysis).

That courts exhibit little or no functional differentiation, and that agencies display a great deal, directly affects the way in which each goes about reconciling the competing claims of rule and equity. In the courtroom, particularity finds a limited sanctuary from the generalizing impulse of the outside world. The dominant judicial ethos holds that parties are entitled to corrective justice meted out to them as individuals, rather than to decisions that merely treat them as instances of an abstract class or category. Particularity looks to what they have done, not to the social interests that they may be said to represent. Rules of evidence, norms of relevance, the generality with which rules are often formulated, the availability of several rules from which the judge may choose, the importance of fact-finding to rule application, and other aspects of the judicial process reinforce this individuated conception of justice; they confine the court's attention to the parties' unique behavior and condition, keep rules at the perimeter of the judge's field of vision, and enlarge the scope of individuated justice.

In a court, the trier of fact also integrates the conflicting claims of rule and equity. As ad hoc decisionmakers without continuing life or responsibilities, juries are probably less preoccupied with maintaining a system of legal rules than with dispensing situational justice.[64] To a lesser extent, this is also true of judges, who do not systematically supervise any specialized policy system and who receive little feedback concerning how their equity-infused decisions affect the integrity or effectiveness of rules.

If courts respond primarily to claims of situational justice, regulatory agencies tend to undervalue or neglect such claims. Most agencies implement policy primarily through rulemaking, rule application, rule enforcement, and activities supportive of these functions, such as research. Some, like the NLRB, formulate their policies almost exclusively through rules adopted in individual case-by-case adjudications.[65] Rules are an agency's most visible, controversial and characteristic product, the focus of its political, legal, intellectual and social concerns. Congress, the media, regulated interests, "public interest" activists, and other attentive groups will evaluate an agency's performance almost exclusively in terms of the presumed consequences of its rules. Rules, in short, are an agency's center of gravity, its raison d'etre.

The agency's pursuit of situational justice, in contrast, is a relatively subordinate enterprise. More a constraint than a defining purpose, equity is the regulator's landfall, not her lodestar. In some agencies, equity receives no special structural expression at all.[66] In others, an exceptions process exists but it is preoccupied with relatively narrow, ad hoc, discrete adjudications decidedly ancillary to the central rule-related activities.[67] Coordination of regulatory equity and regulatory policy tends to occur, if at all, only sporadically at the upper levels of the hierarchy, far from the routinized disposition of exceptions cases. Regulatory equity, therefore, demands more than simply accommodating rule-based and situational justice, difficult as that is. When an agency bureaucratizes the process of justice-seeking and fragments the domains of rule and equity into specialized structures, it has created a formidable organizational problem. Unlike a judge, who combines these strivings in herself, an agency must somehow find a bureaucratic way to integrate the conflicting conceptions of justice that these specialized structures express.

D. Regulatory Equity and Policymaking Through Agency Adjudication

When regulatory equity is pursued in the context of an exceptions process, it takes the form of a particularized adjudication of the rights of individual claimants (or a class of similarly situated claimants) by the agency's exceptions tribunal. Not all agency adjudication, however, is designed to achieve regulatory equity in the "situational justice" sense in which I have defined it. Adjudication may also be used to pursue the agency's broader policy goals. Indeed, as noted above, all regulatory agencies use adjudication to elaborate and enforce their policies to some degree, and a few develop policy almost exclusively through the adjudicatory process.[68]

Despite the important differences in context and norms noted earlier,[69] agency adjudication in pursuit of broader goals resembles common law court adjudication. Like common law judges, agencies often develop rules by a gradual, case-by-case process of inclusion and exclusion, of line-drawing and classifying, as new fact situations come before the tribunal for decision. Through this process, general regulatory principles and policies become more and more determinate, hardening into specific agency rules.

This article will not rehearse the spirited arguments about the virtues and demerits of incremental agency policymaking through common law-type adjudication. Those arguments are well-presented in the scholarly literature.[70] Instead, I wish to emphasize a point that is easily obscured by certain formal similarities between common law-type agency adjudication and exceptions adjudication mentioned earlier. The former, properly understood, has essentially nothing to do with the pursuit of regulatory equity. The purpose of common law agency adjudication is to develop policy that can guide conduct in a relatively large number of future cases, not to avoid an unjust or anomalous outcome in a particular case. Common law agency adjudication thus cannot be legitimated in the same way as equity-seeking exceptions adjudication. The procedures necessary to legitimate the former must be designed to elicit a policy-oriented information base and broad public participation, not a situation-specific record, a narrow party orientation, and an emphasis upon procedural fairness to individuals.

One must be careful, then, not to conflate what are actually two very distinct forms of adjudication that demand very different analytical and normative frameworks. This is difficult, however, for at least two reasons. First, at a formal level, these two types of adjudications resemble one another. Thus, the distinction between regulatory equity through exceptions, on the one hand, and policy development through adjudications, on the other hand, is far clearer analytically than it is empirically. Exceptions process adjudications can be understood as points arrayed on a continuum. Professor Aman has attempted to characterize this continuum by identifying three broad categories of exceptions decisions. Aman calls them "hardship," "fairness," and "policy" exceptions. In Aman's scheme, "hardship exceptions" focus primarily upon individual, unique characteristics of the applicant. "Fairness exceptions" do so as well but take particular account of the applicant's relationship to the program's regulatory goals and of the program's impact upon others similarly situated. "Policy exceptions" emphasize not the plight of particular applicants but the regulatory program's overall goals.[71] Obviously, one could describe numerous intermediate points along the continuum representing hybrid forms.

Typically, the exceptions process is established to adjudicate "hardship" cases, cases in which applying a rule to an individual would work injustice because the rulemaker failed to anticipate such an application and the rule's purpose would not really be served by it. This is regulatory equity proper. But such cases can shade imperceptibly into Aman's "fairness" domain, in which the situational justice considerations animating the decisionmaker are somewhat less weighty and the policy-sensitive considerations are somewhat more so. At some further point, also reached by subtle gradations of motive and orientation, the exceptions decision may seek not merely to achieve that rule's purposes more fully but to achieve agency policy goals that transcend the purposes of the rule from which relief is being sought. I have been at pains to emphasize that this "policy exception" is not regulatory equity, properly understood. But it can easily be mistaken for—and misrepresented as—a "hardship exception," which is regulatory equity proper. Even to the exceptions agency, it will not always be obvious where on the continuum a case should be located, especially in the early stages of adjudication.

The second reason why regulatory equity and policy development through common law agency adjudication are easy to conflate is that both the exceptions applicant and the agency may be tempted to counterfeit the decision process by passing the latter off as the former. This is an especially promising strategy when, as in the DOE, the same bureaucratic unit performs both functions. The applicant's motivation for doing so is not difficult to imagine. The classic canons of adjudication, after all, encourage a litigant to portray his case as one involving a relatively narrow, situational claim rather than a broad policy issue. By exploiting the actual ambiguity of the hardship/fairness/policy exception boundaries, the applicant can often render this portrayal credible. The agency's incentives to adopt a similar strategy are equally powerful but considerably more complex. They require, therefore, a more extended analysis.

To an important extent, largely overlooked by scholars,[72] the use of the exceptions process for policymaking purposes can be understood as an administrative response to a set of constraints upon informal rulemaking under the Administrative Procedure Act. Ironically, these constraints have been imposed largely in the name of "regulatory reform." To a policymaker who wishes to change the prevailing regulatory course quickly, informal rulemaking is increasingly a process to be avoided. The APA requires the agency, at a minimum, to publish a notice of proposed rulemaking inviting written comments from interested parties, to "consider" those comments, and to publish the final rule to be effective at least thirty days thereafter.[73] The resulting rule is subject to judicial review[74] and may be stayed pending such review.[75] Although the notice and public procedure requirements, as well as the 30-day preeffectiveness period, may be waived upon certain agency findings,[76] these findings are themselves subject to judicial review.[77] Particular statutes may augment the APA procedures with additional requirements.[78]

In recent years, a variety of cross-agency "regulatory reform" measures—primarily statutes and Executive Orders—have burdened agency rulemaking with additional analytic procedures and layers of administrative review, including requirements for an environmental impact statement,[79] and a regulatory impact analysis satisfactory to the White House staff.[80] Particular regulatory statutes go even further. The Consumer Product Safety Commission, for example, must consider, analyze and make findings with respect to the effect of each of its rules upon many complex factors, and must publish these analyses along with the rule.[81] These requirements, of course, are themselves directly or indirectly subject to judicial review.[82]

Despite the extensive procedural, analytical, and political hurdles that must now be surmounted before an agency rule may be issued, its survival in the courts is by no means assured. This is true even when the scope of judicial review is narrow, as under the typical "arbitrary and capricious" standard.[83] Indeed, during the 1970's, the lower courts imposed substantial procedural requirements going well beyond those prescribed by the APA.[84] At least some of these additional requirements evidently survived the Supreme Court's decision in *Vermont Yankee Nuclear Power Corp. v. Natural Resources Defense Council, Inc.*, further increasing the vulnerability of rules on appeal.[85] But even where a rule is ultimately upheld on appeal, the delay in confirming—and if a stay pending appeal is granted, in implementing—the rule can be lengthy.

In short, informal rulemaking, which began as an open-ended, discretionary process analogous to a legislative hearing,[86] has evolved into a highly formalized, procedurally complex, rationalistic, and often quite protracted process.[87] This development casts a new light on what has been perhaps the central tenet of administrative reformers for decades—the notion that agencies should be encouraged, and in some instances required,[88] to elaborate agency policy through rulemaking rather than case-by-case adjudication.[89] But as pressures for increased formality, more extensive records, and analytical rigor have dissipated many of the much-celebrated virtues of informal rulemaking, certain advantages of case-by-case adjudication in general, and of exceptions adjudication in particular, have come to seem correspondingly great.

Some of these advantages are intrinsic to agency adjudication. By limiting the impact of decisions to their particular facts, agency adjudication facilitates cautious and flexible policy development and exploits incrementalism's considerable political and intellectual virtues.[90] In principle, agency adjudication limits the scope of factual inquiry, demanding fewer analytical resources than rulemaking and consuming less time. But case-by-case adjudication also has extrinsic advantages, peculiar to particular administrative contexts. In the context of DOE policymaking, for example, these advantages go far toward explaining the power, prominence, and aggressive use of an exceptions process.

First, policymaking by way of adjudication is particularly attractive where an agency's regulatory jurisdiction extends to a broad subject matter or to numerous and diverse regulated firms or individuals.[91] As a practical matter, such an agency must regulate through very general rules which must apply to many firms whose objective circumstances may differ quite radically. Even rules of this character are not infinitely elastic; they cannot be stretched to encompass such diversity without working some injustices. They are inevitably overinclusive. Hardship exceptions must be available to accommodate these "bad fits," and this can only be accomplished on a case-by-case (or perhaps a class-by-class) basis.

This jurisdiction-related temptation to proceed by case-by-case adjudication is even stronger when the program is conceived to be emergency in nature.[92] In such situations, rules must be issued quickly, often in wholesale lots.[93] Hastily prepared, overbroad rules can be disastrous for those who technically are covered by the rules but to whom the rules should not, in justice or sound policy, be applied. Inflexible application of such rules may quickly create grave competitive distortions, perhaps even driving firms out of business before the rules can be refined or eliminated. Again, if relief is to be granted in such cases, adjudication will be necessary to identify the specific situations in which the rule pinches. Furthermore, emergency programs are usually expected to be of short duration, remaining in effect only so long as the exigent conditions persist. Thus, an agency may regard the delay, analytical requirements, personnel demands, and other costs associated with developing a rule as unjustified or simply prohibitive.

Agency adjudication may also seem particularly attractive when the rule-making process is ineffective for any of a number of intellectual, bureaucratic, or political reasons. An agency, for example, may be paralyzed by uncertainty as to what policies to adopt, unable to mobilize the bureaucratic machinery at its command, or unwilling to run the political risks that difficult policy decisions often entail. Where hard choices must be made but the rulemakers cannot or will not make them, the decisions may fall by default or delegation to adjudicators.

Finally, agency adjudication typically enjoys lower visibility and hence greater freedom from outside control than rulemaking. In certain contexts, this may constitute an important advantage to cautious policymakers. Even where policymakers possess the capacity and will to make hard choices, they may nonetheless wish to limit their exposure to political reprisals for unpopular decisions. In such cases, they may search for a bureaucratic cover or buffer that can deflect criticism over controversial decisions away from themselves.[94] Because agency adjudication purports to affect only one or a few firms or individuals, it seldom invites widespread public participation, media coverage, or congressional scrutiny; moreover, it can be readily reversed or limited in future cases if that should seem prudent. Adjudication, unlike policymaking, can also wrap itself in the mantle of judicial legitimacy and independence. Regulatory equity is a more appealing slogan than regulatory change.

Several points about the above discussion should be stressed. First, these particular advantages of the case-by-case approach tend to be distributed in a highly skewed fashion; they accrue almost exclusively to the agency, not to regulated firms or the general public.[95] The disadvantages of adjudication, however, are borne in just the reverse pattern. For example, a body of law or policy is less comprehensible, predictable, or subject to public criticism when it only evolves case-by-case, and when participation may be costly. Adjudication's skewed distribution of benefits and costs, combined with the growing administrative burdens associated with rulemaking, means that agencies—especially those with broad regulatory jurisdiction, politically controversial policies, emergency authority, and a disabled rulemaking apparatus—will often find adjudication a congenial vehicle for policy development. As we shall see, DOE met all of these conditions. Not surprisingly, it adopted this decisionmaking strategy with enthusiasm. Its tactical instrument for doing so was process.

Second, many of the considerations that make rulemaking seem inadequate as a regulatory tool may imply not that case-by-case adjudication is a superior mode for implementing regulatory policy, but that the particular market should not be subjected to regulation of a command-and-control variety at all.[96] In this view, regulatory inequity is so pervasive in such a program that an exceptions process attempts to use band-aids to staunch a massive hemorrhage. In the analysis that follows, however, I shall not question the wisdom or legitimacy of the regulatory program but shall analyze the exceptions process on the assumption that the program of which it was a part was congression-ally mandated and therefore legitimate.

E. Regulatory Equity and the Exceptions Process

In this part, I raise some fundamental questions about the role of exceptions in the regulatory process, questions that the remainder of this study will address. They may be organized around five related problems.

1. The Problem of Functional Integration.   Does the exceptions process simply serve the situation-oriented, particularistic concerns of equity in particular cases, or does it also implicate the agency's larger policymaking functions? If the exceptions process affects both, how does the agency manage to integrate equitable and policy development purposes without sacrificing the distinctive values of each?

2. The Problem of Organizational Integration.   Does the bureaucratic organization of the exceptions and rulemaking processes affect the way in which the agency's rules are formulated, interpreted, and enforced? Does that organizational structure affect the way in which exceptions decisions are actually made? Does it solve the problem of functional integration? What values are served and sacrificed by that particular structure?

3. The Problems of Equitable Criteria and Legitimacy.   How can the exceptions process establish and preserve legitimacy and integrity in a decision context that invites imputations of favoritism, political pressure, ad hoc judgments, and unequal treatment?

4. The Problem of Procedures.   Does the exceptions process employ procedures that are adequate to the kinds of tasks that it undertakes? Are its procedures appropriate both to the pursuit of regulatory equity and to common law-type agency adjudication? In particular, how can it organize what is an essentially adjudicatory process to generate decisions that are not only procedurally fair to individual parties but also expeditious and sensitive to political and policy factors?

5. The Problem of Accountability and Control.   What roles do other institutions—the department, the Congress, the courts, and private groups—play in structuring and influencing the various functions that the exceptions process exercises? How well do these other institutions actually perform them and how should those roles be altered?

After examining microscopically the exceptions process in action in Part II and analyzing those findings in Part III, I shall return to these problem areas in Part IV, using them as analytical foci for evaluating the exceptions process.

•   •   •

IV. Conclusion

It is now possible to offer some answers to the questions about the relationship between the exceptions process and regulatory equity posed at the end of Part I, and to see what meaning can be derived for future administrative design. In the nature of this study, these answers must be tentative, qualitative, and in some cases impressionistic. Moreover, it remains an open question whether and to what extent they can be generalized beyond the kind of regulatory program and exceptions process that the DOE administered. What follows, then, should be regarded as only a first step toward a better understanding of that relationship.

In evaluating the OHA exceptions process and assessing its relevance to the pursuit of regulatory equity in other regulatory settings, three distinctive aspects of the OHA's situation must be borne in mind. First, the OHA purported to make many (though certainly not all) of its decisions under emergency conditions in which expedited decision procedures were thought to be essential and certain external checks, such as rigorous judicial and congressional review, were unavailable as a practical matter. Second, the DOE expected the OHA not simply to achieve regulatory equity, but to help shape a regulatory program of unusual complexity and comprehensiveness. Consequently, the OHA had to operate not on the periphery of regulatory policy but at its very center. The DOE often used the OHA to supplant, not simply to augment, a rulemaking apparatus that appeared to be singularly ineffective. Hence, its policy role was thrust upon it by others, even as it energetically arrogated that role to itself. Finally, the OHA was administered by an unusually experienced and able director, one in whom the DOE's leaders reposed enormous trust. Certain administrative practices that worked tolerably well under Goldstein's administration might, under other leadership and in other circumstances, occasion serious difficulties.

A. The Problem of Functional Integration

DOE exceptions decisionmaking clearly did not confine itself to the conventional goal of such processes—the pursuit of situational justice in particular cases. Instead, the exceptions process constituted a central element, and occasionally *the* central element, of the agency's policymaking apparatus. For many reasons, some more defensible than others, the DOE's leaders delegated to the OHA sweeping discretion and initiative in developing, implementing, and reforming some of the DOE's most important policies, discretion that the OHA aggressively claimed. The direct subsidization of many small refiners and the allocation of ANS crude are among the examples most prominently discussed in this article. These policymaking initiatives by the OHA often took the form, not of equitable criteria, but of what amounted to legislative-type rulemaking.

In general, the OHA managed to perform these broad policy functions without impairing its ability to respond to particular claims of situation-specific injustice. Indeed, the vast majority of its exceptions decisions involved hardship claims of this type, claims having few if any implications for DOE policy generally. It was only during the motor gasoline crisis of 1979, when the ERA's regulatory failures overwhelmed the OHA with myriad hardship claims and related policymaking burdens, that the OHA's ability to dispense regulatory equity was significantly impaired. In this respect, at least, the evidence from the case studies strongly suggests that the mixture of policymaking and equitable functions in one agency was not inherently problematic. Instead, it became problematic only when incompetent policy development and sluggish rulemaking unleashed an avalanche of hardship cases that exceeded the administrative capacities of the exceptions process.

B. The Problem of Organizational Integration

As a matter of formal organizational structure, OHA exceptions decisions and ERA rulemaking were fully integrated. The directors of both units reported to the Secretary and Deputy Secretary of Energy, who were supposed to coordinate the two functions. In practice, however, the OHA and the ERA remained bureaucratically separate to a pronounced degree. The OHA was run with little guidance from or involvement by DOE's politically accountable leadership. Goldstein regarded this autonomy as essential to the OHA's reputation for independent judgment and fairness, and even insisted upon it as a condition of his continued employment. The Secretary and Deputy Secretary seem to have agreed with his assessment.

This separation had significant effects upon the character of both processes. As the case studies reveal, coordination between the OHA and the ERA was often poor. The exceptions process should have been used by the ERA to obtain rapid feedback about the unanticipated consequences of its rules. Instead, the exceptions process was used to perform functions that a more effective rulemaking process would have discharged itself. Some of the OHA's decisions seemed detached and remote from the operational, administrative, and programmatic factors to which the ERA was institutionally sensitive.[97] Moreover, the DOE's promiscuous use of exceptions as an all-purpose "safety valve" probably weakened the ERA, though in an attempt to help it. The DOE was able to put off the hard political and bureaucratic choices needed to rehabilitate the ERA as an effective policy instrument.

It is not at all clear that a greater structural integration of the OHA and the ERA would have produced "better" policies and decisions by each. First, permitting the same official to administer the rulemaking process and to decide exceptions cases might simply lead to a new separation within that official's unit. The advantages of specialized functions, after all, can only be realized by developing different kinds of personnel, operating procedures, performance criteria, and professional-technical skills. Even within a single agency, such differentiations are likely to fragment the organization in ways similar to those that made the integration of the OHA and the ERA so problematic. There are severe limits to the ability of structural reorganization to transcend differences that are deeply rooted in specialized functions, perspectives, operating routines, and training.

Second, informal devices for bridging the structural separation between the OHA and the ERA were readily available.[98] If they were not used effectively, if the well-defined personalities and political dynamics in the DOE policy process neutralized their effects, it is difficult to believe that formal changes alone would have much altered that process or its outcomes.

On the other hand, separation did have some important benefits, especially for the exceptions process, that at least partly offset the disadvantages. Public acceptance of the OHA's more far-reaching exceptions decisions, for example, may have been enhanced by its structural independence, which strengthened its claim to be engaged in an essentially adjudicatory, nonpolitical process. As suggested earlier, this claim was grossly exaggerated in those cases, such as *Delta-Beacon,* in which the OHA was essentially making legislative policy. Even then, however, there was always *something* to the claim.[99] In fact, the OHA *was* relatively free of the political, bureaucratic, and programmatic pressures that shaped (and impeded) decisions in other parts of the DOE. In a situation in which the reform of energy policy seemed paralyzed by political deadlock, the OHA's relative independence doubtless facilitated movement and contributed to the grudging respect with which even most of the OHA's critics regarded its work. The OHA was prepared to make difficult decisions at a time when even a wrong decision might be preferable to continuing uncertainty and inaction. Its willingness to do so was, at least in part, a function of its relative independence.

C. The Problems of Equitable Criteria and Legitimacy

Occasionally, as in its *Delta-Beacon* standards, the OHA did manage to crystallize its decision criteria into rule-like form. The necessity for administering what amounted to a broad subsidy program demanded far more predictability and uniformity of treatment than did the typical OHA "hardship" exceptions. The latter tended to be highly fact-specific and idiosyncratic. But for the most part, the criteria that guided the OHA's broad equitable discretion remained scarcely more specific than the vague statutory criteria: "special hardship," "inequity," and "unfair distribution of burdens." As a result, the exceptions process successfully retained the equitable character, situational orientation, and decisional flexibility for which it was originally created. It did so, of course, at the risk of appearing to decide in an unpredictable and unprincipled manner.[100]

Agency decisions that confer valuable advantages upon one or a few firms vis-a-vis their competitors or the general public can easily be impugned as being motivated by the prospect of narrow partisan advantage, personal favoritism, or otherwise illegitimate reasons. An exceptions process that provides special relief from valid, binding rules with which other firms must comply at considerable cost, is especially open to such criticisms. The OHA, whose decisions often conferred enormous economic, competitive, and political benefits upon particular firms, regions, or sectors, was unusually sensitive to this problem.[101]

In these circumstances, the OHA's reputation for integrity and nonpolitical decisionmaking was a precious asset. If the views of many lawyers who practiced before the agency are a reliable guide, the DOE succeeded rather well in preserving its reputation. The OHA's director and staff earned and retained high marks for administrative competence, analytical rigor, scrupulous honesty, and independence. The merits of some OHA decisions were extremely controversial. Moreover, many of those interviewed complained of the agency's arrogant personnel, informal decision procedures, and eagerness to press its powers to (or even beyond) valid limits. None, however, questioned the integrity or legitimacy of its decision process. By all accounts, the OHA decided cases on its view of the merits, without regard to partisan or other inappropriate considerations.

The absence of vice, of course, is not quite the same as the presence of virtue. The case for an exceptions process like OHA's cannot rest upon mere scrupulousness. Nevertheless, the OHA's reputation for integrity and competence is no trivial matter. It represents a considerable administrative achievement in an era of widely perceived bureaucratic failure and in a regulatory program often denounced for both incompetence and susceptibility to narrow political pressures.

It is also important to recognize, however, that this achievement probably cannot be readily replicated. The OHA's structural separation, adjudicatory image, and relative independence may have facilitated its success, but they could not assure it. The energy lawyers who were interviewed seemed convinced that the OHA's legitimacy would have been in far greater jeopardy had someone less able and scrupulous than Melvin Goldstein been administering the exceptions process. This is both a crucial consideration and a troubling one. Any decision process whose integrity and public acceptability depend critically upon the idiosyncratic personality of the individual who happens to be running it at the time must give one cause for concern. Public officials like Goldstein, many observers emphasized, are in short supply in public agencies today—or in *any* day. The legitimacy of an exceptions process can neither be left to the character of its leadership nor be rendered immune from that influence. It must instead be addressed institutionally, largely by means of adequate procedures and external controls.

D. *The Problem of Procedures*

The earlier discussion of OHA procedures suggests that they are inadequate in certain respects.[102] Each deficiency deserves detailed analysis before a particular remedy is selected, and most plausible remedies would probably slow the decisionmaking process to some extent. Consideration should be given to changes that would: assure timely notice to all interested parties; permit adequate but appropriately controlled discovery at an early stage of the case; regulate ex parte communications; limit hearsay testimony by lawyers, especially when testimony by employees with direct knowledge of the facts is feasible; establish safeguards to minimize the risk that interim exceptions relief, once granted, will become permanent de facto, if not de jure; assure effective administrative review of exceptions decisions; separate the exceptions function from the function of reviewing remedial and enforcement orders; and encourage participation by significantly affected but inadequately represented groups.

Perhaps the most troubling and systematic of the OHA's procedural defects arose from a *substantive* commitment—its simultaneous pursuit of both regulatory equity and policy influence. The process of common law-type adjudication, while reasonably well suited to regulatory equity, was poorly adapted to broad policymaking. First, because the APA's adjudicatory safeguards did not apply to the OHA,[103] this approach engendered numerous legal challenges by regulated firms. Although these challenges were largely unsuccessful, the adjudicatory forms that the OHA employed gave a certain plausibility to many of these complaints. In that sense, the OHA was hoist by its own petard. Having wrapped itself in the mantle of judicial detachment, the OHA exposed itself to claims that it should conduct itself like a court. Second, and probably more important, its adjudicatory procedure, even in the hybrid form that emerged, was incapable of creating the analytical, evidentiary, and political bases necessary to sustain the broad policy development and implementation tasks that it all too eagerly assumed.

This is an inherently difficult problem, one that seems endemic to any decisionmaker that takes on two such disparate administrative tasks and performs them simultaneously—indeed often in the same proceeding. It is especially difficult when circumstances and personalities render the most obvious solution—the distribution of these tasks to two administrative units with different procedures, regulatory responsibilities, and claims to legitimacy—impractical, if not impossible. When the exceptions office undertakes to make broad policy decisions through adjudication, the predictable result is that it will adopt a decision mode that falls between two procedural stools.

The OHA's compromise, developing policy through adjudicatory forms lacking the conventional adjudicatory safeguards, was vulnerable to several different types of criticisms. In *Ashland*, for example, the summary nature of the OHA's decision process raised serious questions about the fairness of the proceedings to those opposing relief.[104] In addition, the need to reduce Ashland's relief substantially on three subsequent occasions suggests that the process yielded a hearing record inadequate to support the complex policy judgments that were required. Similarly, in *Ohio Independents*, the OHA's truncated hearing procedures led to a remedy whose lack of programmatic and political acceptability could be traced, in part, to the narrow focus of the adjudicatory forum in which it was devised. It is almost inconceivable that such a result would have emerged from a rulemaking proceeding, even one conducted under expedited procedures. In that event, the ERA's rule on ANS crude pricing apparently handled the problem.

Such unsatisfactory policy results should not be surprising. As was demonstrated in Part I, a regulatory agency is organized to function as an engine of policy in ways that a court is not.[105] The same, however, cannot be said of the agency's specialized exceptions adjudicators. The OHA's procedures, although adapted in an effort to support its policymaking role, were still constrained and characterized by the narrow, adjudicatory format of its decision process.[106]

Indeed, with respect to the typicality of cases, exceptions adjudication by an agency may be even more poorly suited to broad policy development than traditional common law adjudication by a court.[107] Almost all cases that come before common law courts are those in which both parties claim that they want to be governed by the existing rules. In contrast, those that came to the OHA were, by definition, "exceptional"; they were cases in which the applicant claimed that the existing rules were inadequate or unjust. When adjudicatory records emphasizing such unusual circumstances are the basis for broad policy decisions, those decisions are likely to reflect a somewhat distorted or inadequate view of the relevant social reality.

If policymaking through exceptions adjudication is deeply problematic, it does not follow that informal rulemaking is always superior. Many exceptions decisions may be located toward the center of the hardship/policy exceptions continuum, where adjudicatory procedures may still exert a powerful attraction. Others may have an important policy dimension that becomes apparent only after the exceptions proceeding is well under way or even completed. In still others, policy development through adjudication rather than rulemaking may represent sound social process as well.[108]

The quest for a single solution to this problem is the administrative equivalent of the search for a philosopher's stone. It is doomed to failure. Indeed, even to portray the problem as a procedural one may be quite misleading; as suggested in Part I, the procedural difficulty may merely be epiphenomenal, symptomatic of a fundamentally intractable or misguided substantive regulatory mission.[109]

Even accepting that possibility, however, the general outlines of a "second best" system for exceptions decisions emerge from the OHA's experience.[110] First, Congress or the agencies should establish a richer array of procedural options, a set of alternative decision modes that mirror the diverse mixture of competing values presented by different kinds of exceptions decisions: fairness to individual firms and consumers, accuracy, speed of decision, policy sensitivity, the substantive interests at stake, the kinds of issues to be resolved, the kinds of procedures originally employed to generate the rule from which relief is sought, and political accountability, among others. The formal adjudication and informal rulemaking categories established by the APA are merely end points on a spectrum of procedural formality. They do not begin to exhaust the possibilities for procedural hybrids, much less new species.

Energy regulation had to be conducted in a most extraordinary policy context. It consisted of extremely dynamic, heterogeneous, unpredictable, and interrelated markets and a sluggish political-administrative apparatus paralyzed by a nearly impossible task, overwhelming complexity, and political stalemate. This regulatory world had surprisingly little in common with the one in which the APA was enacted almost forty years ago, or even with those in which the Securities and Exchange Commission or National Labor Relations Board regulate today. Energy policy decisions had to be made and changed much faster than informal rulemaking, as a practical matter, permitted. They also had to be made with a much broader base of information, expertise, political acceptance, and legitimacy than exceptions adjudications could mobilize even with the OHA's innovative procedures.

This kind of regulatory context, at least, seems to call for some new procedural variants. As informal rulemaking becomes increasingly encrusted with judicialized procedures and other extra-APA requirements in the name of "regulatory reform,"[111] the importance of a relatively expeditious, flexible, and discretionary policymaking instrument such as that originally envisioned by section 553 of the APA becomes that much greater. It might, for example, take the form of a more summary rulemaking proceeding leading to temporary rules that would automatically "sunset" after a limited period, thereby ensuring periodic policy review by the agency. Emergency interim relief granted through such rules or in an exceptions proceeding should be conditioned upon creation of an escrow fund, interest obligation, expiration date, or other mechanism to ensure that the status quo ante can be effectively restored in the event that the agency or reviewing court subsequently determines that such relief was erroneous.

If the agency provides more procedural alternatives to administrators, the decision to select among them becomes correspondingly significant. Greater attention, therefore, should be devoted both to the criteria that should guide what must inevitably be a discretionary choice of procedural modes,[112] and to the need for flexible adaptation in the light of new information. If after an essentially adjudicatory exceptions proceeding is commenced, for example, it appears that significant policy issues are implicated, the exceptions office might be required to inform the rulemaking office promptly in order to give the primary policymaking apparatus an opportunity to supplement or supplant the exceptions proceeding.[113] If, however, the exceptions office proceeds with the case, it should seek to broaden public participation in its adjudication, inviting public comments on all significant policy, factual, and remedial issues in the case and conducting the proceeding in much the same way that a rulemaker would. In that event, the exceptions tribunal might be augmented by members drawn from the agency's policymaking organs.

E. The Problem of Accountability and Control

To a degree unusual in public agencies exercising politically controversial and policy-significant power, the DOE exceptions process was autonomous. Neither the administrative review committee nor the departmental leadership was significantly involved in even the most important OHA decision, with the notable exception of the *Ohio Independents* case. The DOE's program offices seldom participated in OHA's proceedings, at least formally. White House clearance of OHA orders, including those carrying broad economic and political consequences, was rare. Congressional oversight of the exceptions process was virtually nonexistent; one committee hearing was held during the motor gasoline crisis, and that had no observable effect. OHA easily deflected pressure from individual members of Congress and circumvented Congress's few statutory directives concerning OHA procedures. The complexity and "emergency" nature of the OHA's exceptions decisions elicited from the courts an abject deference years after the regulatory program had been established and the initial crisis had passed.

The OHA's substantial freedom from external controls had many advantages for the DOE. For that reason, the department's political leaders not only tolerated this autonomy but encouraged it. This reflected both their confidence in Melvin Goldstein's decisions and their perception that a relatively independent OHA constituted a valuable safety valve for a variety of internal and external pressures that had accumulated around the regulatory program. In a different context, of course, stricter bureaucratic controls might well have been imposed.

To the extent that an agency's leaders wish to delegate such autonomy to inferior officials, there is probably little that administrative law can or should do to inhibit that delegation, so long as their ultimate accountability to the politically responsible agency head is preserved. Similarly, there is no way to compel Congress to take greater interest than it chooses to in the decisions of a particular agency. It is probably futile to expect Congress to conduct continuous and effective oversight of an exceptions process, even one as far-reaching as the DOE's. Only the most visible and politically explosive breakdowns, such as the motor gasoline crisis, are likely to engage Congress's sustained attention. Judicial oversight of exceptions decisions is likewise problematic, especially in the context of a perceived programmatic emergency.

If an exceptions process like the OHA's is to be subject to meaningful external checks, if its performance is not to depend excessively upon the unusual talents of one individual, more systematic controls must be devised. These controls should safeguard the full range of values that the exceptions process is supposed to pursue. One possible reform is to encourage greater formal involvement by officials responsible for policy formulation and implementation. The Secretary, for example, could be required to sign off on exceptions decisions that meet certain criteria of significance. Obviously, such a requirement could be routinized and rendered pro forma, thereby defeating its purpose. Even if that occurred, however, accountability for policy decisions would be focused where it belongs. Alternatively, the agency's program offices could be given a formal, party-like role in the adjudicatory proceeding itself, through which they could apprise the exceptions office and the Secretary of important policy differences at a stage in the process early enough to influence the outcome. Reviewing courts, for their part, could take a more skeptical attitude toward "emergency" justifications for otherwise objectionable administrative procedures, especially as the regulatory program matures.

Notes

1. Unless otherwise indicated, subsequent references to the DOE or "the energy agency" may be taken to refer to its predecessor agencies, the Federal Energy Office (FEO) and the Federal Energy Administration (FEA), as well. Unless otherwise indicated, subsequent references to the OHA or "the exceptions office" may be taken to refer to its predecessor offices, the Office of Private Grievance and Redress (OPGR) and the Office of Exceptions and Appeals (OEA), as well.

2. See J. Sellers, Decontrol and Regulatory Legitimacy: The Case of the Entitlements Program (unpublished manuscript, on file with author).

3. The OHA's authorized staffing level for fiscal 1983 was 119, compared to 211 in 1980. Its budget for those years was $5.25 million and $5 million, respectively. Telephone interview with George Breznay, OHA Director, February 16, 1983.

4. The "entitlements clean-up" problem, for example, may involve the disposition of as much as one billion dollars. The OHA has also been given responsibility for effecting billions of dollars in refunds resulting from past overcharges. See 48 Fed. Reg. 50,624 (Nov. 3, 1983) (proposing end to entitlements program).

5. See, e.g., CONGRESSIONAL RESEARCH SERVICE, WESTERN VULNERABILITY TO A DISRUPTION OF PERSIAN GULF OIL SUPPLIES: U.S. INTERESTS AND OPTIONS 78–82 (1983); ENERGY FUTURE: REPORT OF THE ENERGY PROJECT AT THE HARVARD BUSINESS SCHOOL 274–76 (R. Stobaugh & D. Yerkin eds. 1980); Akins, Prospects of Supply Interruptions from OPEC in the Near Future, in POLICIES FOR COPING WITH OIL-SUPPLY DISRUPTIONS 6–9 (G. Horwich & E. Mitchell eds. 1982).

6. Remarkably, the exceptions process has received scant scholarly attention. Apart from studies of the World War II price control program, see, e.g., S. McMILLEN, INDIVIDUAL PRICE ADJUSTMENTS UNDER OPA: A STUDY IN THE DYNAMICS OF FLEXIBLE PRICING (1949); V. THOMPSON, THE REGULATORY PROCESS IN OPA RATIONING 339–43 (1950), it has been essentially ignored until very recently. The first systematic effort to analyze exceptions decisions as a distinctive form of administrative activity appeared in a 1982 article by Professor Alfred Aman. See Aman, Administrative Equity: An Analysis of Exceptions to Administrative Rules, 1982 DUKE L.J. 277 (1982); see also Comment, The Exceptions Process: The Administrative Counterpart to a Court of Equity and the Dangers it Presents to the Rulemaking Process, 30 EMORY L.J. 1135 (1981). A purely descriptive discussion is Cockrell, Federal Regulation of Energy: The Exceptions Process, 7 TRANSP. L.J. 83 (1975). For a general account of economic controls that provides some insights into the problem, see R. KAGAN, REGULATORY JUSTICE: IMPLEMENTING A WAGE-PRICE FREEZE (1978).

7. See Lilley & Miller, The New Social Regulation, 47 PUB. INTEREST 49, 51 (1977).

8. For a discussion of regulatory reform efforts in recent years, see, for example, R. LITAN & W. NORDHAUS, REFORMING FEDERAL REGULATION (1983); Harter, Book Review, 67 MINN. L. REV. 1065 (1983).

9. *See, e.g.*, Schuck, *The Politics of Regulation,* 90 YALE L.J. 702, 724–25 (1981). The strong emphasis upon rules and a legalistic approach to regulation, as distinguished from more flexible, cooperative methods, may be a distinctively American phenomenon. For some interesting international comparisons, see, for example, S. KELMAN, REGULATING AMERICA, REGULATING SWEDEN: A COMPARATIVE STUDY OF OCCUPATIONAL SAFETY AND HEALTH POLICY (1981); Vogel, *Cooperative Regulation: Environmental Protection in Great Britain,* 72 PUB. INTEREST 88 (1983).

10. Not all rules are equally problematic. The form and context of a rule, for example, affect the need for modulation in the interests of justice. Thus, in constitutional law, torts, and contracts, rules increasingly tend to be open-textured, indeterminate, and readily tailored to individual fact situations. In contrast, rules administered by regulatory agencies tend to be more determinate and specific. *Cf.* Kennedy, *Form and Substance in Private Law Adjudication,* 89 HARV. L. REV. 1685, 1686–89 (1976) (distinguishing between "rules," which provide for certainty of results, and "standards," which, by emphasizing underlying policy objectives, allow a more precise result in some cases). Even in regulatory law, however, rules vary considerably along these and other formal dimensions. *See* Diver, *The Optimal Precision of Administrative Rules,* 93 YALE L.J. 65 (1983).

11. Professor Alfred Aman, describing essentially the same phenomenon, has used the term "administrative equity." *See* Aman, *supra* note 6, at 280. Although the terms are functionally interchangeable because any administrative apparatus that applies rules must somehow deal with the claims of equity, I prefer to emphasize the regulatory dimension. This reflects my conviction that this problem is more acute and complex when the body of law that is being developed has crucial competitive market implications, and especially when the agency actually supervises an industry, than it is when the administrative context lacks one or both of these features, as in the Social Security program.

12. ARISTOTLE, NICHOMACHEAN ETHICS, V.10.1137–38 (W.D. Ross trans. 1915).

13. *See, e.g.,* Kennedy, *supra* note 10, at 1685, 1686–89.

14. T. ARNOLD, THE SYMBOLS OF GOVERNMENT 62 (1935).

15. For a discussion of this attribute, see Diver, *supra* note 10, at 67.

16. U.S. CONST. amend. XXVI, s 1 ("The right of citizens . . . who are eighteen years of age or older, to vote shall not be denied . . . on account of age.").

17. ARISTOTLE, *supra* note 12, at V.10.1137a.

18. For a discussion of many of these factors, see Diver, *supra* note 10, at 67, and ADMINISTRATIVE CONFERENCE OF THE UNITED STATES, STATEMENT ON GUIDELINES FOR CHOOSING THE APPROPRIATE LEVEL OF AGENCY POLICY ARTICULATION, 1 CFR s 310.9 (1984).

19. ARISTOTLE, *supra* note 12, at V.10.1137b.

20. The transparency of certain rules renders them constitutionally invalid for somewhat different reasons. *See* Woodson v. North Carolina, 428 U.S. 280, 302–05 (1976) (mandatory capital punishment statute).

21. ARISTOTLE, *supra* note 12, at V.10.1137b.

22. R. DWORKIN, TAKING RIGHTS SERIOUSLY 24–78 (1977).

23. *Id.* at 24.

24. *Id.* at 26.

25. *Id.* at 23–26, 73–78.

26. *Id.* at 22.

27. Duncan Kennedy, using different but somewhat analogous categories, suggests that the introduction of equity (what he calls "standards") into a rule-dominated system may be a way of seeming to humanize an unjust system of law or, alternatively, a way of weakening the hold of such a system, "keeping alive resistance in spite of the capture of the substantive order by the enemy." Kennedy, *supra* note 10, at 1777.

28. *See, e.g.,* Industrial Union Dep't, AFL-CIO v. American Petroleum Inst., 448 U.S. 607, 646–51 (1980).

29. *See* N.Y. Times, May 29, 1982, at 25, col. 6.

30. *See, e.g.,* F. COFFIN, THE WAYS OF A JUDGE 57–58 (1980). There are many situations in which an agency *could* rationalize particular regulatory outcomes in terms of a general rule, but does not. Numerous routine, noncontroversial decisions, such as contract or grant awards, are largely discretionary. Although the lack of standards in such cases does not wholly eliminate the value of giving reasons, it does obviate most of its advantages. This is because giving reasons, if more than a desultory gesture, consumes scarce time and personnel; for some regulatory decisions, these process costs would exceed the value of such benefits as reducing errors, increasing acceptance of adverse decisions, and facilitating review of decisions.

31. The Administrative Procedure Act (APA) requires an agency to give reasons only in connection with formal rulemakings or formal adjudications, 5 U.S.C. ss 556–557 (1982), which account for relatively few agency decisions. In the large, increasingly important category of informal rulemaking, the final rule need only "incorporate . . . a concise general statement of [its] basis and purpose." 5 U.S.C. s 553(c) (1982). That statement, of course, must be sufficiently specific and complete to enable effective judicial review of the decision. Some appellate courts have interpreted this requirement to mean a fairly detailed justification of rules. *See, e.g.,* Kennecott Copper Corp. v. EPA, 462 F.2d 846, 850 (D.C. Cir. 1972). *See generally* Pedersen, *Formal Records and Informal Rulemaking,* 85 YALE L.J. 38 (1975). Still, the requirement was not intended to duplicate the rigor of judicial reason-giving and reviewing courts have tended to demand somewhat less in the way of agency articulation. *See, e.g.,* Kenworth Trucks v. NLRB, 580 F.2d 55, 58–59 (3d Cir. 1978). *But see* Motor Vehicle Mfrs. Ass'n v. State Farm Mut. Auto. Ins. Co., 103 S. Ct. 2856, 2866 (1983). For informal adjudications, which comprise the vast majority of agency decisions, the APA imposes no procedural requirements at all, much less an obligation to articulate reasons. Many commentators have deplored this lacuna. *See* S. BREYER & R. STEWART, ADMINISTRATIVE LAW AND REGULATORY POLICY 524–30 (1979).

32. Reasoning from complex, multifactor premises to a decision is probably more cybernetic and heuristic than formally rational and synoptic. *See generally* J. STEINBRUNER, THE CYBERNETIC THEORY OF DECISION: NEW DIMENSIONS OF POLITICAL ANALYSIS (1974). If one could specify the factors of decision, how they relate to one another and to the real world, the contingencies that bring them into play, and the weight to be applied to each, then one could actually devise a computer program that would yield a decision accurately reflecting those decision ingredients. But to infer or "post-dict" from a complex decision to the ingredients that produced it is a very different matter. In such cases, the reasons decisionmakers articulate cannot fully or accurately reveal the grounds for their decision. Our brains can perform far more complex tasks of integration than we are capable of recapturing and verbalizing. As Polanyi put it, "we can know more than

we can tell." *See* M. POLANYI, THE TACIT DIMENSION 4 (1966); *see also* D. SCHON, THE REFLECTIVE PRACTITIONER viii (1983).

33. *See* United States v. Klein, 80 U.S. (13 Wall.) 128, 140–42 (1871). *But see* Note, *A Matter of Life and Death: Due Process Protection in Capital Clemency Proceedings,* 90 YALE L.J. 889, 905–11 (1981).

34. *See* Vorenberg, *Decent Restraint of Prosecutorial Power,* 94 HARV. L. REV. 1521, 1562–72 (1981).

35. For a discussion of a related issue, see Connecticut Bd. of Pardons v. Dumschat, 452 U.S. 458, 465–67 (1980) (fact that a state board of pardons has granted approximately three-quarters of the applications for commutation of life sentences does not create an entitlement so as to require the Board to justify its denial of such an application).

36. The power of a jury to acquit the accused in a criminal case is another example. *See* M. KADISH & S. KADISH, DISCRETION TO DISOBEY: A STUDY OF LAWFUL DEPARTURES FROM LEGAL RULES 47–50 (1973).

37. In conventional regulatory schemes, treating A "differently" than B may create highly visible competitive distortions and disadvantages, not only creating unfairness but undermining the agency's programmatic goals. But even there, what is being regulated may be so complex and variable that rules alone cannot assure desired outcomes. In such cases, substantially, if not wholly, discretionary decisions may be necessary.

38. *Cf.* G. CALABRESI & P. BOBBIT, TRAGIC CHOICES, 71–72 (1978) ("The reasons for using adopted responsible agencies to make tragic choices may be traced . . . to the desire to make the grounds for decision less direct and perhaps even less obvious, while at the same time trying to make sure that the decisions are based on broadly held social values.").

39. *See* P. SCHUCK, THE JUDICIARY COMMITTEES 242–65 (1975).

40. *See, e.g.,* W.H. BROWN, CONSTITUTION, JEFFERSON'S MANUAL AND RULES OF THE HOUSE OF REPRESENTATIVES, H.R. Doc. No. 398, 96th Cong., 2d Sess. 492–508 (1981); J. SAPP, SENATE MANUAL, S. Doc. No. 1, 96th Cong., 1st Sess. 13–14 (1979).

41. This judicial ambition persists even in the face of rather clear congressional intent to preclude judicial review. *See, e.g.,* Johnson v. Robison, 415 U.S. 361, 366–74 (1974). Even when the courts have acquiesced in a statutory preclusion of review, they have stressed the agency's unique institutional competence to make the equitable, situation-specific decisions that the legislature desires. *See, e.g.,* Hahn v. Gottlieb, 430 F.2d 1243, 1249–51 (1st Cir. 1970).

42. The existence of such a process can mollify not only those to whom the rule may apply but also their political patrons in Congress and the executive branch. *See infra* notes 422–23 and accompanying text.

43. Many court decisions during the 1970's, for example, invalidated overbroad administrative rules that created "irrebuttable presumptions." For a general discussion of these cases, see J. MASHAW, DUE PROCESS AND ITS DISCONTENTS (forthcoming); *see also* FCC v. WNCN Listeners Guild, 450 U.S. 582, 610 n.12 (1981) (Marshall, J., dissenting), and cases there cited; Diver, *Policymaking Paradigms in Administrative Law,* 95 HARV. L. REV. 393, 405 n.62 (1981), and cases there cited.

44. For example, the Nuclear Regulatory Commission exempts from its program for licensing special nuclear materials those licensees that have less than specified quantities of such material. Domestic Licensing of Special Nuclear Materials, 10 C.F.R. ss 71.7–.10 (1982).

In his study of the wartime Office of Price Administration, Victor Thompson found that exceptions appealed to harried administrators for other reasons as well. First, administrators sometimes wished to grant an applicant relief but feared that doing so by rule would open the floodgates. Because exceptions had relatively low public visibility, they hoped to grant the most pressing applications without encouraging others to claim similar treatment. Exceptions also avoided the need to issue narrow-gauged rules that might seem arbitrary and politically motivated. OPA regulators, Thompson found, wished to keep the rules general and "pure." They had an "abhorrence of a rule governing a very small group, especially a named group, in the regulations"; they had fewer qualms, however, if the same group was named in an exception order. V. Thompson, The Regulatory Process in OPA Rationing 342 (1950).

45. K. Davis, Discretionary Justice: A Preliminary Inquiry 4 (1969).

46. Under the Natural Gas Policy Act of 1978, for example, natural gas is divided into more than ten categories, each of which is entitled to separate price treatment. 15 U.S.C. ss 3312–3348 (1982).

47. See Federal Water Pollution Control Act, 33 U.S.C. s 1311(b)(2)(A) (1976), Regulations at 40 C.F.R. s 125.30(a) (1982) (the permits required under the federal Clean Water Act).

48. For a discussion of the distinction between justification and excuse, see Fletcher, *Fairness and Utility in Tort Theory*, 85 Harv. L. Rev. 537, 557–64 (1972).

49. Some agencies have no explicit exceptions process at all. Examples include the National Labor Relations Board and the International Trade Commission. See Letters to Hon. Loren A. Smith, Chairman, Administrative Conference of the United States, from Hugh L. Reilly, Solicitor, NLRB, June 21, 1983, and from Alfred Eckes, Chairman, ITC, June 8, 1983. In such cases, relief from a rule may be obtained, if at all, only by petitioning the agency to repeal or modify the rule, *see* Administrative Procedure Act, 5 U.S.C. s 553(e) (1982), or by successfully resisting its enforcement administratively or in the courts.

50. In the federal government, another common form of exceptions procedure involves a hearing at some point in the exceptions application process before an independent administrative law judge. In such systems, appeals from grants or denials (or both) by the ALJ may ultimately be taken to the agency head (or commission), with review of the final agency decision by the courts. The adjustments process of the Federal Energy Regulatory Commission is an example. See P. Schuck, When the Exception Becomes the Rule, Report to the Administrative Conference of the United States, at app. A (1983). Another model allows for direct application for exceptions relief from a rule to the rulemaker itself (the program office or agency head). *See, e.g., id.* at app. C. The Supreme Court recently had occasion to consider the status of an application for an exception directed to a *court. See* District of Columbia Court of Appeals v. Feldman, 103 S. Ct. 1303, 1313 (1983) (request to court for waiver of bar examination rule requires court to evaluate purposes of rule and therefore requires a "judicial" decision).

51. *See infra* notes 90–94 and accompanying text. Having created an apparatus of logical rules, Thurman Arnold argued, we continue to feel the need to create "separate institutions to represent common sense and benevolence." T. Arnold, *supra* note 14, at 62.

52. *See infra* notes 425–30 and accompanying text.

53. By judicial equity, I refer not to the system of remedial justice traditionally administered by separate courts of chancery, but rather to the process by which courts that engage in common law adjudication integrate conceptions of situational justice into their decisions and thus into the resulting structure of legal rules.

54. These differences are underscored by the fact that regulatory agencies are often created to perform a task that common law courts previously performed but performed (or so the legislature thought) poorly for reasons having to do with limitations imposed by the courts' methodology, values, or institutional character. *See, e.g.,* Clean Water Act of 1977, Pub. L. No. 95–217, 91 Stat. 1566 (codified at 33 U.S.C. ss 1251–1376 (Supp. V 1981)); National Labor Relations Act, Pub. L. No. 74–198, 49 Stat. 449 (1935) (codified at 29 U.S.C. ss 151–166 (1976)).

55. *See, e.g.,* Shepard v. NLRB, 103 S.Ct. 665, 670 (1983) (whereas a court of general jurisdiction will be more likely to grant a successful party's prayer for complete relief, an agency, even in the context of adjudication, need not order complete relief if it has legitimate policy reasons for limiting relief).

56. For an unusual and extremely controversial "exception" to this proposition, one that perhaps "proves the rule," see Roe v. Wade, 410 U.S. 113, 164–65 (1973)(prescribing different substantive standards for each trimester of pregnancy). See also the brace of cases defining the minimal number of jurors constitutionally permitted for criminal prosecutions: Ballew v. Georgia, 435 U.S. 223, 245 (1978)(five are too few); Williams v. Florida, 399 U.S. 78, 103 (1970)(six are enough). In reapportionment cases, the courts, as a result of their "one person, one vote" standard, have felt obliged to make exceedingly fine-grained numerical choices. *See, e.g.,* Karcher v. Daggett, 103 S. Ct. 2653, 2660–65 (1983).

57. *See* P. Schuck, Suing Government: Citizen Remedies for Official Wrongs 196–98 (1983).

58. Of course, the vast majority of discrete decisions that agencies make involve neither the development nor the issuance of rules but rather the application of rules to particular firms or individuals. *See generally* Verkuil, *A Study of Informal Adjudication Procedures,* 43 U. Chi. L. Rev. 739 (1976). This fact, however, only underscores the disproportionate significance to most agency policymaking of the relatively small number of rules that exist or are under development at any particular time, a significance augmented by the fact that agency rules are usually intended to influence a broader range of private decisions than court or agency adjudications.

59. Commentators have almost universally condemned this approach. *See, e.g.,* Mayton, *The Legislative Resolution of the Rulemaking Versus Adjudication Problem in Agency Lawmaking,* 1980 Duke L.J. 103, 103 (1980); Note, *NLRB Rulemaking: Political Reality Versus Procedural Fairness,* 89 Yale L.J. 982 (1980); *see also* sources cited *supra* note 6.

60. *See, e.g.,* NLRB v. Bell Aerospace Co., 416 U.S. 267. 290–95 (1974).

61. For example, agencies may dispense with ALJ decisions, 5 U.S.C. s 557(b) (1982), and, under certain conditions, with cross-examination. 5 U.S.C. s 556(d) (1982). In "informal adjudication," APA procedural requirements do not apply at all. The extreme case may be the Immigration and Naturalization Service. *See* Schuck, *The Transformation of Immigration Law,* 84 Colum L. Rev. 1, 31–34 (1984).

62. By politicization, I mean the circumstances of the agency's creation, its statutory setting, continuous congressional oversight, the appointment and recruitment processes, and its constant and intensive interactions with outside interests.

63. Thoughtful commentators are concerned that this unique condition may be changing. *See, e.g.,* Fiss, *The Bureaucratization of the Judiciary,* 92 Yale L.J.—(July 1983) (forthcoming). *See generally* McCree, *Bureaucratic Justice: An Early Warning,* 179 U. Pa. L. Rev. 777 (1981).

64. *See* G. Calabresi & P. Bobbit, *supra* note 38 at 57.

65. *See supra* note 59. There are combinations of these basic patterns. The Immigration and Naturalization Service, for example, designates certain of its adjudicatory decisions as "precedents," thereby creating the functional equivalent of a rule. *See* Diver, *supra* note 10, at 95.

66. *See supra* note 49.

67. *See e.g.*, P. SCHUCK, *supra* note 50, at app. G.

68. *See supra* note 59.

69. *See supra* note 38 and accompanying text.

70. *See, e.g.*, Strauss, *Rules, Adjudication, and Other Sources of Law in an Executive Department: Reflections on the Interior Department's Administration of the Mining Law*, 74 COLUM. L. REV. 1231, 1258, 1274–75 (1974); *see also* sources cited *supra* note 3.

71. Aman, *supra* note 6, at 293.

72. For an exception, see Strauss, *supra* note 70, at 1245–48.

73. 5 U.S.C. s 553 (1982).

74. 5 U.S.C. s 702 (1982).

75. 5 U.S.C. s 705 (1982).

76. 5 U.S.C. s 553(b)(3)(B) (1982).

77. *See, e.g.*, American Federation of Government Employees v. Block, 655 F.2d 1153, 1155 (D.C. Cir. 1981).

78. These include, for example, requirements that the agency publish advance notice of proposed rulemaking or provide oral hearings with more or less procedural formality, multiple rounds of proposed rules, longer comment periods, or reports to Congress. Legislative veto provisions have also become commonplace. *But see* Immigration and Naturalization Serv. v. Chadha, 103 S. Ct. 2764 (1983).

79. National Environmental Policy Act, 42 U.S.C. s 4332(c) (1976).

80. Executive Order 12,291, 3 C.F.R. 127 (1982).

81. 15 U.S.C. s 2058(c), (f) (1982).

82. 15 U.S.C. s 2058(f)(4) (1982). Rules developed by the DOE, for example, are subject to especially time-consuming procedures. Under the Department of Energy Organization Act, each rule proposed by the DOE must be accompanied by a statement of the research, analysis, and other available information in support of, the need for, and the probable effect of the rule, and a response to the "major comments, criticisms and alternatives offered during the comment period." 42 U.S.C. s 7191(b) (d) (Supp. V 1981). Such requirements are unusual but not unique. *See, e.g.*, Consumer Product Safety Act, 15 U.S.C. s 2058 (1982).

In addition, the Secretary of Energy cannot issue rules until he first notifies the Federal Energy Regulatory Commission (FERC) of the proposed rules. If the FERC determines that the rules may significantly affect FERC functions, the Secretary must refer the rule to the FERC; the FERC must then invite additional public comment on the proposal and publish its recommendations, along with its own explanations of reasons and analysis of comments. Only after the FERC's recommendations are published can the DOE issue the rule. 42 U.S.C. s 7174 (Supp. V 1981). The necessity for formal references under section 7174 is minimized by a process of informal clearance with the FERC. Whether formal or informal, however, the process demands precious time.

If the DOE rules are economically and politically significant, as has often been the case, they must ordinarily be submitted for informal review by the White House policy staff. The regulations altering the base period for motor gasoline allocations during the 1979 shortage is an example. *See infra* notes 268–81 and accompanying text.

83. The Supreme Court recently confirmed this proposition. *See* Motor Vehicle Mfrs. Ass'n v. State Farm Mut. Auto. Ins. Co., 103 S. Ct. 2856, 2866 & n.9 (1983).

84. For an account of this evolution, see Scalia, *Vermont Yankee: The APA, the D.C. Circuit, and the Supreme Court*, 1978 SUP. CT. REV. 345, 348–52 (1979).

85. *See, e.g.*, United States Lines, Inc. v. Federal Maritime Commission, 584 F.2d 519, 534–35 (D.C. Cir. 1978) (agency required to disclose specifically any data relied on in reaching an administrative decision, in order to facilitate judicial review).

86. *See* Scalia, *supra* note 84, at 346–47.

87. Legislation that passed the Senate 94–0 during the 97th Congress, but was not enacted, would have made rulemaking procedures and analytical requirements even more complex, rigorous, and time-consuming than they already are, and would have applied them to the independent regulatory commissions as well as to executive branch agencies. *See* S. 1080, 97th Cong., 2d Sess., 128 CONG. REC. 52,713 (March 24, 1982).

88. *See, e.g.*, NLRB v. Wyman-Gordon Co., 394 U.S. 759, 764 (1969). For a criticism of this approach, see Strauss, *supra* note 70, at 1265–66.

89. *See, e.g.*, K. DAVIS, DISCRETIONARY JUSTICE 54–60 (1969). *See generally* sources cited *supra* note 53.

90. *See* D. BRAYBROOKE & C. LINDBLOM, A STRATEGY FOR DECISION 88, 99–100, 111–12 (1963); *see also* Diver, *Policymaking Paradigms in Administrative Law*, 95 HARV. L. REV. 393, 399 (1981). As Professor Strauss points out, adjudication can also defeat the bureaucratic inclination to defer difficult decisions. Whereas a rulemaking can often be put off indefinitely, a case that is before the agency must be decided. Strauss, *supra* note 70, at 1254.

91. For example, the DOE's regulatory jurisdiction was sweeping with respect to both subject matter and number of firms. Its authority embraced all aspects of the pricing and allocation of crude oil and petroleum products at all levels of production and distribution by literally hundreds of thousands of firms. *See infra* notes 100–26 and accompanying text.

92. Again, petroleum regulation provides a vivid example. *See infra* notes 108–09 and accompanying text. Whether the petroleum regulatory program as a whole responded to or created and exacerbated an emergency situation (or both) is an important question, but one that I shall not address in this article. For sharp criticisms of the program, see sources cited *infra* note 96.

93. The basic petroleum price and allocation regulations under the Emergency Petroleum Allocation Act (EPAA), for example, were issued in a batch within weeks of the law's enactment. They essentially replicated the earlier Phase IV regulations. 10 C.F.R. ss 202–215 (1975).

94. *See, e.g.*, Note, *supra* note 59, at 987–99.

95. Of course, certain other advantages of adjudication—for example, its greater accuracy with respect to so-called "adjudicatory facts"—inure to the public as well as to the agency.

96. Although an evaluation of the merits of regulating the petroleum industry in the manner that Congress directed is far outside the scope of this article, it bears noting that the program was repeatedly criticized by economists and others as being inherently flawed and inevitably counter-productive. *See, e.g.*, K. ARROW & J. KALT, PETROLEUM PRICE REGULATION: SHOULD WE DECONTROL? 46–47 (1979); S. BREYER, REGULATION AND ITS REFORM 120–30 (1982); FEDERAL ENERGY ADMINISTRATION REGULATION: REPORT OF THE PRESIDENTIAL TASK FORCE 139–46 (P. MacAvoy ed. 1977).

97. An example of this is the *Ohio Independents* ruling and the 1979 class exception implementing the "unusual growth" adjustment. Professor Strauss found in the Department of the Interior an even more pronounced isolation of policy-relevant adjudicators from officials with policy responsibility, with similarly problematic results. *See* Strauss, *supra* note 70, at 1254–64.

98. Possibilities include more frequent consultation, a greater willingness or capacity by the Department's political leaders to play a more active coordinating role, or a better system for clearing OHA decisions.

99. *See supra* notes 157–59 and accompanying text.

100. In an earlier study of the Department of the Interior's adjudication of land claims, Professor Strauss identified a similar failure of the adjudicators to state their standards in the form of readily accessible rules, although the standards were susceptible to such codification. He suggested a number of procedural reforms to encourage the adjudicators to do so, including creating a separate office to state policy in rule form, or permitting outside parties to stimulate such codification. As Strauss pointed out, however, such reforms are unlikely as a practical matter to induce rulemaking that the agency wishes to avoid. *See* Strauss, *supra* note 70, at 1266–69.

101. The initial *Ashland* decision alone was worth over $50 million to the company. The *Ohio Independents* decision was worth $14 million, and might have affected President Carter's electoral strength in Ohio. *Delta-Beacon* relief, eventually amounting to $300 million annually, protected some small refiners and their customers from extinction, and significantly drained the valuable entitlements pool. *See supra* notes 192–93 and accompanying text.

102. *See supra* notes 354–410 and accompanying text.

103. *See supra* notes 355–58 and accompanying text.

104. These are questions that the reviewing court might well have resolved against the agency had it known that the "temporary" relief would last two and one-half years.

105. *See supra* notes 63–67 and accompanying text.

106. *See supra* notes 409–10 and accompanying text.

107. This point is developed in a May 1983 letter to the author from Professor Martin Shapiro. Of course, the typicality of cases that come before judges, especially in public law litigation in the federal courts, should not be exaggerated. *See* P. SCHUCK, *supra* note 57, at 157–58.

108. *See, e.g.,* Diver, *supra* note 43, at 399–400, 428–30; *see also* NLRB v. Wyman-Gordon Co., 394 U.S. 759, 770–74 (1969) (Black, Brennan, Marshall, J.J., concurring).

109. *See supra* note 96 and accompanying text.

110. *See also* P. SCHUCK, *supra* note 50, at 187–90.

111. *See supra* notes 86–89 and accompanying text.

112. For a discussion of these criteria, see Aman, *supra* note 6, at 293–322.

113. At least the office should be so encouraged because, in practice, the requirement is unlikely to be judicially enforceable.

6

Law and Post-Privatization Regulatory Reform

Perspectives from the U.S. Experience

Law plays many diverse roles in the regulatory state. It begins by defining property and contract rights. It then specifies the substantive regulatory limitations on those rights, the regulatory structures that impose, administer, and enforce those limitations, the procedures that both the regulator and the regulated must observe in their mutual dealings, and the modes of formal conflict resolution that each can invoke against the other. Law also prescribes the duties that the regulator and the regulated owe consumers, competitors, contractors, governmental entities, and other third parties, and it prescribes the remedies through which the third parties can enforce those duties.

Privatization does not dispense with these roles; it merely alters the precise mix of private and public law through which they are played out. Whether the state spins off a previously state-run activity to private entities (as is now common in Latin America),[1] or it subjects a traditionally private activity to regulation (as has been a common pattern in the U.S.), the state will deploy its public law to exercise some continuing degree of regulatory authority over the activity. The newly-privatizing state will be under political pressure to ensure that the public is served at least as well under the new regime as it was under the old one, while the newly-regulating state in effect declares, as a justification for regulation, that the previously private activity is "affected with a public interest" and that the private regime did not serve this public interest sufficiently well because of market failure or other reasons.

In this paper, I discuss three paradigmatic roles that public law can play in the kind of reformist, post-privatization political and policy environment in which emerging liberal democratic states are now situated. These roles are (1) to create and institutionalize a strong (but rebuttable) presumption in favor of market solutions to social problems; (2) to maximize the effectiveness of regulation where it is used; and (3) to establish extra-regulatory institutions and processes that can help to monitor, augment, and discipline the resulting hybrid system of markets and regulation.

In exploring these three roles, I shall draw largely on the American experience, and the institutions and processes that I shall analyze are largely those at the federal (national) level. I emphasize the American case not because the U.S. is a typical state (it isn't), not because it is a model that Latin America should mimic (it shouldn't and probably couldn't), not simply because it is the system that I know best (though that is certainly true), and not because the U.S. has all the answers (it doesn't). Instead, I do so because I believe that all of us can learn a great deal from America's struggle to construct a political economy that fully exploits the economic advantages of flexible markets, technocratic expertise, and innovation, while also enjoying the social advantages of legality, political accountability, distributional fairness, and other non-market values. This struggle has been a long and difficult one for the U.S.; the necessary institutions, infrastructure, and values that I shall discuss have developed quite slowly and unevenly. The current robustness of the American economy—and, I would argue more controversially, of the American polity (Schuck 1997; Schuck 1998, 354–58)—should not obscure the fact that the struggle is perpetual.

I. The Pro-Market Presumption

A priori, there is no reason to favor markets over regulation—or vice-versa. Only after one specifies a particular society's values and history can one begin to construct a justification for one kind of political economy rather than another. *A priori,* there is no reason to believe that market failures are greater and more harmful than government failures—or vice-versa. Fortunately, however, we do not live not in complete normative, historical, and empirical ignorance but instead inhabit an *a postieri* world that is deeply inscribed with values, history, and knowledge of empirical consequences. Political economies are certainly not path-dependent in any strict sense; a society can choose (or may be compelled) to transform its ways of doing business, as the U.S. has done since the 1960s and as Russia and many Latin American and Asian states are doing now. Nevertheless, different states do exhibit distinct, socially conditioned patterns of political economy.

The political ideology, legal culture, and social institutions of the U.S. today mutually reinforce a presumption in favor of market allocations of goods and services and market solutions to public policy problems, at least where such solutions seem feasible. The presumption is a strong one—and increasingly so—but it is also rebuttable, as I discuss below. This strong presumption in favor of markets has existed for most of American history. Recall that Adam Smith's *The Wealth of Nations* was published in 1776, the year of our independence and a time when it could influence the Framers of our Constitution. (The historical evidence suggests that it, along with other ideas of the Scottish Enlightenment, did indeed influence them).

The U.S. Constitution did not expressly privilege market approaches to public policy problems. In at least four ways, however, it did so indirectly. First, several constitutional provisions explicitly protected property and contract rights against various kinds of government infringement. Second, the Supreme Court for more than a half-century (from the 1880s to 1937) interpreted another provision—the Due Process Clause—to elevate liberty of contract into a constitutional right that even political majorities could not restrict. Third, and perhaps more important in the long run, it created a highly fragmented, decentralized, and internally competitive system of governmental authority that even today fortifies the *status quo,* which in the U.S. has tended to be market-friendly. This governance structure makes it difficult for proregulation forces to assemble political coalitions strong enough to overcome this inertia. Difficult but not impossible, as is demonstrated by the increase in market-constraining regulatory activity during the New Deal and 1960–1980 periods.

What is even more interesting is that the regulatory agenda has flourished even during the recent era of unbridled enthusiasm for the market. For example, political scientist R. Shep Melnick has shown how a dynamic of institutional competition among Congress, agencies, and the courts has increased regulation in some policy areas at the same time that deregulation became a central theme in political economy. (Melnick) Most of the new regulation has been in the nature of "social" regulation—that is, it has pursued non-discrimination, health and safety, and redistributive goals rather than seeking the control of market prices, entry, exit, service, and competition that characterizes traditional "economic" regulation—but there are important exceptions such as the growing restrictions on the marketing of managed care organizations in the health services industry.

Finally, the Constitution entrenches the market by protecting the autonomy and activities of private interests, which in turn strongly influence the political process. Even as these groups often pursue public subsidies, economic rents, and other forms of governmental support for their narrow interests (sometimes called "corporate welfare" or "corporate socialism"), they also seek to minimize governmental interference with private decisionmaking. Their success in doing so thus reinforces the structural and ideological biases favoring market autonomy.

At a sub-constitutional level, the law undergirds this privatistic, pro-market presumption in several ways. Most fundamentally, the law defines individual entitlements and duties, and establishes institutions and procedures for enforcing those entitlements and duties. These entitlements include the rights to hold and use property, exploit original ideas, and engage in voluntary exchanges with others, protected by property, intellectual property, and contract law; rights to physical, economic, and emotional integrity protected by tort law; rights to protection against arbitrary governmental intrusion, protected by public law (constitutional and administrative law); rights to certain public goods such as environmental quality, protected by regulatory law; and so forth. In the course of defining these entitlements and duties, the law in effect marks the boundaries between private and public goods.

One implication of the presumption in favor of markets is that private providers in the U.S. supply many of the goods that are supplied by government in other advanced industrial democracies. Health care and education (especially at the university level) are examples. Private provision is made possible in part by another distinctive, market-reinforcing feature of U.S. law: the nurturing of a vast, rapidly growing non-profit (or "third") sector that provides many of the goods and services that lie near the shifting border between public and private. In addition to health care and education, these include charity for the indigent, other philanthropy, care for pre-school children and the infirm elderly, professional organizations, cooperative activities, scientific research, museums, the performing arts, a vast array of other cultural and social service activities, and community action and advocacy efforts. Even the political parties are, compared to those in other countries, remarkably private in their financing and governance.

This intermediation of nonprofit organizations between the public and private sectors is an important, fascinating, and complex motif in American life. (Hansmann) For present purposes, it suffices to say that the public's trust in the integrity, effectiveness, and selflessness of the non-profit sector has a crucial effect on the American political economy. By providing a "softer", non-market alternative to a public that relies heavily but uneasily on the profit motive to provide certain highly valued social goods, the non-profit sector often deflects and suppresses what might otherwise be strong public demands for direct government provision or regulation. This public trust is sometimes misplaced; in fact, many non-profit providers operate much as private for-profit providers would. Nevertheless, the settled acceptance of, and even preference for, this alternative is a pivotal factor in many debates about the appropriate role of government, such as ministering to the needs of the poor.

It is axiomatic that in order for the law to facilitate the voluntary exchange of property and other rights, it must define them with clarity and precision. To the extent that the law fails to do so, potential buyers and sellers must bear the deadweight losses generated by the transaction costs of ascertaining and negotiating what those rights are, who holds them, and how they can be traded; these costs will deter otherwise socially valuable exchanges. By surrounding the nature and allocation of entitlements with considerable uncertainty, American law often fails this test.

Technical, political, and institutional factors help to explain these failures. (Schuck 1984) First, there are limitations of language; ambiguity pervades legal discourse and much of this ambiguity is irreducible, thereby requiring legal interpretation. Moreover, lawmakers possess only a limited ability to predict the consequences and specific applications of their legal rules; they must therefore use language that is general enough to provide the necessary flexibility to those who must apply these rules. Ambiguity, of course, also has important political virtues. When lawmarkers seek to balance conflicting values and interests, general language helps them to persuade each of the contenders that they have won something and that the law will project their victory into the future. This leaves the resulting definition of entitlements, however, in a compromised and indeterminate form.

Finally, the institutional processes of lawmaking and law application magnify this uncertainty. The common law method of adjudication entails case-by-case development of legal doctrine, which is both defined and limited by the particular facts of decided cases. The highly decentralized American judiciary, further fragmented by the division between federal and state (and often local) courts—not to mention a growing number of private adjudicatory tribunals—is subject to only weak hierarchical controls; thus conflicting lines of authority persist between and within each jurisdiction, resisting authoritative resolution. The ambiguity and compromise of legislation, as I have just explained, is compounded by the intricate, frustrating, and often constitutionally uncertain division of authority between the state and the federal governments. Lawmaking and law administration by executive officials, while usually more specific than statutes, are characterized nonetheless by much ambiguity. More frequently than legislators and judges, bureaucrats use general language in order to maximize their discretion, permit flexible solutions, compromise conflicting interests, and avert legal challenges. All of these uncertainties, of course, are greatly compounded by the separation of powers at each level of American government, which multiplies the number of institutional participants in decisionmaking and requires the constant negotiation of recurrent conflicts with indeterminate and unpredictable outcomes.

The law not only promotes markets by defining private entitlements; it also prescribes the preconditions for government regulation of markets. This further entrenches the presumption in favor of markets and against regulation. As noted earlier, this presumption is often overcome. Vast regulation was imposed during the New Deal and Great Society eras, and the relatively conservative Nixon administration presided over a vast expansion of federal regulation in many areas such as pensions, occupational health and safety, environmental protection, energy, and health care. Under Presidents Ford and Carter, regulation expanded in some other areas such as consumer product safety even as a regulatory reform movement prompted substantial deregulation in the surface transportation and airline industries, and the beginning of energy deregulation. The Reagan and Bush years also brought deregulation to certain policy areas—some agencies were even abolished altogether—yet at the same time Congress and the administration extended the reach of environmental controls, anti-discrimination law, air bag requirements, import restrictions, and other market restraints. Employers were also subjected to new immigration enforcement requirements, assuming a novel gatekeeping role.

During the Clinton years, new regulatory programs have been established with respect to plant closing notification, employee leaves, managed health care practices, and other areas. At the same time, however, Congress and the Federal Communications Commission have taken important steps to deregulate the immense telecommunications industry, and international trade restrictions have been relaxed. Legislation to deregulate the financial services sector has languished in Congress for almost fifteen years but is now moving toward enactment. Without waiting for this legislation, the Federal Reserve Board has administratively facilitated much deregulation of the banks under its jurisdiction, while other financial institutions have in effect dismantled many long-standing regulatory barriers through aggressive competition that pushes against (and sometimes beyond) those barriers. The merger of Citicorp and Travelers Group in April 1998 is expected to accelerate this process, presenting Congress with a *fait accompli* that it will probably have to ratify through legislation. Regulatory reform, including deregulation and privatization, has proceeded even in areas of traditional social regulation; examples include housing (through the expansion of the Section 8 "voucher" program), public education (through federal and state authorization, on a limited scale, of "charter" schools and education vouchers), and affirmative action. Another form of deregulation has occurred as federal courts have gradually lifted long-standing desegregation orders that often had tightly controlled the public school bureaucracies.

Viewed more generally, the last three decades have exhibited a number of common themes. I shall briefly mention six of them. First, an interesting and in some ways puzzling mixture of regulatory expansion, regulatory retrenchment, deregulation, procedural limits on regulation, and other kinds of regulatory reform has occurred throughout the period. In general, *economic* regulation was curtailed; a notable exception is the current movement toward new controls on service and pricing decisions of managed health care firms. In contrast, *social* regulation expanded. (Posner 1997)

Second, many states have expanded their own regulatory authority, especially in areas like health care, insurance, consumer protection, land use, and occupational licensing. This increased diversity in regulatory requirements has generated new conflicts between federal and state regulators, which the courts must resolve by applying certain ambiguous "federal preemption" principles.

Third, federal controls over the decisions of other levels of government increased dramatically during this period. Federal intergovernmental regulation imposed high costs on state and local governments, yet was of doubtful effectiveness. Public institutions generally are more difficult to regulate than private ones, and hybrid forms combining public and private organizational features create their own impediments to regulatory controls. In the 1994 unfunded mandates law, Congress tried to limit this growth of federal intergovernmental regulation, but this reform appears to have been only marginally effective.

Fourth, judicial regulation of a far-reaching but less visible, unsystematic kind has occurred. Courts have expanded common law tort liability in areas such as products liability and employment relationships. (Some observers, however, believe that this expansion may recently have slowed or ceased altogether). Courts increasingly adjudicate disputes in which, although the parties are in a direct or indirect contractual relationship with one another, the plaintiff asserts a common law tort claim as well as, or instead of, a contract claim. Courts often uphold these tort claims, which are more complex to litigate but offer plaintiffs the possibility of more open-ended damages even though the law would traditionally have confined them to a contract claim. There may even be a trend in this direction although many courts[2] and scholars sharply criticize it. Such a trend would contradict the law's traditional preference for contractual allocations of risk, at least where the court views the parties as possessing roughly comparable bargaining power. (Rubin 1993)

Fifth, deregulation, once enacted, has proved very durable; remarkably little re-regulation of previously deregulated industries has occurred. Its staying power is all the more impressive in light of the intense criticisms of deregulation in industries such as airlines, cable broadcasting, telecommunications, and financial institutions.

Finally, much of the federal regulatory reform effort since 1975 has taken the form of procedural controls on the federal regulatory process itself. (Mashaw, Merrill, & Shane, 147–60, 252–85) This development, which is probably less familiar to most regulatory reformers elsewhere, represents a pattern, perhaps distinctive to the U.S., in which reformers attempt to employ process reforms in order to achieve substantive policy ends. This approach is often perceived as more attractive politically and more comprehensive substantively. It constitutes a compromise between pro-regulation and deregulation positions; it seems less threatening to regulated interests; it operates across-the-board rather than applying only to industries; and it seeks to be prophylactic, preventing and improving regulation before it goes into effect rather than undertaking the more difficult task of reforming it after it is already in place.

Through a series of executive orders, all presidents since Gerald Ford have required regulators subject to executive branch control (as distinguished from the so-called "independent" regulatory agencies subject to more congressional control) to submit proposed regulations to various kinds of review by officials in the Executive Office of the President, principally what is now the Office of Information and Regulatory Affairs (OIRA) in the Office of Management and Budget. This review includes preparation of a regulatory calendar disclosing regulatory priorities and timetables, and submission of analyses that seek to compute and compare the private sector costs and benefits of proposed regulations and alternative approaches. Similarly, Congress has imposed a variety of statutory controls on the process of regulatory development. These are designed to force agencies to predict and evaluate impacts of proposed regulations (at least "significant" ones) on the environment (this was the first such requirement, enacted in 1969), small business, competition, paperwork reduction, and other politically popular values. In some cases, these laws require or encourage regulators to adopt the least costly or restrictive regulatory alternative—an emphatic affirmation of the traditional presumption in favor of market approaches to the solution of public policy problems. (Mashaw, Merrill, & Shane, 252–85) Two leading Washington, D.C. think tanks, the Brookings Institution and the American Enterprise Institute, recently launched a project to study the use of regulatory cost-benefit analysis and to improve its effectiveness. (Crandall et al.) Its initial reports are highly critical. (Hahn)

II. Improving the Effectiveness of Regulation

The presumption in favor of markets has foreclosed a great deal of regulation in the U.S. for which there is (always) considerable political support—and that federal, state, and local governments otherwise might been required or permitted to impose. This same pro-market presumption, of course, has driven the movements for deregulation and for privatization of activities that have been publicly administered,[3] such as prisons and education. Important as these market-oriented initiatives have been, however, they have left a vast body of economic and social regulation firmly in place. Indeed, the overall quantity of regulation in the U.S. has probably grown during this era of deregulation as a consequence of growing public concerns about the environment and public health, access to medical providers, occupational health and safety, discrimination, immigration, pensions, land use, and certain other regulated activities. Most regulatory reform is concerned with this body of existing, pending, and future regulation.

This Part discusses how regulatory reformers in the U.S. have attempted to employ legal techniques, rules, and institutions in order to improve the quality of regulation, not eliminate it. I use the question-begging word "quality" here in order to call attention to the fact that regulation, which of course assumes many different forms and operates in many different policy domains, has a number of quite discrete goals, justifications, and constraints. A given regulatory program, however, is likely to be concerned with one or a few but not all of these goals. Moreover, reforms should be tailored to the goals and characteristics of particular regulatory regimes and to the nature of the markets with which the regulations are concerned.

For these reasons, it may be useful to distinguish these goals briefly before I proceed to discuss the legal instruments used to improve regulatory quality.

Regulatory regimes, may seek to: increase the efficiency (as commonly under-stood by economists) of an externality-generating activity by ensuring that ac-tors take into consideration all relevant costs (and benefits); reduce health or other risks, regardless of externalities; control monopoly, oligopolistic, or monopsony market power or the effects of such power; protect certain firms or industries from competition; allocate resources that are thought to be too scarce and precious to be left to unregulated markets; facilitate the functioning of markets by improving information or by redressing inequalities of bargain-ing power; conscript private actors into the government's law enforcement ef-forts; prevent insolvency or increase public confidence; further substantive equality; advance other distributional goals (e.g., regionalism); allocate re-sources and authority among different levels of government; and increase public participation or procedural fairness. This long list of regulatory pur-poses, moreover, is far from complete.

In pursuit of these goals—but also in due recognition of their elusiveness—reformers have devised many specific legal strategies or techniques that are designed to improve regulatory effectiveness, which I define simply as the ability or propensity of a regulatory regime to achieve its goals, whatever those goals may be. I shall briefly discuss twelve of these strategies or tech-niques, in no particular order and without any suggestion that they constitute an exhaustive set of relation-improving approaches:

1. public remedies;
2. private litigation;
3. public advocates;
4. information disclosure;
5. improved regulatory information;
6. gatekeepers;
7. market testing;
8. antitrust law;
9. private regulation;
10. public auction of regulatory rights;
11. private trading of regulatory obligations; and
12. enhancing the credibility of regulatory commitments.

1. Public Remedies

Regulatory statutes almost invariably provide for criminal and civil penalties for regulatory violations. The agency's arsenal of sanctions, which usually re-quire the agency to obtain a court decree enforcing the administrative order, may include fines, imprisonment (for serious, intentional violations), loss of licenses and other regulatory rights, and administrative penalties. The statute may lodge the power to prosecute in the agency, the Department of Justice, or some combination, often leading to disputes about enforcement strategies and priorities. Indeed, such disputes occur even *within* a department or agency.

The argument for public remedies, of course, is that they enable the government to use public power to vindicate public rights by compelling compliance with the regulatory regime. Such remedies are especially important when the putative beneficiaries of the regulatory program are relatively powerless and when their private remedies take a form or are of such a magnitude that private contingent fee lawyers would be unlikely to undertake their representation. Public enforcement, however, is often criticized as being weak, dilatory, unimaginative, and politicized by the "capture" of the regulatory agency by the regulated industry. Hence the case for augmenting them with private remedies.

2. Private Litigation

Certain regulatory schemes are enforceable through private individuals, groups, or firms seeking money damages (compensatory and, in some cases, punitive) or some form of injunctive relief. In order to establish this remedy, the legislature must provide for the private "cause of action" in the statute or for the courts to find such a remedy by implication from the statute. After a brief period during the early 1970s when federal courts found implied causes of action in many statutes, the Supreme Court in *Cort* v. *Ash* and subsequent cases in effect imposed a presumption against implied private causes of action, leaving to Congress the policy choice of whether or not to create such a remedy. (Mashaw, Merrill, & Shane, 1113–1226; Stewart and Sunstein)

As a policy matter, the principal argument in favor of private causes of action is that they can supplement the regulatory agency's limited enforcement resources and enable the intended beneficiaries of regulation to circumvent a passive or "captured" agency and enforce regulatory obligations themselves through the courts. The principal arguments against them are that the legislature and the expert regulatory agency are in the best positions to select the optimal level and pattern of enforcement, while private enforcers pursuing their self-interest may distort these regulatory choices and priorities and actually weaken regulatory effectiveness in the process. In addition, enforcing regulation through a diverse, decentralized system of federal courts will tend to increase inconsistencies in the applicable legal rules and hence magnify regulatory uncertainty. (This objection can sometimes be met, as under the Voting Rights Act, by requiring private litigants to bring their claims in a single court in which the agency also litigates.) Private litigation through the courts may also alter the balance of constitutionally separated powers among the three branches of its development of regulatory principles.

3. Public Advocates

Some jurisdictions create offices of public counsel, ombudsmen, or public advocates in an effort to magnify the voices of interests that would not otherwise be adequately represented, perhaps because of organizational costs, free rider problems, and other reasons well discussed in the literature on public choice. The statutory powers of these advocates vary considerably, as do the definitions of the interests that they are supposed to represent. Some of these agencies are limited to processing citizen complaints, while others are authorized to conduct investigations, obtain information from agencies, testify at legislative and administrative hearings, participate as a party in regulatory proceedings, seek judicial review of agency decisions, and have an opportunity to review regulatory actions before they become final. Most are required to represent the "public interest," citizens, ratepayers, or consumers generally. I am unaware of any rigorous evaluation of the effect of public advocacy organizations on regulatory outcomes, although there are certainly anecdotal reports testifying to their occasional influence.

4. Information Disclosure

Increasingly, regulatory reformers turn to information disclosure as a remedy for consumer ignorance. This, they hope, will reduce search costs by facilitating comparisons among competing products and services and maximizing consumer choice. Proponents view this technique as a means of improving the functioning of consumer markets, perhaps reducing or eliminating the need for command-and-control regulation, which is widely recognized as inefficient and ineffective.

Disclosure has been a core strategy of securities regulation since 1933. In recent years, however, reformers have extended it to many other policy areas. Examples include information about the rates and performance of health care providers, lawyers and other professionals; consumer loan interest rates; insurance premiums; auto leasing terms; brokerage rates; auto fuel efficiency; toxic chemicals; home purchase settlement charges; and unit prices in grocery stores. With the advent of the Internet and other low-cost technologies that facilitate the aggregation, dissemination, and analysis of information, reformers have advanced proposals to adopt new disclosure requirements and to refine old ones. Some important examples include political campaign contributions and auto dealers' costs and sale prices. More conventional information disclosure requirements such as pharmaceutical drug labeling and warning labels on cigarettes, alcohol, and other consumer products have generated an enormous volume of product liability litigation. Judicially-imposed disclosures by health care providers have created a common law right of informed consent that sometimes augments patients' medical malpractice claims. (Schuck 1994)

5. Improved Regulatory Information

In a variety of ways, regulators constantly seek to enhance the quality and quantity of the information that they need to identify and define regulatory problems, lay out alternative approaches, prescribe specific solutions, and monitor outcomes. Efforts to increase public participation, which take many different forms, are intended in part to increase and diversify the flow of information, values, and perspectives to the regulators.

Perhaps the most systematic information-improving technique favored by many regulatory reformers, especially economists, is cost-benefit (or its less demanding cognate, cost-effectiveness analysis), discussed above. (Crandall et al.) However, many consumer, environmental, and other interest groups bitterly oppose it on a number of methodological and other grounds, particularly as a criterion for health and safety regulation.

Many (though certainly not all) objections to cost-benefit analysis might be met by introducing more realistic assumptions about the cognitive capacities and behavioral patterns of individuals facing uncertain choices involving remote risks. A number of American economists and legal scholars are engaged in a broad-ranging effort to refine the conventional law and economics analysis by drawing on experimental and other empirical evidence about the ways in which ordinary people actually make decisions under conditions of uncertainty. This approach, known as behavioral law and economics, brings to the traditional analysis important conceptual modifications such as bounded rationality, bounded willpower, and bounded self-interest. (Jolls, Sunstein, & Thaler) Although this more behavioral approach is quite promising, these fresh concepts inevitably complicate regulatory policymaking by calling on regulators to consider new indeterminacies (e.g., where these boundaries lie) and make new tradeoffs (e.g., between individual irrationality and governmental irrationality). Thus, it remains to be seen whether behavioral law and economies will yield significant regulatory policy payoffs that exceed those produced by the more conventional analysis.

6. Private Gatekeepers

In many markets, government regulators find it prohibitively costly to effectively monitor the behavior of sellers and detect their fraudulent transactions and other legal violations. This may be because the market is highly fragmented (as with sellers of securities) or complex (as with business transactions). In such markets, however, it is sometimes possible for regulators to conscript private professionals, on whom the sellers must rely as "gatekeepers" to the market, into serving as vigilant watchdogs over their clients by requiring them—at risk to their own professional reputations and legal status—to vouch publicly for their clients' honesty and for the accuracy of the information that the clients provide to potential buyers and to regulators. The most common examples of such gatekeepers are accountants who must certify the accuracy of tax returns, accounts and disclosures; lawyers who must provide opinion letters about the legality of transactions; and employers, who must screen potential workers for immigration violations. This gatekeeping greatly economizes on the government's own monitoring and enforcement costs but does so by shifting them to private actors and altering their incentives. (Kraakman)

7. Market Testing

Regulators can also economize on monitoring and enforcement costs by using private individuals or organizations to test the market for possible legal violations. The testers, by representing (actually, *mis*representing) themselves as genuine buyers, can hope to elicit from the sellers their true market behaviors, thereby producing information that regulators can then employ to detect and prosecute those behaviors. This technique, which operates as a kind of random audit, is often used to detect racial or other discrimination in housing, employment, and other consumer markets, and it could readily be extended to others. (Turner, Fix, and Struyk)

8. Antitrust

When firms possess excessive market power, antitrust regulation enables both the government and private competitors to challenge the practices that produce or sustain it. This is done through regulatory promulgation of antitrust guidelines and rules, by regulatory prosecution of criminal or civil violations in administrative or judicial fora, and by private litigation by competitors or others who can demonstrate economic loss as a result of the firm's market power. In recent years, economists have expressed growing skepticism about the theoretical soundness and practical effectiveness of antitrust law, especially in light of the globalization of markets. Many antitrust regulators have come to share that skepticism, limiting their enforcement largely to horizontal mergers and other clearly anti-competitive behavior. The current controversy over the wisdom of the antitrust claims brought against Microsoft by federal and state prosecutors partly reflects this theoretical impasse, especially as it applies to new telecommunications technologies. (Jost)

9. Private Regulation

Government regulators often rely on private entities to exercise some of the functions that public regulation would otherwise have to perform. The U.S. Consumer Product Safety Commission, for example, looks to private, non-profit testing and certification organizations like the American National Standards Institute, the American Society for Testing and Materials, and the National Fire Protection Association to set and (to a limited extent) enforce minimum standards of safety and effectiveness for particular industries and product lines. The National Highway Traffic and Safety Administration sometimes adopts as its own regulatory standards those promulgated by private automotive engineering groups. Building codes frequently incorporate the standards established by private electrical, construction, and other groups whose members are then subject to those standards. Public regulation of hospitals and educational institutions often incorporates the standards of private accreditations groups. The legal authority to make and enforce ethical rules and standards relating to certain other practices of the legal, medical, and other professions is often delegated to professional organizations which then "self-regulate" their members. In the early years of the Occupational Safety and Healthy Administration, most of the agency's important safety standards simply adopted those of the private standard-setting organizations. (Hamilton) The National Association of Securities Dealers (NASD) and the various stock exchanges also combine public regulation and substantial delegation of regulatory authority to private groups. (Banner)

This pervasive system of private self-regulation is subject to obvious risks of conflict of interest and other abuses, and it is often criticized for pursuing the regulated industry's interests at the expense of the public interest—particularly lax standards, self-dealing, and toothless enforcement. Nevertheless, it is widely used, as it serves a number of important public purposes. It mollifies opposition to regulation by co-opting the regulated industry into the regulatory scheme. It draws on technical expertise and regulatory experience that the government cannot readily duplicate. And it reduces the time and public cost entailed in developing and issuing regulations.

10. Public Auction of Regulatory Rights

Traditionally, governments have distributed valuable regulatory rights, such as licenses and exclusive franchises, at no cost to the rights holder (other than the costs of the application process, which can be high). Some reformers have long criticized this allocation system as economically inefficient, distributively unfair, and politically corrupt. The successful applicant receives a windfall—say, an operating license for a television station—of potentially enormous value, while the public fisc receives nothing in exchange for relinquishing it. Applicants have a strong incentive to exercise their political influence, perhaps in improper ways, in order to obtain the valuable right; those without such influence are seriously, perhaps fatally, disadvantaged. The administrative process (especially if the application is contested) can be very costly; it may be protracted and involve substantial expenditures for legal, accounting, consulting, and other services. When an applicant finally wins, its incentive to fulfill the conditions of licensure are reduced because it will enjoy a strong presumption of renewal as a legal or practical matter; renewal will be denied only if the incumbent's performance is unusually poor. An additional defect of the system is that the absence of a market price conceals the right's true value.

For all these reasons, governments in the U.S. have begun to experiment with auctions of some of these regulatory rights, especially in the areas of federally-regulated telecommunications and environmental pollution. Thus, the Federal Communications Commission has auctioned off a number of broadcasting operating rights, often raising substantial revenue in the process. A number of difficulties have arisen in connection with the design and administration of these auctions, such as ensuring that there are enough bidders and that the bidders can actually come up with the cash if they are successful. (Ayres and Cramton) The U.S. Environmental Protection Agency (EPA) has been auctioning off emission rights under the Clean Air Act for almost a decade. And on April 1, 1998, California became the first state to permit the auctioning off of electricity as part of its novel program of deregulation of electric utilities, and some 16 other states plan to follow California's lead. (Salpukas) The auction approach has also been proposed for more exotic policy areas, even including the allocation of human organs and immigrant visas.

11. Private Trading of Regulatory Obligations

Once regulators determine what the regulatory rights and duties are and initially distribute them, they can authorize the rights-holders and duty-bearers to engage in market transactions, subject to more or less constraining regulatory trading rules. The most important policy area in which this approach has been employed is with respect to the trading of emission rights initially distributed to polluters by the EPA under the Clean Air Act. While the market for emission rights has sometimes been thin, there is widespread agreement that the auction approach has been highly effective in reducing the costs of achieving a given level of emission reduction. Given this success, reformers are now proposing to permit such trading in other regulatory areas. The author, for example, has proposed a system for the trading of refugee protection burdens among nations under international rules and supervision. (Schuck 1998, chapter 13)

12. Credible Regulatory Commitments

As noted earlier, a central criticism of the regulatory state is the unpredictability of its decisions and the uncertainty costs that this generates. Regulatory unpredictability, which is common if not ubiquitous in the U.S., probably reflects a number of different factors: the dynamic political environment in which agencies operate; the rapid turnover of their appointed leadership; the fast-changing markets and technologies that they attempt to regulate; the relatively poor quality and provisional character of the information on which regulators must base their decisions; and the multiple, indeterminate, and conflicting nature of most agency's policy goals.

Regulatory uncertainty is especially pernicious in those policy areas in which the agency seeks to encourage the regulated entities to make large, long-term investments in technology, expansion, or infrastructure or other capital assets. (For example, this problem arises with antitrust policies whose twists, turns, and ambiguities have made it difficult for firms to know whether they can adopt certain practices or make certain decisions—often in situations in which delay is very costly). Unless the agency can make credible, durable, and enforceable commitments to adhere to a consistent regulatory policy, however, the entities will try to avoid such investments or will adopt costly strategies for minimizing the regulatory risks associated with uncertainty. For this reason, some reformers emphasize the need for regulators to employ techniques that clearly signal their policy commitments and make deviations from those commitments costly to the agency in political, fiscal, or other terms. Such techniques might include the agency entering into enforceable, long-term contracts with regulated entities; giving fiscal or policy "hostages" to those entities which can only be released if the agency hews to a specified course; developing regulatory policy through rulemaking rather than through case-by-case adjudication; adopting bright-line rules rather than ambiguous standards; announcing policy commitments or fiscal investments that would be politically risky for the agency to reverse; and the like.

An inevitable feature of this approach, of course, is that it limits the agency's future flexibility—indeed, this is its very objective—and it risks locking the agency into a policy that may prove to be misguided either at its inception or as a result of changing circumstances. A prudent agency will therefore search for the optimal balance between regulatory flexibility and predictability, which is difficult because that balance point will itself change as regulatory conditions, needs, and information change.

III. Extra-Regulatory Institutions and Processes

I have been describing a complex system of political economy in the U.S., one that privileges markets both legally and culturally but that also integrates these markets in a multitude of ways with administrative regulation (and private self-regulation) in different combinations and to varying degrees in diverse policy domains. What remains to be discussed, then, are the panoply of other, extra-regulatory institutions and processes that monitor, augment, and discipline this hybrid system.

In the remainder of this chapter, I consider five of the most important of these extra-regulatory institutions and processes: (1) legislative oversight; (2) an independent judiciary; (3) administrative law, including rulemaking, adjudication, and "regulatory equity"; (4) interest group competition; and (5) adversarial media. It is important here to repeat a point made at the outset: all of these institutions and processes were only established and strengthened over a long period of time and after incessant political struggle. None of them has yet fully realized the goals and ideals that have been ascribed to them.

1. Legislative Oversight

Of all the world's parliaments, the U.S. Congress is almost certainly the most powerful. Its power is constitutionally based to some extent but is also a product of other factors: long political tradition, the American party system, a history of strong, skillful, and entrepreneurial parliamentary leaders, and the American public's deeply-ingrained suspicion of concentrated authority, especially when excercised by bureaucrats.

This congressional power is manifested not only through its enactment of authorizing and appropriations legislation but also through the energetic exercise of its power to investigate, monitor, oversee, and influence the views of the key officials in the agencies and other executive branch organs. It is a striking fact that the level of congressional oversight activity appears to have kept up with the rising level of federal regulation. (Strauss, 969) One might imagine that congressional investigations of the executive branch would be more frequent and intense during the periods of divided government when different parties control the White House and Congress. A study by David Mayhew, however, demonstrates that this is not ordinarily true; the level of investigatory activity is unrelated to whether there is divided government.

In part, this may be because Congress has institutionalized the oversight process. The General Accounting Office, acting at the request of members, conducts and publishes numerous studies of agency policies, practices, and performance. The GAO, which also performs financial auditing of agencies for Congress, generally enjoys a reputation for nonpartisanship and in recent years has become one of the most powerful organizations in the federal government; Congress, interest groups, scholars, and the media avidly read its reports. In addition, Congress has established in each of the major agencies an "office of the inspector general" with considerable independence from the agency head and with a duty to inform Congress of most of its investigative findings.

Congress also conducts oversight by influencing agency leadership through its power to confirm most presidential appointees and through its staff's frequent informal interactions with agency officials. It has the right to demand from the executive branch whatever unprivileged information it wants in whatever form it wants, and it can enforce this right by enforcing subpoenas, threatening officials with contempt citations, and withholding funds or legal authority from the agency. Congress's influence, of course, is so notorious that disputes seldom reach that point. In almost all cases, the agency capitulates to the congressional committee or negotiates a compromise with it. (Aberbach) By enacting the Small Business Regulatory

Enforcement Fairness Act of 1996, which requires agencies to lay every new rule before Congress for a period of time for possible disapproval before it takes effect, Congress has forged a new and particularly far-reaching instrument of oversight, one whose significance will be measured not by the number of rules disapproved but by the informal influence over rules that it will afford to congressional committees and staff.

Congress often uses its oversight power over agencies to exert indirect influence over private actors—even (or perhaps especially) after privatization or deregulation when the government is eager to demonstrate that relinquishing its ownership or regulatory control will not harm the public. This indirect influence may occur when a congressional committee seeks to shape an agency's enforcement agenda by pressing it to prosecute (or refrain from prosecuting) a private individual or firm neither owned nor regulated by the government. Recently, for example, Congress was angered by persistent increases in the fares charged by deregulated airlines and urged antitrust and transportation officials to investigate these practices and also prosecute any anti-competitive conduct. Another example is the congressional investigation of the tobacco industry, whose products are sold in private, largely unregulated markets. This investigation, along with a negotiated settlement between the industry and plaintiffs' lawyers, produced pending legislative proposals to regulate its advertising, sales practices, and exposure to litigation.

2. Independent Judiciary

No single institution is more central to the rule of law and to the efficient functioning of markets than an independent judiciary, one in which judges purport to decide disputes on the basis of legal principles rather than narrow partisan or political considerations. Judges' decisions are usually more constrained by principles, precedents, and traditions than are the decisions of legislators and bureaucrats, which tend to be more discretionary, open-ended, and hence unpredictable. It is especially vital that the public *thinks* that judges are independent, as this enhances the legitimacy of, and habitual compliance with, their decisions. Independence, of course, is not an objective fact but is a continuous variable that can be measured along a number of different dimensions. For federal judges, it is encouraged by a constitutional guarantee of lifetime tenure during good behavior and undiminished salary. Perhaps more important, it is also the way in which almost all American judges, even elected ones, think of themselves and their role.

Judicial independence serves the interests not only of judges and of litigants who seek impartial treatment, but also of legislators, bureaucrats and special interest groups. This may seem somewhat paradoxical; after all, courts exercising judicial review often frustrate legislators' desires by in effect rewriting or invalidating legislation on constitutional and statutory grounds. They can also alter bureaucratic rules. In principle, however, independent judges act as the politicians' agents, monitoring for compliance with constitutional, legislative, and bureaucratic norms. By enabling politicians and bureaucrats to make binding, durable agreements, courts help them to bargain cheaply and effectively, which is of course crucial to a fluid, consensual policymaking process. Indeed, public choice theorists like Richard Posner (now a distinguished judge himself) argue that by creating and maintaining an independent judiciary, lawmakers serve their own political interests by ensuring that their promises will be kept and their bargains enforced. "A judiciary that was subservient to the current membership of the legislature," Posner writes, "could effectively nullify, by interpretation, legislation enacted in a previous session of the legislature. Judges are less likely to do this if the terms of judicial tenure make them independent of the wishes of current legislators." (Posner 1992, 533)

Independence in judges, however, does carry some costs to policymakers. Lacking direct accountability to the public, independent judges are more likely to make, find, and interpret law according to their own political preferences—a common complaint in the U.S. If their rulings rest on constitutional grounds, the legislature cannot reverse them without amending the Constitution, but even their statutory rulings, which the legislature can and often does reverse (Eskridge), enjoy the status quo-reinforcing advantage of the political inertia created by those rulings.

3. Administrative Law

Assuming that privatized firms and entities remain subject to regulation, the system of administrative law, applied by agencies and enforced by reviewing courts, is a central lever for controlling both bureaucratic discretion and private compliance in accordance with the rule of law. The vast, complex body of American administrative law is largely based on the federal Administrative Procedure Act (APA), augmented by constitutional principles of due process. Although the daily work of regulation is dominated by informal activity and constant give-and-take between regulator and regulated, the APA is primarily concerned with the more formal decisionmaking processes through which agencies develop most of their regulatory policies. (Mashaw, Merrill, & Shane)

Three of these processes are especially important: adjudication, rulemaking, and "regulatory equity." Agency adjudication is modeled on the judicial process. It consists of an adversary hearing presided over by an administrative law judge, and it employs trial-type evidentiary and procedural rules, albeit often in somewhat looser forms. All agency enforcement proceedings initially takes this form, as do most other formal agency actions that decide the rights or duties of particular entities. Parties to agency adjudications enjoy the right to invoke judicial review and the standard and scope of that review are usually quite broad: *de novo* review with respect to issues of law, and "substantial evidence" review of the record as a whole with respect to issues of fact. In agency adjudication, the agency proceeds on a case-by-case basis that is similar in some ways to common law adjudication, and like a court it is generally, but not wholly, bound in principle by its own precedents. Because adjudication has proved to be a relatively slow, costly, narrow, often unrepresentative, and inflexible process for developing regulatory policy, agencies often prefer to proceed through rulemaking.

Indeed, one of the major thrusts of regulatory reformers during the 1960s and 1970s was to encourage or even require agencies to develop more of their policies through rulemaking rather than through the case-by-case adjudication that most of them were predominantly using. Reformers emphasized that rulemaking has many advantages as a policymaking instrument. It would be quicker, cheaper, more expert, more participatory, more visible and legally transparent, better informed, less "lawyerized" and "judicialized," and more oriented to the pursuit of broad policy considerations. Modeled on the legislative process, the most important form of agency rulemaking is called "informal" rulemaking, which is directed at the development of rules of general applicability. ("Formal" rulemaking, which is more adjudicative in character, is primarily reserved for ratemaking).

An agency usually initiates informal rulemaking by publishing a notice of proposed rulemaking that briefly summarizes the nature and purpose of the rules that the agency intends to promulgate, sets forth the text of the proposed rule, and invites the public to submit detailed written comments on it. Sometimes, the agency will also convene a legislative-type hearing in which members of the public may appear to testify as live witnesses but usually without cross-examination. The agency, having considered these public reactions, may modify its proposed rule and invite another round of public comments before publishing its final rule. Interested parties who are dissatisfied with the final rule may invoke judicial review, usually before it goes into effect or can be enforced against anyone. As the legislation analogy implies, the reviewing court's standard of review of the agency's rule is usually more deferential than in adjudication. The rule presumably is a product of the agency's expertise, and assuming that the rule is not legally defective, the court will ordinarily uphold it unless its policy is found to be "arbitrary and capricious."

Despite the greater deference that reviewing courts are supposed to pay to rules that agencies develop through informal rulemaking, some courts have been so exacting that the agencies have found even rulemaking to be too slow, costly, vulnerable to judicial second-guessing, and otherwise burdensome for effective policymaking. As a result, they have often turned to other, more informal processes or even returned to case-by-case adjudication. Unfortunately, however, these alternative processes lack many of the virtues of rulemaking and entail many problems of their own. (Mashaw and Harfst)

What is desired, of course, is an approach to policymaking that draws on the strengths of both rules and adjudication while avoiding their limitations.[4] At least since Aristotle defined the features of different conceptions of justice, decisionmakers have understood that general rules and individual case-by-case adjudications possess competing advantages and disadvantages as instruments for achieving justice. To vastly oversimplify, rules are more hard-edged and clear-cut, they usually provide more advance notice, guidance, and certainty to both those who are subject to them and those who must apply them in specific cases. Depending on their generality, rules also tend to resolve more cases than adjudication does; hence, they can be an efficient way to order behavior. On the other hand, rules suffer from limitations of form, knowledge, comprehensiveness, and articulation. In contrast, adjudication tends to be more contextual and highly fact-sensitive, allowing the official to tailor decisions to the special circumstances of particular cases. By doing so, however, they provide less guidance for the generality of cases than rules do.

In Anglo-American law, the separation of the highly distinctive courts and doctrines of "law" and "equity" was designed precisely to capture these two competing conceptions of justice. The separate systems of law and equity evinced a recognition not only that each possesses virtues that the other lacks but also that attempting to combine these different conceptions in one system could end up undermining both of them. Nevertheless, the ideal policymaking system would be one that somehow managed to provide clear and coherent direction in the generality of cases while also remaining responsive to the unique and compelling equities of individual situations.

In chapter 5, I called this the ideal of "regulatory equity" and analyzed its nature, the various forms through which it can be pursued, its institutionalization in a particular federal agency, and its relationship to four cognate techniques—discretion, judicial equity, agency adjudication, and an exceptions process—that are designed to make rule-based systems fairer by increasing their responsiveness to special circumstances.

•   •   •

4. Interest Group Competition

Regulation in a post-privatization environment entails a complex system of competition among special interest groups, including government bureaucracies, regulated firms, industry associations, suppliers, employee groups, consumer organizations, and specialized media. To what extent does this group competition produce policy outcomes that are in the public interest?

Beginning with James Madison's justly famous Federalist #10, mainstream democratic theory has vilified special interest groups. The usual critiques emphasize their narrowness of motive and vision, their unfair advantages in the political process, and their promotion of inefficient and inequitable public policies. In chapter 7, I argue that as applied to the U.S. this negative assessment is false, or at least dangerously incomplete and that special interest groups perform vital functions in the American polity.

5. *Adversarial Media*

The role and public responsibilities of the media are heightened in a post-privatization world. In the U.S., at least, the media enjoy very broad access to public records, proceedings, meetings, and decisions as a matter of both legal right (for example, under the First Amendment, the Freedom of Information Act, the Government in the Sunshine Act, the Federal Advisory Committee Act, and state law counterparts) and political cultural tradition. But media access to the transactions of private individuals or groups largely depends on the private parties' willingness to relinquish their privacy and agree to media scrutiny. As previously public functions are increasingly performed by private entities, this scrutiny will become essential to public understanding and assessment of those privatized activities, and indeed, to the very legitimacy of the privatization project itself.

Although Americans often denounce the media for assuming what appears to be an adversarial stance toward the public and private institutions on which they are reporting, such a stance on balance serves the public well. The desire of powerful decisionmakers and institutions to avoid public monitoring and criticism of their activities is probably universal. Only an aggressive media that is independent and by nature suspicious of powerholders can possess both the incentives and the skills to penetrate the shell of privacy and ferret out the information that the public needs to determine where their interests lie. The fact that the media are themselves powerful institutions which prefer secrecy to public exposure simply underscores the importance of the ancient question, "who will watch the watchmen?"

To effectively discharge their public duty, the media must be fiercely independent not only of the government but of the private power centers that they must scrutinize. Industry publications are often dependent on the firms they cover for advertising, subscriptions, patronage, and news; hence they may not be as aggressive as their public responsibilities demand. In a privatized environment, some other means must be devised to develop independent monitors of private activities about which the public needs to be informed. Legal rights of access to those activities are essential but those rights are meaningless without the institutionalization of the monitoring and reporting functions.

Conclusion

Based on the American experience, a democratically accountable, legally controlled regulatory regime in a post-privatization environment will require a private law that scrupulously defines and enforces property rights. It will also require a public law that creates the appropriate mix of market and regulatory solutions to social problems. Where the government chooses a regulatory solution, it must devise regulatory mechanisms and procedures that are fair, efficient, participatory, and subject to the rule of law. This means both establishing political and legal institutions, such as legislative oversight, an independent judiciary, and a body of administrative law, that can monitor and discipline the regulators. It also means protecting social institutions, such as private interest groups and an adversarial media, that can supply regulators with the social intelligence and political legitimacy that they will need for effective regulation.

Notes

1. For a recent journalistic account of the problems of a privatized electric utility industry in Brazil, see Moffett.

2. These claims typically involve economic loss (lost profits) suffered by the plaintiff as a result of an injury inflicted by a third party (usually the defendant in these cases) on someone with whom the plaintiff has a contractual relationship. A classic example was the *Robins Dry Dock* case, decided by Justice Oliver Wendell Holmes in 1927, in which the defendant dry dock negligently damaged a vessel owned by a company that had chartered (leased) the vessel to the plaintiff, causing the plaintiff to lose the economic value of the vessel during the period of its repair. The Court denied the plaintiff's tort claim against the defendant, leaving the plaintiff to pursue a contract remedy against the charterer (or perhaps a contract claim against the dry dock under a "third party beneficiary" theory). Another recent example is *East River Steamship*, a 1986 Supreme Court decision in which the plaintiff had chartered a ship whose defective turbine caused it economic loss. The plaintiff then sued the defendant manufacturer in tort under a products liability theory. The Court barred the tort claim because the plaintiff had a contract with the manufacturer. Contract, the Court reasoned, was a better legal regime than tort for allocating such commercial risks because in contract, "the parties may set the terms of their own agreements."

3. Privatization in the U.S. has proceeded in many different areas of public activity, often in a piecemeal or experimental fashion. For a recent journalistic review of these efforts, see Wessel and Harwood, which discusses the privatization of uranium production, health care, airports, foster care placement, prisons, highways, schools, fire departments, sanitation and janitorial services, social services, welfare eligibility screening, and even a government personnel recruitment agency purchased and privatized by its former employees.

4. The remainder of this section draws heavily on Chapter 5.

5. The remainder of this section draws heavily on Chapter 7.

References

Aberbach, Joel. 1990. *Keeping A Watchful Eye: The Politics of Congressional Oversight.* Washington, D.C.: Brookings Institution.

Ayres, Ian, and Cramton, Peter. 1996. "Pursuing Deficit Reduction Through Diversity: How Affirmative Action at the FCC Increased Auction Competition," *Stanford Law Review* 48: 761

Banner, Stuart. 1998. "The Origin of the New York Stock Exchange, 1791–1860," *Journal of Legal Studies* 27:113.

Crandall, Robert W., DeMuth, Christopher, Hahn, Robert W., Litan, Robert E., Nivola, Pietro S., Portney, Paul R. 1997. *An Agenda for Federal Regulatory Reform*. Washington, D.C.: American Enterprise Institute for Public Policy Research and The Brookings Institution

Eskridge, William N. 1991. "Overriding Supreme Court Statutory Interpretation Decisions," *Yale Law Journal* 101:331.

Hahn, Robert W. "Regulatory Reform: Assessing the Government's Numbers," Working Paper 99-6, July 1999.

Hamilton, Robert W. 1978. "The Role of Nongovernmental Standards in the Development of Mandatory Federal Standards Affecting Safety or Health," *Texas Law Review* 56: 1329.

Hansmann, Henry B. 1980. "The Role of Nonprofit Enterprise," *Yale Law Journal* 89: 835

Jolls, Christine, Sunstein, Cass R., and Thaler, Richard. 1998. "A Behavioral Approach to Law and Economics," *Stanford Law Journal* 50: 1471.

Jost, Kenneth. 1998. "The Microsoft Antitrust Case," *CQResearcher,* June

Kraakman, Reinier H. 1984. "Corporate Liability Strategies and the Legal Controls," *Yale Law Journal* 93: 857

Mashaw, Jerry L. and Harfst, David L. 1990. *The Struggle for Auto Safety*. Cambridge, Mass: Harvard University Press.

Mashaw, Jerry L., Merrill, Richard A., and Shane, Peter M. 1998. *Administrative Law: the American Public Law System*, 4th ed. St. Paul, Minnesota: West Group.

Melnick, R. Shep. 1994. *Between the Lines: Interpreting Welfare Rights*. Washington, D.C.: Brookings Institution.

Moffett, Mark. 1998. "Sour Juice," *Wall Street Journal*, April 27 at A1

Posner, Richard A.

_____1997: "The Rise and Fall of Administrative Law," *Chicago-Kent Law Review* 72: 953

_____1992: *An Economic Analysis of Law*, 4th ed. Boston, Mass: Little, Brown & Co.

Rubin, Paul H. 1993. *Tort Reform by Contract*. Washington, D.C.: AEI Press, 1993

Salpukas, Agis. 1998. "Deregulation of Utilities in California," *New York Times*, April 2, at D4

Schuck, Peter H.

_____1998: *Citizens, Strangers, and In-Betweens: Essays on Immigration and Citizenship.* Boulder, Colo: Westview Press

_____1997: "Against (and For) Madison: An Essay in Praise of Factions," *Yale Law and Policy Review* 15: 553

_____1994: "Rethinking Informed Consent," *Yale Law Journal* 103:899

_____1984: "When the Exception Becomes the Rule: Regulatory Equity and the Formulation of Energy Policy Through An Exceptions Process," *Duke Law Journal* 1984: 163

Stewart, Richard B., and Sunstein, Cass R. 1982 "Public Programs and Private Rights," *Harvard Law Review* 95: 1195.

Strauss, Peter L. 1997. "Presidential Rulemaking," *Chicago-Kent Law Review* 72: 965.

Turner, Margery A., Fix, Michael, and Struyk, Raymond J., 1991 *Opportunities Denied, Opportunities Diminished: Racial Discrimination in Hiring*. Washington, D.C.: Urban Institute Press.

Wessel, David, and Harwood, John. 1998. "Selling Entire Stock!" *Wall Street Journal*, May 14, at A1,

7

Against (and for) Madison

An Essay in Praise of Factions

In James Madison's seminal *Federalist #10*, he famously warned against faction, which he regarded as the greatest scourge of democratic government.[1] Two centuries later, the terminology is different but its normative resonance remains the same. Rather than employ the now-quaint word "faction," modern commentators are more likely to speak of special interests, vested interests, lobbies, pressure groups, and (in certain cases and with particular scorn) single-issue groups. In the spirit of Madison, however, these commentators almost always use these newer terms as pejoratives, hurling them as political epithets so as to discredit them in the public eye.[2] The thundering jeremiad against special interests (as I shall usually call them here) is among the oldest, most common, and most successful techniques in the long history of democratic political rhetoric. Its practitioners remain in full throat today.

But there is an apparent paradox here: The American polity protects special interests as assiduously as it denounces them. The same politician-philosopher who excoriated special interests fathered a constitution that effectively fortifies such groups against their opponents' legal efforts to destroy or disable them. The coexistence of these opposing tendencies of American democracy—the relentless criticism of special interests and the law's remarkable solicitude for them—constitutes one of our system's most striking features. The strength of each tendency—and the fundamental, abiding tension between them—betrays something more than mere ambivalence or confusion, and something less than the pathology of collective schizophrenia. By compartmentalizing our attitudes toward special interests, we have managed to avoid confronting our analytical inconsistencies.

An analogy may help to underscore the point. Suppose that the nation's most distinguished physicians identified a disease so insidious that it posed a continuing threat to the health and lives of all Americans, a threat vigorously denounced at every opportunity by virtually everyone. Suppose further that the physicians thought that they knew how to cure or control this disease—albeit with some possible side effects. In these circumstances, would it not seem exceedingly odd if the nation's leaders not only failed to suppress this disease but actually bound themselves as a matter of constitutional law not to do so in the future?

This Essay seeks to resolve this apparent paradox. In Part I, after disposing of some definitional issues, I describe both the robust constitutional protection that special interests enjoy and the equally vigorous vilification to which the American public has always subjected them. Part II discusses the principal theoretical and empirical claims advanced by the critics of special interests. Part III, the core of the Essay, is a strong but qualified defense of special interests. I conclude in Part IV with a discussion of various reforms that bear on the nature and role of special interests in the political process.

I argue that although special interests pose certain risks for the health of American society,[3] they have actually caused few serious structural problems in recent years.[4] Moreover, they have caused even fewer ills that policy changes are likely to remedy. The provision of strong protection for a strongly reviled system of special interest politics thus appears to be less a paradox than an example, familiar in our system, of a sound political and constitutional commitment to take some risks and to bear some costs in return for larger social benefits. As I shall explain, the pluralist gamble has paid off handsomely. Nevertheless, some changes might improve the system and are worth considering. Overall, however, there is simply no realistic, attractive alternative to special interest groups in a liberal democracy. This reality would remain even if constitutional rights of association and advocacy did not mandate protection for the pluralist system.

I shall make four central claims of my own in the course of this Essay. Two of them are normative. The first is that the central element of Madison's understanding of factions—his objective conception of the public interest—is no longer either plausible or attractive, if it ever was. The second claim is that in the contemporary American polity even the most convincing element of the Madisonian critique—the view that special interests are animated by narrow and selfish motives—does not justify Madison's strong indictment. My third claim is empirical. I argue that the principal weakness of Madison's normative argument, which leading public choice theorists also advance today,[5] is the premise that special interests tend to destroy individual liberty, social welfare, and political health.[6] The dynamic conditions of modern American politics, I maintain, refute this notion. My final claim is prescriptive. Having reaffirmed Madison's most creative and important idea—that only a diverse, competitive, and vibrant civil society can remedy the dangers posed by special interests—I go on to argue that the government's role in nourishing and diversifying the pluralist system ought to be decidedly limited. The government's principal goal, rather, should be to ensure that citizens are educated well enough to discern their own and the community's interests and to make informed, independent choices about the merits of possible public actions.

I. Constitutional Protection and Ideological Demonization

A. *Defining Special Interest*

Madison defined a faction as "a number of citizens, whether amounting to a majority or minority of the whole, who are united and actuated by some common impulse of passion, or of interest, adverse to the rights of other citizens, or to the permanent and aggregate interests of the community."[7] The most striking element of this definition is the proposition that a majority of the citizenry might constitute a faction, with all of a faction's attendant political vices. Madison asserts the objectivity of the public interest ("the permanent and aggregate interests of the community")—a conception that stands above and apart from any special interest or from any combination of such interests—including those of a majority.[8] Such a transcendent conception, of course, was hardly Madison's invention. In one form or another, it had constituted a convention of most political philosophy stretching back through the writings of Rousseau,[9] Aquinas,[10] Aristotle,[11] and Plato.[12] In advancing his conception of the public interest, however, Madison did not adopt the Rousseauian view that this public interest could be discerned simply through the deliberative processes of a small, decentralized, homogeneous, noncommercial republic. Rather, he sought to find a middle ground between the objective conception of the idealists and the more proceduralist conception of the pluralists. He did so through a vision of representation in which, as Cass Sunstein has put it, "legislators were neither to respond blindly to constituent pressures nor to undertake their deliberations in a vacuum."[13] In this view, representation would elevate government above private interests but also keep it accountable to those interests.

Indeed, one of the most significant innovations of liberal political theory, especially of the American variety, is its challenge to the Madisonian conception of the public interest.[14] Much of modern liberalism has repudiated this conception in favor of one defined in terms of process values and political participation through group activity.[15] This procedural notion of the public interest is the dominant one today, essentially accepted even by progressives and social democrats on the left and by market and libertarian conservatives on the right. Commentators of all ideological stripes, of course, criticize the ways in which this model actually operates. They argue, for example, that the process-oriented model systematically favors certain interests and values over others, and that it often produces deplorable policies.[16] Many of these critics, moreover, go beyond simply denouncing particular process failures and outcomes; many invoke a vision of the public interest that purports to transcend such particulars. But these invocations are probably best understood as gambits in a larger rhetorical strategy that is conducted well within the premises of the pluralist system.

To understand the role of special interest groups in the American polity today, then, we must define faction in a way that does not depend—as Madison's definition manifestly does—on a transcendent conception of the public interest that no longer elicits strong defense or justification, even from those who most vehemently condemn pluralism's processes and policies. All definitions of "special" interests can be criticized for being under-inclusive, over-inclusive, arbitrary, or subjective. To characterize any interest as "general," to assert that its goals correspond with those of the community at large, is not simply a presumptuous claim but also inevitably a form of approbation. To characterize an interest as "special," in contrast, is to ascribe to it a partial, parochial, or narrowly self-interested quality; in common parlance this label is almost always deprecatory. If a definition of special interest is to facilitate any useful analytical work, it must be broad enough to include all of those groups that contend for public policy influence and elicit significant opposition. Any such definition will be broad indeed.

Political scientist Paul Peterson has employed a definition of special interest that is probably as serviceable as any. An interest is special, according to Peterson, "if it consists of or is represented by a fairly small number of intense supporters who cannot expect that their cause will receive strong support from the general public except under unusual circumstances."[17] Peterson distinguishes special interests from the major political interests, like those of senior citizens or of the proponents of a strong national defense, whose goals are so widely shared that they have seized the attention of the political parties and helped to shape their policy agendas.

For my purposes, however, even Peterson's broad definition of special interests cuts too finely. In the pages that follow, I mean special interests to include any group that pursues contested political or policy goals, and that is widely regarded by the public as being one contending interest among others. This definition is capacious enough to encompass the political parties themselves.[18] Madison, like the other Framers, viewed parties as factions—as evils to be avoided, if possible, or tamed, if necessary.[19] Two centuries of experience with parties have clarified the nature of their relationship to special interest groups. Today's parties seek to attract such groups into a winning electoral coalition by promising to realize the groups' special-interest goals while simultaneously promising to transcend those goals with a broader vision of the public interest that can appeal to voters unaffiliated with those constituent groups. The fact that a party is, in part, an opportunistic alliance of special interest groups by no means excludes it from my definition of special interest: Each party competes vigorously for public support for its own ideological and programmatic agenda, neither party effectively controls the policy process, and both are widely viewed as, well, partisan (rather than comprehensive) in their appeals.

Broad as this definition is, it is still not broad enough. As I shall note below, the government itself—including politicians, bureaucrats, and even judges—is increasingly seen and denounced by many members of the public as a special interest—indeed, as a special interest of a particularly dangerous kind. This critique, moreover, is by no means confined to anarchists, conspiracy theorists, and revolutionaries; it has become a rhetorical staple of Republican (and some Democratic) politicians, generating important institutional reforms such as term limits, "sunset" laws, and judicial recalls.[20] If much serious, respectable, mainstream political discourse regards government itself as a special interest, our working definition should certainly include it.

One may plausibly object that a definition that excludes virtually nothing is meaningless. In the context of a discussion of public perceptions about special interest groups, however, such an objection misses the point. In truth, the critique of special interests in American politics is so pervasive that it encompasses the institutions of government themselves. Many citizens are convinced that governmental institutions are not merely ineffective in controlling special interest groups but that these institutions actually facilitate those groups' depredations against the public interest.[21] This conviction, that government is part of the problem, has always been both widespread and influential. For that reason, it must be included in our definition and analysis of special interest groups.

Still, most critiques of special interests are concerned primarily with groups that are politically active in pursuing certain economic or ideological issues, such as trade and professional associations, labor unions, commodity groups, religious coalitions, and civil rights groups. While these issues often have far-reaching social implications, they nevertheless occupy only a portion of the full spectrum of issues with which political parties and government are typically preoccupied. Accordingly, the discussion of special interest groups that follows will be primarily concerned with groups pursuing these relatively narrow economic or ideological agendas, although my analysis will usually apply as well to the far broader array of interests that also fall within my definition.

B. The Constitutional Protection of Special Interests

From a political perspective, as Madison recognized, the most important properties of a special interest are its policy goals and the strategic resources that it can effectively mobilize in pursuit of those goals. It is striking, then, that the Constitution protects special interests without regard to their goals or resources.[22] More specifically, it protects people's rights to form special interests, to solicit and expel members, to govern their internal affairs, to define their agendas, to maintain their privacy, to organize their activities, and to deploy their resources for all lawful purposes.[23]

The courts have been especially solicitous of factions that engage in political and legal advocacy.[24] Political parties are accorded very broad protections from government regulation: Under even the narrowest conception of the First Amendment, their representational and advocacy functions lie at the very core of democratic freedoms.[25] The principle that their status as largely private organizations whose autonomy from government influence and funding[26] must be respected contrasts with the conception of parties in most civil law polities, which view them as creatures of public law subject to various regulations and subsidies.

In a series of decisions involving the National Association for the Advancement of Colored People (NAACP), a leading civil rights organization, the Supreme Court recognized a large zone of organizational activity that could not be infringed even to serve otherwise legitimate governmental interests, such as regulating the conduct of litigation[27] and of economic boycotts.[28] More recently, the Court protected the right of nonprofit advocacy groups to make campaign expenditures in support of political candidates that would be illegal if made by business corporations.[29] In these decisions, the Court affirmed that the First Amendment protects not only speech but also the rights to associate with others for common purposes, to seek to influence governmental decisions, and to be free of governmental intrusion on organizational autonomy.

Economic factions also receive broad constitutional protection. In the nineteenth century, the courts recognized the emerging industrial corporations as legal entities possessing most attributes of constitutional personhood, and extended to them broad immunities (later withdrawn) from government regulation.[30] Although corporations, as just noted, are subject to some restrictions on campaign expenditures,[31] they generally enjoy full First Amendment protection for their associations in multi-corporate organizations, and for their political lobbying and public advocacy.[32] Their political activity is also protected against antitrust liability.[33] The same is true of labor unions, which are also permitted to engage in some concerted activities that might otherwise be illegal.[34]

Religious organizations, which are probably more numerous and diverse in the United States than anywhere else in the world,[35] receive special constitutional protection under the Free Exercise and Establishment clauses of the First Amendment, although they are required to comply with "neutral" regulations adopted for health, safety, and other public welfare reasons.[36] The circumstances under which the government may distribute public funds to religious entities (as distinguished from imposing burdens on them) has long been a hotly contested issue in the United States.[37] Secular cultural organizations—those that promote particular languages, traditions, or ways of life—likewise are constitutionally protected in their efforts to exemplify and advance their group values.[38]

C. The Vilification of Special Interests

Given the broad immunities from governmental interference that the Constitution confers on special interests, it may seem surprising that Madison and many other Framers viewed them as inimical to democracy, as groups against which constitutionalists must be especially vigilant. The Framers, ever-mindful of the political conspiracies and intrigues that had (they thought) led to tyranny in ancient Greece and Rome, vilified factions in the strongest terms. This assault on factions, particularly on economic elites, quickly became a central motif of the American political tradition. Although these attacks were almost always engendered by the critics' opposition to particular substantive policies or social conditions, they often took a more general rhetorical form: an indictment of special interests for insidiously deforming and undermining the larger public interest.

During the constitutional period, for example, militant farmers launched Shay's Rebellion against the elites that dominated state and national politics. The Jacksonian Democracy was fueled by a sustained attack on special interests, vividly exemplified by the already moribund Federalists and their Bank of the United States.[39] The Free Soilers, Whigs, Republicans, and abolitionists sought (and sometimes gained) power by demonizing the "Slave Power" and "King Cotton." During the 1880s and 1890s, the Populist movement denounced the railroads, bankers, middlemen, grain elevators, and the emerging industrial corporations,[40] while the Mugwumps broke with the Republican Party over what they viewed as its alliance with corrupt privilege and special-interest politics. A decade later, the Mugwump critique of factions was taken up by the Progressives, who in turn sowed the seeds for the New Deal reform agenda. When industrial interests bitterly opposed that agenda, President Franklin Roosevelt won wide popular support by excoriating them as "economic royalists," even as he legitimated and entrenched them in many of the regulatory institutions that he helped to construct.[41]

In the post-World War II era, this anti-special-interest rhetoric became more or less universal. Not surprisingly, the Democratic Party and many groups on the ideological left of the political spectrum have stressed the nefarious role of "big business" and other special interests in resisting fundamental social change and wealth redistribution and promoting aggressive foreign policies.[42] So widespread and popular has the anti-special interest position become, however, that even middle-of-the-road and right-wing Republicans have joined the chorus of denunciation, from President Eisenhower's warning about the growing domination of the "military-industrial complex," to Patrick Buchanan's accusations that special interests pull the strings on Main Street, Wall Street, and in Washington, D.C. President Reagan, like Prime Minister Margaret Thatcher of Britain, succeeded in positioning himself as the consummate outsider, as a populist elected to do battle with both the federal establishment and the private groups dedicated to preserving the status quo. President Clinton has attempted to do the same.

For a long time, the academy resisted this critique of special interests. As early as the first decade of this century, the pluralist political science of Arthur Bentley explored and celebrated America's unique system of group politics.[43]

Bentley's theory, which was elaborated and empirically supported in the 1950s and 1960s by David Truman,[44] Robert Dahl,[45] Edward Banfield,[46] and other pluralist scholars, was based on a number of propositions about the political significance of interest groups. In this view (setting aside some differences in detail among these scholars), individuals who share common values and interests coalesce easily into groups; such group formation reflects individuals' natural social and political propensities. Politics is a complex process in which these groups bargain with one another, engaging in a combination of argument, resource exchange, threat, protest, and other forms of persuasion. Some groups are more powerful than others in that they possess a richer arsenal of resources. Even so, however, the political bargaining process is exceedingly fluid. New groups face low barriers to entry into this bargaining process, and even small ones participate to some degree. The issues around which bargaining occurs are infinitely varied and the mix of resources possessed by particular groups have different salience and value for different issues. The alliances that form around these issues are remarkably transient, dynamic, and opportunistic.

The pluralist scholars did not intend their portraits of group formation and political bargaining to be merely descriptive accounts. Most of them also viewed these bargaining processes as normatively desirable, claiming that they encouraged forms of participation that succeeded in integrating even marginal groups into the social and political mainstream. This normative celebration of pluralism followed, almost tautologically, from the pluralists' descriptive accounts and from their conception of the public interest as a *process* of group bargaining, accommodation, and conflict resolution. So long as this process was consensual, broadly participatory, and consistent with canons of procedural fairness, it served effectively to legitimate whatever bargains emerged from it. The pluralist logic was that if the process is fair, then its outcomes should be regarded as democratically acceptable, if not necessarily just.[47]

This broad pluralist consensus began to break down in the mid- and late–1960s. The civil rights, welfare rights, anti-war, and environmental movements placed enormous stress on the notion that the pluralist system was operating in a smooth, stable, inclusive, and equitable fashion. The rise of protest politics and the well-publicized spectacles of violence in the streets, on college campuses, and at the Democratic National Convention seemed to belie such smug claims.[48] Theodore Lowi, Grant McConnell, Peter Bachrach, and other political scientists attacked the pluralist model at its foundations.[49] They vigorously denounced the system of "interest-group liberalism" (Lowi's opprobrious term for it[50]) on both descriptive and normative grounds.[51] While these political scientists undermined the pluralist consensus from the ideological left, remarkably similar criticisms of the system were forthcoming from academic conservatives. Mancur Olson, Richard Posner, George Stigler, and other political economists advanced theoretical and empirical accounts of organizational behavior and public decisionmaking that emphasized the distortions that interest-group incentives and behavior created in the polity and economy.[52]

This odd intellectual alliance of left and right was soon joined by the egalitarian, often populist critical legal studies movement, which argued that legal doctrine, especially judicial decisionmaking, was deformed by some of the same organizational and political incentives and dynamics identified by the political scientists and political economists.[53] In the 1970s, these "public choice" critiques of the role of interest groups in American society began to dislodge pluralism as the ruling paradigm in the academy, while discrediting its procedural, functionalist, and often reductionist conception of the public interest. Such critics, however, generally failed to offer a convincing alternative conception.

These intellectual currents were, in part, propelled by the rise of "public interest groups."[54] These groups, typically organized on a nonprofit basis, are dedicated to representing in various public and private for a remarkable array of diverse interests: those of consumers, welfare recipients, the environment, political dissidents, ethnic minorities, women, children, future generations, the elderly, small businesses, worshippers, and countless others. These interests are relatively dispersed and their goals are often non-economic or ideological in nature. For this reason, the increasingly influential critics of pluralism in the academy (and the still-nascent critical legal studies movement) firmly predicted that such interests either would be unable to mobilize and sustain themselves as organizational entities or, once established, would be politically impotent.[55] These predictions were driven by theoretically elegant rational choice models of individual and group behavior, models which posited that such groups were especially vulnerable to the free-rider and other collective action problems.[56]

In the event, public interest groups proliferated and prospered.[57] This was the first major predictive error of the new public choice theorists; I shall mention a second error later on.[58] Many public interest groups, moreover, proved to be remarkably effective political actors, helping to initiate, shape, and reform a broad range of public policies. There are many reasons for their successes; some of them are discussed below.[59] In almost every case, however, an important element of their political effectiveness is their ability to project themselves credibly and persuasively as opponents of the narrowly self-interested "special interests" whose positions jeopardize the public interest.

Ralph Nader was (and remains) the embodiment of the public interest advocacy movement and its chief rhetorician. His work, which first came to public attention in 1965,[60] and that of his colleagues in the consumer, environmental, and civil rights movements, soon expanded to cover vast areas of the domestic policy universe. More importantly, he created a constellation of public interest groups, financed by a combination of his lectures and publications, student fees, foundation grants, and public support. Many of these groups developed alliances and political strategies that continue to wield influence today, more than three decades later. These public interest groups soon augmented and indeed transformed a political bargaining process that their participation rendered far more complex and balanced than the interest-group liberalism that Lowi and others had described and denounced. These groups also engaged in many forms of non-legislative politics, including court litigation, participation in administrative proceedings, and efforts to influence professional groups and academic curricula.

The results of this public interest group activity were nothing short of astonishing. A cataract of new regulatory laws poured out of Congress during the late 1960s and 1970s, unprecedented in American politics. The highly technical character of many of these laws spawned the formation of yet more interest groups hoping to exploit, combat, or at least reach a *modus vivendi* with the new regulatory regimes. Some of these new groups, including a number of industry associations and broader coalitions, were expressly designed to defeat or at least to neutralize the regulatory onslaught that the Nader-type groups had helped to instigate. These organizations exploited the very same levers of influence—litigation, agency proceedings, the Freedom of Information Act, congressional hearings, professional and academic activity, grassroots lobbying, mass media—that Nader and his public interest group allies had successfully deployed against business interests.

Private and public interest groups of both the left and the right shared at least one common theme. This was the perception that *government* itself had become a powerful, independent special interest group in its own right. In this view, the problem was not simply that the government had been bent to the will of private interests. The government's *own* institutional interests—as a bureaucracy committed to a steady expansion of its authority and resources, as an ensemble of career politicians obsessed with self-promotion and re-election, and as an "imperial judiciary" seeking to embed its policy views in the law— were as self-serving and inimical to the public interest as were the profit-seeking, influence-wielding private actors surrounding it. This view came to be held by many on the left who advocated more pervasive and effective control of the market, by many on the right who hoped to liberate the market from interference by governmental or government-sponsored private forces, and by many without strong ideological or partisan leanings who nevertheless perceived the government as an alien, hostile, or needlessly intrusive power.[61]

The attack on "Big Government" as a sprawling, dangerous, uncontrollable special interest was hardly a new one. Madison's definition of faction appears to have referred to private actors and thus did not, strictly speaking, include government. Nevertheless, the *Federalist Papers* (not to mention the vast corpus of anti-Federalist writings) evidence a profound understanding and apprehension of government's oppressive, imperialistic propensities.[62] Although the size of government from the Founding until World War I was small by modern standards, it was nevertheless always large and powerful enough to arouse fear and loathing among those who, for reasons of ideology or interest, opposed its exactions.[63] This government-as-special-interest critique became far more plausible and powerful during the New Deal, of course, but the Great Depression, World War II, and the Cold War blunted the political effectiveness of this position while increasing governmental authority. In the 1970s, however, both Republican and Democratic political rhetoric exploited this theme. Both parties made populist, anti-government (especially anti-Washington) appeals a centerpiece of their post-Watergate strategies to capture Congress and the presidency. In ways that archetypal Washington insiders Lyndon Johnson and Richard Nixon could never have made credible, Jimmy Carter, Ronald Reagan, and Bill Clinton were elected as outsider-reformers determined to clean up the Augean stables fouled by special interests, both private and governmental. They succeeded in making "inside the Beltway" a new, all-purpose political epithet.

During these years, as American politics and the federal government itself became more sharply divided along ideological and partisan lines, a new critique of factions gained prominence. The media, goaded by political reformers from all parts of the political spectrum, excoriated "single-issue" groups as particularly pathological excrescences from the body politic.[64] Some of the critiques, of course, were almost comically hypocritical and self-serving. The American Civil Liberties Union and abortion rights groups denounced the National Rifle Association and the Christian Coalition, which returned the favor by demonizing their detractors. Neither side acknowledged that it, like its opponents, was comprised of narrowly defined interest and ideological groups, nor did most other critics recognize that single-issue groups had produced some of the most important advances in social justice in American history, such as female suffrage and abolition of slavery. Nor did either side grant the possibility that groups with more focused agendas might reflect and represent their members' views more faithfully than those with relatively opaque or diversified appeals. Still less did they concede the pluralist claim, now muted, that this profusion of groups served to enrich and legitimate a more inclusive, participatory system of interest group bargaining.

The proliferation of special interest groups had the paradoxical but entirely predictable effect of spawning new and more effective groups in response.[65] But other factors were also at work in multiplying the number and diversity of such groups. The traditionally broad-based, relatively non-programmatic political parties and other multi-issue organizations such as labor unions declined in importance. Large "peak" trade associations had to share influence with smaller, nimbler, more specialized industry, sub-industry, and market niche groups. The media's institutional need for dramatic confrontations, and hence for organizational representatives of opposing positions, intensified. New communications technologies made it easier and less costly to target narrow public preferences. A more ideological political culture encouraged more combatants to enter the fray.

Ironically, many of those who had long demanded a more issue-oriented, participatory politics to replace the bland, exclusionary consensus—the "insider's game" of interest-group liberalism (as they saw it)—seemed to be even less satisfied with the new ideologically-driven, partisan politics that emerged to take its place. Propelled by the new animus against "single-issue groups," the centuries-old crusade against the special interests continued into the 1990s. It gained additional momentum in the populist presidential campaigns of Ross Perot and Pat Buchanan, in the post-mortems to the Clinton national health plan in 1994 (whose defeat was widely attributed by the left to the machinations of the health care and insurance lobbies), and in the steadily mounting public agitation over the revelation of the campaign-finance abuses before and after the 1996 elections.

I have demonstrated that political rhetoric and political struggle over more than two centuries have centered on a fundamental critique of special interest groups, and never more vehemently than today. Social scientists and legal academics, whose influence over social attitudes has almost certainly grown in recent decades, have provided theoretical models and empirical studies to support that critique. I now turn to a consideration of the particular objections that the critics lodge against special interests.

II. The Claims Underlying the Critique of Special Interests

Three supposed vices of special interest groups are of particular concern-first, that their partiality violates a particular substantive conception of the public interest; second, that the unequal distribution of resources among groups renders political outcomes unfair and hence illegitimate; and third, that quite apart from this unfairness, special interest groups produce undesirable public policies.

A. *The Partiality Objection*

As noted earlier, Western political thought has developed many theories that posit a general or public interest.[66] One version is identified with a discursive ethos of participation and deliberation, as in most versions of civic republicanism. Another version of the public interest, the Madisonian model, is defined primarily in contrast to what it is *not*—private and transitory interests or passions. In each of these (and other) formulations, the public interest remains abstract and indeterminate, at least until a particular policy or arrangement is said to embody it, and its supporter provides an adequate explanation of the reasons for that approbation.

Special interest groups are said to undermine these conceptions of the public interest because they are partial—in three related senses. First, they are animated by selfish motives and transitory passions rather than (as Madison put it) by "the permanent and aggregate interests of the community."[67] A special interest group is self-referential; it seeks to advance its own values or interests, not those of the larger society. Second, such groups think narrowly; they take an incomplete and fragmented view of the good rather than a comprehensive and integrated one, and they have little incentive to look any further.

But special interest groups are partial in a third, more structural sense: They tend to be undemocratic in their self-governance. Although they may not be subject to the rigid "iron law of oligarchy" that Robert Michels posited,[68] it is nevertheless true that relatively few politically active groups are robustly democratic. Some—business corporations, for example—purposefully subordinate participatory values to economic ends.[69] Others, such as labor unions, officially advocate participatory values but seldom achieve them.[70] Many other groups, from political parties to community organizations, have found it difficult to reconcile robust democratic self-governance with their immediate purposes, such as winning elections or influencing government.[71] In still others—the huge American Association for Retired Persons (AARP), for example—members join for essentially instrumental rather than expressive or participatory reasons.[72] In virtually all groups, leaders exercise decisive control over the organization's crucial information, resources, and incentives, making genuine accountability to members unattainable, even if they desire it. Under these conditions, a special interest is likely to be partial from an *internal* as well as external perspective; it will reflect the views and interests of those who effectively control its decisionmaking apparatus rather than those of all its members.

B. The Unfairness Objection

Politically active groups, whether "special" or "public interest," are unequal, and there is simply no way—certainly none consistent with democratic norms—to make them equal.[73] This inequality exists because the resources that can be used to acquire and wield political influence are themselves unequally distributed among different groups. Large corporate interests, for example, tend to have more financial assets than public interest groups and can convert these financial assets into crucial political ones: publicity, access, campaign support, information, lobbyists, and so forth. The values that business groups pursue also tend to be more concentrated and less dispersed than many public values such as the interest in a healthy environment or in protecting future generations. This greater focus may make business interests somewhat easier to organize; it also tends to reduce free-riding and other opportunistic behaviors that impede organizational effectiveness.[74]

Critics of special interests emphasize the dynamic dimension of these organizational and resource inequalities. Political life, the argument runs, does not merely *reflect* these inequalities; it also *reinforces* and *magnifies* them, exemplifying what might be called the law of multiplying advantages. Groups bargaining from a starting point of unequal endowments of influence will inevitably produce political outcomes that will mimic and perhaps even increase that inequality. The powerful will tend to become more powerful, and the rich richer.[75]

C. The Inefficiency Objection

According to public choice theorists, politicians and bureaucrats are entrepreneurs who seek to maximize their wealth or power. Legislators use their votes and bureaucrats use their administrative authority to gain support from special interest groups that can provide them with the campaign funds, policy information, public exposure, reputation, and other resources they need to remain in power and to exercise it effectively. The groups, for their part, "invest" in politicians and bureaucrats in order to induce them to adopt policies that will advance the groups' special interests.[76] Some models of these exchanges, such as those developed by the "McNollgast" trio,[77] tend to be somewhat more complex, politically sophisticated, and institutionally rich than those of most public choice economists, but their general story line is much the same.

The possibilities for bad—in economists' terms, inefficient—policy outcomes become clear when one adds to this public choice story the leading theories of organization and transaction cost economics. These theories stress the differential collective action problems that organizations face in securing the resources they need to maintain themselves and pursue their goals.[78] In these accounts, rent-seeking special interests can solve their collective action problems more easily than public interest groups can and thus are better positioned to influence politicians and bureaucrats.[79] Indeed, *ceteris paribus*, the narrower and more internally homogeneous the group's interests are, the more easily and cheaply it can organize itself and the more effectively it can deploy its political resources to secure its policy objectives. Political influence, then, is a function not only of a group's numbers (indeed, the theory suggests that larger size can magnify its free-rider problems) but also of its internal cohesiveness. This cohesiveness, in turn, is affected by how varied the goals of the group's members are and how effectively the group can control the costs and benefits of membership in order to minimize defections.

If politicians and bureaucrats tend to reward those special interests that support them politically, as these theories claim, then one would expect to find that public policy is replete with anti-competitive regulatory and legal regimes that disadvantage consumers and other diffuse, hard-to-organize, interests.[80] Public choice theorists note the existence of many rules and practices that promote wasteful subsidies, restrict entry and exit, artificially increase prices and reduce quality, and discourage innovation.[81] They claim that information, always a precious resource in policymaking and reform, is distorted by those who can afford to produce, control, and disseminate it in their own interests.[82]

Worse, the critics say, the same disproportionate special interest influences that produce perverse public policies also cause the political system to resist any changes that might reform these undesirable arrangements. The corruption or "hijacking" of government by private interests—a perennial target of reformers in the Mugwump Progressive Nader Perot tradition[83]—becomes endemic. The campaign finance laws promote and legitimate this corruption by encouraging special interests to make their support for particular politicians explicit, thereby facilitating exchanges of favors for contributions.[84] Here again, the law of multiplying advantages applies: Already well-endowed groups are strategically positioned to use their access to politicians to entrench and increase those endowments.

These three indictments of special interest groups—for their narrowness of motive and vision, their unfair advantages in the political process, and their promotion of inefficient and inequitable public policies—together comprise an important element of the American political tradition. These indictments are also propagated by much mainstream academic commentary. If true, they are damning indeed. But to what extent are they true? In the next section, I contend that while there is some truth to these criticisms (this is why my defense is a qualified one), they are vastly exaggerated.

III. A Qualified Defense of Factions

Special interest groups are essential to a vibrant, participatory, technically sophisticated, flexible, and democratically accountable polity. This has never been truer than it is today. My point is not simply that a system like ours that protects special interests is better than the alternative, but also that in a democracy like ours, there really *is* no alternative.

A qualified defense of special interest groups must acknowledge the force of certain of the above criticisms: that these groups always strive to influence public policies to their own advantage, that the policies that would advantage them are often contrary to the social good (at least as I define it), and that they often succeed in getting their way. Their effectiveness in shaping public policy, often in perverse ways, is a brute fact.[85] A qualified defense of the pluralistic system must also acknowledge the danger that politics dominated by powerful special interests will fail adequately to represent voters' diffuse interests in precious collective goods—in the environment, in the welfare of future generations, in the use of public spaces, in a just law, and indeed in the quality of government itself.

Still, it is easy to exaggerate the magnitude of this danger under current conditions. First, diffuse interests of the kind just mentioned do receive considerable recognition in public policy, although not as much as some of us might wish. The constituency for environmental quality is manifestly strong and durable. As noted above, it prospered during the 1980s despite, and perhaps because of, the determined opposition of the Reagan administration, and achieved some significant gains during the Bush and Clinton years.[86] Voters are manifestly committed to the interests of their posterity, as evidenced by the substantial and growing resources devoted to education and child health.[87]

A telling current example of the power of diffuse interests is the strong, bipartisan sentiment in Congress to regulate the managed care industry, which vigorously opposes such regulation and is far better organized in public choice theory terms than are health care consumers.[88] The reality is that many politicians search assiduously for new issues on which they can assail the special interests on behalf of some widely-shared common interest, even at some cost in special interest support. The most successful politicians are those who can fashion that public support when it is still inchoate, winning credit for having had the courage and vision to mobilize that support rather than simply climbing on the bandwagon later.

The representation of such diffuse interests reflects, in part, the growing power of ideas and values (for example, government ethics, economic efficiency, family integrity, non-discrimination, environmental protection) in a more highly educated polity.[89] It also reflects the political reality that the self-interest of well-organized provider groups (for example, pollution-control manufacturers, teachers unions, health care providers) often coincides with these diffuse collective interests.[90] Especially when one considers the far greater complexity of social and political problems today, the United States is probably a better governed, less corrupt, more tolerant, and more just society than at any time in its history.[91]

Second, although well-organized, well-funded groups start with important political advantages, those advantages by themselves are seldom decisive. Political resources take many different forms. They include not only money but also the number and intensity of supporters, quality of leadership, strategic thinking, institutional embeddedness, allies among policymaking elites, name recognition, skill in using the media, political skill, a sense of timing, reputation, rhetorical effectiveness, legal authority or leverage, the appeal of attractive ideas and ostensibly public interest arguments, and just plain luck.[92]

The recent and rapid decline of the political fortunes of the tobacco industry is a dramatic case in point. This industry has long been among the wealthiest, best-connected, effectively organized, legally impregnable, aggressively managed, tactically sophisticated, and politically powerful corporate groups in the United States, indeed in the world. Yet its adversaries—who are poorly endowed in terms of financing, legal precedents, and the support of leading politicians—have nevertheless succeeded in turning public opinion decisively against the industry, transforming its political and economic prospects.[93] This does not mean, of course, that the war against the tobacco industry is over or that the industry will not continue to win some important battles. But the tobacco example indicates the variety of political resources that skillful advocates can press into service and the remarkable openness and fluidity of American politics.

In the United States these resources are distributed widely enough that the vital interests of even poor people—to take what is surely the hardest case for the argument that I am making about the broad distribution of political influence—have gained and sustained a considerable measure of protection despite their relatively low level of political participation and their small share of the population. This is demonstrated by the large growth in overall income and in-kind transfers to the poor (the "safety net") during the last three decades, a growth that was maintained even during the Reagan-Bush years and will remain at high levels even after the implementation of federal welfare reforms enacted in 1996.[94] At the same time, as Paul Peterson has shown, the share of federal spending for programs favored by special interests (as he defines them) declined significantly during the 1980s under the pressure of a more centralized politics of budgetary constraint, tax reform, and programmatic retrenchment: "Although other components of the national budget were holding their own or expanding, these [special interest] programs were being cut by 70%—from 5.3% to 3.7% of GNP—a reduction back down to the levels that had existed in 1962."[95] An important reason for this reduction in special interest influence over the budget has been Congress's imposition of budgetary and tax procedures that require proponents of additional budget or tax expenditures to maintain revenue neutrality by proposing offsetting reductions in other areas.[96] As I discuss below, this establishes a competitive, zero-sum game among special interests that both exposes opportunities for policy improvements and minimizes the inefficiency costs that they can exact through their lobbying activities.[97]

Again, I certainly do not mean to deny that the funds that special interests invest in political influence have an effect on gaining preferred access to decisionmakers. The point, rather, is that many other resources, which special interests may lack, also play their parts in influencing policy outcomes. Even in the area of campaign finance, where the correlation between expenditures and outcome is ostensibly strong, the causal relationship is weaker and far more complicated than the standard account suggests.[98] Political scientist Graham Wilson's finding that economic groups in the United States are less powerful than those in western Europe whereas noneconomic interests in the United States are more powerful,[99] helps us to view the question of special interest influence in a more comparative perspective.

Third, when a group fails to gain approval for a policy change that it advocates, it is hard to know precisely why its effort failed in the absence of a detailed political analysis of the issue. Proponents of rejected reforms tend to blame their defeats on "politics as usual" or "powerful interests," but the truth is usually more complicated. A group may have lost because its support was weak; because its support was strong but too diffuse or unmobilized; because its key sponsors had other, higher priorities; because its ideas were unmeritorious; because its adoption was impeded by its opponents' strategic manipulation of voting rules; because an unexpected political contingency or social event intervened; because its coalition fragmented; because of the inertial force of the status quo; or for any number of other reasons. Too many diffuse, poorly-funded interests have managed to win political struggles and too many concentrated, well-funded ones have been defeated to justify attributing outcomes to any single dimension of politics such as financial advantage. Such a simplistic approach, for example, does not begin to explain either the many victories of consumer, environmental, women's, poverty, economic deregulation, and other reform agendas (again, even in the Reagan-Bush years). Nor can it adequately explain the many recent instances in which traditionally powerful groups such as the chemical industry, the banking industry, the American Medical Association, organized labor, broadcasters, pharmaceutical manufacturers, interstate truckers, defense contractors, and agribusiness failed to get their way. In each of these cases (and in numerous others), reformers successfully mobilized populist, anti-special interest sentiment as well as other political resources to defeat better funded, more highly organized forces. As noted earlier, this sentiment is itself a valuable political asset in American politics.[100]

There are reasons for thinking that the political system today is more resistant to the consistent domination of particular special interests than ever before. A number of recent developments generate strong countervailing pressures. An increasingly global economy has sharply eroded the economic and political power of domestic industries and labor unions traditionally protected by legal and political arrangements. More effective capital markets have imposed harsher penalties on inefficiency. A more competitive political system at all levels of government and in all regions of the country has made the system more responsive and accountable to voters' preferences. The extraordinary proliferation of public interest advocacy groups has provided decisionmakers with a broader diversity of values, information, political pressures, oversight, and coalitional possibilities, as has the more active participation of religious groups in politics. The maturation of a huge nonprofit sector has sustained competition with for-profit providers in many areas of the economy such as health care, long-term care, education, child care, news and entertainment, housing and community development, and many other social services.[101] More critical, professional, and effective mass media, the growing use by citizens of new communication technologies to facilitate political education and action, and the greater limits on groups' ability to make political deals behind closed doors, have increased the public's ability to monitor, expose, and discipline the group bargaining process. A more highly educated citizenry now demands from both the polity and the economy more choices, openness, and competition, as well as higher standards of integrity and superior performance.

I certainly do not mean to suggest that each of these developments is an unalloyed social gain. They have all profoundly reshaped our society in ways that have left some victims in their remorseless wakes, even as they have improved the lives of most Americans. Indeed, they all entail some real social dangers. These changes will inevitably spawn new centers of influence—for example, powerful media conglomerates—whose growing hegemony must be combatted. The changes are also threatening certain values—for example, the idealized doctor-patient relationship and the supply of health care by disinterested providers—whose weakening many of us regret. Higher ethical standards are likely to produce more ethical failures. Politicians who are more closely monitored may display less political courage. My point, rather, is that these developments have made it far more difficult than in the past for a small constellation of special interests to exercise enduring hegemony in contemporary society.

Nevertheless, the traditional American conviction that such special-interest hegemony poses an imminent, mortal threat to our polity and economy is so conventional and deeply entrenched that I shall not belabor it further here. Instead, I shall proceed to discuss the democratic virtues of special interest groups, which are little appreciated by most commentators. These virtues can be grouped into four general categories: participation, social intelligence, liberty, and the public interest.

A. Participation

Modern polities bear little resemblance to the Greek *polis*. Direct democracy through a mass assembly of all citizens is no longer either feasible or even desirable.[102] Despite technological advances that have dramatically reduced the costs of communicating with one another, we still live in a world in which the cost to individual voters of acquiring information relevant to political choice or action remains very high relative to the marginal benefits to them of that information.[103] Special interest groups perform an exceedingly important intermediating function in such a world. They can exploit economies of scale in information by monitoring political developments of interest to their members, conducting research, educating their members, and the like. In addition, they represent their members in the political process by communicating their views to policymakers, forming political alliances, and bargaining on their members' behalf. Finally, factions facilitate participation by providing fora and occasions for purposeful, discursive interaction among members in common undertakings. Values are clarified, social faculties are developed, and political education is advanced through these interactions.[104]

The immensity and anonymity of the polity as a whole encourage free-riding and passivity. The relatively small size of special interest groups enables them to avoid these obstacles to political participation. Although these groups are seldom robustly democratic in their internal governance,[105] many are nonetheless small enough for members to perceive the personal and social consequences of the group's actions and to take some responsibility for them. Precisely because these groups' concerns are more partial and narrowly defined than those of the polity as a whole, they are more likely to engage the interests and energies of voters with severely limited attention spans, time, and political knowledge, and whose most vital concerns are relatively narrow. For the vast majority of citizens—those for whom political action is neither a profession nor a consuming passion—meaningful participation must occur at levels that can effectively engage those limited, specialized capacities and interests. Special interest groups, particularly those organized locally, usually operate at these intermediate levels, which are located somewhere between the generally remote, impersonal realm of issue-oriented politics and public values, on the one hand, and the more affective, parochial domains of family and friendship, on the other.

The size and focus of special interest groups create a deep tension for the polity as a whole. On the one hand, the greater capacity of these groups to elicit citizen involvement is an important democratic virtue. On the other hand, as the earlier discussion of the inefficiency objection suggested,[106] this same capacity confers on such groups advantages in the political bargaining process that may adversely affect the polity. The size of the group may be small enough to make it politically effective in obtaining policies that benefit its members, but large enough that securing these benefits imposes very high costs on the rest of the society.[107] The agribusiness and defense-procurement lobbies exemplify this problem. The solution, however, is not to diminish the activities of special interest groups but to foster a politics in which their attempted depredations are exposed and challenged (as they increasingly are) by other groups pursuing contrary interests and by groups articulating broader ideals of public welfare (in the examples just given, the ideals of social efficiency, environmental protection, and civilian control of the military).

Recent work by political scientist Robert Putnam argues that citizen participation in public life is waning in the United States, and that the stock of "social capital"—the accumulated habits of trust, cooperation, and common purpose in society—is declining. In an article with the evocative, only partly figurative title *Bowling Alone*,[108] Putnam maintains that this depletion of social capital has impaired the vigor of our democratic life. Although some of Putnam's factual claims and inferences are controversial,[109] a more pertinent issue here is whether participation in special interest groups—as distinct from the kinds of local voluntary organizations involving face-to-face encounters and the building of trust that Putnam rightly emphasizes—counts in the stock of social capital. I believe that it should and that the much-remarked profusion of single-issue and other special interest groups, many religiously based and not all locally based, should be welcomed as a sign of greater civic engagement and participation, rather than lamented as a portent of political decay.[110] By raising such questions about Putnam's analysis, however, I do not at all disagree that social capital, understood as civic participation in its many organizational forms, is immensely valuable or that its increase is desirable. The important questions are how and by which institutions the desired increase in social capital can best be achieved, questions that I address directly in Part IV.

Criticism of special interest politics is easy and often warranted; the narrowness, injustice, and inefficiency that this politics sometimes produces are not pretty sights. What is far more difficult, however, is to provide a satisfactory answer to the "compared to what?" question. Some possible alternatives to contemporary pluralism would endanger the democratic project,[111] while other more promising ones seem to elude our grasp. For example, a system that could exploit the political virtues of special interest groups while also promoting effective party organizations with more general, integrative purposes and capacities would be most desirable. Unfortunately, no one has figured out how to generate such a system under contemporary social conditions. Most, though not all, of the measures proposed to regulate or fine-tune special interest influence over the political process—including, notably, many proposals seeking to reform campaign finance—would be unconstitutional, unwise, or ineffective.[112] Given that realistic constraint, participation in special interest groups, despite its flaws, may still be among the best vehicles for sustained citizen involvement in politics.

Special interest groups' growing use of direct marketing techniques to educate and mobilize more citizens through lower-cost information technologies is an important force driving and shaping civic participation today. Many of the risks of these techniques and technologies are clear enough (child pornography and invasion of privacy, for example), but we should not pretend that we can yet understand, much less appraise, all of their effects and implications. Even granting their defects in eliciting democratic participation, the most likely alternative is not a return to the intense civic engagement of the New England town meeting or the Lincoln-Douglas debates.[113] The more realistic prospect is a growing passivity, boredom, and lack of involvement of much of the electorate—a development of which the low voter turnout in the 1996 elections may be a grim harbinger.[114] This disengagement may well constitute a far greater threat to democratic values than the hucksterism of the political marketplace that (technological differences aside) has characterized American politics since the Jacksonian era ushered in mass electoral appeals.

B. Social Intelligence

Sound public policy depends, above all, on a swift, constant flow between citizens and government decisionmakers of accurate, policy-relevant information. Here, information is more than a resource for public participation; it is also an essential ingredient of socially rational policymaking. Special interest groups are among the most important sources of the information that decisionmakers so desperately need. This fact, rather than being a cause for regret, underscores the vitality of the private sector in American life. If, for example, the government wants to know about the nature of housing needs and the cost of expanding or altering the housing stock, it cannot simply consult with public housing authorities, public interest groups concerned with affordable housing, or even the policy research staff at HUD. It must also turn to the private housing market, which utterly dwarfs the public housing sector in information, expertise, analysis, and resources, and possesses powerful incentives to get the information right, at least for its own profit-seeking purposes. The same is true of transportation, health care, education, and virtually every other area of public policy.

Before officials use private information for policy purposes, of course, they should review it for bias due to its possibly interested source. Where feasible, they should also test the reliability of this information against other data. Frequently, however, officials must choose on the basis of a dearth of reliable information rather than having the benefit of competing versions of it; moreover, the best available information may come from an interested source. Officials can sometimes sponsor new policy research and resourcefully seek better, more disinterested information, but these options are not always open to them. Indeed, it is seldom clear what the term "disinterested" means in the highly competitive, adversarial, politicized process in which most important policymaking occurs. Certainly, the fact that research was conducted or sponsored by the government, academics, or public interest groups hardly assures public acceptance of the findings as competent and unbiased.[115] In the end, it is the relative openness of the policymaking process, rather than the exclusion of special interest information or any other alternative, that provides the most effective, publicly acceptable safeguard against bias.

In a democracy, the ability of public policy to reflect voters' preferences is an essential element of social intelligence as well as of democratic responsiveness. But it is not enough for policymakers to know which outcomes voters want. Far more important, they must also discern the *intensity* of voters' preferences—that is, not what voters want in the abstract but how strongly they want it and what they are willing to sacrifice in order to obtain it. This vital political intelligence is hard to obtain. While a competitive marketplace can readily register the intensity of consumers' preferences, only a political bargaining process in which alternative outcomes are "priced" through exchanges among the participants can measure how intensely voters feel about policy outcomes.

Interest groups provide an important index of voters' willingness to "pay" for their policy goals. Being a member of a group usually entails some cost; members' actions on behalf of the group such as writing letters, grass roots work, reading-group materials, and lobbying are even more costly to them. For this reason, voters' group memberships are a crude proxy for the intensity of their policy preferences. So long as "exit" from a group is possible, preference intensity can be viewed as a function of the groups' resources, the costs of membership, their ability to mobilize support, their political effectiveness, and so on.[116] Where members' exit from the group is not feasible[117] or where group membership is virtually costless,[118] the fact of group membership is a much less significant marker of their feelings about its goals, and the same inferences about intensity cannot be drawn. Skillful politicians learn to gauge

these factors as they gain knowledge about the various groups that are actively concerned with particular policy issues. As we have seen, this process of
assessment creates a significant, but not necessarily disabling, political disadvantage for those preferences around which groups cannot easily organize—
either because they are diffusely or weakly held, or because the individuals
who share those preferences lack political resources.[119]

Special interest groups engender social learning, often in dramatic ways. For
example, the insistence of anti-war groups that the Vietnam War was a tragic
error led to President Johnson's decision not to seek reelection and to a rapid
reversal of policy direction. (Ending the war itself, unfortunately, took much
longer). Many different groups—insurers, health care providers, policy analysts, and others—worked to persuade the public that the Clinton national
health plan was misguided, as in some respects it was. Other groups—environmentalists are a notable example—succeeded in marshalling public opposition to central elements of the Republican Party's Contract With America,
which initially dominated legislative activity in the 104th Congress. Groups
advocating the interests of Social Security beneficiaries have educated the
public about long-term threats to the program's financial integrity. Disability-
rights organizations have helped to transform public attitudes toward the
physically and mentally handicapped.

In countless other cases, special interest groups have brought politicians and
the general public around to different views about policy issues. Whether one
regards these as examples of valuable public education or of irresponsible distortion may depend largely on one's views about the merits of these controversies. What is certain, however, is that only special interest groups have both
the incentives and the resources to perform the requisite tasks of analysis, mobilization, communication, and implementation. In a democracy, such groups
are perhaps the main transmission belt for the kind of social learning that is essential to a fluid, responsive policy process not unduly dominated by policymakers parochial interests or myopic, anachronistic perceptions.

C. Liberty

More than 160 years ago, Alexis de Toqueville noted the importance in the
United States of the institutions of civil society,[120] which today are also called
"mediating institutions."[121] Such institutions—the family, churches, and other
voluntary organizations—stand as bulwarks that separate the isolated individual from the powerful state and help to integrate those individuals into the
larger society. These institutions not only represent many of the individual's
interests in state councils, as described above; they also resist the state's encroachments on civil liberties, civil rights, private property, and other interests
that are essential to the preservation and expansion of the individual's liberty
and autonomy.

Special interest groups are important mediating institutions—less central than family, to be sure, but significant nonetheless. They are a source of political intelligence, education, and mobilization, helping members to identify threats to their vital interests, to formulate effective policy responses, and to defend those interests in cooperation with others. Labor unions and community organizations have traditionally played this role, as have the media and a rich variety of lobbying and ideological organizations. By routinizing organized opposition to the proposals and blandishments of politicians and the state, these groups legitimate such opposition and protect the liberties of their members. And by mustering support for proposals that their members favor, they advance the members' conceptions of liberty.

Special interests, of course, can also threaten individuals' liberty if their power over individuals is unchecked. The use of public authority to limit private power is essential to the preservation of liberty to the extent that competition, social and religious values, disclosure and publicity, and other constraining forces are inadequate safeguards. Fortunately, many recent political, technological, economic, legal, and ideological developments make it less likely that special interests can achieve and maintain the level of arbitrary power over individuals' lives that they sometimes exercised in the past. Such changes, for example, have broken the nearly monopolistic hold that network television had for decades on Americans' access to home entertainment and national news. Company towns are largely a thing of the past, marginalized by a more mobile labor force, legal protections, investigative journalism, corporate reputational concerns, and other factors.[122] These same forces have also limited, although certainly not eliminated, race, religion, and gender discrimination in the workplace and most other areas of American life. Legal controls have reduced the ability of government and powerful private groups to punish dissidents for their political views. Again, the important point is not that special interests never oppress individuals but that large social forces are increasingly constraining their power to do so.

D. The Public Interest

Invoking the notion of the "public interest" in support of a policy proposal is a commonplace of political rhetoric. Absent an articulated, more general theory of the public interest, utterance of this phrase usually means little more than that the speaker strongly favors the proposal. Although many political theories, as noted earlier, advance substantive conceptions of the public interest, liberal theories usually define the public interest in terms of fair *process*—a process of representation and bargaining,[123] of dialogue,[124] or of unbiased choice.[125] Such theories sometimes yield substantive principles of justice—for example, Rawls' difference principle,[126] market freedom,[127] or distributive equality[128]—but these principles tend to be highly abstract, and they remain contested even within the community of liberal theorists. Their specific policy implications are even more controversial.

In a procedural conception of the public interest, special interest groups play an essential role. As a practical and perhaps even as a theoretical matter, such groups are necessary to any fair and effective process of representation, bargaining, and political dialogue. I believe that these processes have produced a polity that is more just, diverse, well-governed, economically efficient, inclusive, and dynamic than it was in the past, although it remains plagued by serious problems, especially the persistence of a large, hopeless urban underclass.[129] Even if one views public policy trends more critically than I do (as many readers doubtless will), it would be hard to show that this procedural conception of the public interest, with the role that it assigns to special interest groups, has utterly failed or is responsible for the problems that remain.

IV. Remedies

James Madison, in *Federalist #10,* saw only "two methods of curing the mischiefs of faction: the one, by removing its causes; the other, by controlling its effects."[130] I have maintained here that these "mischiefs" largely turn out either to be exaggerated or to constitute democratic virtues. But even in Madison's own terms, the remedies are decidedly limited: The causes of faction, he concluded, cannot be eliminated in a free society; he focused therefore on controlling its adverse effects. His famous remedy was an extended, commercial republic in which the number of competing interests would be sufficiently large and diverse that they would have to counter one another, thereby preventing the formation of a permanent majority with the power to oppress minorities.

Madison's solution has proved brilliantly prescient. It resembles the remedial mantra of the Supreme Court in First Amendment cases—that the cure for error and falsehood is not government restriction of speech, but *more* speech— which has also served us well. In the same way, Madison seemed to believe that the dangers of special interests could best be minimized if the political process encompassed more of them. I emphatically agree, even as I recognize—as Madison did not—that the multiplication and diversification of interests carries an important cost: They produce an increasingly complex, opaque political process, which ordinary citizens cannot readily understand.[131] The public's bewilderment and confusion may partly explain its growing alienation from government. What can be said with confidence is that the growing incomprehensibility of contemporary politics and policymaking to ordinary Americans would be even more so if special interest groups did not play the intermediation role that I described earlier.[132]

Another risk of multiplying and diversifying interests is that of political stalemate or even breakdown. In such a case, the pluralistic system can simply become overloaded, generating more political energy—more demands, conflicts, and uncertainties—than the institutions of a limited, democratic government can effectively handle. As the number and variety of conflicts for which political solutions are required increases, so too do the risk and adverse social consequences of such a stalemate. This kind of marasmus may be occurring today in France, Germany, and some other advanced welfare states in which the public sectors have grown so large and the conflicts so intractable that even the leaders of these nations seem to recognize that their governance capacities are stretched to the breaking point, making it almost impossible for necessary reform decisions to be made.[133]

To be sure, American commentators frequently warn of possible political paralysis in the United States that would impede necessary reforms.[134] This is certainly a danger worth worrying about, but the important fact is that it has not yet occurred. Indeed, it is striking how many complex, controversial issues Congress has managed to address and resolve (usually for better, sometimes for worse) in the last two decades even as special interest groups—much to the consternation of most commentators—proliferated and became more politically engaged.[135] The period since the early–1970s has been one of truly remarkable policy innovation at all levels of government. The new politics of public policy[136] is unquestionably more complex and hence more difficult than the old, and the growth of special interest groups surely has much to do with this change. The evidence demonstrates, however, that the process remains manifestly viable and effective nonetheless.

In this period, and especially since the Reagan-era recession that ended in 1982, the U.S. economy has been utterly transformed. As it happens, this transformation directly tests—and seems sharply to refute—what is surely the most important and arresting prediction that Mancur Olson and most other public choice theorists have made concerning the putatively pathological tendencies of special interest groups in politics: that such groups would succeed in using their narrow organizational advantages to deform the political process in ways that extract narrow economic benefits for them by imposing massive inefficiencies on the rest of society.[137] *In fact, during precisely the period when special interest groups were rapidly proliferating, many of the most important sectors of the U.S. economy—transportation, automobiles, steel, banking, energy, telecommunications, and (arguably) health care—were growing markedly more efficient.*[138] *Moreover, these efficiency gains, which are an important cause of the persistently low inflation rates experienced in recent years, occurred even as the economy generated new jobs at a rate that is the envy of the rest of the industrialized world.*[139]

Needless to say, the precise causes of this economic transformation are complex,[140] and it is not my purpose here to explore, much less to explain, them. My point is a narrower but nevertheless exceedingly important one: In contrast to the predictions of public choice theorists, the expansion in the number and political activity of special interest groups has not clotted the economy with inefficiency. The evidence strongly suggests that, if anything, the contrary is true. Special interest group expansion has been paralleled by a striking im provement in economic efficiency. Whether this group expansion was one *cause* of the increased efficiency in the economy is an intriguing question that I do not pursue here; I venture only that such a causal relationship, which would be very difficult to prove, is at least plausible.

What does seem clear is that special interest groups cannot subvert the public interest as readily as they could in the past. A relentless growth is occurring both in the mobility of economic resources (capital, labor, information, etc.) and in the options available to firms, interest groups, and individuals concerning the regulatory regimes under which they operate. These developments are steadily reducing the economic and political leeways for governmental and private sector inefficiencies that special interests can spawn and on which they sometimes feed. Special interests have not ceased their traditional efforts to pursue narrow group agendas at public expense. Rather, they are encountering greater political resistance to those agendas and have less freedom to implement them in the face of remorseless market forces.[141]

I have already noted that the proliferation of interest groups since 1965 has accompanied the expansion of the administrative state during this period; indeed, the two developments have been mutually reinforcing.[142] The fact that government action helped to stimulate interest group formation, however, does not necessarily mean that government should affirmatively seek to reduce the risks of partiality, unfairness, and inefficiency created by this proliferation. Indeed, the contrary is true. Although the desire to "level the playing field" of organizational competition will always be a seductive metaphor and a tempting goal, it should be resisted except in unusual circumstances. Even those governmental efforts to improve the functioning of the pluralist process that seem benign and neutral—whatever benignity and neutrality might mean in so intensely competitive a context—are likely to have unpredictable, often undesirable effects.[143]

Government should not be in the business of creating or subsidizing interest groups. By placing its heavy thumb on the scales of organizational competition, it almost inevitably compromises both the integrity and the effectiveness of that competition. Government patronage would tend to stifle the emergence of genuine, grassroots interest groups, delegitimate those groups that government seeks to sponsor, and entrench the status quo in a dynamic society in which flexible responsiveness to change is essential.

Government creation and subsidization of interest groups carries other risks as well. In areas of policy in which government-sponsored and privately sponsored organizations both operate and serve similar populations, the government enterprises are often both inferior and more costly.[144] Where dynamic, complex market forces operate, government's ability to select "winners"—as some proponents of industrial policy envision—is severely limited.[145] Even the well-established policy of encouraging nonprofit activity by granting nonprofit organizations tax-exempt status on a more or less categorical basis raises persistent questions and complaints about the fairness and efficiency of such preferential treatment, given the extent to which nonprofit groups compete with for-profit ones for capital and customers.[146]

Other policy options for encouraging the formation of groups without creating such distortions are limited. The most that government can hope to accomplish in this realm is to foster a dynamic of group competition that, as Madison envisioned, minimizes the damage inflicted by special interests' propensity toward partiality, unfairness, and inefficiency. Even this seemingly modest goal is difficult to achieve. Several examples will suffice to indicate the directions that reforms might take. First, the government can reduce the dangers of special-interest influence over federal budgetary and tax policies by strengthening existing rules, adopted during the last two decades in order to restrain growing federal budget deficits, that require proponents of subsidies or expenditures to propose offsetting reductions in other areas.[147] This approach places special interests in a zero-sum game where any costs that they add must come at the expense of other special interests.[148] This presents a sharp contrast to the logrolling game against which many public choice theorists have warned so wisely and strenuously (but which, as I have explained, has not always had the consequences that they predicted).[149]

A second remedy relates to the first. As these new zero-sum rules increasingly constrain special interests in the tax and budgetary domains, the pressures generated by these groups do not disappear; they are simply channeled into regulations, private sector mandates, special trust funds, borrowing authorities, and other off-budget areas of governmental activity where these constraints do not now apply. By extending the zero-sum rule device to these off-budget areas, the government can further reduce the potential scope of special-interest abuses while still exploiting the social intelligence virtues of those groups for policymaking purposes.

Third, the government should review and rationalize its widespread programs to subsidize the activities of private business interests in the name of such attractive goals as regional development, export promotion, price stabilization, and government procurement. Many of these programs, which take multiple forms, are unfair to beneficiary firms' competitors, costly to taxpayers, and fail to achieve their objectives. Fortunately, this "corporate welfare" is under increasingly intense bipartisan challenge. At a time when traditional welfare for the indigent has been severely curtailed and politicians wish to be perceived by the public as even-handed rather than cruel, such policies may finally be vulnerable.[150]

Fourth, the government can protect the integrity and autonomy of interest groups by preventing, as the courts have generally done, public or private interference with their values and activities.[151] The use of governmental power to harass interest groups is a perennial threat, one magnified by the difficulty of distinguishing between legitimate policy-related investigations and witch-hunts of the kind that characterized the McCarthy era.[152]

The risk of such harassment is particularly great for those groups that depend on government support, such as the local grantees of the federally funded National Endowment for the Humanities (NEH), Legal Services Corporation (LSC), and the Corporation for Public Broadcasting (CPB). Once these groups receive public funds, they are properly subjected to close public scrutiny and demands for accountability. Politics being what they are, this scrutiny and accountability may result in abrupt funding cutoffs, policy changes, personnel controls, and other pressures that jeopardize organizational autonomy. Sometimes those pressures will be legitimate, sometimes misguided, and occasionally illegal, but in a vigorous democratic polity they are inescapable. Nevertheless, the dangers that these pressures pose to group independence (and perhaps effectiveness) constitute a compelling reason for such groups to seek private support whenever possible instead of public subsidies.[153]

Fifth, government can seek to increase the accountability of interest groups both to their members and to the public by requiring the groups to disclose pertinent information about their transactions. Even where disclosure is already required, as with respect to federal-election campaign contributions, much improvement is still possible. Specifically, Congress could require contributors and candidates to file information on the Internet as soon as the contributions are made, in a form that is more comprehensible to journalists and the general public.[154] Similar measures already exist at the state and local level, where many charities soliciting funds from the public must disclose information about their operations, including the amount they spend on fundraising. The disclosure approach is often a better way to protect public values than imposing substantive restrictions on the groups' activities.

Sixth, government can enable voters and consumers to exercise more control over the resources that special interest groups need to survive. Voucher programs and other forms of privatization and decentralization requiring service providers to compete for these resources exemplify this emerging technique. Under the appropriate conditions, this approach might fruitfully be extended to other areas as well.[155]

But a strong caveat is in order. Even the kinds of remedial interventions that I have suggested should be designed and implemented only with great caution. Reformers should approach their meliorative task with a deep appreciation for the integrity, complexity, and fragility of both the processes through which groups form, act, and compete, and the ways that these group processes affect individual values, incentives, and behavior.[156] Clumsy or misguided reforms can easily distort these processes and undermine the legitimacy of the pluralistic system on which liberal democracy vitally depends. Given these stakes, the costs of error are certain to be high.

One of the most important of these costs is the diminished respect for government, a delegitimation that discredits even those governmental actions that are essential or prudent. Much the same political energy and rhetoric that have been so effectively deployed against special interests throughout our history, and which have been particularly successful in reducing the federal government's role since the 1970s, can all too readily be turned against the project of government itself. This may foster a corrosive defeatism and cynicism about politics, impeding the pursuit of social goals—whether cherished by liberals or by conservatives[157]—that cannot be attained without common action undertaken, or at least coordinated or regulated, by government.

This possibility leads to a final remedy, one that government is well-equipped to develop and support. In the end, government's most fundamental responsibility is to see that the public understands the nature and functioning of democratic politics in its increasingly complex contemporary forms. The strongest bulwark of democracy is a sophisticated, enlightened, participatory citizenry, one that thinks critically about changes private and public goals truly require and about how group politics can contribute to the realization of these goals. The revitalization of civic education in this broad sense is the implicit or explicit project of much public commentary today; on this, at least, there seems to be a national consensus. This is among the most urgent tasks of American society as it approaches the twenty-first century.

Notes

1. THE FEDERALIST No. 10, at 77 (James Madison) (Clinton Rossiter ed., 1961).

2. One recent commentator refers to factions as "political parasites." Glenn Harlan Reynolds. *Is Democracy Like Sex?*, 48 VAND. L. REV. 1635, 1643–44 (1995).

3. Although I do not develop the comparative politics point in this Essay, I strongly suspect that special interest groups pose a greater threat to democratic values in other societies whose political and economic institutions, practices, and values are less diverse, competitive, fluid, and participatory than ours. *See, e.g.*, Peter H. Schuck & Robert E. Litan, *Regulatory Reform in the Third World: The Case of Peru*, 4 YALE J. ON REG. 51 (1986) (discussing obstacles to regulatory reform posed by bureaucratic and private interests). My suspicion is supported by the relative inability of other western democracies to cure the "Eurosclerosis" that has long gripped them, raising their tax levels to support expanding public payrolls while drastically limiting their capacity to generate new private employment for their workers. *See* Editorial, *Europe's Year of Reckoning*, WALL ST. J., Dec. 27, 1996, at A6 (lamenting Europe's "well-documented Eurosclerosis, characterized by slow economic growth and rising unemployment"); George Melloan, *Global View: Europe's Gloomier View of the Welfare State*, WALL ST. J., Feb. 14, 1994, at A19 (discussing "renewed Eurosclerosis" and its effects on European attitudes about welfare state).

4. By referring to *structural* ills, I mean to acknowledge the obvious fact that special interests do affect the resolution of particular policy issues, and sometimes do so in ways that I and others regard as undesirable.

5. *See infra* Part II.

6. This was only one of the erroneous premises on which the Constitution was founded. Robert Dahl advanced the point well more than forty years ago: "It is only an index to the pitiful limitations of human knowledge to note that, realistic and gifted as [the Framers] were, many of their key assumptions proved to be false, and the consti-

tution they created has survived not because of their predictions but in spite of them." ROBERT A. DAHL, A PREFACE TO DEMOCRATIC THEORY 141 (1956).

7. THE FEDERALIST No. 10, at 78 (James Madison) (Clinton Rossiter ed., 1961).

8. According to Cass Sunstein, Madison believed that elected representatives, standing above local interests and factions, would deliberate on and produce the common good in the national legislature. *See* Cass Sunstein, *Interest Groups in American Public Law*, 38 STAN. L. REV. 29, 41–42 (1985) (discussing THE FEDERALIST No. 10 (James Madison)).

9. *See* JEAN-JACQUES ROUSSEAU, THE SOCIAL CONTRACT 24–29 (Willmoore Kendall trans., Henry Regnery Co. 1954) (1762) (discussing "general will").

10. *See* Ernest L. Fortin, *St. Thomas Aquinas, in* HISTORY OF POLITICAL PHILOSOPHY 248, 248–58 (Leo Strauss & Joseph Cropsey eds., 3d ed. 1987) (discussing Aquinas's notion of objective order of divine providence).

11. *See* ARISTOTLE, THE POLITICS 99 (Cames Lord trans., Univ. of Chicago Press 1984) (defining "virtue" objectively).

12. *See* PLATO, THE REPUBLIC 189 (G.M.A. Grube trans., Hackett Publishing Co. 1992) (discussing "the form of the good").

13. Sunstein, *supra* note 8, at 47.

14. This innovation, of course, has itself been reviled from many philosophical quarters, most famously in the work of Leo Strauss. *See* LEO STRAUSS, NATURAL RIGHT AND HISTORY 1–8 (1953) [hereinafter STRAUSS, NATURAL RIGHT]: LEO STRAUSS, *Relativism, in* THE REBIRTH OF CLASSICAL POLITICAL RATIONALISM 13, 13–26 (1989) [hereinafter STRAUSS, *Relativism*].

15. This assertion is one axis of the vigorous debate between the natural-rights liberalism of Leo Strauss, who defended an objective, transcendent conception of the public interest, and the pluralist liberalism of Robert Dahl, Edward Banfield, and others, who advanced a bargaining model of the public interest. *Compare* STRAUSS, NATURAL RIGHT, *supra* note 14, *and* STRAUSS, *Relativism, supra* note 14, *with* EDWARD C. BANFIELD, POLITICAL INFLUENCE 7 (1961) (studying government as "patterns of influence"), *and* ROBERT A. DAHL, WHO GOVERNS? (1961) (arguing that political consensus is achieved through continual process of communication between political professionals and population at large).

16. Typically, critics on the left claim that the pluralist process disadvantages the poor and other diffuse groups that find it difficult to organize for political action. *See, e.g.,* THEODORE LOWI, THE END OF LIBERALISM 198–236 (2d ed. 1979). Those on the right often claim that the process disadvantages entrepreneurs and traditional groups in favor of an anti-market alliance of government officials, elite intellectuals, and the mass media, which together comprise a "new class." *See, e.g.,* IRVING KRISTOL, TWO CHEERS FOR CAPITALISM 23–28 (1978): *cf.* JOSEPH WHITE & AARON WILDAVSKY, THE DEFICIT AND THE PUBLIC INTEREST 545–51 (1989) (identifying government officials, intellectuals, and mass media as interest groups affecting political process).

17. Paul E. Peterson, *The Rise and Fall of Special Interest Politics, in* THE POLITICS OF INTERESTS: INTEREST GROUPS TRANSFORMED 326, 327 (Mark P. Petracca ed., 1992) [hereinafter POLITICS OF INTERESTS].

18. Indeed, as the share of voters self-identifying with a political party continues to decline, even the parties might come within the loose size constraints of Peterson's definition.

19. *See* THE FEDERALIST No. 10 (James Madison) (Clinton Rossiter ed., 1961); George Washington, Farewell Address (Sept. 17, 1796), *in* 1 DOCUMENTS OF AMERICAN HISTORY

172 (Henry Steele Commager & Milton Cantor eds., 10th ed. 1988); *see also* Steven G. Calabresi, *Political Parties As Mediating Institutions*, 61 U. Chi. L. Rev. 1479, 1482–83 (1994) (noting that "[t]he Framers of the U.S. Constitution deliberately set up our constitutional regime so that it would be inimical to the spirit of "faction" or of "party"— two terms that they tended to equate"). *But see* Lloyd N. Cutler, *Now Is the Time For All Good Men*, 30 Wm. & Mary L. Rev. 387, 398 (1989) (arguing that Madison's definition of faction "would not appear to cover a broadly based national political party that cuts across narrow interest groups").

20. The fact that such reforms are important does not mean that they are not sometimes misguided, as I believe term limits are. *But see* George F. Will, Restoration: Congress, Term Limits and the Recovery of Deliberative Democracy (1992). Fortunately, Congress now seems unlikely to approve a term limits amendment. *See* Adam Clymer, *House Rejects Term Limits, Bringing Drive to a Dead Halt*, N.Y. Times, Feb. 13, 1997, at A1.

21. For example, a recent CBS News/*New York Times* poll found that 65% of registered voters believe that "most members of Congress are more interested in helping . . . special interest groups" than the people. *CBS News/New York Times Poll, released* Oct. 22, 1996, *available in* WL, Poll Database. In another poll, 85% of registered voters said that "many of [their] elected officials are controlled by contributions from special interests." *Fox News/Opinion Dynamics Poll, released* Dec. 16, 1996, *available in* WL, Poll Database.

22. Even groups with subversive or illegal purposes enjoy such protection, at least up to the point at which they act to effectuate those purposes. *See* Brandenburg v. Ohio, 395 U.S. 444, 447 (1969) ("[T]he constitutional guarantees of free speech and free press do not permit a State to forbid or proscribe advocacy of the use of force or of law violation except where such advocacy is directed to inciting or producing imminent lawless action and is likely to incite or produce such action.").

23. Recently, however, the Supreme Court's remarkably broad constructions of the federal Racketeer Influenced and Corrupt Organizations (RICO) statute have come perilously close to criminalizing behavior that would be valid for entities not statutorily defined as "criminal organizations." *See, e.g.,* NOW v. Scheidler, 510 U.S. 249, 256–61 (1994) (holding that RICO does not require proof that alleged racketeering enterprise or acts were motivated by economic purpose and that RICO can be applied to network of anti-abortion groups).

24. On the other hand, courts do not always accept the policy outcomes generated by constitutionally protected advocacy. As Professor Sunstein argues, courts use certain public law doctrines to require that legislation reflect certain public values and not simply reflect factional political and legal advocacy. A prominent example is the rationality requirement under the Equal Protection Clause. *See* Sunstein, *supra* note 8, at 49–64.

25. *See, e.g.,* Colorado Republican Fed. Campaign Comm. v. FEC, 116 S. Ct. 2309, 2316 (1996) ("The independent expression of a political party's views is 'core' First Amendment activity no less than is the independent expression of individuals, candidates, or other political committees.").

26. It should be noted, however, that federal and state law confer a number of electoral advantages on the two major parties, including public funding for their presidential campaigns, preferred positions on ballots, and special access to regulated media, for which other parties may qualify, but with greater difficulty. The federal equal-time provision for access to media outlets by legally qualified presidential candidates is one specific provision. *See* 47 U.S.C. ss 312(a)(7), 315 (1994); *see also* Fulani v.

FCC, 49 F.3d 904 (2d Cir. 1995) (rejecting complaint by third-party candidate of unequal time); *In re* Complaint of Ross Perot v. ABC, CBS, NBC, & Fox Broad. Co., 11 F.C.C.R. 13109 (1996) (same). Several federal laws grant partial public financing to major presidential candidates. *See* Presidential Election Campaign Fund Act, 26 U.S.C. ss 9001–9013 (1994); Presidential Primary Matching Payment Account Act, 26 U.S.C. ss 9031–9042 (1994); *see also* LaRouche v. FEC, 996 F.2d 1263 (D.C. Cir. 1993) (rejecting third-party candidate's challenge to FEC denial of federal matching funds).

There are numerous state laws granting advantages to the major political parties. *See, e.g.*, ARIZ. REV. STAT. ANN. s 16–571 (West 1996) (allowing representatives of two major political parties, but not independent candidates, to obtain immediately list of people who voted in election); COLO. REV. STAT. ANN. ss 1–6–102, 1–6–109 (West Supp. 1996) (mandating that each major political party supply half election judges); FLA. STAT. ANN. ss 99.092, 99.103(1) (West 1996) (excluding political parties with less than 5% of total registered voters from receiving partial rebate of candidate's quite substantial filing fees); IND. CODE ANN. s 9–18–15–10, 9–18–15–13, 9–29–5–32 (Michie 1997) (mandating preferential distribution to major political parties of $30 "political contribution" fee from each personalized license plate issued by state); N.H. REV. STAT. ANN. s 658:25 (1996) (allowing only members of two major political parties to be designated ballot clerks). For discussions of these and other provisions, see Richard Winger, Election Law Obstacles to Minor Party Success (1996) (unpublished manuscript, on file with author). Recent cases of note involving these issues include *Twin Cities Area New Party v. McKenna*, 73 F.3d 196 (8th Cir.), *cert. granted*, 116 S. Ct. 1846 (1996); *Libertarian Party v. Smith*, No. 87342, 1996 WL 693606 (Fla. Dec. 5, 1996); and *Indiana Republican State Comm. v. Slaymaker*, 614 N.E.2d 981 (Ind. Ct. App. 1993).

27. *See* NAACP v. Button, 371 U.S. 415, 428–29 (1963).

28. *See* NAACP v. Claiborne Hardware Co., 458 U.S. 886, 908–09 (1982).

29. *See* FEC v. Massachusetts Citizens for Life, Inc., 479 U.S. 238, 263–65 (1986); *see also* Austin v. Michigan State Chamber of Commerce, 494 U.S. 652, 661–65 (1990) (upholding *Massachusetts Citizens for Life, Inc.* but finding that chamber of commerce is not exempt organization).

30. *See, e.g.*, Missouri Pac. Ry. Co. v. Nebraska, 164 U.S. 403, 417 (1896) (applying Takings Clause to protect corporation); Minneapolis & St. Louis R.R. v. Beckwith, 129 U.S. 26, 28 (1889) (treating railroad as person under Due Process Clause of Fourteenth Amendment); County of Santa Clara v. Southern Pac. R.R., 118 U.S. 394, 396 (1886) (assuming without discussion that railroad is person under Equal Protection Clause); Insurance Co. v. Morse, 87 U.S. (20 Wall.) 445, 455–58 (1874) (treating insurance company as citizen under Constitution for purposes of diversity jurisdiction). For *Lochner*-era substantive due process decisions that presume that a corporation is a person, see *Coppage v. Kansas*, 236 U.S. 1 (1915), and *Allgeyer v. Louisiana*, 165 U.S. 578 (1897). For discussion of these developments, see Howard Jay Graham, *An Innocent Abroad: The Constitutional Corporate "Person,"* 2 UCLA L. REV. 155 (1955); and Herbert Hovenkamp, *The Classical Corporation in American Legal Thought*, 76 GEO. L.J. 1593, 1640–51 (1988).

31. *See, e.g.*, Federal Election Campaign Act, 2 U.S.C. s 441b (1994).

32. *See, e.g.*, First Nat'l Bank v. Bellotti, 435 U.S. 765, 775–95 (1978).

33. The *Noerr-Pennington* doctrine holds that federal antitrust laws do not regulate the political conduct of private individuals or entities even when they are seeking anticompetitive action from the government. *See* UMW v. Pennington, 381 U.S. 657, 670

(1965); Eastern R.R. Presidents Conference v. Noerr Motor Freight, Inc., 365 U.S. 127, 141 (1961). For a recent discussion and application of the *Noerr-Pennington* doctrine, see *City of Columbia v. Omni Outdoor Advertising, Inc.*, 499 U.S. 365, 379–80 (1991).

34. *Pennington*, 381 U.S. 657, is the classic statement of the labor exemption from anti-trust liability. For a recent application, *see Brown v. Pro Football, Inc.*, 116 S. Ct. 2116 (1996).

35. *See* Gustave Niebuhr, *Death in a Cult: The Landscape*, N.Y. TIMES, Mar. 30, 1997 (reporting that United States has over 2000 distinct religions and that Los Angeles, unlike any country in world, has members of every existing Buddhist sect).

36. *See, e.g.*, Church of the Lukumi Babalu Aye, Inc. v. City of Hialeah, 508 U.S. 520, 531 (1993); Employment Div., Dep't of Human Resources v. Smith, 494 U.S. 872, 879 (1990). These decisions, especially the latter, led to the enactment of the Religious Freedom Restoration Act, 42 U.S.C. s 2000bb–2000bb4 (1994), which is now under constitutional challenge in *City of Boerne v. Flores*, 73 F.3d 1352 (5th Cir.), *cert. granted*, 117 S. Ct. 293 (1996).

37. *See, e.g.*, Michael W. McConnell, *Religious Freedom at a Crossroads*, 59 U. CHI. L. REV. 115 (1992); Michael W. McConnell, *The Selective Funding Problem: Abortion and Religious Schools*, 104 HARV. L. REV. 989 (1991). Today, much controversy surrounds proposals for government-funded vouchers with which parents can pay tuition for religious schools. The Supreme Court is reviewing the status of *Aguilar v. Felton*, 473 U.S. 402 (1985), which barred New York City public schools from sending teachers to provide on-site instruction in parochial schools. *See* Agostini v. Felton, 117 S. Ct. 759 (1997), *granting cert. to* Felton v. Secretary, U.S. Dep't of Education, 101 F.3d 1394 (2d Cir. 1996). This challenge may well succeed. *See* Joseph P. Viteritti, *Choosing Equality: Religious Freedom and Educational Opportunity Under Constitutional Federalism*, 15 YALE L. & POL'Y REV. 113, 165 n.301 (1996).

38. *See* Pierce v. Society of Sisters, 268 U.S. 510 (1925); Meyer v. Nebraska, 262 U.S. 390 (1923). Such groups are actively litigating the constitutionality of states' official English policies. *See, e.g.*, Arizonans for Official English v. Arizona, No. 95–974, 1997 WL 84990 (U.S. Mar. 3, 1997).

39. *See generally* ARTHUR SCHLESINGER, JR., THE AGE OF JACKSON (1945).

40. *See generally* LAWRENCE GOODWYN, DEMOCRATIC PROMISE: THE POPULIST MOMENT IN AMERICA (1976).

41. *See* ARTHUR SCHLESINGER, JR., THE COMING OF THE NEW DEAL 489–507 (1959).

42. At the same time, the Democratic Party, particularly at the national level, has increasingly cultivated big business. *See* E.J. DIONNE, THEY ONLY LOOK DEAD 140 (1996); Alison Mitchell. *The Fund Machine: Building a Bulging War Chest*, N.Y. TIMES, Dec. 27, 1996, at A1.

43. *See, e.g.*, ARTHUR F. BENTLEY, THE PROCESS OF GOVERNMENT (Peter H. Odegard ed., Belknap Press 1967) (1908).

44. *See* DAVID B. TRUMAN, THE GOVERNMENTAL PROCESS (1951).

45. *See* DAHL, *supra* note 15.

46. *See* MARTIN MEYERSON & EDWARD C. BANFIELD, POLITICS, PLANNING AND THE PUBLIC INTEREST (1955).

47. The emergence of a pluralist political science that justified policy outcomes by reference to the fairness of the processes that produced them was hardly an isolated academic development. It paralleled the rise of a more general intellectual paradigm that tended to suppress or marginalize ideological conflict, a paradigm exemplified by

the functionalist sociology of Talcott Parsons, *see* Talcott Parsons, Structure and Process in Modern Societies (1960), and Daniel Bell, *see* Daniel Bell. The End of Ideology (1960), the behavioral psychology of B.F. Skinner, *see* B.F. Skinner, Science and Human Behavior (1953), and the analytical philosophy that increasingly dominated normative political theory.

48. In retrospect, at least, the pluralist system might be viewed as having accommodated protest politics rather comfortably within its dynamic, expansive processes and hence within its self-defining legitimation capacities. Even groups such as war protesters, welfare rights advocates, and environmentalists, whose political resources might have seemed limited to an ability to impede normal governmental processes, asserted compelling moral claims and mobilized media attention. Indeed, these groups were able to extract concessions—in some cases, remarkable victories—from interests that were much more powerful in conventional terms. For accounts of their political struggles, see, for example. Taylor Branch, Parting the Waters: America in the King Years, 1954–63 (1988); Martha F. Davis, Brutal Need: Lawyers and the Welfare Rights Movement, 1960–1973 (1993); Michael Lipsky, Protest in City Politics: Rent Strikes, Housing and the Power of the Poor (1970); and Frances Fox Piven & Richard A. Cloward, Poor People's Movements (1977).

49. *See, e.g.,* Peter Bachrach, The Theory of Democratic Elitism: A Critique (1967); Lowi, *supra* note 16; Grant McConnell, Private Power and American Democracy (1966).

50. *See* Lowi, *supra* note 16, at 50–61.

51. *See generally* Mary Summers, *Putting Populism Back In: Rethinking Agricultural Politics and Policy,* 70 Agric. Hist. 395, 400–09 (1996) (reviewing and critiquing these and other anti-pluralist scholars for their neglect of influence of countervailing populist interest groups).

52. *See, e.g.,* James M. Buchanan & Gordon Tullock, The Calculus of Consent (1962); Mancur Olson, The Logic of Collective Action (1965); Richard A. Posner, *Theories of Economic Regulation,* 5 Bell J. Econ. & Mgmt. Sci. 335 (1974); George J. Stigler, *The Theory of Economic Regulation, in* Chicago Studies in Political Economy 209, 209–33 (George J. Stigler ed., 1988). An important exception is Gary S. Becker, *A Theory of Competition Among Pressure Groups for Political Influence,* 98 Q.J. Econ. 371 (1983), which modeled politicians and bureaucrats as mere agents of interest groups rather than as independent sellers of services, and which predicts that policies that increase efficiency are likely to prevail in pressure-group competition.

53. The critical legal studies scholars also tended to emphasize certain distinctive themes, including the indeterminacy of legal rules and the public mystification effected by liberal ideology. *See generally* The Politics of Law: A Progressive Critique (David Kairys ed., 1982).

54. Because this term has long been conventional in political discourse, I shall not continue to use inverted commas. I do so initially only to call attention to the fact that, although these groups naturally seek to secure the political benefit of such an approbative term, the correspondence between their activities and policy goals, on the one hand, and the public interest, on the other, is largely if not entirely in the eye of the beholder. *See generally* Peter H. Schuck, *Public Interest Groups and the Policy Process,* 37 Pub. Admin. Rev. 132 (1977).

55. The classic account of this argument is Olson, *supra* note 52. *See also* James Q. Wilson, Political Organizations (1973). For a review and critique of this literature, see

DANIEL A. FARBER & PHILIP P. FRICKEY, LAW AND PUBLIC CHOICE (1991); JERRY L. MASHAW, GREED, CHAOS, AND GOVERNANCE: USING PUBLIC CHOICE TO IMPROVE PUBLIC LAW (1997); and Peter H. Schuck, *The Politics of Regulation*, 90 YALE L.J. 702 (1981) (book review).

56. *See infra* text accompanying notes 76–78.

57. On the proliferation in this period of public interest groups and of interest groups generally, see Mark P. Petracca, *The Rediscovery of Interest Group Politics*, in POLITICS OF INTERESTS, *supra* note 17, at 3, 13–18; and Jack L. Walker & Frank R. Baumgartner, *Survey Research and Membership in Voluntary Associations*, 32 AM. J. POL. SCI. 908 (1988).

58. *See infra* text accompanying notes 137–140.

59. *See infra* text accompanying note 65.

60. *See* RALPH NADER, UNSAFE AT ANY SPEED (1965).

61. *See, e.g.,* PAUL C. LIGHT, THICKENING GOVERNMENT: FEDERAL HIERARCHY AND THE DIFFUSION OF ACCOUNTABILITY (1995); INTENSIVE CARE: HOW CONGRESS SHAPES HEALTH POLICY (Thomas E. Mann & Norman J. Ornstein eds., 1995).

62. *See, e.g.,* THE FEDERALIST No. 46, at 298 (James Madison) (Clinton Rossiter ed., 1961) (noting that federalist systems protect against "ambitious encroachments of the federal government on the authority of the State governments"), No. 48, at 308 (James Madison) ("[P]ower is of an encroaching nature and . . . ought to be effectually restrained from passing the limits assigned to it."). But the authors of the *Federalist Papers* were also wary of the dangers caused by governmental weakness, dangers that their experience under the Articles of Confederation had made all too manifest, *See, e.g.,* THE FEDERALIST No. 21, *supra,* at 138 (Alexander Hamilton) ("The next most palpable defect of the existing Confederation is the total want of a SANCTION to its laws. The United States as now composed have no power to exact obedience, or punish disobedience to their resolutions. . . .").

63. *See supra* text accompanying notes 39–41.

64. *See, e.g.,* Tom Mathews et al., *Single-Issue Politics*, NEWSWEEK, Nov. 6, 1978, at 48.

65. *See supra* text accompanying note 60. On the increase in the number of special interest groups in recent decades, see *supra* note 57. A vivid example of this organizational growth was the evolution of environmental policy in the Reagan administration, whose assaults on existing policies and on proregulation environmental groups only succeeded in stimulating additional public support for those policies and groups. An analogous, equally predictable development was that more extensive regulation tended to generate greater political and legal resistance by the regulated industry. *See generally* JOHN M. MENDELOFF, THE DILEMMA OF TOXIC SUBSTANCE REGULATION: HOW OVERREGULATION CAUSES UNDERREGULATION AT OSHA (1988).

66. *See supra* text accompanying notes 7–13.

67. THE FEDERALIST No. 10, at 78 (James Madison) (Clinton Rossiter ed., 1961).

68. *See* ROBERT MICHELS, POLITICAL PARTIES: A SOCIOLOGICAL STUDY OF THE OLIGARCHICAL TENDENCIES OF MODERN DEMOCRACY 377–92 (Eden & Cedar Paul trans., Free Press 1949).

69. Few corporations have successfully introduced substantial worker control without a loss of efficiency. *See* Henry Hansmann, *When Does Worker Ownership Work? ESOPs, Law Firms, Codetermination and Economic Democracy*, 99 YALE L.J. 1749, 1784 (1990) (arguing that efficiency generally improves only in firms with highly homogeneous work forces); *see also* Adam Bryant, *No Longer Flying in Formation: Labor Rifts Return to Employee-Owned United Airlines*, N.Y. TIMES, Jan. 17, 1997, at D1 (discussing difficulties of employee ownership at United Airlines).

70. *See generally* Herman Benson, *Union Democracy and the Landrum-Griffin Act*, 11 N.Y.U. REV. L. & SOC. CHANGE 153 (1982–1983). For a compelling critique by a union lawyer, see THOMAS GEOGHEGAN, WHICH SIDE ARE YOU ON?: TRYING TO BE FOR LABOR WHEN IT'S FLAT ON ITS BACK (1991). Violations of union democracy have sometimes been the subject of Justice Department prosecutions. The recent Teamsters election exemplifies the fragility of hard-won democratic reforms in unions. *See* Steven Greenhouse, *Teamster Counterrevolution: Why It Nearly Won Election*, N.Y. TIMES, Dec. 22, 1996, at A1.

71. *See* NELSON W. POLSBY, CONSEQUENCES OF PARTY REFORM 53–88 (1983).

72. Membership in the AARP is open to anyone over the age of 50 and annual dues are only eight dollars (for which members may receive a variety of benefits, including discounts on drugs).

73. Madison explicitly recognized and addressed this problem. *See* THE FEDERALIST No. 10, at 78 (James Madison) (Clinton Rossiter ed., 1961).

74. This advantage, however, can be exaggerated. Even business interests confront organizational and coalitional difficulties. The classic study demonstrating this is RAYMOND A. BAUER ET AL., AMERICAN BUSINESS AND PUBLIC POLICY (1963).

75. *See, e.g.,* David Cay Johnston, *High Earners Paying No U.S. Income Tax Rise to Nearly 2400 in 1993*, N.Y. TIMES, Apr. 18, 1997, at A21.

76. For a general review and critique of this literature, see FARBER & FRICKEY, *supra* note 55.

77. "McNollgast" refers to the collaborative work of Mathew McCubbins, Roger Noll, and Barry Weingast. *See, e.g.,* Mathew McCubbins et al., *Administrative Procedures as Instruments of Political Control*, 3 J.L. ECON. & ORG. 243 (1987); Mathew McCubbins et al., *Structure and Process, Politics and Policy: Administrative Arrangements and the Political Control of Agencies*, 75 VA. L. REV. 431 (1989); Mathew D. McCubbins et al., *Positive and Normative Models of Procedural Rights: An Integrative Approach to Administrative Procedures*, 6 J.L. ECON. & ORG. 307 (1990).

78. *See, e.g.,* OLSON, *supra* note 52; OLIVER E. WILLIAMSON, MARKETS AND HIERARCHIES, ANALYSIS AND ANTITRUST IMPLICATIONS: A STUDY IN THE ECONOMICS OF INTERNAL ORGANIZATION (1975). The seminal article in this field is Ronald Coase, *The Nature of the Firm*, 4 ECONOMICA 386 (1937).

79. They are also in a better position to shape favorable judicial doctrine by investing strategically in litigation. *See* Marc Galanter, *Why the "Haves" Come Out Ahead: Speculations on the Limits of Legal Change*, 9 L. & SOC'Y REV. 95, 100–03 (1974).

80. *But see* Becker, *supra* note 52 (predicting strong tendency toward more efficient policies, rather than less).

81. Examples include agricultural subsidies, segmented financial-services markets, a bloated tort system, rent controls, and many aspects of environmental policy.

82. Commonly cited examples of such distortion are the misleading information campaigns mounted by both the supporters and the opponents of tort reform. *See* STEPHEN J. CARROLL WITH NICHOLAS PACE, ASSESSING THE EFFECTS OF TORT REFORMS 3 (1987); Marc Galanter, *News from Nowhere: The Debased Debate on Civil Justice*, 71 DENV. U. L. REV. 77 (1993); Marc Galanter, *Real World Torts: An Antidote to Anecdote*, 55 MD. L. REV. 1093 (1996).

83. One cannot easily resist the temptation to point out the hypocrisy of such claims when made by critics such as Ross Perot, whose fortune in part reflects his talent for cultivating and then exploiting this same business-government connection.

84. For an exploration of this and related ethical problems, see Ronald M. Levin, *Congressional Ethics and Constituent Advocacy in An Age of Mistrust*, 95 MICH. L. REV. 1, 84–107 (1996). In an interesting twist, my colleague Ian Ayres and Jeremy Bulow suggest that one remedy for this problem would be to prohibit the disclosure of contributions to candidates. *See* Ian Ayres & Jeremy Bulow, The Donation Booth (Feb. 27, 1997) (unpublished manuscript, on file with author).

85. The Internal Revenue Code is studded with examples. *See* Richard L. Doernberg & Fred S. McChesney, *On the Accelerating Rate and Decreasing Durability of Tax Reform*, 71 MINN. L. REV. 913 (1987) (arguing that tax legislation is a "contract" between legislators and private interests seeking beneficial tax provisions). *See generally* JEFFREY H. BIRNBAUM & ALAN S. MURRAY, SHOWDOWN AT GUCCI GULCH: LAWMAKERS, LOBBYISTS, AND THE UNLIKELY TRIUMPH OF TAX REFORM (1987); MICHAEL J. GRAETZ, THE DECLINE (AND FALL?) OF THE INCOME TAX (1997); Ronald F. Wilson, *Federal Tax Policy: The Political Influence of American Small Business*, 37 S. TEX. L. REV. 15 (1996). The list of special interest influence is hardly limited to tax law, however. The fingerprints of trial lawyers, for example, can readily be found on "tort reform" measures, affirmative action policies reflect the handiwork of civil rights groups and anti-discrimination bureaucracies, and the budget is a compilation of outlays demanded by beneficiary groups. Indeed, one tax law scholar notes that "the Code is much more coherent from a policy perspective than most people believe and less riddled with special interest provisions than many other areas of the law." Letter from Professor Edward Zelinsky, Cardozo Law School, to author (Mar. 10, 1997) (on file with author).

86. Important examples are the Food Quality Protection Act, Pub. L. No. 104–170, 110 Stat. 1489 (1996) (codified at 7 U.S.C. s 136), and the Clean Air Act Amendments of 1990, Pub. L. No. 101–549, 104 Stat. 2399 (codified in scattered sections of 42 U.S.C.).

87. Between 1970 and 1991, public spending on education—per student from kindergarten to twelfth grade—increased from $3431 to $5958 (in 1993–1994 dollars). *See* U.S. DEP'T OF COMMERCE, STATISTICAL ABSTRACT OF THE UNITED STATES 153 tbls. 231–32 (1996) [hereinafter STATISTICAL ABSTRACT].

The number of low-income children actually served under Medicaid has grown rapidly since the mid–1980s, largely due to statutory changes expanding coverage well beyond the traditionally categorically eligible AFDC families. The largest growth in Medicaid spending occurred between 1988 and 1992, when the program grew at over 22% each year, primarily because of expanded coverage of children; nominal dollar expenditures per beneficiary also grew rapidly during this period, increasing by almost 50%. *See* John Holahan & David Liska, *Reassessing the Outlook for Medicaid Spending Growth*, NEW FEDERALISM: ISSUES & OPTIONS FOR STATES (Urban Institute, Series A, No. A–6, Washington, D.C.), Mar. 1997, at 1, 1–2. Although future growth rates in the program may be lower than this, *see id.* at 4–6, several bipartisan bills are pending in Congress that would further expand the coverage of low-income children. *See* Robert Pear, *Senate Bills to Extend Medicaid to Children*, N.Y. TIMES, Apr. 24, 1997, at B8 (describing proposals).

The welfare-reform legislation enacted in 1996, although bitterly and in some respects rightly denounced for its possible effects on low-income children, can best be understood as an effort, perhaps misguided, to improve the long-term prospects of these children by altering their parents' incentives and behavior. *See* Personal Responsibility and Work Opportunity Reconciliation Act of 1996, Pub. L. No. 104–193, 110 Stat. 2105 (codified in scattered sections of 42 U.S.C.).

88. *See* Robert Pear, *Congress Weighs More Regulation on Managed Care*, N.Y. TIMES, Mar. 10, 1997, at A1 (reporting that Congress, anticipating public frustration, is likely to dictate some industry practices, as it did during its 1996 session).

89. Indeed, neo-conservative critics argue that those who propagate the notion of a politics of ideas, rather than of interests, themselves constitute an increasingly powerful special interest—a "new class." *See supra* note 16.

90. *See, e.g.,* R. SHEP MELNICK, REGULATION AND THE COURTS: THE CASE OF THE CLEAN AIR ACT 37 (1983); Bruce A. Ackerman et al., *Toward a Theory of Statutory Evolution*, 1 J.L. ECON. & ORG, 313, 320 (1985).

91. For a comparison of social conditions in 1965 and 1995 documenting significant improvements in these and other areas, see Peter H. Schuck, *Alien Ruminations*, 105 YALE L.J. 1963, 2007–12 (1996) (book review). For a more rueful comparison of the 1950s and the 1990s, one that argues that the decline of authority caused by Americans' obsession with increased personal choice has produced social disintegration, see ALAN EHRENHALT, THE LOST CITY: DISCOVERING THE FORGOTTEN VIRTUES OF COMMUNITY IN THE CHICAGO OF THE 1950s (1995).

92. *See* ETHNIC IRONIES: LATINO POLITICS IN THE 1992 ELECTIONS, at xi–xiii (Rodolfo O. de la Garza & Louis DiSipio eds., 1996) (arguing that luck is important condition for political influence and that it magnified Latino influence in 1992 elections).

93. *See* Kevin Sack, *For the Nation's Politicians, Big Tobacco No Longer Bites*, N.Y. TIMES, Apr. 22, 1997, at A1.

94. The enactment and vast expansion of the food stamp program has virtually eliminated hunger from American life. *See* R. SHEP MELNICK, BETWEEN THE LINES: INTERPRETING WELFARE RIGHTS 183–232 (1994). Although the real value of AFDC benefits eroded during the 1980s, Medicare and Medicaid expenditures grew rapidly, helping many low-income people. *See* Schuck, *supra* note 91, at 2011. Since 1965, the poor have seen an increase in their standard of living. *See* Daniel T. Slesnick, *Gaining Ground: Poverty in the Postwar United States*, 101 J. POL. ECON. 1, 16 tbl.3 (1993). For data on the growth of social welfare spending, see STATISTICAL ABSTRACT, *supra* note 87, at 368–69.

The 1996 welfare reform legislation, which will reduce federal AFDC expenditures, will have relatively little effect on the larger entitlement programs. Indeed, some of these programs, such as Medicaid, Medicare, and Social Security (and possibly food stamps), are expected to grow substantially in the future for demographic reasons. Although President Clinton has proposed capping Medicaid payments, the governors are strongly opposed to such limits. *See* Robert Pear, *Governors Oppose Clinton Proposal for Medicaid Cap*, N.Y. TIMES, Jan. 31, 1997, at A1. Moreover, additional state expenditures on safety net programs may fill some of the gap created by the new legislation. *See* Jennifer Preston, *Trenton Approves Bill Overhauling Welfare System*, N.Y. TIMES, Feb. 21, 1997, at A1 (reporting that New Jersey legislature approved legislation proposed by Gov. Whitman continuing cash benefits and Medicaid for legal immigrants and providing other coverage no longer required or funded by federal government). Hence total safety net expenditures are likely to remain at or near the historically high levels achieved before the 1996 changes were enacted.

Recent research comparing a variety of poverty rate measures across nations indicates that the United States (along with Canada and Luxembourg) has the lowest absolute poverty rate, as measured by equivalent purchasing power, in the world. When measured by relative poverty rates, as determined by incomes below a given percentage of average income, the United States is one of the highest among industrialized nations. *See* McKinley L. Blackburn, Comparing Poverty: The United States and Other Industrial Nations (Feb. 7, 1997) (unpublished manuscript, on file with author).

95. Peterson, *supra* note 17, at 337.

96. *See* Edward A. Zelinsky, *Text, Purpose, Capacity, and* Albertson's, 2 FLA. TAX REV. 717, 729 (1996) (arguing that under constraint of revenue neutrality requirements congressmen otherwise indifferent to granting special interest tax benefits are forced to attack such benefits to pay for desired programs).

97. *See* discussion *infra* Part IV.

98. *See* Bradley A. Smith, *Faulty Assumptions and Undemocratic Consequences of Campaign Finance Reform*, 105 YALE L.J. 1049, 1067 (1996) ("It seems clear that many candidates win despite spending less than their opponents, and that the correlation between spending and success is not as strong as other indicators, such as the correlation between incumbency and success.").

99. *See* Graham K. Wilson, *American Interest Groups in Comparative Perspective, in* POLITICS OF INTERESTS, *supra* note 17, at 80, 95.

100. *See supra* Part I.C.

101. Since 1982, the number of employees in the nonprofit sector has grown by a third, compared with 25% growth in government and private-sector employment. *See* Judith Miller, *Gift Enables Harvard to Establish Center for Study of Nonprofit Sector*, N.Y. TIMES, Apr. 12, 1997, at A12. In 1994, some 16.4 million people worked or volunteered for some 1.4 million nonprofit groups. *See id.*

102. On the other hand, some interesting experiments are seeking to use modern technology to facilitate public deliberation about policies and candidates. *See, e.g.*, JAMES S. FISHKIN, DEMOCRACY AND DELIBERATION (1991).

103. The classic demonstration of this is ANTHONY DOWNS, AN ECONOMIC THEORY OF DEMOCRACY 238–59 (1957).

104. Interacting within special interest groups, individuals learn communication and organizational skills that can be readily transferred to political activities outside those groups. *See* Sidney Verba et al., *The Big Tilt: Participatory Inequality in America*, AM. PROSPECT, May-June 1997, at 74, 79. Although Verba et al. stress that low-income citizens participate at lower rates than more affluent ones, *see id.*, they do not show that the resulting policies adversely affect the interest of the former compared with the policies that might otherwise be adopted.

105. *See supra* text accompanying notes 68–71.

106. *See supra* text accompanying notes 76–84.

107. *See* MANCUR OLSON, THE RISE AND DECLINE OF NATIONS 41–44 (1982). For a critique of Olson's book by the author of this Essay, see Peter H. Schuck, *The Politics of Economic Growth*, 2 YALE L. & POL'Y REV. 359 (1984) (book review).

108. Robert D. Putnam, *Bowling Alone: America's Declining Social Capital*, 6 J. OF DEMOCRACY 65 (1995). Putnam has developed and applied the conception of social capital more extensively in ROBERT D. PUTNAM, MAKING DEMOCRACY WORK: CIVIC TRADITIONS IN MODERN ITALY (1993).

109. *See, e.g.*, Nicholas Lemann, *Kicking in Groups: The Alleged Decline of America's Communal Culture*, ATLANTIC MONTHLY, Apr. 1996, at 22, 25 (arguing that perhaps "the dire statistics in *Bowling Alone* reflect merely a mutation rather than a disappearance of civic virtue, because civic virtue has found new expressions in response to economic and social changes" and citing increase in soccer leagues, number of restaurants, and small businesses as examples): Katha Pollitt, *For Whom the Ball Rolls*, NATION, Apr. 15,

1996, at 9, 9 (arguing that Putnam's "whole theory is seriously out of touch with the complexities of contemporary life").

According to Pollitt, the trend discussed by Putnam is not to be mourned:

> It would be amazing if league bowling survived the passing of the way of life that brought it into being, nor am I so sure we need mourn it. People still bowl, after all. In fact they bowl more than ever,. . . [a]nd despite Putnam's title, they don't bowl alone. They bowl with friends, on dates, with their kids, with other families. The bowling story could be told as one of happy progress: from a drink-sodden night of spouse avoidance with the same old faces from work to temperate and spontaneous fun with one's intimate friends and relations.

Id.; see also Andrew Greeley, *The Other Civic America: Religion and Social Capital*, AM. PROSPECT, May-June 1997, at 68, 73 (showing increase in volunteering since 1981, especially among younger people and much of it through religious organizations).

110. For discussions of religiously based political activity, see STEPHEN L. CARTER, THE CULTURE OF DISBELIEF 67–82 (1993); and JAMES DAVISON HUNTER, CULTURE WARS: THE STRUGGLE TO DEFINE AMERICA 89–95 (1991).

111. One worrisome possibility, for example, is a mass politics mobilized spasmodically by centralized institutions and actors through their skillful, cynical manipulation of the mass media. Some critics have suggested that our political system is moving rapidly in this direction. *See, e.g.,* KEVIN PHILLIPS, ARROGANT CAPITAL at xi–xviii (1994).

112. New disclosure requirements, discussed briefly *infra* at note 154 and accompanying text, could almost certainly improve the system without violating constitutional principles. As I have mentioned, however, mandatory *non*-disclosure, if enforceable, might also be an improvement. *See supra* note 84.

113. Historian David Donald reports that the Lincoln-Douglas debate held at Ottawa, a town of 9000 people, 80 miles from Chicago, attracted 10,000 spectators who journeyed there by foot, horseback, carriage, boat, and rail. As there were no seats, these spectators stood during the three-hour debate. *See* DAVID H. DONALD, LINCOLN 215–16 (1995).

114. Voter turnout in 1996 was 48.8% of the voting-age population. *See* David A. Bositis, *The Farrakhan Factor: Behind the Big Increase in Black Men Voting*, WASH. POST, Dec. 8, 1996, at C1 (reporting turnout decline from 55.2% in 1992 to the lowest rate since 1924). The proportion of Americans who contribute money to campaigns, on the other hand, has almost doubled during the past 20 years. *See* Verba et al., *supra* note 104, at 75.

It should be noted that some studies of non-voting in the United States reveal somewhat less dismaying explanations for this phenomenon (for example, the relatively large number of elections held at inconvenient times, the—correct—belief that one's vote will not affect the outcome, and a degree of acquiescence or satisfaction that lowers the voter's stakes in the outcome). These studies also reveal that the political preferences of voters and non-voters are quite similar, and that non-voters tend to be more ignorant about public issues than voters. The classic study is RAYMOND F. WOLFINGER & STEVEN J. ROSENSTONE, WHO VOTES? (1980). *See also* E.J. Dionne, Jr., *If Nonvoters Had Voted: Same Winner, But Bigger*, N.Y. TIMES. Nov. 21, 1988, at B16.

115. An example is the current dispute over the reliability and objectivity of government-sponsored research on the so-called Gulf War Syndrome. *See* Eric Schmitt. *No Proof, But New Clues on Gulf War Illness*, N.Y. TIMES, Jan. 12, 1997, s 4 (Wneek in Review), at 2 (reporting presidential advisory committee's finding that "Pentagon's initial in-

quiry into [reports of chemical exposure in Gulf War] was so inept that much more research was needed").

116. For the classic discussion of the economic significance of organizational exit, see ALBERT O. HIRSCHMAN, EXIT, VOICE, AND LOYALTY (1970).

117. Examples include "closed shop" unions, corporate contributions to charities or political campaigns, and compulsory contributions to agricultural cooperatives' advertising. On the latter, see Wileman Bros. & Elliott, Inc. v. Espy, 58 F.3d 1367, 1374 (9th Cir. 1995), *cert. granted* 116 S. Ct. 1875 (1996), *and cert. denied* 116 S. Ct. 1876 (1996).

118. *See supra* note 72. The political influence of the AARP, it appears, derives not simply from its number of members but also from its skill in representing and mobilizing them on particular policy issues, such as the swift repeal in 1989 of the mandated catastrophic-care coverage under Medicare, *see* Medicare Catastrophic Coverage Repeal Act of 1989, Pub. L. No. 101–234, 103 Stat. 1979 (codified in scattered sections of 42 U.S.C.) (repealing Medicare Catastrophic Coverage Act of 1988, Pub. L. No. 100–360, 102 Stat. 683), and the periodic easing of the limits under Social Security on retirees' earned income, *see, e.g.*, Senior Citizens' Right to Work Act, 42 U.S.C.A. s 403 (West 1996).

119. *See supra* Part II.B.

120. *See* ALEXIS DE TOQUEVILLE, DEMOCRACY IN AMERICA 513–17 (George Lawrence trans., J.P. Mayer ed., Perennial Library 1988) (1840). Toqueville, who hoped to influence the development of Louis Philippe's bourgeois regime in France, extended his analysis beyond the United States to all liberal polities.

121. *See* PETER BERGER & RICHARD JOHN NEUHAUS, TO EMPOWER PEOPLE: THE ROLE OF MEDIATING STRUCTURES IN PUBLIC POLICY (1977). Indeed, the term is now quite ubiquitous. *See, e.g.*, Calabresi, *supra* note 19.

122. For one example, see Peter H. Schuck & Harrison Wellford, *Democracy and the Good Life in a Company Town: The Case of St. Mary's*, HARPER'S, May 1972, at 56.

123. *See supra* notes 15–16 and accompanying text.

124. *See, e.g.*, BRUCE A. ACKERMAN, SOCIAL JUSTICE IN THE LIBERAL STATE (1980); JÜRGEN HABERMAS, BETWEEN FACTS AND NORMS: CONTRIBUTIONS TO A DISCOURSE THEORY OF LAW AND DEMOCRACY (William Rehg trans., MIT Press 1996).

125. *See, e.g.*, JOHN RAWLS, A THEORY OF JUSTICE (1971).

126. *See id.* at 75–83.

127. *See, e.g.*, ROBERT NOZICK, ANARCHY, STATE, AND UTOPIA 297–334 (1974).

128. *See, e.g.*, RONALD DWORKIN, LAW'S EMPIRE 297–98 (1986); Ronald Dworkin, *What is Equality? Part 1: Equality of Welfare*, 10 PHIL. & PUB. AFF. 185 (1981); Ronald Dworkin, *What is Equality? Part 2: Equality of Resources*, 10 PHIL. & PUB. AFF. 283 (1981).

129. *See* Schuck, *Alien Ruminations, supra* note 91.

130. THE FEDERALIST NO. 10, at 78 (James Madison) (Clinton Rossiter ed., 1961).

131. Interestingly, Madison viewed a complicated, divided government full of checks and balances as a way to curb the influence of factions. *See* Sunstein, *supra* note 8, at 43–45 (discussing THE FEDERALIST NO. 51 (James Madison)).

132. *See supra* Part III.A.

133. *See, e.g.*, William Drozdiak, *German Jobless at Post-WWII High: Recession's Sweep Provokes Calls for Strikes, Concern for Single Currency*, WASH. POST, Jan. 10, 1997, at A28; Thomas Kamm, *French Labor Unrest, Austerity Budget Renew Doubts About Monetary Union*, WALL ST. J., Aug. 29, 1996, at A4; Thomas Kamm & Cacilie Rohwedder, *Continental Divide: Many Europeans Fear Cuts in Social Benefits In One-Currency Plan*, WALL ST. J., July 30, 1996, at A1; Anne Swardson & Charles Trueheart, *French Leaders Face*

Autumn of Discontent: Opposition Groups Plan to Protest Benefit Cuts, WASH. POST, Sept. 1, 1996, at A37.

134. Retiring politicians who have seen the problem first-hand often issue such warnings. *See, e.g.*, David S. Broder, *Three Disillusioned Democrats*, WASH. POST, Nov. 10, 1995, at C7 (quoting Sen. Nunn); Helen Dewar, *Bradley Won't Run for Reelection to Senate in 1996*, WASH. POST, Aug. 17, 1995, at A1.

135. Some examples at the federal level include the substantial, if not total, economic deregulation of basic industries such as telecommunications, financial services, energy, trucking, railroads, buses, and airlines: renovation of the welfare and social security programs entrenched since the New Deal; reform of the federal budgeting and inter-governmental relations systems; a dramatic reduction in the military's share of the national economy and budget; a vast expansion of the national park and wilderness systems; and a fundamental overhaul of the major tax, immigration, housing, agricultural, transportation, campaign finance, environmental, intellectual property, and civil rights laws. Reforms at the state level are equally impressive. *See generally* CARL VAN HORN, THE STATE OF THE STATES (3d ed. 1996); LARRY SABATO, GOODBYE TO GOOD-TIME CHARLIE: THE AMERICAN GOVERNOR TRANSFORMED, 1950–1975 (2d ed. 1983).

136. This phrase is the title of a book that reviews some of the major developments in policymaking during this period. *See* THE NEW POLITICS OF PUBLIC POLICY (Marc K. Landy & Martin A. Levin eds., 1995).

137. *See* OLSON, *supra* note 107, at 44–46 (1982). Olson's theory has been popularized more recently in JONATHAN RAUCH, DEMOSCLEROSIS 23–31 (1994). Earlier in this Essay, I discussed another erroneous prediction of this version of public choice theory: that free-rider problems would prevent the formation, and certainly the political effectiveness, of public interest groups representing diffuse public values. *See* text accompanying notes 52–58.

138. *See* Clifford Winston, *Economic Deregulation: Days of Reckoning for Micro Economists*, 31 J. ECON. LITERATURE 1263, 1274–75 (1993) [hereinafter Winston, *Economic Deregulation*] (observing that in nine industries studied—railroads, trucking, air transport, banking, natural gas, petroleum, telecommunications, cable television, and securities brokerage—which account for about 10% of GDP, deregulation produced price reductions, increased output, and service quality improvements); Clifford Winston, U.S. Industry Adjustment to Economic Deregulation (Sept. 1996) (unpublished manuscript, on file with author) (projecting additional efficiency gains over time in these industries as well as electric utilities, as longer term effects of deregulation occur). A number of studies have demonstrated large efficiency gains in the steel industry. *See, e.g.*, DONALD F. BARNETT & ROBERT W. CRANDALL, UP FROM THE ASHES: THE RISE OF THE STEEL MINIMILL IN THE UNITED STATES (1986); Robert W. Crandall, *From Competitiveness to Competition: The Threat of Minimills to Large National Steel Companies*, 22 RESOURCES POL'Y, 107, 116 fig. 7 (1996) (observing enormous reduction in price of industry's bellweather product, cold rolled sheet steel). Other studies have shown the same with respect to the telecommunications industry. *See, e.g.*, Robert W. Crandall & Jonathan Galst, *Productivity Growth: The Telephone Industry Since 1984*, *in* THE SERVICE PRODUCTIVITY AND QUALITY CHALLENGE 391, 402 tbl.5 (Patrick Harker ed., 1995) (observing that productivity growth has accelerated due to competition and technological change since breakup of AT&T). The same is true for the automobile industry. *See, e.g.*, PAUL INGRASSIA & JOSEPH B. WHITE, COMEBACK: THE FALL AND RISE OF THE AMERICAN AUTOMOBILE INDUSTRY (1994) (discussing resurgence of American auto industry in early–1990s); James Bennet,

Auto Makers Begin to Rethink Prices, N.Y. TIMES, Jan. 23, 1995, at D1 (reporting that "auto makers have achieved enormous productivity gains and other cost decreases in recent years"); James Sterngold, *Facing the Next Recession Without Fear: Newly Leaned Corporations Expect to Do Fine When the Tough Times Come*, N.Y. TIMES, May 9, 1995, at D1 (observing that big three auto makers since 1980s have "sharply reduced costs and shortened the time it takes to get vehicles from the drawing board to the showroom floor").

Judgments about efficiency trends are harder to make in the health care context because the outputs of the system, which constitutes about 14% of GDP, are notoriously difficult to define and measure. Nevertheless, many analysts of the health care industry believe that the industry has become significantly more efficient in recent years. In particular, downsizing, cost controls, and managed care have begun to have substantial effects on excess capacity in the hospital sector, which accounts for roughly 40% of the system's costs. Telephone Interview with Professor Joseph Newhouse, Director, Division of Health Policy Research and Education, Harvard University (Feb. 25, 1997); *see also* Robert Pear, *In Separate Studies, Costs of Hospitals Are Debated*, N.Y. TIMES, Mar. 13, 1997, at D2 (discussing new data from federal commission "show[ing] remarkable reductions in the growth of hospital operating costs in the last three years"). Recent analyses also suggest that the system is delivering at least some kinds of care more efficiently; costs have increased somewhat but the improvements in quality of care and resulting survival rates and life expectancy have improved even more. *See* DAVID CUTLER ET AL., ARE MEDICAL PRICES DECLINING? (National Bureau of Econ. Research Working Paper No. 5750, 1996) (arguing that, according to revised cost of living index, real price of treating heart attacks between 1984 and 1991 may have declined, taking quality into account).

139. Despite these aggregate gains in national wealth and efficiency (or perhaps because of them), inequality in the United States has increased according to some measures. This dismaying rise in inequality appears to reflect a number of complex, interrelated developments: increasing economic returns to education; immigration; the surge of relatively inexperienced young and female workers into the labor force; erosion of the real value of the minimum wage and of AFDC benefits; the extraordinary increase in single, female-headed households; the drop in black male labor-force participation in urban areas; and other structural changes in the economy. On balance, some of these factors seem socially desirable and likely to reduce inequality in the long run even if they increase it in the short run. Higher returns to education, for example, create strong incentives for youths and lower-skilled workers to acquire more education and training and thus improve their economic prospects. And as women who entered the work force in the 1970s and 1980s acquire the additional experience and skills that seniority brings, they will (as they already have) continue to close the gender gap in wages and income. Recent evidence suggests that the income gap may already be narrowing again. *See* Robert Hershey, Jr., *Clinton Aides Say that Income Gap Narrows*, N.Y. TIMES, Feb. 11, 1997, at D3 (discussing annual report of Council of Economic Advisors). For present purposes, however, the relevant point is that the rise in inequality is overwhelmingly the result of deep changes in large, indeed global, economic and social structures rather than the activities of domestic special interest groups.

140. The explanations certainly include deregulation, which was strongly opposed by the major special interest groups (large firms, unions, and trade associations) in

these industries. *See generally* Winston, *Economic Deregulation, supra* note 138. Increased foreign competition, which powerful special interests also seek to restrict, is the main reason for growing efficiency in the automobile and steel industries, which were not deregulated. Foreign competition, however, can explain only part of efficiency gains in the economy as a whole; imports still account for a relatively small share of the U.S. economy. *See* COUNCIL OF ECON. ADVISORS, ANNUAL REPORT, ECONOMIC REPORT OF THE PRESIDENT 300–01 tbl.B1 (1997) (reporting that imports accounted for 12% of U.S. economy in 1995).

141. For an interesting exploration of this theme, see Peter Huber, *Cyber Power,* FORBES, Dec. 2, 1996, at 142. As Huber points out, the relentless squeeze on inefficiency is a global phenomenon in which the industrial nations' inflation rates, tax rates, and regulatory structures seem to be converging under the pressure of these market forces. *See id.* at 147.

142. *See supra* note 57 and text accompanying note 65. This expansion in turn was fueled—but only in part—by the growing economic and social diversity in the United States. *See generally* Peter H. Schuck. *Some Reflections on the Federalism Debate, in* YALE L. & POL'Y REV.-YALE J. ON REG., SYMPOSIUM: CONSTRUCTING A NEW FEDERALISM 1 (1996).

143. For an interesting analysis of the effect of law on group and individual behavior, see Eric A. Posner, *The Regulation of Groups: The Influence of Legal and Nonlegal Sanctions on Collective Action,* 63 U. CHI. L. REV. 133 (1996).

144. For example, most commentators believe that private parochial schools do a better job of educating low-income children than do public schools, although disputes persist over whether the populations served are truly similar. *See, e.g.,* JOHN E. CHUBB & TERRY M. MOE, POLITICS, MARKETS AND AMERICAN SCHOOLS 181, 259–60 (1990). Another example is child welfare services such as adoption and foster care. Prison management may be another example, although the evidence is still incomplete. Private mail service is superior to the U.S. Postal Service, even taking into account the latter's legal duty to serve unprofitable localities. *See* James I. Campbell, Jr., *Politics and the Future of Postal Services, in* PERSPECTIVES ON POSTAL SERVICE ISSUES 194, 195–97 (Roger Sherman ed., 1980); Robert J. Barro, *Let's Play Monopoly,* WALL ST. J., Aug. 27, 1991, at A12.

On the other hand, very recent research on the accuracy of inflation forecasting has concluded that the Federal Reserve's forecasts are superior to those of commercial forecasters; the best explanation is that the Federal Reserve commits far more resources to the effort. *See Federal Reserve Forecasts Would Be Valuable to Commercial Forecasters,* NBER DIG., Jan. 1997, at 1, 1 (citing CHRISTINA ROMER & DAVID ROMER, FEDERAL RESERVE PRIVATE INFORMATION AND THE BEHAVIOR OF INTEREST RATES (National Bureau of Econ. Research Working Paper No. 5692, 1996)).

145. On the other hand, there have been occasional successes, such as the Chrysler and Lockheed bailouts and, more recently, Sematech, *See* Elizabeth Corcoran, *Chip Research Consortium to Drop U.S. Subsidy: Decision to Rely on Corporate Funding Reflects Industry's Comeback,* WASH. POST, Oct. 5, 1994, at F2.

146. See the discussion and references in John G. Simon, *The Tax Treatment of Nonprofit Organizations: A Review of Federal and State Policies, in* THE NONPROFIT SECTOR: A RESEARCH HANDBOOK 67, 91–93 (Walter W. Powell ed., 1987).

147. *See supra* text accompanying notes 96–97. In the tax area, Professor Zelinsky argues that this reduction in special interest influence is caused not only by the revenue neutrality requirement, but also by the structure of tax institutions more generally, including the greater diversity of congressional tax committees' membership compared

to that of the special subject matter committees. *See* Edward A. Zelinsky, *James Madison and Public Choice at Gucci Gulch: A Procedural Defense of Tax Expenditures and Tax Institutions*, 102 YALE L.J. 1165 (1993) (arguing that tax institutions, like Treasury and congressional tax committees, are less readily captured by special interests due to diverse nature of interests affected by tax system).

148. *Cf.* William D. Eggers, *The Incredible Shrinking State*, REASON, May 1997, at 35, 37 (arguing that New Zealand reformers, by proposing changes affecting many different special interests simultaneously, legitimated reform by spreading costs of change and winning special interest support).

149. *See supra* text accompanying notes 52 and 137–139.

150. *See* David E. Rosenbaum, *Republicans in Transition: Corporate Welfare's New Enemies*, N.Y. TIMES, Feb. 2, 1997, at D1. The growing power of John R. Kasich, the Chairman of the House Budget Committee and a fierce, apparently committed crusader against corporate welfare, may augur well for this challenge. *See* Joe Klein, *Balancing Act*, NEW YORKER, Feb. 17, 1997, at 34, 34–35.

151. *See, e.g.*, NAACP v. Claiborne Hardware Co., 458 U.S. 886 (1982) (protecting civil rights group from private interference); NAACP v. Button, 371 U.S. 415 (1963) (protecting civil rights group from public interference).

152. Senator Alan Simpson's crusade against the AARP, for example, may have been undertaken for a combination of partisan and policy-reform purposes. *See* Laurie McGinley, *Sen. Alan Simpson Challenges AARP's Tax-Exempt Status*, WALL ST. J., June 14, 1995. at B3. For Simpson's defense of his challenge to the AARP, see ALAN K. SIMPSON, RIGHT IN THE OLD GAZOO: A LIFETIME OF SCRAPPING WITH THE PRESS 160–61 (1996).

153. Many, if not most, of the grantees of the NEH, LSC, and CPB are, of course, already attempting to do so, sometimes with considerable success. *See* Andrea Adelson, *A Wider Public for Noncommercial Radio*, N.Y. TIMES, Feb. 10, 1997, at D8 (reporting that, on average, public stations rely on federal funds for only 16% of their budgets). Such efforts can also help government-funded groups test and augment the strength of their support in the economic and philanthropic markets rather than in the political one alone. *See* Lawrie Mifflin, *For WNET, a New Fund and a New Security*, N.Y. TIMES, Apr. 17, 1997, at C15 (reporting that station exceeded its goal and established endowment, which is improving its programming).

154. These mandates should also be extended to information about contributions that now escape disclosure requirements altogether. The Internet has vastly increased the potential timeliness and accessibility of such data. *See* Michael Taub, *Government Data At Your Fingertips*, N.Y. TIMES, Feb. 17, 1997, at A45 (describing Websites providing campaign finance information).

155. Without necessarily endorsing the details of the proposal, I note in this regard Bruce Ackerman's interesting scheme to distribute whatever funds are to be used for political campaigns on an equal basis to voters who would then allocate them directly to candidates or parties. *See* Bruce Ackerman, *Crediting the Voters: A New Beginning for Campaign Finance*, AM. PROSPECT, Spring 1993, at 71. For a very brief sketch of my own doubts about limiting campaign spending, see Peter Schuck & Bruce Brown, *Lessons from Lippo*, WALL ST. J., Feb. 27, 1997, at A16. *See also* Smith, *supra* note 98.

156. Antitrust policy is a telling example of how even a relatively uncontroversial justification for governmental intervention in the pluralist system—here, the need to curb aggregations of private power that reduce or threaten competition—can be implemented in ways that frustrate that goal. The "new learning" in antitrust analysis sug-

gests that government antitrust policies have often decreased competition rather than increasing it. *See* INDUSTRIAL CONCENTRATION: THE NEW LEARNING (Harvey J. Goldschmid et al. eds., 1974); Roger Lowenstein, *Trust in Markets: Antitrust Enforcers Drop the Ideology, Focus on Economics*, WALL ST. J., Feb. 27, 1997, at A1; *see also* Posner, *supra* note 143.

157. In order for conservatives to realize much of their political agenda, they too must seek legislative action. The most important examples of this are deregulation, tax reduction, and the reform of existing entitlements.

8

Delegation and Democracy

Comments on David Schoenbrod

I know David Schoenbrod, and he is no Owen Fiss. Yet, if the United States Supreme Court were to resurrect the nondelegation doctrine as Professor Schoenbrod proposes, it would radically increase judicial power over vast areas of American life at the expense of the "political" branches (as we quaintly call them). Fiss, my beloved but occasionally misguided colleague, would probably applaud this change, but Professor Schoenbrod, usually so sensible about such things, would surely deplore it. Fortunately, the Court is most unlikely to adopt Professor Schoenbrod's perverse proposal. Besides, even if the Court did revive the nondelegation doctrine, it would surely want to neuter it. Like Buddy, our First Dog, the Court lacks the balls to do what the doctrine would require. So much the better for the Court—and for the rest of us (though not for poor Buddy).

In explaining why this is so, I have—we all have—the advantage of Jerry Mashaw's recent and excellent book, *Greed, Chaos, and Governance*.[1] There, Mashaw reviews the arguments for and against delegation using the public choice literature and Professor Schoenbrod's book[2] as analytical foils. I do not accept all of Mashaw's claims about delegation. He argues, for example, that voters can more readily discern and police a legislator's preferences through statutory standards like "protect the public health" and "fair and reasonable" than they can through statutory language that prescribes more specific trade-offs of competing values. This claim is quite implausible as a general matter, although it is surely correct in some subset of cases depending on the particular statutes being compared. Additionally, his statement that his point has not been "to decide the nondelegation doctrine issue conclusively one way or the other"[3] strikes me as disingenuous, for his analysis plunges a long, sharp knife deep into the doctrine's heart, leaving it near death's door.

Nevertheless, I accept almost all of Mashaw's arguments. Our agreement, I presume, is not due to something in the New Haven water supply. Instead, it reflects administrative law scholars' familiarity with a wide variety of regulatory schemes and public administration arrangements. It also reflects our common understanding that the ubiquity of broad delegations denotes much more than the undoubted desires of politicians to eat their cake and have it too. In my view, delegation—when backed (as it is in our system) by many powerful institutional and informal controls over agency discretion—constitutes one of the most salutary developments in the long struggle to instantiate the often competing values of democratic participation, political accountability, legal regularity, and administrative effectiveness.

I wish to make some arguments against a robust nondelegation doctrine (and if it is not robust, there is no point talking about it) that Mashaw does not make.[4] In the spirit of Dean Michael Herz's observation that most broad delegations satisfy the formal requirements of Article I legislation and that the merits of a nondelegation doctrine must therefore turn on functional considerations,[5] my arguments in favor of broad delegations in many circumstances are functional in nature. I shall organize my arguments around four questions: What is the nature of the delegation problem?; What should be our goals in seeking to control delegation?; In the absence of a nondelegation doctrine, is agency lawmaking effectively constrained?; What would be the consequences of reviving the nondelegation doctrine?

My answers to these questions can be briefly stated. First, although it is always difficult and costly for a democratic citizenry to monitor, control, guide, and correct the conduct of its governmental agents,[6] this problem has not yet reached the level of serious political dysfunction nor is it the kind of problem for which courts (or even scholars, who are less constrained than judges) can devise an effective doctrinal solution in terms of the desired specificity of statutes. Second, a coherent nondelegation doctrine would not limit itself to the single, simple goal of "responsibility" that is the lodestar of Professor Schoenbrod's analysis; it would also include other goals that exist in profound tension with that of responsibility. Third, agencies are highly constrained to comply with legislative intent as they understand it, and they are further impelled by other powerful forces to understand this legislative intent in much the way that Congress does.[7] In truth, the freedom of agencies "to do as they please"[8] is among the least of their problems—and of ours. Finally, the consequences of a robust nondelegation doctrine would be so pernicious that the Court will either never adopt it or will render it toothless.[9]

I. The Problem

I think that Professor Schoenbrod has the problem wrong. The real problem with delegation is not a lack of political "responsibility," a concept that he deploys frequently but never defines.[10] I understand responsibility to be the accountability of elected officials (and the indirect accountability of their appointed agents) to the electorate for significant policy choices. If anything, our political system produces too much of this kind of responsibility. Our system creates incentives for legislators (especially those with relatively short terms of office, like members of Congress) to think so obsessively about their immediate electoral prospects that they are unduly timorous, lacking the leeway that a more Burkean conception of representation requires. Hence, they may neglect longer term social problems whose solutions require immediate sacrifices for delayed gains, problems that demand as much of the legislators' attention, prudence, and political courage as they can muster.[11]

Whether we have struck the best balance between accountability and stewardship that can be achieved in light of the realistic constraints on democratic governance is a vital question to which no one really knows the answer. But, I feel quite certain that nonaccountability in Professor Schoenbrod's sense is, relatively speaking, a non-problem. The greater dilemma, I think, is that growing social complexity has made it far more difficult for legislators (not to mention voters) to accurately predict the consequences of their choices so that they can reason their way to a conclusion as to the best policy choice. If I am right about this, we may need more delegation to agencies, not less.

I begin with the proposition that in comparative terms, the United States is a well-governed society. I say well-governed, not perfect—and I am comparing it to other large, diverse, and dynamic societies faced with the characteristic problems of post-industrialism, not to Shangri-La or even to a relatively homogeneous, corruption-free country like Denmark. I recently had occasion to adduce some empirical evidence to support the claim that the United States is much better governed than it was in 1965 in the sense that its political processes and policy outcomes are now much more democratic, just, and social welfare enhancing.[12] In the two years since I presented this evidence, the comparative dimension of my claim has also grown stronger. The United States has turned in an extraordinary economic performance (growth in production and wage levels with low inflation and unemployment), while responding to public demands for governmental reform and for fiscal prudence (a budget surplus) and boasting improved social indicators in many policy areas such as crime, health, education, environment, standard of living, poverty, and minority group progress. These achievements are in sharp contrast to the continuing process of Eurosclerosis[13] and the recent freefall of almost all of the Asian economies, with grave threats to their nascent, often fragile political democracies. Such developments belie the image of a dysfunctional lawmaking process that Professor Schoenbrod and many other commentators draw, as well as the persuasive substantive policy failures that public choice pessimists like McNollgast[14] and the late Mancur Olson predict.[15]

I can imagine Professor Schoenbrod responding in several ways. First, as he writes in his Article, "[l]arge majorities tell pollsters that government has somehow eluded their control."[16] I do not doubt this claim, although much of its significance turns on how the pollsters phrased their question and how respondents understood it. The more important point, however, is that

Americans have probably always said this—and that what they say is in a sense true, at least at the level of the individual. What is less clear is that such polling data tell us anything about the desirability of the nondelegation doctrine.

Second, he might argue that if the nondelegation doctrine constrained lawmakers more, the policy processes and outcomes would be even better. Perhaps he is right about this, but I seriously doubt it. At the very least, the post–1965 progress of American society increases the already heavy burden of proof that Mashaw's theoretical analysis imposes on Schoenbrod and the public choice pessimists.

Finally, Professor Schoenbrod might also insist that by discussing policy outcomes, I am addressing the wrong question. The right question to pose about delegation, he might say, is not about its social consequences but about its effects on democratic legitimacy. Here, however, I stand firmly with Dan Kahan,[17] who maintains, along with Mashaw, that these two criteria cannot be separated, that democratic legitimacy is a function of effective governance, desirable policy outcomes, and other political values.[18]

II. The Goals

This leads me to my second point. Professor Schoenbrod has identified the wrong goal, or at least has fastened on one goal to the exclusion of other, equally attractive ones. His sole *desideratum,* it would appear, is what he calls "responsibility." He uses the word no fewer than five times in his one-page introduction, and he mentions no other goal.[19] As noted above, I am not certain what he means by this, although he does associate it with making "hard choices."[20] The closest he comes to defining responsibility is to observe that it is "more meaningfully accountable for what [the administration] does,"[21] in contrast to "responsiveness," which "will give voters what they want."[22] I confess that I thought that giving the voters what they want, and what they thought they voted for, is precisely what democracy is supposed to be about and what advocates of the nondelegation doctrine hope and suppose it will achieve. If that is not Professor Schoenbrod's objective, then I do not know what is.

In any event, political responsibility is no more a self-defining term than is democracy.[23] More to the point, responsibility is only one value among others. Let me suggest some additional constitutional and quasi-constitutional goals that any democratic, just, and effective lawmaking system should seek to both reify and advance. Lawmaking should encourage active, meaningful participation by individual citizens and groups affected by the law. It should facilitate and reflect mature deliberation among members of the public and among the lawmakers themselves. Lawmaking should exhibit instrumental competence, in the sense that it implements a satisfactory level of legislative purposes. Lawmaking, as Mashaw notes, should promote justice in individual cases, not merely at wholesale. It should also achieve responsiveness to public preferences, in Professor Schoenbrod's sense of giving the voters what they (think they) want. Finally, of course, lawmaking in both its procedural and substantive aspects should exemplify and secure the rule of law.

The political responsibility that Professor Schoenbrod wants to achieve through more specific statutes must coexist with these goals and will sometimes conflict with them. Even if the nondelegation doctrine would in fact promote political responsibility, which I very much doubt, it would also frustrate some or all of these other values. Mashaw explains, for example, how more specific statutes can undercut both justice in the individual case and responsiveness to diverse local conditions.[24]

Professor Schoenbrod seems innocent of, or at least unimpressed by, these poignant and inescapable normative and empirical tradeoffs. He assumes that the legislature is the site where the virtues of responsible lawmaking are best achieved; it is there, he suggests, that the public's values should be expressed and the hard policy choices made. He fails to see, however, that the particular attributes of the legislature's delegation—its breadth, type, and level—are themselves fundamental policy choices. Moreover, these issues are hardly peripheral to legislative choice. Along with the closely related issue of the scope of the agency's regulatory authority, they are almost always—and quite explicitly—at the heart of the political debates in Congress over the shape and content of particular pieces of legislation. The optimal specificity and other delegation-related features of the legislation are among the questions on which almost all of the parties to these legislative struggles—congressional committees, legislative staffs, the White House, regulated firms, "public interest" groups, state and local governments, and others—tend to stake out clear positions, for they know the resolution of these questions may well determine the nature and effectiveness of the regulatory scheme being established.[25] The issue of statutory specificity is not resolved *sub silentio* or by default, as Professor Schoenbrod suggests. Rather, it is a focal point of the political maneuvering in the legislature.

Legislation is only part of the process of responsible lawmaking, and it is becoming a less important part. In some important respects, this is for the better. Today, the administrative agency is often the site where public participation in lawmaking is most accessible, most meaningful, and most effective.

The administrative agency is often the most accessible site for public participation because the costs of participating in the rulemaking and more informal agency processes, where many of the most important policy choices are in fact made, are likely to be lower than the costs of lobbying or otherwise seeking to influence Congress. Moreover, the institutional culture of the administrative agency, despite its often daunting opacity, is probably more familiar to the average citizen, who deals with bureaucracies constantly and probably works in one, than the exotic, intricate, unruly (and "un-ruly"), insider's culture of Congress.

The agency is often a more meaningful site for public participation than Congress, because the policy stakes for individuals and interest groups are most immediate, transparent, and well-defined at the agency level. One can scarcely exaggerate the importance of this consideration to the legitimacy of democratic politics and to the substantive content of public policy. After all, it is only at the agency level that the generalities of legislation are broken down and concretized into discrete, specific issues with which affected parties can hope to deal. It is there that the agency commits itself to a particular course of action; because only there does it propose the specific rate it will set, the particular emission level it will prescribe, the precise restrictions on private activity it will impose, the exact regulatory definitions it will employ, the kinds of enforcement techniques it will use, the types of information it will collect, and the details relating to the administrative state's myriad other impacts on citizens and groups. In short, it is only at the agency level that the citizen can know precisely what the statute means to her; how, when, and to what extent it will affect her interests; whether she supports, opposes, or wants changes in what the agency is proposing; whether it is worth her while to participate actively in seeking to influence this particular exercise of governmental power, and if so, how best to go about it; and where other citizens or groups stand on these questions. God and the devil are in the details of policymaking, as they are in most other important things—and the details are to be found at the agency level. This would remain true, moreover, even if the nondelegation doctrine were revived and statutes were written with somewhat greater specificity, for many of the most significant impacts on members of the public would still be indeterminate until the agency grappled with and defined them.

Finally, the agency is often the site in which public participation is most effective. This is not only because the details of the regulatory impacts are hammered out there. It is also because the agency is where the public can best educate the government about the true nature of the problem that Congress has tried to address. Only the interested parties, reacting to specific agency proposals for rules or other actions, possess (or have the incentives to acquire) the information necessary to identify, explicate, quantify, and evaluate the real-world consequences of these and alternative proposals. Even when Congress can identify the first-order effects of the laws that it enacts, these direct impacts seldom exhaust the laws' policy consequences. Indeed, first-order effects of policies usually are less significant than the aggregate of more remote effects that ripple through a complex, interrelated, opaque society. When policies fail, it is usually not because the congressional purpose was misunderstood. More commonly, they fail because Congress did not fully appreciate how the details of policy implementation would confound its purpose. Often, however, this knowledge can only be gained through active public participation in the policymaking process at the agency level where these implementation issues are most clearly focused and the stakes in their correct resolution are highest.

III. The Constraints

If the rule of law is a central goal (as Professor Schoenbrod clearly thinks, although usually calling it "responsibility"), then our *desideratum* should not be statutes of a certain specificity with that level of specificity enforced by courts as a matter of constitutional law. Instead, we should seek to assure that bureaucratic power is checked and effectively bent to the legislative purpose, that the agency, in Professor Schoenbrod's words, is not "free to do as it pleases."[26] Now, no one would suggest that this essential goal of constraining and guiding bureaucratic power is easily accomplished. If it were, Congress could take longer recesses and most administrative lawyers would be out of a job. Developing agency cost theory and other approaches have painstakingly detailed the tensions between this goal and other important goals such as technical rationality, policy flexibility, procedural simplicity, speed of decision, justice in the individual case, individual dignity, and the like.[27]

Federal agencies, however, are hardly at liberty. They are surrounded by watchdogs with sharp, penetrating teeth. Indeed, what most clearly distinguishes the American administrative state from that of other countries is the pervasive public philosophy of mistrust of government bureaucracies and the subordination of bureaucracy to numerous, diverse, external, power-checking institutions and processes. These institutions, moreover, are remarkably powerful; they routinely shape policy and delve into the intricate details of administration. Their broad array of inducements, both positive and negative, enable them to guide and often determine the agency's exercise of discretion. In this fundamental sense, the structural preconditions for democratic delegation are satisfied: the legislature is delegating power to a branch whose decisions the legislature and its other agents—for example, the courts and interest groups—can effectively influence, if not wholly control.[28] I do not claim that this control is complete, nor should it be if the advantages of technocratic administration are to be realized. Agencies enjoy some leeway and sometimes abuse it. The controls, however, are extensive.

Some of these external constraints on bureaucratic policymaking are: (1) Congress; (2) the Executive Office of the President; (3) judicial review; (4) interest group monitors; (5) media; and (6) informal agency norms. It is important, moreover, to remember that these and other constraints on bureaucracy's freedom to "do as it pleases" all operate simultaneously. My consideration of them can be brief, as a vast political science literature exists on each.

A. Congress

Congress possesses numerous formal and informal controls over agency discretion. I shall mention six of them: statutory controls; legislative history; oversight; the appropriations process; statutory review of agency rules; and confirmation of key personnel.

1. Statutory Controls.   Congress, of course, writes the statutes that confer and govern agency authority. In doing so, it prescribes the substantive content of that authority, the structure of agency decisionmaking, the procedures through which it occurs, and the informational, budgetary, and other controls to which the agency will be subjected. As Terry Moe,[29] McNollgast,[30] and many other political scientists have shown, Congress uses these controls to shape the administrative process in ways that serve its electoral and policy interests and make it difficult for agencies to threaten those interests.

2. Legislative History.   Even when Congress enacts vague statutes, it often clarifies their meaning through legislative history. Agencies understand that the committee reports and floor debates serve as important controls on agency discretion. Justice Scalia frequently reminds us, of course, that legislative history can be indeterminate and is often used strategically by members who cannot muster the votes to get their preferences inscribed in the statutory language itself.[31] As Judge Harold Levanthal famously put it, using legislative history is like looking out over a crowd in order to find one's friends.[32] Despite these abuses, or rather because of them, legislative history can dictate which policies agencies may and may not adopt.

3. Oversight.   Congressional oversight of administration is one of the central pillars of the constitutional schemes of checks and balances—or in Richard Neustadt's phrase, "separate institutions sharing powers."[33] While the nature, quality, and intensity of legislative oversight vary from committee to committee, it is often used to signal congressional preferences on agency policy issues and to extract policy commitments from agency officials. Agencies fear intrusive oversight and their decisions and behavior often reflect what political scientists refer to as "anticipatory reaction" to those controls.

4. Appropriations.   The appropriations process sharply constrains the authority and discretion of agencies. These constraints are imposed through the language of the funding legislation, through formal committee and subcommittee oversight hearings, and through the frequent informal interactions between members and agency officials. Despite congressional rules against including substantive legislation in appropriations bills, it is nonetheless a common practice for appropriations committees to engage in this practice and for agencies to acquiesce and abjectly obey. Indeed, substantive controls on agency policymaking are often included even in the increasingly common omnibus budgetary reconciliation legislation.

5. Statutory Review.   In addition to the constitutional power to override presidential vetoes, Congress has over the years enacted a grab-bag of provisions requiring some agency rules to run the gauntlet of various forms of legislative veto before they could become effective. The Supreme Court decision in *INS v. Chadha*[34] invalidated certain forms of legislative veto but left most others, including report-and-wait provisions, in place. In 1996, Congress extended this form of control to all rules of all federal agencies, as defined in the Administrative Procedure Act ("APA"),[35] although the legislation subjects "major rules" to a more intensive review than other rules.

Professor Schoenbrod makes much of the fact that this Congressional Review Act,[36] while comprehensive, has not led to any votes of disapproval by Congress; this inaction shows, he says in a vivid simile, that "legislators react to responsibility as vampires do to garlic—they flee."[37] But it shows no such thing. Numerous empirical studies of the operation of the various kinds of legislative vetoes, both before and after *Chadha*, have found that they generate strong anticipatory reactions by agency officials, often including intensive discussions between those officials and committee members or staff that cause the agency to conform their rules to the wishes of the committee.[38] Indeed, recognition of this powerful informal process of congressional review of agency policymaking outside the statutory procedures of the APA has long caused many consumer, environmental, and other "public interest" groups to oppose legislative veto provisions, including the Congressional Review Act, on the ground that it enables industry interests to use congressional staff to gain an extra bite at the regulatory apple.

6. Confirmation. Finally, Congress frequently uses its constitutional power to confirm or reject presidential nominees in order to shape agency policies. Again, much of this influence operates through the medium of anticipatory reaction, here on the part of the President who must consider congressional policy and personal preferences when determining whose name to send to Capitol Hill. But congressional influence also often operates through the confirmation hearings when members extract from the nominee explicit commitments to adopt or avoid certain policies. These policy commitments can be quite specific; indeed, they may be even more specific than the statutory commitments that Professor Schoenbrod would require of Congress under a revitalized nondelegation doctrine.

B. Executive Office of the President

Even before agency policies and rules see the light of day, the significant ones are vetted with the Office of Management and Budget ("OMB")—and, in a few highly controversial and delicate cases (e.g., FDA regulation of tobacco), with the President and his closest political and policy aides. This may take the form of budgetary review, if the agency action would entail significant fiscal impacts; legislative review, if it requires statutory change; or regulatory review, if it meets the OMB criteria. Once again, the greatest impact of these processes is not so much the reviews themselves as the anticipatory reactions of the agency officials and the reviewers. They are keenly mindful of the policy concerns of the relevant congressional committees and key members, who often are consulted informally as part of these processes and usually receive drafts of the review documents before they are released to the public. Although the review process works somewhat differently with respect to the independent regulatory agencies, their vaunted (but to some extent, illusory) independence is designed to make them even more dependent on Congress and responsive to its policy priorities.

C. Judicial Review

In exercising their review of agency "actions" (not just rules) under the APA, the courts attempt to discipline the agencies by requiring that their actions conform to congressional intent and, where they enjoy a delegated discretion, that the discretion is not abused. Although I and other scholars have questioned the effectiveness and value of this review in many cases, none of us doubts that agencies invariably fear it, that they seek to tailor their actions (at least those that are reviewable) in anticipation of it, and that the courts do attempt to police agency departures from congressional policy choices, which must often be inferred from general statutory language and other interpretive materials. Although it is true that the *Chevron*[39] doctrine in principle increases the deference to agency interpretations of their governing statutes, many commentators have observed that the courts can, and often do, manipulate this doctrine in order to preserve much of their influence over agency decisions, including enforcing agency fidelity to congressional intent.

Toward the end of his book, Professor Schoenbrod quotes then-professor Scalia to the effect that the nondelegation doctrine amounts to a judicial self-denying ordinance. Justice Scalia, of course, was writing before the Supreme Court in *Chevron* curbed judicial authority to interpret statutes without regard to the agencies' own interpretations. In any event, we certainly do not need a nondelegation doctrine to enable Congress to protect its legislative prerogatives from judicial incursion, which was Justice Scalia's concern. As my colleague Bill Eskridge has carefully documented, Congress possesses ample power to overrule judicial rulings and exercises that power frequently.[40] The fact that Congress can do so, however, does not mean that the nondelegation would therefore not create mischief.[41] It would indeed, as I discuss in the final section.

It is noteworthy that the Congressional Review Act expressly provides that the courts may not review any congressional action involved in Congress's review of agency rules,[42] and further provides that Congress's failure to disapprove an agency rule shall not raise any inference concerning "any intent of the Congress."[43] These provisions are the clearest indication, if any were needed, of Congress's determination to maintain its close control over agency rulemaking as against both the courts and the Executive Branch. Indeed, these instruments of congressional control create a paradoxical situation: By preserving and extending its oversight and veto power over agency decisions,

Congress is more willing to delegate power broadly to the agencies, knowing that it can always retrieve and discipline that power if need be.

D. Interest Group Monitors

Agencies' freedom to "do as they please" is further constrained by the close surveillance of their actions by the constellation of interest groups that invariably cluster around them. As students of Congress have pointed out, these groups police the agencies by signaling Congress in a variety of ways whenever the groups think that the agencies are deviating from the policy path that they prefer and that they believe Congress has chosen, regardless of how general or specific the statutory language may be. These groups, of course, further shape agency policies through their participation in formal and informal agency decisionmaking and through their ability to mobilize opposition to these policies. To be sure, these efforts sometimes seek to push the agency to exercise its discretion in a way not intended or permitted by Congress, a circumstance that underlies all concerns about broad delegations. The burden of my comments here, however, is to show that their power to accomplish this end is a highly constrained one.

E. Media

Every agency is surrounded by organs of public communication that focus on its decisions. Some of these media report to a mass audience while others serve highly specialized audiences, including regulated firms, trade associations, consultants, "public interest" groups, Congress, administrative lawyers, and the like. In addition to using conventional journalistic methods of investigation, these media enjoy a legal right of access to agency proceedings under sunshine laws, the Federal Advisory Committee Act,[44] the Freedom of Information Act,[45] and other such laws. In effect, the media help to police the activities of agencies in ways that enable both interest groups and Congress to keep the agencies in line.

Agencies, then, know that their actions are likely to come under public scrutiny and must tailor their conduct and decisions accordingly. This is not to deny, of course, that agencies would often prefer to conduct their business in secret and that they sometimes succeed in doing so. It is to say, rather, that intensive media coverage of agency actions makes it almost impossible to shield from public notice the important decisions that deviate significantly from congressional intent.

F. Informal Agency Norms

Finally, agencies are subject to internal limits on their ability to "do as they please." Or to put the point more precisely, they ordinarily are pleased to do what they think Congress has required—and not only because of the legal and political constraints discussed above. In most if not all agencies, there exists an organizational culture committed to the rule of law. Indeed, as political scientist James Q. Wilson[46] has observed, most of the classic complaints about public bureaucracies are really criticisms of agencies for being too legalistic (too rigid, unimaginative, process-oriented, etc.) in their strict adherence to the statute, at least as they understand it. In addition, management controls are ordinarily designed to reinforce these tendencies. Moreover, agencies are increasingly staffed by individuals who are professionally trained and whose professional norms, which include a commitment to the rule of law, often contradict or transcend the narrow political or bureaucratic interests that might otherwise lead decisionmakers astray.

IV. The Consequences of the Nondelegation Doctrine

The consequences of a robust nondelegation doctrine would not be pretty. First, it would greatly strengthen the power of the federal courts relative to that of Congress and the agencies. Ironically, it would do so in the name of the separation of powers while undermining that very principle. Such a massive shift of power to unelected federal judges should trouble us deeply.[47] It is particularly obnoxious when, as in this case, it is not essential to the vindication of enumerated constitutional rights, and when the courts would be guided by Professor Schoenbrod's principles, which are as unhelpful as "Congress need only state the law"[48] and as slippery, manipulable, and epistemologically incoherent as the distinction between "lawmaking and law interpretation."[49] How general is too general, how specific is specific enough—these are, contrary to Professor Schoenbrod's claim, questions of degree, not kind. They are preeminently questions of politics and of policy that courts are poorly equipped to answer as a functional matter and that they are disabled from resolving as a constitutional matter. Resolution of these questions, moreover, depends entirely on context—or as Professor Schoenbrod recognizes, on a "number of other factors."[50]

To inscribe the nondelegation doctrine in the Constitution, either textually or interpretively, would be little better than having the courts make it up as they go along.[51] This is evident once one tries to imagine how one would draft such an amendment. The line-drawing problems are simply insuperable, which is why the Supreme Court—whether liberal or conservative, textualist or interpretivist—has resisted any robust nondelegation doctrine during more than two centuries of public law adjudication, and especially during the age of statues spanning the last sixty-five years.

It is true, as I noted earlier, that Congress could overturn a court decision invalidating a statute under the nondelegation doctrine by enacting another version of the statute with the requisite degree of specificity. Ironically, of course, the Supreme Court would probably avoid specifying precisely what degree of specificity would pass constitutional muster under a revived non-delegation doctrine, both because it would not know the answer—never having had to grapple with the political and policy problems that animated Congress to draft the statute as it did—and because strategically it would not want to commit itself in advance. Vagueness, it turns out, has its legitimate uses for courts as well as for legislatures. Indeed, the most charitable way to view the doctrine is as an effort to encourage Congress—through a judicially enforced and orchestrated dialogue—to take a second, harder look at the delegation issue. In this view, the nondelegation doctrine would function as a kind of "clear statement" doctrine analogous to the provision of the Canadian Charter of Rights and Responsibilities, which permits Parliament to override certain judicial rulings invalidating statutes on constitutional grounds once the ruling has forced Parliament to confront the constitutional objection squarely and explicitly.[52]

Such a second look requirement certainly has its attractions, but its apparent benignity can be misleading. It means that the court in effect is forcing Congress to bear the burden of inertia, which is always a crucial, and often determinative, factor in legislative politics. It is not enough to say that if Congress enacted the statute once, it can readily do so again—now free of the constitutional taint of inadequate specificity. The political situation may have changed, and it may be impossible to reassemble the winning coalition. Professor Schoenbrod might reply that this is precisely the point; if Congress could not enact the more specific version of the statute, it should not be permitted to enact the less specific one. This argument, however, entirely begs the question before us—whether the nondelegation doctrine is justifiable on other grounds in the first place. To say that it is more justifiable because it can always be overridden by Congress is not simply wrong empirically (the political burden of inertia will have shifted, perhaps decisively, to the supporters of the statute), but is also bootstrapping.

By magnifying the already great uncertainty surrounding the legislative process, the doctrine would further increase the strategic opportunities of politicians and organized interests that hope to shape, derail, or delay new legislation. The risks that courts would invalidate statutes would be vastly greater yet still utterly unpredictable. From the more detached, public interest perspective of one concerned solely with the legitimacy and effectiveness of legislative politics, much would certainly be lost. It is hard to see what, if anything, would be gained.

In the end, then, the nondelegation doctrine is a prescription for judicial supervision of both the substance and forms of legislation and hence of politics and public policy, without the existence or even the possibility of any coherent, principled, or manageable judicial standards. This leads us to three other ironies.[53] The nondelegation doctrine utterly lacks the intelligible standards that it demands of legislation. It invites and empowers judges to render the legislative process even more chaotic and opportunistic than the doctrine's advocates think it already is. And it does so at a cost to democratic politics—the very touchstone of those advocates—that can scarcely be imagined.

Notes

1. Jerry L. Mashaw, Greed, Chaos & Governance: Using Public Choice to Improve Public Laws (1997).

2. David Schoenbrod, Power Without Responsibility: How Congress Abuses the People Through Delegation (1993).

3. Mashaw, *supra* note 1, at 12.

4. I think, however, that Mashaw would agree with them.

5. Michael Herz, Remarks at the *Cardozo Law Review* symposium "The Phoenix Rises Again: The Nondelegation Doctrine from Constitutional and Policy Perspectives" (Mar. 19, 1998) (transcript on file with the *Cardozo Law Review*).

6. *See generally* Peter H. Schuck, Suing Government: Citizen Remedies for Official Wrongs (1983).

7. The notions of congressional understanding and legislative intent are merely metaphors, of course, and somewhat misleading anthropomorphizing metaphors at that; they are images of cognition and purposiveness, necessary fictions for ascribing relatively simple, discrete goals to exceedingly complex institutions.

8. David Schoenbrod, *Delegation and Democracy: A Reply to My Critics,* 20 Cardozo L. Rev. 731, 762 (1999).

9. Such a doctrine moreover would also contradict Professor Schoenbrod's generally sound jurisprudential and political values. He should therefore reject it.

10. *See infra* Part II.

11. *See, e.g.,* David R. Mayhew, Congress: The Electoral Connection (1975). Reform of the Social Security system and global warming are current examples.

12. *See* Peter H. Schuck, *Against (And For) Madison: An Essay in Praise of Factions,* 15 Yale L. & Pol'y Rev. 553 (1997).

13. Eurosclerosis is a term that was coined in the early 1980s to describe the period of sluggishness in the development of the European Union when all issues, however minor, languished until all Member States could agree. *See The Business of Europe,* The Economist, Dec. 7, 1991, at 63. It now applies more broadly to Europe's slow growth, high unemployment, and policy rigidity.

14. *See* Mashaw, *supra* note 1, at 140.

15. Olson might object to being characterized as a pessimist. In a letter written to me six months before his death, Olson said "I don't agree that subsequent experience has gone contrary to any 'predictions' in *The Rise and Decline of Nations.*" Olson also expressed optimism about the role of ideas in improving social outcomes.

16. Schoenbrod, *supra* note 8, at 731.

17. Professor of Law at the University of Chicago Law School. *See* Dan Kahan, *Democracy Schmemocracy,* 20 Cardozo L. Rev. 795 (1999).

18. *See id.*

19. *See* Schoenbrod, *supra* note 8, at 735.

20. *See id.* at 740.

21. *Id.* at 750.

22. *Id.*

23. Professor Kahan emphasizes this point. *See* Kahan, *supra* note 17, at 795.

24. *See* MASHAW, *supra* note 1, at 50–80.

25. *See, e.g.*, Terry Moe, *The Politics of Bureaucratic Structure, in* J. CHUBB ET AL., CAN THE GOVERNMENT GOVERN? (1989).

26. Schoenbrod, *supra* note 8, at 762.

27. *See, e.g.*, JERRY L. MASHAW, BUREAUCRATIC JUSTICE: MANAGING SOCIAL SECURITY DISABILITY CLAIMS (1983); Peter H. Schuck, *When the Exception Becomes the Rule: Regulatory Equity and the Exceptions Process in Federal Energy Policymaking*, 1984 DUKE L.J. 163.

28. The desired level of delegation may vary according to a number of political factors, including the degree to which Congress and the executive branch are controlled by the same political party and the degree of party unity that exists. This is one reason why many New Deal statutes, enacted during a period of unified government, delegated power to the agencies in very broad terms, while many of those enacted during the early 1970s, when government was divided, contained many more controls over agency discretion. *See* DAVID R. MAYHEW, DIVIDED WE GOVERN: PARTY CONTROL, LAWMAKING, AND INVESTIGATIONS (1990); JAMES SUNDQUIST, THE DECLINE AND RESURGENCE OF CONGRESS (1981); *see also* Peter Strauss, Comments at the *Cardozo Law Review* symposium "The Phoenix Rises Again: The Nondelegation Doctrine from Constitutional and Policy Perspectives" (Mar. 19, 1998) (transcript on file with the *Cardozo Law Review*).

29. Senior Fellow at the Hoover Institution and Professor of Political Science at Stanford University.

30. McNollgast is an anagram of Matthew McCubbins, Roger Noll, and Barry Weingast. The authors coined this term for their own joint work, and it has been adopted by others.

31. *See, e.g.*, Morales v. Trans World Airlines, Inc., 504 U.S. 374, 383 (1992); United States v. Nordic Village, Inc., 503 U.S. 30, 37 (1992); *see also* Fort Stewart Schs. v. Federal Labor Relations Auth., 495 U.S. 641, 649 (1990) ("There is no conceivable persuasive effect in legislative history that may reflect nothing more than the speakers' incomplete understanding of the world upon which the statute will operate.").

32. *See* Conroy v. Aniskoff, 507 U.S. 511, 519 (1993) (quoting Judge Leventhal).

33. RICHARD E. NEUSTADT, PRESIDENTIAL POWER AND THE MODERN PRESIDENTS: THE POLITICS OF LEADERSHIP FROM ROOSEVELT TO REAGAN 32 (1990).

34. 462 U.S. 919 (1983).

35. 5 U.S.C. ss 551–559 (1994).

36. *Id.* ss 801–808.

37. Schoenbrod, *supra* note 8, at 739.

38. *See, e.g.*, LOUIS FISCHER, THE POLITICS OF SHARED POWER: CONGRESS AND THE EXECUTIVE (1987).

39. Chevron v. Natural Resources Defense Council, Inc., 467 U.S. 837 (1984).

40. *See* William N. Eskridge, Jr., *Overriding Supreme Court Statutory Interpretation Decisions*, 101 YALE L.J. 331 (1991).

41. Among other things, the politics of restoring a judicially transformed statutory meaning will differ from the polities that produced the original enactment, and may prevent such restoration. *See infra.*

42. *See* 5 U.S.C. s 805 (1994).

43. *Id.* s 801 (g).

44. *Id.* app. ss 1–15 (1994).

45. *Id.* s 552.

46. James Q. Wilson is a professor of management and public policy emeritus at University of California at Los Angeles.

47. In this sense, as Martin Redish points out, an invigorated nondelegation doctrine would be tantamount to a return to substantive due process, another essentially standardless judicial doctrine that reached its zenith at roughly the same time. Redish notes that in other respects, the two doctrines are quite dissimilar, if not opposite. While the nondelegation doctrine is concerned with the form of legislation, substantive due process focuses on its content. And while the nondelegation doctrine demands clearer legislative policy choices, substantive due process denies to legislatures the power to make certain choices at all. *See* Martin Redish, Comments at the Phoenix Rises Again: The Nondelegation Doctrine from Constitutional and Policy Perspectives (Mar. 19, 1998) (transcript on file with the *Cardozo Law Review*).

48. Schoenbrod, *supra* note 8, at 752.

49. *Id.* at 764.

50. *Id.* at 755.

51. Much the same can be said for the balanced budget amendment, but that is another subject.

52. *See* Canadian Charter of Rights and Freedoms s 15 (1994). In a similar spirit, Beth Garrett notes that the rules permitting members to make points of order in the congressional budgetary process enable opponents of majoritarian legislation to encourage the discussion of under-enforced norms such as federalism. She notes further that these rules also give minorities the power to stop the legislation in its tracks for any reason, whether principled or not. *See* Elizabeth Garrett, *Accountability and Restraint: The Federal Budget Process and the Line Item Veto Act*, 20 CARDOZO L. REV. 871 (1999).

53. Peter Strauss notes yet another. Were a robust nondelegation doctrine in place, Congress would find it even more necessary than it already is to delegate its legislative power to its own subcommittees and staff, particularly when it enacts so much substantive legislation through the mechanism of massive budget reconciliation bills. In this connection, Strauss quotes Gordon Crovitz to the effect that members of Congress can walk around these statutes and touch them; the one thing that they cannot do, however, is read them. *See* PETER L. STRAUSS ET AL., ADMINISTRATIVE LAW: CASES AND COMMENTS 195 (9th ed. 1995).

9

To the *Chevron* Station

An Empirical Study of Federal Administrative Law

I. Introduction

We begin with a puzzling fact. Although the study of administrative law began in earnest more than fifty years ago, we still know little about what is perhaps the central question in that field: How does judicial review *actually* affect agency decisionmaking? This question goes to the fundamental nature and quality of the modern administrative state, yet academic specialists have largely neglected it;[1] the subject remains a matter for uninformed speculation.[2]

Despite (or perhaps because of) the lack of data, however, strong opinions on this question are common. Our conversations and our reading persuade us that every self-respecting administrative lawyer has firm, if not always articulate or even consistent, convictions about the effect of judicial review upon agencies. Proof of this assertion abounds. Lawyers and their clients devote vast resources to challenging agency actions in the courts.[3] With Talmudic intensity, legions of legal scholars analyze the language and logic of judicial opinions in administrative law cases.[4] Agencies themselves exhibit great concern about how reviewing courts respond to their handiwork. Manifestly, the "experts" act as if judicial review of agency action were worth fighting, writing, and worrying about. They believe, in short, that what courts say to agencies matters, and matters deeply.

But although there may be widespread agreement that judicial review of agency action matters, there is no consensus about precisely *how* and *under what circumstances* it matters. As Jerry Mashaw and David Harfst recently put it, "The normative expectations of administrative lawyers have seldom been subjected to empirical verification of a more than anecdotal sort."[5] And different observers evidently rely upon different anecdotes.

Virtually all administrative law writers and teachers at one time or another assiduously seek to expand and fine-tune judicial review of agency action, and they usually advocate a variety of institutional and doctrinal reforms for those purposes.[6] They suppose, at least by implication, that what courts do matters substantively—that when a court decides that an agency erred or failed adequately to support its action, the court's ruling actually (and not just normatively) controls the agency's subsequent behavior in that case. This behavioral supposition, after all, is one of the *raisons d'etre* of most of administrative law. The conventional explanation for judicial review of agency action is the need to confine agencies to their legal authority. To deny that courts actually perform this task is to raise dark and difficult questions about the compatibility of the administrative state with the rule of law.[7]

On the other hand, academic discussion of these questions (sometimes by the very same writers) often proceeds as if the axiom of judicial control of agency action were empirically false.[8] Certain inexorable conditions, it is said, limit the capacity of reviewing courts to shape an agency's conduct. Pointing to factors such as the narrow "bite" of legal doctrine, the political context of administrative decisionmaking, judicial deference to agency expertise, the scope of agency discretion, an agency's control of its agenda, the limited resources of litigants, and the protracted nature of agency proceedings, these commentators emphasize that in practice, if not in principle, an agency usually has the last word as well as the first.[9] Writing more than twenty years ago, political scientist Martin Shapiro crystallized this view in the statement that "courts typically let the agency do what it pleases."[10]

Which of these views is correct? We suspect that there is considerable truth in both views—that judicial review "matters" in all cases (if only because review occasions delay and additional cost before the agency's action can be implemented), but that it has different effects which depend upon a variety of factors. That much, of course, can be confidently asserted about virtually any legal phenomenon as complex as the interaction between courts and agencies. The more interesting and challenging question is whether research can identify those factors and effects, discern significant patterns in the relationship between them, and derive systematic conclusions that can illuminate the ways in which reviewing courts actually shape agency behavior.

Believing that the possibility of such research must at least be entertained, we undertook a large-scale empirical study of how federal agency actions fare when they are reviewed directly by appellate courts. Although we were especially interested in the fate of cases that a reviewing court remands to the initiating agency for further proceedings, we anticipated that such a study could also be designed to generate data bearing upon a number of other important, albeit subsidiary, features of administrative law.

In the course of our study, we have come to appreciate all too well how problematic such research inevitably must be. The government does publish data on the number, type, and judicial disposition of the administrative cases that are appealed to the federal courts.[11] But those data, although useful, are too highly aggregated to answer most of the more specific questions that we hoped to answer. We therefore were obliged to gather our own data in ways that are described below in Part II, and we consoled ourselves with the conviction that on questions of this importance and interest, even imperfect information is better than perfect ignorance.

Our report is divided into four parts. In Part II, we describe our study design, organizing the discussion around our four principal goals and explaining the specific procedures that we used to pursue each of them.

We present our findings and analysis of the 1965, 1975, 1984–85, and 1988 data in Part III. We organize this discussion in four general sections. In the first two, we emphasize certain changes that occurred in administrative law during the twenty years between 1965 and 1985. These changes relate to the style of appellate court opinions and the outcomes and certain structural features of judicial review of agency cases (what we call the "ages of administrative law"). In the third section, we draw upon data gathered for 1984–85 and 1988, focusing on how the Supreme Court's decision in *Chevron U.S.A., Inc. v. NRDC*,[12] affected the patterns of appellate court remands to agencies and considering whether those effects had dissipated by 1988, almost four years after *Chevron* was decided. In the fourth section, we analyze a crucial question that has received virtually no attention from commentators: What actually happens to remanded cases after they are returned to the agencies?

In Part IV, we distill the major conclusions of our study. We begin by offering some observations about the strengths and limitations of our general methodological approach as a tool for identifying and understanding changes in the patterns of court decisions. We then summarize our principal findings.

II. Objectives and Study Design

We began our study with four principal objectives in mind. First, we hoped to *describe* the general parameters of judicial review of federal administrative action. Although we recognize the diversity of agencies, agency actions, reviewing courts, and judicial dispositions of agency cases, we attempted to render that diversity manageable by focusing our attention upon some broad categories of information. For example, we wanted to establish the number of agency decisions that are reviewed by the courts of appeals; the proportion of those cases that are affirmed, reversed, and remanded by the courts; the frequency with which cases are remanded for particular reasons; and the distribution of these variables among the different federal agencies and courts of appeals. At the same time, we hoped to shed light upon some ancillary, but potentially interesting attributes of judicial review of agency decisions, such as the length and footnoting of judicial opinions, the number of split decisions, the size of appellate panels, the type of agency proceeding being reviewed, and the frequency with which the courts applied different standards of review.

To that end, we decided to read a large,[13] representative[14] sample of opinions in which federal courts of appeals engaged in direct review[15] of agency action.

Second, we hoped to reveal some of the *dynamic* patterns of administrative law by gathering these kinds of data for cases decided over a period of time that would bracket the two decades, 1965 to 1985, during which judicial review of agency action, by most accounts, experienced fundamental conceptual and doctrinal changes relating to issues of standing, reviewability, standard and scope of review, and other basic issues.[16] We therefore decided to read opinions rendered during five discrete time periods. Four of them were six-month periods: in 1965, just before this transformation of judicial review is thought to have begun; in 1974–75, at a mid-way point during that twenty-year period; in 1984, after the transformation was thought to have concluded and just before *Chevron* was decided; and in 1985, after the Supreme Court reaffirmed and clarified *Chevron*. The fifth time period covered two months in early 1988, which was selected in order to learn whether the changes observed during the 1984–85 period had endured.

The 1984–85 period has the virtue of being close enough to the present to reflect the current state of administrative law (at least as revealed by our data), while also being distant enough from the present to facilitate our third objective—revealing what actually happens when appellate courts remand cases to federal agencies for further proceedings. For this purpose, it was necessary that enough time had elapsed since the remand so that the vast majority of remanded cases could have reached their conclusions in order for us to analyze them as part of our dataset.[17]

In order to learn what had transpired after each of the roughly 180 cases during the 1984–85 period was remanded by a court of appeals to the agency for further proceedings, we conducted interviews by telephone (and occasionally in person) with the lawyer who represented the agency and with the lawyer who represented the petitioner.[18] Those interviews were designed to elicit data bearing upon two "facts" that could not always be resolved by attempting to integrate the lawyers' differing perceptions—the specific post-remand events (about which there was seldom much disagreement between the opposing lawyers), and the parties' evaluation of the outcomes (about which disagreement was more common).[19]

Our final objective explains why we defined and divided the 1985 period as precisely as we did. By doing so, we hoped to learn how the Court's *Chevron* decision, as clarified and reaffirmed eight months later in *Chemical Manufacturers Association v. NRDC*,[20] had affected appellate court review of agency action. We discuss the changes in legal doctrine wrought by *Chevron* in more detail subsequently;[21] for the moment it suffices to say that in *Chevron*, the Supreme Court sent a strong signal to the courts of appeals that they should be more deferential in reviewing interpretations of statutes by administrative agencies. Even before we initiated our study, *Chevron* had occasioned a great deal of published commentary. Most of these commentators viewed (and often denounced) the decision as a watershed administrative law ruling that would encourage reviewing courts to defer to agency interpretations and policy directions. If true, this change would slow, if not reverse, the trend toward more intrusive judicial review that had gathered force during the preceding two decades.[22] In order to test the accuracy of these predictions, we read cases covering the six-month period preceding *Chevron* and the six-month period following *Chemical Manufacturers*.[23]

For purposes of managing and analyzing our dataset, we initially divided it into seven subsets of cases, each with its own computerized data file. These seven files were: (1) the 1965 cases (remand and non-remand);[24] (2) the 1974–75 cases (remand and non-remand);[25] (3) the 1984 non-remand cases (those which an appellate court had disposed of without remanding them to the agency); (4) the 1984 remand cases (those which an appellate court had, in the first instance, remanded to the agency for further proceedings);[26] (5) the 1985 non-remand cases; (6) the 1985 remand cases;[27] and (7) the 1988 cases.[28] To facilitate those analyses for which the distinctions between remand and non-remand cases, or between pre-*Chevron* and post-*Chevron* cases were not relevant, we then aggregated the 1984 and 1985 cases by creating (8) a merged file of all 1984 cases; (9) a merged file of all 1985 cases; and (10) a file further combining all these merged files. These ten files contained data that had been generated in two ways: by analysis of the published opinions (from all 1965 and 1974–75 cases as well as the 1984–85 non-remand cases), and by opinion analysis plus subsequent telephone interviews (for the 1984 and 1985 remand cases).[29]

The 1676 appellate cases from the 1984–85 period that we analyzed were generated in the first instance by almost fifty different administrative agencies.[30] Among other things, we hoped to learn whether different agencies generated different patterns of appellate review and handled remands differently. We found it useful to group the agencies analytically for two reasons. First, a relatively few agencies accounted for a high proportion of the cases studied, whereas the great majority of agencies produced very few.[31] Thus, analyzing the agencies individually often would preclude statistically significant findings, while grouping them into larger clusters might avoid this problem. Second, we believed that certain groupings would help us to discern broad patterns that might otherwise remain obscured. Accordingly, we allocated each agency in our dataset to one of nine agency groups.[32]

The case analyses, interviews, and data recordation were performed under our supervision from early 1987 to March 1989 by a group of law students at Georgetown and then at Yale, each of whom had completed a basic course in administrative law.[33] Once the data had been gathered, coded, and error corrected, they were entered into a computer and preliminarily analyzed.

We, like all teachers and practitioners of administrative law, did not come to the subject without preconceptions. Indeed, we began our work with a variety of beliefs about what we would find and expectations that ranged from weak intuitions to firm convictions. These formed the basis for a number of preliminary hypotheses concerning a range of administrative law phenomena that we hoped our results would illuminate. Most of these hypotheses—and certainly the more important ones, from our point of view—relate to judicial remands. They concern, for example, how court size, agency type, proceeding type, and other such variables affect remands; how agencies respond to various kinds of remands; how long different administrative proceedings take to complete; and how these relationships have changed over time. Our dataset, however, also enabled us to cast some light upon the evolution of certain other features of administrative law. These features, which are not specific to judicial remands, include the "style" of judicial opinions and some of the institutional structures within which administrative law is generated. When we discuss our findings and analysis in Part III, we briefly note these hypotheses and our reasons for initially viewing them as plausible.

Before proceeding to a discussion of the findings and analysis, we wish to emphasize what the earlier description of our methodology should have made clear: Much of our data is in aggregated form. To be sure, we have disaggregated it in many forms—by agency, circuit, proceeding type, court size, time period, and disposition on appeal (itself broken down into several categories and subcategories). Still, our classification of the cases remains aggregated in some respects and irreducibly impressionistic. Its analytical categories are gleaned from the face of the opinions themselves, from the content of those opinions, or (in the case of the discussion of post-remand events) from information obtained from lawyers. We are acutely aware that these variables do not capture all, or even most, of the factors that explain why reviewing courts and agencies decide as they do. The list of other factors that also powerfully shape their decisions would surely be a long one. It would certainly include the following elements: the political environment in which the agency operates; the quality of the agency's personnel and lawyering, as well as the resources of private parties challenging the agency; the legal culture surrounding the agency; the respect with which the agency is held by litigants and reviewing courts; the agency's technical competence; the agency's statutory framework; and other similar factors.[34]

Although identifying such factors unquestionably would help one to predict and to explain agency and reviewing court behavior, we do not discuss them much here because they are tangential to our purposes. Our intention has not been to analyze the behavior of particular agencies or reviewing courts (although we have devoted some attention to trends in the D.C. Circuit). Instead, our purposes have been to uncover broad patterns and general trends in administrative law and, with respect to our discussion of *Chevron*, to gauge how an unusually controversial administrative law decision of the Supreme Court actually has affected reviewing court (and, indirectly, agency) behavior. Our data, we think, are fully appropriate to those goals.

•   •   •

IV. Summary of Principal Findings

This Article has presented a welter of data bearing on numerous hypotheses about administrative law. Lest the most important and intriguing findings be obscured by the lengthy discussions, it may be useful to recapitulate them. We organize this summary of principal findings around the four broad objectives of the study, which in turn defined the four major sections of Part III. First, we hoped to produce some baseline information about parameters such as the character, magnitude, and consequences of judicial review of federal agency decisions. Second, by comparing this information at different points during a period spanning two decades (1965–85) in which the court-agency relationship is widely thought to have undergone a transformation, we hoped to discern changes in these parameters over time. Third, we hoped to learn more about remands, especially about what actually happens when the cases go back to the agencies where they originated. Finally, we hoped to gauge the effectiveness of the Supreme Court's highly controversial effort in *Chevron* to regulate the court-agency relationship through a change in legal doctrine.

Our analysis, we think, increases our understanding on each of these points. As we noted at the end of Part II, however, we regard our findings as more suggestive than conclusive. Some of these findings are incomplete and in some cases impressionistic, as are some of the data on which they are based. They cannot begin to capture the rich complexity and diversity of federal administrative law, nor do they purport to do so. In this regard, detailed case studies can provide far more textured accounts of court-agency relationships than our data permit.[35] But such texture and detail come at a price. Studies that are agency-specific can tell us little about the larger patterns traced on the political-legal landscape by federal agencies and courts. These larger patterns can be discerned only through the kind of panoramic and systemic, but inevitably imprecise bird's-eye view attempted here. This view requires that a much richer database be amassed and a greater analytical effort mounted.[36]

A. *The Changing Style of Appellate Opinions*

Our first finding, based on data published by the Administrative Office of the U.S. Courts (AO), is well known: The administrative law caseload in the circuit courts has increased rapidly and, at least as measured by what the AO calls "termination on the merits" (as distinguished from filings), fairly steadily. Less well known (but also based on that published data) is that this larger caseload constitutes a rather small and steadily shrinking portion of the circuit courts' dockets—only 7% in 1987.

A striking finding that may have wide-spread implications for administrative law concerns the phenomenon of "table decisions"—summary decisions for which no reasoning or factual description is published. Today, the majority of administrative law cases are disposed of in this way. In 1985, almost 60% of all dispositions were by these "table decisions," compared to 38% in 1975, and an unknown number in 1965.[37]

This phenomenon has received relatively little attention or sustained analysis by academic commentators, and its significance for administrative law is not yet clear. It is tempting to speculate on how the predominance of table decisions has affected the affirmance rate, yet even the direction of causality remains uncertain. As we have seen, and as one might expect, all but a handful (albeit a surprisingly large handful) of these table decisions are affirmances. The dramatically increased use of table dispositions may *reflect* an increase in affirmances caused by other factors; in this view, table decisions are simply a less time-consuming way to clear judicial dockets than writing full published opinions. On the other hand, the increased use of table decisions may be a *cause* of a higher affirmance rate, rather than (or as well as) an effect. In this view, docket considerations motivate reviewing courts to dispose of cases summarily, and summary dispositions can be accomplished most readily through affirmance by table decision rather than reversal, remand, or affirmance by written opinion. Unfortunately, our data do not permit us to determine which of these views is correct, although the significant number of table decisions that do *not* affirm tends to undercut the latter view.

The potential importance of table decisions, however, goes well beyond its positive association with the affirmance rate. This method of promulgating decisions raises fundamental questions of the legitimacy and public perception of legal process. When courts dispose of a large number of agency cases summarily and without opinion, administrative law is deprived of the benefits of reasoned justification. In that event, it loses the salutary intellectual discipline and normative significance that opinion writing imposes, and its processes and outcomes appear arbitrary. If courts decide significantly more cases without having to justify their decisions, administrative law becomes increasingly opaque and incoherent. On the other hand, routine cases should be handled routinely and busy courts should not have to expend scarce time and effort belaboring the obvious and familiar. Because the shift toward table decisions as the predominant form of resolution has occurred swiftly and without adequate reflection, it is by no means clear that the current practice strikes the optimal balance between these competing considerations. This phenomenon clearly warrants further investigation.

Our findings concerning opinion length and footnoting are of lesser importance, of course, but a few of them nevertheless are of some interest for what they may reveal about the emerging style of administrative law opinion-writing and the effect of docket pressures.[38] In general, opinions written in the mid–1980s were much shorter on average than those written a decade earlier, although this effect is almost entirely due to the courts' increased use of table decisions. The D.C. Circuit writes longer and more heavily footnoted opinions than the other circuits; in this respect it is even more of an outlier than it was in 1975.

Of greater significance, perhaps, is our finding that consensus within circuit courts, as measured by the proportion of one-opinion cases, increased in all circuits between 1965 and 1975, and remained unchanged a decade later, even when table decisions are excluded.[39] Including them, of course, would dramatically strengthen this consensus index. Even more impressive is the maintenance of this level of consensus at a point (1984–85) well into an administration that was determined to appoint federal judges of a different ideological stripe. Again, the D.C. Circuit was an outlier; in all periods its consensus level was lower than that in the other circuits. Yet even the D.C. Circuit's consensus level appeared to increase between 1975 and 1984–85, although more recent appointments to that court may well have reduced that consensus.

B. The Ages of Administrative Law

The most important finding that emerges from our twenty-year punctuated longitudinal analysis is that the circuit courts are affirming agency decisions at a steadily increasing rate, a rate that approximated 76% in 1984–85, and reached over 81% in 1985—just after *Chevron*.[40] When we measure the petitioners' probability of success—combining the reversals and the 40% of the remands in which the lawyers report a "major change" in the agency's position on remand—we find that it was about 12% in 1985, a figure that our 1988 data suggest may have increased slightly as *Chevron*'s effect weakened. A success rate of only 12% raises an important question as to why petitioners appeal as frequently as they do. In Part III, we speculated that with respect to some but not all agencies, the explanation may be found partly in the possibilities for using appeals to delay the effect of agency action.[41] This question clearly warrants further research.

Our findings concerning the growth of rulemaking were somewhat surprising.[42] Although rulemaking's share of the administrative law caseload increased twenty-fold between 1965 and 1984–85, it still constituted only 6.5% in the latter period. Even more striking is the fact that when we excluded from our analysis agencies that apparently never used rulemaking, and examined only those that sometimes use it, rulemaking's share was still only 9.4% in 1984–85, a share that was actually *lower* than it had been in 1975. We speculated in Part III that reviewing courts' imposition of adjudicatory-type procedural and evidentiary burdens on rulemaking during this period may have had the perverse effect of discouraging its use.

This information relates to our finding concerning the agency composition of the administrative law caseload, which has changed dramatically since 1965.[43] A docket once dominated by labor and patent cases is now dominated by labor, personnel, and immigration cases—virtually all of which are adjudications. Agencies that engage in "social regulation" accounted for less than 4% of the caseload in 1984–85. When we examined the circuit court composition of the caseload, we found that the D.C. Circuit's share of the national administrative law docket remained remarkably stable over the twenty-year period, comprising about 12% in 1984–85.[44] The Federal Circuit's share (36%) was the largest, distantly followed by the Ninth Circuit (15%). Another striking finding was the steady decline in, and the rarity of, en banc decisions, especially outside the Federal Circuit.[45] Even including the Federal Circuit, fewer than 2% of the non-table cases were heard en banc in 1984–85.

C. Remands and the *Chevron* Effect

If our data on dispositions and the use of table decisions indicate a growing tendency of reviewing courts to defer to agencies, our data on remands also suggest that the Supreme Court's *Chevron* decision has reinforced that deference, pushing the overall affirmance rate to levels higher than those that prevailed in 1965, 1975, and 1984—just before *Chevron* was decided.[46] Affirmances increased by almost 15% after *Chevron*, and both remands and reversals declined by roughly 40%. The post-*Chevron* affirmance rates, we found, were bimodally distributed; one group of agencies clustered around 80%, while another group clustered around 60%. We suggested that the different subject matters upon which these two groups of agencies focus—a difference that results in the first group's reliance on adjudication while the other group sometimes uses rulemaking—might help explain this distribution.

When we refined our analysis of remands in order to appraise *Chevron*'s effect more precisely, four findings of interest emerged.[47] First, more of the increased affirmances after *Chevron* "came from" reduced reversals than from reduced remands. This "outcome displacement" effect was fully consistent with the purpose of *Chevron*, which was to make it harder for reviewing courts to reverse for agency errors of law. Second, *Chevron* was immediately followed by a large decline in substantive law remands—the kind that *Chevron* aimed to discourage—while the total number of remands remained constant. Although these data would seem to establish that *Chevron* also had a pronounced "reasons displacement" effect, they actually are more equivocal than that. Third, the increase in affirmance rates after *Chevron* had eroded by 1988; the affirmance rate in 1988 had slipped to 75.5%, roughly halfway between the pre- and post-*Chevron* rates. Fourth, the remand rate increased significantly between 1985 and 1988, although fewer of the increased remands "came from" reversals than *Chevron*'s logic had led us to expect.

These findings suggest that *Chevron* affected outcomes differentially and that those outcome effects differed over time. The expected affirmance-increasing effect occurred immediately but had weakened by 1988, whereas the expected remand-increasing effect did not occur immediately but was evident in 1988.[48] These findings are consistent with the notions that *Chevron* achieved its intended goal in the short run, and that post-*Chevron* developments—including the Supreme Court's own weakening of *Chevron* in subsequent cases and the lower courts' strategic responses to these decisions—frustrated those purposes as time passed.

When we disaggregated the data on the effects of *Chevron* by examining particular circuits and agencies, two other striking findings emerged.[49] First, we found that the D.C. Circuit, whose affirmance rates had been lower than those of the other circuits throughout the twenty-year period and were far lower by the time *Chevron* was decided, responded to *Chevron* by affirming even less often than before, in sharp contrast to the other circuits, which responded to the decision by increasing their already high affirmance rates. And, second, the "outcome displacement" effect of *Chevron* turned out to vary considerably among the agency groups; the affirmance rate actually *declined* for the immigration agency and the "other regulatory" group.

Taken as a whole, our findings with respect to the effects of *Chevron* on remands, although not unequivocal, support a general conclusion of some significance to the analysis of legal process in administrative law. On the evidence of this study, the Supreme Court is sometimes able to effectively shape the court-agency relationship through the kind of relatively broad, open-textured rule adopted in *Chevron*. For reasons that we explained earlier,[50] and because of the quite different conclusion drawn by some commentators following the Court's *Vermont Yankee* decision,[51] this finding was unexpected.

D. What Happens After Remand?

Our data concerning the response of agencies to judicial remands yield one especially interesting finding. Our prediction that agencies would manage to find ways to reaffirm their original decisions—what we called "the agency gets the last word" hypothesis—was *not* borne out.[52] In approximately 40% of the remands, the agencies adopted "major changes," and most agencies appeared to do so primarily *because* of the remand (i.e., on the basis of the old administrative record).

This 40% figure is much higher than we expected. But it does, of course, mean that 60% of the remands did not result in any "major changes." This means that petitioners succeeded in obtaining a major change in the agency's position in only about 12% of the cases—the 8% in which the circuit court reversed the agency outright, plus 40% of the 9% of the cases in which the court remanded, and the agency on remand adopted a major change.

V. Conclusion

We believe that this Article demonstrates anew the value of using large-scale statistical studies of cases,[53] here augmented by interviews with lawyers, to subject important propositions about law and legal change to empirical testing. Although we have deployed this technique in the field of administrative law, its applicability extends as broadly as the phenomenon of adjudication itself.

The traditional method of studying changes in the law—the "leading cases" approach developed by Christopher Columbus Langdell in the 19th century and still used today—is quite unsatisfactory. It posits that the "law" (defined by Oliver Wendell Holmes, Jr. as "what the courts will do in fact"[54]) can be captured in a few supposedly exemplary cases. These cases—cases that are generally selected by academic writers using unconscious, or at least unstated, principles of selection—are in turn assumed to state principles of legal doctrine that explain the results in a much larger number of disputes. As our colleague George Priest has observed, however, this approach to doctrinal analysis has not proved very useful in making predictions about law; better methods are needed.[55] We think that our study confirms Priest's skepticism about the value of forming opinions about trends in the law based on statements in a few leading cases and articles.

Our own methodology, of course, is far from perfect. The conclusions to be drawn can be no better than the data on which they are based, and the data relating to some of the most interesting characteristics of decided cases are impressionistic and subject to competing interpretations. Even apart from these problems, our analysis failed at certain points to accomplish what we had hoped.[56]

Still, this approach seems far more promising than the traditional alternative, especially in the area of administrative law. The state of knowledge about what agencies and reviewing courts actually do in most cases, and about how Supreme Court directives influence their behavior, is so primitive that studies of this kind are likely to produce valuable information *regardless* of what their data show. If it had turned out, for example, that the *Chevron* decision did *not* influence reviewing courts, that would have been just as revealing and interesting a finding as our actual results. As it happens, we are reassured to learn from our study that the Supreme Court's law does indeed matter to reviewing courts, and that their law, in turn, matters to agencies.

Notes

1. The few exceptions in the legal literature involve a consideration of this question in quite particular contexts. *See, e.g.,* Leventhal, *Environmental Decisionmaking and the Role of the Courts,* 122 U. PA. L. REV. 509, 554–55 (1974) (discussing EPA's response to remand in International Harvester Co. v. Ruckelshaus, 478 F.2d 615 (D.C. Cir. 1973)); Williams, *"Hybrid Rulemaking" under the Administrative Procedure Act: A Legal and Empirical Analysis,* 42 U. CHI. L. REV. 401, 425–36 (1975) (discussing responses by three agencies to judicial interpretation of APA requiring more formal procedures in informal rulemaking by EPA). A broader empirical study of the court-agency relationship, Gardner, *Federal Courts and Agencies: An Audit of the Partnership Books,* 75 COLUM. L. REV. 800 (1975), focuses upon judicial strategies of supervision rather than upon how agencies respond to remands. For a critique of the regulatory role of public tort law, see P. SCHUCK, SUING GOVERNMENT: CITIZEN REMEDIES FOR OFFICIAL WRONGS 3–12, 125–81 (1983).

Some political scientists also have examined this question. *See, e.g.,* R. MELNICK, REGULATION AND THE COURTS: THE CASE OF THE CLEAN AIR ACT (1983); S. WASBY, THE SUPREME COURT IN THE FEDERAL JUDICIAL SYSTEM (1988).

2. This irony, of course, is common to all fields, not just law. By some perversity of intellectual inquiry, the most interesting and important questions in life are usually the most elusive and opaque.

3. The number of administrative law cases in the federal appellate courts is large and growing. *See infra* Chart 1.

4. There are several publications devoted exclusively to administrative law doctrine. *See, e.g.,* ADMIN. L. REV. (published by the American Bar Association); ADMIN. L.J. (published by American University). There are also numerous specialized journals concerned with judicial review of agency decisions in particular policy areas, *e.g.,* J. AIR L. & COMM.; J. ENERGY L. & POL'Y; and at least one leading law review publishes an annual administrative law issue, *see* DUKE L.J.

5. Mashaw & Harfst, *Regulation and Legal Culture: The Case of Motor Vehicle Safety,* 4 YALE J. REG. 257, 275 (1987). *See generally* Schuck, *Why Don't Law Professors Do More Empirical Research?,* 39 J. LEGAL EDUC. 323 (1989).

6. *E.g.,* K. DAVIS, DISCRETIONARY JUSTICE: A PRELIMINARY INQUIRY 54–59, 219–22 (1971) (advocating a form of the non-delegation doctrine that would encourage agencies to confine their discretionary power through rulemaking); Strauss, *The Place of Agencies in Government: Separation of Powers and the Fourth Branch,* 84 COLUM. L. REV. 573, 578 (1984) (arguing for the abandonment of "rigid separation of powers compartmentalization" in favor of a more practical analysis in terms of "separation of functions and checks and balances").

7. *See, e.g.,* Monaghan, Marbury *and the Administrative State,* 83 COLUM. L. REV. 1, 6 (1983).

8. *See, e.g.,* K. DAVIS, *supra* note 6, at 27–28, 215–16 (agency discretion limits effectiveness of judicial review).

9. Practitioners, needless to say, find themselves on all sides of this question; their positions depend not only upon their experiences and orientations but also upon whether they are seeking to persuade their clients to challenge or to defend the agency's position.

10. M. SHAPIRO, THE SUPREME COURT AND ADMINISTRATIVE AGENCIES 265 (1968).

11. Data on administrative cases brought before the federal courts can be found in the ANNUAL REPORT OF THE DIRECTOR OF THE ADMINISTRATIVE OFFICE OF THE U.S. COURTS (published jointly with REPORTS OF THE PROCEEDING OF THE JUDICIAL CONFERENCE OF THE UNITED STATES).

12. 467 U.S. 837 (1984).

13. The total number of cases in our 1965–1985 sample is 2325, consisting of 372 decided in 1965, 277 decided in 1974–75, and 1676 decided in 1984–85. The number of cases in our 1988 sample is 147. The grand total, therefore, is 2472 cases. The datasets, and the reasons for constituting them as we did, are explained *infra* text accompanying notes 16–32.

14. Our sample included cases from each of the 16 appellate courts (the D.C. Circuit, the 11 numbered circuits, the Court of Claims, the Court of Customs and Patent Appeals, the Federal Circuit, and the Temporary Emergency Court of Appeals) that heard direct appeals from executive branch agencies during the period under study. A list of the agencies, together with their coding keys, is appended as Appendix A.

15. We excluded all cases, such as Social Security Act adjudications, that had come to the courts of appeals through the federal district courts or through specialized judicial tribunals such as the U.S. Tax Court.

16. *See, e.g.,* Stewart, *The Reformation of American Administrative Law,* 88 HARV. L. REV. 1669, 1670 (1975) (noting that during this period, the Supreme Court had largely eliminated the standing barrier to challenges of agency action in court and that judges had accorded interest groups the right to force the initiation of formal agency proceedings).

17. When we ended the data collection in early 1988, two categories of remanded cases remained incomplete: (1) those in which the lawyers had not provided all of the necessary information during the initial and follow-up interviews, and (2) those that had still been "open" (i.e., post-remand activity was still ongoing) at that point. In an effort to include these cases in our dataset, we made one final pass at them in August 1988, well after we had begun our preliminary data analysis. Even at that late date, some three to five years after the remand, we found that a certain number of cases remained in one or both of these categories. We dropped these from the dataset, at least as far as our analyses of post-remand events and evaluation of outcomes were concerned.

18. At the written request of the ACUS, each federal agency identified a contact person within the agency (usually in the general counsel's office) who would help to facilitate the data-gathering for the study. The identity of the agency's and petitioner's lawyers often was obtainable from the published opinions, as well.

We generally sought to interview the most junior lawyer listed. Our assumption that this would be the lawyer closest to, and most knowledgeable about, the details of the case generally proved to be correct. Sometimes, of course, the lawyers who were in the best position to answer our questions were no longer employed by the agency or firm. In those cases, the interviewer attempted to locate that lawyer, and when that effort failed, the interviewer almost always was able to obtain the desired information from someone else in the agency or law firm who was (or after reviewing the file could become) familiar with the matter.

19. We explain how we handled this problem *infra* Part III(D), "What Happens After Remand?"

20. 470 U.S. 116 (1985).

21. *See infra* Part III(C), "Remands and the *Chevron* Effect."

22. *See infra* Part III(B)(1), "The Outcomes of Judicial Review."

23. Although this means that we actually read cases covering *five* time periods, we treat the two six-month periods during 1985 as a single time period for purposes other than that of analyzing the effects of *Cherron.*

24. The 1965 sample covered cases decided during the six-month period between January 1, 1965 and June 30, 1965.

25. The 1974–75 sample covered cases decided during the six-month period between October 15, 1974 and April 15, 1975. The latter date was selected as the cut-off date in order to immediately precede the Supreme Court's decision on April 16, 1975 in Train v. NRDC, 421 U.S. 60 (1975), a case that anticipated *Chevron* in mandating deference to agency constructions of statutes.

26. The 1984 sample (both non-remand and remand cases) covered cases decided during the six-month period between December 25, 1983 and June 25, 1984, the day *Chevron* was decided.

27. The 1985 sample (both non-remand and remand cases) covered cases decided during the six-month period between February 28, 1985 (the day after *Chemical Manufacturers* was decided) and August 31, 1985.

28. The 1988 sample covered cases decided during the two-month period between March 1, 1988 and April 30, 1988.

29. These data had been recorded by the researchers on individual coding sheets, one for each case. The final coding sheet, which is reproduced as Appendix B, differs from several earlier versions, but only slightly. The changes were made in order to: (1) add some items of information that could be adduced entirely from analysis of the published opinions (e.g., item AA relating to the standard of review); (2) refine some of the data categories (e.g., item K relating to the number of judges; item N relating to the result code); (3) correct obvious errors; and (4) permit computer programming. A coding key also was prepared to facilitate the uniform coding of the data.

30. The number of agencies was smaller during the two earlier periods covered by the study, partly because fewer appellate cases were decided during those periods and partly because there were fewer agencies at that time. Because of the temporal parameters of our dataset, some relatively low-volume agencies (e.g., the Consumer Product Safety Commission) do not have any cases in the dataset.

31. Three sources of agency cases—the Merit Systems Protection Board (MSPB), the National Labor Relations Board (NLRB), and the Immigration and Naturalization Service (INS) (sometimes through the Board of Immigration Appeals)—together accounted for approximately 57% of the cases decided during the 1984–85 study period. Before the creation of the MSPB in 1978, the NLRB generated the most cases, accounting for 31.7% of the total in 1965 and 41.5% in 1975.

32. We formed these groups and assigned particular agencies to them on the basis of a combination of analytical criteria and the frequency with which certain agencies appeared in our dataset. The groups are: (1) the National Labor Relations Board; (2) health, safety and environment regulatory agencies; (3) other regulatory agencies; (4) the Immigration and Naturalization Service and the Board of Immigration Appeals; (5) the Merit Systems Protection Board, which by far accounted for the largest number of cases (27.5% in the 1984–85 period); (6) the Department of Labor; (7) executive departments other than the Department of Labor; (8) the Patent Office; and (9) all other agencies. The agencies included in each group are listed in Appendix A. These designations are arbitrary in the sense that they represent only one of the many ways in which the caseload could have been sliced. The labels used for some of these groups are also crude. Thus, for example, the Federal Mine Safety and Health Review Commission, and the Occupational Safety and Health Review Commission, which are included in group (2), are not really regulatory agencies. Furthermore, although the Federal Aviation Administration and the Occupational Safety and Health Administration certainly fit well in this group, we coded them instead to the Departments of Transportation and Labor, respectively.

33. We took a number of precautions to satisfy ourselves that the students' analyses of the published opinions and their coding of the data were reasonably accurate and uniform.

Most of the data collected from the published opinions was objective and straightforward in nature and there was little risk of error. Only two pieces of data in the opinions required some exercise of judgment in coding: the type of agency proceeding (item M on the coding sheet) and—a more difficult characterization—the reasons for remand (item N).

In order to achieve a high level of uniformity in characterizing the type of agency proceeding, we reviewed with the students the differences between adjudication, rulemaking, and ratemaking, and discussed the kinds of agency actions that might fall into the "other" category. We then instructed each of the students to read a random sample of cases, classify the type of agency proceeding involved in each, and bring any disputed classifications to us, whereupon we met as a group and resolved the few disputes in a way that further clarified the categories for the students.

Characterizing the reasons for remands was more difficult and we therefore felt obliged to be even more circumspect. First, we instructed all students to read a classic article by the late Judge Henry Friendly elaborating the taxonomy of remands that we had found useful and wished to employ in the study. *See* Friendly, Chenery *Revisited: Reflections on Reversal and Remand of Administrative Orders*, 1969 DUKE LJ. 199. We then discussed that taxonomy as a group at some length. Before permitting the students to read any of the cases to be covered by the study, we asked each of them to read and to complete coding sheets for an identical random sample of cases. They were then to meet among themselves to discuss any instances in which some or all of them had classified differently the reasons for a particular remand. After that, we met as a group to discuss those differences as well as any uncertainties that remained. We also encouraged the students to raise with us any questions that might arise when they analyzed the cases covered by the study, and we resolved those questions in weekly meetings that both of us and all of the students (with occasional exceptions) attended. After the students had completed all of the case analyses and coding sheets, we asked a lawyer with extensive administrative law experience in a federal agency to review for accuracy each of the cases and the students' coding sheets, making changes where appropriate. In addition, we reviewed each of the cases and coding sheets as to which the lawyer had raised any question, and we made the appropriate changes.

The authors adopted two additional reliability checks that should be standard procedure for studies of this kind. First, we each read several volumes of the *Federal Reporter* and checked our codings of the cases against those that the research assistants had compiled, going over any discrepancies with them in order to resolve any apparent misapprehensions. Second, we generated a list of key words and phrases that could be the basis for a computerized search for the cases that should be in our datasets. We then tested the reliability of this search technique by comparing its outputs to the cases contained in the relevant volumes of the *Federal Reporter,* enabling us to refine further the list of key words and phrases. Because this technique holds much promise for future research of this kind, we describe it in some detail in Appendix C.

Coding the data generated by the telephone interviews usually required only that the students accurately transcribe what the lawyers told them, not that they exercise independent judgment. The opposing lawyers seldom told them inconsistent things and when they did, the students simply recorded those differences on the coding sheet.

Given the large number of cases in the dataset and the limited experience of the students, we suspect that even these precautions failed to detect some errors. Nevertheless, we believe that the number of such errors cannot be large enough to affect the general conclusions that we have reached from our analysis.

34. To cite just one example, Professor Linda Hirshman notes that the fact that NLRB orders have no effect until they are enforced by a circuit court "creates a culture among labor lawyers of considering all NLRB orders as very tentative, [which] would have a big effect on the statistics throughout [this study]. They should be resisted much more often and reversed . . . more often." Letter from L. Hirshman to E. Donald Elliott (Jan. 18, 1990) (available from authors).

•   •   •

35. *See, e.g.,* Galanter, *Reading the Landscape of Disputes: What We Know and Don't Know (And Think We Know) About Our Allegedly Contentious and Litigious Society,* 31 UCLA L. REV. 4 (1983) (applying statistical analysis to determine the litigiousness of American society); Priest & Klein, *supra* note 68 (applying statistical analysis to the decision of whether to settle or litigate); Wheeler, Cartwright, Kagan & Friedman, *Do the "Haves" Come Out Ahead? Winning and Losing in State Supreme Courts, 1870–1970,* 21 LAW & SOC'Y REV. 403 (1987) (applying statistical analysis to determine whether power and wealth influence court decisions).

36. The data compiled by the Administrative Office of the United States Courts is useful but is only a starting point for analysis. An earlier recommendation by the Administrative Conference urged that the gathering and reporting of such data be improved. ACUS Recommendation No. 69-6, Compilation of Statistics on Administrative Proceedings by Federal Departments and Agencies, 1 C.F.R. s 305.69–6 (1988).

37. *See supra* Part III(A)(1).

38. *See supra* Part III(A)(2).

39. *See supra* Part III(A)(3).

40. *See supra* Part III(B)(1).

41. *See supra* text accompanying notes 68–72.

42. *See supra* Part III(B)(2).

43. *See supra* Part III(B)(3).

44. *See supra* Part III(B)(4).

45. *See supra* Part III(B)(5).

46. *See supra* Part III(C)(1).

47. *See supra* Part III(C)(2).

48. *See supra* Part III(C)(3).

49. *See supra* Part III(C)(4)&(5).

50. *See supra* text accompanying notes 113–20.

51. *See* Scalia, *supra* note 114.

52. *See supra* Part III(D)(2).

53. *See, e.g.,* J. MASHAW, BUREAUCRATIC JUSTICE (1983) (Social Security Administration); J. MASHAW & D. HARFST, THE STRUGGLE FOR AUTO SAFETY (1990) (National Highway Traffic Safety Administration); R. MELNICK, *supra* note 1 (Environmental Protection Agency); *see also* D. Rosenbloom, The Federal Labor Relations Authority (1988) (unpublished manuscript) (available from authors). With the support of the Administrative Conference of the United States, Peter Schuck and Theodore Wang are drawing upon the data and methodology of this study and undertaking a collaborative study of the relationship between a particular agency—the Immigration and Naturalization Service—and the reviewing courts.

54. Holmes, *The Path of the Law,* 10 HARV. L. REV. 457, 461 (1897).

55. Priest, *Selective Characteristics of Litigation,* 9 J. LEGAL STUD. 399, 399–401 (1980).

56. Some of the comparisons that we thought would prove interesting did not bear fruit—either because our database was too small to permit multiple comparisons (e.g., NLRB cases decided by the First Circuit vs. NLRB cases decided by the Second Circuit), or because the factors that we isolated for study turned out not to have as much predictive power as we imagined before we did the study. Thus, for example, our hypoth-

esis that the legal grounds on which courts remanded cases to agencies might be a powerful factor influencing the agency's ultimate decision after remand turned out to have been incorrect: We did not observe significant differences between the final results reached when, for instance, courts remand on a procedural ground than when they remand for further explanation.

10
The Thickest Thicket

Partisan Gerrymandering and
Judicial Regulation of Politics

Few contemporary legal developments are as striking, as unexpected, and as potentially far-reaching as the federal courts' redesign of the fundamental structures, institutions and incentives that frame and fuel political struggle at all levels of government. The courts have become principal regulators of politics.[1]

Judges are now in the business of political reform on a grand scale. During the last twenty-five years, they have altered the political parties' access to voters,[2] the system of legislative representation,[3] candidates' access to the ballot,[4] the scope of patronage in public employment,[5] the structure of campaign finance,[6] and the configuration of electoral districts.[7] And in those areas in which courts have traditionally regulated politics, such as political speech under the first amendment, their interventions are now more conspicuous and complex.[8]

In many areas of adjudication other than politics, lower courts press the Supreme Court to innovate.[9] In contrast, the Supreme Court has usually *initiated* its excursions into the regulation of politics. Rather than yielding deliberately and only incrementally to the importunings of the lower courts, it has often led the charge into political *terra incognita*.[10] Persistent warnings about the Court's limited ability to reform politics and about the dangers that lay ahead have gone unheeded.

The Court's decision in *Davis v. Bandemer*[11] dramatically exemplifies this pattern. In *Bandemer,* the Court held that it would henceforth adjudicate claims of partisan gerrymandering.[12] This phrase denotes a practice in which the party that controls a legislative districting plan's fate[13] deliberately draws district boundaries to its own advantage. It does so by creating a larger number of districts that will be represented by that party than would exist if the districts were drawn without regard to voters' partisan allegiances. This should be distinguished from gerrymandering designed to subordinate racial or ethnic minorities, urban or rural interests, or some division other than party.

We must be clear about what task the Court has now decided to assume. Long before *Bandemer,* the Court had required that state and congressional districting plans meet a constitutional mandate of population equality. Under that standard, all districts within a state must contain substantially the same number of individuals.[14] In addition, the Court had invalidated racial gerrymandering under the fifteenth amendment[15] and the Voting Rights Act.[16] Thus, *Bandemer* really challenges partisan gerrymandering that *already* must satisfy these well-established pre-*Bandemer* limitations on district line-drawing. Moreover, since the Court has been more indulgent toward state redistricting plans like the one in *Bandemer* than toward congressional ones (at least in malapportionment disputes),[17] *Bandemer's* strictures against partisan gerrymandering appear to apply to *all* districting plans.

Bandemer was in some ways a predictable sequel to *Baker v. Carr,*[18] its progenitor a quarter-century earlier.[19] *Baker* seemed to inter the "political question" objection to adjudicating cases like *Bandemer.*[20] But an even more significant link between the cases goes to the merits: partisan gerrymandering, if left unconstrained by the Court, could effectively deny the right that *Baker* and its progeny purported to secure—the right of each voter to have his or her vote carry equal weight in determining the composition of the legislature.[21] In truth, the connection between the cases is even closer and more instructive than that. Ironically, *Baker,* at least as glossed by recent decisions demanding strict population equality among districts, has probably encouraged the kind of partisan gerrymandering that culminated in *Bandemer.*[22]

That connection, however, does not mean that *Bandemer* was necessarily dictated by *Baker* or by any of the Court's other precedents.[23] But in both cases, judicial intervention sprang from much the same concern. For partisan gerrymandering, as for population inequality among districts, a traditional objection to judicial activism—that the remedy for the evil should be sought in the legislature, not in the courts—seems especially impertinent.[24] Both practices are not merely consequences of constitutionally suspect politics. They are also fundamental *causes* of it.

Such concerns are naturally heightened because a partisan gerrymander's animating purpose is to influence not only the districting statute but the entire corpus of legislative decisions enacted in its train. It thus ramifies and perpetuates what might otherwise be a majority's transient political advantage and if successful, may even render future gerrymanders unnecessary. Indeed, by translating a majority's legislative power into administrative and judicial power, a gerrymander may bias all of government. This practice, then, raises especially profound issues concerning the legitimacy of our representational structures and of the public decisions that those structures inevitably shape. Only the federal courts, the argument runs, can provide an effective remedy because only they are institutionally free of that taint.[25]

This is the standard critique of partisan gerrymandering, and as with most standard critiques, there is something to it. Voting rules, districting arrangements, and other representational institutions *do* profoundly influence political behavior. If those basic structures were different—if, for example, our political habits had evolved under a system of proportional representation rather than one in which single-member districts with a plurality voting rule predominates—we would almost certainly observe different kinds of political parties, alliances, leadership, bargaining, and ideological appeals. In that event, the electorate's underlying political preferences might also be altered, for those too are contingent consequences, and not just contributing causes, of these basic structures. But this valuable truth can lead to a false inference. It can suggest that any choice of political institutions is equally arbitrary and thus that such institutions are fungible. And by emphasizing an evil that we know (partisan gerrymandering) while overlooking those greater but less familiar evils that a judicial remedy might entail, it may imply that partisan gerrymandering should be jettisoned.

This leap is both illogical and dangerous. The standard critique's premises are wrong and *Bandemer*'s essential endorsement of that critique is misguided and leads to the wrong rule. The standard critique really derives from three related public norms—what I call the norms of political competition, structural fairness, and fair representation. In principle, these norms support not a general condemnation of partisan gerrymandering but at most a quite narrow scope for judicial disapproval. In practice, they counsel against even that limited intervention because the available judicial remedies would almost certainly create grave political and constitutional risks.

I do not wish to defend partisan gerrymandering. That practice, motivated as it is by narrow, self-interested ends, offends the ideal of a public-regarding politics toward which our polity should strive. But the Constitution does not demand human, much less political, perfection; its tolerance for much that is repugnant to fastidious citizens is a price that we pay for a robust, relatively open-ended political life. Judicial regulation of partisan gerrymandering would be a cure worse than the disease; constitutional change or a more enlightened legislative process would be a better remedy.[26] Until that happy day dawns, however, we ought to regard a rule that *permits* it—that is, one that continues the pre-*Bandemer* constitutional regime—as consonant with our public norms and constitutional traditions and thus as politically legitimate. I argue, in short, that the Court should have held partisan gerrymandering claims to be nonjusticiable. When the Court considers whether and how to regulate politics, it should resist reforms requiring blunt remedial tools that threaten to transform, rather than refine, the American political system.

The Article consists of four principal parts. Part I briefly summarizes the background of *Bandemer* and the Supreme Court's opinions in that case. Part II considers the three strongest principled arguments, each based upon one of the public norms mentioned earlier, against a rule that permits partisan gerrymanders meeting the pre-*Bandemer* districting standards. It concludes that the first two arguments, from political competition and from structural fairness, fail to provide a convincing critique of this practice or a justification for the plurality's constitutional test in *Bandemer*. The third argument, from fair representation, also fails; its account of the American system oversimplifies the problem of representing minorities.

Part III completes my refutation of the third argument. It consists of three sections analyzing some of the methodological problems that the Court must inevitably face if it makes a serious effort to vindicate *Bandemer*'s aspirations for reform. The first section argues that as the Court seeks a meaningful, administrable test of what constitutes a violation and an effective remedy, it will be driven to rely upon some form of party-based proportional representation. The second section shows that proportional representation, like the prevailing system of single-member districting with plurality voting, does not completely solve the problem of representing minorities in the legislature. The final section emphasizes certain changes in American politics that are rendering party divisions increasingly irrelevant and arbitrary as indicators of how fair and effective a districting plan or other representational structure is.

Part IV briefly speculates on why the Court initiated this fresh venture into the judicial regulation of politics, especially under circumstances that are so unpromising. It concludes that the Court's eagerness to launch this new venture (six justices, after all, were willing to underwrite its success) calls into question many legal scholars' core assumption that judicial legitimacy is a fragile wasting asset. I suggest instead that when the Court challenges politicians' pursuit of their self-interest (as distinguished from their more public-regarding policy objectives), it does not draw down its reservoir of public support and perceived legitimacy; it actually replenishes and enlarges it. This is true even (or perhaps especially) when the politicians persist in the face of the Court's challenge.[27] Still, the Court's institutional resilience is no justification for a venture that is so fundamentally unsound.

I. The *Bandemer* Decision

Davis v. Bandemer arose out of a districting dispute concerning the state legislature in Indiana, a state that has oscillated between Democratic and Republican dominance.[28] The Indiana General Assembly consists of 100 representatives elected for two year terms in a mixture of single-member and multimember districts, and of fifty senators elected for staggered four year terms. In 1981, at a time when the General Assembly and the Governor's office were controlled by the Republicans, a reapportionment plan was enacted to accommodate the 1980 census. The Republicans in the General Assembly completely controlled the process by which the plan was adopted, and manipulated it to exclude significant participation by the Democratic minority or the general public. No public hearings were held on the plan; its content was developed in a conference committee in which Democrats lacked all voting power; the plan was based upon a computerized, Republican-funded study of the political effects of different configurations; the Democrats were denied access to this study; the plan was made public only two days before the end of the session; and it was adopted by a party-line vote.

The plan, whose lines cut across a number of political subdivisions and created oddly shaped districts, was designed to maximize the Republicans' partisan advantage. It divided the House into seven triple-member, nine double-member, and sixty-one single-member districts, with some of the more populous metropolitan areas assigned to triple- and double-member districts; the Senate districts, which were all single-member, were not congruent with House district lines. For both chambers, the population deviation among districts slightly exceeded 1%.

Early in 1982, the Indiana NAACP and individual Democratic voters challenged the plan as a partisan gerrymander violative of the equal protection clause. In the 1982 elections held under the new plan, Democratic candidates for the House won 43% of the seats while receiving 51.9% of the popular vote; in the Senate race, Democrats received 53.1% of the vote and won thirteen of twenty-five seats.[29] In certain counties divided into multimember House districts, including the city of Indianapolis, the Democrats received 46.6% of the vote but won only three of twenty-one seats.

In December 1984, a divided three-judge district court invalidated the plan for future elections.[30] Relying on the approach recently taken by Justice Stevens in a population equality case, *Karcher v. Daggett*,[31] the district court emphasized several factors: the vote/seat disparities, the odd configuration of some districts, the use of certain districts to join ostensibly dissimilar communities, evidence of partisan motivation and manipulations by the Republican leadership, and the stacking and splitting of Democrats to maximize the efficiency of Republican votes. The court majority concluded that the plan intentionally and effectively diluted the Democrats' voting power and was therefore unconstitutional.[32] Dissenting, Judge Pell insisted that a plan's validity turned on its effect on voters rather than on its partisan motivation, and found no discriminatory effect. Instead, he attributed the vote/seat disparities to natural partisan advantages and the legislature's pursuit of neutral, legitimate policies.[33]

On appeal, the Supreme Court ruled that claims of partisan gerrymandering were justiciable under the fourteenth amendment, and went on to uphold the plan's validity. Although the Court divided sharply over the particular standard that should be applied to the plan on the merits, Justice White's determination of justiciability commanded the votes of six justices. To support justiciability he pointed to language in earlier racial voting dilution cases suggesting that dilution of political groups' voting strengths was justiciable, and to the Court's decision in *Gaffney v. Cummings*,[34] which adjudicated an equal protection challenge to Connecticut's redistricting law that provided for proportional representation for the major parties. He dismissed as nonbinding a number of earlier summary dispositions of lower court rulings of nonjusticiability with respect to partisan gerrymandering claims. Finally, he refused to apply the political question doctrine, arguing that *Baker v. Carr* and its "fair representation" progeny provided "judicially manageable standards" and established policy premises from which adjudication could proceed.[35]

Turning to the merits, Justice White relied heavily on the Court's racial voting dilution precedents, many of which he had authored. He began by agreeing with certain of the district court's characterizations of the case—namely, that the claim was one of *state-wide* discrimination against Democrats, that both discriminatory intent and effect against an identifiable political group must be shown, and that an intention to achieve the political effects that actually ensued would "most likely" be inferred from the mere fact of redistricting.[36] Rejecting proportional representation of parties as the test of a plan's validity, however, Justice White noted the inevitable "balloon effect" on the majority's representation[37]—and the denial of direct minority representation[38]—that resulted from the system of winner-take-all, single-member districting common in the United States. Although proportional representation was held in *Gaffney* to be permissible, it was not constitutionally required. Nor, Justice White added, was a plan invalid simply because it made it more difficult for a particular group to win; for constitutional purposes, at least, a losing group was presumed to be adequately represented by the winning candidate. The equal protection clause was offended, he wrote, "only when the electoral system is arranged in a manner that will consistently degrade a voter's or a group of voters' influence on the political process as a whole."[39] Such a conclusion, he added, "must be supported by evidence of continued frustration of the will of a majority of the voters of effective denial to a minority of voters of a fair chance to influence the political process."[40]

The district court's findings, Justice White noted, failed to satisfy this test. First, they focused on but a single election; there was no showing that the plan would consign Democrats to minority status in the future. Second, the emphasis on certain multimember districts that elected Republicans disproportionately was misplaced. Although the plan created some "safe" seats, this did not imply state-wide discrimination. Moreover, Democrats had ample opportunity to participate in electing candidates. Finally, the district court had required only a showing of partisan discriminatory intent without also requiring, as in the racial voting dilution cases, that plaintiffs demonstrate an actual, electoral disadvantage continuing (or likely to continue) beyond the results of one or two elections.[41] Here, Justice White concluded, no such threshold discriminatory effects had been shown; hence, it was unnecessary to reach the questions of district configurations or state justifications for the plan.[42]

Justice O'Connor, in an opinion joined by the Chief Justice and Justice Rehnquist, vigorously argued that partisan gerrymandering was nonjusticiable. Extolling the political virtues of the two-party system, she denounced Justice White's opinion as a prelude to judicially mandated proportional representation, a danger "which should inform any sensible jurisprudence of Article III and of the Equal Protection Clause."[43] No prior case, she argued, had established a *group* right to representation except in the case of blacks, the intended beneficiaries of the fourteenth amendment.[44] In contrast, the major parties are dominant groups, and their partisan struggle, through gerrymandering and other strategies, is bounded without the need for judicial intervention. Moreover, any group right would not extend to protection against dilution of state-wide, as distinguished from district-wide, voting power. She argued that the Court's reason for legitimating bipartisan gerrymanders in *Gaffney* actually demonstrated why partisan gerrymanders should be nonjusticiable. As a result, the *Bandemer* majority was in effect preferring the rights of groups (that is, the major parties), whose voting strength would now be substantially protected against dilution,[45] to the rights of individuals, whose votes *Gaffney* allowed to be "wasted" in the service of bipartisan gerrymanders.[46]

Justice O'Connor then turned to the plurality's "consistently degrade" standard for partisan gerrymanders. She contended that vote-dilution analysis becomes more unmanageable as the groups to be protected expand from racial minorities to include the major parties. More constraints imply fewer possible solutions, measuring party strength is more difficult, and courts would almost inevitably turn to proportional representation as a standard for evaluating partisan gerrymanders.[47]

Justice Powell, in a dissenting opinion joined by Justice Stevens, maintained that the plurality's approach would allow excessive latitude for partisan gerrymanders. Under a proper test, he urged, Indiana's plan must be invalidated. Justice Powell controverted two key points in the plurality's analysis. He argued that a partisan gerrymander's effect on a group's state-wide representation could violate equal protection, and that voters whose ability to elect legislators of their choice was limited by a partisan gerrymander could not be said to be fairly represented. He emphasized the importance of "neutral criteria"[48] for districting plans, in addition to population equality across districts, as a necessary safeguard for the fair representation mandated by *Baker v. Carr*[49] and *Reynolds v. Sims*.[50] The district court's finding that Indiana's plan violated these criteria and was designed to perpetuate Republican control, he contended, should be upheld. It was not at all clear how Justice Powell's preferred standard would apply in particular partisan gerrymandering cases; it seemed to require a showing of discriminatory intent based on all circumstances "which bear directly on the fairness of a redistricting plan, as well as evidence concerning population disparities and statistics tending to show vote dilution."[51]

II. The Arguments Against Partisan Gerrymandering

In the best of all possible political worlds, not even partisan gerrymandering satisfying the pre-*Bandemer* districting standards would exist. Legislators would draw district lines without regard to their own electoral prospects or those of their party; instead they would pursue a broad conception of the public interest. They would evaluate the possible plans according to "neutral" districting principles, which could be endorsed without regard to their partisan effects. Applying these criteria, the legislators would converge upon one and only one districting configuration satisfying them. The plan would also be revised periodically to maintain the integrity of the original criteria in the light of changing demographic patterns. These four conditions—legislative selflessness; neutral districting criteria; a uniquely optimal plan; and constant updating—might be thought of as the minimum necessary attributes of a gerrymander-free political world. If even one of them is lacking, a districting plan must, at the very least, generate controversy. If several are lacking, the plan will almost certainly produce gerrymandered districts. In reality, of course, none of these conditions is likely to obtain in the American polity or indeed in any robustly competitive, complex political system.

More important, each of these conditions, with the possible exception of the last, is inconsistent either with our fundamental political values or with the inevitable operation of our political processes. Legislators are manifestly self-interested; indeed, in most modern versions of liberal political theory, the legislator's desire for reelection is the fuel that drives and legitimates democratic representation.[52] Most of the important districting criteria—especially compactness, preservation of political subdivisions, and competitiveness[53]— that courts and other opponents of gerrymandering routinely invoke are not neutral either in the ideal sense defined earlier or in the weaker sense that the criteria do not systematically favor one party or another.[54] Even under the constraint of "one person, one vote," numerous possible districting plans could be drawn; it would require sheer happenstance or skillful agenda manipulation for even selfless, rational legislators to converge on only one. Finally, the ceaseless, rapid flux in demographic and political conditions, as well as the inevitable time lags in legislation, mean that even an "optimal" districting plan would almost certainly become suboptimal by the time it went into effect.[55]

But even if partisan gerrymandering is inevitable under present conditions, that cannot conclude the matter. The Court, after all, has often wielded the Constitution to transform the essential character of our politics. It regards political reality as plastic; for the Court, "is" never implies either "ought" or "always will be." To understand the Court's decision to adjudicate partisan gerrymandering claims, one must consider the standard critique of that practice. It consists of three components. The first is an argument proceeding from the virtues of *political competition*; it relies on a kind of antitrust model of the proper relationships among participants in the struggle for political power. The second is an argument from the norm of *structural fairness*; it invokes the images of the level playing field and the utterly disinterested decisionmaker. The third is an argument based upon a conception of *fair representation*; ultimately, it appeals to a standard of proportional representation.

These three arguments are plausible and appealing; each is grounded in certain widely shared values and powerful metaphors. But individually and in combination, they fail to discredit a constitutional rule that permits partisan gerrymandering meeting the pre-*Bandemer* districting standards. They overlook important complexities and values in our political life, project incomplete visions of democratic representation, and invite innovative political remedies that should not be mandated by federal courts.

A. *The Argument from Political Competition*

Competition among political leaders or parties is the defining characteristic of a real-world democratic polity.[56] Political competition encourages responsiveness to voter preferences, mobilizes citizen participation, infuses new blood into the arteries of government, facilitates policy innovation and flexibility, and inhibits the arbitrariness of entrenched power. According to the argument from political competition, partisan gerrymandering's special vice is that the majority party can forestall its opponents from effectively competing for dominance, perhaps even perpetuating itself in office.

This argument invokes the special economic imagery of the monopolist, which exploits its dominant position to drive existing and potential competitors out of the marketplace. Drawing upon this imagery, the argument seeks to control partisan gerrymandering through an antitrust-type intervention.

If the majority could use an effective partisan gerrymander to bar entry into the political market by new competitors or to deny them any meaningful chance to win, a court *might* be justified in intervening to preserve political competition, just as it might in an antitrust context. Intervention could be warranted if two conditions are met: First, the gerrymandering party's competitive advantage goes beyond the large zone of unrestricted political struggle that the Constitution permits. Second, the court can accurately determine and reliably remedy the violation without unduly infringing upon this zone.

Partisan gerrymanders cannot satisfy both conditions, and the analogy to the economic market helps to explain why. According to contemporary antitrust theory, even monopolies (to say nothing of less commanding market positions) are not economically objectionable per se.[57] If the monopolist dominates the market through consistently superior performance in satisfying consumer preferences or because of scale economies, its power is justified. Even if it achieves its position through aggressive advertising or pricing practices, criticism may not be warranted. So long as these practices do not bar entry, they are presumed to be economically efficient.[58] In the absence of competitive barriers, other firms can expand their market shares, at least in the long run, and exploit any monopolistic inefficiencies.

From society's point of view, of course, the long run may be *too* long.[59] We may be unwilling to tolerate market power for the period necessary to erode the monopolist's advantage. If that is so, we must consider a variety of interventions designed to restore competition in the short run; possible remedies would include antitrust enforcement, abolition of legal or governmentally created restrictions on entry, and subsidization of competitors. Because each of these measures is politically or economically costly, the intervention may not be undertaken or if undertaken, may be unsuccessful. In either case, short run market power would continue. If the intervention succeeds, competition may be quickly restored.

Because political markets differ from their economic counterparts in important respects,[60] the fact that enduring monopoly power is difficult to achieve or maintain in the economic marketplace does not mean that partisan gerrymanders could never create that power in the political marketplace. But partisan gerrymandering is very unlikely to have that result; brief reference to economic analogies helps to explain why.

In the political domain, legal barriers to entry and competition are generally low and presumptively illegitimate.[61] The first amendment guarantees access to voters and to political activity of all kinds.[62] It is true that minor parties and independent candidates do not fare nearly so well at the hands of the first amendment as the major parties; the Constitution permits limited discrimination against them.[63] But partisan gerrymandering is not directed at minor parties or independent candidates. Instead, its target is the other major party, which (even apart from *Bandemer*) enjoys broad constitutional protection from legislative efforts to hobble its ability to compete.[64]

Some barriers to party competition, of course, might be objectionable even though they are not illegal. In particular, financial limitations may sometimes impair a party's ability to win elections. But the history of campaign finance teaches us that private contributions tend to flow to incumbents, regardless of their party.[65] Nor are financial disparities between political opponents the kind of barriers to party competition that are ordinarily regarded as illegitimate. In part, we tolerate them for an important legal and practical reason: it is difficult to design measures that would effectively remedy such inequalities without also offending other constitutional values.[66] We have also learned that financial disparities between the major parties are not decisive. As the Democratic Party's gains in the 1986 elections suggest, political success turns on the interaction of many resources, most of which are more equally distributed than money. A smaller party treasury is often offset by more attractive candidates, the advantages of incumbency, a larger voter base, a more robust ideological or historical appeal, a cadre of volunteer support, national political currents, special local factors, or the errors and exigencies of the other party.[67] Perhaps this is why our polity views parties' differential abilities to secure campaign funds, like firms' differential abilities to raise capital, as an essential element of the pluralistic struggle for public support rather than as a mark of competitive unfairness. So viewed, this larger structure of political competition legitimates the outcomes that it produces.

Other important guarantors of political competition also blunt the damage that partisan gerrymanders can do. One is the fragmentation of party loyalty.

In a weak party system like ours, members of the minority party often possess considerable bargaining power and exert strong influence over the shape of legislation. In such a system, coalitions tend to be fluid, ad hoc and evanescent. Individual legislators or small, ideologically cohesive groups can often extract maximum value for their support by offering to supply the decisive bloc of votes. Even where party cohesion is stronger and one party dominates, interests within that organization will conflict as individual members seek to advantage themselves at the expense of others. Indeed, if the majority coalition is sufficiently fragmented, a cohesive minority faction may actually hold the balance of power on particular issues, even though it is too small to organize the chamber itself.[68]

The potential leverage of minority parties in a system of frequently shifting coalitions is a powerful spur to political competition. Even the closest economic analogies to this phenomenon—the ability of small firms to find a special niche in a highly concentrated market, or the ability of holdouts to use their strategic positions to extract a premium from their bargaining adversaries—do not fully capture its effects. Because legislators bargain continually over a very broad range of matters, they can often translate a decisive or highly valued vote on one issue into significant influence over the outcome of other issues as well, depending on other legislators' intensities of preference and strategic positions.[69] This is especially true if the legislature (as is usually the case) effectively decentralizes its voting function to specialized committees and subcommittees on which minority party members may have greater influence than they do in the chamber or legislature as a whole.[70]

Numerous constitutional and institutional arrangements are designed to frustrate a majority party's exercise of monopoly power. The systems of separated powers and checks and balances, perhaps most dramatically manifested in the executive veto and judicial review, mean that a party's control of one chamber or even both houses of the legislature does not assure that it can implement its will. Formal voting rules that protect minority party interests also buttress political competition in the face of gerrymandering efforts. Familiar examples are the requirements of supermajorities for particular legislative actions, and the rules permitting filibusters.

Practical political considerations also constrain a party's ability to achieve monopoly power through partisan gerrymandering. In order to secure passage of a redistricting plan, a majority party must first attract enough votes to pass the reapportionment bill in both chambers of the legislature, yet that may prove impossible unless the majority party enjoys a large margin of control and party discipline is fairly strong. Even if the party easily controls both chambers of the legislature, it may confront a gubernatorial veto.[71] Even if no veto can be anticipated, the nature of a partisan gerrymander's goal—to obtain a political advantage by maximizing the "efficiency" of its supporters' votes in winning legislative seats—imposes its own limits on the majority party's ability to achieve it, even in the short run.[72] In this context, an "efficient" plan may be defined as one that minimizes the number of its supporters' votes in each electoral district that are "wasted" (that is, not needed to win that district's seat), and that maximizes the number of the opposing party's wasted votes, subject to the constraint of winning only enough seats to assure the majority of reliable, effective control of the chamber.[73]

To increase the efficiency of its support, however, the majority party must incur some significant risks and costs. First, a more efficient seat is also a more competitive one that the opposing party is more likely to win in the next election. Indeed, the Republicans seem to have gained some long-term advantage from the predominantly Democratic partisan gerrymanders of the early 1980s; there was a marked increase in the number of marginal Democratic incumbents and decrease in the number of marginal Republican incumbents in the 1982 elections.[74] Second, a more competitive seat is ordinarily a more costly one to control because each vote becomes more valuable and each candidate must do more to win it. By the same token, the majority party must spend more money if it wishes to contest seats that its plan makes safer for the minority party. Third, making a seat safer for the gerrymandering party does not simply reduce the other party's ability to contest it. Since the value of that seat has not been enhanced, competition *within* the gerrymandering party for that seat may also be intensified, producing more vigorous, divisive and expensive primary battles.[75]

A fourth risk is that the majority party's demographic and political assumptions are simply wrong. These assumptions are inevitably surrounded by some uncertainty and prudent gerrymanderers will prefer to err on the side of safety for their party. Recent evidence, for example, suggests that even in many putatively "safe" districts, the swings in party support from one election to another are substantial.[76] In order to ensure the safety of those seats in the face of this volatility, the gerrymandering party must place an even higher percentage of its supporters in that district, which necessarily leaves fewer surplus votes that can be allocated to other districts. Thus even the most resolute gerrymanderers must waste some of their partisans' votes.[77]

A fifth risk relates to the acute but inexorable conflict of interest between the gerrymandering party (or at least the group that controls its machinery) and some of its members. These members include those whose incumbency would be threatened by the plan, and those whose personal agendas otherwise diverge from the party's goals. The party has two major options available to it—an efficient-majority or inefficient-minority strategy. First, it can attempt to increase the number of its seats by taking those supporters who become "surplus" when districts already under its secure control are made more efficient, and then allocating those supporters to districts in which they will provide the margin of control for seats that the minority now holds or that the majority holds only insecurely. But given even minimal adherence to the pre-*Bandemer* districting standards, the gerrymandering party probably cannot implement this strategy. Indeed, the more stringent those standards—and they are sometimes applied with Procrustean rigidity today, especially in congressional districting cases[78]—the fewer the controlling party's options and the greater its difficulty in successfully gerrymandering.

Alternatively (or in combination with the first strategy), the gerrymandering party can seek to create a surplus of supporters available for redistribution to other districts by moving them out of minority-controlled districts, thereby strengthening the minority's hold on those seats. This strategy is also divisive, for it serves the interests of the majority party's incumbents at the expense of those of its members who aspire to seats now held, perhaps only marginally, by the minority party. It also means, of course, that the minority can retain those seats at lower cost than before.

In either event, a gerrymandering party's attempt to allocate this risk of having to run in a more competitive (or even losing) district among its incumbents or hopefuls is bound to be painful and organizationally divisive. The party's task is especially difficult because it must still pass the redistricting legislation, and it cannot necessarily count upon the votes of incumbents whose seats the plan will jeopardize or make more costly to hold. And if the gerrymandering party seeks to attract the support of some minority party legislators, as it often must, the price may be high: it must make their seats more secure at the expense of the majority's own incumbents and aspirants.

A final risk to the gerrymandering party is that the other party may succeed in making the gerrymander an important, visible campaign issue. Whatever the gerrymander's actual effect on how legislative seats are distributed, many voters are likely to resent both the tactic and its authors.[79] Of course, the gerrymandering dispute (like any other political issue) may turn out not to be salient enough to affect the election outcome, or (as occurred after the successful California referendum) the politicians may manage to reinstate the gerrymander.[80] Still, the dispute is bound to influence some voters at the margin; in a close election, it could be decisive.[81] Voters occasionally punish or even reverse extreme gerrymanders, as they did (with somewhat equivocal effects), in California in 1982.[82]

The argument from political competition, then, does not support a broad-gauged attack on partisan gerrymandering. The argument presupposes an already existing structure of political dominance that is difficult for any party to achieve and even more difficult to maintain over a long period of time absent genuine, enduring voter support.[83] To observe that partisan gerrymanders require a degree of "political market power" that is elusive and transient, however, is certainly *not* to deny that they sometimes succeed.[84] Incentives to gerrymander, after all, are always powerful and the constraints that I have described are not always fully effective. Instead, the analysis suggests that the dynamics of political competition and party organizations strongly inhibit partisan gerrymanders and are likely to limit their effects when they do occur. Even if they increase the party's seats in the next election, many of those seats will be more competitive and expensive than before, sowing the seeds of the gerrymander's own destruction or ineffectiveness.[85]

In short, a party's motive to gerrymander is considerably stronger than its ability to execute and sustain one. That is why some retrospective analyses of recent redistricting cycles have found partisan gerrymandering efforts to have been ambiguous, ineffective or even counterproductive from the dominant party's perspective.[86] Partisan accusations and rhetoric aside, egregious gerrymanders appear to be rare—more feared, hoped for, and talked about than successfully implemented and maintained.

At this point, the analysis of the argument from political competition leads to two conclusions. As an empirical proposition, the argument greatly exaggerates the dangers to competition that partisan gerrymanders present, especially in the long run. On the other hand, the argument may in *principle* justify a judicial response in those unusual situations in which particular gerrymanders do pose actual competitive threats. In *practice,* as we shall see, difficult questions of constitutional standards and remedial methods counsel strongly against judicial regulation of partisan gerrymandering even in those situations.[87]

Although the analogy between political and economic competition helps us to gauge the proper reach of the political competition argument, that analogy should not obscure three crucial differences between the two markets. These differences are highly relevant in deciding what the courts' response to partisan gerrymanders ought to be. First, in principle at least, the conditions of economic efficiency are judicially knowable and remedially feasible.[88] Intense controversy exists over the meaning and implementation of efficiency. But there is widespread agreement on the need for criteria of economic efficiency, on what the alternative measures of efficiency are, and on how they should generally be applied.[89] Drawing upon appropriate evidence and assumptions, antitrust courts can (albeit problematically) identify configurations of firms and market shares that threaten market efficiency. Less ambitiously (but still problematically), they can seek to restore the competitive conditions that prevailed prior to the defendant's illegal practice.

In contrast, the idea of "political efficiency" is incoherent, perhaps even oxymoronic. We *want* political competition to generate political market power because that power is necessary for effective, accountable government. Many different electoral structures might satisfy this requirement, including various districting arrangements and proportional representation systems. But beyond this minimal specification (except at the extremes), we cannot even know what an "efficient" political market would look like. It is one of those things that a liberal polity should prefer to leave indeterminate.

A second difference concerns the way in which preferences are expressed in the two competitive systems. In economic markets, individuals satisfy their preferences through individual purchasing and consumption decisions, which are taken as the ultimate indicia of their preferences. So long as those preferences are met, we do not ordinarily look behind the purchasing decisions for some more ultimate significance beyond the presumed fact of consumer satisfaction. In the political market, however, we do. Partisan labels are largely epiphenomenal. A voter's choice of a Democrat or Republican candidate is usually (and increasingly) a proxy for a set of socially more important preferences about policy, personality, or symbolism. As citizens, we usually care less about whether Democratic or Republican candidates win than we do about whether the outcomes we think they will produce are in accord with our underlying political preferences.

A partisan gerrymander does not really alter the electorate's underlying preferences, except in the special sense that *any* political structure can affect political behavior over time.[90] At most, the gerrymander may alter the partisan identity of the individuals who sit in the legislature to implement those preferences. It may produce some districts that are more liberal than before and some that are more conservative. But the preferences of the electorate as a whole—and thus the voting behavior of the legislators who must seek its votes for reelection—should not be significantly changed. The empirical evidence bearing on the policy effects of gerrymanders tends to confirm this prediction.[91]

A third difference, closely related to the first two, concerns the range of permissible remedies. Because of the normative importance accorded to political actors' autonomy and their freedom from governmental interference, certain judicial instruments that may be uncontroversial in the antitrust context would be intolerable, perhaps even unconstitutional, if employed to regulate political markets. As examples, consider the familiar antitrust remedies of corporate divestiture[92] and mandatory licensing arrangements.[93] These sanctions are designed not only to deprive malefactors of their ill-gotten gains but to create or restore a structure of economic competition that the court concludes will yield efficient market outcomes.

In contrast, a court that adopted the political analogues of those remedies would transgress constitutional limits. It is one thing for a court to remedy a constitutional violation by, say, ordering a party to refrain from discriminating in its membership criteria.[94] It would be quite another thing to issue a decree breaking up a political party or alliance, or compelling one political group to trade votes with another in the interest of enhancing political competition. The former constrains a particular private choice in order to vindicate an independent, well-established constitutional norm. The latter engineers the basic structure of political competition on the basis of some notion of what the outcome of that competition should be; it usurps powers of political association and initiative among private citizens that no organ of government may properly regulate. The difference may be one of degree but if so, it is a difference that seems essential to the survival of a liberal polity.[95]

These distinctions between political and economic markets further undermine the argument from political competition. They call attention to special obstacles that courts must overcome if they are to take up even the limited challenge to particular partisan gerrymanders that that argument may occasionally justify in principle and that *Bandemer* evidently contemplates in practice.

B. The Argument from Structural Fairness

Partisan gerrymandering may also be opposed on the ground that it offends the norm of structural fairness. Where the argument from political competition looks to the practice's effects upon actual political outcomes, the argument from fairness condemns the practice on the basis of a more fundamental principle of political morality. This argument elaborates that principle in the form of a syllogism about the requirements for the essential fairness of representational structures.

The major premise of this fairness syllogism links two propositions, one descriptive-analytical and one normative. The first proposition is that a legislative districting plan establishes a fundamental condition of representative democracy by establishing the terms on which, and the structure within which, political competition is to proceed. The second proposition is that a structure that is fundamental in this sense should be neutral, unbiased, and "outcome blind"; that is, it should not systematically increase the probability that one political claim will prevail over another. The minor premise of the syllogism is that partisan gerrymandering violates this neutrality norm by favoring the majority party and the majority's legislative program. From this logic, the conclusion follows that partisan gerrymandering is an illegitimate way to structure the political process in a representative democracy.

This syllogism, however, is flawed. First, as a descriptive-analytical matter, legislative districting can only in the loosest sense be analogized to those fundamental conditions of representative democracy, such as free political speech and elections. Without them, liberal democratic government as we know it simply could not exist; *no* outcomes worthy of respect could emerge from the process because those conditions are normatively and empirically essential to self-government.[96] But legislative districting lacks that fundamental linkage to representative democracy. Strictly speaking, it is necessary only when representation is not on an at-large basis. Even at that most tautological level, its necessity is limited. As a matter of constitutional design[97] or statutory practice,[98] much political representation in our system, including some legislative representation, is at-large rather than district-based.

But the fact that legislative districting is a contingent element of representative democracy rather than a constitutive one does not suffice to refute the argument from fairness. Perhaps the second proposition in the major premise—that legislative districting should be neutral from a partisan perspective—can stand alone, justified by independent principles of fairness.[99] John Rawls, in his book *A Theory of Justice*,[100] advances one such principle, based on his notion of the "original position."[101] According to Rawls, principles of fairness (and thus of justice) can be derived by considering the rules that rational individuals would choose for society if they were obliged to choose such rules behind a "veil of ignorance" that concealed from them what their individual endowments, both natural and social, would be. Although his conception has been criticized on a number of grounds,[102] it does present a widely accepted, coherent definition of a principle that can be used, as a first approximation, to test the fairness of the kind of structural rules found in the Constitution.

Is it plausible to suppose that rational citizens standing behind the veil of ignorance would choose a rule that permits partisan gerrymandering subject to the pre-*Bandemer* districting standards? One cannot be certain, of course, but there are some reasons to believe that they might. Partisan gerrymandering is clearly objectionable if the criterion of a good districting plan is that every party should win the same share of legislative seats that it receives of the popular vote. But proportionality is not the only possible *desideratum* of a plan. Other criteria, also consistent with the pre-*Bandemer* standards, might also be relevant.

In particular, individuals and parties might prefer to live in a political world in which competitive success confers what I shall call a "victory bonus," than to live in one in which the most that partisan voters can expect is proportional representation. A victory bonus can take a variety of forms—patronage, control over the perquisites of office, greater logrolling opportunities, control of the chairmanship and staff of legislative committees, and so forth. The opportunity to gerrymander might be viewed as just one more variant, no more and no less.

Why might individuals standing behind a veil of ignorance, not knowing which party they would belong to, prefer such a political system? Although much depends upon what knowledge of political life we impute to individuals or parties in that decidedly hypothetical position, several plausible motives for permitting a victory bonus come to mind. By raising the returns to victory (and the costs of defeat), it may attract more talented, entrepreneurial individuals into public life. By increasing the value of electoral support, it may enhance politicians' responsiveness to voters. More speculatively, political groups maneuvering for high-stakes strategic advantage may make political life more interesting for politicians and voters alike, increasing public participation in and attention to politics. Perhaps most important, a victory bonus may be an essential technique for promoting effective governance in a markedly decentralized political system that always skirts the dangers of excessive fragmentation and destabilizing fluidity. Citizens and parties may prefer the stability, power aggregation, and accountability to voters that a victory bonus encourages. By facilitating majority party or coalition formation,[103] a victory bonus thus helps to solve perhaps the fundamental structural problem in American politics.[104]

Reasonable people, of course, frequently disagree about how large a victory bonus ought to be and what margin of victory should be necessary to qualify for it. For present purposes, the important point is that a victory bonus might include partisan gerrymandering opportunities, and that such an arrangement could be supported by citizens and parties who are rational and disinterested in the special, Rawlsian sense.

This does not demonstrate, of course, that Rawlsian political architects would choose a rule permitting this *particular kind* of victory bonus—the opportunity to engage in partisan gerrymandering. They might reject such a rule, for example, on the ground that "neutral" districting plans are possible. An electoral structure or voting rule might be thought to be neutral in at least two senses. Its neutrality might result from (1) the fact that the rule fails to confer any systematic, predictable advantage on any particular party (especially the one sponsoring the rule), or (2) the fact that the rule can be justified by reasons having nothing to do with its advantage-conferring propensities. Neither is true of rules establishing districting plans, at least those in use today.

1. Neutrality of Effects. All rules advantage some players and disadvantage others, and almost all do so more or less systematically.[105] Even a rule to decide an issue by voting favors some individuals and interests over others in the sense that a rule that instead resolved the issue by, say, market processes or brute strength would have advantaged quite different individuals and interests.[106] Ordinarily, one can identify the beneficiaries and victims of a political rule. Experienced politicians are in the business, after all, of trading their own votes for the votes of others. In order to do this effectively, they must possess a detailed, specialized knowledge of the distinctive political biases and electoral impacts of different rules and structures.[107] When politicians choose one rule or structure rather than another, one may reasonably assume that they know (or *think* they know) how it will influence outcomes, at least at the margin.[108]

These propositions are manifestly true as applied to legislative districting decisions. There, certain threshold choices must be made. It must be decided, for example, whether to base representation on geography rather than on some other characteristic, to use districts rather than at-large constituencies, and to use single-member districts rather than multimember districts. These threshold choices fundamentally affect how and which political coalitions are formed, the cost of campaigning, the success of various kinds of appeals to voters, the nature of particular candidates, the salience of specific issues, and many other crucial dimensions of politics.[109] Once these powerful determinants of political outcomes have been settled, the marginal effects of the subsidiary decision to draw district lines in one configuration rather than in another are likely to be relatively small.

If we consider some examples of putatively neutral districting criteria, we see that none is self-defining and most conflict with one another. Although there is general agreement, for example, that compactness is desirable, there is no agreed-upon formula for determining just how compact a district should be. And despite its esthetic appeal, compactness tends to conflict with population equality and with efforts to preserve those so-called "communities of interest" or political subdivisions that happen to be geographically attenuated.[110] The preservation of political subdivisions also is not a neutral criterion; it too conflicts with population equality and tends to promote partisan stability and protect incumbents, which are normatively controversial attributes of a democratic polity.

Even population equality, surely the most universally acclaimed districting standard, can be defined in various ways that may have very different political effects. Because of demographic changes and population mobility, the Census data on which the implementation of this criterion must be based are always imprecise and seldom stable for the decade between redistrictings. Yet there is no satisfactory basis on which to make adjustments nor is there even a consensus about whether such adjustments are appropriate. Indeed, a quarter-century after the Supreme Court mandated population equality, the Court still cannot agree upon what deviations from strict population equality are constitutionally permissible.[111] From a narrow partisan perspective, it may matter a great deal that certain minorities are routinely undercounted by the Census and that the one person, one vote criterion is defined in terms of *population* equality rather than eligible or actual *voter* equality.[112]

2. Neutrality of Reasons. Although districting rules cannot be neutral in their political effects, they might nevertheless be thought to be neutral in the reasons advanced to justify them, a kind of neutrality emphasized by Bruce Ackerman in a recent book.[113] Here, the criterion of a rule's neutrality is whether its defense satisfies certain widely accepted norms of fairness, such as the obligation to give reasoned justifications and the moral equality of individual conceptions of the good. Ackerman calls these norms "conversational constraints" and argues that a rule that is not neutral in this sense is presumptively invalid.[114]

But even this idea of neutrality does not necessarily condemn a rule permitting partisan gerrymandering. Virtually all districting plans, including partisan gerrymanders, either satisfy Ackerman's conversational constraints or render those constraints impracticable. It is surely the rare plan that cannot be rationalized on the basis of a plausibly legitimate districting criterion other than mere partisan advantage.[115] What reasons would satisfy Ackerman's neutrality constraint? His theory does not provide the answer, but there is nothing in that theory to suggest that even the common purpose of protecting incumbents of both parties—a purpose that can be justified (albeit controversially) in the name of legislative expertise and continuity—would not qualify. Moreover, once one acknowledges, as one must, that *all* districting plans have generally predictable, nonneutral political effects, a logical implication follows: society must either be prepared to govern itself without legislative districting, or Ackerman's constraints must be relaxed for this particular conversation.

If politically neutral districting plans simply cannot be drawn (that is, the electoral playing field can never be completely leveled) and if even a partisan gerrymander can satisfy Ackerman's conversational constraints, then Rawlsian citizens might well opt for a rule that permits partisan gerrymandering. They might even believe that once the rule's lack of neutrality is openly acknowledged, it might be transformed into something of a virtue. In a representative democracy, they might rationally maintain, legislators should be assigned clear political responsibility when they adopt districting plans that favor their partisan interests. By promoting candor about partisan advantage-seeking at precisely the point at which it is most certain to occur, such a system may be preferable on balance to one that facilitates evasion of that responsibility by appearing to legitimate what is actually a vaporous pretense of a spurious neutrality. Or so the Rawlsian decision makers might conclude.

As a matter of historical fact, of course, rational citizens *did* make such a choice time and time again when, over the course of the last two centuries, they established the traditional procedures for districting at all levels of government.[116] Those procedures have generally provided for districting through *ordinary* legislation, subject to all of the partisan self-interest and power-seeking that normally attend the legislative process. Indeed, citizens adopted those procedures long before *Baker* and its progeny began to limit the partisan advantage that could be extracted from districting decisions.[117]

What can be made of this clear historical pattern? Obviously, the fact that virtually all jurisdictions have long countenanced partisan gerrymandering and seldom if ever required extraordinary majorities for districting plans cannot dispose of the normative question of structural fairness. People made these choices, after all, not as detached decision makers behind a hypothetical veil of ignorance but as participants in a functioning polity and with knowledge of actual partisan affiliations, policy preferences, and electoral consequences. Their decisions might be viewed as inevitably tainted, reflecting little more than the majority party's earlier self-serving exercise of legislative control.

But just as the historical evidence cannot settle the question of fairness, this reductionist, realpolitik response accords too little weight to that evidence. First, such a response leads to an infinite regress in which no choice can be legitimated because none can be said to be wholly independent of the partisan context out of which it or its antecedents emerged. The mere fact that this response triggers an infinite regress, of course, does not mean that it is wrong, but it should encourage us to look for alternative explanations of the historical evidence. A second, related problem with that response is that it overlooks a striking fact: most, perhaps all, jurisdictions leave, and apparently have always left, the adoption of districting plans to the process of *ordinary* politics.[118] Despite the fact that control of the legislature has often shifted back and forth between the parties through the years, they evidently have not used their intermittent incumbency position to lock in their own gerrymandering—for example, by requiring supermajorities for future changes in districting laws.[119]

This self-denying behavior by the parties may say more about politicians' risk aversion and fear of retaliation than it does about the disinterestedness of Rawlsian citizens once they are in power. Still, the rule permitting partisan gerrymandering has been tolerated for two centuries both by parties, who as erstwhile majorities and minorities have experienced the benefits and the burdens of that rule over the long course of their political history, and by the general public in those jurisdictions in which districting plans favoring certain parties or groups have been adopted by popular referenda.[120] This durable pattern of choice by both parties and by the citizenry at large is not irrelevant to the question of fairness. It strongly supports, although it cannot itself prove, the conclusion that the rule is not fundamentally unfair.

C. The Argument from Fair Representation

A rule permitting partisan gerrymandering might be opposed on a third ground—that it makes fair representation of voters impossible. Since proponents of the argument from fair representation do not ordinarily advance it as a unified, integrated political theory, one must distill it largely from the pre-*Bandemer* gerrymandering and Voting Rights Act cases.[121]

The argument from fair representation focuses upon a set of three political relationships nested within the overall system of legislative representation: the relationship between the individual citizen-voter and political groups; the relationship between the citizen-voter and the district's elected representative; and the relationship between the citizen-voter and the legislature as a whole. I shall call these, respectively, the "group representation," "district representation," and "legislature representation" relationships.

The argument from fair representation consists of a series of claims concerning how these relationships are and should be structured. Descriptively, it holds that partisan gerrymandering impairs or destroys these relationships by reducing the political system's responsiveness to minority party voters. Normatively, the argument from fair representation holds that only a system of proportional representation can fully realize these relationships, and that only such a system can assure voters of a representational relationship to a party, an electoral district, and a legislature that "truly" reflects and secures their political preferences.[122]

1. The Group Representation Relationship. According to the argument from fair representation, the system of legislative representation conceives of voters not as individuals but as members of groups. This conception, which derives from pluralistic theories of politics,[123] includes a normative element. It posits not only that groups are the effective motive forces in the legislative process, but also that the electoral rules that structure that process should be evaluated, at least for purposes of constitutional analysis, according to how well they facilitate group formation and maintenance. In the context of partisan gerrymandering, the crucial aggregations with which the group representation relationship is concerned are of course the majority and minority parties in the legislature at any particular point in time. The gerrymander's special vice, in this view, is that it enables the majority party to impede and distort the processes by which minority parties form, grow and compete to become the majority and represent their members effectively.

2. The District Representation Relationship.   According to the argument from fair representation, a citizen is entitled to fair representation from his or her district's representative in the legislature. The normative content of this entitlement is uncertain, but it includes at least two distinct components. The first extends not only to voters who supported the representative who won the election, but also extends to those who supported losing candidates. At a minimum, it obligates the representative to consider the views and needs of all constituents in the district before deciding upon a course of action, whether they were supporters in the past or not.[124]

The entitlement's second component involves a special obligation toward those constituents who voted for the representative. While not necessarily justifying indifference to the minority party's views, this obligation would accord greater weight to the views of the majority party's members. In terms of district representation, the partisan gerrymander's chief vice is that it encourages the representative to subordinate the first component of the voter's entitlement to the second, thereby depriving minority party members of any expectation that the district representative will protect their interests unless those interests are identical to the majority's.

3. The Legislature Representation Relationship.   According to the argument from fair representation, voters are entitled to a duty of fair representation not only from their district representative but also from the legislature as a whole. The essential structure and substantive content of this entitlement are much the same as in the district representation relationship. The major difference is that the overall relationship between voter and legislature is necessarily more attenuated. In at least one sense, however, that relationship is more direct: the voter's entitlement is affected (that is, protected or threatened) directly through legislative action rather than indirectly through an individual representative's vote.[125] From the perspective of the legislature representation relationship, the partisan gerrymander is objectionable because it enables the majority party, by changing the rules of the political game, to reshape and determine the nature of the other two relationships to the minority party's disadvantage.

While intuitively attractive, the argument from fair representation, like those from political competition and structural fairness, ultimately fails as a critique of a constitutional rule that permits partisan gerrymandering under the pre-*Bandemer* districting standards. Descriptively, its conception of the underlying political relationships results in a radically incomplete and therefore seriously misleading account of political practice. Normatively, its prescriptions concerning those relationships are arbitrary and objectionable in principle.[126]

We have seen that a successful gerrymander can impair the group representation relationship by hindering the minority party's ability to grow, attain control of the legislature, and thus represent its members most effectively.[127] But the partisan gerrymander is not really distinctive in this regard: all of the political rules and institutions that advantage majorities by conferring influence beyond what their mere numbers would warrant interfere with it in precisely the same sense. All victory bonuses—patronage, logrolling opportunities, the opportunity to organize the legislative chamber, the financial and other advantages of majority status, and the like—also create that power-enlarging effect.

Probably the most significant power-enlarging institution in American political life is the system of single-member districting, coupled with a plurality (or "first-past-the-post") election rule for awarding the district seat. That system has always dominated American legislatures. It is difficult to see how one can maintain a fair representation argument against partisan gerrymandering without at the same time challenging single-member/plurality-vote districting; the premises of that argument indict the latter at least as strongly as the former. Like a partisan gerrymander, single-member/plurality-vote districting rejects proportionality in favor of a victory bonus for the majority party. Given the usual distribution of partisans among geographic districts, singlemember/plurality-vote districting produces a balloon effect that provides the majority with more legislative seats, and the minority with fewer, than their shares of the total vote alone would imply.[128]

The size of this balloon effect can be very substantial,[129] and it does not apply neutrally (that is, without regard to which party happens to be in the majority). Indeed, its magnitude is certain to vary depending upon several factors that apply differently to each party. These party-specific factors include the concentration of a party's support within particular districts, the candidates at the top of its ticket, and voter turnout. Other things being equal, for example, a low turnout among low-income, predominantly Democratic voters in urban or other overwhelmingly Democratic districts means that fewer Democratic votes in those districts will be "wasted" relative to more "inefficient" Republican votes in high-income suburban districts where the Republicans dominate and turnout is heavy. This in turn will translate into a higher seat/vote ratio—greater "efficiency"—for such Democratic districts,[130] and the size of the balloon effect in the legislature as a whole will reflect this factor.

The single-member/plurality-vote districting system has three extremely important implications for the argument from fair representation against partisan gerrymandering. First, the system's balloon effect will occur whether or not the majority party has engaged in gerrymandering; the size of the effect depends upon a number of uncontrollable or legitimate factors, such as voter turnout, residential patterns, and permissible population disparities among districts. This means that a high seat/vote ratio cannot properly be used as an index either of partisan gerrymandering or of other forms of majority party maneuvering, for it may easily be attributable to other factors. Indeed, as in the case of low voter turnout, it may in fact reveal that the party is *weak* in its ability to mobilize the electorate (even if it is strong enough in that district to win the seat). This indeterminacy problem provides a compelling reason, along with others to be discussed below, why courts should not intervene to regulate partisan gerrymanders even in those limited situations in which risks to political competition may be thought to exist.[131]

Second, single-member/plurality-vote districting remains a firmly embedded feature of American political life, one that reformers' criticisms have utterly failed to dislodge.[132] Indeed, single-member/plurality-vote districting is not only politically durable; it now amounts to a quasi-constitutional *requirement*. Under the Voting Rights Act of 1965,[133] numerous jurisdictions at the state and local levels have been required to shift from multimember districting and at-large representational systems to single-member districting in order to avoid diluting the voting power of ethnic minorities.[134] The Supreme Court has also indicated its qualified preference for single-member districts.[135] If single-member districting is not merely a permissible but almost sacrosanct system of representation, partisan gerrymandering, which poses a lesser threat to minority groups, seems even less vulnerable to the argument from fair representation.

Third, both single-member/plurality-vote districting and partisan gerrymandering, by creating a similar kind of victory bonus, reinforce the majority party's capacity to govern alone, making it easier to attribute responsibility for political acts, such as legislation, to a single party. For that reason, both practices, like the majority vote requirement in the Electoral College, serve to strengthen party accountability. This is no mean accomplishment in a political system that in many other ways operates to diffuse it.[136] Indeed, a case can be made that fair representation in our system (and perhaps in any complex system) necessitates some degree of party accountability, and that partisan gerrymandering actually *advances* fair representation in that limited sense.[137]

But the fact that partisan gerrymandering is not an *unmitigated* evil, that its majority-reinforcing, accountability-strengthening tendencies are politically functional, does not conclusively refute the argument from fair representation. After all, it is not obvious whether these tendencies should be regarded as a virtue, as too much of a good thing, or as outweighed by the dangers of the practice. The argument from fair representation can only be decisively rebutted by considering the vices of the only alternatives to which it can logically lead. Generally speaking only two alternatives to a rule permitting partisan gerrymandering do not require either constitutional amendment or legislative change. First, courts might review closely either the legislative motives and procedures that led to the enactment of districting plans or the plans' electoral effects, in order to detect and remedy improper partisan influences. Second, courts might impose a requirement of proportional representation in the legislature. These alternatives, however, are unacceptable in principle, unworkable in practice, or both.

III. The Siren's Song of Proportional Representation

My critique of the argument from fair representation has emphasized the inadequacy of its description of the American political system and of the argument's representational model. But the argument's more basic *normative* claim—the claim that parties, electoral districts, and legislatures should embody the proportionality principle rather than facilitating majority-enhancement—requires a normative response. That response consists of three elements. First, *Bandemer,* despite the Court's disclaimer, will encourage proportionality as the standard against which partisan gerrymandering claims will tend to be measured. Second, proportionality's notion of fair representation of minorities is conceptually incoherent. Third, powerful, perhaps irreversible, currents in American political life make the implementation of even a diluted proportionality norm increasingly impracticable.

A. Bandemer *and Proportional Representation*

Although the argument from fair representation leads ineluctably to a system of proportional representation,[138] the connections between the argument and the system are less logical than they are practical and principled. One might suppose that the argument's normative demands for truer, more direct minority representation could be satisfied by institutional changes other than proportionality. This supposition, however, is highly doubtful.

Proportional representation has long appealed to reformers dissatisfied with the structure or outcomes of American politics.[139] In principle, it promises many changes that might seem to make that system more accountable to voter preferences, more responsive to new conditions, and more ideologically coherent and competitive. Most pertinent, proportionality would avoid many of the difficulties that partisan gerrymandering poses for group, district and legislature representation of partisan and other minorities.

In its proponents' view, proportionality would increase existing parties' willingness to promote minorities' interests or would encourage the formation of new parties eager to do so. Coupled with multimember districting or at-large elections, it would reduce, if not eliminate, the wasting of minority votes in the selection of district or at-large representatives.[140] Indeed, given current interpretations of the Voting Rights Act of 1965,[141] proportional representation might be the only way to validate the use of multimember districting and at-large structures in many jurisdictions in which those structures have been judicially condemned. In addition, proportionality could produce a legislature that would contain more minority group members and would more faithfully and effectively represent minority interests. In a society increasingly sensitive to the political claims of racial and other minorities, these are no small virtues.

It is no wonder, then, that calls for proportional representation are always heard.[142] Those calls, however, have seldom been heeded. Proportional representation, especially in the American context, raises concerns that explain the American public's consistent rejection of it.[143] These concerns[144] center on its fragmenting effect on the party system and the legislative process, its encouragement of ideological, single-issue political appeals, its promotion of coalition government and instability, and its relative unresponsiveness to local constituents and individual voters' needs. These and other substantial objections to proportional representation belie any claim that the American resistance to it simply reflects the self-serving strategy of the existing political establishment. That is why the Court in *Bandemer* disclaimed any intention to look to proportionality as the criterion of constitutionality in partisan gerrymandering cases. The plurality and concurring opinions rejected it explicitly[145] and even the dissenting justices agreed that "the Constitution does not guarantee proportional representation."[146]

Saying something, however, does not make it so. There is a dynamic to constitutional adjudication that the Court cannot always control, a dynamic vividly revealed in the steady movement from *Baker* to *Bandemer*. *Bandemer*'s logic requires the Court to devise a judicially manageable test and remedy for partisan gerrymandering. Unless the Court decides to abandon the effort, its search will almost certainly lead it to proportionality as the measure of both. In that event, the Court will doubtless find euphemisms to soften the clear contradiction between its words in *Bandemer* and its subsequent actions. But few will be fooled, least of all the parties. The reality of proportionality will remain.

The links between *Bandemer* and proportionality are straightforward, and are outlined in Justice O'Connor's concurring opinion.[147] Essentially, they amount to this: A court cannot determine whether and to what extent a districting plan "will consistently degrade a . . . group of voters' influence on the political process as a whole"—the plurality's constitutional test[148]—unless the court can compare the group's post-gerrymander representation in the legislature to what the group's "true" representation would be under a "fair" plan.[149] But the latter obviously can be determined only by reference to some norm or benchmark. For a political party, that benchmark can only be its performance at the polls.

But how is that performance to be measured in an actual partisan gerrymandering case? A moment's reflection about how partisan gerrymandering claims would have to be adjudicated must immediately reveal the need to determine both the substantive justiciability and the remedial tractability of such claims. Yet the only feasible way to measure a party's electoral performance[150] for this purpose is to examine the party's past vote totals and the number of legislative seats that it won with those votes, and to decide whether the putative gerrymanding party's seat/vote ratios are "too" high. This analysis must inevitably rely on some notion of "normal" performance, which necessitates use of a "base race". But a "base race," to be a useful construct, must be one in which the effects of issues, candidates' personalities, unusual party effort, and other contingent factors deemed irrelevant to the party's "true" strength are minimal.[151] Judgments about these factors and their effects must be largely subjective and beg questions that lie at the heart of political competition in a democracy.

As a practical matter—as a matter of judicial administrative feasibility rather than of political science theory—this sort of analysis would represent both the beginning and the end of the benchmark inquiry. The reason is that a court will seldom have anything else to go on. It is one thing in a malapportionment case for a political analyst or even a court to attempt to assess the significance of a deviation from population equality by looking to swing ratios and other statistical measures. These indices purport to gauge a plan's sensitivity to party competition, changes in voter support, intensity of voter preferences, or other political variables that may be relevant to whether that deviation is justified or tolerable.[152] But it would be far more problematic for a court to use crude, subjective, question-begging measures to decide partisan gerrymandering claims in cases in which population equality has already been achieved. In effect, the court would be prescribing the partisan configuration of the legislature—the most political of tasks—and doing so on the basis of inevitably conflicting, inconclusive expert testimony about the uses and implications of such tests. This is surely a chilling prospect.

A court sensitive to these difficulties would doubtless seek other criteria, but these alternatives would not be better and might even be worse. The court, for example, might choose to focus on the *legislative process* by which the districting plan was adopted, much as proof of malice in libel cases often looks to the way in which the defendant gathered and analyzed the defamatory material.[153] In *Bandemer* itself, the evidence revealed that the Republican majority in the legislature simply excluded the Democrats from any meaningful participation in the committee process that led to the plan's enactment.[154] It is doubtful, however, whether such egregious tactics are common in the already limited universe of problematic gerrymandering situations. More typically, one supposes, the gerrymandering party would be content simply to rely upon its control of the votes needed to pass the bill and, if necessary, to override the governor's veto.

But even if exclusionary tactics are more common than that, it is difficult to discern constitutionally suitable standards for appraising the adequacy of a legislative process. For the validity of a districting law to turn on whether it was preceded by hearings of a certain type, conducted in a certain spirit, and held before committees of a certain composition would surely offend well-established separation of powers principles, and an injunction compelling the legislature to abide by existing procedural rules would be intrusive and unenforceable.[155] Moreover, interventions like these would necessarily require the courts to reconstruct the legislators' reasons for employing the processes that they did. Yet pre-enactment legislative procedures are notoriously informal and diverse, especially in state legislatures. There, the kind of documentation, such as committee reports and floor debates, that courts typically use to divine the legislative purpose of final statutory enactments seldom exist.[156] The effort to infer the legislative motive for using a particular process, as distinguished from construing a statute's legislative purpose, would plunge the court into the deepest of quagmires.[157]

The benchmark problem, then, is extremely vexing. If there is a judicially manageable solution to it, the *Bandemer* decision does not even hint at what that might be; all but two of the Justices failed even to *acknowledge* the existence of this problem. When the plurality and dissenters *did* divide, it was over an issue that, while methodologically important, was indisputably subsidiary—the question of the number of election cycles over which party performance should be measured.[158]

Once we recognize the striking consensus in *Bandemer* among six Justices as to the centrality of electoral performance in proving a partisan gerrymandering claim, the larger significance of the Court's silence on the methodological issue comes into sharper relief. On the central question of the legal significance that proportionality should have in partisan gerrymandering cases, the Court seemed determined to have it both ways. It scrupulously rejected proportionality as the benchmark of electoral performance that adjudication of such claims requires, yet refused to suggest any other standard that might take its place. By insisting that litigants challenging districting plans as partisan gerrymanders would bear a heavy evidentiary burden[159] while failing to indicate how that burden could be met, the Court simply shoved the problem under the rug.

B. Proportionality and the Representation of Minorities

There are four senses in which it can be said that a legislator "represents" a minority group or party. First, the legislator may have been the direct choice of a discrete group of voters, selected as its designated candidate and elected through bloc voting. Thus a successful candidate is often said to have been the "unions'," "blacks'," or "women's" candidate. Second, a legislator may possess certain personal attributes—race, ethnicity, or gender, for example—that define, or seem especially salient to, the minority, attributes that are thought to assure the legislator's fidelity to the minority's interests. Third, a legislator, although neither the minority group's designated candidate nor a member of that group, may be impelled to promote the group's interests out of a political need to assemble or maintain a winning electoral coalition. Finally, a legislator may seek to advance the minority's interests for moral, public-regarding, or other nonelectoral reasons, such as the pursuit of future career opportunities.

The argument from fair representation emphasizes the first and second of these representational modes—what Hanna Pitkin termed the "accountability" and "descriptive" views of representation.[160] This emphasis is grounded in existing law as well as political theory. It finds support in numerous court decisions under the Voting Rights Act, which equate fair representation of a minority with its ability to elect a candidate of its choice, as evidenced (often conclusively, it seems) by the candidate's own membership in that minority group.[161]

Proportional representation, as Pitkin shows, particularly reifies the "descriptive" view; it is 9the attempt to 'secure a representative assembly reflecting with more or less mathematical exactness the various divisions in the electorate.'9[162] Political accountability is presumed to follow from the formal arrangements under which the representative, elected under proportional representation, must seek reelection.[163] Her descriptive and accountability views merge, then, in a normative conception that is perfectly embodied in a system of proportional representation.

But as we have seen, this conception is not self-evidently correct or desirable. Other, quite different views of representation can also be normatively justified. In particular, the third and fourth notions of representation mentioned earlier emphasize that a legislator may also fairly represent constituents when motivated either by political self-interest or by an altruistic or public-regarding desire to discern and serve their interests.

What is more, a legislator may succeed in representing constituents under these other conceptions even though the legislator and the constituents are quite dissimilar—indeed, even though they have little or nothing in common! This "liberal" view of representation, as Pitkin calls it,[164] is also the most common type of representation for Americans, one that reflects their highly diverse, mobile sociopolitical patterns. It presupposes that interests are rooted in individuals, not groups; that individuals' interests are fluid, subjective, multiple and often conflicting, rather than fixed and determinate; and that even individuals who identify with each other in certain respects (e.g., ethnically or politically) nonetheless conceive of themselves and their interests in distinctive ways that may, and frequently do, cut across these group lines.

In this liberal view, the notion of "wasted" minority votes, so central to the argument from fair representation and to the justification of proportionality, loses most of its descriptive and normative force. Although a minority in a district will usually be unable to elect either its own designated choice or one who mirrors its defining features,[165] that does not imply that minority votes are superfluous or that minority preferences will go unrepresented.

Three problems with the notion of wasted minority votes deserve mention. First, the term "minority," at least when used in discourse about fair representation, contains an important ambiguity. Although the fair representation argument against partisan gerrymandering is of course vitally concerned about protecting of minority *parties*, it is also—and perhaps more fundamentally— concerned with representing racial and other minority interests in society *through* parties. One can easily identify a partisan minority simply by count- ing up the votes that a particular party received and comparing them to the total cast. But one cannot speak so casually about other kinds of minorities in this context, much less about wasting their votes, without making a number of crucial and (as it often turns out) quite arbitrary, question-begging assump- tions. These assumptions concern how members of the group in question ac- tually think of themselves in political settings, how uniform and labile their voting patterns and intensity of preferences are, what kinds of political al- liances they enter into and on what terms, and many other factors.[166] To treat blacks, for example, as if they were political monoliths is to ignore both the ev- idence of significant diversity among their members in precisely these re- spects,[167] and the fact that voting structures can affect, as well as reflect, their political self-definitions.

Second, the analyst who would calculate a minority party's wasted votes in order to judge the adequacy of its representation confronts the same defini- tional problems noted earlier. The only benchmark against which to measure a party's "true" size is the number of votes cast for its candidates, yet even that index is likely to mislead regardless of how many election cycles are used to calculate the base. A party's fortunes wax and wane over time. In a single elec- tion, its success will vary according to the office in question, the attractiveness of particular candidates, coattail effects, salient issues, voter turnout, and many other factors.[168] As one extends the time period backward across a num- ber of elections, these factors interact to make the index less and less relevant for evaluating current party strength and the effect of current conditions and districting configurations.

A third, even more fundamental problem is that minority votes are not ac- tually wasted except in the narrow, almost tautological sense in which that term is used by proponents of proportionality and of the argument from fair representation. So long as candidates must compete for electoral pluralities or majorities in a district, simple political expediency dictates that they take into account the preferences and interests of all constituents whose votes they may need some day, including at least some of those who might ordinarily be ex- pected to support their opponents. For some politicians, considerations of po- litical morality and broad, altruistic conceptions of representational trustee- ship may fortify these self-regarding incentives. Especially in a system in which two broadly based, weakly organized parties contend for power, a can- didate's optimal electoral strategy ordinarily is to appeal not only to her own partisans but also to independents and weakly identifying members of the op- position party.[169]

Proportional representation systems create very different incentives. There, the difficulty of obtaining a majority and the organizational pressures of parties encourage candidates to make ideological, regional, or other narrow or parochial appeals to voters. Under such systems, coalition-building, as Bickel emphasized, tends to occur *after* the election, not before it as in a two-party majoritarian system like ours.[170] Thus, proportional representation does not so much eliminate "vote-wasting" as alter its form and timing. The votes of the supporters of parties excluded from the governing coalition, then, will be wasted just as minority party members' votes are now wasted.[171]

Indeed, in some important respects, that waste seems more complete under a system of proportional representation. There, politicians have less incentive to cast their nets widely in seeking support because voter allegiances to particular parties, for historical and ideological reasons, tend to be more predictable and fixed.[172] Moreover, the at-large or large multimember district representation usually associated with proportionality tends to weaken candidates' concern for geographically localized claims,[173] on which minority and majority interests often coincide. As to those geographically based issues, at least, proportional representation does not even encourage legislators to promote their minority group constituents' interests when those interests overlap, as they often do, with the neighborhood-specific interests of the majority constituents.[174]

C. The Changing Context of Minority Representation

It is puzzling that the concern for minority party representation so evident in all of the opinions in *Bandemer*—a concern that animates the argument from fair representation against partisan gerrymandering and in favor of proportionality—has crested at this particular moment in our political history. In some respects, *Bandemer* comes at the least propitious of times for proportionality or indeed for any representational scheme that attaches a legal significance to party performance at the polls. Understanding why this is so can help to illuminate where the Court went wrong in *Bandemer* and why it matters.

The partisan identification of American voters is probably weaker today than at any time since the founding of mass-based political parties during the Jacksonian era more than 150 years ago.[175] Even this low level of partisan identification, moreover, may diminish further when President Reagan retires from the political scene, unless some other strongly partisan figure emerges to occupy his central place in our contemporary politics. If the 1986 elections are indicative, this erosion of party loyalty is already far advanced. The amount of ticket-splitting (a common measure of declining party identification) for offices at all levels of government and in all jurisdictions has risen to unprecedented levels.[176] Although such changes may be cyclical to some degree, few if any political scientists believe that party identification will ever return to its earlier levels.[177]

This fact significantly weakens the argument from fair representation. As we have seen, the structure of that argument, and the norm of proportionality to which it leads, demand some meaningful concept of "true" minority party support that can be used to define deviations from the representational norm. As a practical matter, they also require that such deviations be objectively ascertainable by a court.[178] But if party identification is already weak and growing weaker, and if widespread and increased ticket-splitting means that a party's electoral performance critically depends upon the particular office on which one focuses, then the party vote becomes an even more arbitrary and unreliable index of party strength. When measuring true party support is a futile effort to solidify the evanescent, the norm of proportionality becomes a shadowy, manipulable thing.

While party identification has been becoming more tenuous, party competition is becoming more robust. There is no contradiction here. Most of the important issues that separated (and in some cases divided) the national parties in the past—the New Deal and the role of the federal government, the Vietnam War, civil rights, fiscal policy, labor relations—have dissolved in a consensus, have been blunted and muted, or have disappeared altogether. The shattering of the New Deal coalition and the rising fortunes of the Republican Party in the South and Southwest, especially in Presidential election years, have reflected, but also generated, more intense party competition between the parties. As they vie for support from voters who previously identified strongly with one or the other of them, they further confound efforts to gauge "true" party support on the basis of any particular electoral outcome.[179]

The factors that cause changes in voting behavior between one election and the next are also becoming more salient, making party performance in one election an even less accurate predictor of its future performance. Candidates, by seeking to detach themselves functionally from their parties, have also complicated such predictions. Although the national parties have recently sought, with modest success, to arrest this fragmentation, the important determinants of electoral victory—fund-raising, issue development, campaign management, media activity, and mobilization of voters—are now handled largely by the candidates themselves.[180] With the spread of primaries and the progressive loss of traditional patronage opportunities, party organizations, especially at the state and local levels, have gradually lost influence. Electorally, candidates are increasingly on their own.

External developments further cloud the picture. Party performance, of course, is always affected to some degree by national issues. But the dramatic political events of recent years—Vietnam, Watergate, the energy crisis, and the severe economic difficulties of the late 1970s and early 1980s—have powerfully affected voter responses, increasing the variation over time in party electoral performances. National developments like these generally exert less influence over the parties' showing at the state and local levels (where districting decisions are made) than local or regional concerns do. Still, such convulsive events further confound efforts to gauge "true" minority party support by resort to historical voting patterns.

A final complication in accurately measuring that support relates to the effects of incumbency. Most political scientists argue that the electoral advantages associated with incumbency today, especially in the House of Representatives on the national level, are already great and probably increasing.[181] The very high reelection rate is said to reflect incumbents' ability to use their perquisites of office (such as free mailings, constituent service, and media coverage) and their superior name recognition and access to campaign funds to discourage primary battles and overwhelm their opponents.[182] Very recently, however, other analysts have refined this view somewhat, observing that the reelection rate in the House has not increased appreciably since the 1950s and that other measures of competition for House seats remain fairly consistent. Although incumbents' vote margins have increased, that has been offset by the volatility of vote swings between elections. According to Gary Jacobson, this "greater heterogeneity of inter-election vote swings explains how vote margins could increase without making incumbents any safer," and may also explain why "House members have been behaving as if they felt more vulnerable than ever."[183]

For purposes of evaluating the wisdom of a judicial attack on partisan gerrymandering, one need not determine whether the "incumbency effect" (as the phenomenon of high reelection rates is sometimes called) is greater now than it was in the past. The more important fact is that it remains very strong. This has at least two important implications for the use of proportionality or any other methodology that relies upon party performance as a criterion for adjudicating the constitutionality of partisan gerrymanders. First, the incumbency effect may dwarf—and in any event is separate from—any electoral advantages that may have been independently conferred by a partisan gerrymander. To put the point another way: unless the court can actually distinguish between that portion of the majority party's seat/vote ratio (or other putative index of gerrymandering activity) that is attributable to the gerrymander and that portion that is instead attributable to the independent advantage that *all* incumbents (regardless of party) enjoy, it cannot know with confidence whether a gerrymander has really occurred and been effective, much less know how to begin to remedy it.

A second implication is that a post-*Bandemer* judicial attack on partisan gerrymanders may be aimed at the wrong target. It may miss the real possibility that gerrymanders are actually concerned less with partisan advantage than with incumbent protection. As Bruce Cain has put it,

> [It] seems logical that in an era when party loyalty counts for less and incumbency counts for more, redistricting tactics should include incumbent considerations. Indeed, if recent trends toward independence from the parties continue, redistrictings in the future could come to focus more on [incumbent] displacement issues and less on the partisan makeup of districts.[184]

Thus, a judicial campaign against partisan gerrymandering might also be a largely meaningless sideshow, diverting attention from what should perhaps be the main event.[185]

When all of these factors are taken into account, one is driven to an important but easily overlooked conclusion: any rule whose application depends upon the variable of party performance (however measured) is bound to be highly erratic, perhaps even random, in its effects. No reliable methodology exists that could enable a court or anyone else to isolate the redistricting plan's actual contribution to the electoral outcome.[186] One would need to control for too many unmeasurable factors that powerfully affect party performance. Incumbency effects might easily swamp party and districting effects. Yet *Bandemer*'s logic leads to just such a rule. If most contemporary gerrymandering activity is not even directed at party performance, then precious judicial energies that are targeted upon partisan gerrymandering—already constrained as that practice is by existing constitutional principles, irreducible political obstacles, and inherent institutional limits—would be tragically misdirected. Moreover, a judicial preoccupation with partisan electoral performance would cast doubt on the legitimacy of election results that may have been influenced only slightly, or not at all, by the gerrymandering effort.

The basic conceptual building blocks of the fair representation argument against partisan gerrymandering—the assumed existence of an identifiable minority party whose "true" strength can be objectively ascertained; the notion that minority votes are "wasted;" and the contention that parties' performances can confidently be ascribed to gerrymandering practices as distinguished from other, potentially more powerful determinants of political outcomes—are highly debatable, if not demonstrably false. These conceptual and administrative dilemmas, moreover, seem insuperable. If the norm of proportionality is applied retrospectively, it presupposes the electoral outcome that "proper" political competition ought to yield, a judgment that no principle can dictate and that no court can legitimately make. If it is implemented prospectively, it would require the most fundamental transformation of political processes, structures and values in our history.

In *Bandemer*, the Court confronted a quintessentially political problem, partisan gerrymandering, for which the courts cannot furnish a satisfactory doctrinal or remedial solution.[187] Court-ordered reform of representational systems based upon *Bandemer*'s formulation of the problem will either be ineffective or it will be *too* effective. The former would be a cause for regret but not for alarm; the Court's legitimacy will survive and may even prosper from another shoot-out or standoff with the politicians.[188] The latter, however, would be a reckless gamble propelling the Court (and us with it) down a path whose destination is proportional representation. A change that is so alien to our political institutions should not be taken at the behest of the Court, an institution that—for better *and* for worse—is neither representative nor accountable in any conventional sense.

IV. The Court and the Perils of Political Success

In *Bandemer*, the Court did not need the clarity of hindsight to recognize what a decision to adjudicate partisan gerrymandering claims portended. Here it had the benefit of prophecy. The predictions of danger from self-interested litigants in *Bandemer* echoed the views of many more detached and well-informed commentators,[189] but these warnings were ignored.

By not heeding them, the Court has chosen to become a combatant in this war, battling with legislators of all partisan stripes.[190] The Court evidently hopes to remain above the fray by limiting its involvement to occasional skirmishes promising high returns and low risks. But alas, this hope may be a vain one. To put it mildly, no bright line separates the legitimate districting plan from the partisan gerrymander now actionable under the *Bandemer* plurality's test: whether a plan "consistently degrade[s]" the plaintiff's "influence on the political process as a whole."[191]

In any event, the intriguing question remains. Why has the Court, in the face of the grave misgivings evinced by many wise judges and thoughtful academics, suddenly decided to encourage a new round of partisan litigation directed at districting plans that already meet pre-*Bandemer* districting standards? The evils of the practice cannot fully explain this decision, especially if those evils are discounted by the high probability that they will not actually come to pass and by the even higher probability that courts cannot effectively remedy them if they do. One's wonder only increases when one considers that the Court has inaugurated its new project at a decidedly inauspicious time—when the parties' electoral performances are increasingly unreliable indices of a districting plan's representational fairness.

Certainly, the *Bandemer* Court operated against a normative background, a public morality of politics, that condemns partisan gerrymandering with a unanimity and gusto generally reserved for denunciations of vote-stealing and ballot box-tampering.[192] The practice is properly viewed as the *locus classicus* of political self-dealing, of politicians up to their old tricks. Thus, the Court could anticipate that few would openly champion this disreputable, if familiar, legislative tactic. At the level of public acceptance, at least, a campaign against partisan gerrymandering must have looked tempting.

But something else was also at work in *Bandemer,* something worth briefly exploring for what it may reveal about contemporary attitudes concerning the judicial regulation of politics. In *Bandemer,* the Court dismissed the doubters by drawing upon an authority that its recent ventures into the regulation of politics have conferred. Viewed from the perspective of that experience, its refusal to take the warnings seriously is not surprising. To the Court, after all, the professors' grim metaphors about political thickets and casualties in battle, their predictable predictions of disaster and their post hoc lamentations, have become numbingly familiar.

More to the point, the Cassandras have frequently, if not invariably, proved to be resoundingly wrong. Consider the constitutional history of the last quarter century. In a long line of cases, the Court has turned aside warnings of just this kind, and has instead proceeded to take on project after daunting project of broad political and social reform. At the time, even sympathetic observers often believed that these projects—school desegregation,[193] control of police misconduct,[194] reapportionment of legislatures,[195] limitations of presidential prerogatives,[196] restriction of pornography,[197] abolition of school prayer,[198] and regulation of abortion,[199] to name just a few—would strain judicial capacities to the breaking point.[200] Yet more often than not, the Court seemed to sustain its projects without losing either perceived legitimacy or prestige.

Indeed, the Court has returned from these engagements bearing the battle ribbons and the public esteem of a military hero. Its struggles with the politicians and the bureaucrats have only served to enlarge its reputation for moral purity, constitutional wisdom, and real-world effectiveness. This towering reputation might seem ironic. After all, some of the Court's rulings overrode social norms that were widely shared at the time.[201] Other of its decisions could not be effectively implemented; the lower courts became mired in litigation, doctrinal uncertainty, and bureaucratic responsibility.[202] Despite these political challenges, however, the Court prevailed at the bar of politics (to use Bickel's phrase[203]), extending and tightening its already extraordinary grip on the popular imagination.[204] In the din of popularity, the objections of a few legal scholars and political scientists were scarcely heard. They stemmed the tide of political influence flowing toward the Supreme Court about as effectively as Canute repelled the sea.

Perhaps nowhere has the Court's political success been more complete than in the area of legislative reapportionment. *Baker v. Carr*[205] was greeted with immense popular approval, attended by a chorus of academic criticism.[206] Yet twenty-five years later, one is most struck by the critics' silence. I do not mean to suggest that the courts' post-*Baker* redistricting crusade has been an unalloyed vindication of democratic values and judicial technique. Political scientists have pointed out, for example, that the advent of computers, more refined political and demographic data, and the emergence of a numbers-oriented constitutional jurisprudence has actually facilitated racial and partisan gerrymandering since *Baker*.[207] Nor is it even clear that the decision forced a redistribution of political power that would not otherwise have occurred. By the time *Baker* was decided, suburban voters' growing influence was already an irresistible long-term trend, one that the Court reinforced but did not itself create.[208]

Instead, the Court's political achievement in *Baker* flowed directly from the popularity of the "one person, one vote" principle to which that decision swiftly led. That principle, so attractive in its manifest simplicity and in its congruence with commonsense notions of fair representation, drained the opposition of credibility; their appeals to legal process values came to seem abstract, petty, even churlish. In retrospect, at least, criticizing the *Baker* decision on process grounds is about as persuasive as denouncing the result in *Brown v. Board of Education*[209] because of defects in its formal legal reasoning. There evidently are moments in our constitutional history[210]—*Baker* and *Brown* are clear examples—when judicial craftsmanship and adherence to precedent are far less important to the polity than judicial statesmanship and innovation.

The line of decisions involving challenges to state and local electoral systems under the Voting Rights Act of 1965[211] was another political triumph for the courts. The original statute authorized federal judges and the Department of Justice to use ambitious, innovative and often intrusive remedial methods[212] in order to eradicate the discriminatory application of literacy tests and other techniques that had denied minority voters access to the ballot. Encouraged by the Supreme Court, however, the statute was soon reshaped into a kind of quasi-constitutional charter[213] aimed at far more sweeping political changes. State and local representational systems throughout the nation were overhauled in order to implement a conception of discrimination that could be remedied only by securing some minority groups more legislative seats.[214] These changes dramatically expanded political participation and officeholding by blacks and Hispanics, especially in the South.[215] In 1982, when Congress carefully reviewed the judges' and administrators' handiwork in this area,[216] it gave this new political vision a resounding vote of confidence, reaffirming and actually reinforcing the main lines of the prior developments under the Voting Rights Act.[217]

In light of these earlier expeditions into the political thicket, one can easily understand why the Court would not shrink from adjudicating partisan gerrymandering claims. Fortified by serviceable legal doctrines, flushed by the public veneration that jousting with politicians only seems to deepen, and driven by a commitment to order, rationality and fairness, the Court might even relish the challenge. By almost any standard, especially a pragmatic political one, the Court has been extraordinarily successful as a governing institution in the public mind.[218] It has managed to turn even the most parlous undertakings to good institutional account and to earn a high return on its precious endowment of moral capital. In a political world in which government is often said to be suffering from a crisis of public confidence,[219] that is no small achievement.

Those who criticize the Court for political myopia and institutional self-abuse, then, have a lot of explaining to do. Indeed, the modern Court's ability to strike boldly at politicians and thrive as a result is so evident that a thorough reevaluation of the academic orthodoxy concerning the sources and durability of the Court's institutional legitimacy seems called for. This Article is not the occasion for such a reevaluation, but the analysis does suggest the need for a better theory of judicial legitimacy than that reflected in much legal scholarship.

The Court's legitimacy is not an undifferentiated resource, unaffected by the particular context in which it is deployed. Different areas of adjudication implicating different actors, policy issues, normative theories, legal traditions and doctrines, political interests, bureaucratic constraints, and remedial requirements are likely to have radically different consequences for the way in which the Court and its performance are perceived. For example, commerce clause cases are likely to generate different political and public responses than institutional reform cases; indeed, within the latter category, prison cases may be perceived quite differently than school desegregation cases.

There is at least one class of cases—those challenging politicians' self-interest defined in narrow, careerist terms—in which the Court's prestige seems to be burnished, rather than tarnished, by its confrontations with legislators, even when those confrontations are inconclusive or unsuccessful. But in other kinds of cases—perhaps those overturning antipornography statutes or school prayer requirements in which the politicians have appealed to lofty principles and widely-shared community norms[220]—the Court may not fare so well in terms of public esteem or institutional influence. The challenge is to develop a richer, more refined understanding of the political, institutional and other variables that shape public responses to court decisions, and of the conditions under which judicial constraints on the basic structures of politics and the behavior of politicians can be both effective and legitimate.

Conclusion

The burden of this Article has been to demonstrate that *this* time, the Cassandras are correct, although perhaps for the wrong reason. This particular thicket—a judicial gravitation toward proportionality as a remedy for partisan gerrymandering—*is* more dangerous than those from which the Court has managed to escape in the past. However, the chief danger here is not, as the critics have supposed, that the Court will fail to root out egregious partisan gerrymandering and thereby risk its legitimacy. If recent past is prologue, the public would simply regard that failure as one more instance in which the selfish politicians defied and confounded the idealistic Court. This disappointment might even be applauded, as noble failures often are, by a people that yearns for principle in its public life.

The greater peril lies elsewhere—in the possibility that the Court will actually "succeed" in its newest project of political reform. It can only do so by adopting a constitutional test, proportionality, that would measure the wrong thing. More important, that test would transform the wellsprings of American politics: the party system, the behavior of voters and politicians, the legislative process, the formation of political coalitions, and the role of ideological divisions. No judge could confidently predict or comprehend the consequences of such changes, and few thoughtful citizens are likely to welcome them.

Notes

1. By regulator, I do not simply refer to its issuance of binding legal rules. All judicial decisions do that. See generally H.L.A. Hart, The Concept of Law *passim* (1961). And by politics, I do not merely mean the process of deciding (in the classic formulation) who gets what, when and how. H. Lasswell, Politics: Who Gets What, When, How (2d ed. 1950). Obviously, all judicial decisions do that as well—and never more so than

today. See, e.g., D. Horowitz, The Courts and Social Policy (1977); Frug, The Judicial Power of the Purse, 126 U. Pa. L. Rev. 715 (1978).

2. E.g., Tashjian v. Republican Party, 107 S. Ct. 544 (1986).

3. E.g., White v. Regester, 412 U.S. 755 (1973).

4. E.g., Munro v. Socialist Workers Party, 107 S. Ct. 533 (1986); Williams v. Rhodes, 393 U.S. 23 (1968).

5. E.g., Branti v. Finkel, 445 U.S. 507 (1980); Elrod v. Burns, 427 U.S. 347 (1976).

6. E.g., Buckley v. Valeo, 424 U.S. 1 (1976).

7. E.g., Karcher v. Daggett, 462 U.S. 725 (1983); Reynolds v. Sims, 377 U.S. 533 (1964).

8. E.g., Pacific Gas & Elec. Co. v. Pub. Util. Comm'n, 475 U.S. 1 (1986); Buckley v. Valeo, 424 U.S. 1 (1976).

9. E.g., Vermont Yankee Nuclear Power Corp. v. Natural Resources Defense Council, 435 U.S. 519 (1978).

10. E.g., Williams v. Rhodes, 393 U.S. 23 (1968); Baker v. Carr, 369 U.S. 186 (1962).

11. 106 S. Ct. 2797 (1986).

12. Id. at 2806. In *Bandemer*, the Court characterized the practice as "political gerrymandering." E.g., id. at 2800. I prefer to use the modifier "partisan" because of the ambiguity of the term "political" when used in this context. All types of gerrymandering—racial, geographical, partisan and other—are "political" in the sense that they alter governmental structures in order to affect the exercise of power.

13. That party will ordinarily win a majority of the statewide popular vote. In principle, however, a party with a bare majority of the popular vote in each of a bare majority of the legislative districts—that is, a minority party with slightly more than 25% of the statewide popular vote—could control the legislature. Nevertheless, for purposes of simplicity, I shall sometimes refer to the gerrymandering party as the "majority."

14. See, for example, discussion in Karcher v. Daggett, 462 U.S. 725, 730–31 (1983). Contiguity, compactness, and respect for political subdivisions are additional norms that, although not constitutionally required, are often deemed to be relevant to whether the inevitable deviations from population equality are constitutionally acceptable, especially in congressional districting. See, e.g., Bandemer v. Davis, 603 F. Supp. 1479, 1493–94 (S.D. Ind. 1984), rev'd, 106 S. Ct. 2797 (1986).

15. See, e.g., Gomillion v. Lightfoot, 364 U.S. 339, 342 (1960).

16. See, e.g., Thornburg v. Gingles, 106 S. Ct. 2752 (1986).

17. See Karcher v. Daggett, 462 U.S. 725, 732–33 (1983) (striking down congressional districts where average population deviation was 0.1384%). See infra note 78 for analogous cases dealing with deviations between state legislative districts.

18. 369 U.S. 186 (1962). See generally Alfange, Gerrymandering and the Constitution: Into the Thorns of the Thicket at Last, 1986 Sup. Ct. Rev. 175 (arguing that the reapportionment cases and standard of one person, one vote were in fact concerned with gerrymandering; Court should abandon simple mathematical tests and squarely face the complex issues of fair representation).

19. *Baker v. Carr* generated considerable political debate and controversy. See, e.g., Drummond, States' Wrongs: The Court and Redistricting, Wash. Post, Mar. 28, 1962, at A2, col. 1 (Senator Strom Thurmond, Senator Herman Talmadge and others call decision "death blow" to states' rights); Kenworthy, President Calls on States to Rush Reapportionment—Kennedy Backs Court, N.Y. Times, Mar. 30, 1962, at A1, col. 2; Capital Is Split on Apportioning, N.Y. Times, Mar. 28, 1962, at A1, col. 1 (President

Kennedy hailed ruling as landmark; Senator Richard Russell of Georgia called it an assault on constitutional system).

Unlike *Baker, Bandemer* was greeted with neither astonishment nor dismay. The gerrymandering decision may have been overshadowed in the press by coverage of that day's Supreme Court decision upholding Georgia's sodomy law, Bowers v. Hardwick, 106 S. Ct. 2841 (1986). For editorial comment on *Bandemer,* see, e.g., . . . And Politics in Court, Wash. Post, July 7, 1986, at A10, col. 1 (ruling does not mean federal courts will take over American politics); The Court Meets the Gerrymander, N.Y. Times, July 7, 1986, at A16, col. 1 (difficult to apply antigerrymandering rule, but may deter partisan abuse after 1990 Census); Will, Two Bad Rulings, Wash. Post, July 6, 1986, at B8, col. 1 (Supreme Court trivialized fourteenth amendment and created confusion). In part, the mild public response to *Bandemer* may reflect the Court's intention—evident in the standard that it announced for evaluating future challenges to districting plans—to invalidate only egregious gerrymanders. See discussion infra notes 39–40 and accompanying text.

There are several reasons to confine my c hallenge to the decision in *Bandemer* rather than extending it to the *Baker* decision itself. First, the "one person, one vote" principle has proved to be judicially manageable, see infra text accompanying notes 208–210, whereas defining and enforcing representational fairness for parties—even if understood as simple proportionality—is not so manageable. See infra text accompanying notes 138–88 (Part III). Second, partisan gerrymandering is politically constrained in ways that pre-*Baker* malapportionment, which often resulted from the legislature simply doing nothing in the face of population shifts, was not. See infra notes 71–82 and accompanying text. Finally, the population equality principle has achieved a public acceptance and settled character in our political system that no merely rational analysis should lightly disregard. *Bandemer* is most unlikely to attain this. See infra notes 138–220 (Parts III & IV).

20. My colleague, Stephen Carter, has recently sought to exhume it. Carter, From Sick Chicken to *Synar:* The Evolution and Subsequent De-Evolution of the Separation of Powers, 1987:3 B.Y.U. L. Rev. (forthcoming in 1988).

21. See, e.g., Reynolds v. Sims, 377 U.S. 533, 562–63 (1964) (Constitution requires equal weight be given to individual votes).

22. The requirement of population equality, of course, somewhat constrains line-drawing and thus reduces the advantage to be gained by a gerrymander. On the other hand, it encourages gerrymandering by necessitating frequent redistricting and the use of computer techniques, while allowing the drawers to subordinate traditional boundaries and political subdivisions in order to satisfy an essentially mathematical criterion. See M. Jewell & S. Patterson, The Legislative Process in the United States 19–20 (4th ed. 1986) (one person, one vote principle generally facilitates racial and partisan gerrymandering); Baker, Threading the Political Thicket by Tracing the Steps of the Late Robert G. Dixon, Jr.: An Appraisal and Appreciation, *in* Representation and Redistricting Issues 21, 26 (1982) (quest for mathematical equality creates potential for extensive gerrymandering); Dixon, The Warren Court Crusade for the Holy Grail of "One Man-One Vote," 1969 Sup. Ct. Rev. 219, 231–33 (irrelevance of political subdivision boundaries will make gerrymandering easier). The Supreme Court anticipated this possibility. See Reynolds v. Sims, 377 U.S. at 578–79 ("Indiscriminate districting, without any regard for political subdivision or natural or historical boundary lines, may be little more than an open invitation to partisan gerrymandering.").

23. Justice White seemed to concede as much in his plurality opinion in *Bandemer,* 106 S. Ct. at 2803–04. But see The Supreme Court—Leading Cases, 100 Harv. L. Rev. 100, 158 (1986) (*Bandemer* "logically" followed from earlier cases) [hereinafter Note]. *Bandemer* was arguably consistent with one of these precedents, Gaffney v. Cummings, 412 U.S. 735 (1973). There, the Court did uphold a *bipartisan* gerrymander, which involves considerations not relevant to a partisan gerrymander and thus could be distinguished from it. *Gaffney* does, however, support the justiciability of a partisan gerrymandering claim.

On the other hand, *Bandemer* does seem inconsistent with other precedents. See cases cited at 106 S. Ct. at 2804. The lower courts, presumably relying upon the Court's earlier refusals to adjudicate partisan gerrymandering claims, had not had the occasion to engage in the process of elaborating and testing judicial standards for adjudicating such claims case by case. Indeed, a "legion" of lower court decisions (as two commentators have recently noted) had consistently eschewed that approach. Lowenstein & Steinberg, The Quest for Legislative Districting in the Public Interest: Elusive or Illusory?, 33 UCLA L. Rev. 1, 3 n.9 (1985). Had such a process occurred, the Court might have been in a better position to anticipate the nature of the project that it agreed in *Bandemer* to begin.

24. John Hart Ely, for example, has analyzed the role of the courts in monitoring the political process wmhen the legislative branch cannot reasonably be relied upon to act fairly. See J. Ely, Democracy and Distrust: A Theory of Judicial Review (1980). See generally, United States v. Carolene Products Co., 304 U.S. 144, 152 n.4 (1938).

25. One may question the implicit assumption that the federal courts are somehow immune from the effects of party politics. Even judges appointed for life are influenced by the partisan composition of the legislature, which can affect courts' jurisdiction, composition, and other factors, as well as the political environment in which they adjudicate. See S. Kelman, Making Public Policy: A Hopeful View of American Government 125–30 (1987); W. Murphy, Congress and the Court (1962). On the relationship between the federal judiciary and party loyalties, see, e.g., R. Carp & C. Rowland, Policymaking and Politics in the Federal District Courts 50 (1983) (partisan loyalties significant in determining case outcomes); Barber, Partisan Values in the Lower Courts: Reapportionment in Ohio and Michigan, 20 Case W. Res. L. Rev. 401 (1969); Ehrenhalt, Reapportionment and Redistricting, *in* The American Elections of 1982, at 44, 51–55 (N. Ornstein ed. 1982).

For an empirical study suggesting that federal judges deciding reapportionment cases may tend to favor the political party of the President that appointed them, see Barnett, Judicial Bias in Partisan Reapportionment Cases (1986) (unpublished manuscript on file at the Columbia Law Review).

26. A constitutional restriction of partisan gerrymandering might take several different forms. One might require a legislative supermajority before a new districting plan could be enacted. Another would establish a bipartisan or nonpartisan commission of distinguished, disinterested citizens to propose plans to the legislature. Each of these solutions, as well as all others, is problematic. See, e.g., T. Mann, Do Incumbency and Gerrymandering Make the House of Representatives Unresponsive to Change? 26–29 (paper prepared for Brookings Conference on Party and Electoral Renewal, Apr. 6–7, 1987) (on file at the Columbia Law Review). For example, the first would favor the plan that is already in effect even where some new plan, due to population and apportionment changes, may be constitutionally required; the second seeks to sanitize what in-

evitably is, and perhaps ought to be, a political decision. Of course, these approaches (or others) may still be preferable on balance to the status quo. The crucial point left is that the selection of a remedy is likely to involve a number of difficult trade-offs.

Changes in legislative process could meet some of the objections to partisan gerrymandering. For example, legislative considerations of districting plans could be made more deliberate and visible through the use of public hearings, multiple votes, alternative plans, and published predictions of the partisan composition of districts under the various plans, but these reforms should not be judicially mandated. See infra notes 153–57.

27. The irony of coupling a criticism of the Court's latest project of political reform with a recognition of the Court's remarkable past success in confounding its critics in the past is not lost upon this author.

28. The statement of facts that follows is taken from Part I of the plurality opinion of Justice White. Davis v. Bandemer, 106 S. Ct. at 2797, 2800–02 (1986).

29. This vote/seat ratio is a very crude measure of whether a plan is a partisan gerrymander. See infra notes 128–30, 150–51 and accompanying text; see also, Lowenstein & Steinberg, supra note 23, at 49–52 (population-based districting does not account for the number of *voters* in the district; thus, one party might win one district with 100 votes while the opposing party wins two other districts with the same number of votes). Nevertheless, this index is widely used by courts and commentators. See, e.g., *Bandemer*, 106 S. Ct. at 2801; Dixon, supra note 22, at 221; Tufte, The Relationship Between Seats and Votes in Two-Party Systems, 67 Am. Pol. Sci. Rev. 540, 549–53 (1973). But see Backstrom, Robins & Eller, Issues in Gerrymandering: An Exploratory Measure of Partisan Gerrymandering Applied to Minnesota, 62 Minn. L. Rev. 1121, 1131–34 (1978) (party strength should be estimated by using figures for either a typical statewide race or a composite of several statewide races, although neither method is perfect); Niemi, The Relationship Between Votes and Seats: The Ultimate Question in Political Gerrymandering, 33 UCLA L. Rev. 185, 204–07 (1985) (finding normal vote very difficult; therefore normal vote will generally be used by defendants to justify a challenged plan).

30. Bandemer v. Davis, 603 F. Supp. 1479 (S.D. Ind. 1984), rev'd, 106 S. Ct. 2797 (1986).

31. 462 U.S. at 744, 754–55 (Stevens, J., concurring).

32. 603 F. Supp. at 1489–95.

33. Id. at 1502–03 (Pell, J., concurring in part and dissenting in part).

34. 412 U.S. 735 (1973).

35. 106 S. Ct. at 2803–07 (discussion of justiciability).

36. Id. at 2807–09.

37. Id. at 2809. The "balloon effect" is the higher seat/vote ratio that the plurality vote, winner-take-all, single-member system produces in the legislature relative to that produced by proportional representation. See discussion infra at text accompanying notes 128–30.

38. Justice White maintained that minorities could be represented in ways not directly reflected in their ability to elect their choices. 106 S. Ct. at 2810; see also infra notes 160–74 and accompanying text.

39. Id.

40. Id.

41. Justice White would allow predictions based upon voting projections. Id. at 2814 n.17, 2815.

42. Id. at 2812–16 (criticism of district court's findings).

43. Id. at 2817 (O'Connor, J., concurring).

44. Id. at 2819–20.

45. The plurality's approach would permit some exploitation of majority advantage. Thus, dilution of group voting strength would only be partly prevented.

46. 106 S. Ct. at 2822.

47. Id. at 2822–25.

48. Id: at 2838 (Powell, J., concurring in part and dissenting in part).

49. 369 U.S. 186 (1962).

50. 377 U.S. 533 (1964).

51. 106 S. Ct. at 2832 & n.13.

52. E.g., D. Mayhew, Congress: The Electoral Connection (1974).

53. See supra note 14.

54. See, e.g., B. Cain, The Reapportionment Puzzle 74–77 (1984) (even political fairness cannot be assured by checking seat/vote ratio).

55. See, e.g., Karcher v. Daggett, 462 U.S. 725, 771–72 (1983) (White, J., dissenting).

56. See, e.g., R. Dahl, A Preface to Democratic Theory 131–33 (1956); J. Schumpeter, Capitalism, Socialism, and Democracy 269–73 (3d ed. 1950).

57. Indeed, that theory denies that monopolies are even possible in the long run, except in a few narrowly defined situations. See, e.g., R. Bork, The Antitrust Paradox 196 (1978).

58. In re Kellogg Corp., [1979–1983 Transfer Binder] Trade Reg. Rep. (CCH) ¶ 21,864, at 22,118 (Sept. 10, 1981) (advertising); In re E.I. DuPont de Nemours & Co., [1979–1983 Transfer Binder] Trade Reg. Rep. (CCH) ¶ 21,770, at 21,960 (Oct. 20, 1980) (pricing).

59. See A. Pigou, John Maynard Keynes, in 32 Proceedings of the British Academy 407 (Quoting J.M. Keynes as saying, "In the long run, we are all dead.").

60. See, e.g., R. Dahl & C. Lindblom, Politics, Economics and Welfare 414–18 (1953) (comparing voting and market choice).

61. Many regulatory programs do impose barriers to entry in economic markets, but the consensus among contemporary liberals and conservatives alike is that such barriers are presumptively unjustified.

62. For the most recent example, see Tashjian v. Republican Party, 107 S. Ct. 544 (1986) (Connecticut's closed primary statute impermissibly interfered with Republican Party's right to define its associational boundaries).

63. E.g., Munro v. Socialist Workers Party, 107 S. Ct. 533, 539 (1986) (Washington statute requiring that minor party candidate receive at least 1% of votes cast in primary election to qualify for general election ballot did not violate first amendment). But see, e.g., Anderson v. Celebrezze, 460 U.S. 780, 793 n.16 (1983) (greater judicial scrutiny may be warranted when interests of minor parties and independent candidates are involved).

64. E.g., Buckley v. Valeo, 424 U.S. 1 (1976).

65. See, e.g., G. Jacobson, Money in Congressional Elections 101–04 (1980). For further discussion of how incumbency affects the arguments against partisan gerrymandering, see infra notes 181–85 and accompanying text.

66. These difficulties are confirmed by the present political stalemate over campaign finance reform. See, e.g., Berke, Senators Propose 5 Election Laws, N.Y. Times, Mar. 6, 1987, at A28, col. 6 (Senators calling for changes in laws regulating campaign financing; leading bill, the Boren bill, would establish campaign spending limits for general elections for candidates electing to receive public funds.).

67. See, e.g., Berke, 107 G.O.P. Millions Didn't Save Senate, N.Y. Times, Feb. 8, 1987, at A28, col. 3.

68. See, e.g., Polsby. Coalition and Faction in American Politics: An Institutional View, *in* Party Coalitions in the 1980's 153–78 (S. Lipset ed. 1981).

69. See, e.g., J. Buchanan & G. Tullock, The Calculus of Consent: Logical Foundations of Constitutional Democracy 131–34 (5th ed. 1974).

70. See, e.g., Weingast & Marshall, The Industrial Organization of Congress, 96 J. Pol. Econ. (forthcoming in Feb. 1988).

71. See Election Boxscore, Pub. Opinion, Jan.-Feb. 1987, at 26; Pound & Jones, Whose Victory?, St. Legislatures, Nov.-Dec. 1986, at 10, 14 (lack of party discipline in several states has led to coalition control of legislative chambers); see, e.g., Robinson. How Redistricting and Reapportionment Will Determine Political Control, Campaigns and Elections, Sept.-Oct. 1986, at 46, 49.

72. The discussion that follows owes much to the analysis in B. Cain, supra note 54, ch. 9.

73. Depending upon the majority party's goals, an efficient plan might be defined instead simply as one in which its seat total is maximized, without a constraint as to the minimum winning coalition; or as one in which certain legislators' seats are retained.

74. Gopoian & West, Trading Security for Seats: Strategic Considerations in the Redistricting Process, 46 J. Pol. 1080, 1095 (1984).

75. Alternatively, a strong party organization may use the seat as patronage and fill it with a relatively weak candidate. See Stern, Political Gerrymandering: A Statutory Compactness Standard As An Antidote for Judicial Impotence, 41 U. Chi. L. Rev. 398, 405 (1974).

76. See, e.g., Jacobson, The Marginals Never Vanished: Incumbency and Competition in Elections to the U.S. House of Representatives 1952–82, 31 Am. J. Pol. Sci. 126 (1987).

77. This consideration qualifies the *Bandemer* plurality's otherwise plausible view, 106 S. Ct. 2797, 2808 (1986), that the actual political effects of a plan must have been intended by the gerrymandering party. E.g., Robinson, supra note 71, at 48 (gerrymandering can misfire, as in Pennsylvania's 1982 Congressional elections, where Republicans hoped to eliminate at least four Democratic seats and yet four Republicans were defeated); see P. Musgrove, The General Theory of Gerrymandering 21–23 (1977) (gerrymanders may result in large number of wasted votes for majority party due to distribution of population and votes).

78. E.g., Karcher v. Daggett, 462 U.S. 725 (1983) (invalidating congressional districting plan with deviation of 0.7% from strict population equality between the largest and smallest districts). The Court is more permissive with respect to state legislative districting plans. See, e.g., Brown v. Thomson, 462 U.S. 835 (1983) (upholding state plan giving each county at least one seat regardless of population; average population deviations were 16% and maximum deviation was 89%); White v. Regester, 412 U.S. 755 (1973) (upholding legislative districts with average population deviations of 2%, and maximum deviations of 10%); Gaffney v. Cummings, 412 U.S. 735 (1973) (upholding legislative districts with average population deviations of 2% and maximum deviation of 8%). This double standard has been criticized by commentators. See, e.g., Grofman, Criteria for Districting: A Social Science Perspective, 33 UCLA L. Rev. 77, 89 (1985).

79. The California Republicans succeeded in overturning the first congressional reapportionment plan (Burton I) by petitioning to get on a statewide ballot and then winning the vote to reject the Democratic plan. See Gurwitt, Redrawn Districts

Expected in Some States, 40 Cong. Q. Weekly Rep. 2894 (1982) (in California, June 8, 1982 referendum vote overturned Burton I; Nov. 2, 1982 initiative vote to establish an independent commission to draw district lines was defeated); California Petitions, 39 Cong. Q. Weekly Rep. 2541 (1981).

80. After California voters rejected the Burton I map, the Burton II map was passed by the legislature in December 1982 and signed by Governor Brown just before he left office. M. Barone & G. Ujifusa, The Almanac of American Politics 1986, at 91 (1985); Gurwitt, Republicans Eye New Attacks on Democratic District Plan, 41 Cong. Q. Weekly Rep. 2040 (1983).

81. Politicians must consider a possible voter backlash before deciding whether and how to proceed with a gerrymander. Voters' perceptions, which include a view about whether the electoral process has been biased or not often upset the plans of those who engineer partisan gerrymanders. Incumbents, for example, often win despite line-drawing designed to defeat them. An example was Barney Frank's victory over Margaret Heckler in a 1982 Massachusetts congressional race despite highly disadvantageous district lines. See Born, Partisan Intention and Election Day Realities in the Congressional Redistricting Process, 79 Am. Pol. Sci. Rev. 305, 317 (1985) (voters now less inclined to behave as desired by drafters of redistricting plans); see also Scarrow, Partisan Gerrymandering—Invidious or Benevolent? *Gaffney v. Cummings* and Its Aftermath, 44 J. Pol. 810, 819–21 (1982) (bipartisan gerrymander eventually resulted in Democratic dominance due to Republican "overkill" and larger swings than anticipated).

82. See supra notes 79–80. For a discussion of the congressional reapportionment battle in California and the state courts' involvement, see Lowell & Craigie, California's Reapportionment Struggles: A Classic Clash Between Law and Politics, 2 J.L. & Pol. 245 (1985).

83. Even where a single party has exercised power for many years, its monolithic facade may conceal deep internal fissures and factional rivalries. Despite the Democratic Party's long dominance in many southern states, for example, competition there was not eliminated or even seriously constricted (except for blacks) but was simply channeled within the party structure. These intraorganizational rivalries often involved profound differences of ideology, geography, patronage, and personality. See, e.g., V.O. Key, Jr., Southern Politics in State and Nation (1984).

84. Although partisan gerrymanders may be in the eye of the beholder, no Justice expressed any real doubt that the Indiana redistricting in *Bandemer* was the genuine article. Another example is California's recent state legislative districting plan. See, e.g., Shuit, State Legislators' Remapping Keeps Most in the Race, L.A. Times, Mar. 11, 1984, at 3, col. 5 (final ed.) (sweetheart reapportionment plan benefitted incumbent legislators by increasing margins of safety, primarily helping Democrats, who were in majority).

85. In this sense, as well as in the senses discussed earlier, see supra text accompanying notes 67–85, partisan gerrymandering, as Justice O'Connor suggested in her concurring opinion, is likely to be "a self-limiting enterprise." 106 S. Ct. at 2820.

86. See T. O'Rourke, The Impact of Reapportionment 55–57 (1980) (in 1970s, parties controlling reapportionment often suffered electoral losses); Born, supra note 81, at 314, 316; Ehrenhalt, supra note 25, at 98 (reapportionment in early 1980s was a "partisan standoff"); Glazer, Grofman & Robbins, Partisan and Incumbency Effects of 1970s Congressional Redistricting, 31 Am. J. Pol. Sci. 680; Ornstein, Genesis of a 'Gerrymander,' Wall St. J., May 7, 1985, at 29, col. 3 ("[O]ne could easily argue that the

redistricting wars of the early 1980s were won by the Republicans—they could have done much worse last year."). But see, e.g., Cain, Assessing the Partisan Effects of Redistricting, 79 Am. Pol. Sci. Rev. 320, 331 (1985) (partisan effects of redistricting in California were "important").

87. See infra notes 138–88 and accompanying text (Part III).

88. See, e.g., R. Posner & F. Easterbrook, Antitrust: Cases, Economic Notes and Other Materials 152–70 (2d ed. 1981).

89. See, e.g., R. Posner & F. Easterbrook, supra note 88, at 152–170; A. Sullivan, Handbook of the Law of Antitrust 2–7 (1977).

90. See supra text following note 25. See, e.g., Bicker, The Effects of Malapportionment in the States—A Mistrial, in Reapportionment in the 1970's, 171–85 (N. Polsby ed. 1971) (studies have not accurately determined whether significant policy effects have resulted from reapportionment); Cain, supra note 86, at 320 ("[A]ttempts to link boundary with policy changes uncovered nothing striking."). But see Y. Cho & H. Frederickson, Measuring the Effects of Apportionment in the American States 97–98 (1976) (evidence shows reapportionment made state legislatures more democratic); T. O'Rourke, supra note 86, at 147–60 (while not revolutionary, reapportionment did affect legislative politics); Saffell, Reapportionment and Public Policy: State Legislators' Perspectives, in Representation and Redistricting Issues, supra note 22, at 203–19 (although evidence is unclear, survey data indicate that state legislators believe legislature is more liberal and urban oriented after reapportionment).

91. See supra note 90.

92. For an analysis of the recent AT&T divestiture, see, e.g., MacAvoy & Robinson, Losing by Judicial Policymaking: The First Year of the AT&T Divestiture, 2 Yale J. Reg. 225 (1985).

93. See, e.g., Communications Act of 1934, 47 U.S.C. s 309 (1982) (awards of licenses must serve "public interest").

94. See, e.g., Terry v. Adams, 345 U.S. 461 (1953) (impermissible state action found in racially restrictive "pre-primary" elections); Smith v. Allwright, 321 U.S. 649 (1944) (blacks must be allowed to vote in Texas Democratic party primary). See generally L. Tribe, American Constitutional Law 1165 (1978).

95. See, e.g., R. Dahl, supra note 56, at 131–33 (discussing need for continuous competition between political parties, or individuals, or both, to preserve democracy).

96. Free speech is necessary to educate citizens, communicate political preferences and lubricate political competition. For this position's classic statement, see A. Meiklejohn, Political Freedom: The Constitutional Powers of the People (1960). Elections are necessary to assure official accountability to the citizenry. See R. Dahl, supra note 56, at 131.

97. U.S. Const. amend. XVII; U.S. Const. art. II, s 1, cl. 1–2.

At the state level, governors are elected at large, while on the federal level, United States Senators represent entire states and the President represents the nation as a whole. See discussion in Whitcomb v. Chavis, 403 U.S. 124, 156–60 (1971).

Legislative districting in Congress is not constitutionally mandated. Article I, ss 2 and 3, of the Constitution only require multiple representatives, not districting. Nevertheless, that has historically been the practice in the House. See Mayhew, Congressional Representation: Theory and Practice in Drawing the Districts, in Reapportionment in the 1970's, supra note 90, at 249–53. Many state constitutions do require districting. For a survey of the 50 states' apportionment laws and practices, see

Reapportionment Politics: The History of Redistricting in the 50 States (L. Hardy, A. Heslop & S. Anderson eds. 1981).

98. Many city council members, for example, are elected at-large.

99. The constitutional counterpart of this logic would be the principle that even a contingent political structure must meet the fairness and rationality demands of the due process and equal protection clauses, especially where minority rights are concerned.

100. J. Rawls, A Theory of Justice (1971).

101. The original position device is used "to determine the content of justice," according to Rawls. J. Rawls, supra note 100, at 584. Under this formulation, rational persons who are placed in an initial situation of equality must choose basic social rules that organize a just society. Rawls argues that the concepts of justice thus chosen would be more reasonable than if selected in other ways. Id. at 19–21.

102. For critiques of Rawls see, e.g., B. Barry, The Liberal Theory of Justice: A Critical Examination of the Principal Doctrines in *A Theory of Justice* by John Rawls (1973); R. Martin, Rawls and Rights (1985); D. Schaefer, Justice or Tyranny?: A Critique of John Rawls's *Theory of Justice* (1979); Reading Rawls (N. Daniels ed. 1975).

103. Professor Douglas Rae has referred to this as "defractionalization" of the parliamentary system. D. Rae, The Political Consequences of Electoral Laws 79–84 (1967). Some political scientists have noted the advantages of traditional party organizations in governance. See, e.g., D. Mayhew, Placing Parties in American Politics 239–45 (1986) (traditional party organizations rank high in autonomy); Greenstone & Peterson, Reformers, Machines and the War on Poverty, *in* City Politics and Public Policy 267–92 (J. Wilson ed. 1978) (antimachine political reformers were less successful in obtaining federal funding and redistributing material benefits).

104. In stark contrast to the American situation, nations suffering from the problem of permanent, implacable majorities that subordinate ethnic or religious minorities sometimes use electoral structures that can help reduce conflict by fragmenting majorities and encouraging formation of multiethnic coalitions. For case studies of such techniques, see D. Horowitz, Ethnic Groups in Conflict 628–52 (1985).

105. My colleague, Akhil Amar, has analyzed a system of representation by lottery that might be thought of as a possible exception to this proposition, depending upon whether advantage is judged by one in the original position or by one conscious of the effect of the status quo. See Note, Choosing Representatives by Lottery Voting, 93 Yale L.J. 1283 (1984). There are many practical objections to Amar's interesting proposal, as he well realizes. Id. at 1308 (noting various difficulties and describing it as a "heuristic device"). I believe that he assigns too little weight to some of its disadvantages, such as its tendency to weaken parties and legislative expertise.

106. In that event, moreover, the issue might well have been formulated in an altogether different way.

107. This is an axiom of public choice theory. See, e.g., J. Buchanan & G. Tullock, supra note 69, at 131–45. For a critique of public choice theory's self-interest premise, see S. Kelman, supra note 25, at ch. 11. Even Kelman, however, does not challenge the notion that politicians possess specialized political knowledge of this kind.

108. Justice White's discussion of intent in *Bandemer* reflects upon this insight. 106 S. Ct. at 2808 (it is likely that those responsible for redistricting probably know the political composition of a district and predict its partisan leanings).

109. For studies of how such choices can affect these political variables, see M. Jewell, Metropolitan Representation: State Legislative Districting in Urban Counties (1969);

Lee & Rothman, San Francisco's District System Alters Electoral Politics, 67 Nat'l Civic Rev. 173, 173–78 (1978).

110. If a polity could agree upon the crucial districting criteria and could define them with suitable precision, computer programs might generate a small number of alternative districting plans satifying those criteria relative to the immense number of original possibilities. Even then, of course, the decisionmaker must choose from among the remaining plans; ample opportunity for partisan gerrymandering will remain. See, e.g., Backstrom, Robins & Eller, supra note 29, at 1134–39. For one computer simulation of this process, see Weaver & Hess, A Procedure for Nonpartisan Districting: Development of Computer Techniques, 73 Yale L.J. 288 (1963). Some criteria (e.g., contiguity and compactness, existing political subdivisions) lend themselves to more precise, agreed-upon definitions than others (e.g., "communities of interest"). Id. As the next paragraph in the text suggests, population equality, despite its superficial determinativeness, falls into the latter category.

At the level of partisan politics, the compactness criterion probably tends to disadvantage Democrats, who are often concentrated in urban areas and can more readily be "packed" into a small number of "inefficient" districts. See, e.g., B. Cain, supra note 54, at 44 (Democratic dominance in inner city area leads to "inefficient" Democratic distribution of votes if compactness criterion is observed). The increasing concentration of ethnic minority voters, overwhelmingly Democratic, in the inner cities also means that compact districts might result in over-concentration of those votes. But see Grofman, supra note 78, at 92 n.67 (suggesting that this "may or may not be true").

111. For a dramatic example of this uncertainty, compare Karcher v. Daggett, 462 U.S. 725 (1983) (population deviation of 0.7% from average district size not justified by state's asserted objective of preserving minority voting strength), with Brown v. Thomson, 462 U.S. 835 (1983) (state's policy of preserving county boundaries justified the 16% average deviation and 89% maximum deviation from population equality), decided by the Court on the same day. The different outcomes may be partly attributed to the different standards applied to congressional and state legislative redistricting plans. See supra note 78.

112. The U.S. Constitution, article I, s 2, speaks of the "People of the several States," not the number of voters. Similarly, the fourteenth amendment requires that congressional seats be apportioned "counting the whole number of persons in each State," and provides for reduction in representation when the right to vote of "male inhabitants" is abridged. U.S. Const., amend. XIV, s 2. Excluding or including groups such as illegal aliens, nonvoters and even children could be significant for the major political parties, since some states have large populations of these groups. Gilford, Causey & Rothwell, How Adjusting Census Counts Could Affect Congress, Am. Demographics, Sept. 1982, at 30, 33 (adjusting census counts to reflect accurately populations of blacks and Hispanics could significantly affect distribution of House seats); Harvison, Speakes & Turner, Drawing the Lines—By the Numbers: The Statistical Foundations of the Electoral Process, 2 Gov't Info. Q. 389, 392 (1985) (Bureau of Census has interpreted clause to include illegal aliens; estimates of over two million illegal aliens in 1980 Census). On the impact of redistribution of Congressional seats according to population, see, e.g., Cohen, The Big Shift, The Nat'l J., Feb. 7, 1987, at 319–21 (1991 reapportionment will move 12–15 seats from Frostbelt to Sunbelt).

113. B. Ackerman, Social Justice in the Liberal State (1980).

114. Id. at 8–10.

115. Even in *Bandemer*, nonpartisan justifications were advanced for the line-drawing. Bandemer v. Davis, 603 F. Supp. 1479, 1504 (Pell, J., concurring in part and dissenting in part) (redistricting protected incumbents and preserved integrity of political subdivisions).

116. On the history of districting in the United States, see, e.g., R. Dixon, Democratic Representation: Reapportionment in Law and Politics 58–91 (1968).

117. Some jurisdictions, to be sure, have established procedures for districting by methods designed to be bipartisan, nonpartisan or at least less partisan than traditional legislative processes. But although these procedures may reduce the risk of egregious gerrymandering, they cannot efface the unmistakable imprint of partisan influence. The partisan members of a bipartisan commission, for example, do not shed their political allegiances simply by being named to a commission, and even nonpartisan members are selected by partisan officials. On the desirability of bipartisan commissions, see, e.g., Dixon, Fair Criteria and Procedures for Establishing Legislative Districts, *in* Representation and Redistricting Issues, supra note 22, at 7, 10–19. Even Dixon, an ardent proponent of the bipartisan commiesion, notes that such plans may have unexpected consequences, e.g., the initial plan for the Connecticut state legislature drafted by Special Master Robert Bork that would have overwhelmingly favored the Democratic Party. Id. at 18–19.

In the recent apportionment dispute in California, the voters rejected a proposal to establish a bipartisan commission to draw district lines for the state legislature. Balzar, Deukemejian, Unfazed by Prop. 39 Loss, Vows to "Reform" State Remapping Laws, L.A. Times, Nov. 8, 1984, at 3, col. 3.

A variant of this problem arises periodically when individuals known to have partisan attachments are named as independents to bodies whose partisan composition is regulated by statute. See, e.g., the dispute concerning Susan Liebeler's appointment to the International Trade Commission. Trade Panel Nominations, N.Y. Times, Feb. 25, 1984, at B32, col. 6 (Liebeler was originally proposed in November 1982 for seat that could not be held by Republican; she described herself as independent).

118. Depending upon the state, these processes in recent years have relied upon redistricting decisions by legislatures, governors, appointed commissions and (in the case of deadlock) courts. See Council of State Governments, Reapportionment in the States (1972); Council of State Governments, Reapportionment in the Seventies (1973).

119. Decisions as to particular districting configurations within a jurisdiction, of course, are reversed whenever a new districting plan is enacted.

120. But see Lucas v. Forty-Fourth Gen. Assembly, 377 U.S. 713 (1964) (popular referendum approving districting plan cannot validate malapportionment violating population equality principle); see also J. Ely, supra note 24, at 239 n.60 (supporting *Lucas'* analysis).

121. See, e.g., Baker v. Carr, 369 U.S. 186 (1962); Gingles v. Edmisten, 590 F. Supp. 345 (E.D.N.C. 1984), aff'd in part and rev'd in part sub nom., Thornburg v. Gingles, 106 S. Ct. 2752 (1986); United Jewish Org. v. Carey, 430 U.S. 144 (1977).

122. Note that I say voters, not citizens. Proportional representation, for example, is based upon vote totals, not upon any other measurement of the level of citizen support.

123. See, e.g., R. Dahl, Who Governs?: Democracy and Power in an American City (1961); D. Truman, The Governmental Process (1962).

124. More robust interpretations of this first component can be imagined, but would be far more controversial. For example, the representative might be thought to be under a duty to represent the views of the average voter in the district, with majority as well as minority party voters included in the pool from which the average is drawn.

An even more demanding obligation would require the representative to oppose legislation that would make it more difficult for a minority party to become the majority.

Richard Fenno describes four constituencies that a member of the House of Representatives perceives—the geographical constituency, the reelection constituency (the member's supporters), the primary constituency (the strongest supporters), and the personal constituency (the intimates). R. Fenno, Home Style: House Members in Their Districts 1–30 (1978). Incumbents may hear from the latter constituencies most frequently, but most feel sufficiently uncertain and vulnerable regarding reelection that they also listen to those whose support they cannot rely upon. Id. at 233–34. Fenno concludes that members' responsiveness to their constituents should be evaluated not only on policy positions, but also in terms of accessibility to constituents. Id. at 241–43.

125. See discussion in Note, supra note 105, at 1306–07.

126. See infra text accompanying notes 138–88 (Part III).

127. Again, even that hindrance is likely to operate only in the short run and at some cost to the gerrymandering party. Lord Keynes' famous dictum, supra note 59, reminds us that the short run matters, especially in politics.

128. See supra note 37. On the inevitability of a balloon effect in plurality single-member districts, see, e.g., D. Rae, supra note 103, passim; Bickel, The Supreme Court and Reapportionment, in Reapportionment in the 1970s, supra note 90, at 57, 69–70. Depending upon the geographical distribution of support among the parties, the balloon effect could conceivably lead to control of the legislature by a party representing a *minority* of voters.

129. In the 1984 congressional elections, for example, Republican candidates received 47% of the vote but won only 42% of the seats. See Ornstein, supra note 86.

130. Id. Ironically, this bias results from the requirement in Reynolds v. Sims, 377 U.S. 533, 568 (1964), of population, rather than voter, equality. See supra notes 112 & 122.

131. See infra notes 138–88 and accompanying text (Part III).

132. See infra notes 142–44 and accompanying text. In this respect, it is like the rule permitting districting plans to be adopted through ordinary legislation. See discussion supra text accompanying notes 116–19.

133. 42 U.S.C. s 1973 (1982).

134. See, e.g., A. Thernstrom, Whose Votes Count? Affirmative Action and Minority Voting Rights 53 (1987); Blacksher & Menefee, At-Large Elections and One Person, One Vote: The Search for the Meaning of Racial Vote Dilution, in Minority Vote Dilution 203–40 (C. Davidson ed. 1984).

135. See Wise v. Lipscomb, 437 U.S. 535, 539 (1978) (single-member districts required in court-imposed plans, although plans designed by legislatures not so constrained); see also Thornburg v. Gingles, 106 S. Ct. 2752, 2764–67 (1986) (analyzing why multimember districts and at-large voting may dilute minority voting strength).

136. See, e.g., E. Banfield, Political Influence 235–62 (1961) (Chicago "machine" a response to extremely decentralized political structure).

137. See infra notes 138–88 and accompanying text (Part III).

138. For purposes of this discussion, the details of proportional representation systems are unimportant, for it is the general contours of such systems that are relevant to the partisan gerrymandering issue.

139. See, e.g., R. Dixon, supra note 116, at 50 (modified proportional representation would serve twentieth-century pluralism better than conventional district systems); J. Pennock, Democratic Political Theory 357 (1979) (proportional representation aims to achieve "mathematically accurate representation of opinions"); Lakeman, The Case for Proportional Representation, *in* Choosing an Electoral System: Issues and Alternatives 41, 45–51 (A. Lijphart & B. Grofman eds. 1984) (proportional representation provides voters with maximum choice); Lijphart, Comparative Perspectives on Fair Representation: The Plurality-Majority Rule, Geographical Districting, and Alternative Electoral Arrangements, *in* Representation and Redistricting Issues, supra note 22, at 143–60 (proportional representation satisfies criteria of fair representation more completely than plurality-majority rule and geographical districts); see also M. Balinski & H. Young, Fair Representation: Meeting the Ideal of One Man, One Vote 87–93 (1982) (proportional representation on a federal level achieves democratic aspirations of Founding Fathers).

140. Its precise tendencies in this regard would depend upon the details of the proportional representation scheme, such as the minimum percentage requirement for ballot access, electoral victory, and allocation of seats in the legislature.

141. 42 U.S.C. s 1973 (1982).

142. Indeed, at least one recent commentator has argued that proportional representation is constitutionally required. Note, The Constitutional Imperative of Proportional Representation, 94 Yale L.J. 163 (1984); see also Rogowski, Representation in Political Theory and in Law, 91 Ethics 395, 411 (1981) ("properly constructed systems of proportional representation . . . can assure both reasonable accuracy and fairness of representation" unlike almost all possible single-member district systems).

143. See, e.g., E. Banfield & J. Wilson, City Politics 96–98 (1963) (proportional representation has not had enduring popularity; political parties have opposed it since it reduces their control); Weaver, Semi-Proportional and Proportional Representation Systems in the United States, *in* Choosing an Electoral System, supra note 139, at 197 (proportional representation remains in effect only for the Cambridge, Massachusetts city council and the New York school committees and has been used primarily at the local government level). For a case study, see Heisel, Abandonment of Proportional Representation and the Impact of 9-X Voting in Cincinnati (paper presented at American Pol. Sci. Ass'n meeting, September 1982) (on file at the Columbia Law Review) But see Grofman, Alternatives to Single-Member Plurality Districts: Legal and Empirical Issues, *in* Representation and Redistricting Issues, supra note 22, at 107, 121 (evidence shows that proportional representation historically worked well in American cities).

144. See Duverger, Which is the Best Electoral System?, *in* Choosing an Electoral System, supra note 139, at 31, 36 (proportional representation generally does not tend to produce stable, strong governments); Hermens, Representation and Proportional Representation, *in* Choosing an Electoral System, supra note 139, at 15, 23 (proportional representation increases fragmentation, making "politics of accommodation" difficult; it also makes success easier for extremists); Riker, Electoral Systems and Constitutional Restraints, *in* Choosing an Electoral System, supra note 139, at 103, 106, 109 (neither proportional representation nor plurality rule perfectly represents the will

of people; proportional representation may produce minority tyranny); Shapiro, Gerrymandering, Unfairness, and the Supreme Court, 33 UCLA L. Rev. 227, 254–56 (1985) (proportional representation would entail constitutional revolution).

145. Davis v. Bandemer, 106 S. Ct. 2797, 2809 (1986) (White, J., plurality opinion) ("Our cases, however, clearly foreclose any claim that the Constitution requires proportional representation. . . ."); id. at 2823–24 (O'Connor, J., concurring) ("The flaw in such a pronouncement [that the Equal Protection Clause requires proportional representation], however, would be the use of the Equal Protection Clause as the vehicle for making a fundamental policy choice that is contrary to the intent of its Framers and to the traditions of this republic.").

146. Id. at 2830 n.7 (Powell, J., dissenting).

147. Id. at 2823 ("[A]ny such intervention is likely to move in the direction of proportional representation for political parties.").

148. Id. at 2810.

149. Although the plurality's test speaks in general terms of "influence on the political process as a whole," 106 S. Ct. at 2810, the test is clearly concerned with representation in the legislature.

150. None of the justices in *Bandemer*, least of all the plurality and dissenters, doubted that party performance was relevant to the constitutional test, however that might be formulated.

151. See, e.g., Backstrom, Robins & Eller, supra note 29, at 1141.

152. For extensive discussions of criteria to be used in apportionment disputes, see generally Symposium: Gerrymandering and the Courts, 33 UCLA L. Rev. 1 (1985); see also B. Cain, supra note 54, at 52–77.

The Supreme Court has repeatedly rejected arguments that rely on these factors to justify population differences between districts, particularly in the context of congressional seats. See, e.g., Kirkpatrick v. Preisler, 394 U.S. 526, 530–33 (1969) (rejecting argument that population variances in congressional districts are needed to account for factors such as interest groups, population trends, proportion of nonvoters, and "political realities"); Lucas v. Forty-Fourth Gen. Assembly, 377 U.S. 713, 738 (1964) (substantial disparities in state legislative apportionment not justified by geographical, historical, topographic, and economic considerations; Court rejected federal analogy when applied to bicameral state legislature). Even here, authors of the ostensibly objective measures warn of serious normative tensions lurking within and among these measures. See, e.g., Dixon, Fair Criteria and Procedures for Establishing Legislative Districts, *in* Representation and Redistricting Issues, supra note 22, at 7–8, 16–18; Lowenstein & Steinberg, supra note 23, at 4 (disputes over proper criteria for redistricting plans "constitute the very stuff of politics").

153. This was suggested by Justice Powell as part of his "factors" approach. 106 S. Ct. at 2832 (Powell, J., concurring in part and dissenting in part) ("Other relevant considerations include the nature of the legislative procedures by which the apportionment law was adopted. . . ."). The number of such factors is large. See Note, supra note 23, at 162 n.60. Powell's approach is to list numerous relevant factors without either defining standards by which they can be applied in particular cases or suggesting how they should be weighted. This seems more calculated to maximize the court's discretion and doctrinal unpredictability than to give legislators clear guidance.

154. 106 S. Ct. at 2832–33 (Powell, J., concurring in part and dissenting in part).

155. The Supreme Court has been traditionally reluctant to intervene with legislative procedures and rules. See United States v. Brewster, 408 U.S. 501, 525 (1972) (speech and

debate clause shields from judicial inquiry acts in legislative process and the motivation for those acts); Field v. Clark, 143 U.S. 649, 671–73 (1892) (declining to review validity of legislative procedures despite claim that legislative journals conflicted with signed, enrolled version of act); Fletcher v. Peck, 10 U.S. (6 Cranch) 87, 123 (1810) ("The validity of a law cannot be questioned because undue influence may have been used in obtaining it.").

156. Legislative history's indeterminacy, manipulability, and occasional abuse are notorious. For a detailed case study, see B. Ackerman & W. Hassler, Clean Coal/Dirty Air, ch. 4 (1981).

157. On the problems of inquiring into legislative motives, see generally A. Bickel, The Least Dangerous Branch: The Supreme Court at the Bar of Politics 208–22 (1962); Colloquium, Legislative Motivation, 15 San Diego L. Rev. 925 (1978); Brest, Palmer v. Thompson: An Approach to the Problem of Unconstitutional Legislative Motive, 1971 Sup. Ct. Rev. 95, 119–30; Ely, Legislative and Administrative Motivation in Constitutional Law, 79 Yale L.J. 1205 (1970).

158. 106 S. Ct. at 2814. Cf. id. at 2831 & n.10 (Powell, J., concurring in part and chssenting in part) (criticizing plurality for failing to enunciate any standard that could guide legislatures and courts, and for its willingness to assume the existence of discriminatory intent). Relying upon only one election would compound the risk of judicial error, while relying upon several might preclude an effective remedy. See Note, supra note 23, at 161 ("In combination with the inherent delays of litigation, the amount of time needed for such evidence to accrue may preclude relief for any given gerrymander before the next decennial apportionment."). Whereas the dissenters were apparently prepared to find a constitutional violation on the basis of predictions about a plan's political effects derived from as few as two elections (before and after the gerrymander), the plurality insisted that any disproportion must continue over more election cycles before a violation might properly be found. It carefully refrained from saying how many more. See id. at 2814 & n.17 ("*Projected* election results based on district boundaries and past voting patterns may certainly support this type of claim, even where *no* election has yet been held under the challenged districting.").

159. 106 S. Ct. at 2810.

160. H. Pitkin, The Concept of Representation 55–91 (1967).

161. The 1982 amendments to the Voting Rights Act sought to codify this understanding by including "the extent to which members of the minority group have been elected to public office in the jurisdiction" as one of seven evidentiary factors probative of a s 2 violation. S. Rep. No. 417, 97th Cong., 2d Sess. 28–29, reprinted in 1982 U.S. Code Cong. & Admin. News 177.

In Thornburg v. Gingles, 106 S. Ct. 2752 (1986), the first Supreme Court case interpreting the 1982 amendments, the Court looked at the degree of black candidates' electoral success in the North Carolina state legislature, as compared with the black population in the state. Id. at 2761–62 (history of black candidates' failure to win elections probative of denial of black voters' opportunities to elect candidates of their choice). A plurality of the Court noted, however, that "the *status* of the candidate as the *chosen representative of a particular racial group,* not the race of the candidate, . . . is important." Id. at 2776. The Court found that sustained success by black candidates might, but would not necessarily, defeat the plaintiffs' claim of discriminatory results under s 2.

See also United States v. Dallas County Comm'n, 739 F.2d 1529, 1539 (11th Cir. 1984) (election of no blacks in modern period supports a finding of racial vote dilution), cert. denied, 469 U.S. 976 (1984); United States v. Marengo County Comm'n, 731 F.2d 1546, 1567 (11th Cir. 1984) (racially polarized voting and historic discrimination have prevented blacks from being elected to public office), cert. denied, 469 U.S. 976 (1984); Jordan v. Winter, 604 F. Supp. 807, 812–13 (per curiam) (black congressional candidates' consistent defeat in Mississippi elections probative of s 2 violation), aff'd sub nom. Mississippi Republican Exec. Comm. v. Brooks, 469 U.S. 1002 (1984).

162. H. Pitkin, supra note 160, at 61 (quoting C. Friedrich, Constitutional Government and Democracy 286 (1950)).

163. Id. at 56.

164. Id. at ch.9.

165. This will depend upon many variables, including the number of candidates, the distribution of votes, the existence of a majority runoff requirement, and the like.

166. For an exploration of some of these issues, see Ackerman, Beyond Carolene Products, 98 Harv. L. Rev. 713 (1985); Schuck, The Graying of Civil Rights Law: The Age Discrimination Act of 1975, 89 Yale L.J. 27, 31–39 (1979) (comparing age and race as group-defining attributes).

167. Significant cleavages among black Americans seem to have emerged recently, particularly along lines based on class or economic status. See, e.g., W. Wilson, The Declining Significance of Race 144–54 (1978); Colasanto & Williams, The Changing Dynamics of Race and Class, Pub. Opinion, Jan.-Feb. 1987, at 50 (blacks increasingly see class differences as greater than racial differences); Lichter, Who Speaks for Black America?, Pub. Opinion, Aug.-Sept. 1985, at 41 (divergence between black leaders and average black Americans, particularly on race relations issues). But see Gilliam, Black America: Divided by Class?, Pub. Opinion, Feb.-Mar. 1986, at 53 (relatively little significant attitudinal difference among black Americans).

168. This variability in partisan success rates has grown over time, since voters increasingly choose candidates on the basis of the politician's personality and issue standards rather than party labels. See, e.g., W. Crotty, American Parties in Decline 26–44, 276 (2d ed. 1984); G. Jacobson, The Politics of Congressional Elections (1983).

169. The declining importance of political parties and the rise of candidate-centered organizations is treated comprehensively in D. Mayhew, Placing Parties in American Politics (1986); see also D. Broder, The Party's Over: The Failure of Politics in America 213 (1972) (responsible party government has declined dramatically in post-Eisenhower era); N. Nie, S. Verba & J. Petrocik, The Changing American Voter 345–56 (1976) (candidate-centered organizations have replaced political parties as basic electoral organization). But see S. Morehouse, State Politics, Parties, and Policy 29–30 (1981) (some parties strong at state level).

170. A. Bickel, Reform and Continuity: The Electoral College, the Convention and the Party System 22 (1971).

171. Supra notes 130 & 140 and accompanying text. For an argument that it is better for that waste to occur in the legislature than in the electorate, see Note, supra note 105, at 1304.

172. There is a chicken-and-egg problem in separating the effects of the sociopolitical cultures in which proportional representation tends to flourish from the effects of the electoral system's special features. Strong socialist parties, for example, often antedated the adoption of proportional representation systems, but the parties' continuation is also encouraged by these systems.

173. See, e.g., E. Banfield & J. Wilson, supra note 143, at 94 (at-large district systems tend to sacrifice neighborhood representation); P. Heilig & R. Mundt, Your Voice at City Hall: The Politics, Procedures and Policies of District Representation (1984) (district

representation is more responsive to local district concerns). It is possible to reduce this effect somewhat by using certain localizing techniques, such as imposing residency requirements on candidates for designated seats in multimember districts.

174. This analysis might suggest that proportionality should be less objectionable as jurisdictions become more specialized in their purposes and powers (e.g., school or water districts). See Ball v. James, 451 U.S. 355 (1981) (approving special district voting system that limited franchise to landowners and apportioned votes on basis of acres owned); Salyer Land Co. v. Tulare Lake Basin Water Storage Dist., 410 U.S. 719 (1973) (approving grant of franchise only to landowners where costs were assessed against land benefited and where activities disproportionately affected landowners as a group).

175. Survey data reveals a marked decrease in the number of voters who identify strongly with either of the two major parties. See, e.g., W. Crotty, supra note 168, at 28. In national surveys conducted at the end of 1986, one-third of the respondents identified themselves as independents. See data in Party ID., Pub. Opinion, Jan.-Feb. 1987, at 35. On the historical decline of party identification, see, e.g., E. Ladd, Transformations of the American Party System: Political Coalitions from the New Deal to the 1970s (2d ed. 1978); J. Sundquist, Dynamics of the Party System (1983).

176. See data in Split Ticket Voting, Pub. Opinion, Jan.-Feb. 1987, at 34. Voters in 11 states chose a U.S. Senator from one party and a governor from another. Apple, Voters' Rebuff to Reagan's Vision, N.Y. Times, Nov. 6, 1986, at A1, col. 2; see also Shribman, Divided Loyalties: How Ticket Splitting Has Become Ingrained in Politics in the U.S., Wall St. J., Sept. 2, 1986, at 1, col. 1 (since 1960s, two-tiered system of politics has emerged, with Republicans dominating executive branch and Democrats dominating Congress).

177. See, e.g., D. Broder, supra note 169.

178. Supra notes 150–59 and accompanying text.

179. See Dionne, After a Battle Bereft of Ideas, No Clear Agenda, N.Y. Times, Nov. 9, 1986, s 4, at 1, col. 1 (1986 elections characterized by an open political agenda and by "partisan brawling"); Mathews & Maraniss, South Offers Contradictions in Otherwise Homogenous Balloting, Wash. Post, Nov. 5, 1986, at A34, col. 1 (southern pattern of voting Republican on national level and Democratic on local level reversed in 1986 elections).

Once again, the 1986 elections exemplify this longer-term phenomenon. In almost every area of the country, competition between the major parties was vigorous. This was especially true with respect to both houses of Congress and state gubernatorial races, but even in state legislative elections in the South, where Democratic dominance has been most persistent, Republican gains have continued. The 1986 elections for senator and governor produced many close races between major party candidates. See Brownstein, The Big Sweep, Nat'l J., Nov. 8, 1986, at 2712; Schneider, Return to Normalcy, Nat'l J., Nov. 8, 1986, at 2708. In Senate elections, many incumbents have lost in recent years. Incumbents of both parties, however, were overwhelmingly reelected to the House in 1986, as 98% of those who ran were returned to office. Calmes, House Incumbents Achieve Record Success Rate in 1986, Cong. Q. Weekly Rep., Nov. 15, 1986, at 2891.

In state legislative races, despite Republican efforts to reverse the historical imbalance of power, Democrats actually gained seats and control of more legislative chambers. Bragdon, Democrats Extend Dominance in the States, Cong. Q. Weekly Rep., Nov. 15, 1986, at 2893. But in the South, where Republican representation has been weakest, the GOP made steady gains. Toner, Democrats Maintain Hold on South, N.Y. Times, Mar. 21, 1987, at A6, col. 1 (Republican share of legislative seats in 11 states of old Confederacy more than doubled in last 10 years, from 10% to 23%). Perhaps more important in the long run, the Republican gains of eight governorships from the Democrats sharply reduced the number of states in which one party holds complete control over the redistricting process. Before the 1986 election, the Democrats had such power in 18 states, and the Republicans held control over only four states. After the 1986 elections, the Democrats enjoy only a 13–6 advantage. Brownstein, supra, at 2713.

180. At the same time, the national parties have increased their aid to state and local parties. See, e.g., L. Epstein, Political Parties in the American Mold 216–25 (1986). The Republican party has been particularly effective at raising money for candidates. Jacobson, The Republican Advantage in Campaign Finance, in The New Direction in American Politics 143 (J. Chubb & P. Peterson eds. 1985). Despite these links between the national parties and the state and local parties, the different levels of party organization are generally detached from one another. See, e.g., L. Epstein, supra, at 343–46.

181. See, e.g., Fiorina, The Case of the Vanishing Marginals: The Bureaucracy Did It, 71 Am. Pol. Sci. Rev. 177 (1977); Mayhew, Congressional Elections: The Case of the Vanishing Marginals, 6 Polity 295 (1974).

The incumbency effect at the state level may also be large. In the 1986 California elections, 139 incumbents sought reelection and all of them won. See, Commentary, 7 Cal. Regulatory L. Rep. 9 (1987).

182. See, e.g., Calmes, supra note 179; Mayhew, supra note 181; Winter, Political Financing and the Constitution, 486 Annals 34, 38 (1986).

183. Jacobson, The Marginals Never Vanished: Incumbency and Competition in Elections to the U.S. House of Representatives, 31 Am. J. Pol. Sci. 126, 133, 138 (1987); see also, T. Mann, Unsafe at Any Margin: Interpreting Congressional Elections 18, 102–03 (1978) (incumbency can usually be translated into an electoral advantage; voters respond primarily to issues, not to party affiliation); T. Mann, supra note 26, at 5–9.

184. Cain, supra note 86, at 331.

185. See, e.g., Common Cause, Toward a System of "Fair and Effective Representation" 17–24 (1977) (incumbent protection undercuts political competition and participation). It further suggests that any judicial challenge to the incumbency effect would have to assume different forms and employ different concepts and techniques than those that would be useful to courts adjudicating partisan gerrymanders. As to the former, notions of party performance and proportionality would be useless, and not simply misleading, to the court. See, e.g., Common Cause v. Bolger, 574 F. Supp. 672 (D.D.C. 1982) (franking privilege upheld against challenge based on denial of privilege to non-members of Congress), aff'd, 461 U.S. 911 (1983). Compare Greenberg v. Bolger, 497 F. Supp. 756 (E.D.N.Y. 1980) (first amendment violated by statutory scheme granting two major political parties reduced mailing rates).

186. On the difficulty of isolating the impact of one such factor in a dynamic electoral process, see, e.g., Lowenstein & Steinberg, supra note 23, at 58 (any uniform method of hypothetically "switching" votes is arbitrary and divorced from any observable political phenomenon).

187. Indeed, by effectively inviting legal challenges of districting plans despite its disclaimer of that purpose, the Court has created a host of new problems for the lower courts and the electoral process. See infra note 191.

188. See discussion, infra notes 189–220 and accompanying text (Part IV).

189. Indeed, only days after oral argument in the Supreme Court, a symposium on gerrymandering and the courts brought together some of the most knowledgeable lawyers, law professors and political scientists in the field. The symposium papers, published several months later, should arouse deep skepticism in any reader about the wisdom and appropriateness of judicial intervention in this area. Professor Martin Shapiro's admonition—"The Court should not enter this battle because the casualties will be too high"—was perhaps the most baleful but the general tenor of his remark was not unusual. Shapiro, supra note 144, at 254.

For earlier proponents of this view, see, e.g., A. Bickel, supra note 170, at 1–3; Elliott, Prometheus, Proteus, Pandora, and Procrustes Unbound: The Political Consequences of Reapportionment, 37 U. Chi. L. Rev. 474, 490–92 (1970).

One commentator advised caution but also encouraged judicial consideration of gerrymandering issues. Compare, R. Dixon, supra note 116, at 491, 493–95 (no reason why Court should not find all gerrymandering justiciable) with Dixon, The Court, the People, and "One Man, One Vote," in Reapportionment in the 1970's, supra note 90, at 7, 35–36 (problems of proof make judicial involvement with partisan gerrymandering difficult; courts should not make it impossible for state legislatures to retain districting function).

Some other commentators have urged the Court forward. See Baker, Gerrymandering: Privileged Sanctuary or Next Judicial Target?, in Reapportionment in the 1970's, supra note 90, at 140–42; Clinton, Further Explorations in the Political Thicket: The Gerrymander and the Constitution, 59 Iowa L. Rev. 1, 47 (1973); Engstrom, The Supreme Court and Equipopulous Gerrymandering: A Remaining Obstacle in the Quest for Fair and Effective Representation, 1976 Ariz. St. L.J. 277, 319.

190. See, e.g., Irving, Court Gets GOP's Gerrymandering Case, San Francisco Examiner, Jan. 25, 1987, at B2, col. 1; Herbers, Court's Ruling Spurs Party Fight for Legislatures, N.Y. Times, July 2, 1986, at B6, col. 3 (Bandemer will encourage parties to challenge state districting plans in federal courts); Gailey, G.O.P. Plans to Cite Ruling in California, N.Y. Times, July 1, 1986, at A17, col. 2 (after Bandemer, Republicans will re-open their legal challenge to congressional districting plan in California).

"Combatant" is not too strong a word. Where judicial remedies are difficult to enforce and may require protracted supervision or repeated involvement by the court, the judicial role can quickly be transformed from arbiter to participant-adversary. See, e.g., P. Schuck, Suing Government: Citizen Remedies for Official Wrongs 150–69 (1983). It seems likely that partisan gerrymandering cases will conform to those specifications.

191. Davis v. Bandemer, 106 S. Ct., 2797, 2810 (1986). Under that standard, it should be child's play for almost any litigant challenging a districting plan to survive a motion for summary judgment. Applying that standard, it would seem, will almost always require a trial, as the court has found in attempting to apply the "good faith" standard in official immunity cases. See P. Schuck, supra note 190, at 93–97. And until the court reaches a final decision and appeals are exhausted, the legitimacy of elections, and thus of government itself, will remain uncertain. That this is no idle speculation is suggested by the Richmond case, City of Richmond, Va. v. United States, 422 U.S. 358 (1975), in which the city council remained frozen for seven years while voting rights act litigation continued. See A. Thernstrom, supra note 134, at 146–49, 158.

192. See, e.g., Squeezing the Gerrymander, Wall St. J., July 3, 1986, at 16, col. 1.

193. E.g., Cooper v. Aaron, 358 U.S. 1 (1958); Brown v. Board of Educ., 349 U.S. 294 (1955); Brown v. Board of Educ., 347 U.S. 483 (1954).

194. E.g., Miranda v. Arizona, 384 U.S. 436 (1966); Massiah v. United States, 377 U.S. 201 (1964).

195. E.g., Reynolds v. Sims, 377 U.S. 533 (1964); Baker v. Carr, 369 U.S. 186 (1962).

196. E.g., Youngstown Sheet & Tube Co. v. Sawyer, 343 U.S. 579 (1952).

197. E.g., Roth v. United States, 354 U.S. 476 (1957).

198. E.g., McCollum v. Board of Educ., 333 U.S. 203 (1948).

199. E.g., Roe v. Wade, 410 U.S. 113 (1973).

200. For critiques of these decisions, see, e.g., Wechsler, Toward Neutral Principles of Constitutional Law, 73 Harv. L. Rev. 1 (1959) (desegregation decisions compromised consistency of constitutional law); Caplan, Questioning Miranda, 38 Vand. L. Rev. 1417 (1985); Neal, Baker v. Carr: Politics in Search of Law, 1962 Sup. Ct. Rev. 252; Corwin, The Steel Seizure Case: A Judicial Brick without Straw, 53 Colum. L. Rev. 53 (1953); Kalven, The Metaphysics of the Law of Obscenity, 1960 Sup. Ct. Rev. 1; Brown, Quis Custodiet Ipsos Custodes—The School-Prayer Cases, 1963 Sup. Ct. Rev. 1; Ely, The Wages of Crying Wolf: A Comment on *Roe v. Wade*, 82 Yale L.J. 920 (1973).

201. See, e.g., Tanenhaus & Murphy, Patterns of Public Support for the Supreme Court: A Panel Study, 43 J. Pol. 24, 24–39 (1981) (public generally rejected Supreme Court approach to school prayer, civil rights, criminal defendants' rights during period 1966–75).

202. See, e.g., Hart v. Community School Bd., 383 F. Supp. 699 (E.D.N.Y. 1974) (New York City school desegregation case), supplemented, 383 F. Supp. 769, aff'd, 512 F.2d 37 (2d Cir. 1975); see also Berger, Away from the Court House and into the Field: The Odyssey of a Special Master, 78 Colum. L. Rev. 707, 733 (1978) (courts not equipped to shape a remedy designed to restructure a neighborhood); Note, Judicial Intervention and Organization Theory: Changing Bureaucratic Behavior and Policy, 89 Yale L.J. 513, 526–36 (1980) (*Hart* court failed to understand organizational context of decision).

203. A. Bickel, supra note 157.

204. See, e.g., Barnum, The Supreme Court and Public Opinion: Judicial Decision Making in the Post-New Deal Period, 47 J. Pol. 652, 662–64, 659 n.13 (1985) (Court's protection of minority rights often reflected either emerging majority view or growing minority view; support for Court's position has generally increased after ruling).

205. 369 U.S. 186 (1962).

206. E.g., A. Bickel, supra note 157, at 193–98 (dangerous for Court to legitimate state apportionment plans); Dixon, supra note 22, at 268–70 (equal population criterion not related to fair representation principle); McCloskey, Foreword: The Reapportionment Case, 76 Harv. L. Rev. 54, 72–74 (1962) (Court should not extend interference beyond vague standards already articulated); Neal, supra note 200, at 326–27 (Court gave no guidance for future courts in reapportionment cases).

207. See supra note 22.

208. R. Dixon, supra note 116, at 85–91 (although rural areas overrepresented in state legislatures on eve of reapportionment cases, urban voters were beginning to exert greater influence through such mechanisms as referenda); see also Shapiro, supra note 144.

209. 347 U.S. 483 (1954).

210. See Ackerman, The Storrs Lectures: Discovering the Constitution, 93 Yale L.J. 1013, 1057–72 (1984) (constitutional interpretation requires recognition of legislative and judicial responses to moments of constitutional crisis in American history).

The occurrence of such moments is a matter of considerable inconvenience and even embarrassment to legal scholars for a very simple reason: we often cannot discern constitutional moments except in the crystalline clarity of hindsight. External events rather than our analyses shape these moments. That reality, however, apparently troubles neither the Court nor other Americans who live and work outside the law schools.

211. Pub. L. No. 89–110, 79 Stat. 437 (1965) (codified as amended at 42 U.S.C. ss 1971, 1973–1973bb–1 (1982)). These cases culminate and are discussed in Thornburg v. Gingles, 106 S. Ct. 2752 (1986), decided on the same day as *Bandemer*. See generally A. Thernstrom, supra note 134.

212. See, e.g., 42 U.S.C. s 1973a (1982) (appointment of federal voting examiners; preclearance of changes in voting procedures).

213. The concept of "quasi-constitutional" provisions developed in Dam, The American Fiscal Constitution, 44 U. Chi. L. Rev. 271 (1977) and Elliott, Constitutional Conventions and the Deficit, 1985 Duke L.J. 1077, refers to legal requirements that although contained in subconstitutional sources of law, prescribe fundamental governmental structures and political relationships of a kind that in other countries (and in many states) are found in constitutions.

214. Allen v. State Bd. of Elections, 393 U.S. 544 (1969); Gaston County, N.C. v. United States, 288 F. Supp. 678 (D.D.C. 1968), aff'd, 395 U.S. 285 (1969). See generally A. Thernstrom, supra note 134. The fact that not *all* minority groups can be simultaneously protected was evident even before the Act's enactment, see Wright v. Rockefeller, 376 U.S. 52, 59 (1964) (Douglas, J., disssenting), and it later became inescapable. E.g., United Jewish Orgs. v. Carey, 430 U.S. 144 (1977). For a development of this point in the context of age discrimination remedies, see Schuck, supra note 166.

215. See, e.g., K. Thompson, The Voting Rights Act and Black Electoral Participation (1983); Morris, Black Electoral Participation and the Distribution of Public Benefits, *in* Minority Vote Dilution, supra note 134, at 271–85.

216. See generally A. Thernstrom, surpa note 134. For extensive commentary on the Voting Rights Act Amendments of 1982, see Report of Senate Committee on the Judiciary, S. Rep. No. 417, 97th Cong., 2d Sess. (1982), reprinted in U.S. Code Cong. & Admin. News 177–410. On the background to the Amendments, see id. at 4–9. On the development of the Voting Rights Act case law, see id. at 19–39; see also McKenzie & Krauss, Section 2 of the Voting Rights Act: An Analysis of the 1982 Amendment, 19 Harv. C.R.-C.L. L. Rev. 155 (1984).

The legislative history's clarity on this point can be compared to the murky legislative history on some other civil rights legislation. See, e.g., Schuck, supra note 166 (on the Age Discrimination Act of 1975, 42 U.S.C. ss 6101–07 (1982 & Supp. 1985)); R. Katzmann, Institutional Disability: The Saga of Transportation Policy for the Disabled ch. 2 (1986) (on s 504 of the Rehabilitation Act of 1973, 29 U.S.C. 794 (1982)).

217. For a somewhat different view of what Congress meant to do, see A. Thernstrom, supra note 134; Blumstein, Defining and Proving Race Discrimination: Perspectives on the Purpose vs. Results approach from the Voting Rights Act, 69 Va. L. Rev. 633, 689–701 (1983) (emphasis on access, not outcome). Some commentators have questioned whether these changes, especially as implemented by the courts and the Justice Department, improve the overall political influence of racial minorities, or simply assure the election of minority candidates. See, e.g., A. Thernstrom, supra note 134; Cooper, Beware of Republicans Bearing Voting Rights Suits, Wash. Monthly, Feb. 1987, at 11; Schuck, What Went Wrong with the Voting Rights Act, Wash. Monthly, Nov. 1987, at 51 (review of Thernstrom).

218. See, e.g., Clymer, Opinion Narrows Over High Court, N.Y. Times, July 13, 1986, at A15, col. 1.

219. On the decline of confidence in public institutions and the political realm, see generally S. Lipset & W. Schneider, The Confidence Gap: Business, Labor and Government in the Public Mind (1983); R. Nisbet, Twilight of Authority (1975). However, some commentators have noticed a recent rise in public confidence in government. See, e.g., Lipset, Feeling Better: Measuring the Nation's Confidence, Pub. Opinion, Apr.-May 1985, at 6 (confidence has risen during Reagan presidency); Confidence in Institutions, 238 Gallup Rep. 2 (1985).

220. E.g., Schad v. Burrough of Mt. Ephraim, 452 U.S. 61 (1981) (live nude dancing); Engel v. Vitale, 370 U.S. 421 (1962) (statute requiring school prayer).

11
Mass Torts

An Institutional Evolutionist Perspective

Introduction

With the benefit of twenty-five years' experience of mass tort litigation,[1] it is time to assess what we have learned. Torts scholars have already arrived at a consensus as telling as it is rare: Although courts have demonstrated considerable resourcefulness in struggling with mass torts issues, the overall performance of the litigation system in this area has been remarkably poor.[2] Some proceduralists have voiced similar criticisms; generally speaking, however, procedure scholars seem to be more confident than torts scholars that reform can be accomplished within the basic tort paradigm.[3] In law as in life, familiarity seems to breed contempt.

Torts scholars charge that mass tort litigation often produces arbitrary results; that it fails to deliver the right compensation to the right victims when it is most needed; that it misallocates risk among consumers, corporations, and governments; that it generates unconscionable waste; and that it does not achieve corrective justice. They argue that the legal actors in the mass tort drama—self-serving, entrepreneurial plaintiffs' lawyers; foot-dragging defense counsel; and overwhelmed, desperately improvising judges—have subordinated important public goals and the needs of individual claimants to their own interests. Notoriously convoluted proceedings enrich lawyers, consultants, and expert witnesses while demoralizing, and often impoverishing, the law's supposed beneficiaries.

Indeed, most torts scholars regard the notion of a mass tort "system" as a misnomer, a convenient but fundamentally misleading rubric for academic conferences, journal commentaries, and occasional texts or courses. Rather, in the dominant view, the field known as "mass torts" comprises a melange of discrete disputes with little in common besides their prodigious procedural complexity, stratospheric transaction costs, and abject dependence on uncertain science.[4]

Many of these criticisms seemed perfectly valid when the first generation of serious mass torts scholarship appeared about a decade ago,[5] and some of these criticisms remain valid today—especially those concerning the risks of injustice when plaintiffs seek essentially unlimited compensatory and punitive damages from sympathetic juries for serious injuries on the basis of changing, easily manipulated scientific evidence. The recent settlement of the silicone gel breast implant settlement[6] and the flood of even weaker claims filed in the wake of that settlement[7] provide anecdotal but dramatic support for the continuing force of these first-generation critiques.

Still, contemporary mass tort litigation has changed a great deal since the torts scholars first returned this indictment. Although some others have noted many of these changes, I hope to bring them into a somewhat sharper, more comprehensive focus. Only by abandoning outdated views of our subject can we come to a fresh understanding of it.

Important questions naturally arise out of this redescription of mass torts: If today's mass tort litigation truly differs from earlier versions, what factors produced these changes? Have these changes been for the better? How does the current mass tort regime compare with other possible approaches? The task of addressing these daunting questions is exacerbated by the difficulties inherent in constructing an empirical test of any answers that might be proposed: No sharp generational line divides yesterday's mass tort litigation from today's,[8] and both are still too recent to afford the scholar much perspective. Accordingly, this Article offers only preliminary answers.

In developing these answers, this Article takes a view of mass torts litigation that differs from the canonical view summarized above. I call this view "institutional evolutionism." The evolutionist emphasis draws attention to, and treats in a more consistent fashion, three distinct but related features of mass torts litigation: (1) incremental system-building, (2) common-law process, and (3) selection by judges and other policymakers among competing institutional designs.

Before detailing the institutional evolutionist view, I wish to define the scope of my analysis. First, I offer it tentatively rather than tendentiously. On a spectrum of persuasiveness, I believe that the institutional evolutionist view lies somewhere between plausible and convincing; only more and better empirical research can determine its exact location.

Second, the term "evolutionist" is meant only to be suggestive, not rigorously scientific. I do not claim that biological metaphors furnish powerful explanations of complex legal phenomena.[9] I claim only that these metaphors evoke gradual processes of conflict, change, differentiation, complexity, and selection in nature which have rough counterparts in the lives of legal systems and sub-systems. These natural processes may therefore have some modest heuristic value in illuminating the character of systems.

Third, while the institutional evolutionist view treats mass tort litigation more charitably than most previous accounts (including my own earlier work),[10] it by no means endorses the status quo. Mass tort litigation continues to yield lower social benefits at a higher social cost than it should. In the world of mass torts, therefore, a Dr. Pangloss is unwelcome. The evolutionist perspective should encourage mass torts scholars to debate the system's character not merely on the basis of old facts and assessments but also in light of the improvements wrought by incremental system-building, common-law process, and selection among competing institutional designs.

Finally, the institutional evolutionist perspective is primarily backward-looking; it seeks to expose the merits and demerits of our current system and to explicate the choices and defaults that have shaped it; it does not support strong prescriptive claims. Nevertheless, this analysis naturally leads to a consideration of alternative ways of handling mass personal injury claims.[11] This consideration is the subject of Part III.

This Article is organized into three parts that track the three distinct aspects of institutional evolutionism: Part I will address incremental system-building. Part II will discuss common-law process. Finally, Part III will describe selection from among competing policy approaches.

I. Building a System

Imagine that it is the summer of 1969. The term "mass tort" has not yet been coined, although it has been loosely applied to airline crashes, large fires, and other single-event accidents that happen to affect numerous claimants.[12] Congress has not yet established a compensation program for coal miners suffering from black lung (although it will do so before the year is out).[13] Clarence Borel has not yet filed his soon-to-be paradigmatic mass tort action against the manufacturers of asbestos insulation materials.[14] With the blessing of the Food and Drug Administration (FDA), physicians routinely prescribe Diethylstilbestrol (DES) to prevent miscarriages.[15] Agent Orange is widely deemed a miracle defoliant that will save the lives of soldiers and civilians rather than putting them at risk of serious illness or death.[16] The newly-designed Dalkon Shield is being heralded as a safe, effective contraceptive.[17] Bendectin is still considered to be a wonder drug by the FDA and by tens of millions of women suffering from morning sickness.[18] Silicone breast implants have been on the market for only a few years; two decades will elapse before the FDA begins to warn women about them.[19] Although the federal government has long engaged in nuclear testing, no one seriously believes that it would knowingly expose soldiers or civilians to dangerous levels of radiation.[20] Repetitive-strain disorders and electro-magnetic field syndromes are not even a gleam in the eye of the most resourceful and creative plaintiffs' lawyers.[21] Cigarette manufacturers have won the first wave of litigation against them by a "knockout," causing the wave to retreat and discouraging further suits by smokers until the 1980s.[22]

Consider further the social and technological changes that will affect the management of public health risks in the future. Industry and government will develop thousands of new chemicals, processes, and technologies. Scientific measurement technology will advance to the point at which even an undergraduate chemistry student can determine human exposures to potential toxins at levels of a few parts per trillion—levels far lower than those at which science could confidently determine actual toxicity. Public fear that these toxins cause cancer and other diseases will intensify, influencing the agendas of legislators, regulators, insurers, corporations, environmentalists, consumerists, the mass media, and other political interests. In response, many new regulatory agencies will be created to tame and prevent the torrent of newly-revealed risks, but their capacity to regulate these risks rationally and effectively will swiftly be overwhelmed. Political and legal decisions will require convincing scientific evidence that even the most sophisticated scientific techniques cannot provide and that the legal system cannot readily process.[23]

A. The Emergence of a New Legal Regime

Tort litigation over occupational, environmental, and product risks burgeoned after 1969—much of it displaying features sufficiently distinctive and recurrent to constitute a discrete legal phenomenon deserving of its own moniker—the "mass tort." This litigation raised novel and complex legal, factual, and policy questions in such diverse legal subdisciplines as civil procedure, choice of law, liability doctrine, evidence, professional ethics, governmental immunity, insurance, bankruptcy, risk assessment and regulation, and court administration.

The volume of mass tort litigation grew in response to the expansion and transformation of tort liability in favor of plaintiffs—particularly in the area of products liability, where strict liability became the dominant rule.[24] Courts recognized new categories of compensable harms, including some merely incipient ones.[25] The level of compensatory damage awards increased, largely but not exclusively due to the rising cost of health care. Moreover, the possibility of punitive damages, seldom awarded in earlier products liability cases, became an important factor in mass tort litigation.

At both the federal and state levels, dramatic procedural and institutional innovations reshaped mass tort litigation. Individual tort actions led to the technique of bringing groups of similar cases, which in turn encouraged more extensive use of multidistrict litigation and case consolidations, certification of class actions, coordination (both formal and informal) of state and federal litigation, and negotiation of global settlements. Congress liberalized the Bankruptcy Code,[26] and many large corporations sought protection in Chapter 11[27] from expanded tort liabilities, among other claims. The personal injury bar itself underwent major changes, with the traditional slip-and-fall claimant's lawyer giving way to a highly sophisticated plaintiffs' bar supported by extensive information exchanges, collaborative techniques, and long-term financing. As the likelihood of having to satisfy enormous judgments increased, liability insurance for many important environmental risks became unavailable, unaffordable, or subject to broad coverage restrictions.

To anticipate these developments would have required a clairvoyance seldom vouchsafed to politicians—or, indeed, to anyone else.[28] Having had little experience with mass exposure torts, legal policymakers probably assumed, like the rest of us, that the future would be rather like the present, only more so. This assumption of continuity, of course, proved to be stunningly false.

B. The Evolution of a Mass Tort System

Once courts began to realize that they were confronting a new, quite different phenomenon,[29] they entered a period of desperate improvisation that has only recently congealed into a system. Compared with the law's traditionally glacial rate of change, some of these innovations in mass tort law occurred with lightning speed.[30] Nevertheless, courts have viewed most of these innovations—including some of the most controversial ones—as incremental, not radical departures from past practices.[31]

The core problem driving the evolution of mass tort litigation was *uncertainty*. Uncertainty typically surrounds the procedural law governing such disputes: questions of choice of law, evidence (especially evidence of general and specific causation), claims aggregation, and the number and nature of present claimants and anticipated future claimants. Uncertainty also shrouds the applicable substantive law of mass torts, whether it be negligence, strict products liability, or governmental liability. Finally, various factors influencing the relief will be uncertain, in particular: the potential compensatory and punitive damages; the availability and extent of insurance coverage; and in some cases, the continuing economic viability of defendants. These multiple uncertainties increase the cost of filing and litigating claims, discourage meritorious claimants, threaten horizontal equity among victims, enlarge the discretion of judge and jury alike, and raise the deadweight costs of insurance.[32]

Although these uncertainties were greatest in the early stages of mass tort litigation, they diminished over time due to the gradual "maturation" of the mass tort system through litigation and settlements, as well as the practical adaptations made by all participants in the mass tort system. Francis McGovern introduced the "maturity" concept into the mass tort lexicon in the late 1980s.[33] In his terms, litigation matures after there has been full and complete discovery, multiple jury verdicts, and a persistent vitality in the plaintiffs' contentions. At the mature stage of mass tort litigation, little or no new evidence will be developed, significant appellate review of any novel legal issues has been concluded, and at least one full cycle of trial strategies has been exhausted.[34] Only at this stage, McGovern contends, can a large number of similar but discrete, high-cost disputes be consolidated into groups of similar cases to facilitate settlement *en masse*.

His leading example of mature mass tort litigation involves asbestos. In its early years, asbestos litigation was so fragmented, chaotic, costly, and unpredictable that it resembled an unruly, erratic adolescent.[35] During that period, relatively few asbestos cases went to trial,[36] but those that did, coupled with the numerous settlements, created patterns that the lawyers discerned and used. Asbestos litigation crossed a kind of developmental threshold in the early 1990s; thereafter cases could be resolved more readily in a more systematic, inexpensive, predictable—and therefore equitable—fashion.

Some disagree with McGovern's advocacy of a maturity criterion as a judicial standard,[37] but the dynamic that this criterion describes seems undeniable. A course of litigation and a pattern of settlements determines the legal consequences of individual torts; this greater determinacy in turn makes it easier to exploit aggregative procedures to refine and establish claim values.[38] It is characteristic of mass torts that their *claim values tend to be highly interdependent*; establishing the value of claim A helps to determine the value of claim B.[39] If claim values can be established within a relatively narrow range of uncertainty, the wholesale settlement of cases can proceed.[40]

McGovern's analysis regarding the maturation of an individual mass tort can be usefully extended to mass tort litigation more generally. The array of mass torts litigated during the last twenty-five years reveals recurrent patterns of litigant behavior, judicial decisionmaking, and institutional change. Whether the tortious agent is asbestos, DES, Agent Orange, breast implants, Dalkon Shield, repetitive stress disorders, Bendectin, or heart valves, the claims are litigated and resolved in strikingly similar ways. Most of these ways are calculated to reduce uncertainty.

The propensity of a maturing mass tort system to reduce uncertainty reflects more than an unfolding, cumulating litigation process; it also reflects relentless efforts by litigants, lawyers, insurers, and judges to manage both risk and compensation in order to achieve transactional efficiency, horizontal equity, and greater predictability. These efforts can be analyzed into five elements: (1) "lawyerizing" mass tort risks; (2) improving loss- and risk-spreading arrangements; (3) adopting new modes of judicial management; (4) making claim values more predictable; and (5) negotiating global settlements. Together, these elements constitute an increasingly coherent legal regime that transcends the particularities of any single mass tort.

1. "Lawyerizing" Mass Tort Risks.   Many regulatory agencies established during the 1960s and 1970s were designed to mobilize technical expertise, identify significant public health risks, and then act to reduce them.[41] Such regulatory schemes were intended to render private tort lawyers ancillary, if not superfluous, to the regulators engaging in risk management.[42]

Alas, as has frequently been the case in the history of the administrative state, this promise proved to be false, or at least vastly exaggerated. Environmental, occupational, and product risks are actually identified through complex processes in which many actors, endowed with different resources, responding to different incentives, and employing different methodologies, play a role. Often, these risks are first revealed by research scientists, public health and environmental organizations, specialized science and health journals, and other private groups. These risk monitors then communicate their research findings to those who are in a position to act upon this information—mass media, industry-specific newsletters, labor unions, policymakers, and services that publish and distribute this information to lawyers.

Sometimes, plaintiffs' lawyers are alerted to litigation-worthy conditions by an accumulation of workers compensation awards, consumer complaints, public health agency reports, or media coverage.[43] This information flow triggers a "lawyerization" of risk. Defense lawyers huddle with their corporate clients to decide how to respond to this information.[44] Meanwhile, plaintiffs' lawyers assess their options: They conduct legal and factual research, contact scientific experts, estimate transaction costs, troll for potential clients, consult with colleagues about possible cost-sharing arrangements, and perhaps generate additional media attention. At some point, plaintiffs' lawyers may contact potential defendants to propose informal settlements, and if the parties cannot come to terms, mass tort litigation may ensue. The plaintiffs' lawyers' powerful "investment engines" propel the process forward toward the settlement conference and perhaps even to the courthouse.[45] Only seldom does formal regulatory agency action spawn mass tort litigation; in cases as diverse as asbestos, Dalkon Shield, DES, Agent Orange, auto safety, and tobacco, the enforcement agency took action only years later, if at all.[46]

Despite the very large volume of mass tort claims, the number of lawyers who undertake long-term commitments to represent mass tort claimants and to litigate on their behalf is relatively small. Tort litigation has become remarkably specialized.[47] The same elite group of plaintiffs' lawyers turns up on the management committees of one mass tort litigation after another. Much the same is true on the defendants' side. This "repeat player" phenomenon creates a high degree of informal coordination, continuity, and learning across different mass torts. It also causes litigators to devote much effort to building and maintaining their reputations and credibility. This further facilitates the lawyerization of mass tort risks.[48]

In sum, an intricate and increasingly efficient private system generates, processes, disseminates, coordinates, and deploys most of the risk information that lawyers need to initiate mass tort litigation. Personal, organizational, and professional incentives fuel this system—a blend of material gain, professional prestige, and ideology. Contrary to the original regulation schemes fashioned in the 1960s and 1970s, government agencies tend to play a subsidiary role in this system. They may sponsor research that aids in risk identification and may gather (or passively receive) evidence that can help personal injury lawyers (and eventually regulators) establish that a significant public health risk exists.[49] But it is the private plaintiffs' lawyers who usually do most of the heavy lifting.

2. Improved Loss- and Risk-Spreading Arrangements. Like so many other complex systems in advanced societies, mass tort litigation depends on practices and institutions that distribute risks and losses. The particular risks at issue here include the liability of those who create dangerous conditions, the losses suffered by those exposed to such conditions, and the risk of economic loss to private lawyers whose profit-driven investments make the mass tort system possible in the first place.

The current system of insurance for potential mass tort liabilities evolved out of the unprecedented, apparently unanticipated environmental liability insurance crisis that crested in the 1980s. Writing in 1988, a leading academic analyst of insurance law summarized the sources of this crisis:

> The new environmental liability tests the limits of insurance in three ways. First, it has created new forms of statutory liability against which it is difficult to insure. Second, judicial strategies of interpretation have made it difficult for insurers to rely on the meaning of insurance policy language designed to avoid covering uninsurable risks. Third, the distinct threat of other, common-law expansions of liability creating additional uninsurable risks that cannot be reliably excluded by policy language renders the scope of an insurer's future obligations uncertain.[50]

Similar developments contributed to analogous upheavals in the products liability insurance market.[51]

Widespread concern about these conditions, heightened through intensive lobbying by the affected industries, produced swift political responses. Legislators in many states enacted tort reform measures designed to increase the availability and reduce the cost of insurance against environmental and product-related mass tort liabilities.[52] Congress moved, albeit haltingly,[53] to improve the Superfund litigation morass.[54] Courts stemmed and then reversed many of the earlier judicial expansions of tort liability.[55] The insurance industry modified its liability policies and marketing practices to eliminate unprofitable lines, reduce moral hazard and uncertainty, and otherwise manage its underwriting risks more effectively.[56] It also established administrative mechanisms to negotiate and coordinate the resolution of its enormous coverage disputes both within the industry itself and with its corporate clients.[57] Nevertheless, some of these coverage disputes could only be resolved through satellite litigation which was very costly and complex in its own right.[58]

Many corporations also took steps to spread their mass tort liability risks and losses through mechanisms other than conventional liability insurance. In the asbestos litigation, for example, some defendant corporations formed consortia to share expenses, reduce transaction costs, and present a united negotiating front with the plaintiffs' lawyers.[59] More commonly, companies such as Johns-Manville Corp. (in the asbestos litigation) and A.H. Robins Co. (in the Dalkon Shield litigation) field for protection under the bankruptcy laws,[60] which allowed them to redistribute their past losses and future risks by reorganizing their capital structures and limiting their vulnerability to litigation.

These recent risk-spreading efforts have produced many of the desired results. Mass tort liability is once again an insurable risk.[61] Although new crises may well occur,[62] the liability insurance market, which is essential to the mass tort litigation and compensation systems, appears to have matured into a more sustainable form.

More efficient risk-spreading and risk-reduction mechanisms for workers and consumers exposed to mass tort risks have also been devised, although the effects of these mechanisms are more indirect and therefore more difficult to measure, than those aimed at corporate liability risks. On the deterrence side, federal and state right-to-know laws have increased the amount and quality of information available to workers and consumers who are at risk of exposure to toxic substances.[63] Environmental and public health standards, most of which have been adopted since the early 1970s, should in time reduce the incidence and severity of long-latency harm such as asbestos-related disease and of traumatic harm such as auto-related injury.[64] Finally Medicaid, Medicare, and disability programs have expanded rapidly during the past decade, effecting a substantial redistribution of health care costs which constitute a major component of mass tort damages.[65]

Plaintiffs' lawyers have also improved their risk-bearing capacity, and hence their ability to act as both the gatekeepers to and the entrepreneurs of mass tort litigation.[66] In recent years, the plaintiffs' mass torts bar has grown far more sophisticated, specialized, and efficient. For example, some lawyers now concentrate on particular kinds of torts, others on particular sites of bodily injury, and still others on particular types of plaintiffs and defendants. The plaintiffs' lawyers have established clearinghouses that help coordinate the exchange of legal briefs, depositions, information on expert witnesses, and other types of costly litigation resources—cooperation that partly reflects the interdependence of mass tort claims values noted earlier.[67] The Trial Lawyers Association of America now distributes a flood of professional development materials and services. Imaginative plaintiffs' lawyers have devised new techniques for running their practices, obtaining and communicating with clients, influencing the media, administering cases, conducting discovery, managing documents, selecting juries, and financing their often protracted litigation. As a result, they have achieved a level of parity with their corporate opponents that was unimaginable as recently as twenty years ago.[68]

3. Adopting New Modes of Judicial Management.   The movement of courts toward managerial judging,[69] spurred by mass tort litigation, has entailed some of the most far-reaching innovations in judicial history.[70] These innovations include novel claims aggregation techniques, statistically-derived outcomes,[71] administration of discovery, damages assessments,[72] advanced courtroom technologies,[73] more systematic alternative dispute resolution efforts,[74] and coordinated federal-state court proceedings.[75] Like the plaintiffs' and defendants' lawyers, a relatively small number of judges (and their special masters) have become repeat players, adept at routinizing the extraordinary.[76] These judges have even established professional organizations and informal consultations that actively facilitate learning and coordination in mass tort cases.

These innovations have already generated an immense body of commentary, both descriptive and prescriptive.[77] Judicial inventiveness in adapting and reshaping the procedural and substantive law of mass torts has led many scholars and some judges to question the legal and ethical propriety of these changes, as well as their practical consequences.[78] Much of this commentary centers on the use of class actions in mass tort litigation, an approach that has increasingly met with judicial approval despite the contrary views of the original Rule 23 draftsmen and the skepticism of many contemporary observers.[79] Signs of judicial, scholarly, and professional acceptance of the use of class actions in mass tort litigation can also be seen in the current proposals to revise Rule 23 which, by setting forth explicit authority to certify mass tort class actions, are likely to make it easier for judges to do so.[80]

However one evaluates these changes, the important point for present purposes is that they constitute a firm, self-conscious judicial commitment to the project of systematizing and refining mass tort litigation into a distinctive genre with its own rules and practices, a project that legislatures have not disturbed.[81]

4. Making Claim Values More Predictable.   The importance of accurate valuation of mass tort claims cannot be overestimated; without it, the system would quickly break down under the pressure of unresolved claims. The number of individual claims currently pending and reasonably anticipated in the future is in some mass tort litigations so large that it is simply not practicable to provide individual trials in the traditional fashion.[82] Even if it were practicable to try all disputes, it would be neither desirable nor necessary.[83] As is well known, the cost and risks of going to trial induces settlement or other dispositions short of trial in over ninety-five percent of all civil claims, mass tort or otherwise.[84] The certification of mass tort class actions, moreover, practically ensures that the litigation will be settled short of trial.[85] Yet negotiated settlements are possible only if the parties' separate estimates of a claim's expected value (net of transaction costs) converge. This convergence, in turn, will occur only if the parties can accurately predict case values.[86]

The mass tort system increasingly generates predictable claim values for particular torts. As noted earlier, this more mature tort system is facilitated by the development of new valuation techniques.[87] Of course, even without any special mechanisms for facilitating the convergence of claims valuations, the maturing of particular mass torts would advance the maturation of other mass torts, and of the system as a whole. Individual cases proceeding through trial, verdict, and appeal in a variety of jurisdictions gradually reveal the behavior of juries and judges, clarify the applicable rules of law, and render the expected value of individual claims more predictable. More accurate information about claim values in turn encourages pre-trial settlements, which further refines and improves the quality of that information, which facilitates still more settlements, and so on. In this way, the litigator acquires an increasingly solid empirical foundation for his estimates of claim values.

But lawyers, courts, and scholars have also developed techniques for predicting claim values that are more sophisticated and systematic then the trial-and-error model outlined above. Some of these techniques are retrospective; they predict future claim values on the basis of a careful review of outcomes in past cases. One such approach employs regression analysis of claim profiles and other statistical methods to model the precise relationship that various claim characteristics bear to claim values in recent litigation and settlements. This approach enables lawyers to estimate more accurately the expected value of pending and future claims.[88] The claims-processing facilities established by mass tort defendants and insurers (as in the asbestos and silicone gel breast implants litigation) and by courts administering settlement funds (as in the Agent Orange and Dalkon Shield litigation) employ some variants of this approach.[89]

Prospective methods have also been developed. Courts sometimes stage non-binding "mini-trials," relying on the hypothetical verdict to induce settlements short of a full trial.[90] Other courts identify "representative" plaintiffs, who are thought to typify larger claimant populations. The claims of these representatives then proceed to full trials, and the outcomes establish patterns that can encourage settlements or (if settlement fails) damages assessments with respect to the claims of the remaining claimants.[91] Another prospective method is statistical or sampling adjudication.[92] Here, the court aggregates a large population of cases, selects a random sample, adjudicates each sample case, and then statistically combines the sample outcomes to yield results for all cases in the population. In contrast to the "representative plaintiff" approach, in which each claimant retains the right to go to trial on his individual claim, the sampling approach requires each claimant in the larger population to accept an average award rather than one that is tailored to the circumstances of his individual claim.[93]

Furthermore, experience gained and techniques developed in the context of a particular mass tort can be used by practitioners specializing in other mass torts, or applied to new species of mass tort as they arise. Information about the value of a Dalkon Shield claim may not be fully transferrable to, say, a breast implant claim, but the information may nevertheless have some utility to breast implant litigators in their efforts to narrow their zones of uncertainty.

5. Negotiating Global Settlements. "Global" settlements of mass tort claims represent the culmination of the system's maturation. Only at the high levels of aggregation, coordination, risk distribution, and legal and factual determinacy, which typify a highly mature system, can global settlements of the kind that have recently been fashioned in mass tort cases become practicable. Even then, global settlements are intricate and extremely difficult to negotiate,[94] and those settlements that are reached are not truly global.[95]

The elusiveness and incompleteness of these settlements, however, should not obscure an extremely important fact: A much higher percentage of tort victims file claims and receive some payment under these mass tort settlements than would sue and recover in tort.[96] The vice of this virtue, however—and it is a great vice indeed—is that mass tort actions attract, and mass tort settlements encourage and pay, a large number of claims that are insubstantial—or, in the words of one experienced plaintiffs' lawyer, "junk."[97] Moreover, these junk claimants may obtain substantial recoveries under the global settlements.[98] Still, the relatively high percentage of *genuine* victims who will recover something under global settlements must be counted as a weighty advantage.

Global settlements can also resolve a variety of complex administrative and policy issues. These agreements establish detailed ground rules to govern the necessary long-term relationship between bitter adversaries, under changing and unpredictable conditions. These rules cover such diverse issues as exposure criteria, medical criteria, claims administration, atypical or extraordinary claims, all aspects of compensation, funding guarantees, opt-outs, case flows, notice, counsel fees, administrative cost, informal dispute resolution, limits on judicial review, and termination of the agreement. In the absence of global settlements, these thorny issues would have to be resolved by further litigation and by courts lacking good information and relevant expertise.

Global settlements provide strong evidence that contemporary mass tort litigation has evolved into a far more coherent and efficient system than its predecessors. All global settlements tend to follow the same general pattern. Imitation being the sincerest form of flattery, this suggests that mass tort litigation has engendered a relatively successful mechanism of dispute resolution. Experiences of litigators, courts, and claims facilities in negotiating and administering global settlements are being accumulated and integrated into patterned, recurrent, and increasingly predictable forms. As a result, new settlements are likely to employ variations on now-familiar themes.[99]

Precisely for this reason, the question of whether these global settlements are fair and reasonable within the meaning of Rule 23(e) assumes crucial importance. In its present form, the Rule supplies judges with no explicit evaluative criteria for making this determination.[100] Courts that have considered this issue focus on the specific terms of the settlement, comparing the treatment of claimants under the settlement against the likely disposition of their claims at trial. In almost all cases, the courts have found the settlements unambiguously fair.[101] These judicial affirmations, however, have not satisfied all doubters; the skeptics tend to focus on the specific terms of particular settlements, the potential for collusion between class counsel and defendants, and the risk of unwarranted preclusion of future claims.[102]

In this Article, I do not assess the fairness of any particular settlement; that task falls to those who have reviewed in detail all of the relevant evidence bearing on this issue. Instead, I suggest two structural criteria that can help frame and inform any fairness analysis: (1) the maturity of the tort, and (2) the conditions of claimant choice among the competing compensation systems—

the tort system and settlement—particularly the quality of information about claim values.

C. Assessing the Fairness of Global Settlements in Mass Tort Actions

1. Maturity of Claims.   The fairness of a mass tort settlement is much easier to assess when a large volume and wide variety of claims have been litigated, adjudicated, and settled by numerous lawyers, judges, and juries. In contrast to an embryonic tort, a mature tort has generated a supply of data which, applying the methods described above, can be used to produce unbiased estimates of claim values. The judge in a mass tort action can use these estimates to compare the value that a claim would have if litigated through the tort system to its prospective value under the settlement (applying appropriate discounts to reflect differences in speed and certainty of recovery, the amount of legal fees, the level of other transaction costs, and so forth). Furthermore, this data assists the judge to make the irreducibly subjective judgments about how to balance the values that each of the competing systems embodies and that a fairness determination requires. Other things being equal, the more mature the tort, the more confident the judge can be that all of the prerequisites for class certification under Rule 23 have been met, that the negotiations were conducted at arm's length and free of actual or potential conflicts of interest, and that the actual settlement terms negotiated by the lawyers are fair.

2. Claimants' Choice Between the Tort System and the Settlement.   In some cases, mass tort claims may be maintained as a class action only if the court certifies a mandatory class.[103] Ordinarily, however, fairness will require that claimants be permitted to protect their individual interests by making a meaningful choice either to remain in the class or to opt out and proceed individually in the tort system. Indeed, all recent global settlements have provided claimants with at least *two* opt-out opportunities. For example, the *Georgine* settlement that resolves future asbestos-related claims first permits a claimant to opt out after the class notice is published, and then (under certain conditions) renews the opportunity after the claims facility has made a specific settlement offer.[104] The silicone gel breast implant settlement, which provides a more determinate schedule of awards at the outset, also provides multiple opt-out opportunities.[105] Current claimants may opt out either at the front end, or subsequently in the event that the settlement fund becomes inadequate to cover all claims (a "ratchet-down" opt-out). Ongoing and future claimants may likewise opt out if and when their benefits are ratcheted down.[106] Defendants in these settlements also insist on multiple opt-out rights, which usually depend on the number of claimants who decide to opt out.[107]

The addition of intermediate and back-end opt-out opportunities constitutes a highly desirable and important innovation for the emergent mass tort system despite the increased uncertainty that these opportunities create in the short term. Indeed, the fairness of a settlement under Rule 23(e) may *require* that such opportunities be extended to claimants. First, they institutionalize and enlarge the central value of claimant autonomy. Second, they permit a dynamic and superior balance to be struck between the competing interests in aggregating and individualizing claims. Each claimant can then choose, from among the alternatives the settlement makes available, the particular mix of collective and individual claiming that best serves her wishes. Third, opt-out provisions furnish a kind of market test of a settlement's fairness and adequacy, particularly of the specific compensation offers that will be made under settlement.[108]

Suppose that a large number of claimants, counseled by their lawyers, conclude that the settlement offers they have received are too low relative to the tort system baseline and therefore decide to opt out.[109] Assuming that these claimants were well-informed, their decisions would constitute the best available (but not necessarily the only) evidence of the settlement's overall inadequacy relative to that base-line. By the same token, of course, if relatively few claimants decided to opt out, their decisions would constitute equally strong evidence of the settlement's overall fairness and adequacy relative to the baseline. The number of opt-outs needed to discredit the fairness of a settlement presents a genuinely difficult question.[110] Moreover, adverse selection within the opt-out process may also occur; claimants with the strongest claims may elect to opt out while those with weaker claims may decide to remain in the class and get paid under the settlement.[111] This may cause the settlement to unravel as defendants find themselves increasingly disadvantaged by it and thus decide to opt out themselves, as they may have reserved a right to do under the settlement agreement. Fortunately, however, the system need not concern itself overmuch with these uncertainties. Assuming that the notice and information were adequate, the parties, counseled by their lawyers, can resolve these issues for themselves.[112]

Because opt-out provisions contribute to fairness and meaningful choice only if claimants are sufficiently well-informed at the time they must decide whether or not to join the class, front-end opt-out provisions, standing alone, may not be enough to warrant a judicial determination that a settlement is fair. Rather, the sufficiency of a front-end opt-out should depend in large part on the maturity or immaturity of the mass tort in question. In all opt-out class actions, Rule 23 requires that claimants receive at the front end adequate notice of the implications of joining the class or not. In cases in which the tort is immature, however, little discovery, adjudication, and settlement of similar claims will have occurred; consequently, little useful information about claim values and other factors, such as the quality of class counsel and potential conflicts within the class, may be available to claimants at the front end. Indeed, the claimant in this situation is trapped in a kind of Catch–22: In order to inform his decision about whether or not to remain in the class, he must remain in the class and see how the information that will subsequently be produced in discovery appears to affect the value of his claim. Should discovery reveal that the claimant's best strategy would have been to proceed alone, however, it will be too late for him to do so if the only opportunity to opt out came at the front end.[113]

The informational void can be even more prejudicial to uninformed claimants in three increasingly common situations. First, an immature tort may produce a "settlement class action," in which the action is simultaneously filed and settled. (This is to be distinguished from a settlement in a conventional class action.) Here, the claimants' information about claim values may be inadequate even at the back end (which Rule 23 does not expressly address), for there will be little or no tort system experience against which claimants can compare their specific settlement offers.

Second, the class may contain future claimants who have been exposed but are not yet injured (as with many asbestos claimants) or have not yet been exposed but may be exposed in the future (as with recipients of heart valves and breast implants that have not yet malfunctioned). Here, claimants may not even know that they have a claim, let alone its value, until after a settlement is concluded. As many commentators have noted, future claims class actions raise many vexing problems of effective notice, adequate representation, litigation management, actual or potential conflicts of interest, legal ethics, and claims administration.[114] I discuss future claims further in Part III.

Third, the information about the number of present and future claims, the value of those claims, and the rate at which they will be filed may be so limited that even those settlements that are reached and approved by the court may ultimately unravel, as may turn out to be the case with the breast implant litigation.[115] This situation may well leave claimants worse off, as a great deal of time will have elapsed without progress toward the resolution of their claims.

A very different situation arises, however, when a mature tort leads to a settlement. The asbestos litigation that culminated in *Georgine* is perhaps the best example. Here, a properly advised asbestos claimant can draw on a twenty-five-year history of jury awards and settlements in a wide variety of litigation contexts before deciding at the front end whether or not to remain in the class and, if so, whether to accept a particular settlement offer at the back end. Moreover, as noted above, the judge will be able to draw on this experience in determining whether to certify a class and whether to approve a settlement under Rule 23.[116]

Accordingly, judges confronted with a Rule 23 fairness determination should require that the settlement contain a back-end opt-out right whenever claimants cannot reasonably predict at the front end[117] the specific settlement offers that they will eventually receive at the back end. This condition will usually exist in a settlement or a settlement class action involving an immature tort and will arise in *any* future claims class action, whether brought before or at the time of settlement.

Assessing the fairness of the particular conditions that a settlement may place on the claimant's exercise of a back-end opt-out right presents further difficulties.[118] From the claimants' perspective, some conditions may clearly be objectionable. Certain conditions may prevent some claimants from exercising the back-end opt-out right immediately or perhaps at all; other claimants may find their rights truncated under the settlement if they choose to return to the tort system. The *Georgine* settlement, for example, places an annual cap on the number of claimants with qualifying asbestos-related medical claims who can return to the tort system or elect binding arbitration, and it bars those who decide to proceed in the tort system from seeking either punitive damages or damages for mere exposure without impairment.[119] In addition, claimants may not know whether these conditions will actually affect them until well after the settlement is in effect, when it will be too late to object. Yet, a settlement may be unattainable unless defendants can impose such conditions on back-end opt outs and can also reserve their *own* opt-out right under certain circumstances. Defendants' need for certainty about their future obligations and cash flows may impel them to reject any settlement that fails to protect these interests.

It is doubtful that courts can deduce general principles to guide them in reviewing the fairness of the conditions placed on back-end opt-out rights. The probable consequences, and hence the fairness of each condition, are likely to be tailored to each settlement—and as always, both God and the Devil are in the details. The settlement terms may subject defendants, and not just claimants, to disadvantages if a claimant decides to return to the tort system. Under the *Georgine* settlement, for example, defendants may not raise noncausal defenses in such a case.[120] These back-end opt-out provisions will embody a variety of tradeoffs, the consequences and fairness of which must be weighed and balanced.

My emphasis here in opt-out rights as indicia of a settlement's fairness should not obscure the larger context in which fairness must be assessed. An opt-out right, of course, is only one element of a complex settlement in which numerous other elements also implicate fairness concerns. It is the settlement as a whole that must be fair, not any particular provision. Finally, the judge must also consider the risk that an entire settlement otherwise conforming to the Rule 23 fairness standard might collapse if she rejects a carefully negotiated opt-out provision—perhaps throwing the parties back into the tort system from which they hoped, perhaps with good reason, to escape.

II. Common-Law Process

The changes to the mass tort system described in the preceding Part were fashioned largely through a process of common-law decisionmaking.[121] Common-law adjudication is a distinctive lawmaking process, with powerful normative claims grounded in the common law's faithful reification of certain ideals, forms, and symbols cherished by American legal-political culture. In this Part, I argue that understanding the common-law character of the mass tort system's development is at least as important to evaluating its performance as is understanding the system's procedural and substantive content.[122]

Before exploring the consequences of the common-law development of mass tort litigation, three categories of *statutory* intervention into the mass torts area should be mentioned. First, Congress and some state legislatures have enacted occupational and environmental regulation measures, right-to-know statutes, special statutes of limitations, and other laws designed to prevent mass toxic harms and facilitate victims' recoveries. Second, Congress has established administrative compensation programs directed at certain mass toxic injuries, most notably the black lung benefits program.[123] The cost and performance of the black lung program, however, have received harsh and sustained criticism from many quarters. Indeed, for critics of the mass tort system who advocate federal compensation statutes as a solution, the black lung program's record has become the ultimate conversation-stopper.[124] Third, as we have already seen, many states adopted "tort reform" statutes in the 1980s,[125] and although most were targeted primarily at medical malpractice litigation, some of the statutes inevitably affected mass tort cases as well.[126] Still, no jurisdiction has even come close to establishing a comprehensive statutory regime to govern the litigation or compensation of mass tort claims.

Like the discovery by the Molière character that he had been speaking prose all his life, the fact that virtually all mass tort law is judge-made seems embarrassingly obvious—once attention is called to it. Even so, it is a striking fact, one that cries out for explanation. The public and private interests involved in mass tort litigation are enormous. Moreover, almost all commentators view the current litigation approach as a costly, tragic, social policy failure. Why, then, have politicians allowed judges to fashion this high visibility, high stakes legal regime without any meaningful political direction, let alone a comprehensive statutory or regulatory framework?[127] To put the question another way: If in 1969 (the very year that Congress enacted the black lung program) we had foreseen the development of a mass torts crisis that defied resolution by even the most imaginative and resourceful courts, would we have also predicted that no comprehensive remedial legislation would have even been considered during the next twenty-five years?

A. Possible Causes of Legislative Inaction

In seeking to account for this legislative inaction, we can quickly dispose of two relatively straightforward explanations. The first possible explanation is that cautious politicians simply refuse to confront so controversial an issue as mass torts policy, involving as it does powerful political interests, enormous sums of money, serious human suffering, conflicting values, and so forth, especially after the black lung program fiasco.[128] But this ignores the fact that, like it or not, politicians simply cannot avoid addressing controversial issues indefinitely: Given sufficient public outcry, they *must* respond one way or another. Mass tort law, moreover, evokes far less controversy and political division than such explosive issues as abortion, taxation, affirmative action, gun control, and health care reform—issues on which legislators routinely must take public positions, even at their political peril. Finally, this argument fails to recognize the *eagerness* with which many politicians position themselves on some of the most controversial issues, including those just mentioned and indeed on tort reform itself. A second explanation—that legislative inaction bespeaks satisfaction with the mass tort system—seems clearly false. Virtually all politicians (and judges) who comment on the mass torts system perceive a crisis and assert that there are better ways to handle mass tort claims; these critics typically suggest that an administrative compensation scheme would be better.[129]

Public choice theory suggests a somewhat more plausible explanation.[130] Perhaps legislators cannot, or do not wish to, assemble a successful coalition in favor of any statutory change. Several factors might support legislative inaction. First, expanding mass tort liability may be highly advantageous to a forum state's citizens (and politicians and judges) in that the plaintiffs tend to be state residents while the defendants tend to be foreign corporations; hence, the benefits of broad liability will inure to the forum state while the costs will largely be borne by out-of-staters.[131] Second, powerful interest groups may prefer the *status quo*. This would be true, for example, if the beneficiaries of the current system were highly organized, with few conflicting interests and large per capita stakes in the outcome.[132] These conditions might, in fact, seem to hold, because plaintiffs' natural allies—the plaintiffs' bar, some "public interest" groups, and many labor unions[133]—which ardently oppose any systemic change in mass tort law,[134] are highly effective lobbyists and shapers of public opinion. Potential mass tort claimants, on the other hand, are difficult to organize politically because they may be unaware that they have been exposed or that they may have valuable tort claims now or in the future. Even claimants with existing claims will experience such difficulties because they constitute a large and diverse group. Their conflicting interests (they differ, for example, in the nature of their exposures, in the strength of their claims, and the quality of their lawyers), and their incentives to free ride on others' organizational efforts would also impede their ability to form a broad reform coalition.[135]

It is true, of course, that mass tort defendants and their insurers strongly advocate some changes. Indeed, they have succeeded in securing state-level tort reform legislation reducing their liability risks,[136] and although they have failed for almost two decades to win broad protection at the federal level, they might finally succeed.[137] Not all mass tort defendants, however, support the same changes. Some, like the powerful tobacco industry, have found the common-law status quo quite congenial.[138]

A convincing public choice analysis would, of course, require a more refined distinction among and consideration of particular group interests.[139] Moreover, such an analysis would also have to consider the role of groups such as judges[140] and investors and the political force of ideology as well as that of economic interests.[141] But enough has already been said to suggest that public choice analysis is complex and points in a number of different directions; it yields no unambiguous explanation of why politicians have allowed the judiciary to initiate, develop, and refine its own mass torts jurisprudence despite widespread public and professional condemnation of the results.

Finally, a legal process or "public interest" explanation is also worth considering.[142] Perhaps legislators have left mass tort lawmaking to the courts because they believe that, all things considered, the courts can do it better. Although many politicians perceive a mass tort "crisis," they might nevertheless conclude that the scientific, legal, economic, political, and social conditions relevant to mass injuries are too complex and fluid to permit an adequate legislative response—a conclusion that the experience with the federal black lung program might well support.[143] In this view, legislators might leave resolution of systemic problems to the courts, the plaintiffs' bar, and corporate defendants, with the expectation that these powerful, well-informed, roughly balanced interests will develop workable solutions on their own as needed—always subject, of course, to the possibility of legislative fine-tuning. As we shall see in the next subpart there are often good reasons for legislators to pursue this strategy—at least to a point—in the area of mass torts.

B. The Pros and Cons of Common Law Policy-Making

Whatever the reasons for legislative inaction during the first twenty-five years of mass tort litigation, the system remains almost entirely a regime governed by common law, developing and implementing policy in the common law's distinctive modalities.[144] Common-law policymaking, however, can be problematic for several reasons.[145]

1. Technocratic and Instrumental Considerations.

First, if political accountability for policymaking is desirable, adjudication may represent a poor vehicle for accomplishing it. The judiciary, which dominates the process, is relatively insulated from the kind of refined public opinion to which legislators and agency policymakers are subject. Moreover, the narrow focus of adjudication tends to diminish the likelihood of political mobilization in response to imprudent or unjust policy decisions. The character and outcome of adjudication is also influenced to a considerable extent by lawyers, who are institutionally and ethically responsible to their clients, not to the general public.

Second, adjudication constitutes a radically decentralized, poorly informed decisionmaking process, which reduces the policy coherence and general applicability of judge-made law. Because tort adjudication tends to be very fact-specific, stare decisis and appellate review are particularly weak coordinating mechanisms in the tort context.[146] Furthermore, rules of evidence limit the kind of policy-relevant information to which judges have access. Adjudication also has a selection bias against the most typical, generalizable behavioral patterns with which policymakers should be primarily concerned.

Third, the institutional competence of the judiciary limits the range of issues that it can address effectively. Common-law judges are generalists, seeing relatively few cases dealing with any given subject and having little control over their issue agendas. In seeking to influence behavior and implement their decisions, common-law judges in mass tort cases can use only the most limited tools: formal rules and money damages. Other deeply embedded common-law tort structures militate against sound, systematic policymaking. These include a vestigial moralism that over a century of functional critiques have failed to displace entirely a glacial accumulation of precedents, a weak and attenuated feedback loop, and a retrospective view transfixed (and perhaps distorted) by the plaintiff's palpable human suffering.[147] This is especially true in the mass torts context, in which the court must confront many complex public policy issues.

But if common-law policymaking is problematic in several important respects, it also exhibits some characteristic strengths, which are often the flipside of its defects. The same geographical, institutional, and analytical decentralization that hobbles systematic policymaking in tort adjudication also stimulates *innovation*, especially in mass tort cases:[148] Unbound by bad precedent in one jurisdiction, mass tort judges and lawyers in other jurisdictions are free to eschew past errors and undertake novel approaches to knotty problems. The small and elite cadre of mass tort lawyers, animated by a contingency fee system unavailable in the legal system of any other nation,[149] has particularly strong incentives to respond quickly, resourcefully, and effectively to any inefficiencies or inequalities resulting from misguided innovations, and to propose remedial changes. These incentives of the bench and bar have driven the evolution of mass tort law, producing many striking instances of both procedural and substantive innovations: market share and proportional liability, various forms of statistical adjudication, medical monitoring damages, personal injury and settlement class actions, compensation schedules, joint federal-state court proceedings, novel uses of adjunct court personnel, and a variety of organizational techniques. Centralized, statutory systems probably would not—and in civil law countries have not[150]—adopted such innovations as quickly, or in some cases at all. The common-law system, however, facilitated not only their creation but also the refinements and new applications that followed.[151] Of course, incremental changes—both good and bad—cumulate almost imperceptibly over time into what amounts to a qualitatively different system. When this occurs, legislative deliberation and negotiation—generally more comprehensive and responsive policymaking processes than common-law adjudication—may reveal systemic problems that adjudication has failed to resolve wisely and that therefore need to be addressed in non-adjudicatory ways.[152]

My point, then, is certainly not to deny a role for legislative regulation or refinement of legal regimes in general or of mass torts law in particular. It is simply to note that the common law of mass torts is likely to be, as a practical matter, more flexible[153] and responsive to contextualized litigation experience than is a statutory solution, which legislatures will revisit only occasionally, often reluctantly, and usually incrementally.[154] This common-law advantage may be especially great during the *maturation* period of mass tort litigation which, as we have seen with the asbestos litigation, may be quite protracted. At least in this area, judicial policy errors are likely to be more confined than legislative ones; more fact-specific and less systemic, judicial errors are usually less firmly entrenched and hence easier for appellate courts and legislatures to correct than legislative policy errors. Furthermore, the political inertia that usually follows a legislative resolution of controversial issues tends not to afflict courts so acutely. Thus even if courts were to err more frequently than legislatures on mass torts issues, the courts' errors might nevertheless be less persistent and less costly to society.

2. Normative and Symbolic Considerations.   The relative advantages of developing a mass tort system through common law courts, subject to periodic legislative review, transcend these technocratic and instrumental considerations. These advantages also extend to the normative and symbolic realms where reifying deeply felt, widely shared norms is of paramount importance. In such realms, the common law's *ethos* matters as much as its actual performance—even when, as is sometimes the case, its ineffectiveness over-shadows that ethos. In the mass torts context, two related aspects of this common-law ethos are particularly salient: (1) commitment to the adversary system and in particular to trial by lay jury, and (2) reliance on a nonbureaucratic mode of legitimating political authority.

a) The Adversary System and the Jury   The canonical elements of the common law model of adversary trial—litigant-controlled proofs and proceedings, neutral and detached judging, and lay jury fact-finding—carry enormous normative force in the American legal-political culture.[155] This observation would appear to apply a fortiori to mass torts litigation. Unlike victims of highway collisions or other determinate harms, mass torts claimants often can only guess at the source of their injury—an invisible chemical, a defective product, something insidious in their food, water or neighborhood, the victim's genome, or mother nature herself. Victims, finding themselves in such a profoundly perplexing and dispiriting position, often desire a knight in shining armor who will come to their aid and ride boldly into battle on their behalf against the anonymous wrongdoers. In an increasingly bureaucratized, often incomprehensible system of justice, the plaintiffs' lawyer seems to play this idealized role, providing a "day in court" before a jury of one's peers.

The lay jury, too, captures the American public's imagination in a way that can scarcely be exaggerated.[156] The groups with the greatest stakes in mass tort litigation—trial lawyers, judges, and litigants—tend to venerate the jury.[157]

Indeed, the jury's popularity continues despite a century of sustained criticism by academics and judges and despite (or perhaps because of) a broad secular trend, extending well beyond mass tort law, toward consolidating and collectivizing claims that were traditionally viewed as individual.[158] The political tide propelling tort reform in virtually every state in the 1980s chipped away at the edges of jury discretion, but left the jury's essential structure and functions largely intact.[159] Two quite recent events—the failed effort to amend the Federal Employer's Liability Act of 1908[160] to substitute a workers' compensation scheme for the long-standing jury-based tort system, and the extension of jury trials to claims alleging sex and disability discrimination in the Civil Rights Act of 1991[161]—demonstrate that public attitudes, far from supporting reforms that would restrict juries, strongly favor *preserving and expanding* the scope of their authority.[162] "Jury reformers are so many voices crying in the political wilderness."[163] In short, any appraisal of a litigation system in the United States must respect the central role that the jury has been assigned and will continue to play in the dominant public conception of justice.

The realities of mass torts litigation, of course, sharply contradict these luminous lay conceptions of legal representation and the day in court. The plaintiffs' lawyer, for example, may represent thousands of other clients whom she regards as more or less fungible, and with whom she communicates only intermittently, impersonally, and unidirectionally. Indeed her own interests may *directly conflict* with theirs, for reasons including: her powerful financial incentives to settle early, the zero-sum competition between the amount of her fee and the funds available for compensation of clients, and her possible control over the compensation fund in the event of a settlement.[164] In all probability, the client's day in court will amount to a written notice of settlement or dismissal; he may never see an Article III judge, much less a jury of his peers;[165] and if there is a hearing he will probably not be permitted to speak. But whatever the distance between ideal and reality, the former retains overwhelming symbolic power. Indeed, the larger the gap, the more enchanting the ideal.

b) Non-Bureaucratic Authority   A commonplace of American legal-political culture is the fear of concentrations of governmental power, especially in its conventional administrative forms.[166] For reasons that are hard to fathom, we regard it as almost unthinkable, perhaps even unconstitutional,[167] that an administrative official might make decisions not reviewable by an Article III judge. Yet, we view as authoritative and legitimate the decisions of a single judge or panel of judges—even when those decisions are essentially unreviewable and hence final.[168] These public attitudes persist, indeed flourish, in the face of two facts which should undermine them: First, the popular, idealized image of judicial process is seldom if ever realized, especially in mass tort litigation. Second, well-managed administrative agencies can and sometimes do achieve impressive levels of accuracy, efficiency, procedural fairness, and political accountability.[169] For present purposes, however, the important point is that Americans are profoundly, and perhaps incorrigibly, antibureaucratic.

The common law's distinctive appeal, then, rests in large part on its role as a nonbureaucratic process for legitimating the exercise of public authority.[170] Moreover, the common law's antiquity, as well as the trappings of the civil courtroom, convey a solemnity, grandeur, and mystery that elicit lay deference and respect, even awe. Paradoxically, although the common law's gradual accretion of precedent imparts to it an opacity that helps to insulate it from lay criticism, lay persons seem to consider judicial rulings to be more transparent, accessible, and acceptable than the fiat of a faceless bureaucracy (to use the common cliche). These features give the common law normative and symbolic advantages over statutory and administrative law.[171]

Sometimes, however, circumstances can overwhelm the common law's advantages in the mass torts area and create openings for administrative solutions.[172] In any event, although the differences between courts and agencies are steadily narrowing,[173] the differences continue to operate at the crucial cognitive, symbolic, and affective levels of lay perception. These perceptions make the emergence of a mass tort system grounded largely in common-law institutions and practices appear less irrational than many commentators (myself included) have previously believed. Indeed, these lay preferences appear even more defensible when one considers the leading *alternative* strategies for achieving mass justice in this context.

III. Selection

Although the mass tort system often seems chaotic and continues to exhibit some decidedly worrisome features, it has actually evolved into a more or less patterned system.[174] This is not a random or adventitious result; rather, the emergent system reflects a selection from among three competing models of legal process and legitimation—common-law, contractual, and bureaucratic. A combination of economic, ideological, institutional, and political pressures and inertias have driven this competitive selection dynamic, resulting in an eclectic, hybrid system dominated by common-law policymaking with some relatively narrow statutory refinements.[175]

Up to this point, my discussion of the new mass tort system has been largely descriptive. In this final Part, I briefly compare this system to three leading reform alternatives.[176] As noted in the Introduction, this comparison is merely suggestive. A rigorous, systematic comparison would require a far more detailed specification of goals, empirical data, and additional analysis. Such an analysis would go well beyond the scope of this Article, which seeks to provoke institutional comparison rather than to proselytize on behalf of any particular solution.[177]

My tentative claim, drawing on the institutional evolutionist perspective, is that despite the mass tort system's many problems,[178] it compares rather favorably to competing models. Specifically, the system already incorporates the most valuable elements of common-law reform proposals ("collective processing"); is perfectly consistent with the contractual approach (a market in tort claims); and is likely to be superior in many respects to the bureaucratic approach (administrative compensation).

A. Collective Processing

Professor David Rosenberg has proposed what he calls a "public law" model of mass tort litigation that would involve a number of innovative procedural techniques and doctrinal changes.[179] Rosenberg's proposals are animated by the same policy goals that have driven the evolution of the mass torts litigation system—to improve horizontal equity and the timeliness of compensation, to reduce transaction costs, to shift some of the burden of causal uncertainty from claimants to defendants, and to increase deterrence of risky behavior.

I will not indulge in a belabored treatment of Rosenberg's model, parts of which I have criticized elsewhere.[180] For present purposes the most striking feature of his model is the extent to which common-law courts have already incorporated its main elements—class actions, proportional liability, damage scheduling, averaged judgments, insurance-fund judgments, fee- and cost-shifting arrangements—into the current mass tort system.[181] Mass tort class actions (especially for settlement purposes) have become more common as courts attempt to protect claimants by assuring adequate notice, by minimizing potential conflicts of interest both within classes and between claimant and lawyers,[182] and by controlling counsel fees.[183] Market share liability, which many courts have adopted, is a form of proportional liability.[184] Forms of damage scheduling and averaged judgments have been widely used, most notably in the Agent Orange, asbestos, and breast implant settlements.[185] The global settlements in *Georgine*[186] and the silicone gel breast implant litigation[187] include damage schedules which are, in effect, insurance-fund judgments for future claims. In these settlements, fee- and cost-shifting have been achieved indirectly and incompletely through court control and reduction of class action costs and contingency fee awards, as well as through agreements by defendants to bear the costs of claims processing and plaintiffs' counsel fees.

B. A Market in Tort Claims

Some scholars have urged the relaxation of traditional legal restrictions on the purchase and sale of tort claims in order to encourage the emergence of a reasonably thick market for tort claims.[188] These proposals seek to exploit the perceived efficiency and transaction cost advantages markets offer as compared to tort law. They also envision some regulation of the proposed market to reduce possible informational asymmetries between the buyers and sellers of mass tort claims.

As to individual claims, one would expect primary markets to develop in which claimants would make initial offerings of their claims in exchange for cash, and secondary markets in which these purchased claims would then be aggregated and sold to others. In such markets, one would expect private sellers of claim valuation services to emerge and compete for claimants' business. One would also expect to see claimants being paid an amount closer to the true, time-discounted litigation value of their claims[189] and receiving that payment more quickly than under the existing system. Plaintiffs' lawyers, defendants, and insurers would be the most likely traders in secondary markets, since they would be in the best position to estimate claim values accurately, to efficiently trade in and settle claims, and to litigate them if necessary.

In the case of a class action, where Rule 23 requires the court to find that the class representatives (which in practice means their *lawyers*) will fairly and adequately represent the class, and where the court in practice determines which plaintiffs' lawyers will control the management of the litigation, the court could convene and administer a second kind of market, auctioning the right to represent the class. The court would not necessarily confer class counsel status on the highest bidder (i.e., the attorney willing to accept the lowest fee), but would take the amounts and terms of the bids into account in making her decision.[190] This approach would have many advantages. In one stroke, it would improve the information available to the court when making its Rule 23 determination of adequate representation for the class, maximize class members' net recoveries, and eliminate what is perhaps the greatest barrier to settlement of class actions—attorneys fee disputes.[191]

New markets in tort claims and in class counsel status, then, would make compensation of claimants fairer and more efficient. By doing so, moreover, they would also tend to optimize deterrence. This general approach would be especially desirable in the mass torts context where there generally are higher agency and transaction costs, higher stakes, more numerous and individualized claims, and more uncertain claim values than in consumer and securities class actions.

Granted, the prospect of markets in tort claims and class representation rights raise some genuine concerns. These include the danger that well-informed traders would take advantage of poorly informed claimants, and that judges would be unable to evaluate class representation claims on the basis of bids in an auction. But then again, the current mass tort system suffers at least as much from these problems as would a market system. I noted earlier that the relationships between mass torts lawyers and their clients, relationships that are attenuated, bureaucratized, commercialized, and conflict-ridden,[192] already present formidable agency problems. Significant informational asymmetries about claim values thus exist now between claimants and their lawyers, and between plaintiffs and defendants. Fair net compensation to claimants under the current system is doubtful; even when paid, it is both skewed and slow in coming. Deterrence is suboptimal. Judges are now even more uninformed in predicting adequacy of representation, as they must in order to certify a class. Thus, in all of these respects, the defects of a mass tort claims market are equalled or surpassed by flaws in the traditional tort system.[193]

Finally, each claim (or, more precisely, one-third or more of each claim) is already "sold" in the current mass tort system. The purchaser, of course, is the claimant's contingent-fee lawyer.[194] Depending on how this lawyer finances her litigation costs, she may use part of her share to secure further financing (which may be tantamount to selling that part).[195] Despite legitimate ethical concerns about such arrangements, invalidating them would probably deny legal representation to all but the most affluent claimants—a proposition that raises equally profound ethical problems at least to American ways of thinking.[196]

Although the current contingent fee and class action financing arrangements already effectively employ a market in tort claims, adopting the proposed market approach would not be superfluous. As we have just seen, existing rules now permit the sale (without calling it that) of only a fraction of the claim. More important, a variety of procedural and ethical barriers inhibit evolutionary reform toward a thick, fully functional market.[197] Finally, of course, courts do not currently auction the right to represent the class, despite the enormous economic value of that right both to the lawyers and to the class members.[198] If enabled by legislative fiat, mass tort claims and class representation markets could, if well-regulated, readily accommodate more complete, well-informed, and efficient trading of claims.

C. Administrative Compensation

The bureaucratic approach to personal injury compensation has received extensive treatment in the literature,[199] in part because schemes such as workers' compensation, disability insurance, and "focused" no-fault plans have been in place for a long time. Professor Robert Rabin has recently reviewed several existing administrative compensation programs. One is the Price-Anderson scheme for nuclear accidents, a "hybrid" plan combining tort and no-fault elements. Another is the National Childhood Vaccine Injury Act of 1986, a narrowly focused no-fault program that also retains a tort option. Rabin also considers several more expansive no-fault plans that have been proposed for toxic-related injuries, plans that would retain tort options.[200] Each of these approaches, Rabin observes, must struggle with the same knotty issues: defining the compensable event, setting compensation levels, deciding the degree to which compensation should be individualized, structuring the tort system's role under the scheme, and specifying how the system should be financed when multiple sources of harm exist.

Rabin finds that the mass tort litigation system remains inadequate even after claims-aggregation, cost controls, and uncertainty-reducing innovations are instituted, but adds that "the superiority of a no-fault approach is far from clear," at least where toxic-related *diseases* are concerned.[201] In such instances, no-fault schemes seem unable to grapple with causation any more effectively than does a reformed tort system, at least so long as the scientific base remains weak. Moreover, these issues become more problematic as the scheme's ambit broadens. His conclusion about the advantages of administrative compensation schemes in the context of many mass torts is decidedly guarded:

> Administrative compensation schemes offer greatest promise when the compensation-triggering "event" features a relatively clear relationship between source, substance, and pathological condition. . . . When one ventures, however, into the unconfined area of mass toxic harms, administrative compensation schemes share many of the burdens that beset a reconstructed aggregative tort liability approach.[202]

Several points can be drawn from Rabin's analysis. First, neither I nor Rabin means to assert that an administrative compensation approach—whether implemented along side the mass tort system or supplanting it altogether—could never be preferable to the status quo. Any meaningful comparison would require significant empirical study and theoretical refinement concerning the appropriate tradeoffs among competing social values. But given the current state of our knowledge, the superiority of an administrative scheme to the contemporary mass tort system is highly debatable.

Second, Rabin's valuable comparison between the litigative and administrative modes of compensation is incomplete in at least one significant respect. Rabin rightly notes that these two modes often interact with and complement one another; thus, he proposes to create a "switching mechanism" that would move tort claims into an administrative compensation system after litigation has reached a certain level of maturity.[203] This proposal is appealing insofar as it seeks to exploit the advantages of both systems—litigation's ability to mobilize information about risk, causation, and other common generic issues, and administration's ability to minimize transaction costs and reduce extreme horizontal inequities once that information has come to light.

Rabin's analysis, however, largely ignores the role of settlement in mass tort litigation—which is rather like analyzing an orchestra without considering the strings. He therefore overlooks the extent to which *today's mass tort system already employs administrative modes of compensation*—a fact that should inform one's comparison of the two systems. In practice, mass tort litigators "batch" claims into broad disease groups for settlement purposes, groups that bear a striking resemblance to the kinds of compensation categories that an administrative scheme might employ. Of course, these batches of claims will be subject to individualizing variables, the number of which will vary depending on the complexity of the settlement structure. The batching may also be distorted by the litigators' strategic considerations.[204] But in general, claimants in a given batch will receive roughly similar settlement amounts—just as they would under the compensation categories that are central features of most administrative schemes.

The hybrid character of the mass tort system[205] is especially striking in the context of the global settlements in which mass tort litigation now often culminates. Indeed, these carefully negotiated settlement plans can be viewed as more tightly drafted, more carefully designed, more scrupulously casted, and more adequately funded versions of administrative compensation statutes. They contain detailed definitions, decision criteria, and distribution protocols. They provide a mix of categorical and individualized treatment of claims.[206] The facilities that the plans establish to process thousands of claims[207] are closely modeled on administrative agencies such as workers' compensation boards. The plans assure long-term funding of the obligations to which the claims will give rise. They seek to anticipate numerous contingencies, while prescribing alternative dispute resolution procedures for those contingencies that cannot be foreseen or immediately resolved.[208] Indeed, in the plans' level of precision and concern to anticipate future developments, they bear more resemblance to bond indentures than to compensation statutes.

This, of course, is no accident; it reflects systemic differences between legislation and contract regimes. When legislators address controversial subjects like compensation, they employ a variety of strategic behaviors: ambiguous drafting, deferring difficult issues, hiding or underestimating costs, and delegating norm elaboration and implementation tasks to agencies and courts.[209] These behaviors magnify the notoriously high monitoring costs that any legislature faces in delegating authority to an agency.[210]

In contrast, litigants who negotiate a global settlement are designing a structure to guide their relationship, manage their actual and potential conflicts, administer their agreements, and distribute their resources over a long period of time during which the incentives to defect may be great and resort to agencies or courts may be costly and otherwise undesirable. Most important, the parties are putting their own money on the line. Accordingly, they take far greater pains than do legislators in drafting the governing document to minimize future uncertainty rather than delegating to others the responsibility for doing so.[211]

Conclusion

Mass tort litigation began to appear in the courts in the late 1960s. Since then, mass tort law has developed gradually through trial-and-error as courts and litigants struggle to adapt traditional legal theories and practices to what only slowly came to be seen as a novel set of problems. The policymakers and judges of the earlier period failed to anticipate many of the dilemmas of legal doctrine, resource allocation, incentives, and institutional design that we now associate with mass tort litigation. Even less predictable was the nature of the system that would emerge in response. Indeed, only in the last decade or so have the general contours of these difficulties become clear enough to elicit serious scholarly attention to the relative merits of possible solutions.

The character of the mass torts system, our understanding of it, and the plausibility of different approaches to its reform are all affected by the path of common-law adjudication along which the system has evolved. By identifying this system with the most precious, evocative symbols and commitments of American legal-political culture, the common law has infused mass tort litigation—for better or for worse—with a powerful normative content and institutional support that it would have otherwise lacked.

In this sense, the common law has favored certain traditional aspects of mass tort law and practice, even as it has quietly and gradually transformed them into a new system. The balance struck by the common law is selective and highly eclectic; it has borrowed from some critiques and remedial approaches, while decisively eschewing others. It has made some functional adaptations while retaining certain features that I and many others view as dysfunctional. From the institutional evolutionist perspective that I have advanced here, the emergent system carries with it some valuable social information that we would be foolish to ignore. The selection of this system in competition with others justifies a presumption that, all things considered, it satisfies important social needs (not just those of the lawyers) better than do the other approaches that have been either tried or seriously considered. As my discussion of a market in mass tort claims suggests, these approaches do not exhaust the universe of plausible alternatives. This presumption of functional superiority, of course, can and should be overcome if the relevant facts (including political ones), values, and needs change. Meanwhile, mass torts scholars should use this selection as an invitation to disenthrall ourselves and thus to think anew about the nature of the competing systems and about their possible reform.

Notes

1. A recent article emphasizes three distinctive features of mass tort litigation: "the large number of claims associated with a single 'litigation'; the commonality of issues and actors among claims within the litigation; and the interdependence of claim values." Deborah R. Hensler & Mark A. Peterson, *Understanding Mass Personal Injury Litigation: A Socio-Legal Analysis*, 59 BROOK. L. REV. 961, 965 (1993). Such definitions usually stress the difficulty of establishing causal responsibility in most, but not all, mass tort actions. This difficulty may arise for any of a number of reasons: claimants' injuries are separated in time and space from their exposures; a number of possible natural and human causes of the injuries exist; particular defendants are not clearly linked to particular plaintiffs; the claims have contacts with a variety of jurisdictions; and other complicating factors. For one taxonomy of mass torts, see JACK B. WEINSTEIN, INDIVIDUAL JUSTICE IN MASS TORT LITIGATIONS: THE EFFECT OF CLASS ACTIONS, CONSOLIDATIONS, AND OTHER MULTIPARTY DEVICES 16–17 (1995).

2. This consensus extends beyond academic tort scholars to analysts at non-academic research organizations such as the RAND Institute for Civil Justice and the Manhattan Institute. *See, e.g.,* Hensler & Peterson, *supra* note 1, at 962–63, 1061 (arguing that the legal system has not responded well to the challenge of mass torts); *see also* PETER W.

HUBER, GALILEO'S REVENGE: JUST SCIENCE IN THE COURTROOM (1991); WALTER K. OLSON, THE LITIGATION EXPLOSION: WHAT HAPPENED WHEN AMERICA UNLEASHED THE LAWSUIT (1991). It even includes scholars such as John Siliciano, who has condemned other critiques of mass tort law both for employing crisis rhetoric and for failing to specify more precisely their benchmark tort system. *See* John A. Siliciano, *Mass Torts and the Rhetoric of Crisis*, 80 CORNELL L. REV. 990 (1995). By contrast, only a few scholars wax optimistic about the possibilities of modifying tort law to accommodate the special difficulties posed by mass tort litigation. *E.g.*, Glen O. Robinson & Kenneth S. Abraham, *Collective Justice in Tort Lata*, 78 VA. L. REV. 1481 (1992); David Rosenberg, *The Causal Connection in Mass Exposure Cases: A "Public Law" Vision of the Tort System*, 97 HARV. L. REV. 849 (1984).

3. *See, e.g.*, Linda S. Mullenix, *Mass Tort As Public Law Litigation: Paradigm Misplaced*, 88 NW. U. L. REV. 579 (1994).

4. *E.g.*, HUBER, *supra* note 2 (1991); PHANTOM RISK: SCIENTIFIC INFERENCE AND THE LAW (K. Foster et al. eds., 1993) [hereinafter PHANTOM RISK].

5. *E.g.*, PETER H. SCHUCK, AGENT ORANGE ON TRIAL: MASS TOXIC DISASTERS IN THE COURTS (enlarged ed. 1987); Peter Huber, *Safety and the Second Best: The Hazards of Public Risk Management in the Courts*, 85 COLUM. L. REV. 277 (1985); Mark J. Roe, *Bankruptcy and Mass Tort*, 84 COLUM. L. REV. 846 (1984); Rosenberg, *supra* note 2; Jack B. Weinstein, *The Role of the Court in Toxic Tort Litigation*, 73 GEO. L.J. 1389 (1985).

6. There, Dow Corning and other manufacturers agreed to pay silicone gel breast implant claimants $4.23 billion for connective-tissue and other diseases, even though these companies knew that their causal responsibility for these diseases could not be proven. Indeed, the best studies yet conducted on this question, released almost before the ink was dry on the settlement agreement, failed to demonstrate a causal relationship between breast implants and these illnesses. *See* Marcia Angell, *Do Breast Implants Cause Systemic Disease?*, 330 NEW ENG. J. MED. 1748 (June 16, 1994) (discussing Gabriel et al. study and others); Gina Kolata, *Study Finds No Implant-Disease Links*, N.Y. TIMES, June 16, 1994, at A18 (discussing Gabriel et al., Hochberg, and other studies); Gina Kolata, *Tissue Illness and Implants: No Tie is Seen*, N.Y. TIMES (National), May 29, 1994, s 1, at 16 (discussing Schottenfeld et al. study); *see also* Phillip J. Hilts, *2 Studies Find No Breast-Implant Tie to Connective-Tissue Illness*, N.Y. TIMES (National), Oct. 26, 1994, at A23 (discussing Hochberg study); Gina Kolata, *A Case of Justice, or a Total Travesty?*, N.Y. TIMES, June 13, 1995, at D1 (reviewing dispute); *FDA Says Risk Minimal From Breast Implants*, WALL ST. J., June 30, 1995, at B8 (follow-up study).

In deciding to settle, the breast implant defendants apparently dreaded the prospect that juries, outraged by internal corporate documents that jurors might interpret as showing corporate irresponsibility or illegality, might award ruinous judgments despite the weak evidence of causation and thereby destroy the firms' goodwill in the consumer products market. Presumably, this reaction by the defendants partly reflected the fact that the breast implant litigation was still "immature" in the sense discussed *infra* part I, but "mature" enough to have produced enormous punitive damage awards. *See* Barnaby J. Feder, *3 Are Awarded $27.9 Million in Implant Trial*, N.Y. TIMES, Mar. 4, 1994, at A16; *$5 Million for Implant Leak*, N.Y. TIMES, Feb. 16, 1995, at A20; *$6 Million Award in Implant Suit*, N.Y. TIMES (National), Feb. 5, 1995, s 1, at 18. Professor Coffee suggests that the size of this settlement was also affected by the rules and procedures governing the settlement process. Their key significance, he argues, was to reduce the opportunity for defendants' and plaintiffs' counsel to collude in a cheap settlement, which he views the asbestos global settlement to be (mistakenly, in my view). *See* John C. Coffee, Jr., *Class Wars: The Dilemma of the Mass Tort Class Action*, 95 COLUM. L. REV. (forthcoming 1995).

The fiscal viability of this settlement, and hence its continued existence, are far from assured. The court recently found that the volume and amount of the existing and future class claims will far exceed the $4.23 billion fund created by the settlement. Under a provision of the settlement authorizing a renegotiation of the amount and structure of the settlement under these conditions, the parties and the court are seeking to come up with additional funds for the present claimants, perhaps by reducing the funds payable to future claimants. The outcome of these negotiations will strongly affect the number of claimants who decide to opt out of the settlement, which in turn will affect the defendants' decisions about whether or not to terminate the settlement, as the settlement permits them to do under certain circumstances. *See* Thomas M. Burton, *Implant Fund Is Too Small to Cover Claims*, WALL ST. J., May, 2, 1995, at A3. Responding to these uncertainties and creating new ones, the major defendant in the case is seeking relief under Chapter 11 of the bankruptcy law, which would stay all breast implant litigation against the company, barring new claims and increasing pressure on the plaintiffs to accept a settlement. *See* Barnaby J. Feder, *Dow Corning in Bankruptcy Over Lawsuits*, N.Y. TIMES, May 16, 1995, at A1.

The Bendectin litigation constitutes another recent example of continuing plaintiff successes—in this instance, at trial—despite very weak causal evidence, adverse rulings in the appellate courts and exoneration of the product by other safety-conscious governments including Britain and France. *See* Peter H. Schuck, *Multi-Culturalism Redux: Science, Law, and Politics*, 11 YALE L. & POL'Y REV. 1, 7–10 (1993). For other examples, see PHANTOM RISK, *supra* note 4, and Schuck, *supra* note 5.

7. Interview with Paul D. Rheingold, Esq., in New York, N.Y. (November 24, 1994) [hereinafter Rheingold Interview]. Rheingold, a prominent member of the mass tort plaintiffs' bar, represents breast implant litigation plaintiffs.

8. *See generally* Judith Resnik, *From "Cases" to "Litigation,"* 54 LAW & CONTEMP. PROBS. 5 (1991) (discussing changes in attitude and practice in mass torts from the 1960s to the 1990s). Even if such a line could be drawn, distinguishing parents from progeny is harder in litigation than in life. Agent Orange, the Ur-case of mass tort class actions, was not finally resolved until early 1994. *In re* "Agent Orange" Prod. Liab. Litig., 996 F.2d 1425 (2d Cir. 1993), *cert. denied*, 114 S. Ct. 1125 (1994). Asbestos litigation—which preceded the Agent Orange class actions by nearly a decade—shows no signs of petering out, notwithstanding the pending settlement by some asbestos defendants of their future claims. Georgine v. Amchem Prods., Inc., 157 F.R.D. 246 (E.D. Pa. 1994).

9. On this question, see, for example, E. Donald Elliott, *The Evolutionary Tradition in Jurisprudence*, 85 COLUM. L. REV. 38 (1985) (tracing the idea of evolution in theories of law); George L. Priest, *The New Scientism in Legal Scholarship: A Comment on Clark and Posner*, 90 YALE L.J. 1284 (1981) (discussing Professor Clark's theory of evolution).

10. *E.g.*, SCHUCK, *supra* note 5; Peter H. Schuck, *The Worst Should Go First: Deferral Registries in Asbestos Litigation*, 15 HARV. J.L. & PUB. POL'Y 541 (1992).

11. One promising reform is the development of a market in mass tort claims. *See* discussion *infra* part III.B.

12. *E.g.*, HENRY S. COHN & DAVID BOLLIER, THE GREAT HARTFORD CIRCUS FIRE: CREATIVE SETTLEMENT OF MASS DISASTERS (1991). As Professor Robert Rabin has noted, empirical studies of aviation litigation demonstrate that more than "massness" is required to pro-

duce the high transaction costs and other difficulties associated with the mass tort litigation problem. *See* Robert L. Rabin, *Some Thoughts on the Efficacy of A Mass Toxics Administrative Compensation Scheme,* 52 MD. L. REV. 951, 953–54 (1993). To underscore this distinction, Professor David Rosenberg has referred to the newer phenomenon as mass *exposure* litigation. *See generally* Rosenberg, *supra* note 2.

13. Federal Coal Mine Health and Safety Act of 1969, Pub. L. No. 91–173, tit. IV, 83 Stat. 742, 792–98.

14. Borel v. Fibreboard Paper Prods. Corp., 493 F.2d 1076, 1086 (5th Cir.), *cert. denied,* 419 U.S. 869 (1974). There were precursors, such as the MER/29 litigation, which antedated but in important respects prefigured, the institutionalized multidistrict litigation that is so common today. *See* Paul D. Rheingold, *The MER/29 Story—An Instance of Successful Mass Disaster Litigation,* 56 CAL. L. REV. 116 (1968).

15. *See* ROBERTA J. APFEL & SUSAN M. FISHER, TO DO NO HARM: DES AND THE DILEMMAS OF MODERN MEDICINE (1984); ROBERT MEYERS, DES: THE BITTER PILL (1983).

16. *See* SCHUCK, *supra* note 5, at 16–20.

17. *See* RICHARD B. SOBOL, BENDING THE LAW: THE STORY OF THE DALKON SHIELD BANKRUPTCY 1 (1991).

18. *See* Schuck, *supra* note 6, at 1–10, and sources cited therein.

19. *See, e.g.,* Hensler & Peterson, *supra* note 1, at 992–98.

20. *Cf.* Nancy Hogan, *Shielded from Liability,* A.B.A. J., May 1994, at 56.

21. *See* Barnaby J. Feder, *A Spreading Pain, and Cries for Justice,* N.Y. TIMES, June 5, 1994, s 3, at 1; Roy W. Krieger, *On The Line,* A.B.A. J., Jan. 1994, at 40.

22. KEETON ET AL., PRODUCTS LIABILITY AND SAFETY (2d ed. 1989), *quoted in* Gary T. Schwartz, *Tobacco Liability in the Courts, in* SMOKING POLICY: LAW, POLITICS, AND CULTURE 131 (Robert L. Rabin & Stephen D. Sugarman eds., 1993). The first such case was Lowe v. R.J. Reynolds Tobacco Co., No. 9673(C) (E.D. Mo., filed Mar. 10, 1954).

23. *See* Schuck, *supra* note 6.

24. Some commentators have observed a recent slowing or even reversal of this pro-plaintiff trend. *See, e.g.,* Theodore Eisenberg & James A. Henderson, Jr., *Inside the Quiet Revolution in Products Liability,* 39 UCLA L. REV. 731, 735 (1992); James A. Henderson, Jr. & Theodore Eisenberg, *The Quiet Revolution in Products Liability: An Empirical Study of Legal Change,* 37 UCLA L. REV. 479, 480 (1990); Gary T. Schwartz, *The Beginning and the Possible End of the Rise of Modern American Tort Law,* 26 GA. L. REV. 601, 603 (1992).

25. Important examples include compensation for the fear of future injury, for medical monitoring costs, and for non-impairing conditions such as pleural plaques due to asbestos exposure. *See* Schuck, *supra* note 10, at 574.

26. 11 U.S.C. ss 101–1330 (1988 & Supp. V 1993).

27. In the asbestos field alone, fourteen companies had done so as of July 1991. *See* Schuck, *supra* note 10, at 555 n.56 (listing companies).

28. This is not to say, of course, that there were no foreshadowing or prophetic voices. *See, e.g.,* Samuel D. Estep, *Radiation Injuries and Statistics: The Need for a New Approach to Injury Litigation,* 59 MICH. L. REV. 259 (1960) (suggesting legal reforms to facilitate resolution of anticipated litigation involving nuclear energy torts); Irving J. Selikoff et al., *Asbestos Exposure and Neoplasia,* 188 JAMA 22 (1964) (linking asbestos to lung cancer). A federal program to compensate black lung victims would be enacted in the last days of 1969. *See infra* notes 123–28 and accompanying text.

29. This dawning consciousness can be glimpsed in Judge Weinstein's assumption of the Agent Orange litigation from Judge Pratt in 1983. *See* SCHUCK, *supra* note 5, at 111–42.

30. For example, Professor Coffee dates the appearance of certified settlement class actions to 1989 (in the Dalkon Shield case), only six years ago. Coffee, *supra* note 6.

31. Perhaps the most controversial current example is the use of settlement class actions in "immature" tort cases such as the Ford Bronco II litigation discussed in Coffee, *supra* note 6, and the certification of class actions for settlement that could not have been certified for litigation, a practice that was recently rejected by a panel of the Third Circuit. *In re* General Motors Corp. Pick-Up Truck Fuel Tank Prods. Liab. Litig., Nos. 94–1064, 94–1194, 94–1195, 94–1198, 94–1202, 94–1203, 94–1207, 94–1208, 94–1219, 1995 WL 223209 (3d Cir. Apr. 17, 1995) [hereinafter *In re* GMC]. For the distinction between mature and immature torts, see *infra* notes 33–36 and accompanying text.

32. Uncertainty, of course, is the *raison d'etre* of insurance. But where the uncertainty surrounding a risk exceeds the level that can be underwritten on a sound actuarial basis, the excess constitutes a cost that the insurer bears at its peril. Howard Kunreuther et al., *Insurer Ambiguity and Market Failure*, 7 J. RISK & UNCERTAINTY 71, 82–83 (1993).

33. Francis E. McGovern, *Resolving Mature Mass Tort Litigation*, 69 B.U. L. REV. 659 (1989) (pointing to asbestos litigation and the Dalkon Shield litigation as examples). A related idea is that of a "congregation" of cases that follows a "career." *See* Marc Galanter, *Case Congregations and Their Careers*, 24 LAW & SOC'Y REV. 371, 390–92 (1990) (citing asbestos litigation as an example).

34. McGovern, *supra* note 33, at 659.

35. *See generally* MARVER H. BERNSTEIN, REGULATING BUSINESS BY INDEPENDENT COMMISSION (1955) (describing a life cycle theory of administrative agencies); ERIK H. ERIKSON, CHILDHOOD AND SOCIETY (2d ed. 1963) (describing a life cycle theory of personal identity).

36. Galanter, *supra* note 33, at 390 n.30.

37. For a strong critique of McGovern in this regard, see David Rosenberg, Comment. *Of End Games and Openings in Mass Tort Cases: Lessons from A Special Master*, 69 B.U.L. REV. 695, 707–11 (1989). Rosenberg does not attack the notion that tort claims can mature over time, but instead criticizes McGovern's argument that maturity should be a prerequisite to the use of collective procedures.

38. The value of a claim equals its expected return, which is a function of the legal and factual contingencies affecting the liability and damages issues, the time and costs needed to liquidate the claim, the risk of defendants' insolvency, and so forth.

But even where the liability issues remain murky and outcomes are therefore difficult to predict, the types of *injury* are relatively fixed; hence, *if* liability is established future damage awards can be more accurately predicted over time on the basis of damage awards rendered in cases already litigated in the same jurisdiction involving similar injuries.

39. Hensler & Peterson, *supra* note 1, at 967–68.

40. *See* George L. Priest & Benjamin Klein, *The Selection of Disputes for Litigation*, 13 J. LEGAL STUD. 1 (1984).

41. The Environmental Protection Agency (EPA), the Occupational Safety and Health Administration (OSHA), the Consumer Product Safety Commission (CPSC), the National Regulatory Commission (NRC), and the Mine Safety and Health Administration (MSHA) are among the health and safety regulatory agencies established during the 1960s and 1970s. The Food and Drug Administration (FDA) was established in 1906 or so.

42. The precise role of the tort bar turned on whether the regulatory statute pre-empted or preserved private tort remedies. *Cf.* Cipollone v. Liggett Group, Inc., 112 S. Ct. 2608 (1992) (holding that certain tort claims were preempted by the federal cigarette package labelling act).

43. Repetitive stress disorders and auto safety defects are examples. *See* Edward Felsenthal, *An Epidemic or a Fad? The Debate Heats Up Over Repetitive Stress*, WALL ST. J., July 14, 1994, at A1 (over 3,000 lawsuits filed; over 1200 newspaper and magazine stories reported in the last year). The causal influence of media reports and plaintiffs' lawyers activity, of course, can be mutually reinforcing. With some consumer products, the media's mention of a dangerous defect can cause reputation-minded manufacturers to act swiftly to remove the product from the market. *See* Hensler & Peterson, *supra* note 1, at 1015–16 (citing other examples).

44. *See* Philip J. Hilts, *Cigarette Makers Debated the Risks They Denied*, N.Y. TIMES, June 16, 1994, at A1. In some industries, product recalls are more feasible because detailed records of purchases and identifiable end-users exist. *See, e.g.,* Warren E. Leary, *Remedy Sought for 22,000 Heart Patients With Risky Pacemakers*, N.Y. TIMES, Jan. 16, 1995, at A9 (describing voluntary recall).

45. The phrase was coined by Francis E. McGovern, *Looking to the Future of Mass Torts: A Comment on Schuck and Siliciano*, 80 CORNELL L. REV. 1022, 1026 (1995).

46. For a discussion of some of the regulatory weaknesses that contributed to the rise of mass torts litigation, especially in the area of medical devices, see Hensler & Peterson, *supra* note 1, at 1017–18; *see also* JERRY L. MASHAW & DAVID L. HARFST, THE STRUGGLE FOR AUTO SAFETY (1990) (documenting that the agency's standard-setting efforts were so sluggish that tort litigation and negotiated recalls became far more significant sources of pressure for enhanced auto safety).

47. *See infra* notes 66–67 and accompanying text.

48. According to Professor Coffee, the diffusion of legal knowledge is rapid within the interconnected defense bar, but not within the far more fragmented plaintiffs' tort bar. Coffee, *supra* note 6. This claim is doubtful given the high degree of coordination and specialization among mass tort plaintiffs' lawyers. *See, e.g.,* Hensler & Peterson, *supra* note 1, at 1025–26; McGovern, *supra* note 45, at 1026; Glenn Collins, *A Tobacco Case's Legal Buccaneers*, N.Y. TIMES, Mar. 6, 1995, at D1 (reporting that a consortium of plaintiffs' lawyers involving almost 60 law firms has amassed a war chest of almost $6 million).

49. Indeed, the role of regulatory standards in the mass tort system is even more attenuated than this. Although defendants' non-compliance with a regulatory standard certainly strengthens plaintiffs' claims in court, the reverse is not necessarily true. Under prevailing tort principles, defendants' compliance with such standards is not binding upon the jury, which ordinarily is permitted to make its own assessment of the challenged conduct. W. PAGE KEETON ET AL., PROSSER AND KEETON ON THE LAW OF TORTS 283 (5th ed. 1984). Pending legislation would modify this rule, at least with respect to punitive damage claims challenging products whose safety has been certified by the FDA. *See* H.R. 917, 104th Cong., 1st Sess. s 6(d) (1995) (the "Common Sense Product Liability Reform Act").

50. Kenneth S. Abraham, *Environmental Liability and the Limits of Insurance*, 88 COLUM. L. REV. 942, 955 (1988).

51. *See, e.g.,* PETER HUBER, LIABILITY: THE LEGAL REVOLUTION AND ITS CONSEQUENCES (1989); George L. Priest, *The Current Insurance Crisis and Modern Tort Law*, 96 YALE L.J.

1521 (1987). *But see* Jon Hanson & Stephen Croley, *What Liability Crisis? An Alternative Explanation for Recent Events in Products Liability*, 8 YALE J. REG. 1 (1991).

52. There is evidence that these efforts succeeded in achieving at least some of their objectives. *See, e.g.,* Glenn Blackmon & Richard Zeckhauser, *State Tort Reform Legislation: Assessing Our Control of Risks, in* TORT LAW AND THE PUBLIC INTEREST: INNOVATION, COMPETITION, AND CONSUMER WELFARE 272 (Peter H. Schuck ed., 1991).

53. *See infra* note 154.

54. *See Cleanup Gets Little of Superfund Settlements,* N.Y. TIMES, Apr. 26, 1992, s 1, at 27.

55. KEETON ET AL., *supra* note 22. The 104th Congress threatens to restrict tort liability even more. *See* Peter H. Schuck, *Tortured Logic,* NEW REPUBLIC, Mar. 27, 1995, at 11–12.

56. *See, e.g.,* Priest, *supra* note 51, at 1570–76 (describing liability insurers' movement to claims-made policies, coverage exclusions, lower policy limits, larger deductibles and coinsurance, and "retro-date" provisions); Thorn Rosenthal, Esq., Remarks at Mass Torts Seminar, Yale Law School (Apr. 21, 1994).

57. *See* Harry H. Wellington, *Asbestos: The Private Management of A Public Problem,* 33 CLEV. ST. L. REV. 375 (1984–85).

58. Insurance Co. of N. Am. v. Forty-Eight Insulations, Inc., 633 F.2d 1212 (6th Cir. 1980), *cert. denied,* 45 U.S. 1109 (1981); UNR Inds., Inc. v. Continental Cas. Co., 942 F.2d 1101 (7th Cir. 1991), *cert. denied,* 112 S. Ct. 1586 (1992).

59. The Center for Claims Resolution, a not-for-profit organization established by a group of asbestos manufacturers to process asbestos-related claims, is an example. For a description of the Center, see Georgine v. Amchem Prods., Inc., 157 F.R.D. 246, 264 (E.D. Pa. 1994).

It must be noted, however, that such cooperation and coordination is atypical. Many mass tort cases, such as Dalkon Shield and Albuterol cases, are brought only against a single defendant. Even where there are multiple defendants, such as in the DES and breast implant litigation, conflict and finger-pointing is far more common than cooperation. *See* Rheingold Interview, *supra* note 7.

60. For a discussion of these bankruptcies, see *In re* Joint E. & S. Dist. Asbestos Litig., 1995 WL 21615 (E. & S.D.N.Y.Jan. 19, 1995) (Johns-Manville Corp.); SOBOL, *supra* note 17, at 51–59 (A.H. Robins Co.).

61. *See, e.g.,* Greg Steinmetz, *Insurers Discover Pollution Can Bolster Bottom Line,* WALL ST. J., August 19, 1992, at B4 (noting the growing availability and profitability of environmental liability insurance).

62. The liability insurance industry is notoriously cyclical, although the reasons for this volatility remain controversial. *See* Scott E. Harrington, *Liability Insurance: Volatility in Prices and in the Availability of Coverage, in* TORT LAW AND THE PUBLIC INTEREST: INNOVATION, COMPETITION, AND CONSUMER WELFARE 47 (Peter H. Schuck ed., 1991).

63. *See, e.g.,* Emergency Planning and Community Right-to-Know Act of 1986, 42 U.S.C. ss 11001–11050 (1988 & Supp. V 1993); OSHA Hazard Communication Standard, 29 C.F.R. s 1910.20 (1994).

64. *See* Schuck, *supra* note 10, at 549 n.37.

65. Medicare benefit payments increased between 1980 and 1991 from $36 to $119 billion. Medicaid benefit payments increased between 1980 and 1991 from $23 to $77 billion. Statistical Abstract of the United States, 1994, Tables No. 156, 162. Disability payments are more difficult to quantify as they include federal, state, workers' compensation, and private programs, but they too have grown rapidly. Between 1980

and 1992, for example, Social Security disability benefit payments more than doubled to $31.1 billion. *Id.* at Table No. 581.

66. The risk-bearing capacity of a plaintiffs' attorney depends on numerous factors, including: the diversification of her litigation portfolio; access to reliable information about the expected value of claims; access to financing; economies of scale in client development, claims processing and litigation; and opportunities to innovate and operate flexibly in these areas. *See* Hensler & Peterson, *supra* note 1, at 1042–43.

67. *See* Galanter, *supra* note 33, at 387 (describing information-sharing and coordination by lawyers).

68. This has produced what two commentators have recently called an "extreme risk aversion" on the part of mass tort defendants as they seek to avoid trials. Hensler & Peterson, *supra* note 1, at 1044. The authors go on to state that "defendants in mass tort litigation may not hold the same advantages over the plaintiff that they have in ordinary tort litigation." *Id.* at 1045.

69. *See* Robert F. Peckham, *The Federal Judge as Case Manager: The New Role in Guiding a Case from Filing to Disposition,* 69 CAL. L. REV. 770 (1981); Judith Resnik, *Managerial Judging,* 96 HARV. L. REV. 376 (1982).

70. *See generally* Stephen C. Yeazell, *The Misunderstood Consequences of Modern Civil Process,* 1994 WIS. L. REV. 631 (providing a rich historical perspective on this development).

71. *See* Robert G. Bone, *Statistical Adjudication: Rights, Justice, and Utility in a World of Process Scarcity,* 46 VAND. L. REV. 561 (1993).

72. *See, e.g.,* SOBOL, *supra* note 17, at 227–28 (describing use of this technique in the Dalkon Shield litigation).

73. *See* Douglas Frantz, *High-Tech Ohio Courtroom Provides Glimpse Of Future (and Preview of the Simpson Trial),* N.Y. TIMES, Aug. 19, 1994, at A23.

74. RAND Institute for Civil Justice, Escaping the Courthouse, Research Brief, Dec. 1994 (on file with author). Perhaps the recent Supreme Court decision in Allied-Bruce Terminix Co. v. Dobson, 115 S. Ct. 834 (1995), which broadly construed the Federal Arbitration Act, making written arbitration agreements in interstate commerce enforceable, will encourage arbitration of some mass tort disputes. *See* Jethro K. Lieberman & James F. Henry, *Lessons from the Alternative Dispute Resolution Movement,* 53 U. CHI. L. REV. 424 (1986).

75. *See* Hensler & Peterson, *supra* note 1, at 1054–55 (citing William W Schwarzer et al., *Judicial Federalism in Action: Coordination of Litigation in State and Federal Courts,* 78 VA. L. REV. 1689 (1992)).

76. Hensler & Peterson, *supra* note 1, at 964, 967.

77. In addition to the pieces included in this symposium, see WEINSTEIN, *supra* note 1; Symposium, *Reinventing Civil Litigation: Evaluating Proposals for Change,* 59 BROOK. L. REV. 655 (1993); Symposium, *Modern American Tort Law,* 26 GA. L. REV. 601 (1992); Symposium, *Modern Civil Procedure: Issues in Controversy,* 54 LAW & CONTEMP. PROBS. 1 (1991).

78. For some examples of scholarly skepticism about these innovations, see SCHUCK, *supra* note 5; Coffee, *supra* note 6; Richard A. Epstein, *The Consolidation of Complex Litigation: A Critical Evaluation of the ALI Proposal,* 10 J.L. & COM. 1 (1990); Richard L. Marcus, *They Can't Do That, Can They? Tort Reform Via Rule 23,* 80 CORNELL L. REV. 858 (1995); Resnik, *supra* note 69; Roger H. Transgrud, *Mass Trials in Mass Tort Cases: A Dissent,* 1989 U. ILL. L. REV. 69. For some skepticism on the part of judges, see *In re*

"Agent Orange" Prod. Liab. Litig., 818 F.2d 145 (2d Cir. 1987), *cert. denied,* 484 U.S. 1004 (1988) *(Agent Orange I);* and *In re* "Agent Orange" Prod. Liab. Litig., 996 F.2d 1425 (2d Cir. 1993), *cert. denied,* 114 S. Ct. 1125 (1994). Even Judge Weinstein, who initiated many of these innovations, has expressed some reservations. *See* WEINSTEIN, *supra* note 1.

79. In addition to settlement class actions, the federal courts have certified opt-out classes in both mass disaster cases and mass toxic exposure cases. Regarding settlement class actions, see, for example, Watson v. Shell Oil Co., 979 F.2d 1014, 1020–21 (5th Cir. 1992), *reh'g granted,* 990 F,2d 805 (5th Cir. 1993) (oil refinery explosion); *In re* Federal Skywalk Cases, 95 F.R.D. 483 (W.D. Mo. 1982) (after vacating mandatory class); Coburn v. 4-R Corp., 77 F.R.D. 43 (E.D. Ky. 1977), *mandamus denied sub nom.* Union Light, Heat & Power Co. v. District Court, 588 F.2d 543 (6th Cir. 1978) (Beverly Hills Supper Club fire). *But see In re* GMC, *supra* note 31 (de-certifying settlement class action). Regarding opt-out classes, see, for example, Sterling v. Velsicol Chem. Corp., 855 F.2d 1188 (6th Cir. 1988) (water contamination); *In re* Copley Pharm., Inc., "Albuterol" Prods. Liab. Litig., MDL Docket No. 1013 (D. Wyo. Oct. 28, 1994) (albuterol); *In re* School Asbestos Litig., 789 F.2d 996, 1009 (3d Cir. 1986), *cert. denied,* 479 U.S. 852 (1986) (asbestos in schools); Jenkins v. Raymark Indus. 782 F.2d 468, 473 (5th Cir. 1986) (asbestos); *In re* "Agent Orange" Prod. Liab. Litig., 100 F.R.D. 718 (E.D.N.Y. 1983), *mandamus denied sub nom. In re* Diamond Shamrock Chem. Co., 725 F.2d 858 (2d Cir. 1984) (opt-out class for compensatory damages, mandatory class for punitive damages); Spitzfaden v. Dow Corning Corp., 619 So.2d 795 (La. 1993) (breast implants).

For a recent rejection of class certification on grounds that may apply to mass torts more broadly, see *In re* Rhone-Poulenc Rorer Inc., No. 94–3912, 1995 U.S. App. LEXIS 5504 (7th Cir. Mar. 16, 1995); *see also infra* note 92.

80. Proposed Amendment to FED. R. CIV. P. 23, under consideration by the Advisory Committee on the Federal Rules of Civil Procedure (1993 draft on file with author); Telephone Interview with Professor Edward Cooper, University of Michigan Law School (Mar. 10, 1995).

81. *See infra* notes 120–40 and accompanying text. Indeed, Congress confirmed and strengthened this judicial project in the Civil Justice Reform Act of 1990, Pub. L. No. 101–650, 104 Stat. 5090 (codified as amended at 28 U.S.C. ss 471–482 (Supp. V 1993)), which encouraged the federal courts to extend their case management innovations. Preliminary evaluation of the Act's effects indicates considerable implementation activity. See RAND Institute for Civil Justice, Evaluating the Civil Justice Reform Act of 1990, Research Brief, Mar. 1995 (on file with author). In general, other countries have not undertaken this project. *See* John G. Fleming, *Mass Torts,* 42 AMER. J. COMP. L. 507, 519–29 (1994).

82. RAND Institute for Civil Justice, Research Brief, *supra* note 74.

83. *See*Michael J. Saks & Peter D. Blanck, *Justice Improved: The Unrecognized Benefits of Aggregation and Sampling in the Trial of Mass Torts,* 44 STAN. L. REV. 815, 827 (1992). *But see* Owen M. Fiss, *Against Settlement,* 93 YALE L.J. 1073 (1984).

84. Michael J. Saks, *Do We Really Know Anything About the Behavior of the Tort Litigation System-and Why Not?,* 140 U. PA. L. REV. 1147, 1213 (1992).

85. Indeed, the strong pressure to settle that class certification exerts on defendants is sometimes considered a vice of mass tort class actions. *See, e.g., In re* Rhone-Poulenc Rorer Inc., No. 94–3912, 1995 U.S. App. LEXIS 5504, at *6 (7th Cir. Mar. 16, 1995). At a recent conference on class actions, none of the large group of knowledgeable participants could think of a single nationwide products liability or property damage class ac-

tion that had gone to trial. Samuel C. Pointer, Remarks at Research Conference on Class Actions, Institute of Judicial Administration, New York University Law School (Apr. 22, 1995).

86. *See* Isaac Ehrlich & Richard A. Posner, *An Economic Analysis of Legal Rulemaking*, 3 J. LEGAL STUD. 257 (1974); Priest & Klein, *supra* note 40. Inaccurate estimates could fortuitously converge, but this is hardly to be expected. On the other hand, there may be a certain class of cases in which uncertainty is so great that it facilitates, rather than impedes, settlements. *See* Marc Galanter & Mia Cahill, *"Most Cases Settle": Judicial Promotion and Regulation of Settlements*, 46 STAN. L. REV. 1339 (1994); Peter H. Schuck, *The Role of the Judge in Settling Complex Cases: The Agent Orange Example*, 53 U. CHI. L. REV. 337, 346 (1986).

87. *See supra* notes 33–38 and accompanying text.

88. *See, e.g.,* Bone, *supra* note 71; Robinson & Abraham, *supra* note 2.

89. *See generally* Symposium, *Claims Resolution Facilities and the Mass Settlement of Mass Torts*, 53 LAW & CONTEMP. PROBS. 1 (1990).

90. *See* Thomas D. Lambros, *The Summary Jury Trial: An Effective Aid to Settlement*, 77 JUDICATURE 6 (1993).

91. Bone, *supra* note 71; Saks & Blanck, *supra* note 83.

92. *Id.*

93. Bone, *supra* note 71, at 564–65. A number of variations on this basic theme are possible. Common to all of these techniques, however, is their suppression of a claim's individual characteristics in the interests of systemic efficiency, a "rough justice" version of horizontal equity, and collective (and perhaps even individual) accuracy. *See generally* Saks & Blanck, *supra* note 83 (finding that aggregation can increase efficiency, accuracy, and equity).

These alternative methods of claims aggregation raise the important question of whether class action treatment of mass tort litigation is really necessary. For a number of commentators, the answer is no. Thus, a panel of the Seventh Circuit recently suggested that such methods reduce the need to resort to class actions in mass tort litigation. *In re* Rhone-Poulenc Rorer Inc., No. 94–3912, 1995 U.S. App. LEXIS 5504, at *13 (7th Cir. Mar. 16, 1995) ("a sample of trials makes more sense than entrusting the fate of an entire industry to a single jury"). In much the same spirit, plaintiffs' lawyer Paul Rheingold argues that asbestos litigation aside, mass torts can be litigated quite effectively without class actions and the many spurious claims that they attract. Paul D. Rheingold, Remarks at Research Conference on Class Actions, *supra* note 85.

94. For a discussion of some of the impediments, see Hensler & Peterson, *supra* note 1, at 1050–52; text accompanying *infra* note 116.

95. For a variety of reasons, a global settlement will probably not resolve literally *all* claims. In the Agent Orange litigation, for example, several hundred claimants opted out of the class action and therefore could not participate in the class action settlement. It is noteworthy, however, that Judge Weinstein did his best to extend the benefits of the settlement to those claimants who opted out of the class. *See* SCHUCK, *supra* note 5, at 226. In the asbestos litigation, the now-pending class action settlement covers only future claims, not present ones, and the number of claimants who will opt out remains to be seen. Georgine v. Amchem Prods., Inc., 157 F.R.D. 246, 298 (E.D. Pa. 1994). In the silicone gel breast implant litigation, the pending settlement covers both present and future claims against the *participating* defendants, but does not cover claims against defendants who declined to join the settlement. *In re* Silicone Gel

Breast Implant Prods. Liab. Litig., No. CV 92-P–10000-S, Civil Action No. CV 94-P–11558-S, 1994 U.S. Dist. LEXIS 12521, at *78–86 (N.D. Ala. 1994). Again, many claimants will opt out, if only because the funds will probably be insufficient to cover all claims. *See* Feder, *supra* note 6; *$5 Million for Implant Leak*, N.Y. TIMES, Feb. 16, 1995, at A20; *$6 Million Award in Implant Suit*, N.Y. TIMES (National), Feb. 5, 1995, s 1, at 18. In the Dalkon Shield litigation, the plan of reorganization confirmed by the bankruptcy court did not cover claims brought against the company's insurers. SOBOL, *supra* note 17, at 209–24.

96. *See, e.g.,* Hensler & Peterson, *supra* note 1, at 1019 (summarizing earlier RAND study of filing behavior in tort system); PAUL C. WEILER ET AL, A MEASURE OF MALPRACTICE: MEDICAL INJURY, MALPRACTICE LITIGATION, AND PATIENT COMPENSATION 73 (1993) (according to a study of New York hospitals, one in 50 negligent injuries yields a malpractice claim).

97. According to Rheingold, 90% of the claims are "junk." Rheingold Interview, *supra* note 7; *see also* McGovern, *supra* note 45 at 1023–24.

98. Note that the *lowest* scheduled award under the breast implant settlement is $140,000. This amount may be reduced, however, if the number and amount of the claims is large enough to deplete the fund, which appears to be the case, *supra* note 6. *See* Schedule of Benefits, Breast Implant Litigation Settlement Notice 6 (Sept. 16, 1994) (on file with author).

99. *But cf.* Coffee, *supra* note 6 (criticizing the use of this model in some recent settlement class actions).

100. *See* William W Schwarzer, *Settlement of Mass Tort Class Actions: Order Out of Chaos*, 80 CORNELL L. REV. 837 (1995).

101. Georgine v. Amchem Prods., Inc., 157 F.R.D. 246, 257 (E.D. Pa. 1994) (per Reed, J.); *In re* Silicone Gel Breast Implant Prods. Liab. Litig., No. CV 92-P–10000-S, Civil Action No. CV 94-P–11558-S, 1994 U.S. Dist. LEXIS 12521, at *72 (N.D. Ala. Sept. 1, 1994) (per Pointer, J.). *But see In re* GMC, *supra* note 31 (decertifying settlement class action and rejecting trial court findings that settlement was fair).

102. *See* Coffee, *supra* note 6; Susan P. Koniak, *Feasting While the Widow Weeps: Georgine v. Amchem Products, Inc.*, 80 CORNELL L. REV. 1045 (1995). John Frank worries that courts in these settlements cannot effectively ensure that class counsel "sell res judicata for an adequate price." John Frank, Remarks at Research Conference on Class Actions, *supra* note 85.

103. *See* FED. R. CIV. P. 23(b)(1), (c)(3).

104. Georgine v. Amchem Prods., Inc., 157 F.R.D. 246, 336 (E.D. Pa. 1994). Access to the back-end opt out is subject to some important restrictions. *See id.* at 281. This is discussed just below.

105. *In re* Silicone Gel Breast Implant Prods. Liab. Litig., No. CV 92-P–10000-S, Civil Action No. CV 94-P–11558-S, 1994 U.S. Dist. LEXIS 12521, at *22 (N.D. Ala. Sept. 1, 1994).

106. *Id.* In addition, the settlement provides an opt-out right for the children of class members and two opt-out rights (including a "ratchet down" provision) for foreign claimants. *See* Breast Implant Litigation Settlement Notice, *supra* note 85, ss 18, 20, 22–24 (on file with author).

107. *See* discussion *supra* note 6.

108. The market-test justification for back-end opt outs was suggested to me by Professor David Rosenberg in a personal conversation sometime in 1993.

109. If the number of opt-outs turns out to be large enough, the defendants may have a right under the settlement agreement to terminate it.

110. Indeed, just counting the number of genuine opt-outs can be a controversial matter, as evidenced by the pending dispute over this question in the *Georgine* litigation. *See* Georgine v. Amchem Prods., Inc., No. CIV. A. 93–0215, 1994 WL 590611 (E.D. Pa. Oct. 21, 1994) (presenting findings of fact and conclusions of law in support of issuance of preliminary injunction).

111. For an explanation of adverse selection in the insurance context, see KENNETH ABRAHAM, INSURANCE LAW AND REGULATION: CASES AND MATERIALS 3–4 (1990).

112. Under Rule 23(e), of course, the court must make a threshold determination of fairness, but this precedes the opt-out decisions by parties to the settlement.

113. This Catch–22 merely reflects the more general fact that information is both costly to acquire and difficult to value until it is in fact acquired. The dilemma is therefore not unique to mass tort class actions; every uninformed plaintiff must invest in discovery *ex ante* in order to learn *ex post* whether the investment was worthwhile. Indeed, plaintiffs in other contexts face an even worse predicament insofar as they lack the option that a class member enjoys to free ride on discovery by the attorneys for the class.

114. *See* Hensler & Peterson, *supra* note 1, at 1045–48; Coffee, *supra* note 6.

115. *See* discussion *supra* note 6.

116. *See supra* part I.C.1 and 2.

117. In a settlement class action, for example, "front end" will usually refer to the time that the settlement is approved.

118. Note that not all settlements condition back-end opt outs. Pfizer did not insist on limiting them in the *Shiley* heart valve settlement, which involved a much smaller number of claims. *See* Hensler & Peterson, *supra* note 1, at 988–92.

119. *See* Stipulation of Settlement, Carlough v. Amchem Prods., Inc., No. 93–0215 (E.D. Pa. filed Jan. 15, 1993, amended Sept. 24, 1993) (part X.A, pertaining to case flow; part X.C, pertaining to procedural rules), *approved sub nom.* Georgine v. Amchem Prods., Inc., 157 F.R.D. 246 (E.D. Pa. 1994).

120. *Id.* at part X.C.3.

121. The common law of mass torts has borrowed extensively from equity jurisprudence, which empowers courts to exercise broad discretion in tailoring old doctrines, procedures, and remedies for application to the new, perplexing problems posed by mass torts. *See* WEINSTEIN, *supra* note 1, at 123–62; Jack B. Weinstein & Eileen B. Hershenov, *The Effect of Equity on Mass Tort Law*, 1991 U. ILL. L. REV. 269. When I refer to the "common law" of mass torts, then, I simply refer to that body of applicable legal doctrines and procedures initiated and then elaborated by the courts largely through incremental (some would say ad hoc), case-by-case adjudication without the guidance of any comprehensive framework or vision.

122. Again, the distinctiveness of this American approach should be noted. Fleming, *supra* note 81.

123. *See supra* note 13. Two more recent examples are the Radiation Exposure Compensation Act of 1990, 42 U.S.C. s 2210 (Supp. V 1993), and the National Childhood Vaccine Injury Act of 1986, 42 U.S.C. ss 300aa–10 to –34 (1988 & Supp. V 1993). Like the neonatal injury reform schemes adopted in Virginia and Florida, these two statutes are narrowly focused. According to a recent report, however, the vaccine program has paid almost $500 million in compensation. *New Whooping Cough Vaccine Is Said to Eliminate Side Effects*, N.Y. TIMES, Nov. 25, 1994, at A20.

I do not discuss state workers compensation statutes in this context because they were designed primarily to address traumatic workplace *accidents,* not chronic occupational *diseases.*

124. The black lung program's arbitrary, unscientific use of presumptions vastly increased the compensation paid. This approach was "the epitome of political manipulation of the pork barrel process under the guise of operating a workers' compensation scheme," according to the most exhaustive study of the program to date. PETER BARTH, THE TRAGEDY OF BLACK LUNG 128 (1987). Kenneth Feinberg, perhaps the leading expert on the politics and administration of mass tort compensation programs, notes that Congress has taken one lesson away from its experience with the black lung program: "Don't do it again." Telephone interview with Kenneth Feinberg, Esq., *cited in* Edward B. Zukoski, The Evolution of the Black Lung Compensation Program and Its Consequences for Mass Torts, at 86 (1992) (unpublished manuscript on file with author).

125. *See supra* note 52 and accompanying text.

126. Examples include changes in rules governing punitive damages, collateral sources, and joint-and-several liability. Congress is almost certain to enact national caps on punitive damage awards in product liability cases, which includes most mass torts. *See* Neil A. Lewis, *Senate Agrees On Bill to Cut Civil-Court Damage Awards,* N.Y. TIMES, May 10, 1995, at A1.

127. If enacted, certain provisions in the tort reform sections of the civil liability legislation now pending in Congress would affect the mass tort litigation. In addition to the punitive damages cap referred to in note 126, these provisions include the FDA safe harbor provision discussed *supra* note 49, and a provision concerning the standard for admitting scientific evidence.

128. In an earlier article, I subscribed to this theory—too readily, I now think. *See* Schuck, *supra* note 10, at 552.

129. For a summary and critique of these views, see Siliciano, *supra* note 2.

130. *See* DANIEL A. FARBER & PHILIP P. FRICKEY, LAW AND PUBLIC CHOICE (1991); Edward Rubin, *Public Choice in Practice and Theory,* 81 CAL. L. REV. 1657 (1993) (reviewing FARBER & FRICKEY, *supra*).

131. For a refreshingly candid defense of this strategy by a state judge, see RICHARD NEELY, THE PRODUCT LIABILITY MESS: HOW BUSINESS CAN BE RESCUED FROM THE POLITICS OF STATE COURTS 1–4 (1988). In such a situation, defendants may seek and obtain a federal statutory solution, a dynamic that contributed to the enactment of the Clean Air Act of 1970. *See* Bruce Ackerman et al., *Toward a Theory of Statutory Evolution: The Federalization of Environmental Law,* 1 J. L. ECON. & ORGANIZATION 313 (1985). It also helps to explain industry's current efforts to federalize products liability law. *See, e.g.,* Schuck, *supra* note 55.

132. *See generally* MANCUR OLSON, THE LOGIC OF COLLECTIVE ACTION (1965).

133. As Judge Reed noted in his fairness opinion, however, the AFL-CIO supported the settlement plan in *Georgine. See* Georgine v. Amchem Prods., Inc., 157 F.R.D. 246, 325 (E.D. Pa. 1994).

134. The word "systemic" is meant to recognize that the plaintiffs' bar has supported some statutory modifications of the common law, such as extensions of the limitations period to revive barred mass tort claims. It also strongly supports modifying the common law to make it easier for smokers (and states paying for smoking-related costs) to prevail in court. *See* Richard Daynard, *Smoking Out the Enemy: New Developments in Tobacco*

Litigation, TRIAL MAG., Nov. 1993, at 16. In general, however, the plaintiffs' bar has viewed most statutory reform proposals as a threat to its interests (and those of its clients).

135. *See* OLSON, *supra* note 132.

136. *See supra* note 52 and accompanying text.

137. The 104th Congress seems likely to enact at least some changes. *See supra* notes 49, 126–27.

138. *See* Schwartz, *supra* note 22. This could change, however, if plaintiffs can substantiate claims left open by Cipollone v. Liggett Group Inc., 112 S. Ct. 2608 (1992) (e.g., fraud), or if new groups of plaintiffs less subject to defenses, such as infants, bring suit against the tobacco companies. *See also* Charles C. Correll, Jr., The Tobacco Industry's Liability for Prenatal and Infant Injuries (October 1994) (unpublished manuscript on file with author). Indeed, several states have already done so. *See, e.g.,* Milo Geyelin, *Tobacco Companies Are Set Back By Actions in Florida, Mississippi*, WALL ST. J., Feb. 22, 1995, at B4. The recent certification of a class action against the companies may also weaken the defendants' commitment to the status quo. *See* Glenn Collins, *Judge Opens Way for Class Action Against Tobacco*, N.Y. TIMES, Feb. 18, 1995, at 1 (*Castano* litigation in federal district court in Louisiana).

139. Most product manufacturers, for example, presumably favor retaining some common-law products liability as a means of fostering consumer confidence in their products which might be reduced if consumers could rely only on contract law and reputation to enforce desired safety levels. The same is probably true of products liability insurers that sell such coverage.

140. Some commentators suggest that the judicial commitment to settlement class actions and other controversial changes in the mass tort system reflects their obsession with reducing their burgeoning caseloads rather than more disinterested motives. *See, e.g.,* Coffee, *supra* note 6; Marcus, *supra* note 78.

141. Public choice theory has difficulty taking account of non-economic values. *See* DONALD P. GREEN & IAN SHAPIRO, PATHOLOGIES OF RATIONAL CHOICE THEORY: A CRITIQUE OF APPLICATIONS IN POLITICAL SCIENCE (1994). The role of ideology in the mass tort system is briefly discussed *infra* part III.

142. *E.g.,* MARTHA DERTHICK & PAUL QUIRK, THE POLITICS OF DEREGULATION (1986); Michael Levine, *Revisionism Revised? Airline Deregulation and the Public Interest*, 44 LAW & CONTEMP. PROBS. 179 (1981).

143. *See supra* notes 123–28 and accompanying text.

144. Indeed, in the traditional view, tort law should not be seen as a policy instrument at all, but rather as an instrument of private law understood as corrective justice. *See* Richard A. Epstein, *A Theory of Strict Liability*, 2 J. LEGAL STUD. 151 (1973); Ernest J. Weinrib, *Corrective Justice*, 77 IOWA L. REV. 403 (1992). Yet, even if one generally views tort law in general as private law, it does not necessarily follow may not follow that one should also view *mass* tort law in the same way. *See* Rosenberg, *supra* note 2. Certainly, the courts have treated mass tort law as a public law problem, even while speaking the language of corrective justice. *See, e.g.,* Lester Brickman, *The Asbestos Litigation Crisis: Is There A Need for an Administrative Alternative?*, 13 CARDOZO L. REV. 1819 (1992).

145. *See, e.g.,* Peter H. Schuck, *The New Judicial Ideology of Tort Law, in* NEW DIRECTIONS IN LIABILITY LAW 4 (W. Olson ed., 1988) (discussing the policymaking weaknesses of common-law judges); James A. Henderson, Jr., *Judicial Review of Manufacturers' Conscious Design Choices: The Limits of Adjudication*, 73 COLUM. L. REV. 1531 (1973) (discussing the difficulties of polycentric decisionmaking in a judicial setting).

146. *See* Yeazell, *supra* note 70, for a discussion of the limits of appellate review. This point applies a fortiori to mass tort litigation, where the trial judge's managerial imperatives are so compelling, and where the appellate court is often presented with a fait accompli that, however legally defective, may be effectively irreversible.

147. *See* Schuck, *supra* note 145, at 15–16.

148. I speculate that some judges in mass tort cases, such as Jack Weinstein, Robert Parker, and Thomas Lambros, sometimes compete to be the most innovative.

149. *See* Fleming, *supra* note 81, at 520, 527.

150. *See* Fleming, *supra* note 81.

151. While many judicially devised mass tort innovations have succeeded, many others have not. Market share liability is an interesting example of the double-edged quality of judicial innovations in mass tort actions. In principle, it is an ingenious, elegant, logically consistent solution to an intractable problem of proof. In practice, however, litigants and courts have found it extremely difficult to implement. In the New York DES litigation, for example, several years and much expense were required to design an acceptable national market share matrix, even though the parties had the advantage of being able to draw on earlier negotiations and settlement patterns in the California DES litigation. In the end, over 99% of the New York claims were settled before the New York matrix was even sufficiently developed to influence the settlement negotiations. Rheingold Interview, *supra* note 7.

152. One example involves the importance of enabling class members to acquire better information about claims values in immature and future claims mass torts settlements. *See* discussion *supra* notes 82–119 and accompanying text. Courts have toiled fruitlessly over this information cost problem for some time in different settlement contexts; it may now be ripe for legislative review. *See also* Linda Silberman, *Judicial Adjuncts Revisited: The Proliferation of Ad Hoc Procedure*, 137 U. PA. L. REV. 2131, 2173–76 (1989) (explaining the need to refine special master procedures). More substantive examples of legislative responses include the narrowly focused administrative compensation schemes established by federal and state statutes. *See supra* notes 123–24 and accompanying text.

153. Professor Richard Marcus correctly notes the possibility that global settlements, which supplant judicial supervision with a detailed structure of long-term governance, will limit this flexibility. Letter from Richard L. Marcus, Professor of Law, Hastings College of Law (Oct. 25, 1994) (on file with author). Although it is too early to tell how the parties will interact under these agreements over time, some flexibility may be retained if, as seems likely, the parties may occasionally negotiate some changes (presumably with judicial approval) and invoke the arbitral or judicial forums which the agreements sometimes provide. For this reason, practice under these agreements may actually permit somewhat more flexibility than under judicially entered consent decrees. *See, e.g.,* David K. Fram, *Recent Development: The False Alarm of* Firefighters Local Union No. 1784 v. Stotts, 70 CORNELL L. REV. 991 (1985) (examining the scope of a district court's power to modify consent decrees).

154. Congress's sporadic and piecemeal review of the Superfund program is an example. *See, e.g.,* John H. Cushman, Jr., *Congress Foregoes Its Bid to Hasten Cleanup of Dumps,* N.Y. TIMES, Oct. 6, 1994, at A1 (failure to enact Superfund amendments). In the mass torts field, as we have seen, Congress's interventions have been both infrequent and narrowly-focused. *See* Rabin, *supra* note 12, and text accompanying *supra* notes 123, 126–27.

155. For experimental evidence on this point, see E. ALLAN LIND ET AL., THE PERCEPTION OF JUSTICE: TORT LITIGANTS' VIEW OF TRIAL, COURT-ANNEXED ARBITRATION, AND JUDICIAL SETTLEMENT CONFERENCES (1989); John Thibaut & Laurens Walker, *A Theory of Procedure*, 66 CAL. L. REV. 541 (1978). For professional and lay opinion about the civil jury, see Valerie P. Hans, *Attitudes toward the Civil Jury: A Crisis of Confidence?*, *in* VERDICT: ASSESSING THE CIVIL JURY SYSTEM 248 (Robert E. Litan ed., 1993).

156. This fascination with the civil lay jury does not extend either to Britain, which has largely abolished it in tort actions, or to civil law countries like Germany. *See generally* Richard A. Posner, *Juries on Trial*, COMMENTARY, Mar. 1995, at 49, 50.

157. Peter H. Schuck, *Mapping the Debate on Jury Reform*, *in* VERDICT: ASSESSING THE CIVIL JURY SYSTEM 329–30 (Robert E. Litan ed., 1993).

158. *See id.; see also* Judith Resnik, *From "Cases" to "Litigation,"* 54 LAW & CONTEMP. PROBS. 5 (1991); Judith Resnik, *Aggregation, Settlement and Dismay*, 80 CORNELL. L. REV. 918 (1995).

159. *See* Schuck, *supra* note 157.

160. 45 U.S.C. ss 51–60 (1988).

161. 42 U.S.C. ss 1981a(c), (d) (Supp. V 1993).

162. *See* Schuck, *supra* note 157.

163. *Id.* at 329.

164. This assumes that she works under a standard contingent fee arrangement. For a critique of these arrangements and a proposal to reduce the conflict of interest they generate, see LESTER BRICKMAN ET AL., RETHINKING CONTINGENCY FEES (1994).

165. Much pretrial adjudication in mass tort cases is handled by magistrates and special masters.

166. *See, e.g.*, JAMES A. MORONE, THE DEMOCRATIC WISH: POPULAR PARTICIPATION AND THE LIMITS OF AMERICAN GOVERNMENT (1990); STEPHEN SKOWRONEK, BUILDING A NEW AMERICAN STATE: THE EXPANSION OF NATIONAL ADMINISTRATIVE CAPACITIES, 1877–1920 (1982) (examining a restructuring of American government in order to accommodate the expansion of the administrative state); James Q. Wilson, *The Rise of the Bureaucratic State*, 41 THE PUB. INTEREST 77 (1975) (explaining the history of and theories driving the rise of the bureaucratic state).

167. *E.g.*, Northern Pipeline Constr. Co. v. Marathon Pipeline Co., 485 U.S. 50 (1982) (holding that Article III bars Congress from establishing bankruptcy courts with exclusive jurisdiction over bankruptcy matters); Crowell v. Benson, 285 U.S. 22 (1932) (holding that the Constitution restricts congressional power to replace Article III courts with administrative courts).

168. Yeazell, *supra* note 70, at 647. Congress's decision in 1988 to impose political review and formal adversary process on the determination of veterans' benefits, one of the very few administrative areas that still lacked these features, is a telling illustration of the point. Veterans' Judicial Review Act, Pub. L. No. 100–687, 102 Stat. 4105 (1988). This hostility to bureaucratic power is not shared by most democratic civil law countries such as France and Germany. On the other hand, these countries seem to be gravitating slowly toward the American model. *See generally* MAURO CAPPELLETTI, THE JUDICIAL PROCESS IN COMPARATIVE PERSPECTIVE (1989).

169. For the classic exposition of this point, see JERRY L. MASHAW, BUREAUCRATIC JUSTICE: MANAGING SOCIAL SECURITY DISABILITY CLAIMS (1983) (demonstrating the success of bureaucracy in dealing with social security claims).

170. More accurately, its appeal rests on its erstwhile lack of bureaucracy. The growing bureaucratization of judicial authority has occasioned concern among commenta-

tors. *See, e.g.,* RICHARD A. POSNER, THE FEDERAL COURTS: CRISIS AND REFORM (1985) (surveying changes in the federal court system); Wade H. McCree, *Bureaucratic Justice: An Early Warning,* 129 U. PA. L. REV. 777 (1981) (examining recent changes in the judicial process to accommodate heavier caseloads). It is unclear, however, whether this development has affected public attitudes toward the courts.

171. These advantages are in addition to the technocratic and instrumental advantages noted *supra* part II.B.1.

172. *See supra* text accompanying notes 148–52.

173. Increasingly—and especially in mass tort litigation—courthouses operate like administrative offices. *See supra* part I.A.3. Many court decisions and settlement decrees are as lengthy and detailed as agency regulations. Courts employ auxiliary staff for routine tasks that judges need not perform. Massive records are accumulated. Even the level of deference that courts and agencies accord to precedent may be converging: Judicial doctrines often entail sharp departures from precedent while administrative ones may be models of stare decisis. Although common law is of course not simply a matter of logical inference pronounced by disembodied oracles, normative claims of precedent are recognized in almost all systems of law, and agencies as well as courts routinely accept their compelling force.

174. *See supra* part I.B.

175. *See supra* part II.

176. I do not wish to discuss the whole host of possible incremental reforms to the current system, some of which have already been adopted in one or more jurisdictions.

177. For a more ambitious project of institutional comparison, see NEIL K. KOMESAR, IMPERFECT ALTERNATIVES: CHOOSING INSTITUTIONS IN LAW, ECONOMICS, AND PUBLIC POLICY (1994), especially chap. 6 on tort reform.

178. *See, e.g.,* Schuck, *supra* note 10, at 553–68.

179. *See, e.g.,* Rosenberg, *supra* note 2; David Rosenberg, *Class Actions for Mass Torts: Doing Individual Justice by Collective Means,* 62 IND. L.J. 561 (1987).

180. SCHUCK, *supra* note 5, at 268–72.

181. Indeed, Rosenberg's writings may have partly prompted these changes. In the seminal Agent Orange fairness decision, for example, Judge Weinstein cited Rosenberg and endorsed much of his model. *Id.* at 270.

182. *See, e.g.,* Nancy Morawetz, *Bargaining, Class Representation, and Fairness,* 54 OHIO ST. L.J. 1 (1993) (discussing distributional conflicts class action lawyers must resolve). *Id.* at 4 n.10 (citing broadly to the legal literature and to judicial authority).

183. *E.g.,* Georgine v. Amchem Prods., Inc., 157 F.R.D. 246 (E.D. Pa. 1994); *In re* Silicone Gel Breast Implant Prods. Liab. Litig., No. CV 92-P–10000-S, Civil Action No. CV 94-P–11558-S, 1994 U.S. Dist. LEXIS 12521 (N.D. Ala. Sept. 1, 1994); *In re* A.H. Robins Co., 880 F.2d 709 (4th Cir.) (finding no abuse of discretion by the district court), *cert. denied,* 493 U.S. 959 (1989); Ahearn v. Fibreboard Corp., Civ. Action No. 6:93CV526 (E.D. Tex.). *See also* Coffee, *supra* note 6.

184. *E.g.,* Hymowitz v. Eli Lilly & Co., 593 N.E.2d (N.Y.) (holding that manufacturers of DES are severally liable to claimants in proportion to their national market share), *cert. denied,* 493 U.S. 944 (1989). Medical monitoring of damage awards based on exposure can also be viewed as a crude form of proportional liability. *See In re* Paoli R.R. Yard PCB Litig., 916 F.2d 829 (3d Cir. 1990), *cert. denied,* 493 U.S. 961 (1991). *See also* discussion *supra* note 151.

185. Georgine v. Amchem Prods., Inc., 157 F.R.D. 246 (E.D. Pa. 1994); *In re* Silicone Gel Breast Implant Prods. Liab. Litig., No. CV 92-7–10000-S, Civil Action No. CV 94-

P–11558-S, 1994 U.S. Dist. LEXIS 12521 (N.D. Ala. Sept. 1, 1994); *In re* "Agent Orange" Prod. Liab. Litig., 611 F. Supp. 1396 (E.D.N.Y. 1985).

186. 157 F.R.D. 246 (E.D. Pa. 1994).

187. *In re* Silicone Gel Breast Implant Prods. Liab. Litig., No. CV 92-P–10000-S, Civil Action No. CV 94-P–11558-S, 1994 U.S. Dist. LEXIS 12521 (N.D. Ala. Sept. 1, 1994).

188. For the main proposals in the area of tort claims, see Robert Cooter & Stephen D. Sugarman, *A Regulated Market in Unmatured Tort Claims: Tort Reform by Contract, in* New Directions in Liability Law 174 (Walter Olson ed., 1988); Jonathan Macey & Geoffrey Miller, *The Plaintiffs' Attorney's Role in Class Action and Derivative Litigation: Economic Analysis and Recommendations for Reform,* 58 U. Chi L. Rev. 1, 105–110 (1991); Marc J. Shukaitis, *A Market in Personal Injury Tort Claims,* 16 J. Legal Stud. 329 (1987). *Cf.* Thomas A. Smith, *A Capital Markets Approach to Mass Tort Bankruptcy,* 104 Yale L.J. 367 (1994) (discussing the feasibility of a market for future claims against mass tort defendants forced to liquidate or reorganize in bankruptcy).

189. This system would minimize, if not eliminate, two problems in the current system that were noted above—the fact that many insubstantial claims nevertheless receive significant payments, *supra* notes 97–98, and the risk of adverse selection in the opt-out process, *supra* note 110.

190. Macey & Miller, *supra* note 188, at 105–10, propose a judicially run auction of the power to control large-scale, small claims class actions and derivative suits. Professor Coffee has criticized this proposal on the ground that it would deter attorneys from conducting pre-filing research, since a late-comer to the auction could free ride on the information that has been produced by others. Weinstein, *supra* note 1, at 263. This problem, however, could be ameliorated by requiring the auction winner to compensate those who have conducted valuable pre-filing investigation and research, perhaps at an hourly rate augmented by a novelty premium. A similar hourly rate arrangement is part of the proposal by Brickman et al., *supra* note 164, to control abuses of the contingency fee system.

191. Judge John Nangle recently observed that fee disputes were the main obstacle to settling class actions. John Nangle, Remarks at Research Conference on Class Actions, *supra* note 85. The implication, however, that this strengthens the policy argument for auctioning the right to represent the class is mine, not his.

192. *See supra* notes 164–65 and accompanying text.

193. As we have seen, these problems may be ameliorated somewhat in global settlements of mature mass torts with effective back-end opt out rights that can function as a market test on settlement claim values. *See supra* notes 104–13 and accompanying text.

194. *See* Geoffrey P. Miller, *Some Agency Problems in Settlement,* 16 J. Legal Stud. 189 (1987).

195. *See, e.g.,* Schuck, *supra* note 5, at 192–206 (discussing the fee-sharing agreement in the Agent Orange case and the ethical issues raised by such arrangements); *see also* Weinstein, *supra* note 1, at 76–82; Vincent R. Johnson, *Ethical Limitations on Creative Financing of Mass Tort Class Actions,* 54 Brook. L. Rev. 539 (1988) (suggesting that novel features of mass tort litigation may require that traditional fee-splitting rules be relaxed in that context.

196. *See* Fleming, *supra* note 81.

197. Geoffrey P. Miller & Jonathan R. Macey, *Comment, A Market Approach to Tort Reform Under Rule 23,* 80 Cornell L. Rev. 909, 915–17 (1995) (listing barriers).

198. The current auctioning of licenses by the Federal Communications Commission, which is required to meet a "public interest" standard roughly comparable to the court's obligation under Rule 23, is an obvious analogy.

199. *See* Symposium, *Future Prospects for Compensation Systems*, 52 MD. L. REV. 893 (1993).

200. Rabin, *supra* note 12, at 955–62. It should also be noted, as Professor Abraham has pointed out, that torts (including mass torts) comprise only a tiny portion of the serious accidents that occur, and that creating an administrative compensation apparatus to deal with them "would be massive overkill." Kenneth S. Abraham, *Individual Action and Collective Responsibility: The Dilemma of Mass Tort Reform*, 73 VA. L. REV. 845, 901 (1987).

201. Rabin, *supra* note 12, at 978–79. Rabin notes that workers' compensation has been far more effective in dealing with traumatic accidents than with long-latency diseases. *Id.* at 980 n.107.

202. *Id.* at 982.

203. *Id.* at 968–69.

204. *See* Schuck, *supra* note 10, at 566–67. For a pending case raising serious ethical questions about batch settlements, see Peter Passel, *Challenge to Multimillion-Dollar Settlement Threatens Top Texas Law Firm*, N.Y. TIMES, Mar. 24, 1995, at B6. Batching also exacerbates the problems of insubstantial claims and adverse selection discussed earlier. *See supra* notes 97–98, 110.

205. As Francis McGovern observes in his Comment on this Article, McGovern *supra* note 45, at 1025, mass tort law can be viewed as a procedural application of Guido Calabresi's characterization of torts as "the law of the mixed society." Guido Calabresi, *Torts—The Law of the Mixed Society*, 56 TEX. L. REV. 519 (1978).

206. Civil law systems of mass torts also appear to be acquiring hybrid forms. Fleming, *supra* note 81, at 519–27.

207. For a detailed examination of such facilities, see Symposium, *supra* note 89.

208. *See, e.g., In re* "Agent Orange" Prod. Liab. Litig., 996 F.2d 1425 (2d Cir. 1993), *cert. denied*, 114 S. Ct. 1125 (1994) (Agent Orange); Georgine v. Amchem Prods., Inc., 157 F.R.D. 246 (E.D. Pa. 1994) (asbestos); Spitzfaden v. Dow Corning Corp., 619 So.2d 795 (La. 1993); *In re* Silicone Gel Breast Implant Prods. Liab. Litig., No. CV 92-P–10000-S, Civil Action No. CV 94-P–11558-S, 1994 U.S. Dist. LEXIS 12521 (N.D. Ala. Sept. 1, 1994) (breast implants); Hensler & Peterson, *supra* note 1, at 989–92 (heart valves).

209. *See, e.g.,* Jonathan R. Macey, *Promoting Public-Regarding Legislation Through Statutory Interpretation: An Interest Group Model*, 86 COLUM. L. REV. 223, 232 & n.47 (1986) (noting that legislatures will attempt to disguise special interest legislation to avoid losing public support).

210. *See* PRINCIPALS AND AGENTS: THE STRUCTURE OF BUSINESS (John W. Pratt & Richard J. Zeckhauser eds., 1985); Matthew D. McCubbins et al., *Structure and Process, Politics and Policy: Administrative Arrangements and the Political Control of Agencies*, 75 VA. L. REV. 431 (1989).

211. Nevertheless, significant agency costs continue to plague and distort the relationship between mass tort plaintiffs' lawyers and their clients, especially in class actions. *See* Macey & Miller, *supra* note 188, at 19–27.

12
Public Law Litigation and Social Reform

I. Introduction

Perhaps the central issue raised by the contemporary public law system is the nature of the relationship between law, courts, and lawyering, on the one hand, and politics and policymaking, on the other. The results of the 1992 election render this concern even more salient.[1] One cannot rule out the kind of fierce interbranch conflicts over constitutional and statutory interpretation that occurred after the elections of 1800 and 1932, although for a variety of reasons they seem unlikely. The academic legal commentary concerning the connection between law, politics, and policy is remarkable in one respect: almost all of it is *normative* in character, consisting of arguments that proceed from one or another conception of justice (often asserted rather than defended). These arguments purport to imply or justify some ideal role for lawyers, law, and courts in the construction of social policy. *Rebellious Lawyering*[2] is a book very much in this tradition, advancing strong claims about how lawyers and clients should relate to one another and to the local cultures and institutions that hold power over them.

Most of the academic legal commentary, however, is preoccupied, even obsessed, with the role of *courts* in legal reform. This line of inquiry invites an obvious follow-up question: to what extent do these normative theories accurately reflect what courts do, and how courts affect social reality? Regrettably, legal scholars seldom ask (much less answer) this question, a fact that should dismay all of us who believe that empirical reality must inform the normative theories that we embrace and teach our students.[3] Fortunately, scholars in other disciplines have attempted to fill the enormous void which we, for reasons that are not altogether clear,[4] have created and then tolerated. Virtually all of the work in this area has been by political scientists.[5]

The Hollow Hope,[6] by lawyer and political scientist Gerald Rosenberg, represents the most recent contribution to this small but exceedingly stimulating and valuable literature. Rosenberg contrasts his book with previous studies of reform litigation which, he says, have "not squarely centered on whether, and under what conditions, courts produce significant social reform."[7] This claim exhibits the common scholarly conceit of uniqueness, but in this case it is, quite simply, false. It ignores, for example, two relatively recent, well-known, book-length studies published by the Brookings Institution on the effectiveness of court-driven reform—books that Rosenberg cites elsewhere in his study.[8] It also ignores a sizable political science literature on the inherent difficulties of policy implementation. This implementation literature applies, *mutatis mutandis*, to court-initiated policies as well as to legislative or administrative ones, and already makes all of Rosenberg's theoretical points.[9] Rosenberg's omissions are highly regrettable as a scholarly matter, and they merit criticism.[10] Nonetheless, *The Hollow Hope* is an important addition to the field, one that all public lawyers and political scientists will read with great profit.

II. Rebellious Lawyering

Rebellious Lawyering, by law professor and legal activist Gerald López, addresses a quite different question than that examined by *The Hollow Hope*: how should a "progressive" or "public interest" lawyer[11] conduct herself both personally and professionally[12] in order to advance the cause of social change? Although this question about modes of lawyering is of direct interest to a much smaller group than that addressed by Rosenberg, the two books are related in at least three important respects. First, López's principal audience consists of a set of actors who initiate much of the "public law litigation"[13] that is Rosenberg's subject. Second, and more interestingly, López seems to share much of Rosenberg's skepticism about the capacity of such litigation to bring about enduring social change.[14]

A third, and more damning, commonality is this: although the notion of "social change" lies at the heart of both books—for Rosenberg it is the dependent variable being analyzed, while for López it is the goal of progressive lawyering—neither book has much to say about its substantive or programmatic content, and neither offers a theory of what causes social change. Rosenberg defines it as "policy change with a nationwide impact" affecting "large groups of people."[15] It is, he says, *liberal* change.[16] Although he does not detail what this means, he implies that it has a decidedly egalitarian, and presumably statist, character.[17] He explicitly renounces any intention to supply a "full blown" theory of what brings social change about, although he does attempt to "assess a host of social, political, and economic changes that could plausibly have led to significant social reform independent of court action."[18]

López is even more Delphic about what constitutes and causes social change. Since his book seeks to instruct lawyers about how to help their clients and communities produce it, this is an astonishing omission.[19] The reader is simply left to infer from several clues what progressive change is, and how it comes about: the facts López uses in his fictional case studies,[20] the groups that he wants progressive lawyers to work with and represent,[21] and the evocative terms that he uses as synonyms for injustice.[22]

López's vivid elaboration of his ideas about progressive legal practice—his "rebellious idea of lawyering against subordination"[23]—constitutes a bold, potentially far-reaching challenge to what he considers the standard practice mode of legal services lawyers, which he calls "the regnant idea of the lawyer for the subordinated."[24] His preferred model, which he characterizes as "teaching self-help and lay lawyering,"[25] contrasts even more sharply with the brand of "public interest law" practiced by organizations such as the Public Citizen Litigation Group, the NAACP Legal Defense and Educational Fund, the Center for Law in the Public Interest, and the Washington Legal Foundation. These organizations, about which López says little, typically are highly professionalized large-city groups strongly oriented toward (and often partly funded by) major impact litigation, which is conducted by lawyers trained at elite law schools who enjoy high status and visibility. Such groups tend to have only the most formalistic relationships with their clients, organizational or individual, and engage in little or no community organizing; they are concerned with client empowerment in only a narrow, legal rights-oriented sense.[26]

The role of these other modes of legal activism in López's world of progressive lawyering remains unclear. Is there room there for the "regnant" and litigation-oriented forms of lawyering? Or are these instead merely degenerate forms which, even when they appear to succeed, further disempower people—both by placing professionals between them and the levers of enduring change, and by fostering the illusion that legal rights are the raw materials of self-actualization? To what extent are these other forms inevitable concessions to limited reformist resources and economies of scale, to the increasing importance of technical and professional know-how in influencing public and private decisionmakers, and to other such realities?

These questions raise some poignant ethical and tactical dilemmas, and López exhibits a good deal of sensitivity to some of these issues as they arise in his imaginary practice settings.[27] But he does not thoroughly canvass or articulate the competing considerations, and his normative assessments rest essentially on plausible but largely unexamined intuitions about human nature and social dynamics, intuitions that he imparts through the storytelling genre now in vogue among some legal scholars.[28] He prefers to argue from *ipse dixit* and personal reflection than from extended, disciplined analysis or available empirical evidence.[29]

The remainder of this Book Review is mostly about *The Hollow Hope*. My reason for confining my discussion in this way, however, is certainly not that *Rebellious Lawyering* is devoid of interest. In fact, it is an engagingly written, insightful, often moving argument in favor of a distinctive conception of professional responsibility by progressive lawyers: more humane, engaged, client-centered, self-abnegating, unheroic, and situational. *All* lawyers, progressive or not, should take up this challenge, for it invites us to "disenthrall ourselves," to "think anew"[30] about how and why we live in the law as we do.

III. The Hollow Hope

Methodologically, *The Hollow Hope* could hardly be more different from *Rebellious Lawyering*. In sharp contrast to López's highly confessional, normative, sometimes epistolary mode,[31] Rosenberg draws heavily on the kinds of data and analytical techniques that social scientists conventionally use.[32] His principal claims are empirical; he purports to be concerned only with the *fact* of judicial effectiveness in producing social change, not with normative judgments about what constitutes desirable change or what the courts' posture toward change ought to be.[33] Commendably, he lays out these claims for all to see, appraise, and criticize. Such an appraisal is my project in the remainder of this Book Review.

Generally speaking, we may distinguish three kinds of scholarly views[34] concerning the effectiveness of court-driven approaches in producing significant social reform.[35] Those I shall call "strong-court" scholars believe that the courts are often effective reformers by reason of their unique institutional features, especially their relative independence from electoral and bureaucratic politics. "Court skeptics" hold that court-directed reform, although not inevitably doomed to failure, is highly problematic. They argue that the most significant effects of such efforts are likely to be unanticipated and often perverse. "Court fatalists" maintain that the effectiveness of social reform depends on factors that courts can perhaps reinforce, but to which they are otherwise either irrelevant or epiphenomenal.[36]

These three views do not correspond to the conventional, often reductionist, polarities of left and right. Most strong-court scholars are liberal; they emphasize the courts' superior ability to articulate and instantiate public values in the face of what they regard as political and bureaucratic abdications. But some—Robert Bork, for example—are militantly conservative. Like the liberals, conservative strong-court scholars believe that court-initiated change is often effective. For precisely that reason, however, they denounce such change, arguing that it is institutionally illegitimate, constitutes lamentable public policy, or both.

The first two views are already well-represented in the literature. Strong-court scholars include commentators like Bork, Owen Fiss, Abram Chayes, and Michael Rebell and Arthur Block.[37] Skeptics are even more numerous; examples include Donald Horowitz, Jeremy Rabkin, Colin Diver, Shep Melnick, Robert Katzmann, and myself.[38] Fatalists, however, are a rarer breed, at least in recent years[39] as popular and professional ambitions for the judicial enterprise, nurtured by the Warren Court during the 1960's and state court expansions of liability law in the 1970's and early 1980's, have grown. Although *The Hollow Hope* sometimes approaches mainstream skepticism, its general thrust is emphatically fatalistic. Thus, Rosenberg in his concluding chapter states that "U.S. courts can *almost never* be effective producers of significant social reform. At best, they can second the social reform acts of the other branches of government."[40] With the publication of *The Hollow Hope*, Rosenberg becomes the leading contemporary exponent of court fatalism.

Rosenberg sets forth his version of fatalism by contrasting what he calls the "Dynamic Court" view (roughly corresponding to what I have called the strong-court view)[41] with a "Constrained Court" view, in which the courts are "weak, ineffective, and powerless."[42] It is hard, however, to think of a single scholar today who adheres to the constrained court view as Rosenberg defines it, nor does he cite any. His organizing scheme, moreover, does absolutely no analytical work for him; indeed, he quickly suggests that both views are partly correct and must therefore be combined to produce a refined understanding of the courts' role. The dichotomy thus turns out to be little more than a temporary placeholder for Rosenberg's own theory, which borrows from each of its halves.[43]

Merging his "Dynamic" and "Constrained" court views, Rosenberg produces a theory of the conditions under which courts produce significant social reform. The effectiveness of courts, he postulates, is limited by three structural constraints: (1) the limited nature of constitutional rights, (2) the low level of judicial independence; and (3) the judicial lack of implementation power. Each of these three constraints can be overcome, however, when three corresponding conditions are met: (1) "ample legal precedent for change"; (2) "support for change from substantial numbers" of congressional and executive officials; *and* (3) "support from some citizens, or at least low levels of opposition from all citizens" *plus* at least one of four other conditions: (a) positive incentives for compliance; (b) costs for noncompliance; (c) court decisions allowing market implementation; or (d) the presence of crucial implementation officials who "are willing to act and see court orders as a tool for leveraging additional resources or for hiding behind."[44]

Several problematic features of this theory should be noted at the outset, for they will recur in the discussion that follows. First, it is radically indeterminate. Virtually every one of the theory's key concepts—court, judicial decision, judicial effectiveness, social change, political support and opposition, incentives for compliance, market implementation, and official willingness to act—is deeply ambiguous and question-begging for Rosenberg's theoretical purposes, which are to explain and predict the consequences of Supreme Court decisions.[45] He disclaims any intention to explicate what is his most indeterminate yet theoretically fundamental concept of all—causality. In sum, Rosenberg cannot escape the inherently complex nature of his subject.[46]

Second, Rosenberg neglects certain dynamic effects unleashed by many Court decisions. In particular, he neglects the repetitive, dialogic nature of the interactions between courts, legislatures, agencies, and other social processes, as well as the political synergy that some litigation engenders.

Third, Rosenberg's measure of court effectiveness appears to give excessive weight to whether litigation advances the avowed agendas of public interest litigators and too little weight to more modest, but still significant, reform goals and to the substantive merits of the policies at stake in the litigation.

Finally, his theory makes no effort to differentiate between constitutional and statutory interpretation decisions. Even if the kinds of reformist court initiatives with which Rosenberg is concerned tend to take the former path, statutory construction remains another significant but quite different route for such efforts;[47] indeed, one of his case studies (environmental litigation) takes precisely this route.[48] Social reform through statutory interpretation has a distinctive dynamic that produces its own patterns of cause and consequence. To note only the most obvious difference, administrative agencies ordinarily play central roles in effectuating statutory regimes. Their relationships to courts, legislatures, and constituencies are pivotal in determining how judicial doctrines are both shaped and implemented.[49] Any theory of court effectiveness that conflates these two reform techniques, then, is bound to miss a great deal.[50]

For all these reasons, Rosenberg's theory is unpersuasive. In themselves, however, these shortcomings do not necessarily render it valueless. After all, a good theory can crystallize important issues, facilitating subsequent resolution through further conceptual clarification or data-gathering. The real test of Rosenberg's approach, then, is whether it can further these processes of hypothesis-refining, prediction-generating, and prediction-testing in the specific contexts to which he seeks to apply it, and hopefully in other contexts as well. As we shall see, his theory and analysis only partly satisfy this criterion, for they fail at many points. On the other hand, they have already succeeded in provoking much scholarly debate,[51] and they provide a (loose) framework around which he can drape some very interesting, significant data that enrich our understanding of the phenomena he discusses. Most important, his work should stimulate more refined theories of judicial effectiveness. Nevertheless (as I suggest in the Conclusion), to expect such theories to do much predictive work is to indulge in a hope as hollow as that which Rosenberg is at such pains to debunk.

A. Brown v. Board of Education

Rosenberg's first and most obvious challenge is *Brown v. Board of Education*.[52] This decision is usually viewed as the most famous instance of judicial activism—and more to the point, of *effective* judicial activism—in the modern history of the Supreme Court. *Brown* has long been celebrated by its supporters[53] and detractors[54] alike as the fountainhead of the civil rights movement and as a milestone of Equal Protection jurisprudence. If Rosenberg can demonstrate that *Brown* actually had little effect, and that the Court's impotence was a result of the constraints and the absence of the conditions identified by his theory, then he will have gone a very long way toward vindicating that theory.

Through a resourceful, imaginative, and pointed marshalling of evidence, Rosenberg succeeds in casting serious doubt on the conventional wisdom about *Brown*. In the end, however, the weaknesses of his theory prevent him from mounting a convincing refutation. After noting the familiar fact that there was little compliance with the decision for over a decade, he shows that when compliance finally did come in the areas of education, voting, transportation, public accommodations, and housing, the trigger was not *Brown* but civil rights legislation authorizing federal program agencies to cut off funding to noncomplying recipients. Anticipating the argument that *Brown* was responsible for this legislation, he notes that its sponsors did not cite *Brown* as a source of inspiration, and that Congress had been considering a similar remedy since the 1940's.[55]

Rosenberg's point is *not* that *Brown* was irrelevant to what followed or that the courts were always ineffective. He surely recognizes (although he does not say) that Title VI of the 1964 Civil Rights Act was legitimated, was rendered compelling policy, and probably passed constitutional muster[56] only because *Brown* had already established desegregated public education as a substantive right protected by the Equal Protection Clause. Nor does he deny that the courts did help to enforce school desegregation after 1968.[57] Rather, his point is that the Court's contribution to the civil rights revolution depended almost entirely on the efficacy of nonjudicial political forces and that *Brown* was largely irrelevant to their emergence. Like becalmed ships, the courts made little real headway until the mid–1960's when favorable winds generated by independent political forces became strong enough to carry them toward their destination. (A quarter-century later, they still are far from reaching it, especially in the area of higher education).[58]

Rosenberg argues that it was the constraints identified by his theory that operated to stymie judicial implementation of *Brown* in its first decade. Political leaders at all levels opposed vigorous enforcement. Public opinion in the South was deeply recalcitrant. The court system's own structure assured judicial impotence. Only when those constraints began to dissolve and some of the conditions for compliance specified by his theory were met—for example, the creation of incentives and the willingness of local actors to use the courts to provide political cover for their compliance—was real progress made. Only congressional and executive branch actions could dissolve these constraints and establish these conditions, but those actions could not be mounted until a decade after *Brown*.

In the meantime, the decision was essentially a dead letter. Rosenberg marshals evidence showing that during that initial decade, press coverage of civil rights—even in the media read by political elites and even in the black press—did not increase or change much; indeed, there was less coverage in those years than in some years of the 1940's. Textbooks continued to portray blacks with the same condescension and out-and-out racism as in the pre-*Brown* period. Elite attitudes appear to have been influenced little by the decision, and the general public remained ignorant of its existence and import.[59] Finding little evidence that *Brown* had much direct effect on civil rights enforcement during its first decade, Rosenberg flatly rejects the traditional view of *Brown* as social apocalypse that American legal scholars have propounded and propagated.[60]

To his credit, however, Rosenberg does not stop there. He goes on to consider the strong-court scholars' obvious fallback position—their contention that *Brown*'s effects were powerful, as advertised, but *indirect*; that subsequent events and additional factors mediated and obscured these indirect effects, rendering *Brown*'s true significance inaccessible to Rosenberg's method of investigation. For the optimist, *Brown*'s real contribution was to put civil rights on the liberal political agenda, force white politicians to respond, raise public consciousness of racial injustice, and inspire civil rights organizations and the black community to take to the streets and the voting booths, thereby producing the long-deferred political gains of the 1960's and 1970's. To exemplify this view, Rosenberg quotes C. Herman Pritchett's rhetorical question: "[I]f the Court had not taken the first giant step in 1954, does anyone think there would now be a Civil Rights Act of 1964?"[61] Rosenberg's intriguing court fatalist's answer is "yes." He recognizes (as he must) that even if the strong-court scholars' indirect effects thesis were in fact false, the complex nature of an encompassing social upheaval like the civil rights revolution would make it hard to rebut and impossible to refute conclusively. Causal pathways for such phenomena are never singular and are seldom clearly marked.[62] He deals with this problem in the only way an empiricist can, seeking to support his fatalistic theory factually by disproving its more optimistic alternatives.[63]

Searching the record for the kind of tracks that even indirect causality would leave, Rosenberg compares the pre- and post-*Brown* eras across a stunningly broad array of political indices: legislative initiatives, congressional debates, presidential pronouncements, political party and other elite attitudes, citizen awareness of *Brown* (and other Court decisions), the volume, motivation, and rhetoric of civil rights demonstrations, relationships among (and funding of) civil rights organizations, and public opinion among both blacks and whites on civil rights issues generally and on *Brown* in particular.[64]

On this evidence (and Rosenberg adduces a great deal of it), *Brown* did *not* "give [civil rights] salience, press political elites to act, prick the consciences of whites, legitimate the grievances of blacks, and fire blacks up to act."[65] Especially revealing in this regard is Rosenberg's discussion of the black community's response to *Brown*. He shows, for example, that the community's knowledge of *Brown* was probably not widespread; that many blacks had a lukewarm response to the decision; that protest actions, far from being sparked by *Brown*, had been more common in the 1940's than in some of the immediate post-*Brown* years; that *Brown* played a negligible role in inspiring the Montgomery bus boycott of 1956, the sit-in movement, or the leading black protest groups other than plaintiff's counsel (the NAACP Legal Defense and Educational Fund); that Martin Luther King, Jr. and other leaders outside the NAACP viewed *Brown*-type court actions as a formalist distraction from a mass protest strategy; and that partly for this reason there was serious conflict between the NAACP and the groups committed to mass protest.[66]

Rather than constituting a watershed in American race relations, then, *Brown* as depicted by Rosenberg was simply one point along an upward trajectory of public sympathy toward civil rights that began in the 1930's and steepened in the wake of World War II. In his fatalist account, this public support achieved political takeoff only in the mid–1960's when nonjudicial factors coalesced to create auspicious conditions for significant legislation and more aggressive enforcement.[67] Although the immediate precipitant of this transformation was the public fear and revulsion aroused by Southern violence against black and white demonstrators, other more structural changes had laid the groundwork. Economic pressures against segregation had mounted; demographic and migratory shifts had concentrated black voters in pivotal, electorally competitive states; the United States' growing international responsibilities made state-sanctioned racism here an embarrassment; the power of mass communications accelerated changes in public opinion.[68] The Court, whose *Brown* decision was already a decade old and unavailing, was merely a midwife of racial progress, not its parent.

Although Rosenberg's data on *Brown* and its aftermath are intriguing and undeniably provocative, they cannot substantiate a theory as open-ended and indeterminate as the one that he offers. At most, the data raise important but ultimately unanswerable questions about causality in a social context in which, as just noted, many factors other than *Brown* were also at work transforming social attitudes. These other factors presumably influenced, and were in turn influenced by, *Brown* in complex ways that are simply impossible to disentangle, though Rosenberg's is an imaginative effort.

B. Roe v. Wade

Rosenberg's analysis of the Court's first major abortion decision, *Roe v. Wade*,[69] is far less persuasive. It purports to exemplify a different aspect of his theory of court fatalism—the proposition (consistent with Rosenberg's "Dynamic Court" view) that courts can effectively propel social change *if* certain conditions are met, especially the existence of widespread public support and of market incentives for the reform. Even here, of course, the public support condition serves to underscore Rosenberg's claim that the Court's reformist role is essentially derivative, reinforcing, and epiphenomenal, not initiatory and causal.

His crucial factual claims center on the observation that the number of legal abortions, although flat in the late 1960's, began a steep, steady rise in 1970 (three years before *Roe*), flattening out again in 1980.[70] From this he argues that widespread availability of abortion, as well as liberal reform activity in state legislatures and relative passivity by conservative politicians on the issue, had already made abortion a mainstream social practice by 1973, when *Roe* was decided. At that time, he says, "there was little political opposition to abortion on the federal level, widespread support for it among relevant professional elites and social activists, large-scale use of it . . . , and growing public support."[71] When the Court rendered its decision in *Roe*, his argument implies, it was sailing comfortably with the wind at its back.[72] Further, since the number of legal abortions increased steadily before and after *Roe*, Rosenberg argues that the decision had little effect.

But *Roe* did, after all, invalidate *forty-six* state laws restricting abortion.[73] Rosenberg's explanation is that the laws that *Roe* struck down had been so massively evaded that their demise had little practical effect. There are several serious difficulties with this argument as a factual matter. As Neal Devins points out, the pre-*Roe* liberalizations of state abortion laws typically had been quite modest, leaving significant restrictions in place.[74] Thus, *Roe* immediately produced far-reaching changes in the law. Nor was the pre-*Roe* liberalization trend as powerful and irreversible as Rosenberg suggests. Indeed, immediately before *Roe*, reform initiatives in Michigan and North Dakota had failed. In qualitative terms as well, *Roe* did not simply continue the pre-*Roe* state of affairs; it appears to have sharply reduced both the maternal death rate from, and the cost of, abortions.[75] To frame *Roe*'s effect another way, it improved the outcomes for even those women who, before the decision, would have successfully evaded the legal restrictions on abortions.

Several interpretations that do *not* support Rosenberg's general theory can explain the data he uses. An alternative explanation for the fact that the post-*Roe* rise in abortions was merely linear might be the effectiveness of new statutory restrictions that states adopted after *Roe* in order to circumvent the decision. The fact that the increase in legal abortions did not flatten until after 1980—*despite* the new state law restrictions—is, under this explanation, what is intriguing about the data. In addition, Rosenberg's comparison is between pre- and post-*Roe*. Perhaps he should instead have attempted to compare the world following the actual *Roe* decision, and the hypothetical world that would have existed had the Supreme Court decided the case the other way. If *Roe* had gone the other way, the abortion rate might have increased at a lower rate or even declined, for evasion of state restrictions might have become more difficult than during the pre-*Roe* period, before the Supreme Court had spoken decisively on the issue. Indeed, had *Roe* upheld state criminalization of abortion, the burden of political inertia would have strongly, probably decisively, favored the pro-life forces; to legalize abortions in certain states might well have required a national constitutional amendment, which a passionate pro-life minority almost certainly could have defeated. Unfortunately, Rosenberg does not pursue these (and other) avenues, which might seriously undermine, or at least require him to refine, his interpretation of *Roe*'s consequences.

Rosenberg notes that *Roe* provoked a severe backlash by abortion opponents[76] but that the number of abortion providers and legal procedures nevertheless continued to increase after the decision, as private clinics proliferated.[77] These clinics provided market alternatives to hospital-based abortions, which were hard to obtain since many hospitals—under pressure from pro-life groups—refused to provide abortions even after *Roe*.[78] From this, Rosenberg infers that the *Roe* decision could not have been effective alone. Rather, effective social change occurred as a result of the *combination* of the decision with public support and the existence of market alternatives capable of neutralizing the unavailability of hospital-based abortions.[79]

This inference is certainly plausible and tends to support Rosenberg's larger theoretical structure of constraints and conditions. But since the issue of clinic versus hospital setting is so important to Rosenberg's analysis, and since the *Roe* Court (like the litigants in the case) largely ignored the question of where abortions occur, the analysis would have been more compelling had he taken account of the post-*Roe* decisions in which the Court actually did grapple with the topic. In looking at those cases, a point and a series of questions emerge. First, to treat the existence of market alternatives as an exogenous factor is hardly accurate; it was the Court, after all, that refused to allow states to confine abortions to hospitals.[80] Second, how is Rosenberg's analysis affected by subsequent court decisions permitting states to regulate clinics that provide abortions?[81] Do those decisions confirm his theory, by showing that the reform is rendered ineffective when market alternatives are restricted? Do they refute it, by showing that as a result of public law litigation and judicial action, the number of abortions did not decrease despite these restrictions?[82] Or do they (as I think) show that the theory's formulation is too ambiguous to be very useful either in clarifying the relevant concepts or in yielding testable, refutable propositions?[83]

Three examples amply illustrate the importance of this last question. First, Rosenberg's theory fails to tell us whether the reformist "court decision" to which he is applying the theory is simply *Roe,* or also includes the series of decisions that have purported to elaborate *Roe,* such as *Webster v. Reproductive Health Services.*[84] Why should his analysis be confined to *Roe* when the legal culture, and most certainly the Court, correctly assumes that such a decision merely initiates a long process through which a principle is elaborated and given content through specific and repeated applications? Second, the theory fails to tell us how to identify the "effects" of a decision like *Roe*—clearly a necessary precedent to appraising its "effectiveness." How did it alter the complex balance of political forces affecting not only future court decisions but state and federal legislative struggles, litigants' strategies, and private behaviors? Again, social reality is far too complex for *post hoc ergo propter hoc* reasoning about causality.

Finally, at the end of his discussion of the abortion cases, Rosenberg draws the following lesson: "[A]s with civil rights, the Court is far less responsible for the changes that occurred than most people think."[85] Yet, once again, if we try to imagine what abortion practices would have been like had *Roe* been decided the other way (rather than merely not decided), it seems plain that neither his theory nor his facts establish even this general proposition. It is one thing to say that *Roe* reinforced pro-abortion forces that were already in train, quite another to say that a contrary decision in *Roe* would not have much affected the course of abortion policy. If Rosenberg is saying the latter when he diminishes the Court's responsibility for the continuing availability of legal abortions, then it is hard to credit the claim.

C. Other Legal Areas

Rosenberg extends his analysis to other categories of cases, but because his treatment of these is more summary and less interesting, I shall discuss them only briefly. His approach in each of these case categories is flawed by one or more of the four problematic features of his theory noted earlier.[86] His discussion of women's rights (other than abortion) suffers both from the indeterminacy of the theory, and from his tendency to depreciate the courts' effectiveness by measuring it according to the agenda of the groups initiating the cases rather than more modest, albeit important, goals. His analysis of these cases is also confusing in other ways. He first contends that although the Court struck down many (but not all) gender-based distinctions during the 1970's and early 1980's,[87] and the other branches moved simultaneously to enlarge and enforce these antidiscrimination principles, little progress was made against wage discrimination because of the persistence of cultural barriers, family structure-based disadvantages, and other factors.[88] He also maintains, however, that a "tide of history" comprised of economic, demographic, educational, technological, ideological, and other factors has produced great gains for women in almost all areas.[89] Finally, he shows that there is little evidence—in media coverage, political activity, public opinion, or the growth and funding of the women's movement—that the Court's decisions had much to do with whatever gains women did make. He argues that this confirms his theory: "[N]one of the conditions allowing for Court effectiveness," he says, "are regularly present with women's rights."[90]

Here again, the theory is so ill-specified that it is hard to know how to evaluate his application of it to women's rights. Is the fact that so-called "comparable worth" claims have not been judicially recognized (Rosenberg's major example of lack of progress) evidence that courts are ineffective reformers, or is it simply evidence that, for better or for worse, they have not chosen to define the right to nondiscrimination to include this conception of pay equity?[91] If the latter, it seems wrongheaded to charge them with being ineffective at achieving a goal, comparable worth, that they never adopted as part of the reform they did embrace, and that many commentators, including some who support that goal, think courts (as distinguished from legislatures or agencies) are poorly equipped to achieve.[92]

Rosenberg's discussion of environmental cases exemplifies all four of the problematic features noted earlier: theoretical indeterminacy, neglect of important political dynamics unleashed by court decisions, measurement of reform effectiveness according to the litigators' most ambitious goals, and the failure to differentiate between constitutional and statutory interpretation by courts. Here too, his discussion is puzzling, and not simply because most of the cases that he cites are (unlike those in the earlier chapters) decisions by lower courts. First, he cites the failure of the courts to *constitutionalize* the right to a healthy environment as evidence of the ineffectiveness of court-initiated reform, predictable on the basis of his theory's constraints and conditions.[93] He does not consider the possibility that no such right was created because it was in fact a demonstrably bad idea, difficult if not impossible to justify on doctrinal, policy, or political grounds.[94] Nor does he consider that the court's role in interpreting environmental *statutes* is altogether different, and far more consequential, than its failure to constitutionalize environmental rights.

Next, he finds that the courts had "varying success" in enforcing environmental laws.[95] As in the gender discrimination area, this mixed verdict enables him to claim vindication for his theory, with its mixture of unspecified (hence analytically slippery) constraints and conditions. Moreover, his notion of judicial effectiveness here seems especially unsatisfactory; the criterion seems to be whether the courts agreed with the claims of environmental groups, not whether the courts' decisions had the beneficial policy results that Congress presumably intended.[96] This latter standard is more appropriate; further, applying it can yield even better, more substantive reasons to doubt the courts' effectiveness than Rosenberg adduces. Some detailed studies of court-regulatory agency interactions, for example, find that courts tend to be poor environmental policymakers whose decisions can often degrade, rather than improve, environmental conditions.[97]

Rosenberg's strategic point—which converges with Gerald López's argument—is that environmentalists (and other reformers) should not look to the courts for much help but should instead invest their resources in political mobilization and legislative lobbying. Courts, he concludes, simply "preserve victories achieved in the political realm from attack. But preservation, while important, is only useful when there are victories to preserve. And environmental litigation, as a strategy for producing a clean and healthy environment, achieved precious few victories."[98] For several reasons, however, this seems a dubious balance sheet on environmental litigation since the early 1970's. First, environmental groups have in fact won many victories in the courts during this period, as industry and government litigators will ruefully attest. The harder, more significant question (as noted above) is whether those victories were actually good for the environment, a question about which Rosenberg shows little sustained interest.[99] Second, there can be little question that environmental litigation was effective in helping to slow, and occasionally to defeat, the Reagan-Bush deregulatory juggernaut, and in helping to build up membership in environmental action organizations.[100]

More generally, his argument moves from the undeniable fact that reformers' resources are limited, so that public law litigation must compete for those resources with other forms of political activity conducted in nonjudicial forums, to what appears to be an implicit but far more doubtful assumption about the *process* of social reform. He writes that "the courts also limit change by deflecting claims from substantive political battles, where success is possible, to harmless legal ones where it is not."[101] The process of social change, however, is not a zero-sum game in which efforts initiated by courts and in other quarters are competitive rather than complementary. It is true, of course, that court-initiated change may generate a political backlash that can defeat or at least impede the reform enterprise, as with the abortion controversy. But this particular dynamic hardly exhausts the range of interactions between courts and politics, many of which are synergistic with respect to both substantive reform and political resources. Here as elsewhere in the book, Rosenberg's agnosticism concerning how social change actually occurs weakens the persuasiveness of his analysis.

In a very brief discussion of reapportionment litigation, Rosenberg likens his findings to those in the environmental area: "A procedural victory was won but one that didn't automatically lead to substantive ends. Legislatures were reapportioned, but the reformers' liberal agenda did not then automatically come to pass."[102] To imply that any reform is ineffective unless it can produce an "automatic" success is patently unreasonable, of course; I know of no reform that would satisfy it. Nevertheless, Rosenberg does make some telling points about how politicians have managed to mute the effects of reapportionment.[103] He goes on, however, to ignore a characteristic aspect of reapportionment litigation that is inconvenient for his theory and conclusion. Compared to the other areas that Rosenberg analyzes, court implementation of reapportionment decrees is easy; the court can either enjoin the election until a satisfactory districting plan is adopted or draw the plan itself.[104]

The final sphere of litigation discussed by Rosenberg is criminal justice reform—more specifically, the rights of prisoners and juveniles, the exclusionary rule, and the right to counsel.[105] Here again, his verdict is that the courts have been only partly effective in these areas ("problems still abound"[106]) and that his theory of constraints and conditions explains why. Indeed, despite the theoretical shortcomings already noted, his analysis seems more persuasive as applied to the criminal justice system—in which all of the effectiveness constraints and none of the conditions prescribed by the theory ordinarily obtain[107]—than to any of the other areas that he considers.

IV. Conclusion

Rebellious Lawyering and *The Hollow Hope* share an important insight. Liberal activist courts are not as effective in producing enduring social change as many of their proponents would wish. Partly because of this, López urges "progressive" lawyers (he tends to avoid the terms "liberal" or "radical") to put their energies and resources elsewhere—into community organizing and political mobilization.[108] He also conjures up a vision of lawyering that *all* lawyers should find challenging and that some will even find inspirational. He makes no large theoretical claims, however, about courts or about their connection to social change.

Rosenberg, in contrast, is preoccupied with these questions. He insists that "a great deal of writing about courts is fundamentally flawed,"[109] and he is correct. His own book is less about courts than about other political forces that surround and intersect with courts: public opinion, other government institutions, the media, and private organizations. Herein lies *The Hollow Hope*'s greatest value. It reminds us of a fact so obvious that only a subculture as parochial and self-absorbed (I am tempted to say autistic) as contemporary legal education and scholarship could possibly miss it: in the world of public law, the problems that reach courts are problems that the larger society has already been working on longer, with richer and more varied instruments, and in more comprehensive, systemic—hence more intractable—contexts.[110] The evidence that Rosenberg mobilizes to illuminate this fact is arresting, resourcefully compiled, and for the most part convincing; so far as I know, use of such evidence in this way is novel. One hopes that other commentators, especially legal scholars who pontificate about the social effects of legal decisions, will emulate and perhaps improve upon his techniques in the future.

When Rosenberg turns to analyzing the relationships between courts and these other political forces, however, his work is of considerably less value and may even be misleading. His court fatalism seems largely oblivious to the dialogic, sequential, iterative quality of court-society interactions in important public law cases,[111] a quality so elegantly elaborated by Alexander Bickel and applied by those scholars who have followed in the Bickelian tradition.[112] Rosenberg's theory of constraints and conditions, while identifying factors that are undeniably significant in determining judicial effectiveness, adds little that scholars literate in the political science of judicial behavior and policy implementation do not already know,[113] and it is in any event too ill-specified to be either fruitful or refutable.

It bears repeating, however, that *any* theory of judicial effectiveness is likely to suffer from these defects—or others at least as disabling. The many threads of causality are simply too tightly knotted to disentangle. The phenomenon of judicial effectiveness is far too complex to be captured in any transparent model. It is too contingent on the social context, political stakes, incentive and enforcement structure, level of rule specificity, power of the court's underlying theory of social action, particular policy domain, and other factors that are too numerous, hard to measure, or even ineffable to lend themselves to social science testing.

This is not a counsel of despair, however—only a plea for caution in the making of strong scholarly claims about causal efficacy, or lack of it, in public law. To say that Rosenberg's theory about judicial effectiveness in large-scale social reform fails to persuade is not to say that some competing theory has thereby been vindicated. Although I believe that the court skeptics, rather than the strong-court scholars or the court fatalists, have the best of the argument, a rueful candor compels me to add that we skeptics, like our competitors, are guided more by our professionally honed, often intuitive grasp of an elusive social reality than by any robust scientific theory worthy of the name.

Notes

1. For the first time since 1933, the same party controls the Presidency and both houses of Congress after a long period (twelve years in both cases) during which the other party had the opportunity to appoint much of the federal judiciary. Indeed the expansion of, and turnover within, the judiciary during the Reagan-Bush years meant that, between them, the two Presidents appointed nearly 600 judges (the total number of federal judgeships is 828). On the other hand, the accumulation of an unusually large backlog of judicial vacancies, coupled with a continuing high turnover rate, is expected to give President Clinton the opportunity to name many more judges to the federal bench during his first term than President Bush did, and almost as many as President Reagan did in his two terms. Stephen Labaton, *Clinton Expected to Change Makeup of Federal Courts*, N.Y. TIMES, March 8, 1993, at A1; Henry J. Reske, *Molding the Courts*, A.B.A. J., Jan. 1993, at 20.

2. GERALD P. LÓPEZ, REBELLIOUS LAWYERING: ONE CHICANO'S VISION OF PROGRESSIVE LAW PRACTICE (1992) [hereinafter referred to as LÓPEZ].

3. There are, however, exceptions. *See, e.g.*, JERRY L. MASHAW & DAVID HARFST, THE STRUGGLE FOR AUTO SAFETY (1990).

4. *See generally* Peter H. Schuck, *Why Don't Law Professors Do More Empirical Research?*, 39 J. LEGAL EDUC. 323 (1989).

5. A number of these political scientists are, however, legally trained or teach in law schools. For example, Martin Shapiro teaches at Berkeley's law school, Boalt Hall, though he has no law degree; Donald Horowitz holds a joint appointment at Duke; Gerald Rosenberg received a law degree from Michigan and a Ph.D. in political science from Yale, and teaches both political science and law at the University of Chicago.

6. GERALD N. ROSENBERG, THE HOLLOW HOPE: CAN COURTS BRING ABOUT SOCIAL CHANGE? (1991) [hereinafter referred to as ROSENBERG].

7. ROSENBERG at 9. Rosenberg cites, but dismisses, the study by Michael A. Rebell and Arthur R. Block, EDUCATIONAL POLICY MAKING AND THE COURTS: AN EMPIRICAL STUDY OF JUDICIAL ACTIVISM (1982), because it is concerned with "admittedly non-controversial areas," ROSENBERG at 10, an odd way to characterize disputes over urban school policies. *See also id.* at 29.

8. The first Brookings book was Donald L. Horowitz's detailed, theoretically informed empirical case studies of reform litigation, THE COURTS AND SOCIAL POLICY (1977). Indeed, three of Horowitz's case studies involve courts' effects on school desegregation, criminal procedure, and juvenile justice, *id.* at 106–70, 220–54, 171–219—areas that Rosenberg examines in *The Hollow Hope*. (Ironically, Horowitz's book was itself criticized for having failed to cite earlier social science studies on the subject. *See* Stephen L. Wasby, Book Review, 31 VAND. L. REV. 727, 733, 740 (1978)).

The second Brookings book was R. Shep Melnick's equally detailed study of environmental regulation, REGULATION AND THE COURTS: THE CASE OF THE CLEAN AIR ACT (1983) [hereinafter MELNICK, REGULATION]. A new book by Melnick. THE POLITICS OF

STATUTORY RIGHTS: THE COURTS AND CONGRESS IN THE AMERICAN WELFARE STATE (forthcoming) (manuscript on file with author) [hereinafter MELNICK, STATUTORY RIGHTS], was unavailable (except, perhaps, in manuscript) when Rosenberg's book went to press. Rosenberg may believe that these books do not meet his criteria. If so, he does not explain why. Perhaps it is because they are case studies rather than systematic, rigorous, empirical analyses; given the limitations of their methodologies, they cannot really isolate the precise contributions of the courts in those cases.

An earlier classic in the field that takes a view roughly similar to Rosenberg's— ROBERT McCLOSKEY, THE AMERICAN SUPREME COURT (1960)—is never specifically cited, although it is included in the general bibliography. In addition, Rosenberg neither cites nor includes in his bibliography a number of other studies of the implementation of particular Supreme Court decisions. For example he omits the literature on school prayer, *see* School Dist. v. Schempp, 374 U.S. 203 (1963), which includes KENNETH M. DOLBEARE & PHILLIP E. HAMMOND, THE SCHOOL PRAYER DECISIONS: FROM COURT POLICY TO LOCAL PRACTICE (1971); WILLIAM K. MUIR, JR., PRAYER IN THE PUBLIC SCHOOLS: LAW AND ATTITUDE CHANGE (1967).

9. *See, e.g.*, EUGENE BARDACH, THE IMPLEMENTATION GAME (1977); JEFFREY L. PRESSMAN & AARON WILDAVSKY, IMPLEMENTATION (1973); Richard Elmore, *Organizational Models of Social Program Implementation*, 26 PUB. POL'Y 185 (1978); Joel F. Handler, *Controlling Official Behavior in Welfare Administration, in* THE LAW OF THE POOR 155 (Jacobus tenBroek ed., 1966); Peter H. Schuck, *Regulation: Asking the Right Questions*, NAT'L J., Apr. 28, 1979, at 711; *Symposium on Successful Policy Implementation*, 8 POL'Y STUD. J. 531 (1980); Donald S. Van Meter & Carl E. Van Horn, *The Policy Implementation Process: A Conceptual Framework*, 6 ADMIN. & SOC'Y 445 (1975); Richard Weatherly & Michael Lipsky, *Street-Level Bureaucrats and Institutional Innovation: Implementing Special-Education Reform*. 47 HARV. EDUC. REV. 171 (1977).

10. Thus, I am puzzled by Professor Powe's apparent effort, in his review of Rosenberg's book, to excuse this failing. Powe observes that fundamentally "Rosenberg's theory is not an implementation theory" and that "the earlier implementation studies are not well known." L.A. Powe, Jr., *The Supreme Court, Social Change, and Legal Scholarship*, 44 STAN. L. REV. 1615, 1631 (1992) (reviewing LEE C. BOLLINGER, IMAGES OF A FREE PRESS (1991) and *The Hollow Hope*). Whatever Rosenberg's theory purports to be, it is plainly a theory about the conditions under which courts seeking to initiate or reinforce social change can "effectively" do so—that is, can *implement* such change, alone or in combination with other forces. And even if Powe's assertion that implementation studies are not well known is true of the general public, this ignorance is either false or irrelevant insofar as social scientists and legal scholars choosing to write in the field are concerned. In either event, it is their duty to know about and, where germane to their arguments, to discuss such studies. In this spirit, Powe observes at the end of his review that lawyers should read more social science; indeed, he criticizes a law professor (whose book was also under review) for having failed to do so. *Id.* at 1641. This criticism must be all the more damning when applied to another social scientist.

11. These labels are used interchangeably throughout the book. They are, of course, somewhat tendentious and self-serving, which is why I put them in quotes. But they are no more so than other labels used by political groups on both the right and the left—for example, "pro-life," "pro-choice," and "libertarian"—which seek to show membership on the side of the angels.

12. López seems to be making the claim that, for these lawyers at least, the two spheres should be integrated—that their personal values and their professional behavior must be consistent. This is interesting but not obviously correct. One argument that might be made against it, for example, is that a lawyer must maintain a certain distance between herself and her client if she is to furnish the sound, professional judgment to which the client is entitled.

13. *See* Abram Chayes, *The Role of the Judge in Public Law Litigation*, 89 HARV. L. REV. 1281 (1976).

14. I say "seems to" because López offers no systematic explanation of what actually constitutes the "social change" to which progressive lawyers should bend their efforts. *See infra* text immediately following this note.

15. ROSENBERG at 4.

16. *Id.* at xi. This is presumably because the Court decisions that he discusses, all in the pre-Reagan years, have generally been characterized as "liberal." He gives no hint as to how his account of judicial effectiveness would have to be altered if more "conservative" changes of the sort sought by the Rehnquist Court were the objects of analysis. This omission is unfortunate.

17. He defines social change as "the broadening and equalizing of the possession and enjoyment of what are commonly perceived as basic goods in American society." *Id.* at 4. Drawing on John Rawls' expansive conception, he speaks of "political goods such as participation in the political process and freedom of speech and association; legal goods such as equal and non-discriminatory treatment of all people; material goods; and self-respect, the opportunity for every individual to lead a satisfying and worthy life." *Id.* (citing JOHN RAWLS, A THEORY OF JUSTICE 42, 440 (1971)).

18. *Id.* at 8.

19. Although López insists (through the mouth of a fictional community organizer) that one must have a vision of the "good life" that includes "a view of the state," he fails to offer even a hint of what such a view would look like. LÓPEZ at 377. A page later, the organizer says that one must also be "programmatic." *Id.* at 378. Again, however, López never mentions, much less defends, any specific agenda.

20. López states at the outset: "*Everything* I describe is fictional." *Id.* at 8. His fictional case studies include legalization efforts on behalf of undocumented aliens, landlord-tenant disputes, the operation of a community law office, disability claims, racial discrimination, and community organizing around a variety of issues. He also refers to the practitioners he describes as "poverty lawyers." *Id.* at 20.

21. These groups include "women, low-income people, people of color, gays and lesbians, the disabled, and the elderly." *Id.* at 37.

22. The most prominent example is "subordination," which he uses to refer generally to a sense of powerlessness but which otherwise remains essentially undefined. *See id.* at 11–82 (ch. I), *passim.* He also writes of "efforts to fundamentally change the world," *id.* at 10, without indicating what this means or entails.

23. *Id.* at 37.

24. *Id.* at 11. López lists twelve characteristics of the "regnant idea" of such lawyering, including formal representation of clients, an emphasis on litigation, and situating the lawyer as primary problem-solver. *Id.* at 23–24.

25. *Id.* at 70.

26. For descriptions of such groups, see ANDREW S. MCFARLAND, COMMON CAUSE: LOBBYING IN THE PUBLIC INTEREST (1984); ANDREW S. MCFARLAND, PUBLIC INTEREST

LOBBIES: DECISIONMAKING ON ENERGY (1976); Robert L. Rabin, *Lawyers for Social Change: Perspectives on Public Interest Law*, 28 STAN. L. REV. 207 (1976); Peter H. Schuck, *The Nader Chronicles*, 50 TEXAS L. REV. 1455 (1972) (reviewing ROBERT F. BUCKHORN, NADER: THE PEOPLE'S LAWYER (1972) and CHARLES MCCARRY, CITIZEN NADER (1972)).

27. *See, e.g.*, LÓPEZ at 14, 18.

28. This genre is especially popular among law professors interested in critical race theory, feminism, literary theory, and related modes of legal theory. *See, e.g.*, Richard Delgado, *Storytelling for Oppositionists and Others: A Plea for Narrative*, 87 MICH. L. REV. 2411 (1989). For a recent critique of the storytelling genre, see Daniel A. Farber & Suzanna Sherry. *Telling Stories Out of School: An Essay on Legal Narrative*, 45 STAN. L. REV. 807 (1993). López defends the narrative approach, LÓPEZ at 39–44, and uses it throughout.

29. Notably absent from his discussion, for example, is any explicit reference to the extensive empirical law-and-society literature on lawyer-client interactions. He does, however, list several such studies in an unannotated bibliography at the end of the book, including, e.g., DOUGLAS E. ROSENTHAL, LAWYER AND CLIENT: WHO'S IN CHARGE? (1974); Austin Sarat, *'... The Law Is All Over': Power, Resistance and the Legal Consciousness of the Welfare Poor*, 2 YALE J.L. & HUMAN. 343 (1990); Austin Sarat & William L.F. Felstiner, *Lawyers and Legal Consciousness: Law Talk in the Divorce Lawyer's Office*, 98 YALE L.J. 1663 (1989); Austin Sarat & William L.F. Felstiner, *Law and Strategy in the Divorce Lawyer's Office*, 20 LAW & SOC'Y REV. 93 (1986).

30. ABRAHAM LINCOLN, *[Second] Annual Message to Congress* (December 1, 1862) *reprinted in* 5 THE COLLECTED WORKS OF ABRAHAM LINCOLN 518, 537 (Roy P. Basler ed., 1953).

31. López makes many of his points through the literary device of fictional memoranda from lawyers, legal investigators, etc. *See, e.g.*, LÓPEZ at 145.

32. But while conventional, these techniques are also quite rudimentary by the standards of quantitative social science. Rosenberg's tables and figures, for example, use simple comparisons of absolute numbers rather than more complex statistics, regressions, or other forms of multivariate analysis.

33. ROSENBERG at xi. Of course, how one defines and measures effectiveness is not simply a matter of objective fact but inescapably involves some value judgments.

34. These are more akin to perspectives than to articulated, systematic *theories*.

35. Rosenberg uses the phrase *"significant* social reform" to apply to nationwide changes in bureaucratic or institutional practices. ROSENBERG at 4. One could quarrel with this definition, but it will serve for purposes of the present discussion. *See also supra* text accompanying notes 15–18.

36. One can be both a skeptic and a fatalist. My colleague Jerry Mashaw places himself in this camp, finding judicial intervention under some circumstances to combine "[i]mpertinence and irrelevance" to social reality. JERRY L. MASHAW, BUREAUCRATIC JUSTICE: MANAGING SOCIAL SECURITY CLAIMS 4 (1983).

37. *See generally* ROBERT H. BORK, THE TEMPTING OF AMERICA: THE POLITICAL SEDUCTION OF THE LAW (1990); REBELL & BLOCK, *supra* note 7; Chayes, *supra* note 13; Owen M. Fiss, *The Supreme Court 1978 Term—Foreword: The Forms of Justice*, 93 HARV. L. REV. 1 (1979).

38. *See generally* HOROWITZ, *supra* note 8; ROBERT A. KATZMANN, INSTITUTIONAL DISABILITY: THE SAGA OF TRANSPORTATION POLICY FOR THE DISABLED (1986); MELNICK, REGULATION, *supra* note 8; MELNICK, STATUTORY RIGHTS, *supra* note 8; JEREMY A. RABKIN, JUDICIAL COMPULSIONS: HOW PUBLIC LAW DISTORTS PUBLIC POLICY (1989); PETER H. SCHUCK, SUING GOVERNMENT: CITIZEN REMEDIES FOR OFFICIAL WRONGS 147–81 (1983)

[hereinafter SCHUCK, SUING GOVERNMENT]; Colin S. Diver, *The Judge As Political Powerbroker: Superintending Structural Change in Public Institutions,* 65 VA. L. REV. 43 (1979); Peter H. Schuck, *The New Judicial Ideology of Tort Law, in* NEW DIRECTIONS IN LIABILITY LAW (Walter Olson ed., 1988).

39. Perhaps the greatest fatalist, though certainly an unconventional one, was Justice Holmes. *See* Yosal Rogat, *The Judge as Spectator,* 31 U. CHI. L. REV. 213 (1964). I thank Owen Fiss for suggesting the Holmes example.

40. ROSENBERG at 338.

41. In Rosenberg's words, the Dynamic Court view "sees courts as powerful, vigorous, and potent proponents of change." *Id.* at 2.

42. *Id.* at 3. Rosenberg intends to confine the contrast to the reform litigation context. "[T]here is no clash between the two views in dealing with individuals." *Id.* at 5. Although he does not discuss the fact that reform cases are often concerned with, and initiated by, individuals, he surely recognizes it.

43. Lest the reader think that I am blind to the shortcomings of my own "trichotomy" (strong-court scholarship, court skepticism, and court fatalism), let me hasten to add that I use it only for the most limited purpose—simply to distinguish at the outset Rosenberg's approach from other scholarly approaches that might otherwise be confused with it.

44. ROSENBERG at 35–36.

45. To cite one striking example, it is not at all clear to which "courts" his theory relates. His two main case studies (school desegregation and abortion) focus on Supreme Court decisions; yet some of his other examples, such as environmental litigation, deal with lower court cases. This is not a trivial ambiguity for, as he himself notes, the Supreme Court enjoys only limited control over the lower courts. Indeed, his own account of the lower courts' early sluggish response to *Brown v. Board of Education,* 347 U.S. 483 (1954) (*Brown I*), 349 U.S. 294 (1955) (*Brown II*), dramatically underscores the need for clarification on this point. *See* ROSENBERG at 42–71. Other examples of fundamental conceptual ambiguity are mentioned throughout this Review.

46. Rosenberg, however, seems to feel that he has avoided this flaw; in this connection, he notes that Stephen Wasby's 1970 book on the impact of Supreme Court decisions "suggested so many hypotheses (one hundred and thirty-five of them) as to be of little practical help." ROSENBERG at 10 (citing STEPHEN L. WASBY, THE IMPACT OF THE UNITED STATES SUPREME COURT: SOME PERSPECTIVES (1970)).

47. For example, in 1978 the Supreme Court reversed a line of circuit court cases holding that the procedures specified in Administrative Procedure Act s 553 provided merely a "floor" of procedural requirements. Vermont Yankee Nuclear Power Corp. v. Natural Resources Defense Council, 435 U.S. 519 (1978); *see also* Antonin Scalia, *Vermont Yankee: The APA, the D.C. Circuit, and the Supreme Court,* 1978 SUP. CT. REV. 345 (1979) (describing and praising Supreme Court's rejection of D.C. Circuit's reasoning). Antitrust law supplies other examples of judicially-initiated reform accomplished through statutory interpretation; for example, early in this century the Supreme Court abandoned per se rules against restraints of trade in favor of a rule of reason, shifting the focus of antitrust law from consumers to small businesses. For a discussion of the relevant cases, see ROBERT H. BORK, THE ANTITRUST PARADOX: A POLICY AT WAR WITH ITSELF 15–49 (1978). Anti-discrimination disability law is yet another field in which the judiciary has attempted reform by means of statutory interpretation. *See, e.g.,* KATZMANN, *supra* note 38.

48. ROSENBERG at 271–92.

49. *See* MELNICK, STATUTORY RIGHTS, *supra* note 8. Indeed, Melnick expressly contrasts his findings with Rosenberg's argument. *Id.* (manuscript at 578 & 660 n.2).

50. Rosenberg does say that the political support necessary (but under his theory, not always sufficient) for judicial effectiveness may exist "when legislation supportive of significant social reform has been enacted and courts are asked to interpret it." ROSENBERG at 31. Although be does not make this point, his claim is supported by the frequency with which Congress overrules judicial interpretations of statutes. William N. Eskridge, Jr., *Overriding Supreme Court Statutory Interpretation Decisions,* 101 YALE L.J. 331 (1991).

51. Reviews of *The Hollow Hope* include Stephen L. Carter, Book Review, 90 MICH. L. REV. 1216 (1992); Neal Devins, *Judicial Matters,* 80 CAL. L. REV. 1027 (1992); Stephen J. Kastenberg, Book Review, 29 HARV. J. ON LEGIS. 589 (1992); David L. Kirp, Book Review, 254 NATION 757 (1992); L.A. Powe, Jr., *supra* note 10; Cass R. Sunstein, N.Y. REV. BOOKS, Oct. 22, 1992, at 47.

52. 347 U.S. 483 (1954) (*Brown I*), 349 U.S. 294 (1955) (*Brown II*).

53. *See, e.g.,* Annual Judicial Conference, Second Judicial Circuit of the United States, 130 F.R.D. 161 168 (1989) (remarks of Justice Thurgood Marshall); Robert M. Cover, *The Origins of Judicial Activism in the Protection of Minorities,* 91 YALE L.J. 1287 (1982); Fiss, *supra* note 37; Jack Greenberg, *Litigation for Social Change: Methods, Limits and Role in Democracy,* 29 REC. ASS'N B. CITY OF N.Y. 320, 337–54 (1974); HARVIE J. WILKINSON, III, FROM BROWN TO BAKKE: THE SUPREME COURT AND SCHOOL INTEGRATION, 1954–1978 (1979).

54. *See, e.g.,* JOHN AGRESTO, THE SUPREME COURT AND CONSTITUTIONAL DEMOCRACY 154 (1984); LINO A. GRAGLIA, DISASTER BY DECREE: THE SUPREME COURT DECISIONS ON RACE AND THE SCHOOLS 18–37 (1976); Herbert Wechsler, *Toward Neutral Principles of Constitutional Law,* 73 HARV. L. REV. 1, 31–35 (1959).

55. ROSENBERG at 42–71 (ch. 2). For a contrary claim on the inspiration point, see Devins, *supra* note 51, at 1041–42. Immediately after, Rosenberg states that "[o]nly after there was a major change in the congressional climate with the passage of the 1964 Civil Rights Act, did the Court re-enter the field." ROSENBERG at 74. This ignores several important Supreme Court decisions decided after *Brown* and before passage of the Act, including Griffin v. County School Board, 377 U.S. 218 (1964) (enjoining public schools from closing to avoid desegregation plan), Goss v. Board of Education, 373 U.S. 683 (1963) (disapproving desegregation plan that allowed any student to transfer out of de-segregated school district), and Cooper v. Aaron, 358 U.S. I (1958) (rejecting district court suspension of Little Rock school board's plan to desegregate schools), all of which Rosenberg discusses in his second chapter.

56. Although much of the Act relied on Congress' power to regulate interstate com-merce, *see* Heart of Atlanta Motel v. United States, 379 U.S. 241, 250 (1964) (upholding Title II, the public accommodations section, as a legitimate use of the commerce power), Title VI, which authorized the termination of federal funds to school districts that discriminated, was premised on the Fourteenth Amendment. *See* United States v. Jefferson County Bd. of Educ., 372 F.2d 836, 856, 882 (5th Cir. 1966) (Wisdom, J.), *aff'd en banc,* 380 F.2d 385 (5th Cir. 1967), *cert. denied,* 389 U.S. 840 (1967). In addition, Title IV provided that the Department of Justice could itself sue to desegregate recalcitrant school districts. Thus, federal enforcement of the norm of desegregation was at least in part directly dependent on *Brown* and its progeny. *See* Swann v. Charlotte-Mecklenburg

Bd. of Educ., 402 U.S. 1, 16 (1971); *cf.* U.S. COMM'N ON CIVIL RIGHTS, TITLE IV AND SCHOOL DESEGREGATION: A STUDY OF A NEGLECTED FEDERAL PROGRAM (Jan. 1973).

57. ROSENBERG at 52–54. Devins apparently misreads Rosenberg on this point. Devins, *supra* note 51, at 1043–46 (discussing judicial role in period following Green v. County School Board, 391 U.S. 430 (1968)).

58. United States v. Fordice, 112 S. Ct. 2727, 2734, 2746 (1992) (a recent extension of *Brown* to desegregation in higher education), documents the still-segregated status of Mississippi State Universities.

59. ROSENBERG at 72–106 (ch. 3).

60. For quotations from sources presenting the traditional view, see ROSENBERG at 39–40.

61. *Id.* at 107 (quoting C. Herman Pritchett, *Equal Protection and the Urban Majority*, 58 AM. POL. SCI. REV. 869, 869 (1964)).

62. Or as Rosenberg puts this indeterminacy point: "Ideas seem to have feet of their own, and tracking their footsteps is an imperfect science. Thus, even if I find little or no evidence of extra-judicial influence, it is simply impossible to state with certainty that the Court did not produce significant social reform in civil rights." ROSENBERG at 108.

63. He employs this technique of proof in his other case studies as well.

64. ROSENBERG at 107–56 (ch. 4).

65. *Id.* at 156. Indeed, by "stiffening resistance and raising fears before the activist phase of the civil rights movement was in place," Rosenberg suggests. "*Brown* may actually have delayed the achievement of civil rights." *Id.*

66. *Id.* at 131–50.

67. *Id.* at 107–56 (ch. 4).

68. *Id.* at 157–69 (ch. 5).

69. 410 U.S. 113 (1973).

70. ROSENBERG at 178–80. Thus the percentage increase, figured annually, declined steadily. Though Rosenberg does not say so, the abortion *rate* (number of abortions per 1000 women age 14 to 44 years of age) and the abortion *ratio* (number of abortions per 1000 live births) followed the same general pattern. Centers for Disease Control and Prevention. *CDC Surveillance Summaries, Abortion Surveillance—United States, 1989*, MORBIDITY & MORTALITY WKLY. REP.; vol. 41, September 4, 1992, at 3 (Figure 1), 12 (Table 2); *Abortion Surveillance—United States 1990*, 41 MORBIDITY & MORTALITY WKLY. REP. 936, 937 (1992). Rosenberg's abortion figures, although compiled in part from CDC data, differ slightly from the numbers reported by the CDC.

71. ROSENBERG at 182. Later, he writes that "[i]n recent times, public discussion [of abortion] did not surface until the 1950s," *Id.* at 258–59, failing to note that nineteenth-century discussion of abortion was extensive, *see, e.g.*, CARL N. DEGLER, AT ODDS: WOMEN AND THE FAMILY IN AMERICA FROM THE REVOLUTION TO THE PRESENT 239 (1980); JOHN P. HARPER, "BE FRUITFUL AND MULTIPLY": THE REACTION TO FAMILY LIMITATION IN NINETEENTH-CENTURY AMERICA (1975); JAMES C. MOHR, ABORTION IN AMERICA: THE ORIGINS AND EVOLUTION OF NATIONAL POLICY, 1800–1900 (1978); Reva Siegel, *Reasoning from the Body: A Historical Perspective on Abortion Regulation and Questions of Equal Protection*, 44 STAN. L. REV. 261, 281–87 (1992) and sources there cited (describing nineteenth-century anti-abortion advocacy of American Medical Association).

72. Even when Congress first passed its annual Hyde Amendment in 1976, severely limiting the use of federal funds to pay for abortions, it took no direct action to prohibit abortion itself, and the pre-*Roe* rate of increase continued. ROSENBERG at 187.

73. *Id.* at 175.

74. Devins, *supra* note 51, at 1057 & n.138.

75. *Id.*, at 1057–58 and sources there cited.

76. ROSENBERG at 185–89. Devins discusses the nature and scale of this backlash in greater detail than Rosenberg. Devins, *supra* note 51, at 1059–60.

77. ROSENBERG at 195–98.

78. *Id.* at 189–90. Although Rosenberg does not cite data on hospital practices prior to 1973, he implies that the limited availability of hospital abortions may have preceded *Roe. Id.* (referring to hospitals that have never performed abortions). This suggests that the post-*Roe* backlash may not have been this pattern's cause.

79. *Id.* at 199–201.

80. Akron v. Akron Ctr. for Reproductive Health, 462 U.S. 416, 434–39 (1983) (state may not require that all second-trimester abortions be performed in a hospital); Planned Parenthood Ass'n v. Ashcroft, 462 U.S. 476, 481–82 (1983) (same).

81. *See, e.g.,* Simopoulas v. Virginia, 462 U.S. 518 (1983) (state may require that second trimester abortions be provided either in hospitals or licensed outpatient clinics); Planned Parenthood v. Danforth, 428 U.S. 52, 79–81 (1976) (upholding recordkeeping requirements for clinics that provide abortions).

82. *See* sources cited *supra* note 70.

83. *See supra* text accompanying notes 45–46 for a list of some of the crucial ambiguities in the theory.

84. 492 U.S. 490 (1989).

85. ROSENBERG at 201.

86. *See supra* text accompanying notes 45–50.

87. The most notable exceptions concerned statutory rape laws, in Michael M. v. Superior Court, 450 U.S. 464 (1981) (upholding statutory rape law that applied only to persons who had sex with females under eighteen years old), and the draft, in Rostker v. Goldberg, 453 U.S. 57 (1981) (upholding Selective Service Act's application to men only). *See* ROSENBERG at 204 n.9.

88. ROSENBERG at 202–27 (ch. 7). The data on women's progress in wages during the 1980's support a far more upbeat view than Rosenberg's. *See, e.g.,* Sylvia Nasar, *Women's Progress Stalled? Just Not So,* N.Y. TIMES, October 18, 1992, s 3, at 1.

89. ROSENBERG at 247–65 (ch. 9).

90. *Id.* at 213.

91. Proponents of comparable worth argue that women are systemically underpaid when they work in typically female job categories, if salaries are compared to typically male jobs of comparable "worth," determined by looking at job skills, duties, etc. The attractiveness of comparable worth as a policy is far more controversial than Rosenberg seems to realize. *See, e.g.,* JENNIFER ROBACK, A MATTER OF CHOICE: A CRITIQUE OF COMPARABLE WORTH BY A SKEPTICAL FEMINIST (1986).

92. *See, e.g.,* HENRY J. AARON & CAMERAN M. LOUGY, THE COMPARABLE WORTH CONTROVERSY (1986).

93. ROSENBERG at 271–73.

94. *See, e.g.,* CASS R. SUNSTEIN, AFTER THE RIGHTS REVOLUTION 89–91 (1990).

95. ROSENBERG at 285.

96. *See, e.g., id.* at 284–85.

97. *See, e.g.,* MELNICK, REGULATION, *supra* note 8; JOHN M. MENDELOFF, THE DILEMMA OF TOXIC SUBSTANCE REGULATION (1988). Rosenberg cites Melnick, ROSENBERG at 278, but ap-

pears not to have read him carefully; Rosenberg sees courts' "lack [of] meaningful independence from the other branches" as the reason for environmental litigation's ineffectiveness, *id.* at 279, while Melnick sees the problem as courts' inadequate attention to the needs of the other branches, especially the implementing agencies. As for Mendeloff's study, Rosenberg does not include it even in his general bibliography.

Scholars have also found perverse, unanticipated consequences from court decisions outside the environmental area. *See, e.g.,* William A. Fischel, *Did* Serrano *Cause* Proposition 13?, 42 NAT'L TAX J. 465 (1989).

98. ROSENBERG at 292.

99. The closest he comes to addressing this question is one paragraph that summarizes the results of environmental action as "decidedly mixed," and a footnote that refers the reader to the Council on Environmental Quality annual reports. *Id.* at 275.

100. *See* JONATHAN LASH ET AL., A SEASON OF SPOILS: THE REAGAN ADMINISTRATION'S ATTACK ON THE ENVIRONMENT (1984); PHILIP SHABECOFF, A FIERCE GREEN FIRE: THE AMERICAN ENVIRONMENTAL MOVEMENT (1993). Again, the extent to which these tactics actually improved the environment and whether they were cost-effective from a purely organizational perspective are separate and quite difficult questions on which Rosenberg sheds little light.

101. ROSENBERG at 341.

102. *Id.* at 297–98.

103. *Id.* at 296–302. On this point, see also Peter H. Schuck, *The Thickest Thicket: Partisan Gerrymandering and the Judicial Regulation of Politics,* 87 COLUM. L. REV. 1325 (1987).

104. I should not be misunderstood as suggesting that enjoining an election is unproblematic (for example, it may keep incumbents in office beyond the term for which they were elected) or that drawing a districting map is straightforward (there are numerous politically sensitive choices to be made). *See* Schuck, *supra* note 103. My point is only that courts can—for better or for worse—do reapportionment essentially alone (with the help of special masters), unlike in the other areas studied. In terms of Rosenberg's theory, then, the third of the structural constraints limiting courts' ability to effect social change, the (normal) judicial lack of implementation power, is not present. *See supra* text accompanying note 44.

105. ROSENBERG at 304–35 (ch. 11).

106. *Id.* at 307.

107. *See id.* at 307–13. Rosenberg discerns more political support for prison reform than I do, at least if reform is not understood as prison construction. *See id.* at 308–09.

108. I say "partly" because I suspect that even if court-ordered change could be more effectively implemented, López might nonetheless prefer the kind of "bottom-up" reform practices that he discusses on the grounds that they are more authentic representations of what community people actually want, more effective techniques for achieving their personal self-realization, and more successful modes of political mobilization.

109. ROSENBERG at 342.

110. *See, e.g.,* sources cited *supra* note 38.

111. For a more detailed criticism of Rosenberg on this ground, see Devins, *supra* note 51, at 1030, 1046–54 (listing examples of effective court-initiated changes in race area effected through dialogic process).

112. *See, e.g.,* ALEXANDER M. BICKEL, THE LEAST DANGEROUS BRANCH: THE SUPREME COURT AT THE BAR OF POLITICS (1962); ROBERT A. BURT. THE CONSTITUTION IN CONFLICT

(1992); HARRY H. WELLINGTON, INTERPRETING THE CONSTITUTION (1990); Fiss, *supra* note 37. *See also* SCHUCK, SUING GOVERNMENT, *supra* note 38, at 169–81.

113. A possible exception to this is his emphasis on the extent to which court decisions allow market alternatives, to which policy analysts are sensitive but many other scholars are not. For an example of legal analysis that recognizes the significance of this factor, see Daniel R. Ortiz, *The Myth of Intent in Equal Protection*, 41 STAN. L. REV. 1105, 1139–42 (1989). As mentioned at text accompanying *supra* notes 79–82, Rosenberg's own discussion of the market alternatives factor is not wholly satisfactory.

Part III
Mapping the Limits of Law

13

The Limits of Law

In the culture of fin de siècle America, law is everywhere. Like the metaphorical fog in Charles Dickens's *Bleak House,* it seeps silently into each nook and cranny of our lives, gradually regulating all social behavior and relationships. And because it is a cultural artifact, law reveals the unique norms, practices, politics, and social psychology of American life.

In this culture, of course, nothing is "law-less."[1] No state of nature devoid of law exists.[2] Indeed, even when law claims to be merely observing or regulating human or physical nature as a distinct, objective thing, law is actually constructing nature.[3] Even the most intimate, spontaneous action is governed by at least one enforceable rule, although the rule is often one that protects privacy or autonomy by barring the intrusion of other rules.[4]

Because law is this pervasive, we should attend more to its possibilities and limits. Gaining such understanding, of course, poses immense methodological and conceptual challenges. I reduce these difficulties only slightly by confining my subject to public law, by which I mean a rule that aims to shape primary behavior by authorizing officials to allocate resources or impose sanctions. Public law (which I shall usually just call "law" hereafter) takes the form of an enforceable statute, an authoritative agency regulation or order, or a court decision. My emphasis here on these familiar forms of public law by no means ignores the vast body of private law, exemplified by the law of contracts, wills, trusts and estates, and property. Quite the contrary. Because much of this private law provides default rules around which parties are usually free to bargain and contract as they pursue greater efficiency or equity than the default rules achieve, the problem for public law is whether and to what extent it should limit this freedom—a problem with which this chapter is centrally concerned. When I say that law is growing more expansive, ambitious, or intrusive, then, I mean among other things that public law is increasingly limiting this freedom of contract, for better or for worse.[5]

The American polity entertains growing ambitions for law. It assigns law redistributive and regulatory roles that are now more expansive than ever.[6] Neither conservative nor neoliberal resistance to this regime has stemmed the tide.[7] Modern public law boasts some remarkable achievements—for example, the virtual elimination of elderly poverty through the Social Security and food stamp programs.[8] Law has waded into domains of choice and intimate relations—euthanasia, informed consent, and the distribution of human organs, for example—that were previously governed largely by custom and professional discretion.[9] Sexual harassment law, a mere gleam in some feminists' eyes only twenty years ago, today regulates much workplace speech and conduct.[10] Disability law now shapes job and building designs, management practices, and educational policies.[11] Environmental law affects activities ranging from indoor smoking to recreation.[12] "Never before," Jonathan Rauch writes, "has the government concerned itself so minutely with the detailed interactions of daily life."[13]

Law's contemporary reach was not inevitable, at least in retrospect. Officials did not extend law inadvertently;[14] they did so only after receiving grim warnings of slippery slopes, unforeseen consequences, and law begetting more law. Despite having been advised "don't go there," they did. Moreover, pressure for more law came both from liberals advocating more state regulation and redistribution and from conservatives eager to criminalize or curtail private conduct[15] of which they disapproved.

This brief sketch of legal expansion, of course, leaves the crucial normative and policy questions on the table: How should we assess law's broader reach? Should we applaud it, oppose it, or say that "it all depends"? How can law be improved, and how do we know what constitutes an improvement?

These questions have no clear, incontestable answers. Law, after all, takes protean forms and pursues diverse and often incommensurate goals in myriad contexts. An analysis of law's potential and limits is useful only if it is both general enough to guide officials who have to address problems in diverse settings yet specific enough to help them find better remedies. This is a tall order indeed.

My account will emphasize law's limits much more than its possibilities. I am not unmindful of law's bright promise; my professional life has been devoted to refining and hopefully redeeming that promise. Nor do I overlook law's great achievements. In principle and often in practice, law can secure order and justice, resolve disputes, facilitate transactions, guide and restrain official power, articulate public values, shape our incentives to our goals,[16] and assure a degree of formal equality among citizens. Every society wanting to pursue these compelling goals has turned to some system of formal rules and sanctions.[17] Moreover, all other social behavior-shaping mechanisms exhibit their own characteristic shortcomings. Neil Komesar notes that an institution like law fails only in the sense that it fails to be perfect. The important question is: failure compared to what?[18]

Why, then, do I focus on its limits? There are a number of sound reasons to do so. First, as we shall see, these limits seriously diminish law's performance and reputation. Those who advocate more law should want to know why so much law disappoints us, why that disappointment is problematic, and what might be done about it. And even if (contrary to fact) law's performance could not be improved, a public that understood the sources of its failures better would entertain more realistic expectations about it and perhaps hold it in higher repute when it fulfills them.

We are unlikely to learn about law's limits, however, either from those who do not want to acknowledge those limits or from those who benefit from them.[19] Success, it is said, has many fathers, but failure is an orphan. It is also true that in the worlds of law and policy the orphans are more numerous[20] but a skewed distribution of information both conceals the orphans' number and obscures their paternity.

Overlooking law's incapacities is also profoundly dangerous. As James Scott has recently chronicled in fascinating detail, all governments exhibit a chronic need to render their societies "legible" so that they can raise taxes, wage war, design and renew cities, control natural environments, reform agricultural practices, and implement other ambitious schemes for social change. Because human communities are highly complex, resistant to change, and opaque to outsiders, states must implement these schemes on the basis of vastly over-simplified models of behavior, environment, and control. Even the most so-phisticated regulators must rely for crucial social and political information on "local trackers," who are then strategically positioned to mislead and subvert official planning and implementation. Scott shows how governments' de-mands for legibility to facilitate social transformation has produced cata-strophic policy failures leading to immense human suffering. Although it is authoritarian and utopian governments that usually cause such disasters, any state determined to effect large-scale social change from above regardless of the cost may create its own calamity.[21]

Greater realism about law's limits is also needed because it is gradually sup-planting religion, family life, and public education as our chief instrument of social reform.[22] Yet law that arouses and then dashes people's hopes discredits the melioristic impulse, leaving corrosive cynicism and mistrust in its wake.[23] Only by realistically assessing law's capacities can we preserve its genuine contributions to social progress[24] while minimizing future policy failures. Paradoxically, a more critical, refined appreciation of these limits might actu-ally increase public support for those reforms that law can successfully imple-ment.

Finally, there is an important ideological reason to respect the limits of law. Traditional liberalism's institutions and ethos placed a thumb on the scales of social policy—a kind of rebuttable presumption against more law. Liberalism demanded affirmative justification for more law not because it opposed change but because its deepest commitment was to individual freedom and autonomy.[25] It preferred to risk too little law than to risk too much. This liberal settlement was profoundly altered, of course, by the Progressive and New Deal eras, by wars hot and cold, and by the post–1960s rights revolution. The question today is whether our greater knowledge of law's limits, gleaned from having experienced them, warrants our striking a new balance.

In order to answer this question, we need to understand what is at stake. I mean to explicate this, first, by advancing three critiques that stress law's intrusiveness, its ineffectuality, and its illegitimacy. I then introduce informal social norms and economic markets—law's two leading rivals in shaping social behavior—and compare them to law and to each other with respect to their capacities to regulate effectively, cheaply, fairly, and with public legitimacy.[26]

I shall want to distinguish from time to time between two types of law, which I shall call "top-down" rules and "bottom-up" rules.[27] I mean this distinction, which of course is only one of degree, to be purely descriptive. Nothing in the analysis turns on how a particular rule is classified, and any normative claim about the superiority of one or the other can only be justified on the basis of some other criteria. I propose such criteria in Part III and then assess top-down and bottom-up rules accordingly, urging lawmakers who are regulating complex, dynamic, and diverse social conditions to consider more closely the advantages (and disadvantages) of bottom-up rules.

Top-down rules reflect the gathering and synthesis of information and values by officials who are sociologically, spatially, or temporally remote from the particular social contexts where those rules will be applied and their consequences felt. The public agencies that create and administer social, economic, and entitlements regulation produce much more law today than the legislatures and courts combined, and most of their legal corpus consists of top-down rules. Top-down rules aspire to a synoptic rationality, a comprehensive approach to problem-solving, that encourage centralized decisionmaking that takes the form of what students of regulation often refer to (almost always disparagingly) as "command-and-control" rules. When these rules are clearly-specified (as they often are), they are relatively easy to understand, apply, and enforce. Their substantive content, however, is likely to suffer from the decisionmakers' remoteness from the information necessary to design and revise law, and from the specific consequences on which the law's soundness depends.

In contrast, bottom-up rules are meant to reflect information and values whose main source is the intended consumers of the rules, those who will most fully experience the rules' positive and negative impacts. Bottom-up rules seek to use and build upon these consumers' informal social norms, revealed preferences, and access to fresh policy-relevant information. Bottom-up rules, for example, might ground their substantive prescriptions in professional customs, community standards, or market tests. The responsiveness of bottom-up rules to the messy, diverse, complex conditions of social life, however, comes at a price. By drawing on and to some extent legitimating these conditions—precisely those that legal reformers at the center wish to alter through synoptic regulation—these rules will tend to reinforce a status quo that may be static (if based on entrenched social norms) or dynamic (if based on competitive markets). In either event, they will likely confound the reformers' more ambitious designs for change.

Comparing top-down and bottom-up law to each other and then to norms and markets serves at least two objectives. First, I want to highlight the positive and normative consequences of choosing law of either type instead of some other form of social control. As Neil Komesar points out, to evaluate one form of social control without also evaluating its competitors (an all-too-common practice that he calls "single institutionalism") is to fundamentally distort policy analysis in the very same way that ignoring opportunity costs distorts economic analysis.[28] So it is with any normative analysis of law that fails to consider how its alternatives might be used to accomplish whatever ends the policymaker decides to pursue.

Second, I want to call attention to how law, norms, and markets interrelate in public policymaking. Anthropologists and sociologists may think of law, norms, and markets as discrete systems, but for the rest of us these systems' very pervasiveness in society obscures the fact that they are alternative, potentially complementary, even synergistic forms of social control. By revealing these possibilities, I hope to encourage lawmakers to augment public law's instrumental repertoire with serviceable new hybrids. In the final section, then, I offer some very broad principles, elaborated in a number of specific, exemplary applications, with which officials might exploit law's great strengths while also keeping it in its proper place.

The theoretically informed and empirically grounded analysis from which I will deduce these principles leads me to two general conclusions. First, law's regulatory efficacy, which is already dismayingly limited, will continue to decline as an activist state demands more and more of law under conditions that are less and less auspicious for law's success. Second, policymakers who understand law's disabilities and hope to improve its performance by "accommodating" them should minimize their reliance on top-down law and draw more on norms, markets, and bottom-up legal rules wherever practically feasible and normatively acceptable.

My project is animated by the comparative and reformist spirit that has infused the magisterial, paradigm-shaping work of scholars like Robert Dahl, Charles Lindblom, Friedrich von Hayek, Albert Hirschman, Robert Ellickson, and Komesar. Although I draw heavily on this extraordinarily rich literature (as my endnotes attest), my goals, methods, and sources are different. Dahl and Lindblom, Hayek, and Hirschman compare politics at a highly abstract, schematic level in order to support normative claims about competing forms of political economy. Komesar's somewhat less abstract comparison of politics, markets, and adjudication is intended to limn the institutional choices that are implicit in different goals and policy approaches. Ellickson compares law and norms (and markets, to a degree) in a very specific social setting—ranchers and farmers in Shasta County, California—in order to reveal how communities can sometimes govern important areas of social interaction through observance of informal norms rather than formal law.

My analysis is closest to those of Komesar and Ellickson, but it is less original and ambitious than either. Whereas Komesar extends the economic theory of transaction (mostly information) costs to the largely neglected domains of institutional choice and design, I neither extend existing theory nor develop new, testable hypotheses. Methodologically eclectic, I instead scavenge for insights about law's limits wherever I can find them. Whereas Ellickson conducts a detailed, almost ethnographic community study that illuminates large but elusive social processes at work, I merely synthesize empirical evidence that he and others have gathered from many different policy realms. My goal, then, is both narrower and more practical than his: to suggest how lawmakers can self-consciously use legal rules, social norms, and economic markets to craft more effective public policies and thus enlarge law's functional and moral limits.

In Part III, I offer five principles to guide this limits-expanding project. The master principle is *comparison*—the necessity to appraise any proposed intervention in the form of a top-down legal rule only after considering the possible use of the major alternative mechanisms of social control: norms, markets, and bottom-up types of law. The other four principles—implementation analysis, process efficiency, responsiveness (sociological, spatial, and temporal), and law minimization—are subsidiary to the comparison principle in the sense that they are chiefly concerned with the effectiveness and ultimately the legitimacy of whichever forms of intervention decisionmakers decide to employ. The last principle, law minimization, is the likely result of pursuing the other four. In a liberal society, it is also presumptively desirable in its own right.

The five principles, I hope to show, can be used to support a number of fairly specific policy interventions. Many of these interventions would strengthen law by using it to prescribe in the form of clearly-specified default rules initial entitlements that people can then redistribute through private exchange transactions—regulated, if necessary, to achieve fairness or efficiency.

I. Critiques of Law

The United States is a relatively law-abiding society.[29] Despite this fact (or perhaps because of it), Americans have always felt free to criticize the law and amply justified in doing so. Even during the Republic's early days, when state and local government dominated public affairs and the federal government had relatively little impact, Americans vigorously contested law's role and scope.[30] Ever since, some have complained of too much law burdening a freedom-loving society while others, with equal conviction, have demanded more law in order to curtail private property and liberty for the common good. The debate became more strident in the Progressive, New Deal, and Great Society eras as law's ambitions grew. It has not abated.[31]

Today, the advocates of more top-down law have won the debate, the battle, and the war. "Over the past half century," Marc Galanter notes, there has been a dramatic change in scale in many aspects of the legal world: the amount and complexity of legal regulation; the frequency of litigation; the amount of authoritative legal material; the number, coordination and productivity of lawyers; the number of legal actors and the resources that they devote to legal activity; the information about law and the velocity with which it circulates.[32]

The river of law has swollen, spilling over its old banks and flooding the surrounding areas. This river ebbs and flows, of course. Since the mid–1970s, the federal government has reduced or ended economic regulation in many basic industries, including transportation,[33] financial services,[34] energy,[35] telecommunications,[36] and ocean shipping.[37] Some states have also reduced their own economic regulation in areas such as hospital rate-setting.[38]

These important deregulatory thrusts, however, have been more than offset by law's continuing expansion, which is occurring in six broad policy domains: (1) economic regulation of specific industries;[39] (2) across-the-board economic regulation;[40] (3) across-the-board "social" regulation to promote health, safety, environmental, civil rights, and other social goals;[40A] (4) intergovernmental regulation;[41] (5) intragovernmental regulation;[42] and (6) social insurance,[43] programmatic entitlements,[44] and other government transfers and benefits.[45]

As these examples indicate, robust demand for more law exists.[46] Even as law's failures proliferate, the clamor for more law continues. One need not resort to fuzzy social psychological theories, such as people's schizoid view of law, in order to explain this. The truth is simpler. As people observe society becoming steadily more complex, crowded, and interdependent, they conclude that only a central authority can manage such interactions, just as police are needed to untangle traffic gridlock. They believe, moreover, that many of the necessary decisions are simply too important to be left to private powerholders who already dominate social hierarchies and pitiless markets.

An ideologically eclectic and reformist culture also demands more law. Even as Americans affirm their privatist, pragmatic, populist, and meliorist values, they also imagine that even an amiably bumbling administrative state may take the rough edges off of ruthless markets and offensive social practices. Can-do and better-not, boldness and risk aversion, have produced a public law marriage of awkward, chronic compromise.[47]

Politicians and issue entrepreneurs skillfully stoke these hopes and fears in order to stimulate more demand for law. Faced with tough budget constraints,[48] they pursue many of their policy goals off-budget or by charging fees for certain activities. By regulating firms rather than increasing taxes, they shift implementation costs from public fiscs to private payrolls.[49] Servicing mass media addicted to vivid anecdote, simplistic moralism, and crisis rhetoric, they fire public feelings of indignation and impatience that in turn generate much irrational, ineffective law.[50] Chronically weak administrative apparatuses at all levels of government further fan regulatory fires by revealing, creating, and exacerbating as many problems as they solve.

Regulation tends to beget more regulation. Like a person attempting to shape a large pillow with only one hand, the law in its effort to fix one problem often spawns new ones that must then be remedied—a kind of perpetual reform machine.[51] The players in this regulatory drama, moreover, consist of a welter of legislative committees and administrative agencies, each with its own subject matter jurisdiction, political culture, problem definition, and policy orientation. It would be miraculous indeed if these fiercely independent law factories produced coherent policies, but such miracles seldom happen. Instead, public law tends to be naive, conflicting, confusing, and sometimes perverse.[52] Its relentless quest for effective control pushes it up to, and often beyond, its political, instrumental, and symbolic limits.

I have been emphasizing the *quantitative* aspect of public law—the sheer number of people and activities it covers and the volume of legal materials it generates. Even more striking, however, is its *qualitative* aspect—its distinctive nature and forms. This qualitative dimension provokes three formidable, analytically separable challenges to public law. Call them the libertarian, functionalist, and illegitimacy critiques.

A. The Libertarian Critique

Resisting constraint in the name of freedom is a universal emotion that stems from our most primordial urges. In all cultures, human rebellion against law is a central, mythic motif; in Judeo-Christian and Islamic cultures it begins with the eating of the forbidden, Edenic apple whereas other cultures have their own parables of hubris and defiance. Lear's rage against the physical, temporal, emotional, intellectual, and spiritual barriers that limit our power and defeat our desires is another archetype of rebellion. With great anxiety but little success, we struggle to transcend these barriers—even as we erect new ones by converting once-unattainable wishes into compelling needs.[53] This imaginative transformation, with its Sisyphean desperation and futility, means that our wants will always exceed our ability to gratify them.[54]

Americans might be forgiven for ignoring this tragic human truth. The conviction that hard work and determination enable one to escape limits is fortified today by a rising standard of living that is fueled by breathtaking technological change and that extends even to most poor families.[55] This conviction of progress is substantiated by the alluring dramas of social mobility,[56] immigrant success,[57] and the safety valve provided even today by new frontiers on a vast but thinly settled continent.[58]

These conditions make the struggle against constraint all the more urgent, intense, and frustrating. Limitations imposed by others are intolerable, of course, but even self-imposed ones are irksome when they bind us. A libertarian, individualistic society like that of the United States[59] harbors a special animus toward legal constraints. The fact that elected representatives enacted them may palliate the pain somewhat but does not eliminate it. Democratic consent to law is abstract, often ascribed, and indirect; in contrast, its fettering of the individual will is deeply felt, personal, and immediate.

To Americans, "legalistic" is an epithet, not a term of approbation. Rules, the paradigmatic form of law, tend to suppress contextual richness and force natural diversity into narrow, artificial legal categories, making them chronically under- and overinclusive.[60] This is often the price of control and predictability, one that often seems to high in an ever-more interactive, heterogeneous society.

Contemporary public law is technocratic in its sources, forms, functions, and main audiences.[61] It projects a synoptic, calculating, rationalizing social vision, not an incremental, exploratory one. It employs the arcane, instrumental argot of specialists, not the common language of common people shaped by a common morality. It often distances the rulemaker from the ruled, alienating the lay public rather than inviting its full participation and comprehension. As Marc Galanter notes, the law that increasingly governs large organizations relies more on formal legal rules and less on informal norms and reciprocities,[62] a formalism that also impedes the flexible corporate entities demanded by today's economy.[63] Finally, these rules are notionally and literally complex; they remind us of the messiness, obscurity, and elusiveness of the realities that they seek to order[64] and deny the simplicities for which people nostalgically yearn.

The libertarian critique, then, mines a deep and rich vein of discontent in American life, one that sees public law at best as a menace to freedom, at worst as a toxic cancer on the body politic.[65] At the libertarian extreme, opponents of law may actually take up arms against it. More moderate opponents may engage in open civil disobedience. Most libertarians, however, do not defy the activist state but are content to mock its laws' pretensions. The ranks of these critics appear to be growing,[66] and their views influence many other citizens who do not think of themselves as libertarians.

B. The Functionalist Critique

Most critics, however, do not object to public law in principle. Even libertarians usually concede that some law is needed to secure basic physical and transactional security in areas where markets are likely to fail. The more common critique is functionalist, holding that much law is costly and ineffective.

Even functionalist critics often fail to appreciate that many of their misgivings derive from the inherent properties of law. The most elemental limitation of this kind is language. Although law's intelligibility, effectiveness, and legitimacy require the use of written words in legal instruments, legal language is a frail support for these goals. Its irreducible ambiguity, magnified by the need for application in diverse contexts,[67] bewilders lay people while bringing lawyers fun and profit. A lawmaker's message, often weak or distorted in transmission, may not be received and comprehended as she intends. Nor can she count on the respectful attention of the receiver, which is usually an implementing bureaucracy with its own agenda and systemic communication defects.[68]

Law's efficacy is also limited by the categories with which it structures legal discourse, doctrine, and responsibility. Ordinarily we assess people and things according to the numerous dimensions along which they vary—for example, size, strength, beauty, speed, intelligence, morality, humor, culpability, and value.[69] In contrast, law—especially regulatory law—usually attempts to govern complex reality through simple binary, yes-or-no categories; it seldom uses the kinds of continuous categories of more-or-less that refine our perceptions and discourse and render everyday life intelligible and nuanced.[70] The citizen beholding law's artificial, reductionist classifications often protests in the name of common sense: "The real world isn't black and white; it is all a matter of degree."

Law knows this, of course, but it pretends otherwise. There are plausible arguments for using simplistic classifications, and they have usually carried the day. Such classifications, however artificial, allow us to make, apply, and comprehend law more cheaply and with higher predictability than if the rules tracked the profuse variety and semiotic complexity of social life.[71] The simple categories of public law promise to facilitate legislators' control of regulators, and regulators' control of the rest of us.

Certain legal techniques can temper this simplicity of rules. For example, lawmakers can include more categories,[72] replace bright-line tests with more-flexible, contextual standards,[73] and permit exceptions.[74] Reforms like these, however, have their own disadvantages. Multiplying categories makes law more complex and costly to understand and apply. Moving from rules to standards delegates discretion to those who apply and enforce them, such as citizens, juries or bureaucrats. Standards also invite arbitrariness, and reduce law's predictability. Exceptions may swallow, weaken, or delegitimate the rule.

Quite apart from law's inherent or "internal" limitations, its effectiveness depends on the consciousness of those whom it seeks to influence, on their awareness of the opportunities that a law creates, and on their efficacy in acting on them. A persistently large fraction of low-income people (and thus their children) who are eligible for public benefits like Medicaid and food stamps still do not claim them, more than three decades after the creation of these programs.[75] The putative beneficiaries of civil rights laws often do not or cannot use them,[76] and even some strong proponents of affirmative action concede that it largely benefits people who are already relatively advantaged, not those who most need special help.[77] Individuals without lawyers seldom avail themselves of their formal legal remedies.[78]

Perhaps law's greatest limitation is its inability to effectively shape behavior driven by diverse and dynamic social conditions. Whereas social change accelerates geometrically, law's capacity to regulate change effectively increases arithmetically or not at all.[79] Its efforts to regulate markets are notoriously reactive, as lawmakers respond to the rapid and fragmenting changes that roil markets long after entrepreneurial traders have impounded them in transactions and moved on. Like a kid brother eager to impress his older, more agile siblings, law is always several steps behind markets, desperately trying to catch up but never quite succeeding. As law's largely futile efforts to regulate Internet abuses illustrate,[80] technologically driven markets are especially elusive. Much the same is true of law's usually feckless attempts to control other such strongly motivated and strategically fluid behavior as tax-minimizing business planning, scientific progress, and illegal migration.[81]

Some of law's limits are endemic to the legislatures, agencies, courts, and legal profession that help to give it flesh and vitality. Law's institutional limits, like its language, deliberate speed, and reactivity, are largely inevitable,[82] often desirable, and sometimes even constitutionally required. These limits secure such vital public values as due process, participation, federalism, accountability, and the separation of powers. Because countless analyses of these institutions' behavior and competence already exist, I shall simply note a few structural factors that deserve more attention.

Legislatures are the most carefully studied of political institutions.[83] On complex subjects, they often write law in broad terms, delegating to agencies and courts the power to fill in details as those delegates apply it in diverse contexts that legislators did not, and often could not, anticipate. Since these details tend to determine both the magnitude and distribution of the law's benefits and costs, the delegates are left with the hardest, most consequential choices. For this reason, some critics find broad delegation troubling, even unconstitutional.[84] Drawing on principal-agent economic theory, they note that legislators' incentives and constraints—reelection, credit claiming, blame avoidance, and short time horizons[85]—differ from those of the delegates. It is costly for legislators to monitor and direct the law's implementation,[86] and even more so for voters, who have little incentive to learn about politics[87] and whose ignorance tempts legislators to pass cost-concealing, unimplementable, or merely symbolic laws.[88]

Legislative delegations to agencies, however, are not always so broad. A recent study reviewed the federal agency requirements that regulated firms specifically cited as unduly burdensome. It found that in about half of these cases, Congress had by statute denied the agencies discretion, requiring them to issue those controversial regulations. Congress had not permitted the agencies in those cases to pursue the regulatory policy goals in other ways, even if those alternative ways would benefit the public and private interests more.[89] If, as is often the case, such alternatives do indeed exist and if this study's findings fairly typify the administrative state as a whole, statutory delegations of discretionary authority to runaway agencies[90] may be less problematic than the statutes' centralism, rigidity, lack of policy imagination, and failure to rationally tailor agency discretion.[91]

Structural criticisms of agencies are if anything even harsher than those aimed at legislatures.[92] The long indictment includes high decision costs, procedural complexity, glacial pace, technical incompetence, technocratic language, narrow participation, nonaccountability, rigidity, "capture" by special interests, hostility to innovation, arbitrariness, and unfairness. Indeed, as agencies' authority has expanded, attacks on their performance and functions in the constitutional order have intensified.[93] Although some agency programs have been reasonably effective,[94] the history of administrative regulation of dynamic markets and complex social contexts is one of almost unrelieved failure.[95]

The effectiveness of courts is harder to assess. Because one of their principal functions is to secure legislative and agency fidelity to law, one cannot appraise judicial performance without also appraising that of the other branches, an enterprise plagued by controversial, elusive normative criteria, immense empirical gaps, and formidable methodological challenges. Not surprisingly, then, the verdict on judicial effectiveness is complicated, contextual, and mixed; assessments tend to vary according to the criteria used, the person doing the assessing, the particular court or courts studied, and the specific legal-policy domain examined.[96]

Many administrative law scholars doubt that judicial review of federal agency decisions is effective, and much empirical work supports their skepticism.[97] Key underlying facts may change during the long review process, rendering court rulings unwise or irrelevant. Judicial doctrine is a crude, weak instrument for controlling agency discretion, especially in the politicized and technocratic context of agency decisions. Because courts have less technical, policymaking, and political skills and resources, they usually defer to agency expertise and judgment.[98] In any case, agencies can deflect or minimize adverse court rulings in a number of ways.

Although the general public continues to hold the judicial system, especially the Supreme Court, in relatively high esteem,[99] judicial effectiveness in constitutional adjudication is equally dubious. Much praise of rights-expanding judicial rulings pays remarkably little attention to causal indeterminacies and implementation barriers.[100] Such insouciance may be justified where the Court's[101] ruling principle is clear and easily understood, enjoys broad public support, and is not stymied by strong market forces, and where noncompliance is easy to detect, challenge, and enjoin. Reapportionment under the "one man, one vote" principle[102] meets these rather stringent conditions, but judicial efficacy in other cases is less impressive.[103]

The difficulty of assessing judicial impact and the ease of exaggerating it are perhaps best illustrated by the Supreme Court's landmark ruling in *Brown v. Board of Education*,[104] which held "separate but equal" schools unconstitutional. *Brown* is often cited as the *locus classicus* of the Court's ability to transcend and transform stubborn social practices in the name of constitutionalism, but empirical evidence on its actual effect supports a considerably more modest, even pessimistic claim. Recent analyses find that *Brown* did not generate reform itself but rather lagged and reflected large reform trends already in train; the

Court, it seems, was swimming with the tide, not against it.[105] *Brown* actually galvanized the remaining white resistance; little desegregation occurred until more than a decade later when federal agencies began to implement Title VI of the Civil Rights Act.[106] Yet even that progress proved to be ephemeral. By the late 1980s, the schools were about as racially identifiable as they had been before the era of court-ordered busing began two decades earlier.[107]

This tragic denouement, of course, has many causes, including market-driven segregated housing patterns, itself exacerbated in some cases by court-ordered busing. But this causal indeterminacy is precisely the point. Courts control few tools for shaping attitudes and behavior other than the injunction, which cannot readily overcome such an embedded social practice. When the judges turned in desperation to busing, one of the few remedies that they *could* order, they aggravated the problem by fueling "white flight" and frustration among minority families that ended up bearing most of the remedial burdens.[108] Indeed, busing's failure in large urban areas has impelled many black parents to seek alternatives to the public schools, such as parochial, private, and charter schools. Whatever the educational merits of these alternatives, they may isolate minority students even more.

Much the same tale of disappointed expectations, thwarted implementation, and perverse, unanticipated consequences can be told in other areas of public law adjudication.[109] *Roe v. Wade*,[110] for example, abruptly ended a strong trend toward state legislation favoring liberalized abortion; it became the *casus belli* driving a militantly conservative grassroots movement that has succeeded in both reversing the liberalizing trend and transforming the face of American politics in ways that abortion rights advocates could not have predicted and which many of them strongly oppose.[111] Thoughtful commentators describe a similar phenomenon in criminal procedure, where judicial expansion of the rights of the accused engendered legislative and prosecutorial reactions that largely undermined those rights and discouraged the recognition of new ones.[112]

When one moves from the rarefied realm of Supreme Court law to the more workaday world of state and lower federal courts, these limits on judicial effectiveness are even more apparent. The institutional shortcomings of courts are evident even in common law tort adjudication, where judicial lawmaking is widely accepted as inevitable.[113] When the courts' main goal in tort cases was corrective justice (i.e., annulling wrongfully inflicted injuries by making wrongdoers pay their victims' losses[114]), judicial competence was assumed; accidents were relatively straightforward and no obvious alternative existed.[115] But when judges came to pursue broad policy goals through instrumental doctrines that treat litigants as proxies for putative social interests, not as ends in themselves as the corrective justice vision posits, they opened a Pandora's box. A loss-spreading rationale enabling injured consumers who misused their products to recover from manufacturers may offend both corrective justice *and* functional goals such as deterrence and insurance.[116] Once courts left the familiar, relatively safe harbor of corrective justice, they sailed into a vast, trackless sea of policy argument in an unseaworthy vessel. Judges are institutionally ill equipped to obtain and integrate the information and values needed for sophisticated policy analysis, to elicit implementing behavior from the relevant social actors, or to learn from and correct their mistakes.[117]

C. The Illegitimacy Critique

Challenging law as illegitimate is an even more foundational critique than charging that it restricts liberty or is ineffective. When the word "illegitimate" is used loosely or rhetorically, it may denote nothing more than the speaker's strong opposition to a law or her belief that it is foolish or immoral.[118] More precisely, people view a law as legitimate if they feel morally obliged to obey it *because it is law,* even though it may severely constrain them and they strongly oppose it on the merits. They view a law as illegitimate if, when they think about it,[119] the law fails to elicit that moral response—or worse, when it elicits moral revulsion or a sense of crisis.[120]

Why do people sometimes accord legitimacy even to law that they regard as unwise, immoral, or possibly even unconstitutional? In the American legal culture, several norms frame the public's view of appropriateness and hence of legitimacy. First, the process that generates and enforces law is at least as relevant to its legitimacy as its substantive content. At the most basic level, appropriateness is measured by the constitutional norms that distribute legal authority and functions between private actors and governmental institutions (and levels), norms that also require decision procedures to be minimally fair, accurate, and participatory.[121] Usually, however, appropriateness turns on perceptions of an institution's political and policy competence rather than its constitutional power. When people deem the lawmaking process legitimate, they will routinely obey laws even if they dislike them and even if their noncompliance would probably escape detection or punishment. Judges often enforce rules simply because the legislature or agency was legally authorized to adopt them, even if the judges think the rules are misconceived.

Second, law's legitimacy is a function not only of its constitutionality and procedural fairness but also of its effectiveness. Although I have distinguished analytically between legitimacy and effectiveness, they are in fact closely linked. Other things being equal, the larger the gaps between a law's promises and its performance and between its costs and its benefits, the less it will elicit the felt moral duty of obedience that is legitimacy's hallmark. Ineffectiveness thus damages law not only by preventing it from achieving its specific goals but more fundamentally by discrediting the legal enterprise itself, a taint that can stigmatize essential and effective laws.

Third, although policymakers can in principle address social problems by actively deploying (or passively relying on) law, markets, informal norms, self-regulation, politics, or other social control techniques, their choices are constrained by some *a priori* normative assumptions concerning the appropriateness of using a certain technique for a specific problem arising in a particular domain. For example, the law prohibits even consenting, well-informed adults from selling their organs. People are convinced that organ allocation is a governmental function from which markets must be strictly excluded, at least (or especially) in principle.[122] These assumptions, which are often morally driven, reflect the socially dominant conceptions of autonomy, equality, obligation, federalism, the proper scope of politics and markets, and other values. These beliefs are by no means fixed; they can change as values and perceptions about the facts change. Nevertheless, they are our points of departure, our background norms, for thinking critically about law's role.[123] Lawmakers cannot violate them without persuasive justification.

A fourth idea affecting law's perceived legitimacy is the widespread notion that law is more imperialistic than other forms of social control. It does not simply share social space with the other forms; it proliferates like weeds in a garden, occupying more and more of the remaining space and crowding out the others. Instances of deregulation and privatization demonstrate that this is not inevitable. But law's strong tendency is to expand, even when this endangers its legitimacy. Law gratifies an official's understandable wish to "do something" (or to *seem* to be doing something) about social problems. Because some conduct subversive of the regulatory scheme always eludes their control, they want to elaborate new law to protect and perfect that scheme. The incentives and processes that motivate politicians and regulators to expand law's empire are well known; those that motivate courts are more obscure.[124] There can be no doubt, however, about the overall pattern.

The legitimacy of law, then, is fragile. Moreover, many of its usual defenders are now attacking it.[125] Citizens disavow a law when it seems to violate their moral principles or their fundamental interests. By challenging a law's moral standing, not just its wisdom, they seek to justify their oppositional stance both to themselves and to others. Their challenge to its legitimacy is reinforced when other stigmata of law are present: ineffectiveness, over- and underinclusiveness, widespread disobedience, slippery slopes, bureaucratic rigidity, high cost, and slow process.

Moreover, people have strong incentives to misrepresent their true reasons for opposing or resisting a law because motives are hard for others to detect.[126] By invoking only public interest grounds for their opposition, they in turn raise the moral stakes in the debate. The common complaint that a law is unwise or unjust merges almost imperceptibly into a more fundamental and corrosive attack on its moral authority. Even a law's critics may be unsure when its folly or injustice rises to the level of illegitimacy.[127] In a rhetorical snowball effect, those who actually oppose a law for "merely" selfish or prudential reasons may be tempted to justify their position under the broader, ostensibly more disinterested rationale. This in turn reduces the costs to others of attacking the law's legitimacy while raising those of obeying it (one cost being the embarrassment of the compliant "sucker"). When the threads of the social fabric that law secures begin to unravel, only nonlegal processes can restore the fabric's integrity and strength. Law will have disabled itself from performing that crucial task.

II. Law's Competitors

In the ancient struggle over how best to motivate and organize human effort, advance well-being, and maintain social order, legal rules compete with robust rivals. Of these, informal social norms[128] and markets are the most important and the most ubiquitous.[129] In this section, I characterize social norms and markets and then discuss how the three systems affect one another. I next compare them along a number of dimensions that are central in deciding precisely how law should figure in the design of public policy. These comparisons in turn will support the principles and applications that I propose in the final section.

Social norms—the shared beliefs, common practices, and mutual expectations among members of a group—are modes of social ordering in all collectivities, including states, families, and friendships.[130] The behavior-shaping power of norms, which may draw on both secular and religious values, does not rely significantly on legal sanctions; indeed, legalizing a norm may actually undermine its power.[131] Instead, norms' salience reflects social-psychological concerns like status, reputation, shame, mutuality, and pride.[132] Norms constitute a kind of social integument, linking people in relationships of trust in which they may forego strategic behavior that would impede the production of public goods and gains from cooperation.[133] But where norms that are sacred to some people deeply offend others—a common occurrence in diverse, polyglot societies like the United States—law cannot easily sustain liberal neutrality. It must often take sides, as it has with abortion, school prayer, drugs, and other sharply divisive social issues.

Even in highly legalistic and market-oriented societies, social norms determine and coordinate a great deal of conduct and thought, much of it subconsciously. But we should not think of norms as a residual category occupying all of the social space not filled by law and markets. Some activities—reflection and imagination, for example—are largely autonomous; they are not really governed by law or markets, and they are only minimally shaped by norms. Instead, activities like these occur within the interstices of, and sometimes in rebellion against, those systems. Many norms, moreover, are relatively limited in coverage, salience, acceptance, or intensity, so that even conduct that falls within their domains remains indeterminate. Even the strongest norms, however, are violated; deviance is common, especially in liberal societies.

Markets are systems of voluntary exchanges through which people buy and sell goods (broadly defined) that they value. Some, like stock exchanges, are highly formal, rule-bound, and institutionalized. Others, like a casual purchase of lemonade from a neighborhood youngster, are entirely informal. The economic value of markets is reflected even in the weakest version of market efficiency, which holds that truly consensual, competitive, and well-informed transactions make some traders better off and none worse off.[134]

A. Interactions among Law, Norms, and Markets

Law's relations to norms and markets are complex, as are their relations to it and to each other. Since people usually operate "in" at least one of them and often in more than one, sometimes simultaneously, their interactions are even more opaque and difficult to disentangle.

Norms are essential to both effective law and efficient markets and are in that sense the most fundamental of the three mechanisms. They support law by securing the felt moral duty to obey on which law's legitimacy ultimately rests, by supplying the substantive standards for many legal rules, and by providing feedback to law—a kind of reality check that helps law to learn and to change. For example, military law concerning extramarital affairs will probably change due to the greater understanding of contemporary sexual practices gained through the investigation of recent scandals involving those practices.

Norms support markets by reducing transaction costs such as information and enforcement, by encouraging traders to deal fairly with one another, and by providing an alternative to inefficient and unfair legal regulation.[135] By coordinating behavior, feelings, and thought, norms also support both law and markets by helping to solve collective-action problems produced by conflicts among self-interested actors. In this way, norms help to determine the nature, effectiveness, and even possibility of different types of property regimes.[136]

Law makes markets both economically possible and socially acceptable. At a minimum, law must define property rights, limit force and fraud, and interpret and enforce agreements. Law can repair market defects by encouraging the production of public goods, reducing externalities, clarifying rules, and removing barriers to competition. It can also redistribute wealth, which of course affects the number, nature, and outcomes of market transactions. On the other hand, law's efforts to improve a market's efficiency or fairness can distort and weaken it. Indeed, law can weaken markets even when it seeks to make its regulations more flexible and responsive to change.[137] Whether law works to improve markets or weaken them, then, will depend on a number of factors, including the nature of its interventions and the institutions that fashion and enforce them.[138]

Robert Post's notion that law reinforces informal norms by "discovering and refreshing them"[139] simplifies what is a far more complex process.[140] Law may sponsor an existing or new norm and may manage to transfer to the norm some of its own prestige and power. This "halo effect," of course, can cut both ways; advocates of legalizing gay marriage want law's legitimating sanction, whereas it is precisely this legitimation that opponents of legal abortion and state-run gambling fear. But there are darker, more paradoxical possibilities than halos. Law's embrace may cast a shadow over norms; indeed, it may kill them with its kindnesses.[141]

Markets likewise affect norms and law in subtle ways. Robert Ellickson's study of ranchers and farmers in Shasta County, California, shows that their norms for managing conflicts have much to do with local understandings, which are wealth maximizing and seen as fair, and have little to do with local law, of which they are quite ignorant.[142] Ellickson finds that these local norms mimic markets, not law—a feature that he also finds in other local cultures[143] and one that surely reflects the market's centrality in U.S. life. Markets also reinforce some norms more than others. Although critics often indict markets for rewarding antisocial, selfish values, Adam Smith was closer to the truth in maintaining that markets may cultivate civility, reputational and relational values, attention to others' needs, and other social virtues that tend to generate, sustain, and improve norms.[144]

Markets affect law differently than they affect informal norms. First, market signals can inform lawmakers about what people want, how much they want it, what it will cost, and what they are likely to do if they are denied it.[145] Second, public fear or dissatisfaction with market outcomes may provoke legal controls even when markets are workably competitive and regulation is unnecessary or counterproductive. Much of the widespread political support for regulating the managed health care industry reflects such demands. Third, strong market forces, particularly when reinforced by norms, may simply overwhelm law, distorting or disabling it.[146] If those forces are strong enough, they will spawn corruption, smuggling, or other illegal markets. Even as law conflicts with markets, however, it often uses market efficiency as a policy benchmark or regulatory yardstick.

Law, norms, and markets possess their own strengths and weaknesses as instruments of complex social ordering. None of them is equal to the task by itself; an effective social policy should consider all three. Before policymakers decide whether and how to use law to influence social behavior, they should always (if they are prudent) ask the question, "compared to what?" I address this question by broadly comparing social norms and markets to law and to each other in light of five vital criteria for policy design: (1) incentives, (2) information, (3) flexibility, (4) transaction costs, and (5) legitimacy.

B. Incentives

A social system's performance fundamentally depends on the power and efficacy of the human motivations that drive, shape, and ultimately legitimate it. Whether individuals acting in a particular context are subject to formal law, are bound by informal social norms, or trade in markets, they almost always seek to get what they think they want as cheaply as they can, given their bounded rationality. In this sense, at least, participants in all three systems engage in purposeful, self-interested, optimizing behavior. But the differences in how self-interest works in the three systems are more striking than this superficial, tautological similarity.

Law appeals to self-interest mainly by creating behavioral incentives that typically take the form of penalties or, more rarely, subsidies. Such incentives generate for law only the grudging respect that fear or duty elicits; this in turn supports a perfunctory, minimal compliance. Laws that must be implemented by administrative officials make self-interest doubly problematic as a motivational force; the self-interest of *either* the enforcer or the regulated may stymie the law's implementation, as often occurs in criminal and regulatory law.[147]

To be sure, law sometimes exploits self-interest more positively and creatively by inducing self-interest to identify with law's spirit and purpose. Widespread public support for Social Security, despite its regressive tax system, and the World War II draft, despite its demand for cannon fodder, are examples. More commonly, however, self-interest rebels against legal constraint; this reflex is checked only, but usually decisively, by habits of obedience, by vaguer, more abstract self-interest in the rule of legitimate law, or by desire to foster cooperation in situations where an unregulated self-interest might prevent it.

Social norms shape behavior through people's desires for social acceptance and communal identity. These desires can be remarkably potent, driving people to great lengths and enormous risk in order to gain psychological well-being and the esteem of others. These solidaristic motives can of course be viewed as self-interested in several senses. Unless these senses are merely tautological, however, it is hard to square them with people's manifest willingness, even eagerness, either to affirm social norms through heroic sacrifices on behalf of other group members (or strangers if that is normative)[148] or to act in ways that would otherwise be deemed antisocial, cruel, or even barbaric.[149]

Markets are driven by self-interest in its simplest form. The foundational axiom of neoclassical economics, that people are motivated by rational self-interest, is either radically incomplete or so elastic as to be meaningless. Nevertheless, this axiom explains and predicts an enormous amount of human conduct, far more than any other testable general theory of behavior that has been proposed. In economic transactions, where the quest for wealth is valorized as normal and legitimate, the motivational force of self-interest is obvious. It fuels not only hard work, creativity, and risk taking but also a compulsive single-mindedness and the sacrifice of other important values.

Markets are more effective in rewarding desired conduct than in punishing unwanted conduct; they are better at providing carrots than sticks.[150] And in social realms where wealth-seeking is less normative and central than it is in commercial transactions, people manifestly leaven self-interest with love, friendship, altruism, social conformity and consensus, public values, and other goals that often confound predictions based on the axiomatic self-interest that economists can readily model.[151] Nevertheless, markets' extraordinary power to harness self-interest is an immensely valuable social resource not only for producing wealth but also for implementing other public policy goals.[152]

Another advantage of self-interested market behavior is that it reveals information to all about individuals' relative intensities of preferences for different goods that compete for the individuals' limited resources. This information, impounded in the goods' relative prices, is valuable not only to the individuals immediately involved but also to the economy as a whole, which must decide through innumerable individual decisions how to allocate scarce resources. More generally, markets create enormous social value by generating ever-fresh, low-cost, and widely accessible information about preferences.

I now compare the informational properties of law, norms, and markets more systematically.

C. Information

Critical determinants of a social system's performance are the cost, value, and distribution of the information that it needs to discharge its functions. Calling them "participatory" costs and benefits, Komesar notes that the economy of information even determines when and how people organize to use information.[153] This economy operates very differently in law, social norms, and markets. Indeed, it varies greatly *within* law itself, depending on the form that rules take and the subjects that they hope to regulate. This variation, moreover, is a potentially powerful lever for the reform of law.

Contemporary law is a highly centralized system of authority and control. In order to legislate, regulate, or adjudicate competently, legal decisionmakers must decide to seek and then gather from many disparate sources a great deal of information bearing on a host of policy-relevant issues: the current legal landscape, the nature and intensity of private preferences, causal and behavioral patterns, moral and public values, and institutional capacities. The officials[154] who compile, interpret, synthesize, distribute, and update this information rely on processes that are in theory open to all but that in practice discourage participation to some degree. The notorious technical, political, and strategic complexity of these adversarial processes bewilder even business executives and other sophisticates encountering them close-up for the first time.[155] The participatory costs of adjudication are especially high. Unlike legislators and regulators, judges do not make it their business to learn how law actually affects the public; they wait for lawyers to come to court and inform them.[156]

The information on which top-down legal rules are based, then, tends to be stale, tendentious, artificially simple, and incomplete; it may even be willfully distorted. As noted earlier, the informational value of legal rules—the quality of the signals they send—is reduced by the inherent limits of legal language, the need to transmit the rules through opaque bureaucracies, and the often-unexpected interactions of rules with social norms and markets. Worse, the feedback loops that could potentially improve information about the law over time are slow and attenuated, especially for courts, and suffer from many of the same informational defects that produced the original, deficient rule. Once legal rules are adopted, the status quo's inertia makes them structurally conservative even when they are meant to be substantively progressive.

Social norms use information quite differently. Unlike law, they are not artifacts of centralized, synoptic rationality and self-conscious regulatory processes; rather, they are distillates of evolving custom, reflexive repetition, and behavioral reinforcement. Because the justification of norms is seldom articulated, the behavior they prescribe is clearer than the social functions they serve. They need only be known and observed, not understood or rationalized. One gains the necessary knowledge of a norm simply by living in the culture in which it is conventional.[157] One observes the norm out of a comfortable conformity, a natural wish to avoid stigma and exclusion, and a habituation to and mimicry of the familiar. Since many norms are implicit patterns based on subtle clues rather than explicit principles articulated as such, one can easily misread their often intricately coded information, especially if one is an outsider or a newcomer to the normative community. Legal rules, of course, can also be misread, even by lawyers. But the nature and sources of misreading, and the sanctions against it, are quite different in the two systems.

Social norms, then, impose fewer informational demands than law does. Indeed, conservatives in the tradition of Edmund Burke and Friedrich von Hayek value norms precisely because they resist the rationalizing ambitions of law or of any group short of society itself.[158] But this resistance or embeddedness of established norms, reinforced by many of the same collective-action problems that encourage the resort to law, makes it difficult to change norms even when they seem dysfunctional.[159] Norms are probably more labile now than ever before. Quite apart from fads and fashions, change in modern societies has become itself a self-conscious, profit-maximizing industry, not merely an observable phenomenon or a widely shared value. Normative insularity is harder to maintain. Even so, norms' stability does limit their utility as policy instruments in dynamic social environments.

Market signals possess most if not all of the advantages that legal signals lack. They economize on information by viewing it like any other good entailing benefits and costs in both production and use. Whereas law must rely on centralized political institutions to gather, process, interpret, disseminate, and correct information, markets radically decentralize it to individuals and firms, minimizing what each of them must know about the complex world in order to make decisions that are individually rational and efficient, and that, *mutatis mutandis*, may be socially desirable.[160] If property rights in information are well defined, assigned, and priced—important conditions given information's public good aspect and burgeoning social value—markets can produce information that is relevant, accurate, and almost instantaneously responsive to changes in facts and opportunities. Because feedback loops are as short as proximity to customers can make them, correction is constant and relatively cheap.

From society's point of view, however, the comparatively efficient economy of information found in markets and norms may be problematic. Some people are always able to obtain, interpret, and deploy information more quickly or fully than others because they are smarter, faster, more responsive, or have better access to key sources. When society views this advantage not as earned or natural but as manipulated and unfair, it may use law to curb it—for example, by regulating insider trading in stock markets and job networks that favor coethnics over strangers.

D. Flexibility

I noted earlier that law paradigmatically takes the form of rules employing simple, often binary categories that map reality very crudely, and that all remedies for this defect, such as looser standards or an exceptions process, entail other problems that may be even greater. Lawmaking institutions, we saw, reinforce these rigidities, as do law's informational deficiencies, tradition of *stare decisis*, procedural morass, and responsiveness to well-organized political interests favoring the status quo. For these reasons, law tends to stifle innovation even when it aims to stimulate it, as with technology-forcing environmental rules,[161] and also tends to delay the correction of even manifest policy errors, as with New Deal–type economic regulation.[162]

Social norms are also slow to change, except in unusual circumstances. I noted that norms by their very nature appeal to long usage and habit and to the esteem of norm compliers. Thus they tend to resist rationalization, innovation, and reform. To discredit and revise norms usually requires a sustained and unusually energetic effort, as the examples of temperance, feminism, smoking, and civil rights movements reveal.[163] A society that admires and richly rewards the very *idea* of novelty creates rich opportunity for entrepreneurs of change who hope to create new norms (Internet behaviors and pattern of dress, for example) and to transfigure old ones. The recent, substantial, and somewhat unexpected changes in teenage sexual practices—less sex and more effective contraception—suggests that new technologies and (less well understood) social learning can accelerate the process of normative change.[164] Nevertheless, one is impressed by the tenacity and resilience of established norms, as well as their defenders' crusading zeal.

Markets are by far the most flexible of social systems. The individualistic race for wealth (and the celebrity, power, and honor that often go with it) releases a kinetic energy that can dislodge and transform settled norms, practices, perceptions, and institutions. This "creative destruction" (in Joseph Schumpeter's phrase)[165] can induce a radically reductionist, economistic consciousness that respects traditional values only insofar as they are profitable, while threatening ruin to those who react slowly or predict poorly. In this remorselessly unstable environment, firms can survive only by being as nimble, innovative, self-critical, and useful as markets demand.[166] Although social norms are valued in part because they change more slowly,[167] they cannot survive long in such an environment unless they become functional.

E. Transaction Costs

Transaction costs are the process costs that decisionmakers incur in reaching and implementing decisions, as distinct from those that flow from the decisions' consequences. Even if one assumes, contrary to fact, that law, norms, and markets could each elicit the same desired social behavior, each system would still occasion different transaction costs along the way. These differences, moreover, might be large enough to affect a prudent sociopolitical decision about which system(s) should be used.

Law's transaction costs tend to be relatively high in terms of time, money, bargaining, and the like. These costs reflect the elaborate routines—institutional, procedural, consultative, and professional—through which people make, learn, communicate, apply, enforce, and review law. Some of these routines are constitutionally required; others seem conducive to democratic legitimation or sound policy. In either event, their high cost requires law to rely heavily on voluntary compliance. At the same time, however, the nature of public goods and services prevents law from relying merely on reputation, informal norms, and other lower-cost, nonlegal remedies for error and abuse. But even where the benefits of legal routines fully justify the entailed transaction costs, law might reduce those costs by using norms, markets, or bottom-up or other lower-transaction-cost legal forms to pursue the policy goals.[168]

Our most important social norms have evolved through a slow, laborious, and costly struggle by many generations of parents to transmit values, meanings, and practices to their children. No single family could possibly initiate and execute this effort itself, unaided by the enormous, cumulative stock of social learning with which the past endows us. Because parents, peers,[169] and the larger society transmit and constantly reinforce this normative endowment, children usually internalize and reflexively conform to it at an early age. In this way, the cost of this normative endowment is spread across yet another generation. Although entrenched norms evolve with little public awareness or effort, such change is usually slow. Self-consciously altering or overthrowing them, however, requires that reformers unearth, discredit, and replace them with new ones. The long struggles of feminism and civil rights illustrate how costly such campaigns can be, almost regardless of the movements' merits.

Markets economize on transaction costs, just as they do on information (one such cost), in order to maximize profits. Unlike lawmakers and enforcers, however, market traders bear those costs personally. Their strong incentives to minimize them shape countless business practices such as Internet trading, incomplete and form contracts, alternative dispute resolution, "just-in-time" inventories, standardized procedures, default and bright-line rules, and reliance on reputation and custom. Indeed, transaction costs are often the difference between market success and failure.

F. Legitimacy

The public perception that law is legitimate constitutes a social resource of incalculable value. It nourishes respect for both polity and principle and hence for the claims of one's fellow citizens. It induces people to comply with law even when, as often occurs, narrow self-interest counsels disobedience. Indeed, it invites people to broaden their conception of what their interests are and perhaps to identify them with the interests of others. It reflects an often compelling vision of social justice.

Yet as I noted earlier, law's legitimacy is always fragile in a vibrant, liberal society. Political and economic actors attack laws that constrain them while supporting those that constrain their competitors.[170] Law's moral claim to obedience rests ultimately on the public's perceptions of its procedural fairness, substantive justice, and practical efficacy. Because the process of lawmaking invariably compromises these values, its legitimacy is always contestable.

Law is most vulnerable when it takes on the ambitious task of social reconstruction,[171] for here the gap between its promise and its performance is widest. This gap contributes to the decline in the public's respect for government.[172] It also helps explain why judges, whose usual task is the relatively simple one of applying given rules to a single set of facts, are more highly esteemed than politicians and bureaucrats, who must devise effective policies addressing complex, fluid problems and then face the cost-bearers at the polls.[173]

A social norm is morally acceptable and legitimate within its domain almost by definition, for people conform to it with little conscious thought. When its domain is insular or parochial, those outside that normative community may contest or even punish it,[174] as the United States does in opposing the practice of clitoridectomy here and abroad.[175] Socially diverse polities that protect local and minority rights while also enacting the majority's values into law are increasingly roiled by these normative conflicts.[176]

We have seen that although norms do evolve, the process of change is usually opaque[177] and slow.[178] Old norms enjoy the benefit of an inertia created by indolence, tradition, habit, and other economizing and community-affirming behaviors. Law may try to accelerate normative change by lending its incentives and legitimacy to new or different norms, but its actual effect is uncertain. Often we cannot tell whether legal change is a cause or a consequence of social change, or both.[179] People almost always react to law in ways that its authors neither expected nor desired, as occurred with Prohibition.

Indeed, law's adoption or encouragement of a norm can actually discourage the desired act (for better or worse) by altering the social meanings that people convey when they comply with or violate it.[180] When law compels an act—

charity or patriotism, for example—observers are unable to distinguish spontaneous, voluntary behavior from compulsory performance of the act. This blurs the act's signal to others. Even when law merely rewards an act—subsidizing organ donations, for example[181]—it may change the values that people ascribe to the act and thus alter their behavioral responses to it. Law may in effect cut off the norm's oxygen supply, smothering the spontaneity, authenticity, and autonomy of will that gave the norm vitality, thereby endangering precisely what the law hoped to promote.[182] William Stuntz has noted a similar paradox in criminal law enforcement. When the community perceives enforcement as unfair or overzealous, criminals suffer less social stigma, lowering the effective price of their crimes.[183] Finally, the fact that the state has adopted a norm may actually encourage some people to defy and violate it, especially if it is only weakly enforced,[184] as with laws against teenage smoking or drinking.

The legitimacy of markets arouses much ambivalence.[185] Even among Americans, who embrace markets ardently[186] and design institutions pragmatically,[187] this ambivalence is striking. For example, Americans endorse markets in food, securities, education, and blood while viewing markets in sex, human organs, and childbearing as improper, even criminal.[188] One can glimpse a society's distinctive moral constitution in the way in which it defines, evaluates, and regulates different markets.[189]

Talk of the global hegemony of markets, a dominant motif today, might seem to signal their inevitable dominance and burgeoning legitimacy.[190] The truth, however, is more complex. Since earliest antiquity, people have denounced markets on religious and humanistic grounds. Many critics have simply feared that markets threatened their social control or authority, but many others have had more idealistic or disinterested objections. Markets, they claim, produce atomized, selfish, amoral, Godless, acquisitive individuals who undermine hopes for genuine communities of common purpose and compassion.[191] These criticisms of markets resonate especially powerfully among elites whose prosperity is relatively insulated from market changes, find materialism debasing, and desperately want to think better of themselves and their society.[192]

The most common critiques, however, are more functional than moral. They indict not markets in general but particular markets deemed inefficient or unfair. (They may raise the rhetorical stakes by challenging markets in moral terms as well).[193] The persistence of these attacks and their embodiment in law make market triumphalism both premature and perverse; its smug arrogance feeds popular resentments about the fairness of markets, resentments that lie just beneath the surface of an anxious, competitive society and that can easily be inflamed by populist rhetoric. Perhaps ironically, the market system's remarkable success in raising consumer welfare, generating wealth, promoting political and economic freedom, accelerating social mobility, and stimulating technological change by no means assures its moral legitimacy. For better or worse, justified or not, many Americans take these marvels for granted and focus instead on what they see as the market's failures: rampant commercialism, economic insecurity, enduring poverty, environmental pollution, moral decline, and a persistently skewed distribution of wealth. For remedies, they look to government and hence to law.

III. General Principles and Specific Applications

This complex accounting of the advantages and disadvantages of law, social norms, and markets is all well and good, the reader might say, but where does it lead and what practical difference can it make?

I offer a cautiously optimistic answer. At a minimum, the analysis teaches that law is not the only, or always the best, technique available to even an activist government that wishes to self-consciously shape and coordinate social behavior. This lesson might make both official and popular judgments about public policy more intelligent and fruitful. If I am correct that our habits, incentives, and impulses lead us almost reflexively to design policy in the form of law, and often top-down law at that,[194] then we need a broader approach that promises to make us more aware of these properties.

Such self-criticism does not come easily or naturally. Law, after all, is the most visible of policy instruments. Its public processes, political contestation, and credit claiming call attention to itself whenever it moves to adopt or apply a rule. In contrast, we are as embedded in webs of norms and markets as we are immersed in the air we breathe. For all their ubiquity and vitality—indeed, *because* of their ubiquity and vitality—we scarcely notice them as such. Even less do we think comparatively and systematically about how we might leverage them for public purposes.

It remains, then, to propose some general principles that encourage officials to view norms and markets not just as obstacles that law must overcome or regulate but also as policy tools that government can use creatively to refine or complement law or, more rarely, to avoid it altogether.[195] At least five such principles can be drawn from the earlier analysis. Comparison, the first of them, is the master norm; the other four—implementation analysis, process efficiency, responsiveness, and law minimization—are more specific, reform-oriented applications of the comparison principle.

I hasten to add that these are decidedly modest principles. None of them can itself provide a substantive solution to a particular policy problem. Such solutions can be devised only after detailed, painstaking, and systematic analysis of the issues in all of their empirical and normative specificity. Nevertheless, this framework can help lawmakers to think "outside the box" about policy instruments and provide them with some structural or "meta-analytical" criteria for deciding how to use law, norms, and markets in the policy designs of the activist state.[196]

A. Comparison

When policymakers decide whether and how to use law, norms, and markets for policy purposes, they can look to three highly imperfect systems, each with its paradigmatic values, structures, and incentives.[197] The comparison principle holds that a rational decisionmaker should systematically assess the relative strengths and weaknesses of each of them before deciding whether and how to proceed.[198]

This principle is self-evident—indeed it defines rationality[199]—yet many officials appear not to observe it. Lawmakers are drawn to top-down forms of law such as command-and-control rules, which seem authoritative, clear, rigorous, and relatively easy to interpret and enforce. In contrast, markets and social norms are often the problems that policymakers want law to solve by supplanting or modifying them, yet both are notoriously hard to control.[200] As for regulators and courts, they may have little or no choice in the matter; the law may require regulators to issue such rules and courts to apply them.[201] Even regulators who are not precluded from using markets seem to prefer top-down rules that promise bureaucratic security and stability,[202] and common law courts often craft their own rules even in cases where market values should predominate, although these rules tend to be more flexible and contextual than those crafted by legislators and regulators.[203]

This persistent preference for top-down rules over nonrule forms of social control is not simply habitual; it is also driven by strong political and institutional incentives. One approach to inducing regulators to think in more comparative terms—requiring officials to explicitly consider and analyze the merits of alternative forms before deciding to issue rules—does not really alter those incentives.[204] A more direct reform strategy is to press public service providers to adopt market efficiencies by forcing them to compete with private providers for resources and clients under suitable, market-improving regulation. Many policymakers already use this approach to generally good effect for education, sanitation, security, child welfare, health care, and other local public services.[205]

B. Implementation Analysis

Some law is flawed conceptually. It cannot possibly succeed if it is conceived on false premises and widely abhorrent values and lacks public legitimacy. Most important laws, however, are based on plausible premises and arouse only the usual political and policy objections, which do not bring their moral legitimacy into question. If they fail, they fail not at their inception but because they cannot be implemented at a socially acceptable cost—or perhaps at all—in the real world. The vast majority of law's failures are probably of this kind.

Law's long, tortuous path from adoption to fulfillment is strewn with obstacles, detours, and pitfalls (a minefield may be a truer metaphor), which social scientists have analyzed in great detail.[206] Although some of these political, bureaucratic, informational, legal, fiscal, motivational, cultural, and other barriers would elude even the most diligent, prescient lawmaker, many are readily predictable. For those, systematic attention to the problematics of policy implementation would enhance the quality and effectiveness of law.

Like the comparison principle, implementation analysis seems obvious. Further, one might expect that during the often-laborious process of developing law, opponents and skeptics would identify potential obstacles to implementation in order to persuade lawmakers to oppose the proposal or to at least take these problems into account. For several common reasons, however, this does not always happen. A proposal's advocates will tend to downplay implementation obstacles, while lawmakers who underestimate the law's significance will devote little time to predicting them.[207] Even when lawmakers do consider possible future problems, however, they often assume them away by imagining a fully implemented law. Some laws are adopted so quickly and surreptitiously that those in a position to foresee implementation problems have little chance to sound the alarm. A legislative juggernaut under a full head of steam is hard to stop.

Implementation analysis is designed to minimize these omissions. It suggests that a formal agency or process be given responsibility, before lawmaking is completed, to analyze the probable barriers to implementation, the steps and costs needed to surmount them, the distribution of those costs, and (in the spirit of the comparison principle) other, perhaps better ways of accomplishing the same ends. This analysis should also identify possible inconsistencies and overlaps with existing laws that may, and often do, render the larger regulatory system incoherent.[208]

In an earlier work, I proposed that courts, before issuing complex, far-reaching remedial orders (often called "structural injunctions"), require a similar analysis. I did not minimize the difficulty of such analyses but argued that the alternative—decisions that obscure or neglect such crucial questions until it is too late—was worse.[209] This is even truer of statutes and regulations, as they are often broader in scope and more difficult to modify than court orders. Some analogous analytical requirements—what I call "metaregulation"—have been adopted in recent years by Congress and executive order.[210]

C. Process Efficiency

An important, sometimes decisive consideration in deciding whether and how to use law, norms, and markets in policy design is the kind of process that each of them entails. The process efficiency principle holds that this decision should minimize the policy's transaction costs, *ceteris paribus*.

The earlier discussion suggested that law, norms, and markets tend to differ significantly in this respect.[211] Law imposes high transaction costs. Norms, in contrast, entail very low ones within their domains but potentially high ones beyond those domains, where resistant outsiders must somehow be persuaded to accept them. Markets, unlike law and norms, rigorously economize on transaction costs; if such costs exceed the expected gain from a transaction, the transaction is not undertaken.

Three important implications follow for our purposes. First, if policymakers analyze alternative regulatory modes in accordance with the comparison principle but fail to include in the analysis each mode's transaction costs, they are likely to make poor policy design decisions. Second, the transaction cost differential between a top-down legal rule and a market may be so large that even policymakers who are determined to issue rules should consider incorporating even concededly imperfect markets into the legal regime, for such a policy may still be superior on balance.[212] Third, policymakers should search for other ways to minimize the transaction costs of their interventions, as through public information, improved management and enforcement, privatization, and pursuit of the responsiveness principle.

D. Responsiveness

Several structural criteria for deciding whether and how to use law, norms, and markets in policy design remain to be discussed. Some of these criteria are sociological, stressing the diverse social conditions that government seeks to regulate. Some are spatial or geographic; they concern the extent of a policy's domain or coverage and the level of government (or private) action at which primary responsibility for policy choice and administration should be lodged. And some are temporal, focusing on how policy might be reconsidered and revised over time. The "responsiveness principle" simply gathers these very different criteria together under one encompassing rubric. It holds that policymakers should, *ceteris paribus*, use policy instruments whose responsiveness is well calibrated to the kinds and magnitudes of diversity and dynamism exhibited by the particular environments they want to regulate.

1. Sociological. Americans and their communities are extraordinarily diverse.[213] This fact has always astonished observers from abroad, for it occurs in every conceivable dimension: political, economic, religious, cultural, linguistic, national origin, demographic, topographical, and even climatological.[214] Though nationally oriented mass media and high residential mobility encourage some convergence, most of these diversities are increasing as America's consumer- and technology-driven society rapidly fragments and differentiates on both the supply and demand sides of the market[215] and in other realms such as religion.[216] However one views these diversities,[217] they clearly challenge law's efficacy as a regulatory instrument.

Law is diversity's mortal enemy in many respects. I noted earlier that law characteristically employs reductionist categories and analysis; it suppresses complexity and diversity in order to advance legal system values.[218] But even when law seeks to promote diversity, it may succeed in producing only an unwanted or spurious variety. Antitrust law, for example, promotes market diversity, but at a price that consumers may be unwilling to pay if they prefer more standardization or network efficiency to a costly differentiation.[219] Consider also the racial classifications that law creates for census, affirmative action, and other administrative purposes, classifications that many private groups also use. Although the groupings are usually benignly intended, they are in fact scientifically incoherent ("race" is not a valid biological concept), illogical ("Hispanic" is a language group, not a race), ahistorical (census groupings constantly change), insensitive (racial categories exclude people who identify themselves as multiracial), arbitrary (why only five groups?), dangerously misleading (each group is internally heterogeneous), and easily manipulated.[220]

Such groupings conceal and debase genuine diversity. Law can promote or protect authentic, vibrant social diversity only by proscribing invidious discrimination and then getting out of the way. Its effort to compel or affirmatively create social diversity where it is not genuinely valued or where none actually exists, however, is instead more likely to stifle, deaden, or discredit it.

2. Spatial.   In principle, law's domain can be more readily circumscribed spatially than the domains of norms and markets can. By their nature, the rules that impose controls define their own regulatory ambits. In contrast, norms and markets are more spontaneous and uncoordinated, and so cannot be segmented in the same way that rules can. A norm's domain, unlike that of a rule, is defined not top-down by a central authority but bottom-up by a community of adherents that may cross conventional geographic boundaries. The difference is suggested by the Supreme Court's reliance on "community standards" in reviewing state and local regulation of pornography, a notoriously arbitrary and difficult norm to apply.[221]

Law has even less leeway in defining markets because the domain of markets is determined by people's desire to trade with others, which is constantly changing and has little or nothing to do with the boundaries of geographical or normative communities. If this desire to trade is great enough, restriction of a legal market's domain will both distort transactions in that market and spawn an illegal market outside it.[222] Throughout history, schemes to regulate informal markets have foundered on this reality.[223]

Another important spatial criterion for deciding how to use law concerns the level of government that should design, impose, finance, and administer it.[224] The general principle of spatial responsiveness, subject to qualification below, is this: Law should be imposed by the level that is closest geographically to those who will mainly bear the law's costs and enjoy its benefits. Distributing responsibility for law in this way subjects voters and lawmakers alike to salutary democratic disciplines. First, they must balance taxation, limits on freedom, compliance duties, enforcement and transaction costs, and other burdens entailed by the law against the social benefits that it promises to confer. Second, they must constantly review these trade-offs as perceptions and conditions change. It is striking, then, that the Clinton administration proposed federalist guidelines that repudiate this principle in favor of criteria that would almost certainly centralize lawmaking power in Washington,[225] while the European Union has at the same time been implementing a "subsidiarity" norm that allocates such power to the lowest possible level (usually the member state), except where common interests predominate.[226]

My proposed principle for allocating lawmaking authority makes it more likely that a law will be both efficient (i.e., its benefits will exceed its costs, both broadly defined) and fair (i.e., it will distribute those costs and benefits in ways that taxpayers and any other cost-bearers consider just). The notion that lower levels of government should exercise lawmaking power because they are "closer to the people" expresses this allocation norm in the form of a political piety. Whether the implicit empirical claims underlying it—that lower levels of government are easier to participate in, more knowledgeable about people's needs, more flexible and responsive, and so forth—are true or not,[227] the principle can and should accommodate such considerations.

This spatial-political principle, of course, is only a first approximation. The main qualifications concern externalities—the effects of the law on those outside the political community that adopts it. Most polities are defined geographically and historically,[228] yet law's effects are not so neatly confined. Thus, outsiders may also bear some of its costs, receive some of its benefits, or both. In addition, people belong to state, federal, and even international polities and nonpolitical communities, not just a local one; to some extent, people have interests in, feel responsible to, and are prepared to make sacrifices for their countrymen in other localities and for people outside their own country.[229] In addition to these externalities, we may pursue scale economies to increase the law's benefits or reduce its costs by moving responsibility for a law to a higher level of government. Constitutional constraints, of course, also affect the particular level to which a lawmaking power is allocated. Moreover, society's historical, symbolic, and emotional commitments have compelling logics of their own.[230] These and other spatial-political factors render the optimal location of lawmaking power somewhat indeterminate and highly controversial.

This indeterminacy and controversy in turn are reflected, and uneasily resolved, in our remarkably messy and complex federal system.[231] This system must cope with many normative conflicts that law cannot easily settle. One is the fear that opportunistic behavior by individuals and jurisdictions may lead to socially undesirable "races to the bottom" as states compete to attract business by lowering taxes, relaxing regulatory controls, and encouraging out-migration by the poor by eliminating their safety net benefits.[232] Although the race-to-the-bottom possibility merits policymakers' attention, there are theoretical, empirical, and normative reasons to doubt that this possibility alone will often dictate responsibilities to the national government for program design, funding, and administration.[233] In theory, the size and nature of any such effect will depend on many complex, interacting factors and thus vary from program to program. In fact, a race to the bottom has not occurred in environmental or post–1996 welfare policy, where one would most expect to observe it.[234] As a normative matter, a world of difference exists between a race to the bottom, on the one hand, and competition among states with persistently distinctive demographic patterns, social attitudes, economic bases, and political cultures, on the other. The former may induce less regulation and welfare spending than citizens and governments truly prefer. The latter, however, may induce desirable (or at least acceptable) levels of interstate diversity; this can also help to restrain the political incentives for government at all levels, especially the national, to overregulate and overspend.[235] Policy designers allocating programmatic responsibilities among different levels, then, must balance any risk of a race to the bottom against other political, sociological, spatial, and (as we see next) temporal factors.

3. *Temporal.* A wise lawmaking system will revisit, and probably revise, public policies over time as the environment changes in ways that call for policy adjustment. In general, the pace of social change has been accelerating remorselessly. Some environments (e.g., parenting and pedagogical techniques) change more slowly than others (e.g., currency markets and computer technology). The more dynamic a policy environment is, the more responsive the adjustments must be in order to advance social goals rather than distort or retard them.

A policy instrument's temporal responsiveness turns on how quickly, accurately, and persuasively it can perform three essential functions: learn about environmental changes, educate others about them, and revise policies accordingly. The first depends on the length and quality of an instrument's feedback loop; the second on the instrument's ability to transmit its learning to others in persuasive ways; and the third on how quickly it can decide about policy change and mobilize the actors who must implement it.

Law and norms, as we saw earlier, tend to be less responsive than markets in these three respects.[236] Markets register almost instantaneously any changes in the supply or demand for goods. Traders have strong incentives to predict, learn about, and verify such changes and then to capitalize on the information before their competitors can. By affecting prices, these actions immediately communicate this learning to other traders. In contrast, top-down law's feedback loop is longer, slower, costlier, and more vulnerable to distortion and error. By the time officials get around to revising a law and implementing the revision, the dynamism of the regulated environment may have already made the revisions irrelevant, unfair, or unwise. In the increasingly vital domains involving fast-changing technologies and robust markets, law's valiant catch-up efforts are likely to be futile; they are rather like trying to nail jelly to a wall.[237]

Decentralizing policy initiative and implementation responsibilities, discussed earlier as a spatial issue, can also reduce the temporal aspects of law's disability, though it cannot wholly eliminate it. Almost all federal domestic policy innovations have drawn upon earlier state or local models.[238] Decentralization can telescope policy innovation, learning, and reform by shortening feedback loops as well as changing incentives.

The responsiveness criterion forces law to make a challenging and in a way ironic choice, one that markets do not face in the same way. One of law's singular strengths is its capacity to project a future order credible and stable enough to encourage the kinds of social expectations whose satisfaction demands long-term investments of human, economic, and social capital. In order to fulfill this need, the modern administrative state creates legal entitlements and social programs aimed at improving our health, safety, economic security, and well-being. Yet at the same time—and often for the very same purposes— the state also exercises broad regulatory and taxing authority, using rules whose applications are both uncertain and subject to change (sometimes retroactively) depending on the vagaries of transitory politics. This regime, by unsettling expectations as it pursues attractive regulatory goals, reduces the security of these socially desired investments for the future—which of course, reduces people's willingness to make them and reinforces a vicious cycle of uncertainty and legal ineffectiveness.

The administrative state thus faces an inescapable temporal dilemma. By facilitating law's revision, the state can make law more responsive to future social changes, but only at some cost in long-term investment and market efficacy. Alternatively, the state can make law more stable, which will encourage investment and strengthen markets, at least in the short run. The resulting law, however, may be less flexible, responsive, and just.

Some constitutional scholars argue that the Takings Clause of the Fifth Amendment resolved this dilemma once and for all by protecting property rights from regulatory incursion.[239] As a constitutional matter, however, a democratic polity must remain free to decide within very broad limits[240] on the precise trade-off between dynamic regulation and redistribution, on the one hand, and secure property rights, on the other, that best serves its political values, social institutions, and policy goals.[241] It must also remain free to alter this choice from time to time, while recognizing that this freedom comes at a price.[242]

E. Law Minimization

We have seen that law, norms, and markets are distinctive but subtly related social systems, that they can be combined in countless ways in order to maximize competing policy values, but that lawmakers have institutional and political reasons to favor top-down rules as policy instruments. Ideally, however, a lawmaker would not decide on policy design until she asks and answers three basic questions: What tasks must be performed in order to implement a particular policy goal in a given policy environment? In order to perform these tasks well, what features must a policy instrument possess? And which among the available instrumental forms will maximize these desirable properties?

The law-minimization principle offers a partial answer to these questions.[243] It holds that the limits of law, most pronounced in its top-down form but also visible elsewhere, disable it for many of the regulatory tasks required by contemporary social policies, that the severity of law's disability will continue to grow, and that policymakers should devise forms of social control that reduce law's adverse effects or avoid them altogether.

We can briefly develop these claims by arraying law, norms, and markets along a spectrum of regulatory forms defined by the degree of reliance on legal commands *simpliciter,* a spectrum bounded at one end by top-down law and at the other by pure markets. The same properties that attract lawmakers in the administrative state to top-down forms—its characteristic but often illusory certainty, clarity, cheap enforcement, and control of administrative discretion and through it, of social behavior—explain why such forms are increasingly unsuitable as mechanisms for regulating complex, diverse, and dynamic environments. Regulating uncontroversial, readily measured, and stable policy variables such as the eligibility age for public officials is one thing; regulating a metropolitan area's airshed, technologies, a large, specialized profession, and markets is quite another. In contexts like these, simple and certain rules egregiously distort reality. If they also produce unjust results and encourage citizens or officials to evade the law, as the federal sentencing guidelines apparently have,[244] they may even delegitimate it. Top-down law, then, is only a desirable regulatory form where its precision produces vast administrative gains while its simplicity and rigidity are unproblematic.

These conditions, however, do not describe most regulatory environments today. As the pace of social change and differentiation quickens, a rational policymaker should consider moving to more bottom-up forms of law, hoping to exploit the advantages of social norms—their embeddedness, low administrative costs, and high legitimacy—by dragooning them into law's service. Because these, hybrid forms eschew clear, definitive rules on which consensus may be hard to reach in favor of more ambiguous standards, they can also possess the important political virtue of facilitating compromise.

Such hybrid legal forms may draw on or incorporate societywide or narrower community norms. For example, many common, statutory, and constitutional law doctrines use "reasonableness" as the standard of care.[245] Legislators, agencies, and courts sometimes adopt occupational or professional group norms or the standards set by technical organizations, rather than trying to devise their own.[246] Thus they defer to "business judgment" in corporate law, "professional custom" in medical malpractice cases, "the needs of the service" in military law, and "the custom of the trade" in commercial disputes.[247] A growing body of laws channeling disputes to informal dispute resolution in effect looks to process norms that favor conciliation and compromise; these in turn rest on substantive norms of fairness.[248]

Even lawmakers who use social norms to augment or soften legal rules, however, may find that effective regulation demands more. They may need to mobilize stronger incentives, stimulate more innovation, generate cheaper, more accurate data on costs and preferences, and obtain better, faster feedback about performance and changing conditions. Such lawmakers may be attracted to markets' comparative advantages in information, speed, incentives, and administrative costs and seek to capture those advantages by substituting default rules for mandatory ones, or by grafting onto the legal rules any of a growing number of market-mimicking regulatory devices: auctions of public rights, recognition of new (or newly alienable) private rights, unbundling of existing rights, emissions trading and pricing of other externalities, user charges, competitive bidding, market tests or yardsticks, cross-risk optimizing techniques such as regulatory bubbles, and the like.[249] In the same spirit, the leading Social Security and Medicare reform proposals seek to protect or improve benefit levels by combining markets, norms, and law in new ways: authorizing market investment vehicles and performance criteria, mobilizing and educating informal investment practices, and adopting legal rules to prevent undue market risk taking.[250]

Law can recruit market incentives to enhance not only its substantive standards of conduct but also its sanctioning systems. Most top-down regulation relies largely on public enforcement, yet prosecutorial motivation and resources are often weak and poorly aligned with social goals, leading to underenforcement and thus to regulatory failure. Regulators, however, could deploy bounties, counsel fee awards, and other market incentives to attract "private attorneys general" who are more highly motivated to monitor and sanction violators.[251] Top-down regulation of child-support obligations,[252] campaign finance,[253] and other chronically underenforced programs could be bolstered in similar ways.

Lawmakers may approach the other end of the spectrum by relinquishing more prescriptive power to the market and confining law's domain to market-perfecting and equity-enhancing sanctions, incentives, rules, and subsidies. Recent deregulation and privatization measures by no means exhaust law's opportunities to exploit the structural and efficiency advantages of workably competitive markets while reaffirming core collective values like public safety, nondiscrimination, and social insurance.[254] New balances are always being struck.[255]

Federally subsidized insurance, for example, constitutes an immense public undertaking that is often both inefficient and distributively perverse.[256] Private insurers could cover bank insolvency, crop failure, loan default, flooding, clouds on residential title, and many other risks if government would let them compete for customers. Private provision can co-exist with regulations assuring insurer solvency, consumer information, and controls on adverse selection, moral hazard, and other market defects. Lawmakers could promote any equity goals through direct subsidies in the form of cash, vouchers, or tax credits.

Still closer to the market end of the spectrum, lawmakers might generate even greater social gains through programs[257] aimed at freeing citizens, especially low-income families, from the often benignly intended but nonetheless oppressive tyranny of traditional public service monopolies. The most important current examples are education vouchers to benefit school-age children and housing vouchers for low-income families.[258]

In principle, however, this model can be extended, *mutatis mutandis,* to other services: health and long-term care under Medicare, Medicaid, and state-funded programs; veterans benefits; adult and vocational education; job training by employers; transportation for the disabled; English-language schools for immigrants; campaign finance; support for museums and other cultural resources, and so forth. Although the devil is always in the details, such programs should assure several vital elements: provider competition for consumer-citizens' patronage; no governmental favoritism toward particular providers; direct payment of service fees by consumer-citizens, not officials; adequate information on service characteristics and performance; and laws securing nondiscrimination and other overriding public values.[259]

IV. Conclusion

The rule of law is humanity's greatest creation, the essential precondition of a civilized, just society. Precisely because law is an artificial contrivance, not "the natural flowerings of behavior in its customary forms,"[260] we are drawn to view it, and increasingly inclined to use it, as perhaps the chief instrument in our self-conscious struggle to gratify both immediate wants and more elusive aspirations. This is not the first time that the Anglo-American legal tradition has embraced the contemporary conceit that law can effectively meet these challenges.[261]

Perhaps it can, but not without substantial assistance from informal norms and especially from markets. Law's limits are measured by its irreducible needs: to mobilize political will, institutional rationality, fresh and accurate information, socially productive incentives, energy and ardor, speed and efficiency, flexibility in the face of diversity, learning and corrigibility in the face of constant change and frequent error, and public confidence and legitimacy. These needs, seldom satisfied in contemporary policymaking, are bound to increase in the future. The failure to fulfill them will become all the more glaring and disabling, and delegitimating.

The central question is, and will always be, not which of these flawed mechanisms is the right one but how they all can be refined, integrated, and institutionalized in the service of an effective, legitimate, and just administrative state. The first step is to understand that (and why) this is indeed the vital question and consider how we might go about answering it.

Notes

1. "Law-lessness" here denotes not criminality but the absence of a formally applicable rule of law. Behaviorally speaking, all societies exhibit lawlessness. Some commentary on the penetration of law fails to distinguish clearly between these two meanings. *See, e.g.*, DONALD BLACK, THE BEHAVIOR OF LAW 123–24 (1976) (social life without law ["anarchy"] has existed everywhere to some degree).

2. *See* PAUL H. RUBIN, THE STATE OF NATURE AND THE EVOLUTION OF POLITICAL PREFERENCES (Emory Univ. Working Paper, 1999). The prepolitical, prelegal "natural rights" posited by some theorists are no less law's artifacts. In a consent-based constitutional democracy, such rights are either recognized and protected by law, or they are merely aspirational ("nonsense on stilts," in Jeremy Bentham's dismissive formulation, *see* Jeremy Bentham, *Anarchical Fallacies, in* 2 WORKS OF JEREMY BENTHAM 489, 501 (James Bowring ed., 1843)).

3. Examples include the law's construction of race, *see, e.g.*, Ariela J. Gross, *Litigating Whiteness: Trials of Racial Determination in the Nineteenth-Century South,* 108 YALE L.J. 109 (1998); IAN HANEY LOPEZ, WHITE BY LAW: THE LEGAL CONSTRUCTION OF RACE (1996), and of gender, *see, e.g.*, JUDITH BUTLER, GENDER TROUBLE (1990). Law also constructs our ideas of physical nature, even wilderness. *See, e.g.*, UNCOMMON GROUND: TOWARD REINVENTING NATURE (William Cronon ed., 1995).

4. Legal rules, whether derived from a constitution, statute, regulation, or common law principle, may protect autonomy or privacy by enforcing private choices (as with the common law of contracts), by denying courts jurisdiction over certain matters, and by immunizing conduct from legal controls or effects. The common law conferred many tort immunities as well as establishing narrow legal duties and other such limitations on liability tantamount to immunity. *See, e.g.*, Robert L. Rabin, *The Historical Development of the Fault Principle: A Reinterpretation,* 15 GA. L. REV. 925 (1981). Constitutionally protected liberties, such as political speech, are immunized, as are statutorily created immunities, such as Good Samaritan laws.

5. The interaction between private law and public policy has always been far-reaching, *see, e.g.*, Adrienne D. Davis, *The Private Law of Race and Sex: An Antebellum Perspective,* 51 STAN. L. REV. 221 (1999) (interaction of law regulating racial and sexual relations and estate law), and has become even more so in the modern administrative state. Although the boundary between public and private law is sometimes blurry, little or nothing in my analysis turns on a precise demarcation.

6. *See generally* BRUCE A. ACKERMAN, RECONSTRUCTING AMERICAN LAW (1984). For a history of the development of this regime, *see, e.g.*, ALAN BRINKLEY, THE END OF REFORM: NEW DEAL LIBERALISM IN RECESSION AND WAR (1995).

7. See, *e.g.*, PAUL PIERSON, DISMANTLING THE WELFARE STATE? REAGAN, THATCHER, AND THE POLITICS OF RETRENCHMENT (1994) (Reagan administration failed to roll back welfare state). Social spending and overall government spending both rose in real terms during the Reagan-Bush years. *Id.*, at 144. This growth continued in some respects even in the "devolutionary" 104th Congress. See *GOP Confounds Expectations, Expands Federal Authority,* CONG. Q., Nov. 2, 1996, at 3117; *cf.* THE BURGER COURT: THE COUNTER-

REVOLUTION THAT WASN'T (Vincent Blasi ed., 1983) (continuity in Burger Court era belied popular rhetoric about conservative retrenchment). *See also,* Chapter 7 of this book, at n. 94.

8. The United States no longer records starvation as a statistically significant cause of death among any group. STATISTICAL ABSTRACT OF THE UNITED STATES, 1998, at 100–102 (hereinafter "1998 STATISTICAL ABSTRACT"). Indeed, more than 30 percent of Americans in all income categories are "overweight." *Id.,* at 154. Still, Americans do occasionally die of starvation. *See, e.g.,* Nina Bernstein, *Placing the Blame in an Infant's Death,* N.Y. TIMES, Mar. 15, 1999, at B1 (infant death from malnutrition).

9. The law, of course, always proscribed the murder or assisted suicide of patients, and it still does. Dirk Johnson, *Kervorkian Sentenced to 10 to 25 Years in Prison,* N.Y. TIMES, Apr. 14, 1999, at A1. State law will largely shape the contours of the new "right to die." See Quill v. Vacco, 521 U.S. 793 (1997). See also Sam H. Verhovek, *Oregon Reporting 15 Deaths in 1998 Under Suicide Law,* N.Y. TIMES, Feb. 17, 1999, at A1 (discussing implementation of Oregon's new assisted-suicide law, only law of its kind in world). On informed consent, see Peter H. Schuck, *Rethinking Informed Consent,* 103 YALE L.J. 899 (1994). On organ distribution, see *Fight over Organs Shifts to States from Washington,* N.Y. TIMES, Mar. 11, 1999, at A1.

10. *See, e.g.,* Vicki Schultz, *Reconceptualizing Sexual Harassment,* 107 YALE L.J. 1683, 1685–86 (1998) (describing rapid development and expansion of sexual harassment law over past twenty years). For a critical assessment of the current contours of sexual harassment law, see Jeffrey Rosen, *I Pry: Paula Jones and the End of Privacy,* NEW REPUBLIC, Mar. 16, 1998, at 21.

11. Cedar Rapids Community School District v. Garret F., 119 S. Ct. 992 (1999) (school must provide continuous nursing services to quadriplegic student under Individuals with Disabilities Act).

12. For a good overview of the reach of modern environmental law, *see, e.g.,* GREGG EASTERBROOK, A MOMENT ON THE EARTH: THE COMING AGE OF ENVIRONMENTAL OPTIMISM (1995); AARON WILDAVSKY, BUT IS IT TRUE? A CITIZEN'S GUIDE TO ENVIRONMENTAL HEALTH AND SAFETY ISSUES (1995).

13. Jonathan Rauch, *Tunnel Vision,* NAT'L J., Sept. 19, 1998, at 2153.

14. Legislative tacticians often try to hide controversial policy decisions in committee reports; in budget, appropriations, and tax provisions; or in committee reports that are technical and less visible except to lobbyists and committee staff. Still, opponents are wise to this game—they may play it themselves—and endeavor to expose it, as do some media.

15. Whether the behavior is characterized as public or private, of course, is often a key element of the political debate. Abortion, homosexuality, drug use, flag burning, gambling, and some union activities are common examples. Left and Right also confound conventional political categories when agreeing to privatize regulated activities (e.g., airlines) or regulate private ones (e.g., patients' rights).

16. Prisoner's dilemmas and other opportunistic and strategic behaviors by private actors often prevent them from reaching the outcomes that they would presumably prefer absent such behaviors. *See generally* ROBERT M. AXELROD, THE EVOLUTION OF COOPERATION (1984). By coordinating private choices in such situations, law can help overcome these obstacles; indeed, some commentators think that this is its principal function. For a provocative recent example, *see* ROBERT H. FRANK, LUXURY FEVER: WHY

Money Fails to Satisfy in an Era of Excess (1999) (urging progressive consumption tax to control overconsumption motivated by status competition).

17. *See* Leopold J. Pospicil, The Ethnology of Law 54–55 (2d ed. 1978). For a useful review of different mechanisms of legal influence in contemporary society, see the essays in How Does Law Matter? (Bryant G. Garth & Austen Sarat eds., 1998).

18. Neil K. Komesar, Imperfect Alternatives: Choosing Institutions in Law, Economics, and Public Policy 103 (1994).

19. *See* David R. Mayhew, Congress: The Electoral Connection (1974); *see also* Michael Hayes, Lobbyists and Legislatures: A Theory of the Political Process (1981) (demand for legislation particularly strong where benefits concentrated).

20. As is well known, the vast majority of market entrepreneurs fail. Although public programs seldom go out of business, there is every reason to expect that they are even more problematic than private ones. *See, e.g.,* Charles Wolf, *A Theory of Non-Market Failures,* 55 Pub. Interest 114, 120 (1979).

21. James C. Scott, Seeing Like a State: How Certain Schemes to Improve the Human Condition Have Failed (1998).

22. Prohibition offers only the best-known example of the manner in which American law manifests popular reformist instincts. *See generally* Edward Behr, Prohibition: Thirteen Years That Changed America (1996). It also offers the best-known example of law's *failure* in the United States, although some commentators argue that Prohibition's failings have been exaggerated. *See, e.g.,* Thomas R. Pegram, Battling Demon Rum: The Struggle for a Dry America 1800–1933, at 163–65 (1998) (Prohibition successful in certain respects); *cf.* Donald J. Boudreaux & A. C. Pritchard, *The Price of Prohibition,* 36 Ariz. L. Rev. 1 (1994) (decline in tax revenue, not Prohibition's perceived failures, major impetus for repeal).

23. For example, the obvious failure of the 1971 campaign finance law, Federal Election Campaign Act of 1971, Pub. L. No. 92–225, 86 Stat. 3 (codified as amended at 2 U.S.C. ss 431–56), to curb money's influence in politics has contributed to the difficulty of enacting new reforms. *See, e.g.,* Joseph Cantor, *Campaign Financing* (Cong. Res. Serv. Issue Brief, Feb. 1994); Hanna Rosin, *Teamwork: Killing Campaign Finance Reform in Congress,* New Republic, Mar. 10, 1997, at 11 (bipartisan effort to scuttle McCain-Feingold bill). The Federal Election Commission chronically underenforces the law. *See* Todd Lochner & Bruce E. Cain, Equity and Efficacy in the Enforcement of Campaign Finance Laws (1999) (unpublished manuscript).

24. I support this proposition with data in Peter H. Schuck, Citizens, Strangers, and In-Betweens: Essays on Immigration and Citizenship 354–58 (1998), and also in Chapter 7 of this book.

25. This concept is much the same as Isaiah Berlin's "negative liberty." *See* Isaiah Berlin, *Two Concepts of Liberty,* in Four Essays on Liberty 118 (1969).

26. In earlier work, I have compared the conflicting cultures of science, law, and politics. See Chapter 2 of this book.

27. For examples of both types of law, see *infra,* at Section III.E. I am not concerned here with procedural law, which has tended to become more contextual, borrowing heavily from principles of equity. *See* Stephen N. Subrin, *How Equity Conquered Common Law: The Federal Rules of Civil Procedure in Historical Perspective,* 135 U. of Penn. L. Rev. 909 (1987). Possible distinctions between different forms of norms and of markets would add little to an analysis of law and its limits, so I do not develop them here.

28. KOMESAR, *supra* note 18, at 50.

29. Even the notorious U.S. homicide rate has been declining and is now lower than that in many other countries where it is still rising. Indeed, South Africa's rate is now eight times that of the United States. *See* Daniel J. Watkin, *Mandela Offers Hope in Last Major Speech*, GLOBE AND MAIL (Toronto), Feb. 6, 1999, at A17.

30. LAWRENCE FRIEDMAN, A HISTORY OF AMERICAN LAW (1985).

31. For a discussion of the historical forces that impelled these heightened ambitions, *see generally* BRUCE A. ACKERMAN, WE THE PEOPLE: FOUNDATIONS (1991), and BRUCE A. ACKERMAN, WE THE PEOPLE: TRANSFORMATIONS (1998).

32. Marc Galanter, Planet of the Apes: Reflections on the Scale of Law and Its Users 8 (1999) (unpublished manuscript).

33. *See, e.g.*, Civil Aeronautics Board Sunset Act of 1984, Pub. L. No. 98–443, 98 Stat. 1703 (codified as amended in scattered sections of 49 U.S.C.) (eliminating CAB); Airline Deregulation Act of 1978, Pub. L. No. 95–504, 92 Stat. 1729, 1731 (codified as amended in scattered sections of 49 U.S.C.). For an excellent study of the causes and implications of deregulation in the transportation sector, see MARTHA DERTHICK & PAUL J. QUIRK, THE POLITICS OF DEREGULATION (1985).

34. Some piecemeal deregulation has occurred, and more comprehensive deregulation is finally progressing through Congress. Stephen Labaton, *Bill to Overhaul Financial System Passes the House*, N.Y. TIMES, July 2, 1999, at A1. This reform, however, has been stymied in Congress for more than a quarter-century. *See, e.g.*, Thomas H. Hammond & Jack H. Knott, *The Deregulatory Snowball: Explaining Deregulation in the Financial Services Industry*, 50 J. POL. 3 (1995).

35. The regulation of petroleum products, which was eliminated in the early 1980s, had been imposed on a temporary basis in 1973. Federal regulation of natural gas wellhead pricing effectively began after a Supreme Court decision in 1954, *see* Phillips Petroleum Co. v. Wisconsin, 347 U.S. 672 (1954), and was eliminated in 1989 by the enactment of the Natural Gas Wellhead Decontrol Act. Pipeline regulation, imposed by the Hepburn Act in 1906 and expanded significantly during the New Deal, persists.

36. See Telecommunications Act of 1996, Pub. L. No. 104–104, 110 Stat. 56 (codified in scattered sections of 47 U.S.C.). *But see* Robert W. Crandall, *The Telecom Act's Phone-y Deregulation*, WALL ST. J., Jan. 27, 1999, at A22 (ostensible deregulation is actually new and misguided regulation in disguise).

37. See Ocean Shipping Reform Act of 1998, Pub. L. No. 105–258, 112 Stat. 1902 (partial deregulation but retention of antitrust immunity).

38. For example, New York largely eliminated rate-setting for hospital charges in 1996. *See New York Hospitals, Payers Face Repeal Problem*, WASH. HEALTH WK., Dec. 9, 1996.

39. Examples include cable broadcasting, nursing homes, managed care, occupational licensure, and low-income banking. Additional regulation of banking is also likely. *Greenspan Says Giant Banks Will Face New Regulations*, N.Y. Times, Oct. 12, 1999, at C12. In October 1999, California reinstated accident victims' right to sue recalcitrant insurers for punitive damages. Pending legislation to enact various consumer bills of rights would impose regulation (in the case of patients) or restore some that had previously been repealed (in the case of airline passengers). Support is mounting in Congress to delay the scheduled deregulation of cable TV rates in light of rate increases. *Cable Rates Rising As Industry Nears End of Regulation*, N.Y. TIMES, Mar. 8, 1999, at A1.

40. For example, government-mandated pension funds were established by the Employment Retirement Income Security Act of 1974 (ERISA), Pub. L. No. 93–406, 88 Stat. 829 (codified as amended at 29 U.S.C. ss 1001–1461). The duties of employers to employees under federal law were expanded further by the Family and Medical Leave Act of 1993, Pub. L. No. 103–3, 107 Stat. 7 (codified as amended in scattered sections of 29 U.S.C.). Even conservative states are establishing statewide superagencies to control development and urban-suburban sprawl. *See, e.g.,* David Firestone, *Georgia Setting Up Tough Anti-Sprawl Agency,* N.Y. TIMES, Mar. 25, 1999, at A20.

40A. See, e.g., The Americans with Disabilities Act of 1990, Pub. L. 101–336, 104 stat. 327.

41. The proliferation of this kind of regulation—in which higher levels prescribe the decisions and processes of lower ones—prompted Congress to enact a statute limiting unfunded federal mandates imposed on state and local governments. *See* Unfunded Mandates Reform Act of 1995, Pub. L. No. 104–4, 109 Stat. 48 (codified in scattered sections of 2 U.S.C.).

42. Legislatures have traditionally regulated administrative procedure and substance, but with the notable exception of the Administrative Procedures Act of 1946 and state law counterparts, they have regulated it on a programmatic, agency-by-agency basis. Recently, however, comprehensive legislative regulation of agency procedure ("metaregulation," as it were) has been common. *See, e.g.,* Regulatory Flexibility Act of 1980, Pub. L. No. 96–354, 94 Stat. 1164 (codified at 5 U.S.C. ss 601–612) (agencies must consider alternatives to rulemaking and determine rulemaking's impacts on small business); National Environmental Policy Act of 1969, Pub. L. No. 91–190, 83 Stat. 852 (codified as amended at 42 U.S.C. ss 4321–47) (agencies must assess environmental impact of proposed rules). Moreover, the executive branch has required agencies to submit cost-benefit analyses of proposed regulations to the Office of Management and Budget. *See, e.g.,* Exec. Order No. 12,291, 3 C.F.R. 127 (1982), reprinted in 5 U.S.C. s 601, at 557–61 (1994) (Reagan-Bush requirements); Exec. Order No. 12, 866, 3 C.F.R. 641 (1993), reprinted in 5 U.S.C. s 601, at 558–61 (1994) (Clinton requirements). Indeed, the proposed Federalism Accountability Act, which enjoys considerable support in Congress, would in effect make it harder for Congress itself to enact laws that limit state regulatory authority. *See* Stephen Labaton, *Anti-Federalism Measures Have Bipartisan Support,* N.Y. TIMES, Sept. 6, 1999, at A8 (New Eng. ed.).

43. *See, e.g.,* C. Eugene Steuerle & Jon M. Bakija, *Retooling Social Security for the 21st Century,* SOC. SECURITY BULL., Jan. 1, 1997, at 37 (continued increases in real value of Social Security benefits since program's inception and rapid growth since 1970).

44. Despite the small-government rhetoric of the Reagan and Bush administrations, many social programs were expanded markedly during the 1980s and early 1990s. *See, e.g.,* Mickey Leland Childhood Relief Hunger Act, Pub. L. No. 103–66 (1993) (codified at 7 U.S.C. s 2011) (expanding Food Stamp program eligibility and benefit levels); Housing and Community Development Act of 1987, Pub. L. No. 100–242, s 145, 104 Stat. 1815, 1852 (1988) (codified as amended at 42 U.S.C. s 1437f (r)) (expanding portability of Section 8 housing vouchers); Low-Income Home Energy Assistance Act, Pub. L. No. 97–35, 95 Stat. 893–902 (1981) (codified as amended at 42 U.S.C. ss 8621–8629); PIERSON, *supra* note 7, at 125–126 (expansion of Earned Income Tax Credit during Reagan administration); *Development in Policy: Welfare Reform,* 16 YALE L. & POL'Y REV. 221, 245 (1995) (expansion of childcare and family support programs in 1980s); Collette Fraley, *States Guard Their Borders As Medicare Talks Begin,* 53 CONG. Q. WKLY. REP. 1637,

1639 (1995) (increase in Medicaid spending from $20 billion in mid–1980s to $75 billion in 1995). Even the controversial 1996 welfare reform provided incentives for states to fund job training and childcare programs. *See, e.g.,* 42 U.S.C. s 604 (c); *see also Welfare Check,* NEW REPUBLIC, Sept. 28, 1998, at 9 (1998) (General Accounting Office [GAO] found higher welfare expenditure in several major states); Gene Koretz, *States Ante Up for Workfare,* BUS. WK., July 6, 1998, at 20 (similar findings of National Governor's Association study).

45. *See, e.g.,* Augustus F. Hawkins Human Services Reauthorization Act of 1990, Pub. L. No. 101–501, 104 Stat. 1222 (codified as amended in scattered sections of 42 U.S.C.) (expanding Head Start program). In addition, many government programs in this category, such as educational loans, are effectuated through tax expenditures and off-budget regulations as well as through direct fiscal subsidies.

46. This demand, moreover, is even greater outside the United States. *See, e.g.,* Fareed Zakaria, *Passing the Buck,* N.Y. TIMES REV. BOOKS, Apr. 25, 1999, at 16 (steady growth in regulation and governmental share of gross domestic product [GDP] in many countries despite, and in some cases because of, neoliberal policies).

47. *See, e.g.,* JAMES MORONE, THE DEMOCRATIC WISH: POPULAR PARTICIPATION AND THE LIMITS OF AMERICAN GOVERNMENT (1994).

48. The prospect of large budget surpluses in the future has not eliminated these constraints, as politicians in both parties have agreed to commit a large portion of them (though differing on the precise sums) to financing future Social Security benefits. *See* Richard W. Stevenson, *Congress Passes G.O.P.'s Budget Voting Largely Along Party Lines,* N.Y. TIMES, Mar. 26, 1999, at A1 (parties agree on setting aside bulk of surpluses for Social Security)

49. These impositions on the private sector not only evidence a strong demand for new law but often confound public choice theory as well. *See, e.g.,* Chapters 4 and 7 of this book. *See generally* DANIEL A. FARBER & PHILLIP P. FRICKEY, LAW AND PUBLIC CHOICE: A CRITICAL INTRODUCTION (1991); JERRY L. MASHAW, GREED, CHAOS, AND GOVERNANCE: USING PUBLIC CHOICE TO IMPROVE PUBLIC LAW (1997). Commentators have also noted the inverse phenomenon: *deregulation* where public choice theory would least expect it. *See, e.g.,* DERTHICK & QUICK, *supra* note 33.

50. *See, e.g.,* STEPHEN G. BREYER, BREAKING THE VICIOUS CIRCLE: TOWARD EFFECTIVE RISK REGULATION 37–39 (1993) (media coverage distorts public perceptions of risk).

51. The late Aaron Wildavsky called this phenomenon "policy as its own cause." *See* AARON WILDAVSKY, SPEAKING TRUTH TO POWER: THE ART AND CRAFT OF POLICY ANALYSIS 62–85 (1979). For some examples from property law and environmental regulation, see Carol M. Rose, *The Several Futures of Property: Of Cyberspace and Folk Tales, Emission Trades, and Ecosystems,* 83 MINN. L. REV. 129 (1998).

52. For discussions of laws with perverse results, *see* Jonathan R. Macey, *Derivative Instruments: Lessons for the Regulatory State,* 21 J. CORP. L. 69, 82 (1995) (derivatives regulation); Rena I. Steinzor, *The Legislation of Unintended Consequences,* 9 DUKE ENVIR. L. & POL'Y F. 95 (1998) (Superfund program); Cass R. Sunstein, *Political Equality and Unintended Consequences,* 94 COLUM. L. REV. 1390 (1994) (campaign finance); *see generally* ALBERT O. HIRSCHMAN, THE RHETORIC OF REACTION: PERVERSITY, FUTILITY, JEOPARDY 11–12 (1991) ("perversity" thesis asserting that "attempts to push society in a certain direction will result in its moving . . . in the opposite direction").

53. *See, e.g.,* ABRAHAM H. MASLOW, MOTIVATION AND PERSONALITY (1954).

54. From this obvious but far-reaching fact, of course, all economic theory ultimately derives. Not all goods are scarce, at least in the same sense. Some religious ethicists claim that sanctity—God's abundant grace and forgiveness—"may be a rare good but not a scarce one." Peter Steinfels, *Belief,* N.Y. TIMES, Jan. 30, 1999, at B7 (reviewing work of Jon P. Gunnemann).

55. *See, e.g.,* W. MICHAEL COX & RICHARD ALM, MYTHS OF RICH & POOR 14–17 (1999) (steadily growing share of poor own homes, automobiles, and other nonnecessities, and spend steadily declining share of income on food, clothing, and shelter). This is true despite (according to some measures) increasing income inequality. *See* FRANK LEVY, NEW DOLLARS AND DREAMS: AMERICAN INCOMES AND ECONOMIC CHANGE 60–68 (1998).

56. *See* University of Michigan Panel Survey on Income Dynamics, discussed in COX & ALM, *supra* note 55, at 72–78 (statistical evidence of significant social mobility since 1970s).

57. *See, e.g.,* THE NEW AMERICANS: ECONOMIC, DEMOGRAPHIC, AND FISCAL EFFECTS OF IMMIGRATION (J. Smith & B. Edmonston eds., 1997).

58. The classic discussion is FREDERICK J. TURNER, THE FRONTIER IN AMERICAN HISTORY (1920). Even today, despite public concerns about overpopulation and "suburban sprawl," the United States, even in large cities, remains thinly settled compared to other highly industrialized countries; *see Letter from Peter H. Schuck to Dan Stein,* 1 AMERICAN PROSPECT 20–22 (1991) (data), and the amount of open space is actually increasing. *See* Gregg Easterbrook, *Suburban Myth,* NEW REPUBLIC, Mar. 15, 1999, at 18 (data).

59. For prominent criticisms of this individualist strand in U.S. life, *see, e.g.,* ROBERT BELLAH ET AL., HABITS OF THE HEART (1985), and MICHAEL J. SANDEL, DEMOCRACY'S DISCONTENT (1996).

60. Even those scholars who are critical of a positivist, rule-centered understanding of law, however, recognize that rules should guide legal interpretation when they are settled and unambiguous. *See, e.g.,* RONALD M. DWORKIN, TAKING RIGHTS SERIOUSLY 17–22 (1977). Dworkin argues, however, that standards and principles underlying statutory and constitutional provisions are sources for judicial decisionmaking and are as legitimate as rules. *Id.; see also* Ronald M. Dworkin, *The Model of Rules,* 35 U. CHI. L. REV. 14 (1967).

61. Most public law rules are aimed not at ordinary individuals but at the public agencies that must implement these rules and the private corporate bureaucracies that these agencies must regulate. See Galanter, *supra* note 32.

62. Galanter, *supra* note 32, at 6.

63. *See* discussion *infra,* at Section III.E.

64. *See* Chapter 1 of this book.

65. Conor Cruise O'Brien, *Thomas Jefferson: Radical and Racist,* ATLANTIC MONTHLY, Oct. 1996.

66. See Gerald F. Seib, *Less Is More: Libertarian Impulses Show Growing Appeal Among the Disaffected,* WALL ST. J., Jan. 20, 1995, at A1.

67. As usual, Justice Oliver Wendell Holmes Jr. put the point well: "A word is not a crystal, unchanged and transparent, it is the skin of a living thought and may vary in color and content according to the circumstances and the time in which it was used." Towne v. Eisner, 245 U.S. 418, 425 (1918).

68. *See generally* PETER H. SCHUCK, SUING GOVERNMENT: CITIZEN REMEDIES FOR OFFICIAL WRONGS 4–13, 161–63 (1983). Similar problems afflict large private bureaucracies, though to a somewhat lesser extent.

69. I am not concerned here with how these attributes are distributed in a population (a statistical issue) or with whether they are immanent or imputed (an epistemological issue).

70. In law, defendants are guilty or not guilty, liable or not liable. Gain is taxable or not. Documents are privileged or not. Official immunities are absolute or qualified. Companies have limited liability or they do not. The list of these dualities could be extended indefinitely.

71. For a rigorous articulation of the virtues of bright-line rules, *see* RICHARD A. EPSTEIN, SIMPLE RULES FOR A COMPLEX WORLD (1995). *See also* Antonin Scalia, *The Rule of Law as a Law of Rules,* 56 U. CHI. L. REV. 1175 (1989).

72. The historical evolution of the two-category examples in the text demonstrate the point and further suggest the courts' reluctance to promote flexibility by using more than three categories. States permit juries to find criminal defendants innocent, guilty, or guilty by reason of insanity. In a civil tort case, a negligent plaintiff is no longer barred from suing a defendant; comparative fault rules give the jury a third option. To limited and full liability of partnerships and corporations, respectively, states sometimes permit a third, hybrid category.

In contrast, administrative agencies sometimes proliferate regulatory categories in order to fine-tune their controls, though not always enough to satisfy critics.

73. For a discussion of this development, *see* Duncan Kennedy, *Form and Substance in Private Law Adjudication,* 89 HARV. L. REV. 1685 (1976).

74. For my analysis of this and related developments, *see* Chapter 5 of this book.

75. For example, a 1990 GAO study found that more than 50 percent of eligible food stamp recipients do not take advantage of the program. U.S. GENERAL ACCOUNTING OFFICE, FOOD STAMP PROGRAM: A DEMOGRAPHIC ANALYSIS OF PARTICIPATION & NONPARTICIPATION (1990). The rigors of the 1996 welfare reforms may have magnified this pattern. *See* Jason DeParle, *Leftover Money for Welfare Baffles, or Inspires, States,* N.Y. TIMES, Aug. 29, 1999, at 20.

76. *See, e.g.,* William N. Eskridge, *Reneging on History? Playing the Court/Congress/President Civil Rights Game,* 79 CAL. L. REV. 613, 613–15 (1991) (recent Supreme Court decisions limit ability to recover under civil rights laws); *see also* SCHUCK, *supra* note 68. A closely related problem is people's limited "legal consciousness" about their legal rights. *See* Austin Sarat, *Studying American Legal Culture: An Assessment of Survey Evidence,* 11 L. & SOC. REV. 427, 450–51 (1977) (knowledge of rights among poor "quite low"); *cf.* SALLY ENGLE MERRY, GETTING JUSTICE AND GETTING EVEN: LEGAL CONSCIOUSNESS AMONG WORKING-CLASS AMERICANS (1990) (even middle-class litigants often believe courts do not take their claims seriously).

77. *See, e.g.,* ORLANDO PATTERSON, THE ORDEAL OF INTEGRATION: PROGRESS AND RESENTMENT IN AMERICA'S "RACIAL" CRISIS 115 (1997) ("top-down" strategy benefiting middle class). William G. Bowen and Derek Bok's recent study shows that 86 percent of disadvantaged minorities matriculating at twenty-eight selective colleges were middle- or upper-class. WILLIAM G. BOWEN & DEREK BOK, THE SHAPE OF THE RIVER: THE LONG TERM CONSEQUENCES OF CONSIDERING RACE IN COLLEGE AND UNIVERSITY ADMISSIONS 49 (1998). However, Bowen and Bok further argue that a class-based affirmative action program would be inadequate due to test score disparities between low-income whites and low-

income African Americans. *Id.*, at 46–47. *See also* RICHARD D. KAHLENBERG, THE REMEDY: CLASS, RACE, AND AFFIRMATIVE ACTION (1996) (favoring class-based benefits); Steven A. Holmes, *TV Station Deal Draws Opposition*, N.Y. TIMES, Apr. 11, 1999, at 26 (Federal Communication Commission [FCC] affirmative action in award of broadcasting licenses allegedly induces sham arrangements with black front groups to enable wealthy whites to evade other FCC restrictions); Holmes, *What Is a Minority-Owned Business?*, N.Y. TIMES, Oct. 11, 1999, at C6 (affirmative action program limits minorities' access to capital).

78. See Sarat, *supra* note 76; MERRY, *supra* note 76; Marc Galanter, *Why the "Haves" Come out Ahead: Speculations on the Limits of Legal Change*, 9 L. & SOC. REV. 95 (1974) (one-time, nonwealthy parties disfavored).

79. Since 1980, despite the increased regulation discussed *supra*, text accompanying notes 39–45, government spending has declined as a percentage of GDP at both the state and federal levels. 1998 STATISTICAL ABSTRACT, *supra* note 8, at 307, 341. During that period, federal employment has remained constant in real terms. *Id.*, at 331.

80. *See, e.g.*, Stephen Labaton, *U.S. Cracking Down on Internet Information Brokers*, N.Y. TIMES, Apr. 23, 1999, at A14 (Federal Trade Commission [FTC] suing investigators who offer to sell confidential data).

81. *See generally* George Cooper, *The Taming of the Shrewd: Identifying and Controlling Income Tax Avoidance*, 85 COLUM. L. REV. 657 (1985); *see also* MICHAEL GRAETZ, THE DECLINE (AND FALL?) OF THE INCOME TAX 41–51 (1997) (use and abuse of tax shelters); Holcomb B. Noble, *Of Life, Death, and the Rules of Liver Transplants*, N.Y. TIMES, Apr. 6, 1999, at F6 (federal and state limits on eligibility of hepatitis B patients for transplants lag behind advances in medical treatment); SCHUCK, *supra* note 24, at 46 (more illegal aliens now live here than before 1986 law).

82. I say "largely" because although some reforms can and probably should be made, they are likely to be at the institutional margins.

83. Much recent work takes "public choice" and "rational actor" theories of governmental processes, which model politics as the interaction of utility-maximizing behaviors by voters, interest groups, candidates, and officials, as the leading source of testable hypotheses. For foundational works in the "rational choice" theory *see* KENNETH J. ARROW, SOCIAL CHOICE AND INDIVIDUAL VALUES (2d ed. 1963) and ANTHONY DOWNS, AN ECONOMIC THEORY OF DEMOCRACY (1957); *cf.* DONALD GREEN & IAN SHAPIRO, PATHOLOGIES OF RATIONAL CHOICE THEORY (1992) (criticizing methodology of rational choice theorists). Other recent students of the legislative process employ "positive political theory," which derives its methodology from rational choice in certain respects but also stresses the strategic relationship between legislatures and other lawmaking institutions. *See, e.g.*, William N. Eskridge & John Ferejohn, *The Article I, Section 7 Game*, 80 GEO. L.J. 523 (1992); McNollgast, *Administrative Procedures as Instruments of Political Control*, 3 J.L. ECON. & ORG. 241 (1987).

84. Indeed, the nondelegation doctrine, long dormant in the federal courts, has found some recent support in the U.S. Supreme Court, *see, e.g.*, Clinton v. City of New York, 524 U.S. 417 (1998); Loving v. U.S., 517 U.S. 748 (1996), and among some commentators. *See* DAVID SCHOENBROD, POWER WITHOUT RESPONSIBILITY: HOW CONGRESS ABUSES THE PEOPLE THROUGH DELEGATION (1993). I join some others in viewing this concern about delegation as vastly exaggerated. *See* Chapter 8 of this book (criticizing Schoenbrod's argument).

85. Term limits may further shorten the time horizon as lawmakers scramble to move on to higher offices where their terms can begin anew. The arguments for and against

term limits are developed in GEORGE F. WILL, RESTORATION: CONGRESS, TERM LIMITS, AND THE RECOVERY OF DELIBERATIVE DEMOCRACY (1992), and MORRIS P. FIORINA, DIVIDED GOVERNMENT 53–58 (1996), respectively.

86. *See generally* PRINCIPALS AND AGENTS: THE STRUCTURE OF BUSINESS (John W. Pratt & Richard Zeckhauser eds., 1985).

87. In fact, scholars have observed that rational citizens have little incentive to *vote*, let alone to educate themselves extensively about the political process. See DOWNS, *supra* note 83, at chap. 13. Recent studies on voter knowledge confirm this theoretical suspicion, showing that most voters lack even the most basic political information. *See, e.g.*, MICHAEL X. DELLI CARPINI & SCOTT KEETER, WHAT AMERICANS KNOW ABOUT POLITICS AND WHY IT MATTERS (1996); *see also* PHILIP E. CONVERSE, THE NATURE OF BELIEF SYSTEMS IN MASS PUBLICS, IN IDEOLOGY AND DISCONTENT 206 (David E. Apter ed., 1964).

88. *See, e.g.*, Peter H. Schuck, *The Graying of Civil Rights Law: The Age Discrimination Act of 1975*, 89 YALE L.J. 27 (1979). *See generally* MAYHEW, *supra* note 19. A recent example of a well-intended, bipartisan-supported law imposing higher-than-expected costs and having perverse consequences is the Americans with Disabilities Act (AWDA) of 1990, which apparently caused a sharp decline in employment for the disabled—a clear break from the pre-AWDA employment trends. See DARON ACEMOGLU & JOSHUA ANGRIST, CONSEQUENCES OF EMPLOYMENT PROTECTION? THE CASE OF THE AMERICANS WITH DISABILITIES ACT (National Bureau of Economic Research Working Paper No. 6670).

89. U.S. GENERAL ACCOUNTING OFFICE, SOME AGENCIES' CLAIMS REGARDING LACK OF RULEMAKING DISCRETION HAVE MERIT (GAO/GGD–99–20, Jan. 1999).

90. *See, e.g.*, SCHOENBROD, *supra* note 84. *Cf.* Chapter 8 of this book.

91. Public choice theorists explain the distribution of under- and overdelegation in different policy areas according to how the benefits and costs to politicians and their constituents are distributed. See FARBER & FRICKEY, *supra* note 49, at 52–58 (using MAYHEW, *supra* note 19, and HAYES, *supra* note 19, to develop typology of legislative supply and demand).

92. Arguments that agencies are vulnerable to "capture" by the industries they regulate (and, in some instances, by public interest groups) are common in the regulatory literature. *See, e.g.*, ROGER NOLL, REFORMING REGULATION 40–42 (1971) ("capture" phenomenon). Criticisms of agencies have also stressed their lack of political accountability. *See, e.g.*, Hugh Heclo, *Issue Networks and the Executive Establishment, in* THE NEW AMERICAN POLITICAL SYSTEM 87 (American Enterprise Institute ed., 1978). For other general assessments and criticisms of the administrative state in the United States, *see* MARTHA DERTHICK, AGENCY UNDER STRESS: THE SOCIAL SECURITY ADMINISTRATION IN AMERICAN GOVERNMENT (1990); JAMES Q. WILSON, BUREAUCRACY: WHAT GOVERNMENT AGENCIES DO AND WHY THEY DO IT (1989); THE POLITICS OF REGULATION (James Q. Wilson ed., 1980).

93. *See, e.g.*, Cynthia R. Farina, *The Consent of the Governed: Against Simple Rules for a Complex World*, 72 CHI.-KENT L. REV. 987, 987 (1997) ("In no period . . . has the energy and intensity devoted to the reconciliation [of regulatory government with constitutional ideals] effort been greater than at present.")

94. *See, e.g.*, MARTHA DERTHICK, POLICYMAKING FOR SOCIAL SECURITY 17–37 (1979) (Social Security Administration); CHARLES C. MOSKOS, ALL THAT WE CAN BE: BLACK LEADERSHIP AND INTEGRATION THE ARMY WAY (1996) (military); JAMES Q. WILSON, BUREAUCRACY: WHAT GOVERNMENT AGENTS DO AND WHY THEY DO IT 367 (1989) (discussing several successful agencies). For a very recent example, *see* Michael M.

Weinstein, *Economic Scene: New York Blazes a Trail on How to Handle Local Phone Access,* N.Y. TIMES, Mar. 25, 1999, at C2 (Public Service Commission forged politically and technically complex compromise).

95. *See generally* RICHARD A. POSNER, ECONOMIC ANALYSIS OF LAW 523 (4th ed. 1992); DANIEL F. SPULBER, REGULATION AND MARKETS 21–69 (1989). This negative assessment has befallen even the more popular agencies that regulate markets and market activity. *See, e.g.,* George J. Stigler, *Public Regulation of the Securities Market,* 37 J. BUS. 117 (1964) (failure of Securities and Exchange Commission [SEC] disclosure requirements); *see also* Jonathan R. Macey, *Administrative Agency Obsolescence and Interest Group Formation: A Case Study of the SEC at Sixty,* 15 CARDOZO L. REV. 909 (1994) (broader critique).

96. For example, *compare* Burt R. Neuborne, *The Myth of Parity,* 90 HARV. L. REV. 1105 (1977) (theoretical justifications for lack of parity between state and federal courts) *with* Paul M. Bator, *The State Courts and Federal Constitutional Litigation,* 22 WM. & MARY L. REV. 605, 633 (1981) (rebutting Neuborne's arguments); *see also* Michael E. Solimine & James L. Walker, *Constitutional Litigation in Federal and State Courts: An Empirical Analysis of Judicial Parity,* 10 HAST. CONST. L. Q. 213 (1983) (empirical study finding no disparity between state and federal courts); Susan N. Hermann, Comment, *Why Parity Matters,* 71 B. U. L. REV. 651, 664 n.29 (1991) (criticizing Solimine & Walker's methodology). After nearly a decade of debate about state courts, "the debate over parity is a stalemate because parity is an empirical question—whether one court system is as good as another—for which there can never be any meaningful empirical measure." *See* Erwin Chemerinsky, *Parity Reconsidered,* 36 U.C.L.A. L. REV. 233, 236 (1988).

More generally, litigants' behavior makes such comparisons extremely difficult even under ideal circumstances. *See* George L. Priest, *Selective Characteristics of Litigation,* 9 J. LEG. STUD. 399 (1980) (percentage of plaintiffs winning in any jurisdiction should gravitate toward 50 percent as litigants impound information on legal rules, making it hard to learn from interjurisdictional comparisons of winners and losers).

97. *See, e.g.,* JERRY L. MASHAW AND DAVID L. HARFST, THE STRUGGLE FOR AUTO SAFETY (1990); R. SHEP MELNICK, BETWEEN THE LINES: INTERPRETING WELFARE RIGHTS (1994); R. Shep Melnick, *Administrative Law and Bureaucratic Reality,* 44 ADMIN. L. REV. 245 (1992); Martin Shapiro, *APA: Past, Present, and Future,* 72 VA. L. REV. 447 (1986). My own empirical study of this question produced mixed results. See Chapter 9 of this book. *See also* William S. Jordan, III, Ossification Revisited: Does Arbitrary and Capricious Review Significantly Interfere with Agency Ability to Achieve Regulatory Goals Through Informal Rulemaking? (1999) (unpublished manuscript) ("hard look" review does not interfere). Some commentators, though conceding that much review is ineffective, nevertheless urge courts to do more of it. *See, e.g.,* Cass R. Sunstein, *Factions, Self-Interest, and the APA: Four Lessons Learned Since 1946,* 76 VA. L. REV. 271, 291–95 (1986) (despite problems with judicial review, urges "moderately aggressive judicial role" in agency oversight); *see also* Alan B. Morrison, *The Administrative Procedure Act: A Living and Responsive Law,* 72 VA. L. REV. 253, 260–63 (1986).

98. The Supreme Court's decision in Chevron, Inc. v. Natural Resources Defense Council, 467 U.S. 837 (1984), was meant to reinforce this deference. *See* Chapter 9 of this book.

99. *See* Linda Greenhouse, *47% in Poll View Legal System as Unfair to Poor and Minorities,* N.Y. TIMES, Feb. 24, 1999, at A12 (public confidence in judicial system has increased since 1978 while declining for most other institutions; Supreme Court at top of list, with 50 percent expressing strong confidence in it).

100. For examples of such praise by scholars, see Abram Chayes, *The Role of the Judge in Public Law Litigation*, 89 Harv. L. Rev. 1281 (1976); Owen M. Fiss, *The Forms of Justice*, 93 Harv. L. Rev. 1 (1979). I discuss the problem of implementation in Suing Government, *supra* note 68, chaps. 6–8. *See also* Michael J. Klarman, *What's So Great About Constitutionalism?*, 93 Nw. U. L. Rev. 145 (1998) (on causation of social changes).

101. State courts, although understudied, are also important policymaking institutions. Indeed, some attempts by state courts to solve complex social problems offer valuable insights into the structural limitations of "public law litigation." *See, e.g.*, Jesse Dukminier & James E. Krier, Property 1105–31 (3d ed. 1993) (decade-long attempts by New Jersey courts to solve exclusionary zoning problem in Mount Laurel); Caroline M. Hoxby, All State Finance Equalizations Are Not Created Equal (National Bureau of Economic Research Working Paper No. 6792, 1999) (perverse effects of equalization programs).

102. See Baker v. Carr, 369 U.S. 186 (1962) and Reynolds v. Sims, 377 U.S. 533 (1964). Some commentators applaud the Court's implementation of these decisions. *See, e.g.*, Martin Shapiro, *Gerrymandering, Unfairness, and the Supreme Court*, 33 U.C.L.A. L. Rev. 227, 252 (1985) ("great victory"); Schuck, Chapter 10 of this book (same).

103. *See, e.g.*, Robert A. Kagan, *Adversarial Legalism and American Government, in* The New Politics of Public Policy 88 (Mark K. Landy & Martin A. Levin eds., 1995) (case study of litigation's negative impact on efficiency and policy coherence); R. Shep Melnick, Regulation and the Courts: The Case of the Clean Air Act (1983) (criticizing role of judicial review in environmental policymaking); *see generally* Jeremy Rabkin, Judicial Compulsions: How Public Law Distorts Public Policy (1989); Schuck, *supra* note 68, at chap. 6 (reviewing implementation literature); Klarman, *supra* note 100 (same). A recent study of problems in implementing structural injunctions in New York City, see Ross Sandler & David Schoenbrod, Government by Decree (forthcoming 2000).

104. 347 U.S. 483 (1954).

105. "[By] the time of the Court's intervention, half the nation no long supported racial segregation." Klarman, *supra* note 100, at 161. *See also* Gerald N. Rosenberg, The Hollow Hope: Can Courts Bring About Social Change? (1991), at 39–71.

106. Klarman, *supra* note 100, at 177; Rosenberg, *supra* note 105, at 49.

107. David J. Armor, Forced Justice: School Desegregation and the Law 208–09 (1995).

108. The degree to which busing contributed to the problem of white flight is hotly debated in the social science literature. Compare *id.*, at 208–09 (busing a major factor) *and* James Coleman et al., Trends in School Desegregation, 1968–1973 (Urban Inst., 1975) (same) *with* Gary Orfield & Susan E. Eaton, Dismantling Desegregation: The Quiet Reversal of *Brown v. Board of Education* (1990) ("white flight" attributed to other factors). Furthermore, many minority group members now oppose busing, which they view as ineffective. *See* Derrick Bell, Race, Racism, and American Law 581 (3d ed. 1992) (citing studies).

109. For a penetrating analysis of other examples, *see* Donald L. Horowitz, The Courts and Social Policy (1977) and Melnick, *supra* note 103.

110. 410 U.S. 113 (1973).

111. *See, e.g.*, Rosenberg, *supra* note 105, at 175–201; *see also* Ruth Bader Ginsburg, *Speaking in a Judicial Voice*, 97 N.Y.U. L. Rev. 1185, 1205 (1992) (before *Roe*, most state leg-

islatures were expanding abortion rights, but in *Roe*'s wake "a well-organized and vocal right-to-life movement rallied and succeeded, for considerable time, in turning the legislative tide in the opposite direction"); Peter Beinart, *Private Matters,* NEW REPUBLIC, Feb. 15, 1999, at 21 (Roe v. Wade a major impetus for political organization of religious conservatives).

112. For a trenchant analysis of this pattern in the law and practice of criminal procedure, *see* William J. Stuntz, *The Uneasy Relationship Between Criminal Procedure and Criminal Justice,* 107 YALE L.J. 1 (1997); *see also* AKHIL REED AMAR, THE CONSTITUTION AND CRIMINAL PROCEDURE chap. 1 (1997) (criticizing Fourth Amendment doctrine); Klarman, *supra* note 100, at 162.

113. The necessity for courts to choose among competing legal rules is generally understood by scholars and practicing lawyers. Bitter controversy arises, however, over which considerations should guide their choices.

114. *See* JULES L. COLEMAN, RISKS AND WRONGS (1992).

115. Workers compensation for industrial accidents was, and remains, the great exception.

116. An example of such critiques is George L. Priest, *The Current Insurance Crisis in Modern Tort Law,* 96 YALE L.J. 1521 (1987).

117. *See* Peter H. Schuck, *The New Judicial Ideology of Tort Law, in* NEW DIRECTIONS IN LIABILITY LAW, at 16(W. Olson ed., 1988).

118. *See, e.g.,* PHILIP K. HOWARD, THE DEATH OF COMMON SENSE: HOW LAW IS SUFFOCATING AMERICA (1994).

119. With law, as with other types of authority, some zone of indifference exists within which people do not question its authority; they may simply take no notice of it, experiencing it as routine, a part of the background noise of social life. *See* CHESTER A. BARNARD, THE FUNCTION OF THE EXECUTIVE (1938) (on zones of indifference in the industrial bureaucratic setting).

120. Civil disobedience on the part of civil rights and abortion protesters on both sides exemplify this moral revulsion. My late colleague Arthur Leff noted another, more existential kind of crisis—that people may doubt law's legitimacy when they realize, as in a secular legal culture they eventually must, that its ethical grounding is not revelation or nature but human choice. "To put it as bluntly as possible," Leff asks, " if we go to find what law ought to govern us, and if what we find is not an authoritative Holy Writ but just ourselves, just people, making that law, how can we be governed by what we have found?" He answers with vintage Leff: "Much of the time one can act as if there is, for constitutional determinations, a God, though He may occasionally mumble." Arthur A. Leff, *Unspeakable Ethics, Unnatural Law,* 1979 DUKE L.J. 1229.

121. On litigants' perceptions of procedural fairness, *see, e.g.,* E. ALLEN LIND & THOMAS R. TYLER, THE SOCIAL PSYCHOLOGY OF PROCEDURAL JUSTICE (1988); JOHN THIBAUT & LAUREN WALKER, PROCEDURAL JUSTICE: A PSYCHOLOGICAL ANALYSIS (1975); Robert P. Roper & Albert P. Melone, *Does Procedural Due Process Make a Difference? A Study of Second Trials,* 65 JUDICATURE 136 (1981); *cf.* Jerry L. Mashaw, *The Supreme Court's Due Process Calculus for Administrative Adjudication in Mathews v. Eldridge: Three Factors in Search of a Theory of Value,* 44 U. CHI. L. REV. 28 (1976) (procedural fairness affects individual dignity).

122. *See* GUIDO CALABRESI & PHILIP BOBBITT, TRAGIC CHOICES 78–79 (1978). *See also* discussion *infra,* at Section II.A.

123. For a current example to the north, *see* Anthony DePalma, *Western Canada Is Up in Arms over Gun Control*, N.Y. TIMES, Mar. 28, 1999, at 3 (civil disobedience movement extraordinary for law-abiding Canada).

124. Government's abhorrence of a legal vacuum is a common theme in analyses of the policymaking process. *See, e.g.*, Hammond & Knott, *supra* note 34, at 3–5 (reviewing literature). Observers of Congress note that members have incentives to seek opportunities to claim credit in ways that often generate more law. *See* MAYHEW, *supra* note 19; *see also* HAYES, *supra* note 19 (demand for legislation particularly strong where benefits concentrated). *Compare* Richard A. Epstein, *The Independence of Judges: The Uses and Limitations of Public Choice Theory*, 1990 B.Y.U. L. REV. 827, 827 (public choice theory relatively unsuccessful in explaining judicial behavior) *with* JEFFREY A. SEGAL & HAROLD J. SPAETH, THE SUPREME COURT AND THE ATTITUDINAL MODEL 65 (1993) (judges motivated by desire to impose policy preferences) and McNollgast, *Politics and the Courts: A Positive Political Theory of Judicial Doctrine and the Role of Law*, 68 S. CAL. L. REV. 1636, 1646 (1995). Though the theoretical arguments are inconclusive, anecdotal evidence suggests that courts, like legislatures, tend to expand their authority. *See, e.g.*, Marbury v. Madison, 5 U.S. (1 Cranch) 137 (1803) (Court finds judicial review power); MELNICK, BETWEEN THE LINES, *supra* note 98 (courts use statutory construction to expand rights and remedies); CASS R. SUNSTEIN, AFTER THE RIGHTS REVOLUTION (1990) (courts expanded individual rights in 1960s and 1970s).

125. For instance, certain religious and cultural conservatives suggest that the "undemocratic" character of such recent Supreme Court decisions as *Roe v. Wade* call the federal government's legitimacy into question. *See, e.g.*, Russell Hittinger, *A Crisis of Legitimacy*, FIRST THINGS, Nov. 1996, at 25.

126. These informational asymmetries resemble those presented in certain market situations. *See, e.g.*, George A. Akerlof, *The Market for "Lemons": Quality Uncertainty and the Market Mechanism*, 84 Q. J. ECON. 488 (1970).

127. The current attacks on the Supreme Court of Israel are an example. *See* Deborah Sontag, *Plans for Rival Rallies on Religion Issue Stir Fears in Israel*, N.Y. TIMES, Feb. 12, 1999, at A3 (leading politicians and religious leaders describe Chief Justice Aharon Barak as an "enemy of Judaism").

128. "Norms" here thus excludes legal norms, which are formal and authoritative and are discussed as "law."

129. I do not include politics as a distinct rival because law, norms, and markets ultimately mediate the social influence of politics. (In Chapter 2 of this book, however, I analyze politics as a distinct system, comparing it to law and to science.) I also exclude as rivals other important ordering systems such as education because they are epiphenomena, creatures of law, norms, or markets. *See* Donald R. Matthews & James W. Protho, *Southern Racial Attitudes: Conflict, Awareness, and Political Change*, 344 ANNALS 108, 114–15 (1968). Group self-regulation is another epiphenomenal ordering system. *See* Diana B. Henriques, *When Your Rival Is Also the Referee*, N.Y. TIMES, Mar. 7, 1999, at sec. 3, p. 1 (competition to U.S. stock exchanges from unregulated electronic communications networks and foreign stock exchanges); Andrew Pollack, *For Coders, a Code of Conduct*, N.Y. TIMES, May 3, 1999, at C1 (challenges to self-regulation by computer programmers).

130. Even violent authoritarian regimes ultimately depend on patterns of informal deference to and acquiescence in the use of force. *See, e.g.*, DANIEL J. GOLDHAGEN,

HITLER'S WILLING EXECUTIONERS: ORDINARY GERMANS AND THE HOLOCAUST (1996); GRESHAM M. SYKES, THE SOCIOLOGY OF CAPTIVES (1958).

131. See discussion *infra* at text accompanying notes 180–184.

132. Norm theorists differ somewhat as to whether norms originate in internal concerns like guilt arising from a wish to conform or in external concerns like the wish for esteem. *Compare* Richard H. McAdams, *The Origin, Development, and Regulation of Norms*, 96 MICH. L. REV. 338, 352–76 (1997) (offering external "esteem" theory of norm creation) *with* Robert D. Cooter, *Decentralized Law for a Complex Economy: The Structural Approach to Adjudicating the New Law Merchant*, 144 U. PA. L. REV. 1643 (1996) (offering "internalization" theory of norm origin). The difference is subtle. A purely "internal" theory of norm origin does not ground norm creation and perpetuation in others' ability to detect and sanction defectors. Moreover, norms arising from external, rather than internal, sources may be more susceptible to rapid change than "internalization" theorists have supposed. *See* McAdams, *supra* at 376–381. Even external theorists, however, acknowledge that an internal theory is needed to explain some persisting social norms. *Id.,* at 378–79. Because a wish to conform is usually based on a wish for the esteem of others who subscribe to the norm, these different accounts may have similar behavioral or policy implications.

133. The term "social capital" is commonly used to describe the stock of such norms. *See, e.g.,* ROBERT D. PUTNAM, MAKING DEMOCRACY WORK: CIVIC TRADITIONS IN MODERN ITALY (1993); FRANCIS FUKUYAMA, THE GREAT DISRUPTION chap. 2 (1999) (discussing social capital and reviewing criticism of Putnam's approach to it).

134. Even this "Paretian" concept of efficiency—a policy is efficient if it makes one person better off and leaves no one worse off—has its critics. *See, e.g.,* AMARTYA K. SEN, COLLECTIVE CHOICE AND SOCIAL WELFARE 22 (1970) (society can be Pareto-optimal even though "some people are rolling in luxury and other are near starvation"); Jeffrey L. Harris, *Class, Personality, Contract, and Unconscionability*, 35 WM. & MARY L. REV. 445, 468–80 (1994) (Pareto-optimality ignores psychological impact on person who is materially no worse off when another is made better off).

135. *See, e.g.,* Lisa Bernstein, *Opting Out of the Legal System: Extralegal Contractual Relations in the Diamond Industry*, 21 J. LEG. STUD. 115 (1992). *But see* LISA BERNSTEIN, THE QUESTIONABLE EMPIRICAL BASIS OF ARTICLE 2'S INCORPORATION STRATEGY: A PRELIMINARY STUDY (John M. Oliver Law and Economics Working Paper No. 74, 2nd series).

136. *See supra* note 16. Social norms help to solve prisoner's dilemmas and other collective-action problems by imposing shame "taxes" on defectors from cooperative arrangements. *See, e.g.,* Cass Sunstein, *On the Expressive Function of Law*, 144 U. PA. L. REV. 2021, 2029–33 (1996). This occurs whether the "tax" be internally or externally imposed. For a discussion of how norms shape real property regimes, including common property and communal ones, see Robert C. Ellickson, *Property in Land*, 102 YALE L.J. 1315 (1993).

137. See discussion *infra*, at Section III.D.

138. *See, e.g.,* Andrei Shleifer & Robert W. Vishny, *A Survey of Corporate Governance*, 52 J. FIN. 737 (1997).

139. Robert Post, *The Social Foundations of Privacy: Community and Self in the Common Law Tort*, 77 CAL. L. REV. 957, 970 (1989).

140. Indeed, Edmund Burke insisted that the relationship is the reverse: "Manners are of more importance than laws. Upon them, in a great measure, the laws depend. The law touches us but here and there, and now and then." Quoted in MARK CALDWELL,

A SHORT HISTORY OF RUDENESS (1999). For a thoughtful discussion of the "expressive function" of law on social norms, *see* Sunstein, *supra* note 136.

141. See discussion *infra*, at text accompanying notes 180–184..

142. ROBERT C. ELLICKSON, ORDER WITHOUT LAW: HOW NEIGHBORS SETTLE DISPUTES (1991).

143. For example, he details behavior patterns in whaling communities. *Id.*, at 191–206. See also JAMES ACHESON, THE LOBSTER GANGS OF MAINE (1988) (describing how social norms and extralegal enforcement mechanisms resolve the common pool problem in lobster-fishing communities).

144. ADAM SMITH, AN INQUIRY INTO THE NATURE AND CAUSES OF THE WEALTH OF NATIONS 15–16 (Edwin Cannan ed., 1976) (1776). *See also* Albert O. Hirschman, *Rival Interpretations of Market Societies*, 20 J. ECON. LIT. 1463 (1982).

145. Tax law provides many instances. For example, estimates of the behavioral and revenue effects of higher alcohol or cigarette taxes derive from observed demand elasticities. Immigration law must tailor enforcement policy to the false document, smuggling, and sham marriage markets.

146. *See, e.g.*, E.E.O.C. v. Consolidated Service Systems, 979 F. 2d 233 (7th Cir. 1993) (hiring through ethnic networks has both efficiency and normative advantages); Lisa W. Foderaro, *Many Hospitals in New York Quit Plan for Fewer Doctors*, N. Y. TIMES, Apr. 1, 1999, at A1 (incentives to train more physicians overwhelm regulation to reduce supply).

147. *See, e.g.*, JAMES Q. WILSON, THE INVESTIGATORS: MANAGING FBI AND NARCOTICS AGENTS (1978); *see also* SCHUCK, *supra* note 68, at chap. 6.

148. *See, e.g.*, MOSES BEN MAIMON, THE LAWS OF THE HEBREWS RELATING TO THE POOR AND THE STRANGER 67–68 (James W. Peppercorne trans. & Pelham Richardson ed., 1840) (praising anonymous charity). History is replete with examples of soldiers, police officers, and ordinary citizens who sacrificed themselves on behalf of strangers. On a more mundane level, self-interest cannot explain why people commonly return found wallets and give tips to people they do not know and will never see again. *See, e.g.*, William Grimes, *Tips: Check Your Insecurity at the Door*, N.Y. TIMES, Feb. 3, 1999, at F1 (studies on tipping).

149. *See, e.g.*, GOLDHAGEN, *supra* note 130 (obedience to Nazis); MALCOLM H. KLEIN, THE AMERICAN STREET GANG, ITS NATURE, PREVALENCE, AND CONTROL (1995) (gang psychology); *see generally* STANLEY MILGRAM, OBEDIENCE TO AUTHORITY: AN EXPERIMENTAL VIEW (1974) (habitual systems of obedience can override ethics and sympathy).

150. I am indebted to Bob Ellickson for pointing this out. Even granting his point, however, markets are sometimes used to punish conduct, as in boycotts, and legal sanctions against wrongdoing can be structured to exploit market incentives, as with antitrust treble damages and punitive damages.

151. This is not to say that economics has nothing interesting to say about those realms and goals. *See, e.g.*, RICHARD A. POSNER, SEX AND REASON (1992).

152. *See* discussion *infra*, at text accompanying notes 248–257.

153. KOMESAR, *supra* note 18, at 8.

154. All judges, many legislators, some regulators, and many government staff are generalist lawyers ill equipped to interpret specialized or technical information. However, there are signs that the proportion of lawyers in legislatures is declining. *See, e.g.*, Richard Perez-Pena, *Making Law vs. Making Money: Lawyers Abandon Legislatures for Greener Pastures*, N.Y. TIMES, Feb. 21, 1999, at sec. 4, p. 3.

155. *See, e.g.*, MARVER H. BERNSTEIN, THE JOB OF THE FEDERAL EXECUTIVE (1958).

156. KOMESAR, *supra* note 18, at 127–28.

157. In a highly pluralistic society, especially one with many recent immigrants from disparate cultures, it may be harder or take longer for newcomers to acquire such knowledge. *See* Schuck, *supra* note 24, at 341–46.

158. EDMUND BURKE, REFLECTIONS ON THE REVOLUTION IN FRANCE 76 (Pocock ed., 1987) (1791) ("We are afraid to put men to live and trade each on his own private stock of reason, because we suspect the stock in each man is small, and that individuals would do better to avail themselves of the general bank and capital of nations and of ages."); FRIEDRICH A. VON HAYEK, LAW, LEGISLATION, AND LIBERTY: A NEW STATEMENT OF THE LIBERAL PRINCIPLES OF JUSTICE AND POLITICAL ECONOMY (3 vol. ed., 1973–79).

159. I say "seem" because (as with teenage smoking) social norms' latent functions (in Robert Merton's phrase) may outweigh their apparent dysfunctions, at least to those who are members of the normative community.

160. I say *"mutatis mutandis,* may be socially desirable" in recognition of the well-known problems of externalities and imperfect markets, "second best" theory, and indeterminate social welfare functions, all of which confound our ability to extrapolate social efficiency from individual efficiencies. *See generally* ARROW, *supra* note 83 (inherent indeterminacy in extrapolating social welfare functions through aggregation of individual preferences); A. C. PIGOU, THE ECONOMICS OF WELFARE (Macmillan 4th ed. 1932) (externalities as reason for government intervention); Richard S. Markovits, *Second-Best Theory and Law and Economics: An Introduction,* 73 CHI.-KENT L. REV. 3 (1998) (theory of second best undermines law and economics).

161. *See, e.g.,* Bruce A. Ackerman & Richard B. Stewart, *Reforming Environmental Law,* 37 STAN. L. REV. 1333 (1985). A particularly egregious example is the federal government's paralysis over adopting a uniform bullet-tracing system despite available technology with great crime-reduction potential. *See* Barry Meier, *Deadlock over Bullet-Tracing System,* N.Y. TIMES, Aug. 1, 1999, at 20. *But see* Fox Butterfield, *Instant Check on Gun Buyers Has Halted 100,000 of Them,* N.Y. TIMES, Sept. 9, 1999, at A25 (report claiming effective instant background-checking system).

162. *See, e.g.,* Robert Pear, *Audit of V.A. Health Care Finds Millions Are Wasted,* N.Y. TIMES, Aug. 1, 1999, at 1 (despite repeated criticism of wasteful and antiquated health care, agency fails to change). Indeed, opponents of ostensibly popular reforms in health insurance, campaign finance, the regulation of financial institutions, and other policy areas have easily blocked them for years. *See* sources cited *supra* notes 23 and 34, and *infra* note 193.

163. *See, e.g.,* FLORA DAVIS, MOVING THE MOUNTAIN: THE WOMEN'S MOVEMENT IN AMERICA SINCE 1960 (1991); JOSEPH R. GUSFIELD, SYMBOLIC CRUSADE: STATUS POLITICS AND THE TEMPERANCE MOVEMENT (1963); RICHARD KLUGER, SIMPLE JUSTICE: THE HISTORY OF BROWN V. BOARD OF EDUCATION AND BLACK AMERICA'S STRUGGLE FOR EQUALITY (1976); RICHARD KLUGER, ASHES TO ASHES: AMERICA'S HUNDRED-YEAR CIGARETTE WAR, THE PUBLIC HEALTH, AND THE UNABASHED TRIUMPH OF PHILIP MORRIS (1996).

164. *See* Sheryl Gay Stolberg, *Birth Rate at New Low as Teen-Age Pregnancy Declines,* N.Y. TIMES, Apr. 29, 1999, at A26 (studies showing sharp decline in teenage birth rate after six straight years of decline and estimating 20 percent of decrease due to reduced sexual activity and 80 percent due to better contraception). *See also* McAdams, *supra* note 132, at 393–97 (new technologies can accelerate norm change by making information more readily available and reducing risk of deviation being detected).

165. JOSEPH A. SCHUMPETER, CAPITALISM, SOCIALISM, AND DEMOCRACY 83 (3d ed. 1950). For a recent, more hyperbolic example of such critiques, *See* JOHN GRAY, FALSE DAWN: THE DELUSIONS OF GLOBAL CAPITALISM (1999).

166. *See, e.g.,* ARNALDO BAGNOSCO & CHARLES F. SABEL, SMALL AND MEDIUM SIZED ENTERPRISES (1995) (market pressures produced more decentralized management structures).

167. Andrew Sullivan illustrates this in *There Will Always Be an England,* N.Y. TIMES MAG., Feb. 21, 1999, at 44.

168. *See, e.g.,* laws and executive orders cited *supra,* at note 42.

169. JUDITH RICH HARRIS, THE NURTURE ASSUMPTION: WHY CHILDREN TURN OUT THE WAY THEY DO (1998) (emphasizing the role of peer groups).

170. This is an important source of the long deadlock among politicians over campaign finance reform. *See* Cantor, *supra* note 23 (more than 70 percent of political action committee [PAC] contributions go to incumbents), although other causes exist. *See* Chapter 7 of this book, at note 98. In the economic area, anticompetitive motives fuel much antitrust and intellectual property litigation and economic regulation. *See, e.g.,* WILLIAM NISKANEN, BUREAUCRACY AND REPRESENTATIVE GOVERNMENT (1971); Richard A. Posner, *Theories of Economic Regulation,* 5 BELL J. ECON. 335 (1974); George J. Stigler, *The Theory of Economic Regulation,* 2 BELL J. ECON. 3 (1971). These motives are most evident in the telecommunications policy wars, where local telecommunications providers struggle to exclude long-distance carriers from local markets. *See* Crandall, *supra* note 36.

171. See ACKERMAN, *supra* note 6. Tort law's subordination of corrective justice to a policy-oriented functionalism is an example. *See* discussion *supra,* at text accompanying notes 113–117.

172. *See* MORONE, *supra* note 47.

173. For a discussion of this comparison, *See* Schuck, *supra* note 117.

174. *See* Robert M. Cover, *Foreword: Nomos and Narrative,* 97 HARV. L. REV. 4 (1983).

175. *See In re* Kasinga, Interim Decision No. 3278 (B.I.A. en banc, 1996). California has criminalized this practice, 73 Interp. Rel. 1461 (1996), and Congress has moved against it. Illegal Immigration Reform and Immigrant Responsibility Act of 1996, Pub. L. No. 104–208, ss 644–645, 110 Stat. 3009–708 (codified in 8 U.S.C. s 1374).

176. *See, e.g.,* Barbara Crossette, *Testing the Limits of Tolerance as Cultures Mix: Does Freedom Mean Accepting Rituals that Repel the West?* N.Y. TIMES, Mar. 6, 1999, at B9. This tension is exemplified by controversies over whether Muslim women may wear head scarves in public institutions. *See* Jon Henley, *Muslim Scarf Dispute Hits French School,* GUARDIAN (London), Jan. 11, 1999, at 11; Stephen Kinzer, *Islamic Woman in a Head Scarf Suddenly Galvanizes Turkey,* N.Y. TIMES, May 4, 1999, at A7 (excluded from taking seat in Parliament).

177. Changes in education, technology, utility, status, demography, markets, and politics all play a part in altering social norms. *See supra* note 163.

178. *See* HIRSCHMAN, *supra* note 52.

179. *See* discussion *supra,* at text accompanying notes 104–108.

180. For many examples and an elegant explanation of this corrosive effect, *See* ERIC A. POSNER, LAW, COOPERATION, AND RATIONAL CHOICE (forthcoming). *See also* William S. Landes & Richard A. Posner, *Salvors, Finders, Good Samaritans, and Other Rescuers: An Economic Study of Law and Altruism,* 7 J. LEG. STUD. 83 (1978); Lawrence Lessig, *The Regulation of Social Meaning,* 62 U. CHI. L. REV. 943 (1995). For an interesting current ex-

ample, *see* ELI BERMAN, SECT, SUBSIDY, AND SACRIFICE: AN ECONOMIST'S VIEW OF ULTRA-ORTHODOX JEWS (Falk Institute for Economic Research in Israel Discussion Paper No. 98.08, Oct. 1998).

181. *See* Sheryl Gay Stolberg, *Pennsylvania Set to Break Taboo on Reward for Organ Donations*, N.Y. TIMES, May 6, 1999, at A1 (state will contribute $300 to donor's funeral expenses).

182. *See* E. POSNER, *supra* note 180; Landes & R. Posner, *supra* note 180.

183. William J. Stuntz, *Race, Class, and Drugs*, 98 COLUM. L. REV. 1795, 1826 (1998).

184. *See, e.g.,* Sunstein, *supra* note 136, at 2033–34 (studies of rebellion norms in certain communities, particularly among younger people).

185. I say the legitimacy of "markets" rather than "the market" because most people seem to ascribe different moral and social meanings to different markets depending on the specifics of what is being traded, by whom, and on what terms.

186. CHARLES E. LINDBLOM, POLITICS AND MARKETS (1977). For a current example of this ardor, *see* Michael Janofsky, *Financial Aid Bargaining Drives Admissions Frenzy*, N.Y. TIMES, Apr. 5, 1999, at A12 (students bargain with prospective colleges for better aid packages).

187. *See, e.g.,* BELLAH ET AL., *supra* note 59, at 32–35 (describing "pragmatic utilitarianism" as a persisting cultural theme in U.S. history).

188. The economic virtues of market transfers in some of these traditionally uncommodified areas are explored in, e.g., R. POSNER, *supra* note 151; RICHARD TITMUSS, THE GIFT RELATIONSHIP: FROM HUMAN BLOOD TO SOCIAL POLICY (1971). *See* Stolberg, *supra* note 181 (paying organ donor's funeral expenses may violate federal law).

189. Other societies view some of these markets very differently. TITMUSS, *supra* note 188. Canada's refusal to allow the sale of fresh water is another example. *Free Trade in Fresh Water? Canada Says No and Halts Exports*, N.Y. TIMES, Mar. 8, 1999, at A9.

For a theory opposing market transfers of things that constitute one's "personhood," *see* Margaret Jane Radin, *Market-Inalienability*, 110 HARV. L. REV. 1849 (1988). Enforcing such market-denying norms may effectively prevent people without other options from using the market to advance their interests as they define them, which certainly raises competing moral concerns. *See, e.g.,* SCHUCK, *supra* note 24, at chap. 13 (on trading refugee protection burdens); Henry Hansmann, *The Economics and Ethics of Markets for Human Organs*, 14 J. HEALTH POL. POL'Y & L. 57 (1989); Arthur A. Leff, *Unconscionability and the Code: The Emperor's New Clause*, 15 U. PA. L. REV. 485 (1967); Peter H. Schuck, *Some Reflections on the Baby M Case*, 76 GEO. L. REV. 1793 (1988) (defending surrogate motherhood under regulation). Enforcing these norms may also induce people in that position to resort to black markets, often to their legal, moral, economic, and other disadvantage.

190. A rather hyperbolic account is FRANCIS FUKUYAMA, THE END OF HISTORY AND THE LAST MAN (1992). *But see* SAMUEL P. HUNTINGTON, THE CLASH OF CIVILIZATIONS AND THE REMAKING OF THE WORLD ORDER (1996).

191. Such critiques come from a wide range of ideological sources. *See, e.g.,* Karl Marx, *Alienated Labor, in* KARL MARX: SELECTED WRITINGS 56–68 (1844) (Lawrence H. Simon ed., 1994); SANDEL, *supra* note 59; Brook Larmer & Rod Nordland, *Preaching to the Masses*, NEWSWEEK, Feb. 2, 1998, at 54 (Pope John Paul II criticizes "excesses of capitalism" during visit to Cuba).

192. *See* RICHARD H. THALER, QUASI-RATIONAL ECONOMICS 201 (1991).

193. A good recent example is the contentious rhetorical debate over the Clinton health care plan. *See generally* THEDA SKOCPOL, BOOMERANG: CLINTON'S HEALTH SECURITY EFFORT

AND THE TURN AGAINST GOVERNMENT IN U.S. POLITICS (1996). This parallels the stakes-raising rhetorical tactic of law's critics. *See supra* text accompanying notes 125–128.

194. This reflex is itself a robust social norm. *See supra* text accompanying notes 46–52, 161–162.

195. Law, of course, can never literally be avoided. *See* discussion *supra,* at text accompanying notes 1–4, but it can be minimized or softened. *See infra,* at Section III.E.

196. In much the same way, Komesar's illuminating analysis of *participatory* costs and benefits can help them to choose self-consciously among politics, markets, and adjudication. KOMESAR, *supra* note 18.

197. In Chapter 2 of this book, I compare the discrete social systems of law, science, and politics.

198. Unless, of course, undertaking the comparison itself would be more costly than any resulting policy gains, which seems unlikely in most cases.

199. I say "defines rationality" because even officials who merely "satisfice," seeking a satisfactory result rather than an optimal one, are not rational if they fail to weigh alternatives. HERBERT A. SIMON, ADMINISTRATIVE BEHAVIOR: A STUDY OF DECISION-MAKING PROCESSES IN ADMINISTRATIVE ORGANIZATION 61–78 (3d ed. 1976). I say "appear" because legislators, who enjoy the most policy discretion, often make their real decision processes opaque to outsiders.

200. The Occupational Health and Safety Act, 29 U.S.C. ss 651–678, and the Endangered Species Act, 16 U.S.C. ss 1531–1544, are only two examples of classic command-and-control regulatory statutes. Command-and-control regulation is also common in environmental law, where it has been much disparaged for its inefficiency and inflexibility. *See, e.g.,* Ackerman & Stewart, *supra* note 161.

201. *See, e.g.,* the statutes discussed *supra,* at note 89. The Delaney Clause, *see* 21 U.S.C. s 348 (c) (3) (A), also exemplifies inflexible statutory mandates on regulators. It requires a ban on food additives containing *any* carcinogens. Not surprisingly, the Delaney Clause has often been criticized. *See, e.g.,* Richard A. Merrill, *FDA's Implementation of the Delaney Clause: Repudiation of Congressional Choice or Reasoned Adaptation to Scientific Progress?,* 5 YALE J. ON REG. 1 (1988).

202. Regulators' tendency to prefer strict rules to discretionary standards stems partly from many officials' pronounced risk aversion. *See, e.g.,* SCHUCK, *supra* note 68, at 73–75; *See also* Stephen G. Breyer, *Analyzing Regulatory Failure: Mismatches, Less Restrictive Alternatives, and Report,* 92 HARV. L. REV. 548, 573 (1979).

203. *See* Charles J. Goetz & Robert E. Scott, *Liquidated Damages, Penalties, and the Just Compensation Principle: Some Notes on an Enforcement Model and a Theory of Efficient Breach,* 77 COLUM. L. REV. 554 (1977) (criticizing judicial hostility to negotiated remedies for breach); Schuck, *supra* note 117. *But see* ANTHONY T. KRONMAN & RICHARD A. POSNER, THE ECONOMICS OF CONTRACT LAW (1979) (common law rules are efficient).

204. Regulatory Flexibility Act of 1980, 5 U.S.C. ss 601–612. The law's enforceability and effectiveness remain uncertain.

205. *See* DAVID OSBORNE & TED GAEBLER, REINVENTING GOVERNMENT: HOW THE ENTREPRENEURIAL SPIRIT IS TRANSFORMING THE PUBLIC SECTOR (1992); *Symposium: The New Private Law,* 73 DENV. L. REV. 993 (1996) (privatization and hybrid public-private regulation). This is not to deny, however, that this strategy has sometimes led to abuses, as in the case of some privatized prison and detention facilities. *See infra* note 255.

206. *See, e.g.,* EUGENE BARDACH, THE IMPLEMENTATION GAME (1977); JEFFREY PRESSMAN & AARON WILDAVSKY, IMPLEMENTATION (3d ed. 1984); SCOTT, *supra* note 21; MORONE, *supra* note 47.

207. Legislators often overlook the fact that courts may construe statutes in a manner that Congress did not anticipate. *See, e.g.*, ROBERT A. KATZMANN, INSTITUTIONAL DISABILITY: THE SAGA OF TRANSPORTATION POLICY FOR THE DISABLED (1986); MELNICK, BETWEEN THE LINES, *supra* note 98. For a general discussion of the problem of implementation, *see* SCHUCK, *supra* note 68, at chaps. 6–8.

208. Environmental law provides many examples. *See, e.g.*, E. Donald Elliott & Gail Charnley, *Toward Bigger Bubbles*, FORUM FOR APPLIED RESEARCH & PUB. POL'Y 48, 49 (Winter 1998) (fragmentation into separate regulatory programs prevents rational comparative risk priorities).

209. SCHUCK, *supra* note 68, at 188–89.

210. *See supra* note 42. These requirements, however, assume that the laws being analyzed have been fully implemented and focus instead on certain specific impacts. See, e.g., Robert W. Hahn, *Regulatory Reform: Assessing the Government's Numbers*, Working Paper 99–6, AEI-Brookings Joint Center for Regulatory Studies, July 1999 (criticizing quality of and compliance with, these analyses).

211. *See supra*, at text accompanying notes 168–169.

212. For example, the high transaction costs of command-and-control modes of spectrum allocation led to market-based FCC auctions of broadcast licenses despite some problems with the use of such auctions. *See, e.g.*, Pablo T. Spiller & Carlo Cardilli, *A Property Rights Approach to Communications Spectrum*, 16 YALE J. ON REG. 53 (1999) (discussing the efficiency of broadcast spectrum auctions and proposing more market-based deregulation of spectrum allocation). I have proposed a market in refugee protection burdens among nations. *See* SCHUCK, *supra* note 24, at chap. 13.

213. This discussion of diversity draws on, and is extended in, Chapter 3 of this book.

214. Even the nature of slavery in the United States differed from region to region. ORLANDO PATTERSON, RITUALS OF BLOOD: CONSEQUENCES OF SLAVERY IN TWO AMERICAN CENTURIES 31–32 (1998). *See also* Alan Finder, *Upstate Prosecutors Often Turn to Death Penalty*, N.Y. TIMES, Jan. 21, 1999, at A1 (geographic distinctions in application of death penalty even within individual states).

215. In one small but revealing example of market fragmentation, large corporations are increasingly using "tracking stock" to allow investors in a company to tie their fates to the performance of one or another of its product lines rather than to the company as a whole. *See, e.g.*, Claudia H. Deutsch, *Latest DuPont Formula Turns One Company into Two Stocks*, N.Y. TIMES, Mar. 11, 1999, at C1. *See also*, David Barboza, *Pluralism Under Golden Arches*, N.Y. TIMES, Feb. 12, 1999, at C1 (McDonald's allowing more local control and variation by franchisees).

216. *See* Gustav Niebuhr, *Makeup of American Religion Is Looking More Like Mosaic, Data Say*, N.Y. TIMES, Apr. 12, 1998, at 14; Russell Shorto, *Faith Is an Option: Belief by the Numbers*, N.Y. TIMES MAG., Dec. 7, 1997, at 60 (of roughly 1,600 religions and denominations in United States today, about half founded since 1965).

217. I discuss them in Chapter 3 of this book and also in SCHUCK, *supra* note 24, chap. 14.

218. *See* discussion *supra* in text accompanying notes 69–74.

219. Economic historians debate whether the economic virtues of standardized technology, even where it seems suboptimal, is exemplified by the survival of the typewriter keyboard's "QWERTY" sequence. *Compare* Paul A. David, *Clio and the Economics of QWERTY*, 75 AM. ECON. REV. 332 (1985) (yes), *with* S. J. Leibowitz, *Fable of the Keys*, 33 J. L. & ECON. 1 (1990) (no). *See also* Marcel Kahan & Michael Klausner, *Standardization and Innovation in Corporate Contracting (Or "The Economics of Boilerplate")*, 83 VA. L. REV.

713 (1997) (discussing trade-offs between standardization and innovation in corporate contracting context). The benefits of standardization have been a theme of the "new learning" in antitrust policy, *see, e.g.,* INDUSTRIAL CONCENTRATION: THE NEW LEARNING (Harvey J. Goldschmidt et. al eds., 1974), and have been invoked by Microsoft's defenders in its ongoing litigation with the Justice Department. *See, e.g.,* Paul Kedrosky, US v. Microsoft: Neuter Microsoft? Does the World Need More Unix?, WALL ST. J., June 10, 1998, at A18.

220. *See, e.g.,* Stephan Thernstrom, *American Ethnic Statistics, in* IMMIGRANTS IN TWO DEMOCRACIES: FRENCH AND AMERICAN EXPERIENCE 80 (D. Horowitz & G. Noiriel eds., 1992); YEHUDI O. WEBSTER, THE RACIALIZATION OF AMERICA (1992); Christopher A. Ford, *Administering Identity: The Determination of "Race" in Race-Conscious Law,* 82 CAL. L. REV. 1231 (1994); Steven Holmes, *U.S. Officials Are Struggling to Measure Multiracial Heritages,* N.Y. TIMES, June 14, 1998, sec. 1, p. 32; Holmes, *supra* note 77.

221. Miller v. California, 413 U.S. 15 (1972) (current test); *cf.* Roth v. US, 354 US 476, 488 (1957) (origin of test). Similar difficulties arise in other contexts, such as defamation law, where law defines norms by reference to "community" or other geographic terms. The jury sometimes provides a crude but workable approximation of "community."

222. This was the unhappy fate, for example, of federal efforts to regulate natural gas rates by separate, artificially defined geographic areas. The Permian Basin Area Rate Cases, 390 U.S. 747 (1968) (affirming Federal Power Commission use of area-based rate-setting) contributed to the natural gas shortages of the 1970s. *See* STEPHEN G. BREYER & RICHARD A. STEWART, ADMINISTRATIVE LAW AND REGULATION 645–47 (3d ed. 1992).

223. *See, e.g.,* PAUL A. SAMUELSON & WILLIAM D. NORDHAUS, ECONOMICS 76–77 (16th ed. 1998).

224. These are discrete policy functions; they need not all be assigned to the same level. As noted in the very next sentence in text, however, program responsibility should ordinarily follow cost-bearing (mostly fiscal) responsibility.

225. Executive Order No. 13,083, *Federalism,* May 14, 1998, *reprinted in* 63 Fed. Reg. 27,651–55. This order aroused severe criticism in Congress and was suspended on August 5, 1998. This may have contributed to the support in Congress for legislation protecting state regulatory authority from federal preemption. *See* Labaton, *supra* note 42. But see James Brooke, *Clinton Jolts Canadians With a Plea on Federalism,* N.Y. Times, Oct. 10, 1999, at p. 4 (praising decentralization in light of diversity).

226. *See* Treaty on European Union, Feb. 7, 1992, Art. 3b, 31 I.L.M. 247. *See, e.g.,* Paul A. Marquandt, *Subsidiarity and Sovereignty in the European Union,* 18 FORDHAM INT'L L.J. 616, 617 (1994). The current move toward a unified currency and other common policies may threaten the principle's vitality.

227. They are largely true, especially at a time when the quality of state government has improved significantly. *See* Chapter 3 of this book, at note 10. These claims are supported in surveys showing that Americans have substantially more confidence in state and local governments than in the federal government. *See, e.g.,* Andrew E. Busch, *Political Science and the 1994 Elections: An Exploratory Essay,* 28 PS: POL. SCI. & POL'Y 708, 709 (1995) (citing studies). The preference for local government is found in the origins of American federalism. *See* THE FEDERALIST NO. 46 (Alexander Hamilton).

228. Some, such as water and improvement districts, are defined not geographically but by special subject matter interests. *See, e.g.,* Salyer Land Co. v. Tulare Lake Basin Water Storage District, 410 U.S. 719 (1973).

229. For a review of this phenomenon and its implications for citizenship law, compare Peter J. Spiro, *The Citizenship Dilemma*, 51 STAN. L. REV. 597, 617–38 (1999), with SCHUCK, *supra* note 24, chap. 10.

230. *See* Chapter 3 of this book.

231. *See generally* PAUL PETERSON, THE PRICE OF FEDERALISM (1995). I discuss this in Chapter 3 of this book.

232. *See* Peterson, *id.*, at 121–26 (some evidence of race to the bottom in welfare policy between 1969 and 1990); *see also* Daniel C. Esty, *Revitalizing Environmental Federalism*, 95 MICH. L. REV. 570, 638 (1996) (predicting race to the bottom).

233. I am among the doubters. *See* Chapter 3 of this book, text accompanying notes 50–52. *See also*, Adam B. Jaffe et al., *Environmental Regulation and Competitiveness in U.S. Manufacturing: What Does the Evidence Tell Us?*, 33 J. ECON. LIT. 132 (1995) (reviewing studies); Richard L. Revesz, *The Race to the Bottom and Federal Environmental Regulation: A Response to Critics*, 82 MINN. L. REV. 535 (1997) (refuting environmental race to the bottom); Ralph K. Winter, *State Law, Shareholder Protection, and the Theory of the Corporation*, 6 J. LEG. STUD. 251 (1977) (finding "race to the top" in corporate law rather than to bottom); ROBERTA ROMANO, THE GENIUS OF AMERICAN CORPORATE LAW (1993) (same). Paul Peterson shows that races to the bottom are more likely when state and local governments adopt "redistributive" as opposed to "developmental" functions. *Supra* note 231, at 72–73.

234. *See, e.g.*, Revesz, *supra* note 233; *see also* JAN K. BRUECKNER, WELFARE REFORM AND INTERSTATE WELFARE COMPETITION: THEORY AND EVIDENCE 23–25 (Urban Inst., Assessing the New Federalism, Occasional Paper No. 21, Dec. 1998) (evidence is "mixed"); JOHN HOLAHAN ET AL., HEALTH POLICY FOR THE LOW-INCOME POPULATION: MAJOR FINDINGS FROM THE "ASSESSING THE NEW FEDERALISM" CASE STUDIES 58 (Urban Inst., Occasional Paper No. 18, Nov. 1998) (little evidence of race to bottom relating to health care for poor); SUSAN A. RIEDINGER ET AL., INCOME SUPPORT AND SOCIAL SERVICES FOR LOW-INCOME PEOPLE IN NEW YORK 11–12 (Urban Inst., Assessing the New Federalism, Feb. 1999) (most states continuing to provide cash and Medicaid benefits to immigrants even without federal funds).

235. *See supra* note 124, and Chapter 3 of this book, at text accompanying notes 50–53.

236. *See* discussion *supra*, at Sections II.B, II.C, and II.D.

237. For an important example, *see* Lynn M. LoPucki, *The Death of Liability*, 106 YALE L.J. 1 (1996) (technology facilitates corporate strategy of becoming judgment-proof).

238. For a current example, *see* Peter T. Kilborn, *Tennessee Talks of Paring Plan for "Uninsurables,"* N.Y. TIMES, May 1, 1999, at A1 (government health coverage for uninsured). For a discussion of states as engines of policymaking innovation, *see* DANIEL ELAZAR, AMERICAN FEDERALISM: A VIEW FROM THE STATES (3d ed. 1984) The Clinton administration's pre–1996 grants of waivers from uniform federal requirements to states wishing to try new welfare reform approaches provided fresh, valuable information to both federal and state policymakers.

239. *See, e.g.*, RICHARD A. EPSTEIN, TAKINGS (1985). This view is anomalous for several reasons, particularly given its acknowledgment that property rights can be limited by the common law principles of nuisance, which are notoriously open-ended and would give judges, who often are unelected, more power to restrict property rights than elected legislators or their regulatory agency delegates. An example of the continuing vitality of these common law principles despite more-aggressive Supreme Court enforcement of the Takings Clause is the Court's decision in Lucas v. California Coastal Comm'n, 505 U.S. 1003 (1992).

240. In addition to the Takings Clause, such limits include the Contracts, Due Process, and Equal Protection clauses.

241. In a highly (and in my view, excessively) influential article, Charles Reich proposed that policy discretion concerning one's access to public benefits be subject to "new property" rights similar to those that limit public takings of traditional property. *See* Charles Reich, *The New Property*, 73 YALE L.J. 733 (1964). For a critical analysis of Reich's position, *see* Robert L. Rabin, *The Administrative State and Its Excesses*, 24 U. SAN FRAN. L. REV. 273 (1990).

242. To some, destabilization is not merely a price that the administrative state must sometimes pay but a positive good that the law should promote and protect. *See* ROBERTO MANGABEIRA UNGER, KNOWLEDGE AND POLITICS (1975) (urging "destabilization rights").

243. Cass Sunstein's praise of "judicial minimalism" has much in common with my argument here, though it is concerned with judicial methodology, not law more generally. CASS R. SUNSTEIN, ONE CASE AT A TIME: JUDICIAL MINIMALISM ON THE SUPREME COURT (1999).

244. *See* KATE STITH & JOSE A. CABRANES, FEAR OF JUDGING: SENTENCING GUIDELINES IN THE FEDERAL COURTS (1998).

245. The classic instances are the negligence standard in tort law and the Fourth Amendment's prohibition of "unreasonable searches and seizures."

246. *See, e.g.*, Associated Builders and Contractors Inc. v. Brock, 862 F. 2d 63 (D.C. Cir. 1988) (Occupational Safety and Health Administration [OSHA] authorized to adopt private organization's standards to set exposure levels under Occupational Safety and Health Act).

247. *See* Model Bus. Corp. Act s 8.30 (1991) (business judgment rule); U.C.C. s 2–103 (1) (b) (merchants must observe "reasonable commercial standards of fair dealing" in contract performance); Orloff v. Willoughby, 345 U.S. 83, 92 (1953) (judicial deference to "needs of the [military] service"); W. PAGE KEETON ET AL., PROSSER & KEETON ON THE LAW OF TORTS s 32, at 189 (5th ed. 1984) (malpractice law incorporating community medical standards). *But see* BERNSTEIN, *supra* note 135 ("customs of trade" do not consistently exist, even in close-knit merchant communities).

248. *See, e.g.*, Christine Jolls et al., *A Behavioral Approach to Law and Economics*, 50 STAN. L. REV. 1471, 1489–93 (1998) (discussing literature and reporting on new experiment showing that individuals who have optimizing opportunities in one-on-one bargaining situations often select "fair" outcome instead).

249. For an overview of various market-based regulatory strategies and a proposal for using "administrative markets" as a regulatory enforcement device, *see* Michael Abramowicz, *Market-Based Administrative Enforcement*, 15 YALE J. ON REG. 197 (1998); *See also*, Elliott & Charnley, *supra* note 208, at 50 (new "bubble" applications in environmental law).

250. *See, e.g.*, Robert Pear, *Politically and Technically Complex, Medicare Defies a Sweeping Redesign*, N.Y. TIMES, Mar. 18, 1999, at A23.

251. For example, I have urged the U.S. Immigration and Naturalization Service (INS) to consider partially privatizing its notoriously feckless efforts to apprehend aliens who abscond pending their removal hearings, which is in turn a critical element of that agency's larger policy failure. Standards must be imposed, of course, to prevent private prosecutorial abuse. *See* Peter H. Schuck, *INS Detention and Removal: A White Paper*, 11 GEO. IMM. L.J. 667, 682–85, 698, 700–01 (1997). *See also*, Marjorie Valbrun,

Cleaning Firm's Suit Says Rival Broke Law by Hiring Illegal Immigrants, WALL ST. J., Jan. 25, 1999, at B2.

252. *See* Jack Colwell, *Going After Deadbeats,* SOUTH BEND TRIB., Feb. 25, 1999, at A1 ($59.8 billion in outstanding custody payments owed by noncustodial parents in 1997).

253. *See, e.g.,* Lochner & Cain, *supra* note 23.

254. *See, e.g.,* MARTIN FELDSTEIN & DANIEL ALTMAN, UNEMPLOYMENT INSURANCE SAVINGS ACCOUNTS (National Bureau of Economic Research Working Paper No. 6860, 1999) (plan to reduce moral hazard of unemployment insurance without decreasing protection for unemployed).

255. *See, e.g.,* Pam Belluck, *As More Prisons Go Private, States Seek Tighter Controls,* N.Y. TIMES, Apr. 15, 1999, at A1 (approximately twenty-six states have privatized some prison operations, but some states are regulating the private providers more closely).

256. Indeed, Congress and the executive branch have studied the possibility of privatizing public insurance programs, including "Fannie Mae" and "Freddie Mac." *See, e.g.,* CONGRESSIONAL BUDGET OFFICE, ASSESSING THE PUBLIC COSTS AND BENEFITS OF FANNIE MAE AND FREDDIE MAC (1996); DEPARTMENT OF HOUSING AND URBAN DEVELOPMENT, PRIVATIZATION OF FANNIE MAE AND FREDDIE MAC: DESIRABILITY AND FEASIBILITY (1996).

257. The particular level of government designing, funding, and administering such programs would be guided by the responsiveness principle, discussed *supra,* at Section III.D.

258. Since the focus here is on encouraging alternatives to public service monopolies, not on increasing consumer purchasing power in private markets, I do not include food stamps.

259. For a discussion of the current debate on school vouchers, *see* Paul E. Peterson et al., *School Choice in Milwaukee,* PUB. INTEREST, Fall 1996, at 38 (favorable assessment of voucher programs); Jonathan Rauch, *Choose or Lose,* NEW REPUBLIC, Nov. 11, 1997, at 4 (generally favorable assessment); Tamar Lewin, *Few Clear Lessons from Nation's School-Choice Program,* N.Y. TIMES, Mar. 27, 1999, at A10 (Milwaukee program). School voucher programs have survived constitutional challenges in Ohio and Wisconsin, but not in Maine. Moreover, constitutional questions persist, especially if such programs provide benefits to religious schools. *See* Alan Finder, *State Constitution Poses High Hurdles for Voucher Proposal,* N.Y. TIMES, Mar. 5, 1999, at B12 (Establishment Clause objections to proposed New York City program).

260. Pokora v. Wabash Railway Co., 292 U.S. 98, 105 (1934) (Cardozo, J.) (characterizing informal norms and distinguishing them from rules of law).

261. *See generally* LAW AND GOVERNMENT UNDER THE TUDORS (Claire Cross et al. eds., 1988) (describing system of extensive regulation).

Index